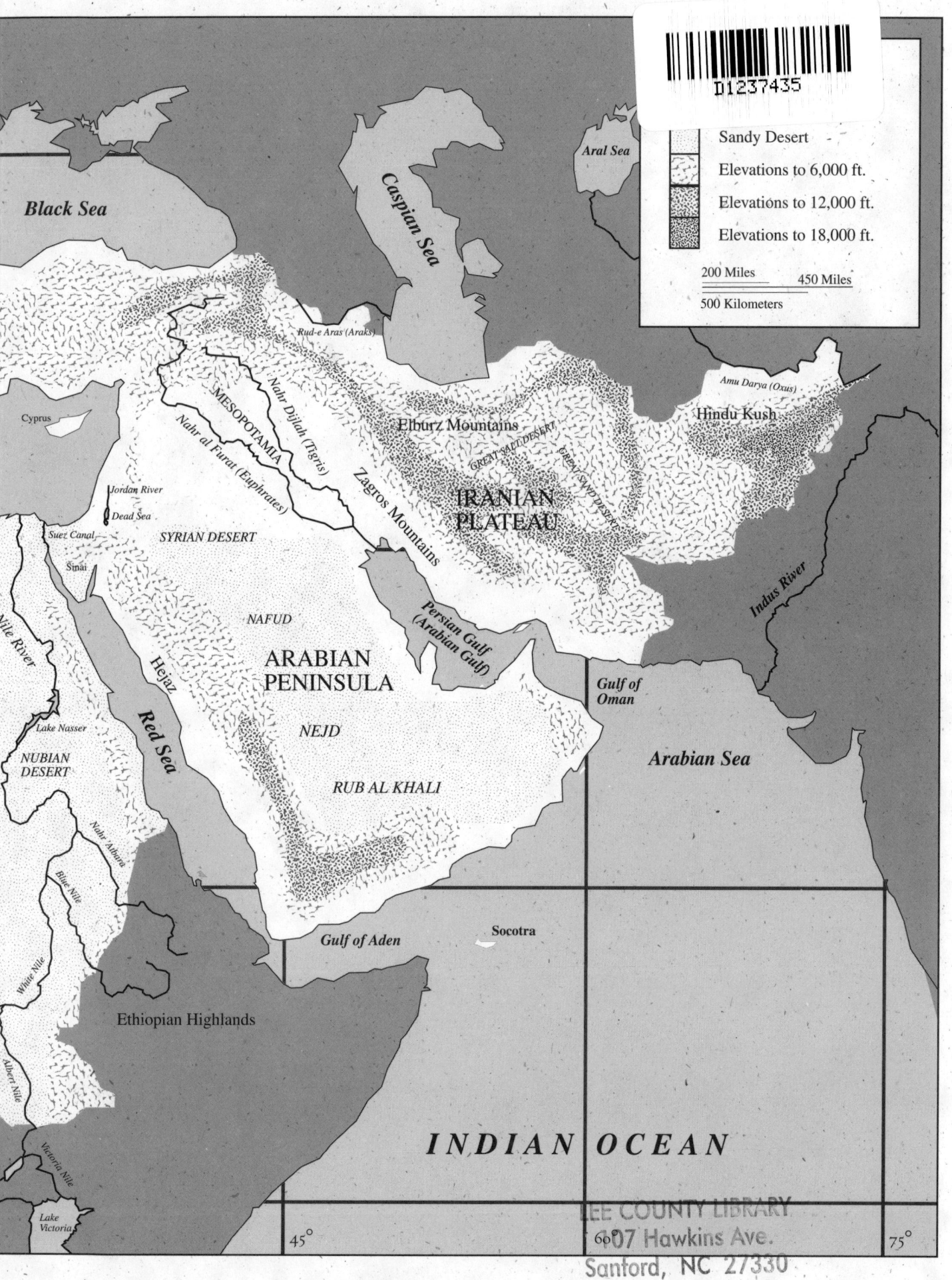

Black Sea

Caspian Sea

Aral Sea

Sandy Desert

Elevations to 6,000 ft.

Elevations to 12,000 ft.

Elevations to 18,000 ft.

200 Miles   450 Miles

500 Kilometers

Rud-e Aras (Araks)

Amu Darya (Oxus)

Cyprus

MESOPOTAMIA

Nahr Dijlah (Tigris)

Elburz Mountains

Hindu Kush

Nahr al Furat (Euphrates)

GREAT SALT DESERT

GREAT SAND DESERT

Jordan River

Dead Sea

Zagros Mountains

IRANIAN
PLATEAU

Suez Canal

SYRIAN DESERT

Indus River

Sinai

NAFUD

Persian Gulf
(Arabian Gulf)

Nile River

ARABIAN
PENINSULA

Gulf of
Oman

Lake Nasser

Hejaz

NEJD

Arabian Sea

NUBIAN
DESERT

Red Sea

RUB AL KHALI

Nahr Atbara

Blue Nile

Gulf of Aden

Socotra

White Nile

Ethiopian Highlands

Albert Nile

INDIAN OCEAN

Victoria Nile

Lake
Victoria

45°   60°   75°

ENCYCLOPEDIA
OF THE
MODERN
MIDDLE EAST

ENCYCLOPEDIA
OF THE
MODERN
MIDDLE EAST

VOLUME 4

Edited by

Reeva S. Simon
Philip Mattar
Richard W. Bulliet

MACMILLAN REFERENCE USA
SIMON & SCHUSTER MACMILLAN
NEW YORK

SIMON & SCHUSTER AND PRENTICE HALL INTERNATIONAL
LONDON   MEXICO CITY   NEW DELHI   SINGAPORE   SYDNEY   TORONTO

Simon & Schuster Macmillan
1633 Broadway
New York, NY 10019-6785

PRINTED IN THE UNITED STATES OF AMERICA

printing number

1   2   3   4   5   6   7   8   9   10

LIBRARY OF CONGRESS CATALOGING-IN-PUBLICATION DATA

Encyclopedia of the Modern Middle East / edited by Reeva S. Simon,
    Philip Mattar, Richard W. Bulliet.
        p.   cm.
    Includes bibliographical references (p.   ) and index.
    ISBN 0-02-896011-4 (set : lib. bdg. : alk. paper). — ISBN
0-02-897061-6 (v. 1 : lib. bdg. : alk. paper). — ISBN 0-02-897062-4
(v. 2 : lib. bdg. : alk. paper). — ISBN 0-02-897063-2 (v. 3 : lib.
bdg. : alk. paper). — ISBN 0-02-897064-0 (v. 4 : lib. bdg. : alk.
paper).
    1. Middle East—Encyclopedias.   2. Africa, North—Encyclopedias.
I. Simon, Reeva S.   II. Mattar, Philip, 1944–   .   III. Bulliet,
Richard W.
DS43.E53   1996
956′.003—dc20   96–11800
                                                              CIP

This paper meets the requirements of ANSI/NISO Z39.48-1992
(Permanence of Paper)

S

(Continued)

Sha'arawi, Huda al- [1879–1947]

Egyptian feminist and nationalist.

Huda al-Sha'arawi was born in Minya in Upper Egypt and raised in Cairo. Her father was Sultan Pasha, a wealthy landowner, provincial administrator, and later, president of the Chamber of Deputies. Her mother, Iqbal, was Circassian. Al-Sha'arawi married an original member of the WAFD, Ali Sha, and was closely associated with Wafdist politics. In 1919, al-Sha'arawi organized women protesters in an anti-British demonstration. In 1920, she founded the Wafdist Women's Central Committee, which led a boycott of British goods in 1922. In 1925, al-Sha'arawi founded the Egyptian Feminist Union, and established *L'Egyptienne,* a journal that called for enlightened attitudes toward women. She established another journal, *al-Misriyya* (The Egyptian Woman) in 1937, and in 1938, chaired the first ARAB WOMEN'S CONGRESS. In 1946, she participated in the founding of *al-Mar'a al-Arabiyya* (The Arab Woman), the newsletter of the Arab Feminist Union. Her memoirs were published in Arabic in 1981, and translated into English in 1986 under the title *Harem Years: The Memoirs of an Egyptian Feminist.*

BIBLIOGRAPHY

BADRAN, MARGOT, and MIRIAM COOKE, eds. *Opening the Gates: A Century of Arab Feminist Writing.* Bloomington and Indianapolis, Ind., 1990.

WUCHER KING, JOAN. *Historical Dictionary of Egypt.* Metuchen, N.J., 1984.

David Waldner

Sha'b, al-

Newspaper of the Socialist Labor party in Egypt.

Al-Sha'b was founded by former Young Egypt leader Ibrahim Shukri in 1978. President Anwar al-Sadat closed it in the September 1981 crackdown that led to his assassination. Resuming publication under President Husni Mubarak, *al-Sha'b* reflected the party's drift toward an alignment with the Muslim Brotherhood. Its attacks on Zionism, corruption, and American hegemony frequently displease the Mubarak regime.

BIBLIOGRAPHY

HINNEBUSCH, RAYMOND A., JR. *Egyptian Politics under Sadat.* Boulder, Colo., 1985.

Donald Malcolm Reid

Shabak

See Shin Bet

Shabaka, al-

Magazine published in Lebanon.

Al-Shabaka first appeared in the early 1960s. It was founded by Sa'id Furayha, head of the Dar al-Sayyad publishing firm. It is devoted to news about society and celebrities throughout the Arab world, especially featuring articles about and interviews with singers and actors. It is sold all over the world.

As'ad AbuKhalil

Shabbi, Abu al-Qasim al-   [1909–1934]

Noted twentieth-century Tunisian poet.

Born in the southern Tunisian oasis town of Tozeur, al-Shabbi had a mobile childhood because of his father's judicial career. The constant traveling familiarized him with the Tunisian countryside and people and induced in him a profound and lifelong infatuation with both that permeated his later poetry. Studies at Tunis's eminent Zaytuna Mosque university and law school also influenced al-Shabbi, but they clashed with his penchant for European and Arabic literature and with his budding rebellion against the French colonial system and the restrictions of the Arab poetic tradition.

His entire poetic career was compressed in a seven-year period that occurred between age eighteen, when he began publishing his poetry, and age twenty-five, when he succumbed to heart disease. The pressures of family obligations caused by his father's untimely death in 1929 and the additional responsibilities occasioned by his marriage are thought to have contributed to his early demise in October 1934.

New currents in Arab poetry from the Middle East and North America stirred al-Shabbi's imagination, as did the European Romantics. Al-Shabbi sought to break the bonds of convention and tradition and to revolutionize both poetry and society. Although he opposed the French colonial regime, he also castigated traditional Tunisian mores and called for social transformation, freedom, and progress. For this imaginative poet, the city contrasted unfavorably with nature, where he felt he could escape into a solitary utopia and indulge in his pursuit of idealized womanhood.

Al-Shabbi's revolutionary stance appealed to a later generation of Tunisian and Arab nationalists. Along with other Tunisians of his generation, al-Shabbi contributed to the literary renaissance of his country, at the same time that other Tunisians heralded a social renaissance (for example, Tahir al-HADDAD in his ep-ochal work on Tunisian women) and a political renaissance (for example, Habib Bourguiba through his founding of the Neo-Destour party in the year of al-Shabbi's death). Al-Shabbi helped Tunisian poets break with traditional forms and find a more impassioned poetic expression that could help move the Tunisian people toward social awakening and a modern outlook. Many of his poems were set to music and became patriotic or popular songs. During October 1994, which marked the sixtieth-anniversary commemoration of the poet's death, celebrations were held in the towns al-Shabbi had visited or resided in, such as Tozeur (his birthplace and the site of his mausoleum), Majaz al-Bab, Gafsa, and Kebilli. Al-Shabbi is known as the "poet of life," after his most famous collection of poems, *Songs of Life.*

BIBLIOGRAPHY

AL-SHABBI, ABU AL-QASIM. *Selections from the Poetry of Abu Al-Qasim Al-Shabbi (1909–1934): Songs of Life.* Tr. by Lena Jayyusi and Naomi Shihab Nye. Carthage, Tunisia, 1987.

Larry A. Barrie

Sha'bi Family

Prominent Yemeni clan.

Originally from al-Sha'b, Qahtan and Faysal Abd al-Latif al-Sha'bi were prominent in the origins of the Yemeni branch of the Arab Nationalist Movement as well as the National Liberation Front of South Yemen. Until deposed by more radical elements, Qahtan was president of the People's Republic of South Yemen (1967–1969), while Faysal served briefly as prime minister and foreign minister. Shortly thereafter, Faysal was assassinated.

Manfred W. Wenner

Shader, Joseph   [1907–1977]

Former Lebanese minister, deputy, and vice president of the Phalange party.

Born and educated in Beirut, Joseph Shader was a prominent Armenian Catholic lawyer who was elected to the Chamber of Deputies in 1951, when he became the first parliamentary representative of the PHALANGE party. In parliament, he joined Camille Chamoun, Kamal Jumblatt, Raymond Eddé, and others who sought to force President Bishara al-Khuri to resign. He successfully competed in every single parliamentary election held until his death in 1977 and was therefore a deputy for Beirut in the parliaments elected in 1953, 1957 (when he also became deputy speaker of the chamber), 1960, 1964, 1968, and 1972. Under President Chamoun (1952–1958), he supported the government's pro-Western and anti-Nasser foreign policy, and in March 1958 he became minister of planning in a cabinet headed by Sami al-Sulh. A specialist of public finance, he once was president of the Parliamentary Commission for Finances. He held the vice presidency of the Phalange party for several years and is remembered as one of that party's most influential members.

BIBLIOGRAPHY

SALIBI, KAMAL S. *The Modern History of Lebanon.* New York, 1965.

Who's Who in Lebanon. Beirut, 1970.

Guilain P. Denoeux

Shafi'i Law School

One of the four systems, or schools, of thought in Sunni Muslim law.

The Shafi'i Law School was founded by Muhammad ibn Idris al-Shafi'i (died 820), a disciple of Malik ibn Anas (died 795) and Muhammad ibn Hasan al-Shaybani (died 805). Bringing about a synthesis between the rationalists and the traditionalists, Shafi'i elaborated a system of positive law and a rudimentary legal theory that attracted a number of scholars who propagated his teachings, thus creating the first personal school of law (*madhhab*) in Islam. His two chief treatises that survived are *al-Umm,* a collection of treatises mainly concerned with positive law and disagreements among the early jurists, and *al-Risala* (also known as *al-Kitab*), a work on legal theory with particular emphasis on Prophetic *hadith* (traditions) as a binding source of law.

The immediate students of Shafi'i who were responsible for propagating his teachings, and thus for laying the first roots of the school, were al-Buwayti (died 846), Harmala (died 857), Muzani (died 878), al-Za'farani (died 874), al-Karabisi (died c. 859), and al-Rabi ibn Sulayman al-Jizi (died 870). Al-Rabi ibn Sulayman al-Muradi (died c. 884) is known as the transmitter of most of Shafi'i's extant works. Other scholars, such as Ibn Hanbal (died 854) and Abu Thawr (died 855), initially the disciples of Shafi'i, became themselves the founders of independent law schools.

The widespread influence of the Shafi'i school must be credited to the work of Ibn Surayj (died 918), significantly nicknamed the "Little Shafi'i." He was responsible for harmonizing the teachings of the school and for training a generation of influential Shafi'i scholars who guaranteed not only the survival of the school but indeed its success. Among the most important of these scholars are Abu Bakr al-Sayrafi (died 942) and al-Qaffal al-Shashi (died 948), who are considered two of the first major authors of complete works on Shafi'ite legal theory (*usul al-fiqh*).

Among the many names that dominated the later history of Shafi'ism are: Abu Bakr al-Baqillani (died 1013), Abu Ishaq al-Isfara'ini (died 1015), Abu Muhammad al-Juwayni (died 1046) and his son Imam al-Haramayn (died 1085), Bayhaqi (died 1066), al-Mawardi (died 1058), Abu Ishaq al-Shirazi (died 1083), Ghazali (died 1111), Abu Bakr al-Shashi (died 1113), Fakhr al-Din al-Razi (died 1209), Rafi'i (died 1226), Izz al-Din b. Abd al-Salam (died 1262), Muhyi al-Din al-Nawawi (died 1277), and Suyuti (died 1505). The positive law (*furu*) treatises of Juwayni, Shirazi, Ghazali, Rafi'i and Nawawi became standard for the later period, whereas in legal theory, the works of Juwayni, Ghazali and Razi gained popularity.

Today the Shafi'i school has followers in Egypt—mainly in rural areas—as well as in Syria, Lebanon, Palestine, Jordan, Iraq, Hijaz, Bahrain, Yemen, Pakistan, Iran, India, and Indonesia.

BIBLIOGRAPHY

HALLAQ, WAEL B. "Was al-Shafi'i the Master Architect of Islamic Jurisprudence?" *International Journal of Middle East Studies* 4 (1993): 587–605.

MAHMASSANI, SUBHI. *The Philosophy of Jurisprudence in Islam.* Tr. by Farhat J. Ziadeh. Leiden, 1961.

SCHACHT, JOSEPH. *The Origins of Muhammadan Jurisprudence.* Oxford, 1975.

Wael B. Hallaq

Shafiq, Durriyya   [1908–1975]

Egyptian writer and feminist.

Durriyya Shafiq was born in the town of Tanta in Egypt's Nile delta, where she was educated by Roman Catholic nuns. With the support of Huda al-Sha'arawi, she received her doctorate from the Sorbonne in Paris, where she wrote a dissertation entitled "La femme Egyptienne et l'Islam." In 1945 Shafiq returned to Egypt, founded *Majalla Bint al-Nil* (The Magazine of the Daughter of the Nile), and in 1948 established the Union of the Daughter of the Nile, an association which called for political rights for women and female literacy. A later political party, which she founded in 1953, was banned in 1954. In the 1960s Shafiq's public opposition to President Gamal Abdel Nasser led to her being placed under house arrest. Among her writings are *Al-Mar'a al-Misriyya min al-Fara'ina ila al-Yawm* (The Egyptian Woman from the Pharaohs until Today) and *Al-Kitab al-Abyad li Huquq al-Mar'a al-Misriyya* (The White Paper for the Rights of the Egyptian Woman).

BIBLIOGRAPHY

BADRAN, MARGOT, and MIRIAM COOKE, eds. *Opening the Gates: A Century of Arab Feminist Writing.* Bloomington, Ind., 1990.

David Waldner

Shahabi, Hisham al-

Bahraini labor leader.

Since 1970, Hisham al-Shahabi has been a member of the Bahraini reformist-leftist group and has advocated democratization. While al-Shahabi and his group boycotted the elections to the Constitutional Assembly in 1972, a year later they participated in the election to the National Assembly. Hisham al-Shahabi, an architect by training, has also been a leading member of the Bahraini labor movement since the 1960s.

BIBLIOGRAPHY

NAKHLEH, EMILE. *The Persian Gulf and American Policy.* New York, 1982.

Emile A. Nakhleh

Shahada, George   [1910–1989]

Lebanese playwright and poet.

Born in Alexandria, Egypt, of an old Lebanese family imbued with French culture, George Shahada completed his primary studies at the Jesuit school in Beirut before moving to Paris where he received most of his secondary education and all of his university training. After obtaining a French *licence* (bachelor of arts) in law, he returned to Beirut, where he first worked as cultural attaché at the French embassy. He later became a professor and then the secretary-general at the Ecole Supérieure des Lettres, which had emerged as a center for the promotion of French avant-garde poetry in the region.

His first collection of poems, *Poésies I,* published in Paris in 1938, showed very clearly the influence of surrealism on his work and gained him the attention of French and international critics. Repeated stays in Paris enabled him to maintain a close friendship with André Breton, a leader in the surrealist movement, whom he had met during his student days. He also developed friendships with Cocteau, Eluard, St.-John Perse, Supervielle, and other leading French intellectuals. By the early 1950s, he already had established himself as one of the leading neosurrealist poets and the foremost representative of Lebanese poets writing in the French language. It was then that he started writing plays, which soon brought him more recognition than his poetry and indeed established him as the best-known French-language dramatist outside France.

During the 1950s and 1960s, Shahada wrote more than a half-dozen important plays; the best-known of these are *Monsieur Bob'le* (1951), *La Soirée des Proverbes* (1954), *Le Voyage* (1961), and *L'Emigré de Brisbane* (1965). Although Shahada always wrote in French and spent a great part of his life in France, his work reflects his emotional attachment to his native land and an unmistakable Eastern influence. Its emphasis on magic and fantasy has even led some critics to compare it to Oriental fairy tales and to describe Shahada as a storyteller in the tradition of Scheherazade. His heroes (for instance, M. Bob'le and Vasco) are usually good-natured, naive figures who had been able to preserve a childlike innocence and the ability to wonder at the marvels of nature and life. They identify mysteries behind the appearance of the ordinary and are usually led from banal, everyday situations into increasingly unexpected, odd, and captivating adventures. Far less preoccupied with understanding the world than with experiencing its beauty, they are sometimes shown communicating not only with other human beings, but also with the animals and objects that surround them.

By placing such strange but charming characters at the center of his humorous plays, Shahada seeks to evoke the harmony that men and women can find with nature and among themselves. He invites the members of his audience to look for the mysteries of life, and to listen to their intuitions and dreams instead of being driven by their minds. Shahada's plays thus constitute a plea for feeling before understanding, and they exhibit an unmistakable Oriental sensitivity to the wonders of nature.

Although Shahada's suspenseful, funny plays highlight the comical, incongruous, and tragic aspects of the human condition and draw on technical devices that were used in the avant-garde theater of the 1950s, they nevertheless differ from the so-called Theater of the Absurd. Unlike plays by Ionesco or Beckett, for instance, they betray an optimistic outlook on life. Beckett's characters tend to feel helpless, frustrated, and bitter, and live only in their minds, whereas Shahada's heroes are spontaneous individuals who still display the simple happiness and purity of childhood. In sharp contrast to the way Beckett emphasizes the chaotic and meaningless aspects of life, Shahada invites his audience to appreciate what he sees as the intrinsic harmony and beauty of the world and to look at one's surroundings with the innocent, uncorrupted eyes of a child.

In 1973, Shahada returned to poetry. In December 1986—a year after his last collection of poems, *Le Nageur d'un Seul Amour,* was published in Paris—the Académie Française awarded him the Grand Prix de la Francophonie during a summit of French-speaking countries held in Paris. By becoming the first recipient of this prestigious honor three years before his death, Shahada obtained well-deserved recognition of his unique place in the world of Francophone literature; other leading members of this world include such well-known literary figures as Aimé Césaire, Tahar Ben Jelloun, Léopold Senghor, and Kateb Yacine. He will be remembered as the twentieth-century author who best blended Western surrealist literature and avant-garde dramatic techniques with the Oriental tradition of storytelling.

BIBLIOGRAPHY

BERNDT, BARBARA ANN. "The Franciful World of Georges Schehadé." Ph.D. diss., University of Wisconsin–Madison, 1979.

KHALAF, SAHER. *Littérature libanaise de langue française.* Ottawa, 1974.

ROBIN, PIERRE. *Poésie et théâtre de Georges Schehadé.* Beirut, 1957.

Guilan P. Denoeux

Shahbandar, Abd al-Rahman   [1880–1940]

Syrian politician.

Born in Damascus, Abd al-Rahman Shahbandar attended the Syrian Protestant College (later the American University of Beirut). He received his medical degree in 1906 and became a professor of medicine. He was one of the most prominent nationalists in Damascus after World War I, serving Emir Faisal as chief liaison with Britain, and as an interpreter for the King–Crane Commission in 1919. Shahbandar was appointed minister of foreign affairs in 1920 by the newly crowned King Faisal. The French promptly disbanded this government, and Shahbandar fled to Egypt. He returned to Damascus under French amnesty in 1921 and founded the first nationalist organization in Syria, the Iron Hand.

Shahbandar was arrested and sentenced to twenty years in prison for nationalist activities in 1922. The sentence was changed to exile, and after seeking support for Syria's independence in the West, with the help of his friend Charles R. Crane, he returned to Damascus in 1924.

In 1925, Shahbandar organized and led the PEOPLE'S PARTY, which played a central role in the revolt (1925–1927). He spent ten years in Cairo, then returned to Damascus in April 1937. His pro-Hashimite stance put him in direct confrontation with the ruling National Bloc, and he was placed under house arrest in 1938. Shahbandar's quest for Britain's support for a confederation of Syria, Transjordan, Palestine, and Lebanon under Emir Abdullah ibn Husayn, and his denunications of his more hard-line nationalist rivals, led to his assassination in Damascus (June 1940). Ultimate responsibility for the assassination was never fixed, though National Bloc members may have been involved.

BIBLIOGRAPHY

KHOURY, PHILIP S. *Syria and the French Mandate: The Politics of Arab Nationalism, 1920–1945.* Princeton, N.J., 1987.

Charles U. Zenzie

Shahin, Tanyos   [1815–1895]

Leader of the Lebanese peasant revolt.

Shahin was born into the Sa'adah family in Rayfun, Kisrawan. When peasant protests against the feudal landlords swept parts of Mount Lebanon in 1858, Shahin was approached by armed peasants and asked to become a local leader in Rayfun; his influence quickly spread through the Kisrawan region. He succeeded Salil Sfayr, who feared the consequence of his role and resigned. Shahin articulated the grievances of the peasants to the Mashayikh (heads of Maronite landowning families) and was not reluctant to use violence to achieve his aims. The Maronite patriarch Bulus Mas'ad accused Shahin of intensifying the conflict between the peasants and the landlords. When the landlords tried to ignore the demands of the peasants, Shahin made clear his willingness to use force. At one point he tried to arrest leading landlords who were meeting in a monastery, but the presence of clerics stopped him.

Shahin called for the confiscation of property and crops owned by the landlords and in 1859 seized silk and wheat belonging to landlords and put it in his own house. His power allowed him to punish and reward individuals. By the spring of 1859, he had expelled all members of the Khazin family from Kisrawan. At the end of the year, the Maronite peasant rebellion had become interwined with the Maronite–Druze conflict, which led to the civil war of 1860. The appointment of a Mutasarrif in 1861 led to the defeat of Shahin, although he was allowed to remain in Kisrawan as local leader.

As'ad AbuKhalil

Shahin, Yusuf [1926–]

Egyptian film director.

Born in Alexandria, Egypt, to a middle-class Christian family, Shahin studied at Victoria College and Alexandria University, and later studied acting in California. He directed his first film, *Baba Amine,* in 1953, at the age of twenty-four. Considered to be one of the most important directors of Egypt and of the Third World, his films have provided critical insight into the evolution of Egyptian society while remaining accessible to wide audiences. Shahin's criticism of government policies led to his voluntary exile in Libya between 1965 and 1967. Shahin has directed over twenty films, and is the subject of numerous books and articles.

BIBLIOGRAPHY

THOMAS, NICHOLAS, ed. *International Dictionary of Films and Filmmakers.* Vol. 2, *Directors.* Chicago, 1991.

David Waldner

Shah-People Revolution

See White Revolution

Shahpur Ahmadzai

Emir of Afghanistan, 1842.

Shahpur Ahmadzai was placed on the Afghan throne by the British in October 1842 as they began their disastrous retreat from Kabul. Shahpur was the youngest and weakest son of Shah Shuja, who ruled Afghanistan from 1803 to 1809 and from 1839 to 1842. His reign was brief, and he fled to Peshawar by the end of 1842, following the British in their retreat.

BIBLIOGRAPHY

DUPREE, LOUIS. *Afghanistan.* Princeton, N.J., 1980.

Grant Farr

Shahyad Square

Memorial to the Pahlavi dynasty of Iran.

Shahyad square, renamed Azadi (freedom) square after the Iranian Revolution of 1979, is located in the western part of Tehran, close to Mehrabad International Airport. The Shahyad monument, sitting in the square's center, was designed by Hoseyn Amanat, a young Iranian architect. It is an arch of white marble built by Mohammad Reza Shah Pahlavi in 1971 to honor himself and his dynasty and to celebrate 2,500 years of Iranian kingship.

BIBLIOGRAPHY

HANAWAY, WILLIAM L., JR., "The Symbolism of Persian Revolutionary Posters." In *Iran since the Revolution,* ed. by Barry M. Rosen. Boulder, Colo., 1985.

Neguin Yavari

Shakkur, Yusuf [1928–]

Syrian army general.

Born in Homs, Yusuf Shakkur studied at the military academy in Homs. In 1949, Shakkur was sent on a mission to France and the USSR. Between 1961 and 1964 he was consul general in Venezuela and Brazil. In 1964, he became chief of intelligence, a post he held until he became general chief of staff in April 1972. He participated in the Arab–Israel wars of 1967 and 1973. He has served as Syria's ambassador to France and has been assistant to the Syrian foreign minister since the early 1990s.

George E. Irani

Shalom Achshav

See Peace Now

Shaltut, Muhammad [1893–1963]

Grand Shaykh of al-Azhar.

Shaykh Muhammad Shaltut studied and taught at al-Azhar until he became Grand Shaykh of al-Azhar in 1958. Shaltut emphasized commitment to combining the modern sciences with traditional religious studies; consequently, his work is frequently cited in Egypt and the Arab world today by Islamist modernists and moderates.

Raymond William Baker

Sham'a, Rushdi Bey al-   [?–c. 1916]

Syrian politician.

Born the son of Ahmad Rafiq Pasha al-Sham'a into a prestigious Damascus family, Rushdi Bey al-Sham'a was connected with the Decentralization party as deputy for Damascus in 1910. He was arrested for conspiring with French authorities against the Ottoman Empire and was executed by 1916.

BIBLIOGRAPHY

KHOURY, PHILIP S. *Urban Notables and Arab Nationalism: The Politics of Damascus 1860–1920.* Cambridge, U.K., 1983.

Charles U. Zenzie

Shami, Ahmad Muhammad al-

Yemeni political leader.

A prominent member of a large family of Sayyid aristocrats in Yemen, al-Shami joined the early opposition to the imamate in the 1940s. As a founding member of the FREE YEMENIS in 1944, he was among those imprisoned in Hajja after the aborted 1948 revolution. Thereafter refusing to cast his lot with the republicans, al-Shami served as royalist foreign minister during the civil war following the 1962 revolution, which produced the Yemen Arab Republic (YAR). He finally led the moderate royalists into the republican–royalist reconciliation in 1970, after which he joined the YAR's plural executive. He withdrew from politics and moved to London for medical treatment in the mid-1970s.

Robert D. Burrowes

Shami, Muhammad Abdullah al-

Agent of North Yemen's Hamid al-Din family in the 1940s.

Al-Shami served as frontier officer in the eastern border town of al-Baydha for Imam Yahya and Imam Ahmad of the Hamid al-Din family. He conducted border negotiations with the British and repeatedly subverted South Yemeni tribes with money and arms.

Robert D. Burrowes

Shamir, Moshe   [1921–   ]

Israeli writer and political activist.

Shamir was born in pre-state Palestine, in Safed, and raised in Tel Aviv. From 1941 to 1947, he was a member of Kibbutz Mishmar ha-Emek. In 1944 he joined the Palmach and fought in the Arab–Israel War (1948). Shamir is a leader of the first generation of native Israeli writers and best known for his novels of the 1940s and 1950s, which depict in rich detail and glowing terms the development of the new state and the sabra character. *Hu Halakh Ba-Sadot* (1947; He Walked in the Fields), *Ad Eilat* (1950; Until Eilat), and *Kilometer 56* (1949) were all written in this vein. His adulatory attitude toward Israeli society metamorphosed into a critical one such as is found in his novels *Ha-Gevul* (1966; The Border) and *Yonah Be-Hazer Zarah* (1975; Pigeon in a Strange Yard). His historical novels, *Melekh Basar Va-Dam* (1954; King of Flesh and Blood [1958]) and *Kivsat Ha-Rash* (1956; David's Stranger [1964]) also criticize contemporary Israel, albeit indirectly.

Shamir is the most political of Israeli writers, and following the Arab–Israel War (1967), he helped found the Greater Land of Israel movement, advocating the retention of land captured during the war. In 1973, he joined the Likud party under Menachem Begin and became a member of Knesset (Israel's parliament). In 1979, he became a leader of the right-wing Tehiyah party and a member of the ninth Knesset.

Ann Kahn

Shamir, Yitzhak   [1915–   ]

Israeli prime minister, 1983–1984, 1986–1992.

Shamir, whose name means "hard stone," was born in 1915 in eastern Poland. He emigrated to Israel in 1935, where he studied at the Hebrew University and in 1937 joined the Irgun Zva'i Le'umi (IZL). In 1940 he joined the extremists who split from IZL to form Lohamei Herut Yisrael (LEHI). One of the three chief LEHI leaders by 1942, he headed the organization's operations, which included the assassination, in November 1944, of the British minister of state for the Middle East, Lord Moyne.

Because of his involvement with LEHI, the mandate police seized Shamir in December 1941 and incarcerated him in the Mazra prison camp, from which he escaped in August 1942. During the summer of 1942, he negotiated with Menachem Begin, who wanted to reunite IZL with LEHI, but Shamir found himself unable to accept Begin's terms. In July

Yitzhak Shamir. (Israel Office of Information)

1946, he was imprisoned again, and again he managed to escape. In May 1948 Shamir returned to Palestine and led LEHI operations in Jerusalem—including the assassination, in September 1948, of the UN mediator Count Folke Bernadotte—until LEHI was outlawed in late 1948. Shamir was one of the disbanded LEHI leaders who formed the political party Fighters' List, which gained one seat in the first Knesset. During the party's convention in 1949, Shamir supported its nationalist platform and also its "neutral" pro-Soviet orientation and leanings toward a socialist ideology; he soon retreated from the latter position, however.

Engaged in private business until 1955, Shamir was thereafter recruited by the MOSSAD. As head of the Israeli intelligence agency's special operations in Europe until 1964, he sought to prevent the Egyptian government from employing German scientists to develop missiles and unconventional weapons. When Mossad director Isser Harel retired and was replaced by Meir Amit, Shamir left the service and returned to private business. In 1970, at age fifty-five, he joined the LIKUD party (then known as the Herut party), becoming its director of organization.

He was elected a Knesset member of parliament in 1974 and chairman of the Likud party in 1975. When the Likud party came to power in 1977, Shamir became speaker of the Israeli parliament. In March 1980, Moshe Dyan resigned as foreign minister and Shamir replaced him. The Kahan Commission, appointed in 1982 to investigate the murders in the Sabra and Shatila refugee camps in Lebanon, reprimanded Shamir for not having attempted to verify the information about these events given him by the deputy defense minister.

With the retirement of Prime Minister Begin and the departure from the political arena of old leaders of the Likud, Shamir was regarded as the natural successor. He was elected prime minister on September 15, 1983. After the 1984 general elections, he formed a National Unity Government with the Labor party, which won by a narrow majority. By prearranged plan, he switched roles as foreign minister, deputy prime minister, and prime minister with Shimon Peres and, accordingly, served as prime minister from 1986 to 1988. In 1988, he won election on his own and became prime minister for four more years, again as part of a National Unity Government. The Labor party withdrew from the coalition in 1990 after a dispute with the Likud party over the peace process. In 1992, the Likud party, led by Shamir, was defeated. With this defeat, Shamir's political career came to an end.

Shamir's tough ideological and political policies were reflected in his refusal to grant any territorial concessions to the Arabs and his support for increased Israeli settlements in the occupied territories. He was for reaching peace agreements with Syria and Jordan but believed these treaties should be based on Israel's territorial gains after the Six-Day War. Although Shamir led the Israeli delegation in the direct peace talks between Israel and its Arab neighbors that opened in Madrid in the fall of 1991, he firmly opposed the principle of exchanging land for peace, established in the CAMP DAVID ACCORDS.

Shamir's many diplomatic accomplishments while in office included the renewal of diplomatic relations with many countries and the opening of relations with what was then the USSR and with China. Shamir advocated using a strong hand against the Intifada and refused to set limits on new construction of Israeli settlements, even at the risk of losing the American loan guarantees he needed to take in the Jewish immigrants coming from the Soviet Union in very large numbers.

While prime minister, Shamir was often jeopardized by Mossad-related controversies, such as the Folard affair and the Shabak affair, and his policies demonstrated both his determination to preserve the political status quo and his minimal concern with social and economic issues.

BIBLIOGRAPHY

ENDERLIN, CHARLES. *Shamir.* Paris, 1991.

Yaakov Shavit

Shamlan, Abd al-Aziz

Nationalist labor leader and politician of Bahrain.

Together with two other Bahrainis, Abd al-Aziz Shamlan was exiled in 1956 by the British to St. Helena because of his political activity. Upon his release from St. Helena in the 1960s, Shamlan resided in Kuwait. Following independence in 1971, the Bahraini ruler invited Shamlan back to Bahrain where he was elected to the Constitutional Assembly in 1972. He also became the deputy speaker of the assembly. However, he was defeated in his election bid to the National Assembly. He later served as Bahrain's ambassador to Tunisia and to the Arab League in that country. He died in the mid-1980s.

BIBLIOGRAPHY

NAKHLEH, EMILE. *Bahrain: Political Development in Modernizing Society.* Lexington, Mass., 1976.

Emile A. Nakhleh

Shamlu, Ahmad [1925–]

A leading Iranian exponent of she'r no poetry (i.e., new poetry; specifically, modernist poetry).

Ahmad Shamlu comes close to the rejection of the bases of Persian verse rhythms and metrical patterns in his poetry. The late 1950s through the 1960s marked Shamlu's most productive years as an engagé (politically concerned) modernist poet.

After several years of self-exile in exasperation at life in the late Pahlavi era, Shamlu returned to Tehran in early 1979, full of optimism about the new social order emerging in the aftermath of the Iranian Revolution. He founded a weekly called *Ketab-e Jom'eh,* which the Islamic republic banned a year later. Shamlu's collected poems were published in Germany in the mid-1980s.

In April 1990 at the University of California at Berkeley, during an extended stay in the United States for health reasons, Shamlu delivered the most controversial lecture in the field of Persian literature.

He attacked Ferdowsi (940–1020), author of Iran's national epic called *Shahnameh* (Book of Kings, c. 1010), as a feudal writer perpetuating royalist myths. Hundreds of responses to Shamlu's speech subsequently appeared in Persian publications throughout the world.

BIBLIOGRAPHY

An Anthology of Modern Persian Poetry (1979) offers English translations of Shamlu poems. L. ALISHAN, "Ahmad Shamlu: A Rebel Poet in Search of an Audience," *Iranian Studies* (1985), investigates the poet's unswerving *engagement* and modernism since the 1950s.

Michael C. Hillmann

Shammar

A tribe of north-central Saudi Arabia.

The Shammar are a sharif tribe (a tribe claiming noble descent), centered in northern Najd in the region of Ha'il, Jabal Shammar, and the Nafud. The Shammar are led by the Al Rashid family, former rulers of Ha'il who captured Riyadh in 1891 and were ousted by Ibn Sa'ud in 1902. Divided into four sections—Abde, Aslam, Al Sinjara, and Tuman—the Shammar tribe was primarily camel-herding bedouin. Some few lineages live in farming villages. Many of their lineages, including the ruling Al Rashid, were seminomadic, maintaining oasis gardens during part of the year and grazing their animals in the desert in the wake of winter rains. In the nineteenth century, the Al Rashid were active proponents of the Muwahhidun reform movement, though they opposed the extension of Al Sa'ud family rule into their territory, encouraged Qur'anic education for boys and girls, and required Friday attendance in the mosque by men. In the twentieth century, the Shammar intermarried with the Al Sa'ud family and benefit today from the patronage of the ruling family, although they have been generally excluded from governing posts.

Eleanor Abdella Doumato

Shammas, Anton [1951–]

Israeli novelist, poet, and nonfiction writer.

Shammas is an atheist who defines himself as a Palestinian citizen of Israel who identifies with Muslim culture. He writes in Hebrew and English. His works are characterized by an attempt to challenge the definition and test the tolerance of the Israeli discourse from within the Hebrew language. His highly praised first novel *Arabesqot* (1986; Arabesques, 1988) was written in Hebrew and deals with the residents of the Israeli Christian Arab village of Fassuta and, more specifically, with the Shammas family. Interwoven with their lives are historical events and associations that highlight the conditions of the Arabs residing in Israel.

Ann Kahn

Shammas, Ibrahim al-

Palestinian politician and businessman.

Born to a Greek Orthodox family in Jerusalem, Shammas became a wealthy merchant and lived in England briefly before World War I. After the war, he became a leading Palestinian nationalist as a member of the Muslim–Christian Association and the moderate Nashashibi opposition. He urged cooperation with Britain, holder of the mandate over Palestine, and opposed the boycott of the 1922 Palestine elections.

BIBLIOGRAPHY

Muslih, Muhammad Y. *The Origins of Palestinian Nationalism.* New York, 1988.

Elizabeth Thompson

Sham'un

See under Chamoun

Shapira, Hayyim Moshe   [1902–1970]

Israeli political leader; active in the Ze'irei ha-Mizrachi Zionist movement.

Born in Russia, Hayyim Moshe Shapira studied at the Grodno Yeshiva in Russia and at the Hildesheimer Rabbinical Seminary in Berlin. He attended the fourteenth Zionist Congress and later was elected to the Zionist General Council as a representative of Ha Po'el ha-Mizrachi. In 1925, he emigrated to Palestine, where he became a leader in the Zionist Executive.

After the *Anschluss* of Austria and Germany in 1938, Shapira went to evacuate Austrian Jews to Palestine. Throughout his life, he sought to facilitate the emigration of religious Jews to Israel. From the time that the State of Israel was proclaimed in 1948 until

his death, Shapira was a minister in the Israeli cabinet as part of the National Religious party.

Bryan Daves

Sharabati, Ahmad   [1905–?]

Syrian politician.

Ahmad al-Sharabati, the son of nationalist Damascene merchant Uthman al-Sharabati, studied engineering at the American University of Beirut and at the Massachusetts Institute of Technology. He started his career by running a tobacco factory for his father and later became involved in import trade, especially motor vehicles. His political career started in the early 1930s when he joined the National Action League, a pan-Arabist movement that was anti-communist. Harassed by the French mandatory authorities in Syria, Ahmad fled to Transjordan (now Jordan), where he stayed for several years. In 1943, he became a member of the Syrian parliament, running as a nationalist. In 1945, he became minister of education and then minister of national economy in the ministry of Faris al-Khuri. After his resignation from the cabinet that year, in 1946 he was appointed minister of national defense in the cabinet of Jamil Mardam. In 1948 he resigned as a result of the poor performance of the Syrian army in the Arab–Israel War. In 1951, he was implicated in a conspiracy against Adib Shishakli, the military ruler in Syria, and was sentenced to two years and four months in prison.

BIBLIOGRAPHY

Khoury, Philip. *Syria and the French Mandate: The Politics of Arab Nationalism, 1920–1945.* Princeton, N.J., 1987.
Seale, Patrick. *The Struggle for Syria: A Study of Post-War Arab Politics, 1945–1958.* New Haven, Conn., 1987.

Abdul-Karim Rafeq

Sharaf, Abd al-Hamid   [1939–1980]

Government official in Jordan.

Sharaf, a cousin of the Hashimite kings of Jordan and Iraq, was born in Iraq, and grew up in Istanbul and Amman. In 1955, he was sent to the American University of Beirut (AUB), where he joined the Movement of Arab Nationalists (MAN) and became the editor of its newspaper.

Sharaf left MAN soon after it moved further to the left in 1961. He was reconciled with King Hussein and returned to Amman, where he joined the Foreign Ministry. He rose quickly in the ministry and later became minister of information and culture. He was ambassador to the United States (1967–1971), and then Jordan's permanent representative to the United Nations (1971–1976). In July 1976, he returned to Amman to head the Royal Court.

King Hussein asked Sharaf to form a government in December 1979. Sharaf liberalized the system and decentralized power by introducing regional self-government and giving undersecretaries executive responsibilities. He supported reform of the educational system and women's rights and was concerned with stamping out corruption and reforming the tax system.

Jenab Tutunji

Sharef, Ze'ev [1906–1984]

Israeli political leader.

Having emigrated to Palestine from Romania in 1924, Sharef eventually became the secretary of the central committee of the Haganah. After statehood (1948), he served in various capacities in and out of the Israeli government including secretary of the political department of the Jewish Agency and secretary of the Emergency Committee and the National Administration (which established the Israeli civil service). From 1948 to 1957, Sharef was the first secretary of the Israeli government, and in the early 1960s he was director of state revenues, and administrator of the Weizmann Institute. He also held several ministerial portfolios, including commerce and industry, and finance and housing.

Bryan Daves

Sharett, Moshe [1894–1965]

Israeli politician; prime minister, 1953–1955.

Sharett was born Moshe Shertok. His family migrated from Russia to Palestine in 1906. He attended school in Herzliyya and Tel Aviv, and after graduating in 1913, he entered the University of Istanbul to study law. When World War I broke out, he was drafted into the Turkish army.

At the end of the war, Sharett attended the London School of Economics, graduating in 1924. He returned to Palestine and became a journalist; from 1929 to 1931 he was editor of *Davar*, a daily newspaper in Tel Aviv.

In 1931 Sharett became the political secretary for the Jewish Agency for Palestine; in 1935 he was named director of its political department, a position of leadership of the government of the Yishuv, the Jewish population in Palestine. In 1946 he participated unofficially in talks in London to negotiate Zionist goals.

Sharett was a representative of the Jewish Agency in the 1947 negotiations with the UN Special Committee on Palestine. He sought UN support for the creation of an independent state for the Jews in Palestine. In December 1947 he was among Jewish leaders lobbying for American support in the United Nations.

In May 1948, Sharett (who had hebraized the name Shertok at the time of the creation of the State of Israel) was named foreign minister in the Jewish provisional administration. In that capacity he negotiated support for Israel's statehood with U.S. Secretary of State George Marshall.

Once the State of Israel was in existence, Sharett became its first foreign minister, a position he held until 1956. In that post he emphasized that proceeds from the sale of lands belonging to absentee Arabs would be applied to a fund to resettle the refugees elsewhere, not to repatriate them in Israel. He argued that the problems of the Palestinian refugees were just like the problems of refugees around the world. In that sense, there was no legal precedent requiring their repatriation to the lands they had occupied before the war.

In March 1949, Sharett introduced the "principle of nonidentification" to indicate that Israel would not be aligned with either the East or the West. Israel's intention was to work with all nations to develop peaceful links and support for its existence. However, by 1951 it had become clear that the Soviet Union would support the Arab bloc against Israel, and Israel's foreign policy became clearly aligned with the West.

Prime Minister David Ben-Gurion resigned in December 1953, and Sharett became prime minister. In June his cabinet was overturned by the withdrawal of the General Zionist party from the coalition. He remained as acting prime minister until the scheduled elections for the third Knesset took place. After the elections, Ben-Gurion took over the government again with a MAPAI-dominated cabinet.

In 1956 tensions increased between Ben-Gurion and Sharett over the appropriate response to Egypt's actions in and around the Suez Canal. Sharett argued that Israel should act with great restraint, while Ben-Gurion was in favor of a more drastic strategy. When Ben-Gurion felt that the tensions were growing too great, he asked for Sharett's resignation as foreign minister in June 1956, replacing him with Golda Meir.

BIBLIOGRAPHY

BEN-GURION, DAVID. *Israel: A Personal History.* New York, 1971.

SACHAR, HOWARD M. *A History of Israel: From the Rise of Zionism to Our Time.* New York, 1981

Gregory S. Mahler

Shari'a

Arabic for "the trodden path leading to a water hole." In Islam, the regulations of God's law as transmitted through a prophet; the dominant law in Islamic societies.

Muslims, Christians, and Jews each have "a law (*shir'a*) and a normative way to follow," the Qur'an attests (verse 48). In the Middle Ages, Islamic discourse referred not only to this strict definition of *Shari'a* as law but also to all that which Allah has revealed—whether it pertained to actual religious practice or to belief. In Islam, those aspects relating to practice belong to the province of law (FIQH); those that concern belief belong to theology (*ilm al-kalam* or *ilm al-tawhid*). Law, however, depends on theology, since the contents and validity of law rest on textual sources, whose divine origins and truth are known. Furthermore, all sciences that are used to attain a knowledge of law and theology are considered *Shari'a* sciences, even if their subject matter is not legal or theological. Therefore, the Arabic language, *hadith* (verbal statements of Prophetic traditions), exegesis (interpretations), and even logic are deemed *Shari'a*—even if designating logic this way has always been controversial.

The use of the term *Shari'a* has actually, in practice, been restricted to the realm of law, and particularly to those aspects that bear upon the conduct of the individual in both worldly and religious matters. *Shari'a* may be equated, therefore, with *fiqh* in both its components: (1) positive law (*furu*) and (2) legal theory (*usul*). Positive law delineates legal obligations, ranging from rituals to personal and penal law; contracts; sales; hunting; and more. Legal theory demonstrates how positive law is derived through legal reasoning and interpretation, which results in the law stipulating the legal and moral responsibility thrust upon Muslims.

The legal and moral elements in the *Shari'a* are evident in the individual rulings classified in accordance with five norms (*ahkam*): (1) the obligatory (*wajib*), (2) the recommended (*mandub*), (3) the permissible or indifferent (*mubah*), (4) the prohibited (*haram*), and (5) the repugnant (*makruh*). The obligatory represents an act whose performance entails reward and whose omission entails punishment. It is commonly divided into those acts that are binding on all and those that are binding on the Muslim community as a whole but which are discharged once a sufficient number of individuals perform them. The recommended act requires a reward for performance but does not involve a punishment for omission. In the permissible, both omission and commission are equally legitimate. The prohibited is an act that entails punishment upon commission. The repugnant act is rewarded when omitted but not punished when committed.

The nature of reward and punishment supports the permeating moral element in Islamic law. Reward is always bestowed in the hereafter; punishment—in rituals and in several other spheres of the law—is nothing but divine punishment to be meted out at the resurrection. As a comprehensive system of law, imbued with religious mores, the rules of the *Shari'a* are not always enforceable.

As a system of legal rights and obligations that governs public and private life, *Shari'a* has always been the dominant law in Islamic societies. No doubt secular organs of justice, such as the early and medieval *mazalim* courts and the QANUN of the Ottoman Empire, have always supplemented *Shari'a*; however, their jurisdiction was confined mainly to administrative and penal law, and they were, more often than not, run by *Shari'a* judges and jurists.

Judges and jurisconsults (*muftis*) have played the central role of developing *Shari'a* since the first century of Islam. Immediately after the death of the Prophet MUHAMMAD in 632 C.E., the Qur'an provided the main source of the law that may be considered Islamic. To be sure, customary Arabian law and the later Umayyad dynasty's administrative practices supplemented Qur'anic legislation, but these were not yet imbued with a religious character. The Prophet's *sunna* (his utterances and idealized practice as expressed in *hadith*) was to gain importance as a source of law only gradually. It was not until the end of Islam's first century (c. 700 C.E.) that his *sunna* became a source of law, supplementing the Qur'an and the still prevailing popular and administrative practices of the Umayyads. Islam's second century (ending c. 800 C.E.) witnessed a gradual yet definite process whereby these practices were idealized as the consensus of the geographical schools—a consensus seen to reflect the ideal practice of the Prophet Muhammad and the early caliphs who succeeded him. Thus imbued with a religious element, these practices, expressed through verbal statements of *hadith*, were gradually and constantly projected back to the earlier generations until they have come to be connected with the Prophet himself. By the beginning of Islam's third century (the ninth century C.E.), the process of back-projection was virtually completed, and the law, now elaborated to its fullness, was recognized to have been exclusively derived from the Qur'an and the *sunna* and sanctioned by the authoritative instrument of consensus (*ijma*).

By the eighth and ninth centuries, the body of *Shari'a* law was elaborated by a variety of legal schools, ranging from those that resorted to free reasoning and expediency in elaborating their positive law—such as the Hanafi Law School—to those standing on the other end of the spectrum, such as the Zahiris, who interpreted the texts literally. Such radical tendencies and their schools, including the Zahiri, soon disappeared; but liberal tendencies were not sufficient to bring the Hanafi school to extinction. Nevertheless, they had to be rationalized and modified to be admitted by mainstream jurisprudence. A classical example of this process of adjustment may be seen in the concept of *istihsan*, which represented to the eighth-century Hanafis a means of formulating law on the basis of practical considerations, without being restricted by the imperatives of the religious texts. Whereas problems of law solved by *istihsan* were largely accepted, even in later centuries, the procedure of *istihsan* had to be, and indeed was, restructured by the likes of Dabusi and Sarakhsi—this was based on the proposition that the *sunna* and the Qur'an were the ultimate sources of the law and that no human intervention can be allowed in the unraveling of divine law.

The Sunni schools of law thus came finally to acknowledge a common legal theory, though differences among them continued to exist—partly as a reflection of the legacy they inherited from their early development within differing geographical schools. Be that as it may, in addition to the Shi'a schools, only four Sunni schools survive and they provide, in effect, a comprehensive system of *Shari'a*.

Shari'a continued to dominate the life of Muslims until the nineteenth century, when, because of influences and pressures from the West, changes in the law were deemed necessary. Formally, the most notable legal change was the introduction of the code system, which was foreign to *Shari'a*, a law based on interpretation of religious doctrine. Substantively, several attempts were made to wholly substitute European codes for a number of *Shari'a* laws. Thus, during the Ottoman Empire, commercial and penal codes based on their French counterparts were promulgated in 1850 and 1858, respectively. A more important codification of this period was the *Majalla* (1876), which represented the first attempt ever to codify Islamic law. Selectively codified, Hanafi law was restricted to contracts, some torts, and a law of procedure. The last part, however, was soon replaced by the *Code of Civil Procedure* (1880), again based on French law.

A more drastic set of reforms was adopted in Egypt in 1875. In addition to new penal, commercial, and procedural codes based on French law, a new court structure was introduced. It incorporated into the Egyptian court system the MIXED COURTS, with a majority of non-Egyptian judges, one of whom presided over the bench.

In 1917, the first attempt at reforming family law was made by the Ottomans, without resorting to European codes. It promulgated the *Ottoman Law of Family Rights,* which regulated matters of personal status and was based on a comprehensive amalgamation of legal doctrines belonging to the Maliki, Shafi'i, and Hanbali law schools, and sometimes weak authorities from the Hanafi school. One of the main concerns in this promulgation was the improvement of the legal status of married women.

Legal reforms, introduced by national legislation, have become an ongoing process in the Muslim states since the beginning of the twentieth century (based on Sunni and Shi'a principles). In these reforms, *Shari'a* law was to some extent preserved in the area of family matters, but even here it was applied in a new system of courts and administered through a modern law of procedure. With these sweeping changes, the officials of the traditional court virtually disappeared, and the traditional role of the *qadi* (judge) has been drastically diminished.

BIBLIOGRAPHY

ANDERSON, NORMAN. *Law Reform in the Muslim World.* London, 1976.

FYZEE, A. A. *Outlines of Muhammadan Law.* Oxford, 1949.

KHADDURI, MAJID, and HERBERT LIEBESNY, eds. *Law in the Middle East.* Washington, D.C., 1955.

SCHACHT, JOSEPH. *An Introduction to Islamic Law.* Oxford, 1979.

———. *The Origins of Muhammadan Jurisprudence.* Oxford, 1975.

SMITH, WILFRED CANTWELL. "The Concept of Shari'a among Some Mutakallimun." In *Arabic and Islamic Studies in Honor of Hamilton A. R. Gibb,* ed. by George Makdisi. Cambridge, U.K., 1965.

Wael B. Hallaq

Shari'ati, Ali [1933–1977]

Iranian Islamic ideologue, whose lectures and writings on secularly educated youth helped prepare the way for the Islamic Revolution of 1978/79.

Shari'ati was born in the village of Mazinan in northeastern Iran but soon moved with his father, Mohammad Taqi Shari'ati, a reformist cleric of Islam, to the city of Mashhad. There he attended high school and teachers' training college as well as pursuing a religious education under the aegis of his father. He then began working as a teacher, studying at the same time at the Mashhad Faculty of Letters and beginning his long career of oppositional activity; his first arrest came in 1957. After a year's delay, he was permitted to travel to Paris in 1960 for his doctoral studies. While in France, he came under the influence of scholars and thinkers, such as Louis Massignon and Jacques Berque, became politically involved in the struggle for Algerian independence and the organization of Iranian students in Europe, and, most importantly, acquired the ideological orientation that was essential to his thought.

Immediately on his return to Iran in 1964, Shari'ati was arrested and detained for several months before being allowed to take up a post at the University of Mashhad. His tenure there was shortlived, and it was outside the academic environment that he exercised the greatest influence. Moving to Tehran, he began lecturing on Islam in a variety of settings, most importantly the Hosayniyeh-ye Ershad, a modernist religious institution established in 1969 that attracted large crowds to its functions. Shari'ati's name became virtually synonymous with the institution, and when it was closed by the government in 1973, he was arrested for a third time. Released in 1975, he spent two years under house arrest in his native village before being allowed to leave for England. He died there on June 19, 1977, soon after his arrival, under circumstances that led to widespread suspicion of involvement by the Iranian secret police. His body was taken to Damascus for burial.

Central to Shari'ati's understanding and presentation of Islam were an emphasis on the social and civilizational functions of religion; an impatience with the niceties and abstractions of traditional Iranian Islamic culture; and a bold if often unconvincing use of themes and terms eclectically derived from non-Islamic sources. His legacy has been varyingly assessed in postrevolutionary Iran, being sometimes denounced for its syncretic nature and its implicitly anticlerical message.

BIBLIOGRAPHY

SHARI'ATI, ALI. *On the Sociology of Islam.* Tr. by Hamid Algar. Berkeley, Calif., 1979.

Hamid Algar

Shariatmadari, Kazem [1904–1986]

One of Iran's most important clerics.

Ayatollah Sayyid Kazem Shariatmadari, born in Azerbaijan, was a MARJA' AL-TAQLID (source of emulation) from 1962 until his death in 1986.

Ayatollah Shariatmadari was not inclined to political activism. But throughout the Pahlavi period, the scholars affiliated with his Center for Islamic Study and Publication rivaled Ayatollah Ruhollah Khomeini's more activist followers. Shariatmadari was briefly imprisoned in 1963, following the June uprisings. In general, he viewed the Pahlavi regime as dictatorial and favored restoration of constitutional rule in Iran. With the triumph of the Islamic Revolution in 1979, Shariatmadari again called for restraint and the rule of law, denouncing the revolutionary tribunals and summary executions of the early days of the revolution. He also confronted the regime on the issue of a referendum to decide the form of the post-Pahlavi state. Rather than a simple vote of yes or no on an Islamic republic, Shariatmadari, as well as most secular parties, supported at the least a choice between an Islamic, democratic, or just simple and plain republic. Shariatmadari was also associated with the Islamic People's Republican party (IPRP), the main contender to Khomeini's Islamic Republican party. The IPRP favored collective rule of the *ulama* (Islamic clergy), a more democratic constitution, and an elected rather than an appointed assembly of experts empowered to draft the constitution of the nascent Islamic republic. The IPRP was dissolved in 1980, over the first presidential elections, a victory for Khomeini and the Islamic Republican party.

Shariatmadari continued to oppose the excesses of the Khomeini regime and, in 1982, was implicated in a coup against the Islamic republic, organized by Sadeq Qotbzadeh, was stripped of his title of marja' al-taqlid, and was placed under house arrest, where he remained a marginal player in the political life of his country until his death in 1986.

BIBLIOGRAPHY

AKHAVI, SHAHROUGH. *Religion and Politics in Contemporary Iran.* Albany, N.Y., 1980.
BAKHASH, SHAUL. *The Reign of the Ayatollahs.* New York, 1986.

Neguin Yavari

Sharif

An Arabic word that literally means "noble" or "illustrious," especially by virtue of one's lineage.

In the first few centuries of the Muslim era, *sharif* (pl., *ashraf* or *shurafa*) was used to refer to members of the prominent Arab families that made up the typically landed aristocracy of the expanding Muslim domains. However, much like its rough equivalent SAYYID, use of sharif as an honorific was gradually limited to scions of the clan of the Prophet Muhammad (i.e., the Banu Hashim), and eventually was further restricted to Muhammad's direct descendants through his grandsons Hasan and Husayn. In Mecca, Medina, and their environs, the custom developed of applying the title sharif almost exclusively to descendants of Hasan. Under Ottoman rule the senior member of the Arabian sharifs was recognized as the semiautonomous governor of Mecca and the keeper of its sacred sanctuary.

Scott Alexander

Sharif, Aziz [1904–]

Iraqi leftist politician.

Born in Ana and educated at Baghdad Law College, Sharif founded the People's party in 1943 and subsequently joined the Communist party. He was a candidate member of its central committee (1958–1963), and secretary-general of the Partisans of Peace, a leftist umbrella organization. Sharif was minister of justice under the Ba'th government (1970–1971) and a key intermediary in the Ba'th–Kurdish negotiations. Sharif served as minister without portfolio until 1976.

Marion Farouk-Sluglett

Sharif, Haram al-

See Temple Mount and Haram al-Sharif

Sharif, Umar [1932–]

Egyptian movie star.

The son of a wealthy merchant of Lebanese descent, Sharif was born Michel Chalhoub on April 10, 1932. Educated at Victoria College in Alexandria, he converted to Islam and changed his name to Umar al-Sharif (Omar Sharif) before making his Egyptian film debut in the film *The Blazing Sun* in 1953. Between 1953 and 1958, he appeared in twenty-four Arabic-language films. Sharif became internationally known after playing a lead role in the film *Lawrence of Arabia,* a part for which he received an Academy Award nomination for best supporting actor. Sharif appeared in many English-language films, including *Doctor Zhivago* and *Funny Girl*.

BIBLIOGRAPHY

KATZ, EPHRAIM. *The Film Encyclopedia.* New York, 1979.

David Waldner

Sharif-Emami, Ja'far [1910–]

Iranian statesman.

Ja'far Sharif-Emami was the son of Hajj Mohammad Hasan (known as Sharif), a member of the religious establishment of Iran who worked as an aide to Sayyid Muhammad Emami, the leader of Friday prayers in Tehran. Sharif-Emami attended college in Germany and worked at the Railroad Office of the Ministry of Roads. In 1943, the British forces accused him of belonging to a German fifth column in Iran and incarcerated him for one year. He was elected to the senate as a deputy from Tehran in 1953 and became minister of industries and mines in 1957 and prime minister in 1960. In 1961 he was made head of the Pahlavi Foundation, the largest corporation in the country, and amassed a great fortune as a consequence. In 1962, he was also appointed speaker of the senate. It was widely believed that Sharif-Emami led the German Freemasonry Lodge in Iran. In an effort to quell the Islamic Revolution by choosing a reformist leader, Mohammad Reza Shah Pahlavi reappointed him premier in the turbulent days of 1978. Sharif-Emami failed in his mandate, however, and the military government of General Gholam Reza Azhari was declared in November 1978. Sharif-Emami left Iran in 1979 and resides in the United States.

BIBLIOGRAPHY

AQELI, BAQER. *Iran's Prime Ministers from Moshir al-Dowleh to Bakhtiyar.* Tehran, 1991.

Neguin Yavari

Sharifian Dynasties

Rulers of Morocco since the sixteenth century, when the modern principle was first established that they be sharifs—descendants of the Prophet Muhammad, founder of Islam.

The cult of the Sharif was introduced in Morocco under Idris II in the early ninth century but went into abeyance. Sharifism became established in Morocco as a response to the crises of the sixteenth century—occasioned by Christian efforts to extend the *reconquista* (reconquest) of the Iberian peninsula into Morocco; large-scale tribal migrations in North Africa; the fragmentation of the Moroccan polity following the decline of the Merinid dynasty; the rise of regional Sufi powers; and the conquest of Algeria in 1517 by the Ottoman Empire.

Both the Sa'dians (1548–1641) and the ALAWI (1668–present) were Alids, and traced their descent

to Muhammad through his son-in-law Ali, but they were Sunni rather than followers of Shi'ism. Both assembled powerful political coalitions that combined tribal solidarities, rural Sufism, and Sharifism. Both rose to power after first securing control over southern Morocco and then conquered the cities and Atlantic plains. Both were responses to the long-term crisis of legitimization caused by the fragmentation of Islam's power in the Maghrib (North Africa) and al-Andalus (Iberian province) and especially to the threat posed by the Spanish and Portuguese, who had driven the Moors from the Iberian peninsula and unified their countries under Catholic monarchs.

The Sa'dians emerged in the period 1514–1548 as opponents of the Portuguese in southern Morocco and revivers of Islam. Under Muhammad al-Shaykh, they defeated the reigning Wattasids, conquered Fez and Marrakech, and stabilized Morocco's frontiers at roughly their present borders. Under Ahmad al-Mansur (1578–1603), the state was reorganized along Ottoman principles, including notably a force of musketeers, financed by the production of sugar for export on royal estates. The conquest of Timbuktu in 1591 briefly gave Morocco direct access to the salt and gold of the sub-Saharan zone. With the help of an alliance with Elizabethan merchant adventurers, the Sa'dians were able to defeat the Iberians and confine them to a few coastal enclaves. Following the death of Ahmad in 1603, the Sa'dians went into a long decline, as the result of dynastic conflict, a resurgence of Iberian threat, and the reemergence of regional power centers of which the *zawiya* (community) of Dila in the Middle Atlas mountains and the Andalusian corsair republic of Sala were the most important.

The rise of the Alawis, cousins of the Sa'dians, took place under Muhammad al-Sharif and Rashid, who were able to defeat the Dila Marabouts and assert their control over Morocco by 1668. The consolidator of the dynasty was Isma'il (1672–1727), a remarkable ruler who by incessant warfare and systematic organization was able to bring the disparate regions of the state under control. Isma'il restructured the army around a contingent of musket-wielding black slaves, defeated the Sufi brotherhoods, and imposed a system of heavy taxation. He expelled foreign occupiers, notably the Spanish from Larache and the British from Tangier. Henceforth, Moroccan sultans styled themselves as "Commander of the Faithful," an implicit claim to the caliphate otherwise also claimed by the Ottomans. Following Isma'il's death, however, the army revolted, and power once again fragmented.

After the turbulent reign of Abd Allah, who was deposed five times between 1727 and 1757, the state was reorganized under Muhammad III (1757–1790),

the architect of "modern," i.e., precolonial, Morocco. By deemphasizing the tax on agricultural produce and increasing trade (and thus customs revenues), Muhammad III provided an alternate basis for the state finances without disturbing the potentially volatile rural populations. The port of Essaouira was founded in 1767 to place the foreign trade of the Atlantic coast of Morocco under government control.

By emphasizing the religious aspects of his leadership as sultan, caliph, and sharif, Muhammad III sought to counter the reassertion of the maraboutic forces in the countryside. By constant diplomatic negotiation with foreign powers and constant bargaining with local authorities, he devised a precarious balance for the Moroccan state. Its dependence upon foreign commerce made it vulnerable to foreign intervention, however, while the absence of a strong army deprived it of any means to reassert its control over the population.

Under Sulayman (1792–1822) and Abd al-Rahman ibn al-Hisham (1822–1859), Morocco entered into a precolonial phase, increasingly dependent upon foreign trade and increasingly vulnerable to European pressure, notably signing after 1856 a series of treaties granting most-favored nation status to leading European powers. In retaliation for Moroccan support of the Algerian resistance leader Abd al-Qadir, Moroccan ports were shelled by the French navy, and a Moroccan army was defeated at Isly in 1844. A war with Spain in 1859–1860 over the city of Tetuan was settled only after Morocco agreed to pay a sizable indemnity and make other concessions.

Hassan I (1873–1894) sought to reverse the decline, with mixed results. His military and administrative reforms failed to survive his death, although his adroit diplomacy managed to buy time for Morocco in the face of rising European imperialist ambitions. His successors Abd al-Aziz and Abd al-Hafid also sought to introduce needed reforms and to play off the European powers, but with less success. The MOROCCAN QUESTION (1900–1912) marks a period of increase in European rivalries over Morocco. In 1912 the Treaty of FES with France and the Spanish–Moroccan accords marked the formal end of Moroccan independence.

The protectorates of France and Spain lasted from 1912 to 1956. During this period, Moroccan sultans Mulay YUSUF (1912–1927) and MUHAMMED V (1927–1961) were formally incorporated into the French colonial administration, their titles confirmed, but their powers largely alienated to the European occupiers and their local Moroccan agents through a factional delegation. With the rise of nationalism in the 1930s and 1940s, Muhammed V began increasingly to show his sympathy for the nationalists. In 1946 he publicly broke with the French and assumed leadership of the nationalist movement.

Since 1956, independent Morocco has continued to be governed by the ALAWITE DYNASTY. The present sultan, Hassan II, assumed power in 1961 upon the death of his father.

BIBLIOGRAPHY

ABUN-NASR, JAMIL. *A History of the Maghrib,* 2nd ed. Cambridge, U.K., 1976.
JULIEN, CHARLES-ANDRÉ. *History of North Africa.* Tr. by John Petrie. London, 1970.
LAROUI, ABDULLAH. *The History of the Maghrib.* Berkeley, Calif., 1975.

Edmund Burke III

Sharifian Revolt

See Arab Revolt

Sharif of Mecca

The local, hereditary rulers of Mecca from about 965 to 1916.

Although the sharifs never enjoyed complete independence from distant powers, their remoteness from the imperial capitals of Cairo and Constantinople (now Istanbul) helped them maintain effective rule in Mecca, as did their claimed descent from the Prophet Muhammad. The last sharif, HUSAYN IBN ALI (1852–1931), tried to establish an independent Arabian kingdom, leading the ARAB REVOLT in 1916 against the Turks in the Hijaz, but he was overthrown by the Saudis in 1925. Founder of the modern Arab Hashimite dynasty, Husayn died in Amman, the capital of his son Abdullah, then ruler of Trans-Jordan (now Jordan). His third son, Faisal I, founded the royal line of Iraq.

BIBLIOGRAPHY

GAURY, GERALD D. *Rulers of Mecca.* London, 1951.

Khalid Y. Blankinship

Sharja

One of the United Arab Emirates.

Sharja is the third largest of the United Arab Emirates (U.A.E.) with an area of one thousand square miles (2,590 sq. km). Most of its 100,000 people live in the capital city of the same name on the Persian/Arabian Gulf coast, just north of Dubai. Three exclaves on the Gulf of Oman coast belong to Sharja and make it the only one of the seven emirates to share borders with all the others. It has the extreme summer heat and aridity of its neighbors, but some agriculture is possible in the Dhaid Oasis and in the exclave territories.

In the late eighteenth and nineteenth centuries Sharja and its northern neighbor, Ra's al-Khayma, formed the most powerful state of the lower Gulf under the al-QASIMI FAMILY, still the ruling clan in each emirate. Subsequently the Qasimi were eclipsed by the Banu Yas tribal confederation of Abu Dhabi—then, as now, led by the Al Nahayyan family. Ra's al-Khayma split from Sharja in 1869 and gained formal British recognition as a separate emirate in 1921. Sharja enjoyed moderate prosperity in the early twentieth century, boosted by the presence of a Royal Air Force base in World War II. After the war, however, its creek became silted and, with the decline of maritime commerce, it lost its position of importance in the lower Gulf. In 1971, Dubai achieved near political parity with Abu Dhabi in the new union; Sharja was given the same status as its poorer neighbor, Ra's al-Khayma. Moreover, on the eve of independence, Iran forced Sharja to agree to shared sovereignty over Sharja's island of Abu Musa, an act that precipitated a coup attempt that killed the ruler, Shaykh Khalid ibn Muhammad.

Although subsequent oil and gas discoveries brought a measure of prosperity, excessive spending in the 1970s brought a downturn in the economy. This was in part responsible for another coup attempt in which Shaykh Abdul Aziz ibn Muhammad tried to overthrow his brother, Shaykh Sultan, who had come to power in 1972 on the death of Khalid.

Since then, the economy has been largely stabilized, and Sharja is developing a modest tourist industry to supplement its other sources of income. Reflecting the academic bent of the ruler, who holds a doctorate from Exeter University, Sharja leads the U.A.E. in the development of literature and the arts. Its press tends to be the most outspoken in the Gulf, and *al-Khaleej* (the Gulf) is the most respected newspaper in the region.

BIBLIOGRAPHY

HEARD-BEY, FRAUKE. *From Trucial States to United Arab Emirates.* New York, 1982.
PECK, MALCOLM C. *The United Arab Emirates: A Venture in Unity.* Boulder, Colo., 1986.

Malcolm C. Peck

Sharm al-Shaykh

Town opposite Tiran island, on the southeastern tip of the Sinai peninsula.

The cove and town of Sharm al-Shaykh control access to the Strait of Tiran from the Sinai peninsula. In 1954, Egypt fortified the cove to block Israeli shipping from the port of Eilat, but in the Arab–Israel War of 1956 it was captured by Israel. A UN emergency force was stationed at Sharm al-Shaykh from 1957 to 1967, when Egypt requested they leave. Its removal in May 1967 precipitated the Arab–Israel War of 1967. Occupied by Israel during that conflict and used as the Israeli naval base of Ophira, the town was returned to Egyptian sovereignty in 1982, after the signing of the Camp David Accords (1979).

BIBLIOGRAPHY

BRAWER, M., ed. *Atlas of the Middle East.* New York, 1988.

SHIMONI, YAACOV, ed. *Political Dictionary of the Middle East in the Twentieth Century.* New York, 1974.

Zachary Karabell

Sharon, Ariel [1928–]

Israeli army commander and politician.

Ariel Sharon was born in Kfar Malal. He joined the Haganah in 1945 and took part in the 1948 Arab–Israel War as a platoon commander and intelligence officer; he fought in Jerusalem and the northern Negev. In 1952, he formed a special commando force geared for retaliatory operations in enemy territory. It set the standard for the elite commando units of the Israel Defense Forces (IDF). In 1954, this unit was integrated into IDF's paratroop divisions, with Sharon as commander. From 1956 onward, Sharon and his paratroopers executed Israel's defense strategy, which entailed inflicting retaliatory actions more severe than the original provocations.

Sharon's performance as military strategist during the 1956 Arab–Israel War earned him a reputation as one of IDF's most brilliant field commanders. At the same time, his military activism made him a controversial figure and drew criticism from his superiors. Sharon was a major general during the 1967 Arab–Israel War, and the unit he commanded won many crucial battles. In 1970, he became commander of the South Command, despite his initial opposition to the Bar-Lev line, a defense system that contravened IDF's preference for mobile armed units. The harsh measures Sharon took in 1971 to suppress Palestinian commando activity in the Gaza Strip were met with disapproval by some Israelis.

After retiring from the army in June 1972, Sharon was influential in establishing the Likud party. He was back in uniform for the 1973 Arab–Israel War, during which he led Israeli forces in penetrating Egyptian defenses to cross the Suez Canal. During this period, in a bitter dispute with the military chief command over tactics, he was accused of insubordination but was not relieved of his command because of his reputation as a military leader and because of political considerations. Elected in December 1973 to the Knesset, he resigned after a year to accept an appointment with the IDF. From June 1975 to March 1976, he served as Prime Minister Yitzhak Rabin's special adviser on terrorism. He founded a new political party, Shlomzion, which gained two Knesset seats in the 1977 elections; shortly thereafter, he rejoined the Likud party, which had won the elections, and was appointed agricultural minister.

Sharon was a determined supporter of increased Jewish settlements in the occupied territories and of Gush Emunim. He opposed the peace treaty reached with Egypt in 1977, and yet he favored returning Sinai and initiated and administered the destruction of the Jewish settlements there. In 1981, he was appointed defense minister in Prime Minister Menachem Begin's government. He planned and led Israel's war in Lebanon, which began in June 1982, and was thought to be responsible for extending the war's objectives far beyond those originally proclaimed by the government. The Kahan Commission concluded that Sharon was culpable for not preventing the murders at the Sabra and Shatila refugee camps in Lebanon. As a consequence, he was forced to resign the defense ministry but allowed to remain as a member of Begin's cabinet. In 1984, and again in 1988, he was appointed minister of industry and trade in the National Unity government led by Prime Minister Yitzhak Shamir. A libel claim he filed against *Time* magazine led to the court's conclusion that there had been no grounds for accusing him of endorsing the Phalangists' mass killing of civilians in the refugee camps. The jury nevertheless found that the article had been published without malicious intent, so Sharon was not awarded the fifty million dollars in compensation he had sought.

One of the most controversial politicians in Israel, Sharon is considered by some people to be a brilliant commander and statesman. He is objectionable to other people because of what they term his "dictatorial tendencies." He regards Jordan as the "Palestinian state" and believes that Gaza and the West Bank should be annexed to Israel. Some observers contend, however, that he lacks any ideological basis for his public rejection of territorial concessions, and that he would support pragmatic steps for ending Arab–Israeli conflicts.

BIBLIOGRAPHY

BENZIMAN, UZI. *An Israeli Caesar.* Tr. by Louis Roussol. New York, 1985.

HILMI, ANSMAR. *Sharon, malik al-irhab.* Amman, 1987.

SHAVIT, MATY. *Arik: The Commando's Commander.* Tel Aviv, 1969. In Hebrew.

Yaakov Shavit

Sharqawi, Abd al-Rahman al- [1920–1987]

Egyptian novelist and playwright.

A graduate of the Law School in Cairo, Egypt, al-Sharqawi is one of the most important dramatists of the postwar generation of Egyptian realists. His work is characterized by social and political commitment to the popular struggle against corrupt rulers, landlords, and foreign invaders. His novel *al-Ard* (The Earth), published in 1954, depicts village life in the 1930s and the struggle of peasants against oppression. The novel was made into a film directed by Yusuf Shahin.

BIBLIOGRAPHY

BECKA, JIRI, ed. *Dictionary of Oriental Literatures.* Vol. 3, *West Asia and North Africa.* New York, 1974.

David Waldner

Sharqi, Hamad ibn Muhammad al-

Ruler of Fujayra.

Shaykh Hamad ibn Muhammad, a member of the Sharqi family, was minister of agriculture and fisheries in the first cabinet of the United Arab Emirates in December 1971. He was proclaimed ruler of Fujayra emirate and member of the Supreme Federal Council of the United Arab Emirates on September 18, 1974, after his father's death. During his reign, Fujayra has enjoyed a modern renaissance.

BIBLIOGRAPHY

MORSY, MUHAMMAD A. *The United Arab Emirates.* London, 1978.

Persian Gulf Gazette and Supplements, 1953–1972. London, 1987.

M. Morsy Abdullah

Sharqi Family, al-

Ruling family of the Emirate of Fujayra, one of the United Arab Emirates.

The ruling family of the Sharqiyyin tribe inhabits both the al-Hajar (al-Hijr) mountains and the coastal region of the Shimailiyya district on the Gulf of Oman. This warlike tribe dominates the main passes of Wadi Ham and Wadi al-Qur. The port city of Fujayra is the family seat.

The family began as a member of the Qasimi federation, but because they had different tribal politics and a different religious attitude, they were inclined toward independence. In this they had the backing of the shaykh of Abu Dhabi, who later founded the United Arab Emirates.

Shaykh Hamad ibn Abdullah (1870–1932) began to lead a series of revolts in 1870 and became the founder of the Fujayra independence movement. The British, who had a nineteenth-century protectorate in the Gulf based on treaties with the shaykhs, denied the independence of Fujayra in 1903. Shaykh Muhammad ibn Hamad (1932–1974) continued his father's independence movement, however, and the British recognized Fujayra's independence in 1951. In 1952, he joined the Trucial States Council; in 1971, when the British withdrew, he joined the United Arab Emirates. His son Hamad succeeded him in 1974.

BIBLIOGRAPHY

HEARD BEY, FRAUKE. *From Trucial States to United Arab Emirates.* New York, 1982.

MORSY, MUHAMMAD A. *The United Arab Emirates.* New York, 1978.

REICH, BERNARD, ed. *Political Leaders of the Contemporary Middle East and North Africa.* New York, 1990.

M. Morsy Abdullah

Sharqiya

An Egyptian delta province (governorate).

Located in Egypt's delta, Sharqiya has a land area of 1,615 square miles (4,180 sq. km) and a 1986 population estimated at about 3.5 million. Its capital is Zagazig (al-Zaqaziq).

BIBLIOGRAPHY

Europa World Yearbook, 1994, vol. 1. London, 1994, p. 1024.

Arthur Goldschmidt, Jr.

SHAS

Israeli political party founded in 1984 to better represent ultraorthodox Sephardim.

SHAS, an acronym that means Sephardi Torah Guardians, is a religious Zionist party, begun by disaffected Sephardim of AGUDAT ISRAEL. It was led initially by ultraorthodox Ashkenazic Rabbi Eliezer Schach. When he made a speech in 1990 that Sephardim considered humiliating, SHAS was taken over by followers of former Sephardic Chief Rabbi Ovadiah Yosef, who is also considered one of Israel's leading Sephardi Torah scholars. SHAS won four Knesset seats in 1984, six in 1988, and six in 1992. It held the Ministry of Interior portfolio in the National Unity government of 1984, and SHAS deputy Aryeh Deri received the same post when SHAS became the only religious party to join the coalition led by the Labor party following the 1992 election.

Walter F. Weiker

Shashlik

Grilled lamb on a skewer.

Shashlik is a Turkish dish of marinated lamb. The marinade usually consists of onions, olive oil, and paprika. The lamb is skewered and grilled and served with scallions.

Clifford A. Wright

Shatt al-Arab

The narrow waterway that forms the southern border between Iran and Iraq.

Shatt al-Arab, or Arvandrud, as known in some Iranian sources, provides Iraq with its only means of access to the Gulf. Issues of joint sovereignty over the waterway have long been a source of hostility between Iran and Iraq. In 1975, the Algiers Accords were signed by Mohammad Reza Shah Pahlavi of Iran and Vice President Saddam Hussein of Iraq, demarcating the THALWEG LINE along the Shatt al-Arab as the border between the two states. In September 1980, Iraq launched an offensive against the Islamic Republic of Iran and professed as one of its intentions to restore the Shatt al-Arab to sole Iraqi sovereignty.

BIBLIOGRAPHY

PELLETIERE, STEPHEN C. *The Iran-Iraq War: Chaos in a Vacuum.* New York, 1992.

Neguin Yavari

Sha'ul, Anwar   [1904–1984]

Iraqi writer and journalist.

Sha'ul was born into a Jewish family in the city of al-Hilla in southern Iraq; they moved to Baghdad when he was in his early teens. He studied at the Alliance Israélite Universelle and later obtained a law degree. Between 1924 and 1938 he was a journalist, first editing the Jewish weekly *al-Misbah* (the Lantern) and in 1929 launching his own weekly magazine, *al-Hasid* (the Reaper).

Sha'ul's knowledge of foreign languages enabled him to translate literary works from English and French. A volume of original and translated fiction appeared in 1922 under the title *al-Hisad al-Awwal* (The First Harvest). It was followed in 1955 by *Fi Ziham al-Madina* (In the Crowded City) and in 1956 by a volume of poetry, *Hamasat al-Zaman* (Whispers of Time).

Sha'ul stayed in Iraq after the mass exodus of its Jewish community in 1951 and 1952. In 1971 he left Baghdad and settled in Kiron, near Tel Aviv. In 1981 he published his collected poetry in *Wa Bazagha Fajr Jadid* (And a New Dawn Has Risen). He also published an autobiography, *Qissat Hayati fi Wadi al-Rafidayn* (My Life in Mesopotamia), in 1980.

BIBLIOGRAPHY

SOMEKH, SASSON. "Lost Voices: Jewish Authors in Modern Arabic Literature." In *Jews and Arabs: Contacts and Boundaries,* ed. by Mark R. Cohen and Abraham L. Udovitch. Princeton, N.J., 1989.

Sasson Somekh

Shawarma

A lamb-based meatloaf sold by street vendors and in restaurants.

Shawarma is a popular Levantine Arab specialty. A combination of lean and fatty sliced or ground lamb is seasoned with onion, garlic, allspice, cinnamon, coriander, or other ingredients and molded in conical form around a large skewer that is adjusted to a vertical rotisserie. The outside becomes crusty brown as it cooks, is sliced off and wrapped in flat bread and served with chopped onions, tomatoes, and cucumber-yogurt sauce. Shawarma is also popular in Greece and Turkey where it is called *gyro* and *döner kebab,* respectively. Shawarma is sold by street vendors and restaurants but rarely made at home.

Clifford A. Wright

Shaw Commission

A British commission of inquiry into a 1929 disturbance in Palestine.

A commission of inquiry, led by Sir Walter Shaw, was sent to Palestine by the British government to investigate the August 1929 WAILING WALL DISTURBANCES, which caused the deaths of 249 Jews and Arabs. The commission's report, issued in March 1930, stated that the fundamental cause of the political violence was "the Arab feeling of animosity and hostility towards the Jews consequent upon the disappointment of their political and national aspirations and fear for their economic future." The Palestinians feared that by "Jewish immigration and land purchases they may be deprived of their livelihood and placed under the economic domination of the Jews." The commission's report called for an explicit policy regulating land and immigration that would have, in effect, curtailed the Zionist program in Palestine. The British government, however, postponed consideration of any change in policy until after another commission, which it appointed in May 1930 under Sir John Hope-Simpson, had studied land settlement, immigration, and development.

BIBLIOGRAPHY

PALESTINE GOVERNMENT. *A Survey of Palestine for the Information of the Anglo-American Committee of Inquiry.* 2 vols. Jerusalem, 1946. Reprint, Washington, D.C., 1991.
SMITH, CHARLES D. *Palestine and the Arab–Israel Conflict.* New York, 1988.

Philip Mattar

Shawkat, Naji   [1891–?]

Iraqi government official in the 1920s and 1930s.

Naji Shawkat, brother of Sami Shawkat (prime minister of Iraq for six months in 1932/33), was born in Baghdad. After fighting in the armies of the Ottoman Empire and the Sharifian dynasty in World War I, Shawkat returned to Iraq. He served frequently as minister of interior in the 1920s and 1930s, but his political career ended when he sided with Rashid Ali al-Kaylani in 1941.

Peter Sluglett

Shawkat, Sami   [1893–?]

Iraqi prime minister for six months in 1932/33.

Sami Shawkat, brother of Naji Shawkat, was born in Baghdad in what is now Iraq. Director general of education several times in the 1930s, Shawkat was an ardent pan-Arab nationalist and militarist (see his polemic, "The Profession of Death"), who advocated shedding blood for one's country. His tract *Hadhihi Ahdafuna* (These Are Our Aims) was published in 1939.

Peter Sluglett

Shawqi, Ahmad   [1868–1932]

Egyptian poet and author.

Shawqi was born in Cairo into a prominent family of mixed Arab, Turkish, Greek, and Kurdish extraction, and educated in Egypt where he graduated from law school. He wrote three historical novels glorifying ancient Egypt and Persia, the first appearing in 1897. His poetry, collected in the three-volume *Shawqiyat,* was in the classical tradition, characterized by extensive imagery, incisive expression, and rhythmic sensitivity. Known as the "prince of poets," Shawqi's support for the royal family led his critics to dub him "poet of the princes."

BIBLIOGRAPHY

BECKA, JIRI, ed. *Dictionary of Oriental Literatures.* Vol. 3, *West Asia and North Africa.* New York, 1974.

David Waldner

Shawwaf, Abd al-Wahhab al-   [1916–1959]

Lieutenant colonel in Iraq's army.

Shawwaf joined the clandestine Free Officers organization in 1956. After the overthrow of the monarchy in July 1958, he was appointed commander of the Fifth Brigade, stationed in Mosul. Offended at his exclusion from political influence, he began to plot against the regime of Abd al-Karim Kassem. In March 1959, Shawwaf led a revolt against Kassem. He was killed during the revolt, which failed.

BIBLIOGRAPHY

DANN, URIEL. *Iraq under Qassem.* Jerusalem, 1969.

Michael Eppel

Shaykh

A general title of respect.

The term *shaykh* (also sheikh), can be applied to an elderly man, a tribal chief, a ruler of a shaykhdom

Marsh Arab shaykh in Iraq, 1942. (D.W. Lockhard)

thority to issue a formal legal opinion (*fatwa*). In fact, although the more elitist, quasi-official usage of this title has continued into the modern period (particularly in the form of posthumous conferral), the later medieval and early modern periods witnessed an increasingly widespread attachment of the title to official positions in state-controlled judicial administrations. The office of Shaykh al-Islam seems to have reached its apex as part of the Ottoman imperial establishment. By the time of Süleyman I (ruled 1520–1566), the chief jurisconsult of Constantinople (now Istanbul) was designated as the unique Shaykh al-Islam and recognized as the highest-ranking and most powerful member of the extensive imperial judiciary with exclusive direct access to the sultan himself. In 1916, however, the Committee for Union and Progress transferred much of the power of the former Ottoman Shaykh al-Islam to a secular Ministry of Justice, and by 1924 the new Turkish republic completely abolished the office. It is important to note that the office of Shaykh al-Islam has been much more widely and systematically instituted in Twelver Shi'a contexts than in Sunni contexts. It was first introduced into the Iranian Shi'a judicial system by the Safavid Shah Abbas I (ruled 1588–1629) and remains today the official title of the presidents of municipal religious courts in the Shi'a communities of Iran and the former Soviet Union.

Scott Alexander

along the Persian Gulf, a village chief, a religious scholar, a senator, or a Sufi master. The early caliphs were known as shaykhs. Shaykh al-Islam was the title given to the chief mufti (jurist) of the Ottoman Empire, who had direct access to the sultan and served as the highest-ranking legal administrator.

Marilyn Higbee

Shaykh al-Islam

Honorary title for Muslim jurists.

Shaykh al-Islam (literally, Elder of Islam) is an honorific title that has been historically applied to prominent Muslim jurists, theologians, and spiritual masters in recognition of outstanding knowledge and/or piety. In the early medieval period (c. 800–1200), the title was quasi-official and conferred on an elite few through acclamation by disciples or peers. Over time, however, the title was adopted by certain highly trained jurists (i.e., muftis, or "jurisconsults"), who could legitimately claim the au-

Shaykhi

Follower of Shaykh Ahmad al-Ahsa'i (1853–1826), a Twelver Shi'ite Islamic thinker who emphasized the esoteric and intuitional aspects of the religion.

Shaykh Ahmad personally cultivated religious followers in al-Hasa in eastern Arabia, Bahrain, Basra and Karbala in Iraq, as well as in Yazd and Kermanshah in Iran. A separate school of Shi'ism did not coalesce around his name until after his death, when he was succeeded by Sayyid Kazim Rashti (died 1844) in Karbala; for a time it seemed possible that esoteric Shaykhism would emerge as the major alternative to the scholastic orthodoxy of the Usuli school of Shi'a Islam.

After Rashti's death, though many Shaykhis became BABIS, important Shaykhi communities continued to exist in eastern Arabia and Basra, and in Kerman, Milan, and Tabriz. The Tabriz Shaykhis diminished their doctrinal and ritual differences with the majority Usuli school, and under the leadership of Thiqat al-Islam played a progressive role during Iran's Constitutional Revolution (1905–1911). The

Kerman Shaykhis, led by Karim Khan Kermani (1810–1871) and his descendants, retained more unabashedly the esoteric doctrines of al-Ahsa'i. Some among the Qajar nobility showed an interest in Shaykhism, and Mozaffar al-Din Shah (reigned 1896–1906) converted to this school. Karim Khan was a Qajar noble and a landed magnate; his branch of Shaykhism proved socially and politically conservative and was often supported by Kerman governors related to him. This privileged position helped provoke Shaykhi–Usuli riots in 1905.

In the twentieth century, Shaykhism became marginalized, as a sectarian group within Twelver Shi-'ism, and Shaykhis suffered some persecution under the Islamic Republic of Iran after 1979.

BIBLIOGRAPHY

BAYAT, MANGOL. *Mysticism and Dissent: Socioreligious Thought in Qajar Iran.* Syracuse, N.Y., 1982.
NICOLAS, A. L. M. *Essai sur la chéikhisme,* 4 vols. Paris, 1910–1914.

Juan R. I. Cole

Shazar, Shneour Zalman   [1898–1974]

Third Israeli president.

Shazar's last name is actually an acronym for Shneour Zalman Rubashov, his original name. Shazar was born in Minsk, Russia, and raised in Stabsty where he was educated in a Habad Heder, a Lubovitch Hasidic school. He joined the Po'ale Zion (Labor Zionist) movement in 1905. In 1911, Shazar went to Palestine for the first time and worked on Kibbutz Merhavia, but he did not emigrate there until 1924. He became a member of the Secretariat of the Histadrut (General Federation of Labor) and was on the editorial board of its newspaper, *Davar.*

In 1947, he served as a member of the Jewish Agency delegation to the United Nations. After statehood Shazar ran and was elected on the MAPAI (Labor) list for the Knesset in 1949 and served there until 1957. He was appointed to be the minister of education and culture in 1949, and two years later he became a member of the executive of the Jewish Agency. In 1963 he was elected Israel's third president, to succeed Yizhak Ben-Zvi, and served two terms.

BIBLIOGRAPHY

WINER, GERSHON. *The Founding Fathers of Israel.* New York, 1971.

Bryan Daves

Shazli, Sa'd al-Din

Egyptian military officer and opposition politician.

Shazli was educated at Cairo University and the Military and Staff colleges in Cairo, and received training at the infantry school at Fort Benning in the United States. Shazli was chief of staff of Egyptian armed forces during the 1973 Arab–Israel War. Shazli broke with President Anwar al-Sadat over Sadat's 1977 peace initiative with Israel, and was sent as ambassador to the United Kingdom and to Portugal. In 1978, he called for the overthrow of Sadat. In 1980, he went into exile in Algeria, where he formed an opposition party. Shazli has published books on military strategy and the Arab–Israeli conflict.

BIBLIOGRAPHY

Who's Who in the Arab World, 1990–1991. Beirut, 1991.

David Waldner

Sheba

Ancient pre-Islamic trading state of South Arabia.

Based in Marib, Sheba (also Saba) sat astride the frankincense trail on the edge of the desert a short distance after it turned north toward the Najran oasis and the rich markets of the ancient world. The great prosperity and strength of Sheba, which probably reached its peak between 500 and 200 B.C.E., was based on its control of the passage of trade and on its extensive system of irrigated agriculture, which in turn was based upon the huge, fabled Marib Dam. Although Ethiopians and some scholars dispute this, Saba is almost certainly biblical Sheba, the fabled queen of which was Bilqis (or Balkis). If Bilqis is the Queen of Sheba, she did more than woo and win Solomon. Unlike the leaders of neighboring Main, who focused on the development and protection of the trade routes, Saba and its Sabaeans were vigorously expansionist. For about a century around 400 B.C.E., the five major Yemeni trading states were united under a single Sabaean regime. Karib il-Watar was the king who first extended Saba's hegemony over the neighboring states.

Robert D. Burrowes

Shekel

Name of Israeli currency.

Until 1970, the Israeli currency was called the lira or pound. In 1984, following a steep devaluation, the name of the currency was changed to the new Israeli shekel (NIS).

The word *shekel* derives from biblical times, when coins were called shekels. *Shekel* was the term used by leaders of the Zionist movement to denote the price of membership. For the purpose of designating this cost of membership, attendees at the First Zionist Congress pegged the shekel to a fixed rate of certain major Western currencies.

Bryan Daves

Sheli

See Avneri, Uri

Shemer, Naomi

Israeli singer and songwriter.

Educated at the Academy of Music in Jerusalem, Shemer is most noted for the song "Yerusalayim shel Zahav" (Jerusalem of Gold), which she wrote just before the 1967 Arab–Israel War when Israel captured the Old City of Jerusalem. Israelis quickly adopted the song as a national anthem.

Bryan Daves

Shenhar, Yitzhak   [1902–1957]

Hebrew writer.

Yitzhak Shenhar was born in Ukraine and became active in the He-Halutz movement before moving to Palestine in 1921. He published his first poetry in 1924 and held a number of manual labor jobs until he began his literary career. In the 1930s, he worked as a writer, editor, and translator for the Schocken publishing house. He wrote short stories and poems about the life of Jews in Eastern Europe and in Palestine.

Bryan Daves

Shenouda III   [1923–   ]

Patriarch of the Coptic Orthodox Church since 1971.

Few Coptic patriarchs have had as much experience in both secular and ecclesiastical affairs prior to their election as Shenouda III (born Nazir Jayyid). A graduate of Cairo University and the Egyptian Reserve Officers' School, Shenouda took part in military actions against Israel in 1948. He received a bachelor of divinity degree in 1950 from the Coptic Orthodox Theological Seminary. Within the church, he was successively a monk, a secretary to Cyril VI, and a bishop. As a bishop, Shenouda was a professor of Old Testament studies at the Coptic seminary and editor of its magazine. He has been a prolific writer for both the popular and theological press. Shenouda is the highest-ranking cleric of the Coptic Orthodox Church, which represents the largest denomination of Christianity in the Middle East.

Shenouda was one of more than fifteen hundred Muslims and Christians who were accused by President Anwar al-Sadat in September 1981 of "sectarian sedition," that is, alleged extremist religious activity. Exiled and replaced by a council of five bishops, Shenouda fled to the monastery of Anba Bishoi in the Wadi Natrun, a desert area northwest of Cairo. Despite Sadat's description of Shenouda as "the most dangerous man in Egypt," the worst complaint actually leveled against the patriarch was that he "want[ed] to be a political leader of the Copts and [to] achieve certain personal objectives."

The reasons for Shenouda's arrest and exile in September 1981 remain unclear. Although religious turmoil had increased in the late 1970s and early 1980s, primarily on the part of Muslims dissatisfied with Sadat's historic peace treaty with Israel at the 1978 Camp David Accords, many of Sadat's charges went unproven, including those against Shenouda. Sadat's actions were widely regarded as a thin disguise for silencing his political opponents. Although some people punished by Sadat were employed in religious professions, such as the Coptic and Muslim clergies, and thus superficially gave credence to his allegations, others had secular occupations—lawyers, writers, journalists, broadcasters, politicians—and appear to have been guilty of no crime more severe than disagreeing with the president. Sadat also used the occasion to proscribe several religious and political publications that had been critical of him.

Sadat's actions may have been a delayed response to the protest that Shenouda lodged in September 1977 against a proposed imposition of Islamic jurisprudence (*Shariʿa*) on all aspects of Egyptian life. The proposal would have made apostasy—in this case, the abandonment of Islam—a capital offense. Shenouda had worried about the potentially troublesome applications of the law for Egyptian Christians and other non-Muslims. At the very least, it would have diminished even further the lowly social position of the COPTS. Shenouda was temporarily successful, and the recommendation was withdrawn. (*Shariʿa* was reintroduced, however, in 1980.) Because Muslim fundamentalists then unleashed a murderous round of terror against the Copts, Shenouda ordered a series of demonstrations that enraged many Muslims and later served as "proof" of the patriarch's political agenda. Shenouda's repeated requests for a meeting with the president were to no avail. Consequently, in 1981 the patriarch refused to accept the government's Easter greeting and humiliated Sadat, who supposedly used the September detentions as revenge.

Some Copts believed that Shenouda's dismissal was a political move to balance Sadat's incarceration of many Muslims. By another explanation, during a 1980 meeting between Sadat and U.S. President Ronald Reagan in Washington, D.C., a group of Coptic expatriates staged a protest, which Sadat blamed on Shenouda. No connection was proved.

The censure of Shenouda for "sectarian sedition" was both ironic and unfortunate. Although he has been a vigorous, even aggressive, defender of the Coptic Church and has not hesitated to take action against Muslim fundamentalists, he has never been antagonistic toward Islam per se. Throughout his career, he has been sympathetic to Muslim causes and to Egyptian national interests. Some of his theological writings, particularly his important 1967 work *Al-Khalas fi al-mafhum al-Urthuduksi* (Salvation in Orthodox Understanding), are as critical of aspects of Protestantism as of Islamic fundamentalism. Shenouda has specifically denounced the intrusion of religion into political affairs. A major result of his historic meeting with the Roman Catholic Pope Paul VI in May 1973, the first visit by an Egyptian patriarch to his Roman counterpart since 325, was a joint statement of concern about the Palestinian problem in the West Bank. In November 1977, Shenouda sent Sadat a message of confidence for his forthcoming peace talks with Israeli officials. In May 1986, Shenouda sent a representative to the funeral of a leader of the fundamentalist group the Muslim Brotherhood.

Shenouda's plight improved slowly after Sadat's assassination on October 6, 1981. However, on April 12, 1983, an administrative court upheld Sadat's actions against Shenouda and ordered the Coptic Orthodox Church to hold a new papal election; not until January 2, 1985, did Shenouda regain his office, thanks to a decree by President Husni Mubarak.

BIBLIOGRAPHY

FERNANDEZ, ALBERTO M. *The Coptic Orthodox Salvation Theology of Anba Shenuda III*. Master's thesis, University of Arizona, 1983.
HIRST, DAVID, and IRENE BEESON. *Sadat*. London, 1981.
New York Times. Various articles dated September 15, 1977; September 3 and 8, 1981; October 11, 1981.
PENNINGTON, J. D. "The Copts in Modern Egypt." *Middle Eastern Studies* 18 (1982): 158–179.

Donald Spanel

Shepheard's Hotel

British gathering place in Cairo from 1841 to 1952.

In 1841 a British farmer's son named Samuel Shepheard built Shepheard's Hotel in Cairo. As Britain became more involved with the finances of khedival Egypt and especially after the establishment of an informal British protectorate in 1882, Shepheard's became the center of British social life in Cairo. Renovated in 1891, 1899, 1904, 1909, and 1927, the hotel was famous for its opulence.

British officers and administrators often retired to the bar at Shepheard's at the end of the day, and the Moorish Hall attracted tourists from Europe and America. After World War II, the relationship between Britain and Egypt deteriorated and, on Saturday, January 26, 1952, riots erupted in Cairo, which led to the destruction of numerous British and foreign establishments. Singled out by the crowd for particular attention was Shepheard's Hotel. The hotel was destroyed in an explosion, and although rebuilt on another site in 1957, it never regained its former stature.

BIBLIOGRAPHY

HOPWOOD, DEREK. *Egypt*. London, 1987.

Zachary Karabell

Sheshbesh

One of several names for a board game, known in the West as backgammon, played with two dice and thirty pieces (fifteen per side).

Sheshbesh pieces are usually black for one player and white for the other. The origins of the game are obscure; while some experts argue for its invention in Persia, others suggest that it originated in southwest Asia. In 1927, Sir Leonard Wooley discovered a board game in the ruined city of Ur that was marked off into elaborately inlaid squares (twenty in all) accompanied by two sets of dice and two sets of discs, seven white and seven black. This places sheshbesh variants in Sumeria as early as 2600 B.C.E. Although it is not known how this game was played, experts assume that movement of the pieces over the board was governed by rolling the dice. The Ur game appears somewhat related to modern ludo, which in turn is related to backgammon.

The traditional game consists of balancing the elements of skill and chance while playing on a board marked with twenty-four chevrons in alternating colors of black and white. The pieces, fifteen to a player, are arranged on the trays according to a specific pattern, or are held off the board. Entry or movement begins according to the roll of the dice. The pieces move the full distance around the board in a race to the home tray, and are then borne off. Most commonly, players try to prevent and delay one's opponent from bearing off. If a hit has been made the player will attempt to block the entry of the piece by making homes—covering a chevron with a minimum of two pieces.

Shesbesh is known by a large variety of names. These include *takht-e nard* in Iran, *plakato* and *tawali* in Greece, *tric-trac* in France and Germany, *tables reales* in Italy and Spain, *mahbuseh, yahudiya farangiya,* or *tawla al-Zahr* in Syria and Arabia, and *boola* in Egypt.

BIBLIOGRAPHY

GROSVENOR, N. *Modern Backgammon.* New York, 1928.

Cyrus Moshaver

Shi'a National Resistance Movement

Shi'a militias in southern Lebanon.

The member militias of the movement launch military attacks against Israelis and their allies in the Israel-occupied part of southern Lebanon. Their activities have forced the government of Lebanon to spare the Party of God (Hizbullah) from its disarmament campaigns. The Party of God, the backbone of the resistance, has used the issue of Israel's occupation of southern Lebanon as its rallying cry.

As'ad AbuKhalil

Shiberghan

City in northern Afghanistan.

The capital of the Afghan province of Jowzjan, Shiberghan is located about eighty miles (129 km) west of Mazar-e Sharif. The city has a population of about 15,000 inhabitants and is in a predominantly Uzbek area, although the city itself has a sizable Turkoman and Tajik population. After natural gas was discovered in 1931, Shiberghan was developed into a modern city, with the help of Soviet workers. The Soviet workers left when the Soviet Union withdraw from Afghanistan in 1989.

BIBLIOGRAPHY

ADAMEC, LUDWIG. *Historical Dictionary of Afghanistan.* Metuchen, N.J., 1991.

Grant Farr

Shidyaq, Ahmad Faris al-   [1804–1887]

Lebanese writer, linguist, and literary critic who played a leading role in the Arabic literary revival of the mid-to-late nineteenth century.

A Maronite who converted to Protestantism in 1826 after witnessing the Maronite clergy's persecution of his brother As'ad, Faris al-Shidyaq was sent to Egypt by the American Protestant missionaries in Lebanon so that he could pursue his studies in Cairo. From 1834 to 1848, he taught at the American Protestant mission school in Malta, undertook a new Arabic translation of the Bible, and edited the publications of the American press there. For several years afterward, he traveled widely through Europe and the Near East, and worked as editor of the official Tunisian journal *al-Ra'id al-Tunisi* between 1854 and 1860. He converted to Islam during his stay in Tunis and adopted the name Ahmad Faris. In 1860, he relocated to Istanbul at the invitation of the Ottoman authorities. While there, he undertook his most important project: the publication of the Arabic-language newspaper *al-Jawa'ib,* a mouthpiece for OTTOMANISM which soon became a leading forum for the discussion of the political and cultural issues of the time and can be considered a pioneer of modern Arabic journalism. In addition to the many pieces of literary criticism that he wrote for this journal and others, Ahmad Faris al-Shidyaq is also remembered for his own writings in prose and verse and for his travel writing. A writer whose influence was felt throughout the region, he was one of the architects of modern literary Arabic.

BIBLIOGRAPHY

SALIBI, KAMAL. *The Modern History of Lebanon.* New York, 1965.
SHARABI, HISHAM. *Arab Intellectuals and the West.* Baltimore and London, 1970.

Guilain P. Denoeux

Shihab

See under Chehab

Shi'ism

Branch of Islam that traces its leadership to Ali ibn Abi Talib, cousin of Muhammad.

Shi'ites constitute the largest Islamic community after that of Sunni Islam, numbering close to 90 million worldwide. Iran is the only predominantly

Shi'a country; significant Shi'a minorities exist in Iraq, India, Pakistan, Afghanistan, Yemen, Kuwait, Bahrain, eastern Saudi Arabia, Lebanon, and various Western countries. Shi'ism rests on a belief that the right of succession to political and religious leadership of the community belongs solely to the Prophet Muhammad's cousin, Ali ibn Abi Talib, and his progeny. The Prophet was first succeeded by three of his companions—Abu Bakr, Umar, and Uthman—who ruled successively (632–656).

Origins. The assassination of Uthman in 656 opened a split in the Islamic community. Soon after the accession of Ali to the caliphate, Mu'awiya, governor of Syria, kinsman of Uthman, and among the last generation of companions of the Prophet, declared his opposition to Ali's leadership. His opposition soon gained support among tribal groups in Syria and Mesopotamia. In response, Ali moved the Islamic capital to Kufa (in southern Iraq) and engaged Mu'awiya in a protracted rivalry that ended in an armistice known as *al-Tahkim,* which left Mu'awiya sovereign in Syria, Egypt, and northern Mesopotamia, while Ali ruled the Arabian peninsula and the east. Those who supported Ali were known as Shi'at Ali (the partisans of Ali); hence the name Shi'ism. Ali was assassinated in 661; subsequently, Mu'awiya consolidated his rule over the territories formerly under Ali and moved to make the line of political succession that of his family, the Umayyads.

Ali had two sons, Hasan and Husayn, from his marriage to the Prophet's daughter, Fatima. They quickly inherited Ali's leadership and attracted the loyalty of the Shi'ites. Exasperated by the political deadlock, Hasan abandoned his claim to succession, leaving Mu'awiya free to extend his control. Mu'awiya was succeeded in 680 by his son Yazid, who lacked the political acumen of his father. Yazid's hereditary route to power upset an Islamic community accustomed to a strong consultative element in political election and viewing senior companions of the Prophet as worthier candidates to rule.

In 680, the residents of Kufa invited Husayn, who lived in Medina, to assert his right to succeed his father, and pledged to support him. Husayn left Medina with his family and close associates, but before he could reach Kufa, an Umayyad force attacked and killed him and most of his family. This unprovoked attack on the youngest of the Prophet's grandchildren increased opposition to the Umayyads. The cause of Shi'ism then expanded to include other branches of the larger family of the Prophet, the Banu Hashim, or Hashimites. There were a number of Hashimite revolts, primarily in Iraq and the east. Pivotal revolts were those of Zayd ibn Ali ibn al-

Husayn in Kufa (743), and of his son Yahya in Transoxania. Zayd's movement formed an early current of Shi'ism espousing political activity to further the Alid cause, and did not restrict the imamate to one particular branch of the Alid family. (The Zaydi sect still survives in Yemen.)

In 750 a broadly based movement originating in Khorasan toppled the Umayyad caliphate. Succession to the caliphate passed to the Abbasids, a Hashimite branch named after Abbas, an uncle of the Prophet. Feeling betrayed, the Alids staged several revolts, the most notable of which was the one in Medina by Muhammad al-Nafs al-Zakiyya (762), a descendant of Hasan. By then, however, the Abbasids had consolidated their control.

Theology. Shi'ism originated as a political movement supporting the rights of Ali to the caliphate. Since leadership in the early Islamic community was associated to a great extent with religious merit, Ali was considered the rightful ruler not only because of his early conversion to Islam and close family ties to the Prophet, but also because of his religious knowledge. Shi'a tradition states that the Prophet always referred to Ali as the preeminent expert on spiritual matters among his companions, and that at Ghadir Khumm, Muhammad reportedly declared to his companions that Ali was his *waliyy* (rightful and trusted successor), and blessed him with special prayers. The earliest concrete evidence of Shi'ism as a spiritual sect, however, did not appear until the 750s or 760s. In the era immediately following the revolution, a divergence emerged among those supporting the cause of Ali's family. Shi'ism came to be associated increasingly with descendants of Husayn, and in particular, the sixth descendant, Ja'far al-Sadiq.

Although little historical fact is known about Ja'far al-Sadiq, it is generally believed that it was in his time that the rudiments of Shi'a theology were first formed. These consisted of the belief that the imam (presumably from the Husaynid line) holds the secrets of religious knowledge (*ma'rifa*), that he has the authority to pass on this knowledge to a designated successor through a process of investment known as *wasiyya,* and that the followers of the imam must not challenge the authority of the established state in support of the Alid imamate until the imam declares the historically assigned time for such a political revolution. From the time of Ja'far al-Sadiq, the Shi'ites became closely clustered around the line of his descendants. However, a significant division took place within his lifetime. Ja'far's son Isma'il was supposed to be the spiritual successor to his father, and thus began to attract followers. Either because Isma'il died during his father's lifetime or because Ja'far decided to transfer the succession to another of his sons, Musa, during Ja'far's last years another group began to recognize Musa as his only successor.

This latter group continued to recognize the transmission of the authority of the imamate in a line of twelve successors, the last of whom, a child, is believed to have disappeared in the city of Samarra in 873. Shi'ites believe that the last of the twelve imams will one day reveal himself as the leading religious and political guide (the Mahdi), reestablish his leadership over the whole Islamic community, and usher in an age of justice and righteousness. Recognition of twelve descendants of Ali as imams led to this larger Shi'a community being known as Twelver Shi'ites or Imamis. The other group, which refused to accept Musa as successor and maintained its religous loyalty to Isma'il, the seventh imam, is hence known as Isma'ilis or Seveners. Like the Twelvers, some Isma'ilis believe in occulation (*ghayba*), but they consider Isma'il to be the vanished imam destined to usher in a righteous age.

The Growth of Shi'ism. In the late ninth century, competing Shi'a missions emerged. For some time, Isma'ili *da'wa* (mission, propaganda) had its strongest support in North Africa, where it was the religious affiliation of the Fatimid dynasty (909–1171), which came to rule North Africa, Egypt, Hijaz, and Syria. Establishing the city of Cairo (969) as their capital, the Fatimids hoped to turn Egypt into the center of Isma'ili propaganda and for this purpose founded al-Azhar seminary. The Fatimids' religious enterprise had little success, for the majority of their subjects adhered to Sunni schools of thought; Isma'ilism became the ideology of the state and a minority in society. Elsewhere in the Islamic world, the Buyid dynasty, which ruled Iran and Iraq between 932 and 1062, declared its loyalty to Shi'ism but chose to follow the Twelver branch. Although Shi'ism did not become the religious affiliation of the majority under Buyid rule, the dynasty did much to promote it. For example, Husayn's murder was commemorated with public ceremonies on the tenth of Muharram, the events at Ghadir Khumm were celebrated, and steps were taken to protect Shi'ism.

The next stage of substantial elaboration of Twelver Shi'a thought occurred in the sixteenth century under the Safavid dynasty in Iran. Until their arrival, Iran had been primarily a Sunni region. Locked in a mortal conflict with two Sunni dynasties, the Ottomans to the west and the Uzbeks in Transoxania to the east, Isma'il al-Safawi (1494–1524), founder of the dynasty, found it politically helpful to underline the ideological particularity of his government by adopting Shi'ism as the state religion. At the time, Safavid Shi'ism consisted largely of an affiliation to Sufi movements in Azerbaijan. Under his successor, Tahmasp (1524–1576), however, the state moved toward a more institutional and hierarchical structure guided by a clergy and an established law, rather than by the esoteric propensity of Sufi masters. This change fostered the alliance between the state and the clergy, the latter bolstering the legitimacy of the state and the former supporting Shi'a propaganda. The Safavids sought to make Shi'ism the law of the land and the only religious affiliation in society. Under Abbas I (1588–1629), they built theological seminaries and attracted renowned scholars from Iraq, southern Lebanon, and Bahrain to help systematize Shi'a learning. Sunni Islam was all but eliminated in the Safavid territories.

Shi'a Scholars and Differences with Sunnism. The idea of the occultation of the imam deprived Shi'ism of binding authority in spiritual matters. This inevitably called for the presence of religious scholars who could guide the community. Kufa was the earliest center of Shi'a thought, and in later times Qom in Iran emerged as a preeminent center of Shi'a learning. Among the most prominent of scholars in Qom were Abu Ja'far al-Kulayni (d. 941) and Ibn Babawayh al-Saduq (d. 991). Noted scholars in the later theological schools of Baghdad were Shaykh al-Mufid (d. 1022) and Sharif Murtada Alam al-Huda (d. 1067). The greatest Shi'a scholar, however, was perhaps al-Majlisi (d. 1699), who contributed the most toward changing a Sufi form of Shi'ism to a dogmatic and formal legislative form. Since the nineteenth century there has been a debate between two main currents in Shi'ism: the Akhbari, which seeks to establish Shi'a jurisprudence on the authority of tradition (*akhbar*), and the Usuli, which emphasizes the primacy of rationalist principles (*usul*) and the need to exercise *ijtihad* (reasoned speculation). Since the debate has been resolved in favor of the Usuli current in the twentieth century, the authority of the *mujtahid* (expert scholar capable of exercising reasoned speculation) has taken on greater importance. Although Shi'ites and Sunnis agree on core matters of ritual, dogma, and law, they differ on details. Whereas Sunnis, for instance, permit the occasional practice of wiping the foot covering with water (*al-mash ala al-khuffayn*) during ablution, Shi'ites reject the practice. The institution of temporary marriage (*mut'a*), accepted under Shi'a law, is rejected in Sunnism. The most prominent area of difference, however, remains historical. The Shi'a rejection of the caliphate of the first successors to the Prophet—viewed as equals according to Sunni historical reading—and the insistence on the sole right of Ali ibn Abi Talib to the succession has long formed the most visible difference between the two communities.

BIBLIOGRAPHY

ALGAR, HAMID. *Religion and State in Iran, 1785–1906: The Role of the Ulama in the Qajar Period.* Berkeley, Calif., 1980.

ARJOMAND, SAID AMIR. *Authority and Political Culture in Shi'ism.* Albany, N.Y., 1988.

———. *The Shadow of God and the Hidden Imam: Religion, Political Order, and Societal Change in Shi'ite Iran from the Beginning to 1890.* Chicago, 1984.

DABASHI, HAMID. *Theology of Discontent: The Ideological Foundation of the Islamic Revolution in Iran.* New York, 1993.

DAFTARY, FARHAD. *The Isma'ilis: Their History and Doctrines.* Cambridge, U.K., 1990.

KEDDIE, NIKKI. *Religion and Politics in Iran: Shi'ism from Quietism to Revolution.* New Haven, Conn., 1983.

MOMEN, MOOJAN. *An Introduction to Shi'i Islam.* New Haven, Conn., 1985.

MOOSA, MATTI. *Extremist Shiites: The Ghulat Sects.* Syracuse, N.Y., 1988.

SACHEDINA, A. A. *Islamic Messianism: The Idea of the Mahdi in Twelver Shi'ism.* Albany, N.Y., 1981.

———. *The Just Ruler in Shi'ite Islam: The Comprehensive Authority of the Jurist in Imamite Jurisprudence.* New York, 1988.

Tayeb El-Hibri

Shilluk

Non-Muslim Sudanese people.

The Shilluk are a linguistic group belonging to the Western Nilotic subgroup of the Eastern Sudanic branch of the Nilo-Saharan family. They are concentrated along the west bank of the White Nile in southern Sudan. Because Shilluk political organization is centered around the king (*reth*), the Shilluk have experienced greater unity than other tribes in the region. Enjoying access to good agricultural land along the Nile, the Shilluk are more settled than other tribes and rely more on cultivation and fishing than on cattle raising. The Shilluk numbered about 150,000 persons according to the 1983 census.

BIBLIOGRAPHY

VOLL, JOHN. *Historical Dictionary of the Shilluk.* Metuchen, N.J.: 1978.

David Waldner

Shim'un, Mar   [1908–1975]

Patriarch of the Assyrian (Nestorian) community.

Ishai Mar Shim'un XXIII was born in the Ottoman Empire (now Turkey) and educated in England in the 1920s. In 1918/19, some twenty thousand Assyrians (NESTORIANS) who had fled southeastern Turkey were settled in Iraq by the British authorities. Fearing the consequences of British withdrawal in 1932, the Mar Shim'un attempted to set up a separate enclave for his people with himself as politico-spiritual leader. The Assyrians were told that they should either become assimilated as Iraqis or leave, and in a confrontation between the community and the Iraqi army in August 1933, at least six hundred Assyrians were killed. The Mar Shim'un left Iraq, eventually reaching the United States; though he returned briefly to Iraq in 1970, he died in the United States in 1975.

Peter Sluglett

Shin Bet

Israel's General Security Service (Shabak), responsible for preventing hostile secret activity within the state.

The Shin Bet was founded at the outset of the State of Israel in 1948, for the purposes of preventing foreign espionage, internal and external sabotage, and illicit acts of violence. It carries out extensive security checks on candidates for sensitive posts and decides the rules for safeguarding information. The Shin Bet uses offensive measures as well, neutralizing the actions of those involved in hostile operations. The first head of the Shin Bet was Isser Harel, who served until 1954. Until 1996, the name of the current head was never revealed for security reasons.

The Shabak affair (1984–1986) brought a wide-scale examination of the Shin Bet's practices. In 1984, after terrorists hijacked an Israeli bus and the IDF (Israeli Defense Forces) stormed the bus, two of the terrorists were taken into custody. The two Palestinians taken prisoner were said to have been killed during the rescue, but media pictures showed them leaving the bus alive, and it became clear that they had been killed afterward. Several committees were formed to investigate the incident, and Attorney General Yitzhak Shamir recommended that Avraham Shalom, head of the Shin Bet, be removed from his post. The left wing accused Yitzhak Shamir of covering up for the Shin Bet and for using the rescue unit's commander as a scapegoat. Israel's President Hayim Herzog pardoned Shalom and eleven other Shin Bet officers in June 1986, starting a new round of protests. The new attorney general, Yosef Harish, appointed a three-person committee to investigate the entire working procedures of the Shin Bet. Though the Yariv Committee's recommendations were never made public, they were implemented. A final report in December 1986 found that Shamir had not attempted to cover up the killing and recommended that the eleven Shin Bet officers implicated in the affair should not be brought to trial, as they had already been pardoned.

BIBLIOGRAPHY

BLACK, IAN, and BENNY MORRIS. *Israel's Secret Wars: A History of Israel's Intelligence Services.* New York, 1991.

Julie Zuckerman

Shinui

Israeli political party founded in 1977 as a faction of the Democratic Movement for Change.

Shinui (Change) was established by law professor Ammon RUBENSTEIN. After the breakup of the Democratic Movement for Change, Shinui became an ally of the Labor party and a strong voice for electoral and constitutional reform and for a more flexible policy in the Arab–Israel dispute. In 1992, Shinui, MAPAM, and the Civil Rights movement joined to form MERETZ, which won twelve seats and became the main coalition partner of the Labor party.

BIBLIOGRAPHY

ROLEF, SUSAN, ed. *Political Dictionary of the State of Israel.* New York, 1987.

Walter F. Weiker

Shipbuilding, Bahrain

Shipbuilding flourished in Bahrain throughout the eighteenth and nineteenth centuries.

Shipbuilders of Bahrain specialized in constructing the long-prowed, square-sterned *sambuq,* which was used for pearling, and the larger *boom,* which was used as long-distance transport both in the Persian/Arabian Gulf and between regional ports and the East African coast. Timber was imported from India and became more and more expensive during the 1930s. World War II disruptions in trade dealt a massive blow to local shipbuilding. By the 1950s, only a handful of masters was left on the islands, concentrated along the quay at Muharraq. It was perhaps Bahrain's tradition as a shipbuilding center that persuaded the members of OPEC, the Organization of Petroleum Exporting Countries, to set up a large-scale drydock capable of repairing supertankers, the Arab Shipbuilding and Repair Yards, off the tip of al-Hidd in 1972.

BIBLIOGRAPHY

AL-RUMAIHI, MOHAMMED GHANIM. *Bahrain: A Study on Social and Political Changes since the First World War.* Kuwait, 1975.

Fred H. Lawson

Shiraz

A provincial capital in southwestern Iran.

Shiraz, the capital of Fars, today has a population of around 600,000. The city was probably founded in Aechemenid times, and by the late seventh century it had developed into an important commercial and military base, one of medieval Persia's significant urban centers. From the tenth century onward, Shirazi traders were active along the East African coast. Famous for its gardens and wines, Shiraz is also home to two of Iran's greatest poets, Sa'di and Hafez. Shiraz flourished in the late eighteenth century, when it was made capital of the Zand dynasty. Karim Khan Zand built the Vakil mosque in Shiraz in 1773. The brother of the eighth Shi'a imam, Ali al-Reza, is buried in Shiraz. His shrine, known as the Shahcheragh, is a popular visiting site. Apart from many Islamic monuments, such as the Old Mosque (Masjed-e Atiq) dating to the Safavid period, Persepolis, Naqsh-e Rostam, and Pasargad, magnificent archaeological remains from Iran's pre-Islamic past, lie near Shiraz. In the late Pahlavi period, an annual arts festival was held there, attended by performers, artists, and musicians from all over the world.

Neguin Yavari

Shirazi, Mirza Hasan   [1815–1897]

Nineteenth-century Iranian cleric.

Born in Shiraz to a well-established clerical family, Shirazi embarked on vigorous religious training that took him first to Isfahan and then Iraq. He has become most notable for a religious decree (*fatwa*) in 1892 against the use of tobacco. The decree read as follows: "In the name of God the merciful, the usage of tobacco in any way is equal to denouncing God and fighting against the divinely guided messianic leader [i.e., the Mahdi, the Imam of the Age]." Shirazi's decision to issue such a proclamation is said to have stemmed from the allocation of exclusive rights of tobacco production and sales to the British by Naser al-Din Shah and his prime minister. The effect of the decree was that the government was forced to annul its agreement with the British. It is said that even the wives of the shah refused to use and serve tobacco during the period of the decree.

BIBLIOGRAPHY

ALGAR, HAMID. *Mirza Malkam Khan: A Study in the History of Iranian Modernism.* Berkeley, Calif., 1973, pp. 206–237.

Farhad Arshad

Shiraz University

A private university established in 1956 in Shiraz, Iran.

The Pahlavi University of Shiraz, Iran, was established by a special law passed by the parliament in 1956 as a nongovernment university under the trust of the king, the queen, and the crown prince. Its name was changed to Shiraz University after the 1979 Iranian Revolution. It included 9 colleges or faculties at the start and by 1977 totaled 648 faculty and 5,129 students. It was one of the first universities created along American lines, offering courses in English and including among its faculty a number of foreigners. Its curriculum includes courses in literature, natural sciences, medicine, agriculture, and engineering. It had 11,500 students and 360 teachers in 1990.

BIBLIOGRAPHY

LENCZOWSKI, GEORGE. *Iran under the Pahlavis.* Palo Alto, Calif., 1978.

Parvaneh Pourshariati

Shishakli, Adib   [1909–1964]

President of Syria, 1953–1954.

Shishakli was born in Hama, in west-central Syria. He was a volunteer in the Troupes Spéciales (Syrian Legion), an army commanded by French officers with a rank and file from various French colonies, including North Africa. During the Palestine war, Shishakli, a senior officer in Jaysh al-Inqadh, Fawzi al-Qawuqji's "Army of Deliverance," was one of the more successful Syrian commanders. In early manhood he was a member of Antun Sa'ada's PARTI POPULAIRE SYRIEN (PPS). Shishakli was one of Husni al-Za'im's fellow conspirators, leading the infantry and armored units that carried out Za'im's coup in March 1949. Following his quarrel with Za'im, Shishakli was retired from the army with the rank of lieutenant colonel on 6 August 1949, only to be

reinstated by Sami al-Hinnawi, after Hinnawi's coup that overthrew Za'im later that month.

On 19 December of that year, Shishakli moved on Damascus and overthrew Hinnawi, ostensibly to save Syria from British influence and union with Iraq, but in reality to fulfill his own political ambitions. Being an outsider with only grudging support from the political elites of Syria, he allowed the formal parliamentary government established by Hinnawi to form a cabinet, though in fact he ran the show from his position as deputy chief of staff. In November 1951, Shishakli staged a second coup, this time arresting Prime Minister Ma'ruf al-Dawabili; members of the government; the People's party secretary-general, Nazim al-Qudsi; and a number of Hashimite sympathizers who favored union with Iraq. Having silenced his critics, particularly the People's party, which was entrenched in parliament, he dissolved parliament and assumed the functions of head of state by military decree.

Shishakli's political ambitions benefited from his shrewdness, toughness, and political ability. In December 1951, he appointed a figurehead president and prime minister, Col. Fawzi Selo. As his influence grew, he distanced himself from the PPS and gained the support of al-Hizb al-Arabi al-Qawmi (the Pan-Arab party) and, with the support of its leader, Dhafir al-Rifa'i, in 1952 set up a new party, Harakat al-Tahrir al-Arabi (Arab Liberation movement). The principles of Arab nationalism and social reform embodied in the program of the new party were meant primarily to realize his political ambitions. Syria's agricultural output, particularly of cotton, peaked toward the end of Shishakli's rule, thanks in part to the founding of the Cotton Bureau in 1952.

In June 1953, Shishakli became premier and had himself elected president in a controversial referendum that also approved a new constitution. On 25 February 1954 a coup forced Shishakli to resign, and he fled to Lebanon. Later he lived in Saudi Arabia and France. In 1960 he immigrated to Brazil, where a Druze named Nawas al-Ghazali assassinated him in September 1964, apparently in revenge for Shishakli's repression of the Druze community in Syria.

Muhammad Muslih

Shishakli, Salah

Syrian military officer.

Salah Shishakli, an army captain from Hama, Syria, and member of the Syrian National Social party (Parti Populaire Syrien, PPS), was an important aide and intermediary to his brother, the authoritarian president Adib Shishakli. Salah Shishakli was exiled and indicted in December 1956 for his involvement in attempting to restore his brother to power (he had been ousted in 1954).

BIBLIOGRAPHY

SEALE, PATRICK. *The Struggle for Syria.* London, 1965.

Charles U. Zenzie

Shish Kebab

Meat roasted over open fires on skewers.

The origin of shish kebab is lost in antiquity, but given the swordlike skewers so common in the Middle East, it probably originated with Turkish horsemen cooking wild game over open fires. In Turkish, *shish kebab* means "gobbets of meat roasted on a spit or skewer"; the Arabs call it *lahm mishwi,* grilled lamb.

The threading of vegetables—onions, mushrooms, tomatoes, and peppers—onto the skewer, interspersed with meat, appears to be a modern restaurant introduction.

Clifford A. Wright

Shitreet, Bebor   [1897–1967]

Israeli Sephardic leader.

Bebor Shitreet was born in Tiberias into a family that had emigrated from Morocco to Palestine in the eighteenth century. He was educated as a rabbi and taught Hebrew, Arabic, and French in the Alliance (French) school system in Tiberias. An organizer of the police force set up in Palestine by the British in 1919, he later was a police commander in lower Galilee and head of the Tel Aviv police force in 1927. After the founding of the State of Israel in 1948, he was elected to the Knesset as a member of the MAPAI party and served as minister of police. During his lifetime Shitreet sought to improve relations between religious minorities in Israel.

Bryan Daves

Shlonsky, Avraham   [1900–1973]

Hebrew poet, editor, and translator.

Born in Russia, Shlonsky was sent to Palestine at the age of thirteen to study at the Herzliah high school in Tel Aviv. Prior to World War I, he returned to Russia to complete his studies and in 1921 emigrated to Israel. Although Shlonsky's literary output was not restricted to poetry, his fame rests primarily on his verse. He is considered Israel's revolutionary poet and the originator of a new school of poetry. In his works, he rebelled against the classicism of previous Hebrew poetry and sought to create a new poetic language by amalgamating the old and the new.

Although occasionally optimistic, as in his post-Holocaust *Ki Tashuv* (You Shall Return), Shlonsky's poetry is for the most part deeply pessimistic. His poems reflect the world he inhabited. The horrors of the Russian pogroms and the revolution are described in *Elef Yegonot* (One Thousand Griefs), *Devai* (1924, Sorrow); his reaction to the Arab riots in Palestine in the1920s are dealt with in *Be-Eleh ha-Yamin* (In These Days); the horrors of Nazism are expressed in *Shirei ha-Mapolet Ve-Ha-Piyus* (1938, Poems of Defeat and Appeasement); observations on life and death constitute the subject of *Mishirei ha-Prozdor ha-Arokh* (1968, Poems of the Long Corridor). In addition to the nine major collections of poetry that he published, Shlonsky also translated over seventy major European works into Hebrew.

Ann Kahn

Shomer Ha-Tza'ir, ha-

Zionist socialist youth movement founded in Vienna in 1916.

During World War II, some members of ha-Shomer Ha-Tza'ir (Young Guard) fought in various partisan resistance movements and in the Red Army of the Soviet Union. In Israel since 1927, it founded several kibbutzim and emphasized educating youth for kibbutz life. It was also active in settlement and illegal immigration activities before the founding of the state. Since that time, it has been affiliated with MA-PAM and has been a vigorous proponent of both Zionism and socialism.

BIBLIOGRAPHY

ROLEF, SUSAN, ed. *Political Dictionary of the State of Israel,* 2nd ed., New York, 1993.

Walter F. Weiker

Shorfa

North African title for all descendants of the Prophet Muhammad.

In Morocco, since the rule of the Idrisid dynasty, descent from the Prophet Muhammad became a source of legitimacy for establishing political power. All the founders of the religious brotherhoods claimed such origin to gain authority and credit among disciples. A genealogical tree linking the Shorfa to the Prophet would assess the claim. The Sa'di (sixteenth century) and Alawi (seventeenth century to the present) dynasties that ruled or have ruled Morocco are considered shorfa dynasties.

[See also: Sharif]

Rahma Bourqia

Shrine of the Book

See Dead Sea Scrolls

Shuf

Region of Lebanon.

Shuf is the region (in administrative terms it is the *qada*) located in southern Lebanon between Qada al-Matn and Qada Jizzin, and between the Mediterranean Sea and the Biqa' valley. It has more than 220 towns. The main city is the predominantly Druze Ba'aklin, which was, for a while, the seat of government for the Ma'nids. The Shuf was made part of the governorate of Mount Lebanon because a sectarian balance between Maronites and Druze was desired. Historically, the electoral battles in the region were between the candidates of Kamal Jumblatt and of Camille Chamoun, but the presence of a number of sects in the region forced both leaders to seek support among nonaligned sects to win election. For example, the Shuf had a Sunni seat, and even Maronite Chamoun had to field a Sunni candidate to win election. Druze leader Walid Jumblatt has been demanding the division of the Mount Lebanon governorate into two sections to achieve a degree of sectarian parity. He does not feel he should have to seek support among the Maronites, who constitute a majority in the northern part of the governorate.

As'ad AbuKhalil

Shufman, Gershon   [1880–1972]

Hebrew writer.

Born in Belorussia, Shufman received a traditional Yeshiva education and taught himself Hebrew and Russian. In 1902, he enlisted in the Russian army, which coincided with the publication of his first collection of short stories. From 1913 to 1938 he lived in Austria and from there emigrated to Palestine. His brief articles and short stories are his best literary creations. They describe life in Galicia, Austria, and in Israel and focus on day-to-day experiences that, in turn, reflect reality.

Shufman's writings are considered forerunners of modern Hebrew literature. A four-volume revised version of his collected works appeared between 1946 and 1952, and a fifth volume was added in 1960. He received the Israel prize for literature in 1957.

Ann Kahn

Shukri, Mohammad   [1935–   ]

Moroccan novelist.

Shukri was born in Beni Shiker in the Nadhor region of Morocco. He learned to read and write only at the age of twenty. He lives in Tangier.

Shukri's first autobiographical novel, *Al-Khubz al-Hafi Sira Riwa'iyya, 1935–1956,* details the difficulties he encountered as a child and stirs the admiration of the reader for his efforts to overcome his difficult circumstances. The extreme realism of Shukri's writings, reproducing the life of hunger, theft, drugs, and prostitution as he either lived it or observed it around him, delayed the publication of his novel in Arabic for many years. The English translation by Paul Bowles, *For Bread Alone* (1973), appeared first. His collection of short stories *Majnun al-Ward* (1979, Enamored with Roses) depicts city life in Morocco with the same harsh realism and a camera-eye technique; the words seem even more poignant than the pictures and have a stronger impact on the reader.

Shukri wrote a book on Jean Genet and Tennessee Williams' visit to Tangier; it was later translated into French by Mohammed el-Ghoulabzouri under the title *Jean Genet et Tennessee Williams à Tangier* (Paris, 1992).

[See also: Literature, Arabic, North African]

BIBLIOGRAPHY

"Littérature marocaine." *Europe* (June–July 1979): 68–71.

Aida A. Bamia

Shumayyil, Shibli   [1850–1917]

Syrian medical scholar.

Born in Syria to a Christian family, Shibli Shumayyil was one of the first graduates of the Syrian Protestant

College's medical school in Beirut. He completed his medical studies in Paris and settled in Egypt to practice medicine and write numerous articles on medicine and on social and scientific theories. He was particularly influenced by Charles Darwin, using the evolutionist's ideas to formulate his ideas on the unity of being and natural laws in human society. He denounced despotism as unnatural and false. Also influenced by the thought of philosophers Herbert Spencer and Ludwig Büchner, Shumayyil criticized nationalism and all forms of exclusive solidarity because they divided human society. He preached universalism and liberalism and so gave measured support to the Young Turk movement. Like his contemporary, the Lebanese Farah Antun, Shumayyil sought the theoretical basis for a secular state that would promote a society where Christians and Muslims would be equal.

BIBLIOGRAPHY

HOURANI, ALBERT. *Arabic Thought in the Liberal Age, 1789–1939.* New York, 1984.

Elizabeth Thompson

Shuqayr, Shawkat

Syrian military officer.

An army officer of Druze and Lebanese descent who was loyal to Syria's President Adib Shishakli, General Shawkat Shuqayr was appointed chief of staff in 1953 and deputy governor early in 1954. He played a key mediating role in the downfall of Shishakli, in late February 1954, that brought Hashim al-Atasi to power. Shuqayr was appointed minister of defense later that year, but he abruptly resigned from his post as chief of staff on July 7, 1956, and returned to Lebanon. There he became involved in the military organization of the PROGRESSIVE SOCIALIST PARTY headed by Kamal Jumblatt.

BIBLIOGRAPHY

SEALE, PATRICK. *The Struggle for Syria.* London, 1965.

Charles U. Zenzie

Shuqayri, Ahmad   [1908–1980]

Diplomat, activist; first head of the PLO.

Shuqayri was a Palestinian born in Tibnia, Lebanon, while his father, the Islamic judge Shaykh As'ad Shuqayri, was living there in exile. Ahmad returned to the family's hometown of Acre in 1916. After studies there and in Jerusalem, he entered the American University in Beirut in 1926 but was expelled by French mandate authorities the following year for Arab nationalist activities. Following his return to Palestine, he studied law and wrote for a newspaper; eventually, after graduating from college, he went to work in the law offices of the nationalist figure Awni Abd al-Hadi and became involved in the pan-Arab nationalist Istiqlal party.

During the 1930s Shuqayri put his legal skills to work on behalf of Palestinians charged with security offenses. He fled Palestine for Cairo following the end of the Arab Revolt, to return only at the end of World War II. During the late 1940s he was appointed head of the Arab Higher Committee's Arab Information Office in Washington and later headed the central Arab Information Office in Jerusalem. He fled to Lebanon during the 1948 fighting.

In exile, Shuqayri rose to become a leading Arab diplomatic figure during the 1950s and early 1960s. He served in the Syrian delegation to the United Nations from 1949 to 1950 before being appointed assistant general secretary of the League of Arab States (the Arab League) from 1950 to 1957. He then served the government of Saudi Arabia as minister of state for UN affairs and as its UN representative until he was dismissed in 1963 for disagreeing with the Saudis over Egyptian intervention in the first Yemeni Civil War.

Shuqayri began to play a major role in Palestinian nationalist affairs in September 1963, when he was asked to serve as the representative of Palestine at the Arab League. At the Arab summit of January 1964, he was asked to begin investigating the possibility of creating a uniquely Palestinian organization. That February Shuqayri called for the convening of a Palestinian National Council in East Jerusalem for just such a purpose. At that meeting the Palestine Liberation Organization (PLO) was created with Shuqayri as its head. The PLO thereafter sought to mobilize Palestinians politically and militarily. It established offices in several Arab countries and worked to raise men to serve in the PLO's fighting force, the Palestine Liberation Army, brigades of which were attached to the armies of Syria, Iraq, and Egypt.

Shuqayri and the PLO remained close to Egyptian President Gamal Abdel Nasser and the Arab regimes. Far from a revolutionary organization, the PLO consisted of conservatives and nationalists willing to work with the regimes in liberating Palestine in coordination with overall Arab strategies vis-à-vis Israel. Younger Palestinian militants, such as those in the Fath organization, believed instead in a policy of independent, guerilla-style struggle.

Israel's massive defeat of Arab forces during the June 1967 Arab–Israel War rendered the policies of the Arab states and the PLO bankrupt in the eyes of many Palestinians. For them, Shuqayri's elegant and sometimes heated rhetoric about liberation contrasted starkly with his failure and that of the established Arab elites. Associated with Nasser and the catastrophe of defeat and facing criticism for his administration of the PLO, Shuqayri resigned on December 24, 1967.

He lived thereafter in Cairo until his opposition to the 1978 Camp David Accords prompted him to move to Tunisia. He died in Amman, Jordan, while receiving medical treatment on February 25, 1980.

Michael R. Fischbach

Shuqayri, As'ad al-   [1860–1940]

Palestinian religious scholar and politician.

Born in Acre in Palestine, Shaykh Shuqayri attended al-Azhar in Cairo. Before World War I, he became mufti of Acre and a member of the Shari'a Inquiries Court at Istanbul. He was elected to the Ottoman parliament in 1908 and 1911. An Ottoman loyalist, Shuqayri wrote many articles opposing Arab nationalism. During World War I, he served as mufti to the Fourth Army. In the 1920s, Shuqayri served on the Supreme Muslim Council and helped make Acre a center of opposition to the Husayni-led Arab Executive party. As'ad al-Shuqayri was the father of Ahmad Shuqayri, founder of the Palestine Liberation Organization (PLO).

BIBLIOGRAPHY

MANDEL, NEVILLE, J. *The Arabs and Zionism before World War I.* Berkeley, Calif., 1976.
MUSLIH, MUHAMMAD Y. *The Origins of Palestinian Nationalism.* New York, 1988.

Elizabeth Thompson

Shuqayri Family

Prominent Palestinian family from Acre.

In the late nineteenth century, the Shuqayris emerged among the elites of Acre, one of the fastest-growing Palestinian cities of the time. They were landowners, Ottoman administrators, and religious officials. The family's prominence continued into the twentieth century. As'ad Shuqayri, mufti of Acre, served on the Shari'a Inquiries Court at Istanbul and as mufti for the Fourth Army during World War I.

Opposed to the anti-Zionist movement, As'ad sold several hundred *dunums* of the family's land near Haifa to Zionists in the 1930s.

The family was associated with the Nashashibi-led National Defense party. Another member of the family, Dr. Anwar al-Shuqayri, was assassinated by members of the opposing Husayni party in 1939. As'ad's son Ahmad Shuqayri, a lawyer, edited the newspaper *Mir'at al-Sharq* for two years and was a founder of the ISTIQLAL PARTY in 1931. In the 1940s Ahmad became known as a feisty nationalist, taking on several leading political roles. In the 1950s he represented Syria and Saudi Arabia at the United Nations and in the 1960s was chosen Palestinian delegate to the Arab League. He founded the Palestine Liberation Organization (PLO) in 1964.

BIBLIOGRAPHY

KHALAF, ISSA. *Politics in Palestine: Arab Factionalism and Social Disintegration, 1939–1948.* Albany, N.Y., 1991.
MANDEL, NEVILLE J. *The Arabs and Zionism before World War I.* Berkeley, Calif., 1976.
MUSLIH, MUHAMMAD Y. *The Origins of Palestinian Nationalism.* New York, 1988.

Elizabeth Thompson

Shura

A consultative council.

The first recorded *shura* in Islamic history was called by Caliph Umar in 644 to choose his successor. The choice of later caliphs, although usually designated by their predecessor, was customarily ratified by a shura of family members and political leaders. The shura soon became generalized as an Islamic tradition of leaders consulting members of a community or family and asking them to reach consensus on troublesome issues.

The term *shura* has been used throughout the Middle East in the nineteenth and twentieth centuries to confer traditional legitimacy on a variety of modern representative councils. The Ottomans applied the term to many of the administrative councils created by the nineteenth-century Tanzimat reforms. Political groups in twentieth-century Arab states, particularly around the Gulf, have based their demands for representative bodies on injunctions in the Qur'an that men should conduct their affairs through shura, or consultation, with others.

BIBLIOGRAPHY

LAPIDUS, IRA M. *A History of Islamic Societies.* New York, 1988.

PETERSON, J. E. *The Arab Gulf States: Steps toward Political Participation.* New York, 1988.

Elizabeth Thompson

Shuster, Morgan   [1877–1960]

Financial adviser to Persia in the early twentieth century.

W. Morgan Shuster, an American publisher, financier, and lawyer, was born in Washington, D.C. After attending Columbia College and Law School, Shuster worked for the War Department and the Cuban Customs Service from 1898 to 1901. He then served in a variety of posts in the Philippines from 1901 to 1909, after which he became a banker. From May 1911 to January 1912, he was treasurer general and financial adviser in Persia (now Iran). In 1915 Shuster became president of the Century Corporation in New York City, a post he held until 1933 when he became the president and chief executive officer of Appleton-Century-Croft. In an effort to rationalize Persia's finances, the Majles (legislature) hired Shuster upon the recommendation of the U.S. State Department and with the consent of Russia. Described by some as lacking in tact and courtesy, Shuster immediately organized a Treasury Gendarmerie to collect taxes, some from prominent Russian officials. Shuster chose Major C. B. Stokes, a devoted friend of Persia and former British military attaché, to head this new treasury police force. The Russian legation opposed this appointment, leading the British to post Stokes to India. Shuster's successful opposition to the Russian-supported restoration of Muhammad Ali as shah earned him additional enmity from that quarter.

The British also viewed Shuster's activities as hostile to Anglo–Russian understandings regarding Persia, dating from the agreement of 1907. This opposition came to a head in November 1911 when Shuster ordered the confiscation of property owned by the former shah's brother, Shoa al-Saltana, then living in exile in Russia. The Russian consul general, claiming that Saltana's assets were owed to the Russian bank, sent an armed force of ten Russian-trained Persian cossacks to prevent Shuster from taking control of the property. Shuster responded with a larger force. This led to the Russian demand of November 5 for an apology; Persia apologized, but then Russia demanded Shuster's removal. For a time the Majles rejected this demand, and Persian nationalists attacked Russian troops in Tabriz and Rasht. There was also a boycott of Russian goods and the assassination of a pro-Russian minister. Russia responded with force, hanging a number of nationalists and sending troops to Tehran. In early December, the Majles again rejected the demand of Shuster's removal, but it finally yielded to Russian pressure and that of the powerful Bakhtiari tribe on December 20. Shuster left Persia in January 1912 to pursue his other interests.

BIBLIOGRAPHY

SHUSTER, W. MORGAN. *The Strangling of Persia.* New York, 1912.

Daniel E. Spector

Shuttle Diplomacy

Term used by the media to describe U.S. Secretary of State Henry Kissinger's trips to the Middle East in the wake of the Arab–Israel War of 1973.

KISSINGER flew back and forth between Israel and its Arab neighbors, offering his services as an intermediary and applying pressure to secure what he termed "step-by-step" agreements between the belligerents. He succeeded in negotiating two disengagement agreements between Egypt and Israel—Sinai I (January 1974) and Sinai II (September 1975)—and one between Syria and Israel (May 1974).

Jenab Tutunji

Shu'un Filastiniyya

Monthly journal of the PLO.

Shu'un Filastiniyya is the monthly Arabic-language journal published by the Palestine Research Center, the research department of the PALESTINE LIBERATION ORGANIZATION (PLO). The first issue appeared in Beirut, Lebanon, in March 1971 under the editorship of Dr. Anis Sayigh. After the PLO's departure from Beirut in 1982, the journal continued publication from Nicosia, Cyprus. In addition to articles on Palestine, the Arab–Israel conflict, and related issues, it regularly publishes political documents concerning the Palestinian national movement, analyses of Israeli affairs, a chronology, and a bibliography. *Shu'un Filastiniyya* suspended publication in 1993 because of the financial crisis within the PLO, but it still officially exists.

Mouin Rabbani

Sib, Treaty of

Treaty between the sultanate and imamate in Oman.

A British-mediated undertaking signed September 25, 1920, by the rival sultanate and imamate governments in Oman. Ending seven years of warfare, it recognized both regimes' mutual autonomy and initiated a peace lasting until 1955. Subsequently, it was used unsuccessfully to justify the creation of a fully independent imamate in Oman's interior.

BIBLIOGRAPHY

LANDEN, ROBERT G. *Oman since 1856: Disruptive Modernization in a Traditional Arab Society.* Princeton, N.J., 1967.

Robert G. Landen

Siba'i, Hani al-   [1893–?]

Syrian lawyer and politician.

Hani al-Siba'i was born in Homs in 1893 and educated at Damascus University. As a member of the People's party, he became minister of education in Khalid al-Azm's 1950 cabinet, and again in 1951 under Ma'ruf al-Dawalibi. He was appointed to the same post in 1957 as an independent under Sabri al-Asali.

BIBLIOGRAPHY

SEALE, PATRICK. *The Struggle for Syria: A Study of Post-War Arab Politics, 1945–1958.* London, 1958.

Charles U. Zenzie

Siba'i, Mustafa al-   [1915–   ]

Syrian lawyer and professor.

Born the son of Hosni al-Siba'i in Homs in 1915, Mustafa al-Siba'i received a doctorate of laws from al-Azhar University in Cairo. He became a professor at the University of Damascus, and served as deputy for Damascus in 1949. He represented Syria at the Islamic Congress in Karachi in 1951. Siba'i was a leader both of the Muslim Brethren and of the Islamic Socialist Front. In these capacities, and as he was of great influence also in the chamber of deputies, he continually worked against the secularism of the state.

BIBLIOGRAPHY

SEALE, PATRICK. *The Struggle for Syria: A Study of Post-War Arab Politics, 1945–1958.* London, 1958.

Charles U. Zenzie

Sick Man of Europe

See Eastern Question

Sidara

Iraqi headgear.

Introduced by Faisal I, the *sidara* is commonly made of black velvet. It is an overseas cap.

Marilyn Higbee

Sidon

Coastal city in south Lebanon known as one of the oldest crossroads of Mediterranean civilization.

Sidon (or Saïda in French) derives its name from the Semitic word *sayd,* which means fishing, mainly for the murex shell, from which the famous purple dye was extracted. Sidon is mentioned in many ancient stone inscriptions, such as the Tell Amarna letters in Egypt to the Hittites and the inscriptions found in the city of Ugarit. Sidon is also mentioned in Homer's *Iliad.*

Sidon's golden age came about in the seventeenth century, under the rule of Emir Fakhruddin II; at this time, Sidon became the capital of the Lebanese Ma'an dynasty and an important center for the dyeing and silk industries. Fakhruddin built several inns for foreign tradesmen like the *ifranj* inn, the rice inn, and the soap inn. In addition, the emir built several castles surrounded by beautiful gardens.

During this period, Sidon was an important city in which several peoples of different religions (especially Christians and Muslims) coexisted. This coexistence is reflected today in Sidon's Great Mosque of Omar and the Maronite church, whose foundations go back to Roman times.

Today, Sidon, with its suqs and its narrow streets, is a bustling city. In addition to the markets within the city, there are agricultural products such as citrus fruit and vegetables growing in the groves in and around the city. There is also a petroleum refinery plant, and fishing is an important source of livelihood for many of Sidon's inhabitants. Rafiq Hariri, Lebanon's prime minister, was born in Sidon and has been investing in several projects in the city.

George E. Irani

Sidqi, Bakr   [1885–1937]

Iraqi soldier and government official.

Bakr Sidqi carried out the first military coup in the period between the two world wars in the Arab Middle East. Sidqi fought in the Ottoman army in World War I and joined the Iraqi army in 1921. In

August 1933, he gained national prominence as the commander of an army unit that killed some six hundred Assyrian villagers in Sumayl.

Sidqi's ruthlessness and decisiveness in putting down the RUMAYTHA REBELLION in 1935 served to enhance his prestige further. At the same time, he formed a secret alliance between himself and Yasin al-Hashimi's main rivals, Jama'at al-Ahali, the AHALI GROUP, led principally by Hikmat Sulayman. This culminated in a coup d'état, organized by Sidqi and Sulayman, which forced Yasin's government out of office on October 29, 1936. Sulayman became prime minister and appointed a largely Ahali or pro-Ahali cabinet, while Sidqi remained the power behind the regime. However, Sidqi's dictatorial style gradually lost him the confidence of al-Ahali, most of whom had resigned by May 1937. By this time, Sidqi had also managed to alienate many of his colleagues in the army, who organized his assassination at Mosul in northern Iraq on August 11, 1937.

Peter Sluglett

Sidqi, Isma'il   [1875–1949]

Egyptian politician and prime minister.

Sidqi was born into a bourgeois family in Alexandria. His father was a high government official. Sidqi graduated from the School of Law in Cairo, and began a career in government. He was a colleague of Sa'd Zaghlul, the leader of the Wafd party favoring autonomy for Egypt, and was exiled with the other Wafdists in 1919, but soon broke with Zaghlul and joined the Liberal Constitutionalist party in 1924.

When King Fu'ad dismissed the Wafd government in 1930, Sidqi was asked to form a new government. Sidqi quickly renounced his membership in the Liberal Constitutionalist party, suspended parliament, instituted press censorship, and abrogated the 1923 constitution, replacing it with a more conservative constitution. He next formed his own political party, al-Sha'b (The People), which he used to run in the 1931 elections. The Wafd and other liberal parties boycotted these elections in protest of Sidqi's autocratic rule. Throughout Sidqi's term as prime minister, there were frequent protest by nationalist politicians demanding the restoration of the 1923 constitution. Sidqi's policies, combined with the effects of the 1929 depression, made his rule very unpopular in Egypt, but the lack of unity among his opponents kept him in office.

By 1933, King Fu'ad felt that he had sufficiently weakened the Wafd and strengthened his own power that he could rule without Sidqi. Sidqi stepped down

in September of 1933 and immediately joined the National Front,which called for the reinstatement of the 1923 constitution.

In February of 1946, Sidqi was again invited to form a government, which lasted until December of 1946, when he resigned on the grounds of bad health. During this year, Sidqi conducted negotiations with Britain about troop withdrawals. These negotiations were widely condemned by nationalists, particularly with regard to the threat to Egypt's position in the Sudan.

BIBLIOGRAPHY

Africa Who's Who, 1st ed. London, 1981.

David Waldner

Sidra, Gulf of

A body of water on the coast of Libya.

The Gulf of Sidra is located on the Mediterranean cost of Libya. Its coastline, 310 miles (500 km) of barren desert, forms an important geographical boundary between Libya's two major populated areas: Tripolitania, the western coastal region that shares many historical features with the Maghrib, and Cyrenaica, the eastern coastal region that has been more closely associated with the Arab states of the Middle East. This gulf then provides an important dividing line for the culture of the Maghrib and that of the Mashriq.

Stuart J. Borsch

Sihnawi, Antoine   [1903–1989]

Lebanese politician and parliamentarian.

Sihnawi was born in Damascus and died in Lebanon in September 1989. An economist by training, he held several managerial positions in the banking and industrial sectors in Lebanon. He was elected twice as member of the Lebanese parliament (1960 and 1964) and was a member of the government headed by Prime Minister Hussein al-Uwayni (1964/65). He was a recipient of the Vatican's medal as Knight of the Great Cross of Saint George and honorific medals from Tunisia and Belgium.

BIBLIOGRAPHY

Arab Information Center, Beirut.

George E. Irani

Silk

Fiber taken from the wrapping of silkworm cocoons.

Silk became an important textile product and luxury commodity in the Middle East from antiquity. Silk textiles came into the Middle East by trade from India and China. While Indian and Arab merchants sailed the Indian Ocean, Chinese merchants sent the fine cloth along the famous four thousand-mile (6,400 km) Silk Road—through central Asia and northern Iran to Europe. (Except for a few traders, rarely did any travel more than a short distance of the entire route.)

In the sixth century C.E., the Byzantines smuggled Chinese silk cocoons to Istanbul to begin their own mulberry groves and silkworm industry. Lebanon, Iran, and Iraq cultivated mulberry trees and silkworms as well. While part of the Ottoman Empire, Bursa and Mount Lebanon were important centers of silk-cocoon farming, and their fine silk textiles were loomed throughout the empire for both trade and imperial use. In the late nineteenth and early twentieth centuries, many Middle Eastern silk weavers lost their trade because of French intervention during the mandate period and the appearance of increasingly inexpensive silk goods that were being produced in the industrialized nations and in Asia for world markets.

BIBLIOGRAPHY

OWEN, ROGER. *The Middle East in the World Economy 1800–1914.* New York, 1981.

QUATAERT, DONALD. "The Silk Industry of Bursa, 1880–1914." In *Contributions à l'histoire economique et sociale de l'empire ottoman.* Paris, 1983.

"Silk Route." *Encyclopedia of Asian History.* New York, 1988.

Elizabeth Thompson

Silver, Abba Hillel   [1893–1963]

U.S. rabbi and Zionist leader.

Born in Lithuania, Silver was brought to America as a child. From 1917, he was rabbi of the temple in Cleveland, Ohio. Between 1938 and 1948 he was head of the Zionist Organization of America, the American Zionist Emergency Council, the United Jewish Appeal, the United Palestine Appeal, and the Central Conference of American Rabbis. Silver was one of the chief Zionist spokesmen at the UN Palestine hearings in 1947. His writings include *History of Messianic Speculations in Ancient Israel* (1959) and *Where Judaism Differs: An Inquiry into the Distinctiveness of Judaism* (1956).

BIBLIOGRAPHY

RAPHAEL, MARC LEE. *Abba Hillel Silver: A Profile in American Judaism.* New York, 1989.

Mia Bloom

Simavi, Sedat   [1896–1953]

Turkish newspaper and magazine publisher.

Simavi, born in Istanbul, was the son of a governor of Samsun and was descended on both sides of his family from grand viziers of the Ottoman Empire. After graduating from Galatasaray Lycée, he worked as a teacher for a few years, then in 1917 made two of Turkey's earliest films, *The Claw* and *The Spy.* He began his publishing career in 1916, with magazines like the political-humor weekly *Hande* and, in 1919, the slick, progressive monthly women's magazine *Inci.* Simavi published a variety of popular magazines between 1918 and 1939 on women, fashion, health, humor, and cinema.

Simavi is best known for founding the daily newspaper HÜRRIYET, in 1948. The first of the boulevard-type newspapers, emphasizing slick style, sensation, and personal stories, it reached a circulation of 30,000 in its first year and by the 1950s was Turkey's largest paper (it had supported the winner—the new Democrat party—in the 1950 elections). While *Hürriyet's* circulation approached 700,000 in the 1970s, it declined in the 1980s to about 450,000, with stiff competition from newer newspapers like *Sabah* and the Simavi-owned *Günaydın.* After Simavi's death, his son Erol became editor of the paper. With other family members, including grandson Sedat Simavi, he heads a publishing empire that includes several top daily newspapers and magazines.

BIBLIOGRAPHY

ÖZKÖK, ERTUĞRUL. "The Turkish Press, 150 Years of Controversy." In *The Transformation of Turkish Culture,* ed. by Günsel Renda and C. Max Kortepeter. Princeton, N.J., 1986.

Elizabeth Thompson

Sinai Peninsula

Triangular peninsula between the Mediterranean and Red seas.

The Sinai is the desert area of northeast Egypt that forms the land bridge between Africa and Asia. It has flat dry surfaces in the north and rugged mountains in the south, including the plateaus of al-Tih and Egma and the Jabal Musa hills. The Sinai peninsula is bordered on the east by the State of Israel and the Gulf of Aqaba and on the west by the Suez Canal and the Gulf of Suez.

The population was estimated at about 38,000 in 1948, mainly bedouin; it had grown to about 140,000 by 1970, with the development of petroleum and manganese deposits plus the influx of Palestinian refugees. The manganese was discovered at Umm Bugma, and the oil at Ra's Sudar, Abu Rudeis, and the Alma Field on the Gulf of Suez. The Sinai is hot year round, with temperatures similar to those of the Negev (which is its northern extension)—average highs of about 90° F (32°C) and average lows of about 60° F (15° C), but lower in the mountains. The largest cities of the Sinai are al-Arish on the north coast, with an estimated population of 80,000; Port Said at the north end of the Suez Canal; Suez at the south end of the canal; Sharm al-Shaykh, a port at the southern point of the peninsula on the Red Sea; and Eilat, an Israeli port at the head of the Gulf of Aqaba.

Sinai has mainly been part of Egypt—its gateway to Asia, the Levant, and Mesopotamia. According to the Bible, it was the site of the forty years of wandering by the Israelites who followed Moses out of Egypt—and the site of Mount Sinai (Jabal Musa), where Moses received the Ten Commandments. When the Ottoman Turks formed their empire, they ruled the area from 1517 until 1840. After their appointed governor Khedive Muhammad Ali broke with the Ottoman Empire, he was assigned rule over Egypt by his British allies in the Treaty of London, but the Sinai remained basically Ottoman. The British Colonial Office exerted its own rule over Egypt from 1882 and clashed with the Ottomans over specific areas of the Sinai; they managed to establish the eastern boundary as a line from al-Arish or Rafa to Aqaba. Rafa–Aqaba became the southern boundary of the British mandate territory of Palestine from 1922 to 1948. It remained the international border between Egypt and the new State of Israel from 1949 through 1967, when, through the winning of the ARAB–ISRAEL WAR (1967), Israel occupied the Sinai until the 1980 to 1982 staged withdrawals, based on the CAMP DAVID ACCORDS and the Egyptian–Israeli peace treaty. During Israel's occupation, Jewish settlements were established in the Sinai, two major air force bases were constructed, and the Alma Oil Field was discovered and developed.

BIBLIOGRAPHY

ROLEF, S. H., ed. *Political Dictionary of the State of Israel.* New York, 1987.

SHIMONI, YAACOV. *Political Dictionary of the Arab World.* New York, 1987.
VATIKIOTIS, P. J. *The History of Egypt.* London, 1969.

Elizabeth Thompson

Sinai War

See Arab–Israel War (1956)

Şinasi, İbrahim   [1826–1871]

Ottoman intellectual.

İbrahim Şinasi's father was an army officer for the Ottoman Empire, and Şinasi himself became an army scribe after completing elementary school. He learned French, and in 1849 he was sent to Europe by the leading Tanzimat reformer, Mustafa Reşid Paşa. There he was influenced by such luminaries as Ernest Renan and Albert Lamartine, but when he returned to Turkey, he was unable to advance in the government and devoted himself to literary endeavors. The author of several plays and books of poetry, he was also a prominent journalist and the editor of TASVIR-I EFKÂR (Description of Ideas), which began in 1862 and acted as a clearinghouse for the liberal Young Ottoman ideas then in vogue. Like many of the Young Ottomans, Şinasi found himself at odds with the more autocratic Tanzimat officials of the day, including Ali Paşa and Fuad Paşa, and he was forced to leave Istanbul in 1864. He remained in Paris until his return to Istanbul shortly before his death.

BIBLIOGRAPHY

LEWIS, BERNARD. *The Emergence of Modern Turkey.* New York, 1961.
MARDIN, SERIF. *The Genesis of Young Ottoman Thought.* Princeton, N.J., 1964.
SHAW, STANFORD, and EZEL KURAL SHAW. *History of the Ottoman Empire and Modern Turkey.* New York, 1977.

Zachary Karabell

Şirket-i Hayriye

Nineteenth-century Istanbul ferryboat company for the Bosporus Straits.

This was the first substantial joint-stock company established in the Ottoman Empire. It was founded in 1849 with two thousand shares and sixty thousand Turkish lire in capital with the support of Mustafa Reşid Paşa, one of the leaders of the mid-nineteenth-century reforms called Tanzimat. Created to provide ferry transport on the Bosporus in Istanbul, the company bought its boats for seven thousand Turkish lire each from a British company.

The company was promoted by Reşid Paşa as an example of new economic forms. To demonstrate the security of joint-stock companies, he encouraged several other government officials to invest in the ferryboat firm. Similar companies were soon founded in the 1850s, including the Bank-ı Osmanı, the Aydın–İzmir Railroad, and Şirket-i Osmaniyyesi.

BIBLIOGRAPHY

LEWIS, BERNARD. *The Emergence of Modern Turkey*. New York, 1969.

Elizabeth Thompson

Sirte

See Sidra, Gulf of

Sistan

Province in the southeast of Iran.

The boundaries of the Sistan portion of the province in the east of Iran, formerly also known as Sijistan, were formed in 1872, after protracted war, by an agreement between Persia (Iran's name before 1935) and Afghanistan. Sistan united with the Iranian portion of Baluchistan in 1959 to form one province. (The other part of Baluchistan is a province of Pakistan.) In medieval times, Sistan comprised a much larger area. Its name derives from Sakistan, or land of Sakas (Scythians), who invaded the region in 128 B.C. The region is fertile but has a hot, arid climate. The Helmand is the principal river and main source for agriculture in the region. The capital is Zahedan. In 1986, the population of the province was 1,197,059.

BIBLIOGRAPHY

BOSWORTH, C. E., ed. *An Historical Geography of Iran*. Princeton, N.J., 1984.

Parvaneh Pourshariati

Sitra

One of the thirty-three islands in the Bahrain archipelago.

Sitra lies in the Persian/Arabian Gulf, just off the northeast corner of Bahrain, the main island, to which it is connected by a short bridge. On Sitra are located the petroleum loading terminal and tank farm belonging to the Bahrain Petroleum Company, as well as a small number of date palm gardens and a limited amount of cropland at the northern end of its eleven square miles (28 sq. km).

BIBLIOGRAPHY

CLARKE, ANGELA. *The Islands of Bahrain*. Manama, 1981.

Fred H. Lawson

Sitt

Title for a woman; it means "lady" in Arabic.

Sitt, the equivalent of *sayyida*, is often used in royal titles to signify the sisters and daughters of the caliph, sultan, or emir.

Marilyn Higbee

Sivas Congress

Convened (September 4–11, 1919) to resist plans of the Triple Entente to dismember the Ottoman Empire; a significant step in the progression of events leading to the Turkish revolution.

The official communiqué issued by the Sivas Congress was the first Turkish declaration against the partitioning of lands under Ottoman sovereignty that had taken place when the MUDROS ARMISTICE was signed. The same document summoned the sultan to call for a general election and announced the creation of the Association for the Defense of the Rights of Anatolia and Rumelia, whose Representative Committee was designated to act as a provisional government in Anatolia until May 1920.

Ahmet Kuyas

Siwa Oases

Group of oases in northwest Egypt.

The Siwa oases, located at 29° 12′ N, 25° 31′ E, or 186 miles (300 km) west of Marsa Matruh, had a population of 5,169 in 1966. In ancient times, Siwa was the seat of the oracle of Jupiter Ammon, visited by Alexander the Great in 331 B.C.E. It has historically served as both Egypt's western boundary and the easternmost area inhabited by Berbers. The spoken Siwan dialect is a Berber language heavily influ-

View of part of the Siwa oases in the Eastern desert region of Egypt. (Mia Bloom)

Overview of Siwa and the Eastern desert of Egypt. (David Rewcastle)

Siwa surrounded by the craggy terrain of Egypt's Eastern desert. (David Rewcastle)

enced by Arabic. In the nineteenth century it was one of the centers of the Sanusi Order, and some fighting took place there during World War I. It is a center for date palm agriculture. Siwa is also the name of the town in the southern part of the oases.

BIBLIOGRAPHY

SEARS, CONSTANCE S. "The Oasis of Siwa: Visited and Revisited." *Newsletter of the American Research Center in Egypt* 165 (Spring/Summer 1994): 1–10.
VIVIAN, CASSANDRA. *Siwa Oasis: Its History, Sites, and Crafts.* Ma'adi, Egypt, 1991.

Arthur Goldschmidt, Jr.

Six Arrows

See Kemalism

Six-Day War

See Arab–Israel War (1967)

Slave Trade

The buying and selling of humans for servitude was an old tradition in the Middle East as in many other parts of the world.

Since antiquity, slavery was an integral part of the various societies that inhabited the Middle East. Men, women, and children were enslaved within these lands or imported into them from neighboring and faraway regions. From the early sixteenth to the early twentieth centuries, the Middle East was part of the Ottoman Empire, in which slavery was legal and the slave trade active. The traffic in slaves was substantially reduced toward the end of the nineteenth century, and slavery died out in most of the Middle East during the first decade of the twentieth. In certain parts of Arabia, the practice lingered on well into the second half of this century, and various forms of slavery continue to exist even today.

"Slavery" in Middle Eastern—and other—societies can be difficult to define. Some attempts to answer the question "who is a slave?" have resulted in "one whose labor is controlled and whose freedom is withheld," a person "in a state of legal and actual servility or [who is] of slave origins," or a "natally alienated and generally dishonored person" under "permanent, violent domination." In Islamic legal terms, slavery grants one person ownership over another person, which means that the owner has rights to the slave's labor, property, and sexuality and that the slave's freedoms are severely restricted. But in sociocultural terms, slavery sometimes meant high social status, or political power, for male slaves in the military and bureaucracy (MAMLUKS and *kul*s) and female slaves in elite harems. Even ordinary domestic slaves were often better fed, clothed, and protected than many free men and women. In any event, slavery was an important, albeit involuntary, channel of recruitment and socialization into the elite and a major—though forced—means of linking into patronage networks.

Slavery gradually became a differentiated and broadly defined concept in many Islamic societies since the introduction of military slaves into the Abbasid Caliphate in the ninth century. In the Ottoman Empire, military-administrative servitude, better known as the *kul* system, coexisted with other types of slavery: harem (quite different from Western fantasy), domestic, and agricultural (on a rather limited scale). While the latter types of slavery remained much the same until late in the nineteenth century, the *kul* system underwent profound changes.

From its inception, the *kul* system was nourished on periodical levies of the unmarried, able-bodied, male children of the sultan's Orthodox Christian subjects, mostly from the Balkans. This child levy was known as the *devşirme*. The children were reduced to slavery, converted to Islam, and rigorously socialized at the palace school into various government roles, carrying elite status. However, freeborn Muslims gradually entered government service, and the *kul* system evolved to accommodate this change. Ultimately, the child levy was abandoned during the seventeenth century, the palace school lost its monopoly on the reproduction of military-administrative slaves, and a new, *kul*-type recruitment-cum-socialization pattern came to prevail.

With the evolution of the *kul* system, the classification of *kul*s as slaves was gradually becoming irrelevant. Ottoman officials of *kul* origins and training held elevated, powerful positions with all rights, privileges, and honors, and cases in which the sultan confiscated their property or took their life became increasingly rare. Whereas *kul*s and non-*kul*s were subject to the sultan's "whims" to the same extent, the intimacy and mutual reliance of the master-slave relationship often provided the *kul* with greater protection than that enjoyed by free officials. Harem women of slave origins were in much the same predicament, playing a major role in the reproduction of the Ottoman elite. Toward the nineteenth century, the servility of persons in the *kul*/harem category becomes more a symbol of their high status and less a practical or legal disability. All that has led some scholars to question the very use of the term "slaves"

for such men and women. In any event, the HATT-I ŞERIF OF GÜLHANE of 1839 freed government officials from the last vestiges of servility attached to their status.

In the Ottoman Middle East, and with local modifications also in other Muslim societies, there was a continuum of various degrees of servility rather than a dichotomy between slave and free. At one end of that continuum were domestic and agricultural slaves, the "real slaves" in Ottoman society, while at the other were officeholders in the army and bureaucracy, with little to tie them to actual slavery. In between, but close to officeholders and far from domestic and agricultural slaves, came officials of slave origins (*kul*-type) and then harem ladies of slave origins.

The overwhelming majority of the slaves living in the Middle East during the Ottoman period were female, black, and domestic; they served in menial jobs in households across a broad social spectrum. A smaller number of white female slaves also worked in similar circumstances, as did a number of black and white male slaves. African male slaves were employed in the Red Sea, Persian/Arabian Gulf, and Indian Ocean as pearl divers, oarsmen, and crew members in sailboats, in Arabia as agricultural laborers (in date, coffee, and other plantations) and outdoor servants, and in Egypt as cotton pickers in the 1860s. African men were used as soldiers in scattered instances in Yemen and other parts of Arabia, as in Egypt where the experiment of Muhammad Ali Pasha to recruit Sudanese slave soldiers failed. *Kul* and harem slaves were a relatively small minority among Middle Eastern slaves in the nineteenth century.

At the time, a fairly steady stream of about eleven thousand to thirteen thousand slaves per year entered the region from central Africa and the Sudan, from western Ethiopia, and from Circassia, Abkhazia, and Georgia. They were brought in by caravan and boat via the Sahara desert routes, the Ethiopian plateau, the Red Sea, the Nile river valley, the Mediterranean, the Persian/Arabian Gulf, the Black Sea, and the pilgrimage routes to and from Arabia. After raids, sales, and resales, they reached their final destinations in the great urban centers of the Middle East, where they were sold in markets or in private homes of slave dealers.

Whereas slaveholding was still legal at the beginning of the twentieth century, the slave trade into the region had already been prohibited by law for several decades. The traffic in Africans and Caucasians practically died down, although it would pick up from time to time on a small scale. Slavery was gradually being transformed into free forms of service-cum-patronage, such as raising freeborn children (mostly female) in the household, socializing them into lower- or upper-class roles—as talent and need determined—and later marrying them off and setting them up in life. Ottoman elite culture was articulating a negative attitude toward the practice and gradually disengaging from it on moral grounds. This was a significant development, given the fact that slavery enjoyed Islamic legitimacy and wide social acceptance in the Middle East and that, except for cases of cruelty and ill-usage, it was a matter over which no serious moral debate ever arose.

The profound change that occurred was part of a major reform program introduced into the Middle East during the nineteenth century. Much of this happened during the TANZIMAT (loosely covering the 1830s to the 1880s), generally regarded as a period of change in many areas of Ottoman life, although it is not certain how deeply the reforms affected the overwhelming majority of the population or even the peripheral groups within the Ottoman elite. Visible changes in the army, the bureaucracy, the economy, law and justice, education, communication, transportation, and public health went along with the reinvigoration of central authority. This was the work of a strongly motivated, Ottoman-centered group of reformers, who implemented their own program and political agenda and were not merely the tools of Western influence. While the government came to possess more efficient means of repression, its reforms also sowed the seeds of political change, giving rise to a strong constitutional movement, although the extent to which Western ideas—not just technology and fashion—were assimilated into Middle Eastern culture is still under debate.

Having abolished slavery by the end of the first third of the nineteenth century, the powers of Europe now turned their zeal to slavery in the Americas. But in the 1840s, the British government and public opinion were already beginning to take an interest in the abolition of slavery in the Ottoman Middle East. Attempts to induce Istanbul to adopt measures to that effect soon proved futile. Instead—and as an alternative method that would ultimately choke slavery for want of supply—a major effort was launched to suppress the slave trade into the region. The essence of that long-term British drive was to extract from the Ottomans, on humanitarian grounds, edicts forbidding the trade in Africans and Caucasians. The implementation of such edicts was then carefully monitored by British diplomatic and commercial representatives throughout the Middle East and reported back to London. In turn, London would press Istanbul to enforce the edicts, and so on.

This pattern yielded the prohibition of the slave trade in the Gulf in 1847, the temporary prohibition of the traffic in Circassians and Georgians in 1854–1855, the general prohibition of the African slave trade in 1857, the Anglo–Egyptian convention for the suppression of the slave trade in 1877, and the Anglo–Ottoman one in 1880. The campaign reached its climax in the Brussels Act against the slave trade, which the Ottoman government signed in 1890. From the mid-1850s onward, Caucasian slavery and slave trade were excluded from the realm of Anglo–Ottoman relations. In that area, the Ottomans initiated some major changes, acting alone and according to their own views.

One of the most important factors that shaped Ottoman policy toward Caucasian slavery was the large number of Circassian refugees—estimates run from 500,000 to 1 million—who entered Ottoman territory from the mid-1850s to the mid-1860s. That Russian-forced migration contained about 10 percent unfree agricultural population, which put the question of non-African slavery into a different perspective. Increased tensions between refugee owners and slaves, at times causing violence and disturbance of public order, induced the Ottoman government in 1867 to design a special program for slaves who wished to obtain their freedom. Using an Islamic legal device, the government granted the slaves the land they were cultivating in order to purchase manumission from their own masters.

In 1882, the authorities moved further in the same method to facilitate the conscription of Circassian and Georgian slaves. Such a step was necessary because only free men could be drafted into the army. Measures were also taken from the mid-1860s onward to restrict the traffic in Circassian and Georgian children, mostly young girls. Thus, by the last decade of the nineteenth century, the trade in Caucasian slaves was considerably reduced. The remaining demand was maintained only by the harems of the imperial family and the households of well-to-do elite members. The imperial harem at the time contained about 400 women in a wide array of household positions quite different from those consigned to them by Western fantasy. Those harems also continued to employ eunuchs, and as late as 1903, the Ottoman family alone owned 194 of them. In the nineteenth century, a perceived decline occurred in their political influence, both as individuals and as a distinct corps in court politics. Whether officially abolished by the 1908 revolution, or only later by the new Turkish republic, Ottoman slavery died piecemeal, not abruptly, with the end of the empire.

Except for the issue of equality for non-Muslims, the call for the abolition of slavery was perhaps the most sensitive and culturally loaded topic processed in the Tanzimat period. Although it was rarely debated in the open, this was a matter of daily and personal concern, for both the public and private spheres of elite life were permeated by slaves on all levels. Faced with British diplomatic pressure to suppress the slave trade into the Middle East and with the zeal of Western abolitionism, Ottoman reformers and thinkers responded on both the political and the ideological planes. However, that response came when slavery was already on the wane, doomed to disappear with other obsolete institutions.

BIBLIOGRAPHY

BAER, GABRIEL. "Slavery and Its Abolition." In *Studies in the Social History of Modern Egypt.* Chicago, 1969.

LEWIS, BERNARD. *Race and Slavery in the Middle East.* New York, 1990.

PIERCE, LESLIE. *The Imperial Harem.* New York, 1993.

TOLEDANO, EHUD R. "The Imperial Eunuchs of Istanbul: From Africa to the Heart of Islam." *Middle Eastern Studies* 20, no. 3 (1984): 379–390.

———. "Ottoman Concepts of Slavery in the Period of Reform (1830s to 1880s)." In *Breaking the Chains: Slavery, Bondage and Emancipation in Africa and Asia,* ed. by Martin A. Klein. Madison, Wis. 1993.

———. *The Ottoman Slave Trade and Its Suppression, 1840–1890.* Princeton, N.J., 1982.

———. "Slave Dealers, Women, Pregnancy, and Abortion: The Story of a Circassian Slave-Girl in Mid-Nineteenth-Century Cairo." *Slavery and Abolition* 2, no. 1 (1980): 53–68.

Ehud R. Toledano

Smilansky, Moshe   [1874–1953]

Israeli author and agricultural pioneer.

Smilansky was born in Kiev province in the Ukraine to a family of farmers. He emigrated to Palestine in 1891 and worked as an agriculturalist at various places before settling in Rehovot in 1893. There he spent the remainder of his life as a citrus plantation owner and writer. A fierce advocate for developing the land, Smilansky led various agricultural organizations, for example, the Histadrut ha-Ikarim (The Farmers' Association).

He was also a prolific author and began writing in 1898 as a publicist for the fledgling settlements in Palestine and for the cultivation of its soil. A unique literary contribution of Smilansky was his stories, in Hebrew, depicting Arab life, written under the pseudonym Khawaja Moussa, which were collected in a single volume entitled *Benei Arav* (1964, Arab Sons). He described in great detail the pioneer movement in Palestine of which he was an active participant. His most famous works on the topic are the

six-volume *Perakim Be-Toledot Ha-Yishuv* (1959; Chapters in the History of the Yishuv) and the four-volume *Mishpahat Ha-Adamah* (1943–1953; Family of the Soil).

Ann Kahn

Smolenskin, Peretz   [1842–1885]

Hebrew writer of the Haskala period, forerunner of Zionism.

Born in Russia, Smolenskin moved to Vienna in 1868 and became editor of the Hebrew monthly *Ha-Shahar* (the Dawn), in which most of his writings were published. He helped found Kadima, the first national Jewish students' organization, in Vienna. Following the Russian pogroms of 1881, he advocated the idea of a Jewish "return to Zion."

BIBLIOGRAPHY

HERTZBERG, ARTHUR. *The Zionist Idea.* New York, 1979.

Martin Malin

Smyrna

See İzmir

Sneh, Moshe   [1909–1972]

Israeli politician and statesman.

Born in Poland where he was an active Zionist, Sneh emigrated to Israel in 1940. He was chief of the Haganah High Command from 1941 to 1946 and later head of the "illegal" Immigration Department of the Jewish Agency. From 1949 to 1965, he was a member of the Knesset from Maki, the moderate faction of the Israeli Communist party, and editor of its daily newspaper.

Walter F. Weiker

Sobol, Yehoshua   [1939–   ]

Israeli playwright.

The plays of Yehoshua Sobol reflect common Israeli themes including the Holocaust and the Arab–Israeli conflict. A graduate of the Sorbonne in Paris, Sobol has worked as artistic director of the Haifa Municipal Theatre since 1984, where most of his plays have premiered. His most famous work is *Ghetto,* one of three related plays about the Vilna ghetto. Other works include *Soul of a Jew, The Days to Come,* and *Shooting Magda.* Many of his plays have been produced all over the world in many languages.

BIBLIOGRAPHY

Modern Israeli Drama in Translation. Portsmouth, N.H., 1992.
SOBOL, YEHOSHUA. *Ghetto.* London, 1989.

Julie Zuckerman

SOCAL (Standard Oil Company of California)

See Arabian American Oil Company

Social Democratic Party of Azerbaijan

Political party in Iranian Azerbaijan.

The Firqa-ye Ijtima'iyun-e Ammiyun (Social Democratic party), also called *Mujahid,* was active mainly in Iranian Azerbaijan. It may have been an offshoot of the ADALAT (Justice) party, a nominally social democratic, but actually anticolonial, organization formed in 1904/05 by Azerbaijanis in Baku (on the Caspian Sea) who were involved in the social democratic party Hümmet (Endeavor). Adalat was created for workers from Iran employed in the Baku petroleum industry.

In August or September 1906, members of the founding committee of the party established a "secret center" in Tabriz, then cells in Ardebil, Rasht, and Enzeli; these organizations apparently remained under the direction of a central committee in Baku. The party program demanded a constitution in Iran, ministerial responsibility to the Majles (Iran's legislature), establishment of universal suffrage, and civil liberties. It pointed to Qur'anic precedents and the example of "every civilized state of Europe and Asia."

The party was apparently suppressed around 1909 but served as a model to the later Communist TUDEH PARTY.

BIBLIOGRAPHY

BAYAT, MANGOL. *Iran's First Revolution: Shi'ism and Constitutional Crisis, 1905–1909.* Oxford, 1991.
SWIETOCHOWSKI, TADEUSZ. *Russia and a Divided Azerbaijan: Foreign Conquest and Divergent Historical Development.* New York, 1994.

Audrey L. Altstadt

Social Democratic Populist Party

Turkish political party formed in the mid-1980s.

This party was formed by the merger of the Social Democratic and the Populist parties, both of which had been established in 1983 in the wake of the military coup of 1980. As its name implies, it is a moderate center-left party. It also claims the Kemalist ideological heritage of the pre-1980 REPUBLICAN PEOPLE'S PARTY. In the 1987 parliamentary elections, the first in which it competed, the party came in second with 25 percent of the vote and 99 of the 450 seats at stake. In 1991, it slipped to third place, polling 21 percent of the vote and winning 88 seats. It then became the junior partner in a coalition government led by Süleyman DEMIREL and the True Path party.

BIBLIOGRAPHY

LANDAU, J. M. "Turkey." In *Political Parties of the Middle East and North Africa,* ed. by F. Tachau. Westport, Conn., 1994.

Frank Tachau

Socialist Cooperative Party

Syrian political party.

The Socialist Cooperative party was founded in 1948 by Faysal al-Asali. The small, right-wing group preached a strong pan-Islamist message and valued an ascetic, secretive lifestyle of study and military drilling.

BIBLIOGRAPHY

SEALE, PATRICK. *The Struggle for Syria.* London, 1965.

Charles U. Zenzie

Socialist Labor Party

Egyptian political party.

The Socialist Labor party was established in September 1978 by Ibrahim Shukri, the former leader of Misr al-Fatat (Young Egypt), following Egyptian president Anwar al-Sadat's party law of June 1977 allowing a controlled return to the multi-party system. Shukri and his right-hand man, Mahmud Abu Wafia, both from large landowning families, and the members of the party, generally middle-class, are urban professionals, state employees, and some rural notables. Sadat had intended the party to be a loyal opposition on the left, but in 1981 he had the entire leadership of the party arrested. In 1982, the party was legalized again after successfully supporting Husni Mubarak for president after Sadat's assassination in 1981. The party supports economic liberalization (*infitah*) and peace with Israel. In the 1987 parliamentary elections, the party formed an alliance with the Liberal Socialist Party and the Muslim Brotherhood and received 17 percent of the votes. The party's weekly paper, *al-Sha'b* (The People) is edited by Adil Husayn, a former Marxist and now a neo-Islamist economist.

BIBLIOGRAPHY

HINNEBUSCH, RAYMOND. *Egyptian Politics under Sadat: The Post-Populist Development of an Authoritarian-Modernizing State.* Cambridge, U.K., 1985.
SAID ALI, ABDEL MONEM. "Democratization in Egypt." *American Arab Affairs* 22 (1987): 11–27.

David Waldner

Socotra

South Yemen's largest island.

Measuring twelve hundred square miles (3,100 sq. km), Socotra is located in the Arabian Sea not far from Somalia. The ruler of the Mahra Sultanate of Qishn and Socotra resided there under British rule, before the National Liberation Front (NLF) took over upon South Yemen's independence in 1967. Thought to be of strategic significance to Western counties from time to time over the centuries, Socotra most recently lost its importance in this regard with the end of the Cold War in 1990. Socotra has a mountainous interior; its inhabitants engage in agriculture and fishing.

Robert D. Burrowes

Soheyli, Ali   [?–1954]

Iranian politician.

Ali Soheyli was born in Tabriz and studied at the military school in Tehran. After several cabinet positions, he was named minister of foreign affairs in 1937 and served three times as prime minister during the tenure of Mohammad Reza Shah Pahlavi. In 1947, because of pressure from the parliamentary faction loyal to Mohammad Mossadegh, Soheyli, a royalist, was put on trial. He was charged with mishandling of public funds, illegal intervention in elections in the south of the country, disrespect for the constitutional provision of free speech and a free press, and conspiracy against the nationalist govern-

ment. After being acquitted of all charges, Soheyli resumed political activity as a minister without portfolio. Famous for his skill in handling foreign diplomats in Iran, he enjoyed amicable relations with both the Russian and the British legations in Tehran. In 1953, he sought appointment as prime minister but failed to get it. The shah appointed him ambassador to Britain, where he died of leukemia.

BIBLIOGRAPHY

AQELI, BAQER. *Iranian Prime Ministers from Moshir al-Dowleh to Bakhtiyar.* Tehran, 1991. In Persian.

Neguin Yavari

Sokolow, Nahum   [1859–1936]

Hebrew journalist, author, and Zionist leader.

Born in Poland, Sokolow received a traditional Jewish education and distinguished himself as a Talmudic scholar. He moved to Warsaw in the late 1870s and was a journalist for the Hebrew language paper *Ha-Tzfira,* of which he became editor and owner in 1885. Sokolow also published books on anti-Semitism and the Jewish enlightenment and biographies.

Following the first Zionist Congress (Basel, 1897), Sokolow became a principal spokesperson for the Eastern European Zionist movement. He was appointed secretary-general of the World Zionist Organization in 1907, and in 1911 he was given the political portfolio on the Zionist Executive. He traveled extensively in that capacity, meeting with leaders throughout Europe and with Arab leaders in Lebanon and Syria. Sokolow worked closely with Chaim Weizmann in England during World War I, laying the groundwork for the Balfour Declaration. In 1921, he was elected head of the Zionist Executive. He was president of the World Zionist Organization from 1931 to 1935.

Martin Malin

Solel Boneh

See Histadrut

Solh, Alia al-

Daughter of Lebanese Prime Minister Riyad al-Sulh.

Choosing journalism as her profession, Alia al-Solh (also, al-Sulh) interviewed Arab and world leaders

for *al-Nahar*. She later became editor of the weekly publication *al-Hasna*. She was known for her strong political opinions, which ranged from her support of Palestinian militancy to, later, her approbation of Bashir Jumayyil and Michel Aoun.

Bassam Namani

Solh, Kazem al-   [1909–1977]

Lebanese politician, diplomat, and journalist; former ambassador to Iraq; member of parliament, 1960–1964.

Kazem al-Solh (also al-Sulh) was born into a prestigious Sunni family that was active in the Arab nationalist movement at the turn of the century. He emerged in the 1930s as one of the most articulate advocates of an independent, sovereign Lebanon that would be free from French control but would also remain separate from Syria. In defending the territorial boundaries that the French mandatory power had established, he went against the dominant opinion of people in his community, who still favored reintegrating into Syria those regions the French had annexed to Mount Lebanon in 1920.

Unlike many of his Muslim contemporaries, Kazem al-Solh understood very early on that independence from France could only be gained by reaching out to moderate Christians, particularly Maronites. He argued that the Maronites would more easily loosen their ties to France and join the nationalist cause if they could be reassured that independence would not be followed by absorption into Syria, or by policies that would undermine Lebanon's political autonomy vis-à-vis other Arab countries. He aspired to create an independent Lebanon based on Muslim–Christian accommodation. It would be possible to achieve this goal, he believed, if the Sunnis agreed to a historic compromise: if they would shed their traditional demand for reunification with Syria in exchange for the Maronites' abandoning their call for a Christian Lebanon and renouncing French protection and interference in Lebanese affairs.

To promote these ideas, Kazem al-Solh created a group called al-Nida al-Qawmi (The National Appeal), which attracted moderate Sunnis and became a political party in 1945. Although it never was able to develop a mass following, the group played an important role in mobilizing Sunni support for an independent Lebanon. It also strengthened the hand of Maronite leaders like Bishara al-Khuri who were arguing within their own communities for the very kind of cross-confessional compromise that Kazem al-Solh and like-minded Sunni notables and intellec-

tuals were advocating. Some measure of the influence of Kazem al-Solh and groups such as al-Nida al-Qawmi can be gotten by noting that the aspirations they articulated were eventually embodied in the 1943 NATIONAL PACT. Kazem and his brother Taki al-Din are usually credited with facilitating the conversion of their first cousin Riyad al-SULH to the cause of an independent, sovereign Lebanon managed through a Maronite–Sunni partnership.

Although his ideas had a critical impact on the course of Lebanese history, Kazem al-Solh played only a marginal role in post-independence Lebanese politics. Although he was a gifted writer and political thinker, he never was a particularly effective politician. By the late 1950s, al-Nida al-Qawmi had ceased to function, a victim to the rising tide of Arab nationalism. Kazem al-Solh's politics had always been based on compromise, tolerance, and conciliation, and this approach had become increasingly inappropriate in the context of an Arab world that, caught in the ferment of the 1950s and 1960s, witnessed the radicalization of the Sunni masses. Kazem al-Sohl served as Lebanese ambassador to Iraq during the 1940s and 1950s, and he was criticized by pan-Arab intellectuals and politicians for the part it was alleged he played in designing the ill-fated BAGHDAD PACT. Thanks to Christian votes, he was elected a Sunni representative from Zahle to the parliament (1960–1964). Kazem al-Solh ended his career as a relatively uninfluential politician, largely discredited within his own community.

BIBLIOGRAPHY

GORIA, WADER R. *Sovereignty and Leadership in Lebanon, 1943–1976.* London, 1985.

HUDSON, MICHAEL C. *The Precarious Republic: Political Modernization in Lebanon.* Boulder, Colo., 1985.

JOHNSON, MICHAEL. *Class and Client in Beirut: The Sunni Muslim Community and the Lebanese State, 1840–1985.* London, 1986.

Guilain P. Denoeux

Solh, Rashid al-   [1926–   ]

Lebanese politician; prime minister, 1974–1975 and 1992.

Al-Solh, born into a minor branch of the prestigious Sunni Solh (sometimes Sulh) family, was brought up in the house of former prime minister Sami al-Sulh. After receiving a law degree from St. Joseph University in Beirut, he became a lawyer and a judge. Elected deputy for Beirut in 1964 and 1972, he inherited the political mantle of Sami al-Sulh following the latter's death in 1968. Considered a moderate among Sunni leaders in the 1970s, Solh nevertheless developed a reputation as a champion of the working class and maintained a close relationship with Kamal Jumblatt. While still a relative newcomer among Sunni political bosses, he was chosen as prime minister by President Sulayman Franjiyya in October 1974; he held the premiership until May 1975, when he resigned. He thus presided over the outbreak of the Lebanese Civil War, which he was unable to prevent or stop. Before stepping down, Solh denounced the inertia of Lebanon's society and the political and administrative corruption and nepotism that, he claimed, had thwarted the implementation of his reforms. He warned that unless the entire political system was overhauled, the country was headed toward political chaos and disintegration.

In May 1992, Solh became prime minister again, following the demonstrations and riots that brought down the government of Umar Karami. He held the position until October, when he was replaced by Rafiq Hariri. During his short tenure, he was frequently criticized for subservience to Syria. In particular, his insistence on proceeding with parliamentary elections in the summer of 1992 alienated many Lebanese, who opposed the timing of these elections. Beirut's electorate severely punished him for this and other decisions that were seen as bowing to Syria's wishes. The electoral list he headed was soundly defeated by that led by Salim al-HOSS. Although he managed to win a seat in parliament, Solh received the fewest votes (11,428) of all Sunnis elected, and no other Sunni on his list was elected (three Armenian Orthodox candidates and one Armenian Catholic were).

BIBLIOGRAPHY

JOHNSON, MICHAEL. *Class and Client in Beirut: The Sunni Muslim Community and the Lebanese State, 1840–1985.* London, 1986.

Guilain P. Denoeux

Solh, Taki al-Din al-   [1909–   ]

Lebanese journalist and politician; former prime minister and minister of finance, 1973–1974.

A first cousin of Riyad al-Solh, Taki al-Din al-Solh (also al-Sulh) was born in Beirut and educated at the American University of Beirut, where he studied literature and history. During the 1930s, he worked as a journalist, literature teacher, and director of the Ministry of Information. With his brother Kazem,

he founded the al-Nida al-Qawmi (The National Appeal), a group of moderate Sunni politicians and intellectuals who advocated a free and sovereign Lebanon, independent from the French and separate from Syria. A traditional, nonideological politician, he proved either unwilling or unable to build a strong political machine and consequently did not develop a wide base of popular support. He nevertheless—because of his connection to a prestigious family—occupied several important political positions in the 1960s: he was a member of parliament (1964–1968) and a minister of the interior (1964–1965). His career reached its zenith in July 1973 when President Sulayman Franjiyya called upon him to become Prime Minister. During his fifteen months in office, he was unable to prevent Lebanon's slide toward political disintegration. His tenure was marked by economic crisis and political turmoil, student and labor unrest, a growing rift between Muslims and Christians, repeated clashes between the Lebanese army and Palestinian commandos, and numerous Israeli raids in southern Lebanon. He resigned in September 1974 and was replaced by Sa'ib Salam.

BIBLIOGRAPHY

HUDSON, MICHAEL C. *The Precarious Republic: Political Modernization in Lebanon.* Boulder, Colo., 1985.
SALIBI, KAMAL S. *Crossroads to Civil War: Lebanon, 1958–1976.* Delmar, N.Y., 1976.

Guilain P. Denoeux

Somekh, Abdallah   [1813–1889]

Iraqi rabbi.

Somekh, one of the most venerated rabbinic authorities in Baghdad in the nineteenth century, was instrumental in renewing Jewish religious studies in that city. In 1840 he established its first modern rabbinic seminary, Beit Zilkha. He wrote a commentary on *Shulhan Arukh* and a number of volumes of responsa that often addressed problems arising from the incursion of technology and modern education into the life of Oriental Jewish communities—for instance, whether a telegraphic message can be used as evidence in a Torah court. Somekh often dealt with religious questions addressed to him by Iraqi Jews who had settled in India, China, and other Far Eastern nations. In the 1860s, when the Alliance Israélite Universelle was established in Baghdad, he sent his son to study there, ignoring the protestations of conservative rabbis who strongly disapproved of secular education. Somekh died in Baghdad during a plague epidemic.

BIBLIOGRAPHY

SASSON, D. S. *A History of the Jews in Baghdad.* Letchworth, U.K., 1949.

Sasson Somekh

SONATRACH

Holding company for the state's interests in Algeria's hydrocarbon sector.

In the events leading up to the independence of Algeria in 1962, the French government attempted to create a number of arrangements for continued access to Algerian oil, which had been discovered in the Sahara regions of the country a few years earlier. As part of its strategy to put the proceeds from oil sales into its industrialization strategy, the government of Algeria formed SONATRACH (Société Nationale de Transport et de Commercialisation des Hydrocarbures). It was headed initially by Abdessalam Belaid, who would become the country's head of centrally guided industrialization—a strategy in which SONATRACH was seen as the financial cornerstone. The initial difficulty faced by SONATRACH was that all production and marketing of hydrocarbons in the country had been geared toward the requirements of France's economy, a goal now incompatible with the socialist and inward-oriented new development strategy of the Algerian government. Initially restricted to pipeline development and marketing abroad in an effort to break the French monopoly, SONATRACH eventually branched out into all aspects of oil exploration, refining, and marketing, often entering into joint ventures with foreign oil companies for exploration and production. By the early 1970s, SONATRACH had become a giant state enterprise and the single largest employer in the country. It exercised control not only over the recovery of oil but managed the major refineries in Algiers, Arzew, and Skikda, and it was the domestic distributor for Algerian oil. In addition, the state enterprise also controlled a large number of oil-related subsidiaries that fueled much of the country's industrialization drive.

Under President Houari Boumédienne (1965–1978) the Algerian government attempted to index the price of natural gas to that of petroleum, since Algeria was estimated to possess the fourth largest gas reserves in the world. At the same time SONATRACH increased its exploration activities substantially, at a time when the world demand for Algerian natural gas was stagnant or declining. The strategy necessitated heavy investments, among other items, in liquefaction plants built at the Algerian coast, for which the country borrowed extensively on the international market, starting in the mid-1970s. Neither the indexing nor the investments proved sound decisions, and by the early 1980s SONATRACH was forced to renegotiate most of its major contracts and accept lower prices for its natural gas exports. By 1970 SONATRACH directly controlled an estimated 30 percent of Algerian oil production, which accounted for some 34 percent of the country's gross domestic product. By 1977, after a series of nationalizations that ended in 1971, its participation had increased to approximately 75 percent.

The death of President Boumédienne in 1978 brought to a halt the socialist experiment that Algeria had adopted after independence in 1962. The June 1980 party congress, guided by the new president, Chadli Benjedid, stressed the need for increased privatization and liberalization in the Algerian economy. Benjedid advocated a reorganization of the huge national enterprise to make it more competitive internally and more efficient internally. By 1985, SONATRACH was the sole national enterprise that continued to show profits; nevertheless, the giant company was divided into thirteen smaller companies, each of which would compete for clients. By 1990, the Algerian government was searching once more for foreign partners to participate in the exploration for and production of its oil and natural gas.

BIBLIOGRAPHY

AMIN, SAMIR. *L'Economie du Maghreb.* Paris, 1966.
ECREMENT, MARC. *Indépendance politique et libération économique: Un quart de siècle du développement de l'Algérie, 1962–1985.* Grenoble, 1986.

Dirk Vandewalle

Sousse

Northeast coastal town in Tunisia on the Gulf of Hammamet.

Sousse (also Susa; ancient Hadrumetum) was founded as a Phoenician commercial post and became the center of Sousse province under French colonialism (after the protectorate of 1881). After the independence of Tunisia in 1956, it was made the center of the Sousse governorate. In 1984, it had a projected population of 83,500. It is a busy port, handling mostly phosphates and olive oil, and the tourist trade centers on a well-preserved medieval Islamic fortress.

Corner tower of a medieval Islamic fortress at Sousse. (Mia Bloom)

BIBLIOGRAPHY

Tunisia: A Country Survey. Washington, D.C., 1988.

Matthew S. Gordon

Soustelle, Jacques   [1912–   ]

French statesman.

A faithful adherent of General Charles de Gaulle, Jacques Soustelle was governor-general of Algeria (1955–1956), where he combined social reforms with harsh repression of the Front de Libération Nationale (National Liberation Front, FLN). He broke with de Gaulle in 1960 over concessions to the FLN, and following the failed army coup of 1961, Soustelle left France under the threat of arrest because of his hardline *pied noir* sympathies. He remained in exile until 1968.

BIBLIOGRAPHY

HORNE, ALISTAIR. *A Savage War of Peace.* London, 1977.

Zachary Karabell

South Arabian Armed Forces

Short-lived army of the Federation of South Arabia.

The armed forces of the ill-fated Federation of South Arabia were created by the merger of the Federal National Guard and the Federal Regular Army in mid-1967, on the eve of South Yemen's rushed independence. By this time, however, the national struggle had rendered these forces unreliable, and they were to play no real part in the collapse of the federation and the transfer of power from the British to the National Liberation Front (NLF).

Robert D. Burrowes

South Arabian League

Group promoting independence of Britain's protectorates in southern Arabia.

The league was the oldest (founded 1950) of the major nationalist groups created to change the status of Britain's possessions in southern Arabia. Its goal was to unite the various principalities of Aden and the Protectorate States into an independent state, to be called South Arabia.

The league's politics tended to be reformist and conservative, and it received much of its support from Saudi Arabia during the 1960s, when the conflict over the future of the protectorates and Aden became a major issue. In 1967, they became part of South YEMEN.

Manfred W. Wenner

Southeastern Anatolia Project

A massive integrated regional development scheme for the Euphrates and Tigris river basins in Turkey (in Turkish, Güney Anadolu Projesi, or GAP).

The project area covers about twenty-seven thousand square miles (70,000 sq. km) in six provinces of the Anatolia region of Turkey, lying between the Anti-Taurus mountains and border with Syria: Adıyaman, Diyarbakır, Gaziantep, Mardin, Sanliurfa, and Siirt. The project is designed to create economic, social, and spatial changes through the construction and integration of dams, hydroelectric power plants, irrigation projects and infrastructural improvements in transportation, health, education, and nonagricultural employment opportunities. Estimated completion is 2013.

GAP is composed of thirteen subprojects, of which seven are on the Euphrates and six on the Tigris. These comprise fifteen dams, fourteen hydroelectric power stations, and nineteen irrigation projects. The completed project will also incorporate the already completed Keban Dam and will vastly increase the extent of irrigated land in what has been the most economically depressed region of Turkey. As of the early 1990s, only some 315,000 acres (about 127,000 ha) were irrigated in this region—or about 4 percent of the total irrigated land in Turkey. Upon completion, almost 5 million acres (some 2 million ha) will be irrigated. The project will also double Turkey's electrical output by generating 22 billion kilowatt hours of electricity each year.

The World Bank refused to provide project loans until an agreement had been reached with Syria and Iraq on sharing the water of the two rivers. Because foreign currency has been in great shortage in Turkey, international contractors who had been awarded contracts were replaced by Turkish firms. Since Turkish firms have proven themselves capable of completing the project, international financial circles have been persuaded to make loans. In 1985, the Export-Import Bank of New York and Manufacturers-Hanover Trust lent Turkey 111 million U.S. dollars for the Atatürk Dam, and European banks are providing another 440 million dollars for equipment purchases.

GAP has caused friction with Turkey's neighbors. The Euphrates and Tigris rivers are important sources of water for both Syria and Iraq, and the governments of both countries have expressed reservations about the project. The official Turkish position is that year-long regulation of the flow of the rivers will increase the amount of water available to Syria and Iraq. In July 1984, Turkey and Iraq signed a protocol guaranteeing a minimum flow of 654 cubic yards (500 cu. m) per second, which did not include Syria. In July 1987, a similar agreement was signed with Syria, and further negotiations were held in March 1991. The agreements have not ended the political tensions created by GAP: Turkish forces stood guard in January of 1990 when the Euphrates river was cut to divert water into the reservoir for the Atatürk Dam, which reduced the flow of water into Syria and Iraq by 75 percent.

A number of problems have delayed completion of the project. Because the dam sites are located in remote mountainous areas, roads, worker accommodations, and other infrastructure services must be provided. There are also shortages of skilled labor and engineers. Finally, the reservoirs created by just the two Karakaya and Atatürk dams will force the relocation of an estimated seventy thousand people, with more relocations to come in the future.

BIBLIOGRAPHY

KOLARS, JOHN R., and WILLIAM A. MITCHELL. *The Euphrates River and the Southeast Anatolia Development Project.* Carbondale, Ill., 1991.
Middle East Economic Digest. March 29, 1991, p. 21.
New York Times, January 14, 1990, p. 15.
PITMAN, PAUL M., III. *Turkey: A Country Study,* 4th ed. Washington, D.C., 1988.

David Waldner

South Lebanon Army

Israeli-supported militia in southern Lebanon.

This organization originated with Israel's 1978 invasion of southern Lebanon, based on concerns about the Palestine Liberation Organization (PLO) and its activities from southern Lebanon across the Israeli border. To provide a buffer zone, Israel transferred a one-hundred-kilometer-long (62-mi.) area along its northern border to a militia headed by Sa'd HADDAD, a Lebanese Greek Catholic. Haddad headquartered his Israeli-funded two-thousand-man militia at Marjayun, Lebanon.

In 1979, Haddad declared his Free Lebanon Army autonomous from the Lebanese armed forces. In 1980, he changed its name to the South Lebanon Army. His troops were 60 percent Shi'ites and 35 percent Christians, but many of the officers were Israelis. Haddad died in January 1984; he was replaced by General Antoine LAHAD, with the approval of the Maronite Christian leader Camille Chamoun. By 1985, many Shi'a troops defected from the militia as it came under attack from the Muslim militias in the region.

Following Israel's withdrawal from south Lebanon in 1985, a security zone was established and controlled by the South Lebanese Army.

BIBLIOGRAPHY

FISK, ROBERT. *Pity the Nation.* New York, 1990.
GRESH, ALAIN, and DOMINIQUE VIDAL. *A to Z of the Middle East.* Atlantic Highlands, N.J., 1990.
PETRAN, TABITHA. *The Struggle over Lebanon.* New York, 1987.
SCHIFF, ZE'EV, and EHUD YA'ARI. *Israel's Lebanon War.* New York, 1984.

Elizabeth Thompson

South Persia Rifles

British-organized paramilitary unit in Iran during World War I.

The South Persia Rifles (S.P.R.) were a largely indigenous, paramilitary force raised, trained, and paid by the British to police their imperial interests in southeastern Iran during World War I. Organized in 1916 by Major Percy Sykes as a totally autonomous unit, they reached a peak strength of eight thousand men. They were summarily disbanded by Reza Khan, the future shah, in 1921.

BIBLIOGRAPHY

SYKES, PERCY MOLESWORTH. *A History of Persia.* London, 1930.

Jack Bubon

Spain and the Middle East

The Islamic conquest reached Spain in 710 C.E. and lasted until the Catholic reconquest in 1492.

Because of the seven centuries of Islam and Arab civilization based in Spain, this country retains an Arabic legacy in language, culture, and especially architecture. The Arabs came in 710 by way of North Africa with Berbers and Syrians. In 711, they established the first Andalusian caliphate, which lasted until 1492, when the united Catholic kingdoms of Castile and Aragon, after centuries of warfare in the Iberian peninsula, reconquered the last Moorish stronghold at Grenada and expelled the last of their Islamic conquerors (the Moors), as well as the long-resident Jewish population (Sephardim). Many formed new communities in North Africa and the Levant.

The Andalusian Arab civilization had been cosmopolitan, urban, tolerant, and intellectually rich. The arts and sciences flourished at Cordoba, Grenada, and Seville, housed in magnificent architecture. The courts patronized scholars—Arab, Jewish, and Christian—who produced major original works as well as translations from the Greek and Latin. A prolific Judeo-Arabic literature included philosophical and theological treatises and studies of advanced astronomy, mathematics, and medicine.

Waves of mostly Berber troops, motivated by Islamic religious reform, sought to check the Christian reconquest of Spain. The Almoravids (1056–1147), from southern Morocco, and the Almohads (1130–1269), Berbers from the Atlas mountains, stopped the Christian advance for a time. As Moorish Spain lost its dynastic unity and the local kingdoms were formed, the reconquest steadily advanced from north to south. By the late 1400s, Spain had not only taken back the entire peninsula but had established control over the Moroccan port cities of Ceuta and Melilla, settling them with Spanish colonists.

After 1492, Spain's attention became focused on the New World and its mineral wealth. The Ottoman Empire confined Spain's expansion in North Africa to a few Moroccan sites and to Oran (Wahran), which remained under Spanish rule from 1509 to 1792. With pronounced economic and political problems from 1700 on, Spain was content to coexist with the Ottomans and a nominally independent Morocco.

In the late nineteenth century, European imperialism advanced in North Africa, and Spain was challenged by France for influence over Morocco. The results were a Spanish share in the governance of the then-international city of Tangier; a Spanish protectorate established in 1912 over northern Morocco (then called Spanish Morocco) and fought for in the Rif wars of 1919 to 1926; and a colony in the desolate Spanish Sahara, now Western Sahara.

The nationalists, under Francisco Franco Bahamonde, in July of 1936, launched their revolt against the Spanish republican government with Moroccan troops. A veteran of the Rif wars, Franco coveted parts of Algeria, opposed Arab nationalism, and reluctantly relinquished Spanish influence and territory in Morocco. In 1975, his deathbed decolonization of the Spanish Sahara led to the peaceful Moroccan GREEN MARCH and occupation of the former Spanish colony.

Thus, the leaders of the post-1975 Spanish transition to democracy inherited a legacy of conflict with Morocco; with Algeria embittered by a dispute over a natural-gas contract; and over differences between the conservative nationalism of Franco and the radical ideologies of many Arab leaders. First under Christian Democrat leaders and then, from 1982, under Socialists, Spain has tried with considerable success to establish cooperative working relations with Arab states, especially those of North Africa.

The basis for changed relations has been Spanish acceptance of diverse Arab political regimes, provision of export credits, modest technical assistance and some arms sales to Arab countries, and noninvolvement in the Western Sahara War. Spain, however, has written sovereignty over Ceuta and Melilla into its 1978 constitution and has insisted on keeping them.

Complex bilateral relations with Morocco, including issues of fishing rights, immigration, and a possible tunnel or bridge across the Straits of Gibraltar have received careful management, as have relations with Algeria. Tunisia has become a close supporter of Spain, while relations with Libya have been erratic. The Spanish presence in the Gulf, Egypt, Saudi Arabia, and Lebanon is modest. Taking an objective line on the Arab–Israel conflict and related issues while recognizing Israel has earned Spain a respected role.

Since 1975, Spain has achieved the status of a significant minor power in the Middle East. Its diplomacy and trade are directed primarily at Morocco and Algeria, where its fears of Islamic fundamentalism lead to support for status-quo regimes.

BIBLIOGRAPHY

BALTA, PAUL. *Le grand Maghreb: Des indépendances à l'an 2000.* Paris, 1990.

HODGES, TONY. *Western Sahara: The Roots of the Desert War.* Westport, Conn., 1984.

HOURANI, ALBERT. *A History of the Arab Peoples.* Cambridge, Mass., 1991.

PAYNE, STANLEY. *The Franco Regime, 1936–1975.* Madison, Wis., 1987.

SEGAL, AARON. "Spain and the Middle East: A Fifteen-Year Assessment." *Middle East Journal* 45, no. 2 (1991): 250–264.

Aaron Segal

Spanish Morocco

Portions of northwest Africa held by Spain from the 1500s until 1975.

The presence of Spain along the coast of northwest Africa was initially manifested during the 1400s and 1500s—after centuries of Muslim rule in the Iberian peninsula had been overturned by warfare and the Moors retreated to North Africa. The Mediterranean port cities of Melilla and Ceuta came under Spanish rule in 1496 and 1578, respectively, and remain so today, as do three tiny islands off the Mediterranean coast of Morocco. In the late nineteenth century, Spain joined the European scramble for overseas territories. Spain expanded its Ceuta and Melilla enclaves, asserted itself militarily in the Rif mountains, and temporarily occupied Tetuan in 1860; an 1860 treaty committed Morocco to ceding land along its southern coast for the establishment of Spanish fisheries, eventually resulting in Spain staking claim to Ifni. Further south, Spain established coastal trading stations at Villa Cisneros (Dakhla), Cintra, and Cape

Stamp from Spanish Morocco commemorating the seventy-fifth anniversary of the Universal Postal Union in 1949. (Richard Bulliet)

Blanca. In December 1884, a Spanish protectorate was declared along the Saharan coast, a claim recognized by the Berlin Conference in 1885.

Spanish holdings in both the north and south were expanded by three treaties between Spain and France, the last in 1912. Spain then nominally held full sovereignty over Saguia el-Hamra and Rio de Oro (Spanish Sahara, now Western Sahara), 102,703 square miles (266,000 sq. km) of territory, below the twenty-seventh parallel, wedged in between the Atlantic Ocean and what are today the internationally recognized boundaries of Morocco, Algeria, and Mauritania. Implementation of Spanish authority came in stages: control of Tarfaya, north of the 27th parallel, was taken in 1916; La Guera, in the extreme south of Rio de Oro, in 1920; the 580-square-mile (1,502 sq. km) Ifni zone, between Tarfaya and Agadir, in 1934; and Smara, in the Saharan interior, also in 1934. Spanish Sahara and the Ifni and Tarfaya areas were governed between 1934 and 1958 as parts of Spanish West Africa, whose military governor was based in Ifni.

The Spanish protectorate in the north, established in 1912, was one-twentieth the size of the French zone. Tangier was made part of the Spanish zone from 1940 to 1945, but then reverted to its previous international regime. The Spanish zone's population in 1955, including Europeans, was about one million, nearly ten percent of Morocco's total population. Economic resources were few and the area underwent little development, constituting an economic liability to Spain.

Spain was both a competitor and sometimes junior partner of France, often working in tandem politically and militarily—the latter during the Rif rebellion led by Muhammad ibn Abd al-Krim from 1921 to 1926; in the southern campaigns in 1934; and again in 1957/58 against the irregular Moroccan Army of Liberation, following Morocco's achieving independence in 1956. Nonetheless, Spanish rule was both weaker and often less dominating than that of France. Spain returned Tarfaya and its surroundings to Morocco in 1958 and the Ifni enclave in 1969.

Phosphates were first discovered in Spanish Sahara during the 1940s, and proved to be of high grade and large quantity. Exports began in the early 1970s. By 1975, exports stood at 2.6 million tons (2.36 million metric tons), the sixth largest in the world. In 1974, the Spanish presence numbered just over 26,000; a 1974 census of the native Sahrawi population counted 73,497 persons, most of whom had been sedentarized from their nomadic life.

In 1973, Spain decided to introduce internal self-government, to deflect international pressure for decolonization. But by mid-1974, following the collapse of Portugal's Africa empire, Madrid promised to implement United Nations calls for a referendum in the territory during the first half of 1975. In September 1975, Spain's foreign minister and POLISARIO representatives agreed on a mutual release of prisoners and the principle of an independent Sahrawi state in return for fishing and phosphate concessions to Spain. But following Morocco's GREEN MARCH in the Western Sahara War, and with Spain's Generalissimo Francisco Franco on his deathbed, Spain, Morocco, and Mauritania signed a tripartite agreement in Madrid on November 14, 1975, administratively dividing the region into Moroccan and Mauritanian zones and setting up a transitional tripartite administration. The final Spanish departure from its Saharan colony came on February 26, 1975.

BIBLIOGRAPHY

ABUN-NASR, JAMIL N. *A History of the Maghrib in the Islamic Period.* Cambridge, U.K., 1987.
HODGES, TONY. *Western Sahara: The Roots of a Desert War.* Westport, Conn., 1983.
MERCER, JOHN. *Spanish Sahara.* London, 1976.

Bruce Maddy-Weitzman

Spanish Sahara

See Western Sahara

Special Forces of the Levant

Military group under the French mandate in Lebanon.

After France gained control of Lebanon through the mandate from the League of Nations, it formed the Troupes Spéciales du Levant, which recruited Lebanese and Syrian soldiers and was commanded almost exclusively by French officers. It was devised to legitimize French police and military activities in the region and to give the impression of local rule. The percentage of officers who were Lebanese or Syrian increased over the years although the power of command and control remained in French hands. By 1945, 90 percent of the officers in the 14,000-strong Special Forces were Arabs.

During World War II, Lebanese Special Forces troops were ordered to fight on the side of the Vichy French against the British and Free French. When the Vichy forces in the Middle East surrendered in 1941, volunteers from the Special Forces were recruited by the Free French to fight actively in North Africa, Italy, and southern France. In 1945 three thousand Lebanese troops in the Special Forces formed the nucleus of the Lebanese Army.

As'ad AbuKhalil

Spectateur Oriental

French newspaper.

Established in İzmir in 1821 by Alexander Blacque, a French lawyer, *Le Spectateur Oriental* was one of the first newspapers published in the Ottoman Empire. Although published in French by a Frenchman, the paper supported the Ottoman state and opposed French policy toward Greece, thus angering the French consul, who ordered the paper closed.

BIBLIOGRAPHY

Tanzimat'tan cumhuriyet'e türkiye ansiklopedesi. Istanbul, 1984.

David Waldner

Sphinx

Mythological human-headed lion carved from rock at the pyramids of Giza.

The Sphinx is 190 feet (27 m) long and 66 feet (20 m) tall at its highest. It probably represents the pharaoh Khafre (c. 2550 B.C.E.), whose pyramid is nearby. Arabs called it Abu al-Hawl, "father of terror." Like the pyramids, it has become a symbol of Egypt, first appearing on postage stamps in 1867 and replacing the bust of King Farouk (1936–1952) on coins in the 1950s.

The Sphinx and one of the three pyramids near it. (Mia Bloom)

BIBLIOGRAPHY

HASSAN, SELIM. *The Great Sphinx and Its Secrets*. Cairo, 1953.

Donald Malcolm Reid

Sports

Traditional and modern athletic activities.

Most sports practiced in the past century in the Middle East are the result of colonial contacts. Games and sports of a Western nature were encouraged by two types of institutions: mission schools of Christian denominations, which transmitted ideals of sportsmanship, and sporting clubs, which were primarily the preserve of the British. Through such institutions, the local elite, and other social classes, not only learned Western sports, but also were co-opted into a Westernized outlook.

Colonizers and colonized played both team and individual sports. Team activities included basketball, volleyball, polo (almost exclusively among military officers), and soccer. Soccer acquired tremendous popularity in the region primarily because of the success of Egyptian teams in the Olympics and the African Games and of Saudi teams in the Asian Games. Individual sports in the Middle East are usually the preserve of the elite who can afford membership in clubs and private coaching. Tennis, squash, swimming, shooting, and golf are among the more popular and are evidence of the lingering influence of the colonial sporting clubs. Three exceptions of individual sports in terms of colonial influence are wrestling, both free and Greco-Roman, long-distance running, and weight lifting. Athletes from Morocco, Algeria, Tunisia, Egypt, and Lebanon have consistently performed well at the Olympics in these sports. Israel has also successfully participated in tennis and judo on an international level. Beginning in the 1990s, Arab women athletes, notably Hassiba Boulmerka from Algeria and Ghada Shouaa from Syria, achieved world-class success in track and field competitions.

Falconry remains the traditional sport throughout the Arabian peninsula, where it is practiced by the bedouin, as well as by some of the ruling families. Traditional wrestling has a long history in Turkey, while Iranian men exercise in traditional gymnasiums called *zurkhaneh*.

The nadir of Middle Eastern sports occurred at the 1972 Olympic Games in Munich. The Israeli team was taken hostage by militant Palestinians seeking to draw international attention to their political plight. In a shoot-out between the Palestinians and German police sharpshooters, the Israelis and most of their captors died. The event cast a pall over the games, which, nonetheless, resumed after a day's mourning.

BIBLIOGRAPHY

OPPENHEIM, JEAN-MARC R. "Athletics: Politics and Play." In *The Columbia History of the Twentieth Century*, ed. by Richard W. Bulliet. New York, 1996.

Jean-Marc R. Oppenheim

Sprinzak, Joseph   [1885–1959]

Israeli political leader.

Born in Moscow, Joseph Sprinzak was one of the founders of Tze'irei Zion in Russia (1905) and was a delegate to Zionist Congresses.

He began medical school at the American University in Beirut but then settled in Palestine in 1908, where he was an early activist in the Labor movement. He was a founder of the HISTADRUT and the MAPAI party and served in leadership positions in both organizations. Unanimously elected speaker of the first Knesset in 1949, he served in that capacity until his death. He also was acting president of Israel while Chaim Weizmann was ill and after Weizmann's death (1952), until the election of Yizhak Ben-Zvi.

BIBLIOGRAPHY

MERHAV, PERETZ. *The Israeli Left: History, Problems, Documents*. San Diego, Calif., 1980.

Bryan Daves

Srvantziants, Garegin   [1840–1892]

Armenian ecclesiastical leader, ethnographer, and folklorist.

Garegin Srvantziants was born in Van and educated in local parochial schools. He became a teacher and was ordained a celibate priest in 1867. While assigned ecclesiastical responsibilities in Van, Erzurum, Bitlis, and Harput, he organized a number of schools and was the assistant prior of the Armenian monastery of *Surp Karapet* (Holy Precursor), one of the most hallowed sites of Armenian religious pilgrimage, at Moosh. After his investiture as a bishop in 1886, he was appointed prior of Surp Karapet. A fervent preacher and exponent of Armenian emancipation, he was removed from office and placed under surveillance in Istanbul.

Well before his confinement to the Ottoman capital, Srvantziants had published what in the aggregate may be considered the most important ethnographic data on the Armenians yet gathered at the time. As an associate of Mkrtich Khrimian, he had traveled with the later catholicos through the Armenian provinces in 1860 and 1861. Recognized much like his mentor for the kinship he felt with his own people, Srvantziants was instructed by the Armenian patriarch of Istanbul, Nerses Vazhapetian, to investigate and report on the condition of the Armenian communities in eastern Anatolia after the Russo–Ottoman War of 1877 and 1878, while Khrimian prepared to plead the Armenian cause at the Congress of Berlin.

During these trips, and at all other opportunities, Srvantziants tirelessly recorded the folklore of the Armenian rustic population. He released the results of his expeditions in a series of works issued in the 1870s and 1800s. In *Grots u brots* (The Written and the Spoken, 1874), he published popular Armenian folk stories and traditions. In *Hnots yev norots* (From the Old and the New, 1874), he published Armenian stories from manuscript records. *Manana* (Manna, 1876) included proverbs, riddles, songs, and epigraphs from the Van region. In *Hamov-hotov* (The Flavorful and the Colorful, 1884), he described the topography, climate, and monuments of Armenia. The most significant of his discoveries was the first cycle of what was later recognized as the Armenian national folk epic *Sasna Tsrrer* (The Daredevils of Sasun), more popularly known by the name of its hero. Srvantziants recorded the section called "Sasuntsi Davit kam Mheri tur" (David of Sasun, or the Gate of Mher). Srvantziants also published important studies on the subjects he recorded and was elected an honorary member of the Imperial Academy of Antiquities in Saint Petersburg. He died in Istanbul.

Rouben P. Adalian

Stack, Lee [1868–1924]

Governor-general of the Sudan and sirdar (commander) of the Egyptian army.

Sir Lee Stack was assassinated in Cairo as part of an Egyptian nationalist campaign to gain complete independence from Great Britain. He had joined the Anglo–Egyptian army in the Sudan in 1899 (when it became an Anglo–Egyptian condominium after its conquest, 1896–1898). As governor-general, he contributed to the economic and political development of the Sudan.

BIBLIOGRAPHY

MARLOWE, JOHN. *Anglo–Egyptian Relations, 1800–1953.* London, 1954.

Oles M. Smolansky

Stalin, Josef [1879–1953]

Soviet political leader, 1924–1953.

Stalin was a pseudonym for Iosif Vissarionovich Dzhugashivili. He was born in Georgia and was a revolutionary in Czarist Russia. He emerged as the leader of the Soviet Union after Lenin's death in 1924, and through ruthless politics, he remained in power until his death in 1953. Stalin had established a Soviet-dominated empire of satellite states in Eastern Europe; he attempted to add Asian, African, Latin American, and Middle Eastern states during his postwar rivalry with the United States and the West for world leadership. Stalin aided Communist parties throughout the Middle East, including Palestine until 1948. Other than limited success in Iraq, Syria, and Egypt during World War II and with the Tudeh party in Iran, Stalin was unable to generate a mass communist movement in the Middle East.

In 1939, before World War II, Stalin signed a non-aggression pact with Nazi Germany but joined the Allies after Germany invaded the USSR in June 1941. He cooperated in a joint Allied occupation of Iran, but at the war's end, he refused to evacuate Soviet troops from Azerbaijan. The resulting AZERBAIJAN CRISIS culminated in a Soviet withdrawal in early 1946. Pursuing a more aggressive foreign policy after the conclusion of the war, Stalin pressured Turkey to amend the MONTREUX CONVENTION (1936), thus providing the Soviet Union with easier access to the Mediterranean Sea. It was partly in response to this pressure on Turkey that the United States announced the TRUMAN DOCTRINE in 1947.

Although hostile to Zionism, Stalin supported the UN partition plan (1947) for Palestine in order to hasten the end of British imperialism. He extended diplomatic recognition to the new state of Israel in 1948, and he gave military aid to Israel when it was attacked by the Arab states in the Arab–Israel War (1948). Stalin then turned against Israel and began repressing Soviet Jews because of their allegiance to Israel and all it represented to them.

BIBLIOGRAPHY

SAFRAN, NADAV. *Israel: The Embattled Ally.* Cambridge, U.K., 1981.
ULAM, ADAM. *Stalin.* New York, 1973.
WIECZYNSKI, JOSEPH, ed. *Modern Encyclopedia of Russian and Soviet History.* New York, 1981.

Zachary Karabell

Stamboul

See Istanbul

Standard Oil

See Arabian American Oil Company

Stanhope, Hester   [1776–1839]

English noblewoman who settled in Lebanon.

Niece of and, for the last three years of his life, adviser to William Pitt, Lady Hester Stanhope is said to have been admired for both her beauty and her political acumen by George III, who granted her a pension upon Pitt's death in 1806. Thus financed, Stanhope departed for points east in 1810. Following a shipwreck near Rhodes, she adopted Turkish men's dress and traveled extensively in Egypt, Palestine, and Syria before settling in 1814 with her retinue in the mountains above Beirut. There she became the "prophetess" of a messianic astrology of her own devising. A supporter of the sultan, she joined Druze and other local resistance to Ibrahim Pasha and sheltered refugees from Acre after its fall to him in 1832. She also engaged in intrigue against local British officials on behalf of her protégés.

Stanhope has been a favorite of orientalists from her own day to the present. She was acquainted with the English poet Lord Byron and the French poet Lamartine. She was written of admiringly by the latter as well as by several other nineteenth-century travel memoirists, including Alexander Kinglake. She was also the subject of Mary Stewart's 1967 novel *The Gabriel Hounds*. Stanhope died in 1839, impoverished after her royal pension, which had never been sufficient for her needs, was diverted on petition of her creditors. Despite her well-known rejection of traditional Christianity, her burial in the garden of her home on Mount Lebanon was presided over by an American missionary specially recruited for the occasion by the British consul in Beirut.

BIBLIOGRAPHY

CHILDS, VIRGINIA. *Lady Hester Stanhope: Queen of the Desert.* London, 1990.
KINGLAKE, ALEXANDER WILLIAM. *Eothen.* New York, 1901.
PASTON, GEORGE. *Little Memoirs of the Nineteenth Century.* London and New York, 1902.

Alison R. Steiner

Stark, Freya   [1893–?]

British explorer and author.

After World War I, Stark studied Arabic at the School of Oriental and African Studies in London and then worked for the *Baghdad Times* in Iraq. She traveled extensively through the Middle East, mapping remote regions of the Arabian peninsula and the Valley of the Assassins in Luristan, western Iran. She is the author of more than thirty books, including *The Southern Gates of Arabia* (1936).

BIBLIOGRAPHY

BRENT, PETER. *Far Arabia.* London, 1977.

Zachary Karabell

Star of North Africa

The first Algerian political movement to call openly for independence.

The Star of North Africa, also known as the Etoile Nord-Africaine (ENA) was founded in 1926 in Paris by Hadj Ali Abd al-Qadir and Messali al-HADJ. With a base in the large Algerian immigrant community that was influenced by the Communist-dominated French labor movement, it also propounded a leftist social and economic agenda.

The movement was banned in 1929 but grew clandestinely until it reappeared in reorganized form in 1933. Messali al-Hadj returned to Algeria in the summer of 1936 to address the Algerian Muslim Congress that was designing a program of reforms within the Colonial framework. Before that audience, he became the first individual to speak openly of independence within Algeria itself. He then turned to organizing ENA cells across the country. Authorities in January 1937 banned the ENA. Its successor was the Parti du Peuple Algérien (PPA), which was outlawed, in its turn, in September 1939.

BIBLIOGRAPHY

KADDACHE, MAHFOUD. *Histoire du nationalisme algérien: Question nationale et politique algérienne, 1919–1951.* Algiers, 1981.

John Ruedy

State Planning Organization (SPO)

Organization set up in Turkey in 1960 to administer national economic development.

Within the framework of the constitutionally anchored principle of etatism (state economic enterprise), Turkey first experimented with central planning in the 1930s but only with a focus on industrialization. During the 1950 to 1960 legislative period, the Democratic party governments were strongly criticized for their opposition to any kind of economic planning. After the military takeover in 1960, strong pressure reversed this approach. Accordingly, the principle of indicative, not compulsory, planning was written into the 1961 constitution, via Article 129, which stated that "economic, social and cultural development is based on a plan. Development is carried out according to this plan." Article 129 was first enacted in September 1960, laying down the structure and functions of the State Planning Organization (Devlet Planlama Teşkilati). The main function of the SPO was to create five-year plans, covering all aspects of economic development, along with long-term plans and annual programs.

The institutional structure of the SPO was designed to create a degree of independence and security for the technical experts charged with preparing the plans and to facilitate cooperation between them and political authorities. Unfortunately, the elaborate machinery specified in Law 91 did not prevent arguments among the politicians and planners concerned with the degree to which plans might direct private-sector investments and the role of public and private enterprise in the development process.

After 1965, representatives of the private sector, who had been virtually excluded from the preparation of the first plan, were fully consulted on the second, which was to run from 1968 to 1972. In the introduction to the second plan, it was stated that it would be "imperative" for the public sector but only "indicative" for private enterprise.

Turkey's 1982 constitution also adopted the mechanism of long-term planning. Article 166 states:

> The planning of economic, social, and cultural development, in particular the speedy, balanced, and harmonious development of industry and agriculture throughout the country, and the efficient use of national resources on the basis of detailed analysis and assessment and the establishment of the necessary organization for this purpose are the duty of the State.
>
> Measures to increase national thriftiness and production, to ensure stability in price and balance in foreign trade transactions, to promote investment and employment, shall be included in the plan; in investments, public benefit and requirements shall be taken into account; the efficient use of resources shall be aimed at. Development activities shall be realized according to this plan.

A 1984 decree reorganized the SPO and attached it to the office of the prime minister. If necessary, the prime minister can delegate authority to another member of the cabinet. The SPO is headed by an undersecretary. It consists of eight departments: Economic Planning; Coordination; Priority Regional Development; Relations with the European Economic Community; Economic Cooperation with Islamic Countries; Credit Allocation; Foreign Capital Investment; and Free Zones. The SPO maintains permanent representatives in international economic organizations and major foreign capitals.

The goals for economic, social, and cultural development and the related policies are discussed and decided upon by the High Planning Council. The finalization of each five-year plan is prepared by the SPO in accordance with the directives determined by the goverment. The long-term plans, after being discussed and decided upon by the cabinet, are submitted for approval to the Turkish Grand National Assembly. The yearly programs are prepared by the SPO, discussed at the High Planning Council, submitted to the council of ministers, and enter into force upon approval of the council.

Because of repeated military interventions since 1960, the net results of the first three five-year plans have been uneven growth and surplus labor in both rural and urban areas. The fourth plan (1978–1983) did recommend better coordination and observance of market forces. Accordingly, import substitution was replaced with export orientation; productivity and competition were stressed; and foreign capital and transfer of technology have been encouraged. The fifth five-year plan (1984–1989) listed three priorities: energy; infrastructure; and export-oriented industries. The sixth five-year plan (1989–1994) was an exact continuation of its predecessor.

BIBLIOGRAPHY

İLKIN, S., and E. İNANÇ, eds. *Planning in Turkey*. Ankara, 1967.

Nermin Abadan-Unat

Stern, Abraham   [1907–1942]

Jewish underground leader during the British mandate of Palestine.

Abraham Stern was born in Poland but spent many of his formative years in Russia. He moved to Palestine in 1924 where he studied Latin and Greek at Hebrew University and later began to study for his doctorate in Florence, Italy. Stern served in the Haganah starting in 1929 but broke off in 1931 to form the IRGUN ZVA'I LE'UMI, through which he smuggled weapons into Palestine and established contacts with the Polish military. In 1934 he gave up his academic interests to devote himself fully to the underground.

Stern returned to Palestine in 1939, following the publication of the British White Paper, to organize resistance to the British. He was detained by the British for ten months, until his friends in the Revisionist movement arranged for his release. In 1940 he broke with the Irgun and its leader, David Raziel, and formed a new group, LOHAMEI HERUT YISRAEL, also known as Lehi, or the Stern Gang, because he did not feel the Irgun was militaristic enough. His ideological manifesto, "Eighteen Principles of Renaissance," included many controversial ideas, including that the new Zionist goals should be a land of Israel extending from the Nile to the Euphrates rivers.

During World War II, unaware of the realities of the Holocaust, Stern sought links with Fascist Italy and Nazi Germany, although they did not result in anything. Stern, who appeared on British "wanted" posters for bank robbery and murder, was found and killed by British policemen in 1942.

BIBLIOGRAPHY

BEN-YEHUDA, NACHMAN. *Political Assassinations by Jews: A Rhetorical Device for Justice*. Albany, N.Y., 1993.

Julie Zuckerman

Stern Gang

See Lohamei Herut Yisrael

Stock Market

Most Middle East stock markets have little influence on the countries' economies.

Except for the stock market of Turkey and of Israel, the exchanges of the Middle East are small and of minimal importance in the economic life of their respective countries. Even in countries where economic liberalism is embedded in the economic life, such as Saudi Arabia, capital markets are heavily regulated and have not had any major influence in helping nongovernment firms raise capital from the public at large. Exchanges suffer from a lack of reliable information on and from the companies, insider trading is common, and accounting practices are not demanding. Government interference is constant and regulation tends to be overwhelming. In most countries, the markets have no depth and are totally closed to foreign investors.

Bahrain. The market in Bahrain is still very small and highly regulated. It is, however, beginning to open

TABLE 1

Major Stock Markets within the Middle East

Country	Shares Traded (in millions of U.S. \$/year)	Number of Companies Traded	Capitalization (in millions of U.S. \$)
Israel	13,505	600	45,000
Turkey	12,435	1,304	27,145
Saudi Arabia	4,615	78	62,400
Kuwait	2,640	47	10,000
Jordan	1,375	110	5,000
Iran	247	112	1,344
Egypt	170	670	2,500

up to foreign investors if they reside in Bahrain. Each foreign investor is limited to a maximum 1 percent stake in a company. If markets become more deregulated in Bahrain and if Saudi Arabia, as the main center for private industrial ventures, approves, this stock market could become an important place for Gulf industries to raise capital.

Iran. In the liberalization of 1992, the Iranian stock market was expected to be the transmission belt between Iranian capital at home and abroad and the companies to be denationalized. Foreign capital was permitted to buy minority positions. However, as of 1994, only thirty-two new companies had been listed. The move toward liberalization seems stalled and the market is not very active.

Israel. The Israel stock exchange is located in Tel Aviv. It lists about 600 companies and has a capitalization of 45 billion U.S. dollars. The market is open to foreign investors. Technically, the market is quite advanced with computer support similar to that of U.S. markets. However, volumes traded are relatively low, in the average range of 37 million U.S. dollars per day in 1994. The market tends to be somewhat volatile due to the low number of buyers and sellers. The progress of the markets is marked by the "two-sided index," which stood at 166.14 as of August 12, 1994.

Jordan. The Jordanian market, which was started in 1977, is still small in terms of volume but has a good reputation among investors. Foreign investors need to be approved by the government, which greatly limits the liquidity of the shares and the potential growth of the market.

Kuwait. Until 1982, the Kuwaiti capital markets were the largest in the Middle East. After the crash of the SUQ AL-MANAKH, the government enforced old regulations and introduced new ones. The number of brokers, the number of companies eligible to be traded, and the daily volumes are limited. The Gulf War, which caused many industrial companies to disappear, limited the number of tradable issues to the financial institutions. Kuwaiti-owned companies based in Bahrain and elsewhere in the Gulf are also traded. No foreigners are allowed to trade in Kuwaiti shares, except Gulf Cooperation Council nationals.

Saudi Arabia. Saudi Arabia, despite having the largest volume of shares traded in the Gulf, does not have a stock exchange or trading floor. All shares are exchanged and cleared through the banks. To have shares traded, companies must be registered as "Sharikat Mosahhama," a registration somewhat similar to a U.S. corporation C. To obtain this status, companies must be vetted by the Saudi Arabian Monetary Agency and, until 1992, also needed approval by the king. Only firms not involved in defense or oil are allowed to register. Thus, Saudi firms have a very difficult time raising money directly from the public through the stock market. No foreign capital is allowed to trade in Saudi shares, except in limited circumstances if originating from within the Gulf Cooperation Council.

Turkey. The stock exchange in Turkey got its impetus from a 1989 law on investments. The law strongly restricts insider trading, provides for proper financial reporting by companies, and authorizes foreigners to invest. By 1993 the Turkish market had become one of the leading emerging markets with investments from many U.S. and European mutual funds.

Jean-François Seznec

Storrs, Ronald [1881–1955]

British colonial official.

After studying classics at Pembroke College, Cambridge, Storrs served as Lord Horatio Kitchener's Oriental secretary in Egypt prior to and during World War I. In this capacity, he met with Amir Abdullah ibn Husayn in April 1914, one of the Hashimites' early attempts to determine Britain's attitude toward their ambitions. Storrs later played an important role in the Anglo–Hashimite dialogue and the Arab Re-

volt, traveling from Egypt to the Hijaz on several occasions in 1916, including a journey with T. E. Lawrence, to cement Britain's relationship with the Hashimites.

In December 1917, Storrs was appointed the first military governor of Jerusalem after Allied troops entered the city. He believed that the role of Britain's military government in Palestine was simply to administer the country, not to introduce fundamental social or political changes. However, Britain had pledged to support Zionist settlements in Palestine through the BALFOUR DECLARATION. In April 1918, Storrs formally received the Zionist commission, headed by Chaim Weizmann, that had traveled to Jerusalem to begin making arrangements for implementing the Balfour Declaration. He felt that the commission's dismay at the negative attitude displayed toward it and Zionism in general betrayed a fundamental naïveté about the Palestinians and their understanding of Zionism.

Palestinian nationalist frustrations were manifested in the Nabi Musa disturbances (April 1920). As governor of Jerusalem, Storrs subsequently dismissed the mayor of Jerusalem, Musa Kazim al-Husayni, for his role in the affair. Husayni went on to become the senior Palestinian nationalist figure in the 1920s, as head of the Arab Executive.

Storrs took an interest in cultural preservation in Jerusalem, forming the Pro-Jerusalem Society to restore historic monuments in the city. He arranged for Armenian artisans to produce tiles for the Islamic shrines at the Haram al-Sharif as part of these efforts.

Following the introduction of civil rule in Palestine in the mid-1920s, Storrs was Jerusalem's first civilian governor. After leaving service in Palestine, he became governor of Cyprus in 1926 and of Northern Rhodesia in 1932. He retired from colonial service in 1934.

BIBLIOGRAPHY

STORRS, RONALD. *Orientations: The Memories of Sir Ronald Storrs.* London, 1945.

Michael R. Fischbach

Straits, Turkish

A strategic 200-mile (320 km) natural waterway that joins the Black and Aegean seas.

Less than 30 percent of the length of the Straits—the Bosporus, starting in the Black Sea, and the Dardanelles, ending in the Aegean—are natural straits; between them lies the inland Sea of Marmara. So long as the Black Sea was Ottoman and the only

Bosporus strait shown on a postage stamp from Turkey. (Richard Bulliet)

approaches flowed through the sultan's domain, he alone decided what ships might visit what parts of his realm. Foreign naval vessels did not enter Ottoman inland waters except on calls of courtesy or for repairs—unless in time of war they sought to breach the sultan's naval defenses. At the Straits and in the Ottoman-dominated river mouths of the Black Sea, attempting such a breach would have entailed overwhelming risks.

The fact that at its southern end the Bosporus divided the imperial capital between Europe and Asia enhanced the Ottoman security planners' sensitivity to the movement of foreign vessels through the Straits. By the eighteen century, commercial ships arriving from the Mediterranean were permitted into the Sea of Marmara only as far as Constantinople. From that point north, all trade with Black Sea ports moved on Ottoman ships.

Once Russia captured primary river outlets to the Black Sea (such as the Dnieper and the Don—the latter connected to the Black Sea by the Sea of Azov), and thus could validly claim riparian status, the situation changed. The Treaty of KUÇUK KAYNARJA, which in 1774 ended a six-year war with the Ottoman Empire, opened all water lanes with outlets on the Black Sea to Russian commercial shipping. The Ottomans subsequently bestowed the privilege of free merchant navigation through the Straits upon other seafaring powers of Europe and even the United States. This was done by separate act for any Western state enjoying capitulatory (extraterritorial) privileges that requested it. The Ottoman government in 1822 notified all powers that "the passage of the Bosporus is closed to the ships of nations to whom the Porte never accorded the right of entry to . . . [the Black] sea." Not until the Treaty of Paris in 1856 was commercial freedom conferred on all flags.

The transit of war vessels was also resolved by international agreement, starting with the STRAITS CONVENTION, signed in London on July 13, 1841. Article 1 expressed the sultan's firm resolve "to maintain . . . the principle . . . [whereby] it has . . . been prohibited for the Ships of War of Foreign Powers to enter the Straits . . . ; and . . . so long as the Porte is at peace . . . [to] admit no foreign Ship of War into the said Straits." In the same article the powers of Europe pledged "to respect this determination." In Article 2 the sultan reserved "to himself . . . to deliver f[e]rmans [edicts] of passage for light vessels under flag of war . . . employed . . . in the services of the Missions of foreign powers."

The defeat in World War I of the Ottoman imperial government ended the 1841 agreement. Under the Armistice of Mudros in 1918, the victors (chiefly Britain, France, and Italy) imposed a naval occupation on the Sublime Porte, and in 1922 on its successor, the Republic of Turkey. The powers of Europe assumed the role of Straits traffic regulator until the ratification in 1923 of the Treaty of LAUSANNE. For a dozen years, an International Straits Commission oversaw the flow of all Straits traffic. In 1936 the MONTREUX CONVENTION restored sovereign authority to the Republic of Turkey.

In conferences with Britain and the United States at Tehran in 1943 and at Yalta in 1945, the Soviet Union declared the Montreux Convention prejudicial to its security interests. It acknowledged that in wartime Turkey had acted with goodwill in defense of the Straits. Nevertheless, Moscow demanded revision of the 1936 convention to assure its warships free movement through the Straits at all times.

When the issue was reviewed at Potsdam in mid-1945, the Western powers agreed that each of the Big Three would hold talks with the Turkish government on revising the 1936 instrument "to meet present-day conditions." After a year of diplomatic exchanges, Moscow's insistence on sharing in the defense of the Straits led to a stalemate in August 1946. The Soviet Union refused to modify its demands, and Britain and the United States gave full support to Turkey. Seven months later, President Harry Truman promulgated the U.S. strategy for the global containment of the Soviet Union "and international communism" thereby marking the formal start of the Cold War.

[*See also:* Capitulations]

BIBLIOGRAPHY

HUREWITZ, J. C. *The Middle East and North Africa in World Politics: A Documentary Record,* 2 vols. New Haven, Conn., 1975–1979.

———. "Russia and the Turkish Straits: A Revaluation of the Origins of the Problem." *World Politics* (July 1962): 605–632.

SHOTWELL, JAMES THOMSON, and FRANCIS DÉAK. *Turkey at the Straits*. New York, 1940.

J. C. Hurewitz

Straits Convention

International agreement, signed in 1841, on access to the Black Sea; it denied passage in peacetime to non-Ottoman warships through the Straits connecting the Mediterranean and Black seas.

Until 1774, when the Russian Empire under Catherine the Great acquired territory on the north shore of the Black Sea, there was no question concerning passage of ships between the Black and Mediterranean seas because the Black Sea was essentially an internal Ottoman sea. After 1774 access to the Straits presented a persistent problem in international affairs. Russia sought to ensure its right to passage while opposing similar rights for other maritime powers; Britain, in particular, wanted to restrict Russian access to the Mediterranean as a threat to its aspirations in the Levant. The Ottoman Empire considered its control of the Straits essential to its sovereignty and a guarantee of its security and independence.

The Straits Convention of 1841 resulted from internal Ottoman problems and imperial rivalries. The Ottoman Empire had been wracked by the aspirations of Greece for independence and the threat posed by Muhammad Ali of Egypt in his efforts to establish control over Syria and possibly to replace the Ottomans as head of the empire. Russia and most other European powers supported the Greek cause. France supported Muhammad Ali in hopes of reaping benefits as his ally. Russia wanted unhampered access to the Mediterranean and acknowledgment of its claim of protection over Christian Orthodox subjects of the Ottoman Empire. Britain and Austria-Hungary were suspicious of Russian designs.

Muhammad Ali originally supported the Ottomans in their struggle against the Greeks seeking independence; he sent his son Ibrahim ibn Muhammad Ali with an army to help the Ottomans subdue the Greeks in 1825. The venture was not successful, and by 1828 Ibrahim's army had withdrawn from Greece. Muhammad Ali then turned his attention to Syria in an attempt to expand his control of the eastern Mediterranean, launching an army led by Ibrahim against the Ottomans in the first Syrian war (1831–1833). France tacitly supported this effort; Britain, distracted by other international problems (particularly Belgium), did not; the Russians supported the Ottomans. Ibrahim's forces came within 150 miles of Constantinople, but in February 1833 Russia sent a naval force and troops to support the Ottoman defense of the city. France and Britain, fearing the prospect of Russian influence in the Ottoman Empire, called for mediation. The Convention of Kütahya (April 8, 1833) conceded Ottoman Syria to Egypt but prevented Egyptian control of the empire as a whole. Because of its support, Russia retained its position as the Ottomans' principal ally. This was reflected in the Treaty of Hunkâr-Iskelesi (July 8, 1833), in which Russia and the Ottoman Empire pledged mutual support in any future conflict. The treaty also called for closure of the Straits to any naval forces threatening Russia.

The agreements of 1833 did not last long. In 1839 Sultan Mahmud II decided to deal with Muhammad Ali's threat by sending a military force against his son, Ibrahim, in Syria; thus began the second Syrian war. In spite of a force developed by Helmuth von Moltke of Prussia, the Ottomans were defeated at Nesib on June 24, and the Ottoman fleet defected to Egypt. Fearing that the breakup of the Ottoman Empire would not be in the best interests of Britain, Lord Palmerston, foreign minister and later prime minister, called for talks with Russia, Austria, and Prussia in London in 1840. In July the ambassadors of the four powers persuaded the Ottomans to recognize Muhammad Ali as hereditary pasha of Egypt and grant him control of Palestine (southern Syria) in return for a cease-fire within ten days. France, although now under a government more favorable to Britain, was noncommittal, and Muhammad Ali refused the compromise. The British, with help from Austria, occupied Beirut and Acre in October and November and helped the Ottomans defeat Ibrahim's forces in Syria. Muhammad Ali, no longer counting on French help, was forced to accept Egypt as a hereditary domain and return the Ottoman fleet to the control of Constantinople.

Russia, Austria, Prussia, Britain, and France then signed the Treaty of London on July 13, 1841, ratifying these agreements. Appended to the treaty was an agreement on the Straits question: "Warships of foreign powers have always been forbidden to enter the Straits of the Dardanelles and of the Bosporus." Lord Palmerston had succeeded in strengthening Britain's position in the Middle East, preventing France from gaining influence in Syria, and containing Russian advances in the Ottoman Empire. That empire was thus preserved for a time, its existence now guaranteed by the five major European powers. Muhammad Ali remained in control of Egypt, with special rights in the Sudan. Although all parties seemed to have gained something, the stage was set for continued jockeying for position in the Middle East.

[*See also:* Straits, Turkish]

BIBLIOGRAPHY

ARNAKIS, GEORGE G. *The Near East in Modern Times*, vol. 1: *The Ottoman Empire and the Balkan States to 1900*. New York, 1969.

HUREWITZ, J. C. *Diplomacy in the Near and Middle East*, vol. 1. Princeton, N.J., 1956.

Daniel E. Spector

Stratford de Redcliffe

See Canning, Stratford

Struma

Ship on which Jewish World War II refugees died, in part because of Britain's wartime refugee policy.

In October 1941, the 180-ton Romanian coastal vessel *Struma,* which normally carried one hundred passengers, sailed for Haifa with almost one thousand Jewish refugees. The ship broke down at Istanbul on December 16 because of overloading, a leaking hull, and defective engines. Turkey would not permit the passengers to land without British certificates for Palestine, but the British refused to issue them.

Since the refugees could not go forward and could not return to Romania, the *Struma* remained in port for ten weeks. The British refused the appeal of the Jewish Agency to permit the refugees entrance to Palestine—if only for later transport to Mauritius, an island in the Indian Ocean. On February 24, Turkey towed the *Struma* with its passengers out to sea, where six miles from shore it sank; it is not known whether it capsized, struck a mine, or was hit by a torpedo. Some 70 children, 269 women, and 428 men drowned—only 2 swam to safety.

This event became the symbol for the Jewish community in Palestine (the YISHUV) of Britain's unrelenting World War II policy toward the Jewish refugees of Nazi-occupied Europe.

BIBLIOGRAPHY

MORSE, ARTHUR D. *While Six Million Died*. New York, 1968.

SACHAR, HOWARD M. *A History of Israel: From the Rise of Zionism to Our Time*. Oxford, 1979.

Miriam Simon

Students in the Line of the Imam

An unofficial organization of radical Islamic students.

Students in the Line of the Imam, formed after the Islamic revolution in Iran, was largely blamed for the takeover of the American Embassy in Tehran in November 1979. The students, directed by their mentor Mohammad Musavi Khoeyniha, were instrumental in bringing to an end the presidency of Abolhasan Bani Sadr, Iran's only nonclerical head of state, and the closure of Iranian universities in April 1979. With the war with Iraq, which had begun in September 1980, and the subsequent resolution of the hostage crisis in January 1981, the Students in the Line of the Imam had outlived their utility and were relegated to the margins of Iranian political life. They have since converted the American Embassy compound in Tehran to a publication site, printing embassy documents in a series called "Documents from the Nest of Spies."

It is interesting to note that Abbas Abdi, who was one of the leaders of the Students in the Line of the Imam, is currently the editor in chief of the daily newspaper *Salam* (Hello), which publishes frequent and vociferous attacks on the policies of the government in Tehran.

BIBLIOGRAPHY

BAKHASH, SHAUL. *The Reign of the Ayatollahs*. New York, 1986.

IRAN RESEARCH GROUP. *Who's Who in Iran*. Meckenheim, Germany, 1990.

Neguin Yavari

Suarès Family

Prominent Sephardic family, influential in Egyptian society and economy.

The family settled in Livorno, Italy, then went to Egypt during the first half of the nineteenth century. Menachem Suarès della Pegna settled in Alexandria while his brother Isaac settled in Cairo. In the mid-1870s Isaac's sons—Joseph (1837–1900), Félix (1844–1906), and Raphael (1846–1902)—created the Banque Suarès, which until 1906 served as mediator for European capital investment in Egypt. Given Raphael Suarès's connections with British industrial investors, he channeled British investments into such enterprises as the construction of the first Aswan Dam, the National Bank of Egypt, and the khedivial estates (*al-da'ira al-saniya*). The Suarès family was not only involved in banking and finance but also transportation, establishing in Cairo the first public transportation company and building railway lines between Cairo and Helwan, Qina and Aswan. Members of the family owned real estate in the heart of Cairo where Suarès Square bore Félix Suarès's name (Maydan Suarès was renamed, in 1939, Maydan Mustafa Kamil).

One family member, Edgar Suarès, was involved with a major shareholders' company. Owing to his initiative vast areas of land—several thousand *feddan* (a *feddan* is approximately one acre)—were purchased in Upper and Lower Egypt. Edgar Suarès reclaimed them and introduced modern irrigation facilities for large-scale agricultural development. He subsequently sold the land as small holdings to rural Egyptians at low prices and long-term credit. The Suarèses were not very active in Jewish communal affairs; only Edgar Suarès served very briefly as president of Alexandria's Jewish community during World War I. Their influence in Egyptian society and the economy declined after the 1930s.

BIBLIOGRAPHY

KRÄMER, GUDRUN. *The Jews in Modern Egypt, 1914–1952.* Seattle, 1989.

MIZRAHI, MAURICE. "The Role of Jews in Economic Development." In *The Jews of Egypt: A Mediterranean Society in Modern Times,* ed. by Shimon Shamir. Boulder, Colo., 1987.

Michael M. Laskier

Sublime Porte

Residence/office of the Ottoman sultan.

In the Ottoman Empire, the sultan would appoint a grand vizier to head the government. Just as the prime minister of Great Britain resides at 10 Downing Street, the grand vizier of the Ottoman Empire lived and worked in the Sublime Porte. This term is a French translation of *al-Bab al-Ali,* which means literally "the High Door." In the nineteenth century, it became common to refer to the entire Ottoman government as "the Sublime Porte," as it is common today to refer to the U.S. government as "the White House."

BIBLIOGRAPHY

LEWIS, BERNARD. *The Emergence of Modern Turkey.* New York, 1961.

Zachary Karabell

Sudan

A country of northeast Africa located south of Egypt on the Nile.

Known in the past as *bilad al-sudan* (the land of the black people), Sudan is the largest country in Africa, covering one million square miles. Its nearly twenty-five million residents, who live scattered across the wide expanse, differ along lines of ethnicity, language, and religion. The country's political instability is, in part, a result of this diversity. Moreover, given its geostrategic location astride the Nile, it has been vulnerable to foreign pressure.

Sudan has more than fifty ethnic groups, which are subdivided into at least 570 tribes. The principal groups in the north are Arab, Beja, Nuba, Nubian, and Fur. Nearly half the population identifies itself as Arab, generally meaning peoples who speak Arabic and reflect its cultural heritage. The Arabs along the Nile valley tend to dominate Sudanese political and economic life. The Beja, who comprise 5 to 6 percent of the population, are concentrated in the east along the Red Sea and coastal mountain ranges; they are Muslim but do not speak Arabic. The Nuba, residing in the Nuba mountains of southern Kurdufan, are 5 percent of the population and speak their own languages, not Arabic; some are Muslim, others Christian or adherents of traditional African religious beliefs. About 3 percent are Nubians, who traditionally lived along the lower reaches of the Nile, merging into Egypt. In the early 1960s, most had to move to central Sudan when the construction of the Aswan

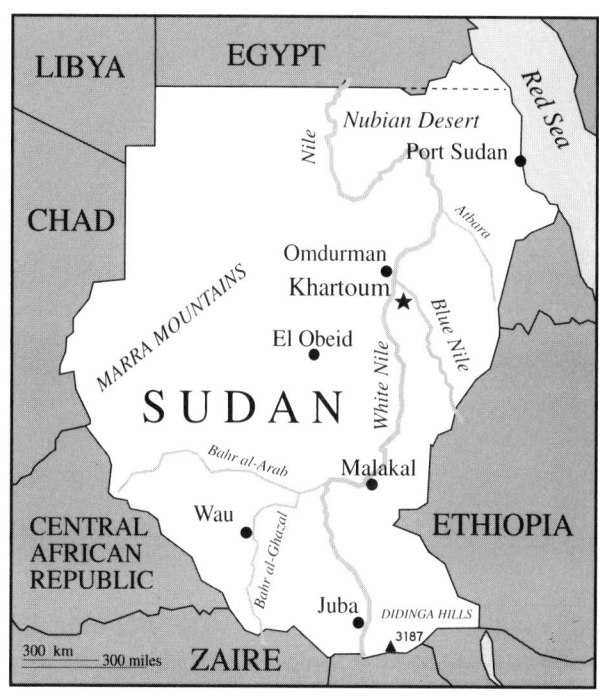

Sudanese cattle herding on the banks of the Upper Nile. (D.W. Lockhard)

High Dam resulted in the flooding of their homes. They too speak their own languages but are Muslim. The Fur, 2 percent of the population, live in the far west; like the Nubians they have a tradition of independent kingdoms. The Sultanate of Fur lasted from the fifteenth century until the early 1890s. In the southern third of Sudan, the Dinka are 40 percent of the local population (10 percent of the Sudanese as a whole), the Nuer are 5 percent of the whole, and the Shilluk are 1 percent. None of those groups are homogeneous, and they compete for territory, cattle, and trade routes. Numerous groups live in Equatoria, the southernmost province, and they differ in language, customs, and religion. Overall, the ethnic fragmentation in the south is greater than in the north.

Language overlaps with ethnicity as a basic distinguishing trait among the Sudanese. Half the population speaks Arabic as its native tongue. At most, 20 percent of the adults are literate, and indigenous languages remain important. Arabic serves as the lingua franca only among the educated classes in the north. Residents of the south resisted learning Arabic but were taught in English in the missionary schools. Nevertheless, Arabic has made inroads in the south in recent decades. Religion also divides the population—about 70 percent are Muslim, 25 percent follow traditional beliefs, and 5–6 percent are Christian. The north is overwhelmingly Muslim, with pockets of Christians in the Nuba mountains and in urban areas. Many Muslims belong to the networks of Sufi *tariqas* (brotherhoods) that formed originally around holy men and came to serve economic, social, and

political as well as religious functions. The brotherhoods cut across tribal allegiances, but otherwise most of the divisions reinforce cleavages, particularly the Arab/Muslim separation from the African/non-Muslim.

Sudan is predominantly rural, with about 25 percent of the population in urban areas (that share is growing as people flee famine in the outlying provinces). Eighty percent of the labor force works in agriculture or herding and 33 percent of the gross national product comes from agriculture. Northern Sudan is largely flat savannah and desert, where cattle, camels, and sheep are raised, sorghum and sesame are grown, and gum arabic is harvested. Along the Blue and White Nile, south of Khartoum, cotton and peanuts are grown for export on large-scale agricultural holdings, called schemes. Rains are heavier in the tropical south than in the north, but development in the south has been hampered by civil war and difficult conditions, such as the vast swamp known as the Sudd (barrier). Industry in Sudan is based on agriculture, notably canning and textile factories. In 1979, the Chevron Oil Company discovered oil in Bentiu (Upper Nile) and Muglad (southern Kurdufan). Extraction was blocked by the civil war, which resumed in 1983. As a result, all of Sudan's petroleum must be imported, at substantial expense.

The urban population is centered in the Three Towns—Khartoum, Omdurman, and Khartoum North—which serve as the political and economic capital. Port Sudan, built by the British in 1910, remains the only port on the Red Sea, although ef-

Sudanese in traditional battle garb at ceremonial reception. (D.W. Lockhard)

forts are being made to revive the historic port at Sawakin. Kassala and Qadarif are the main towns in the grain-growing east, and Wad Medani is the capital of the cotton-growing Gezira area. In the west, al-Ubayyad serves as the capital of Kurdufan, and al-Fashir is the capital of Darfur; both are important trading centers. Juba, the capital of Equatoria, was the capital of the south when it was unified from 1972 to 1983; it has been isolated from the surrounding countryside by the rebel forces of the Sudan Peoples Liberation Army (SPLA) since 1985. Virtually all the rest of the south is controlled by the SPLA.

The territory that now comprises Sudan was not unified until the Turko–Egyptian invasion of 1821, which imposed centralized control over most of the north relatively quickly. The Turko–Egyptian forces did not conquer Darfur until 1874 and never subdued the southern tribes. The indigenous politico-religious movement called the Mahdiyya overthew the Turko–Egyptian government in 1885 and ruled until 1898. British forces, marching south from Egypt, overran the country in 1898 and imposed the Anglo–Egyptian condominium. One enduring legacy of British rule was the virtual separation of the south from the north; from 1922 to 1946 the southern provinces were isolated from the rest of the country.

When Sudan gained independence on January 1, 1956, parliamentary rule was established. The two leading religious orders—the Ansar and the Khatmiyya—predominated in the governments, although their authority was challenged by secular nationalists, communists, southerners, and religious fundamentalists. The democratic institutions had not had time to take root by the time General Ibrahim Abbud instituted military rule on November 17, 1958. His rule lasted until November 1964, when a popular uprising led to a renewed democracy. That, too, proved unstable as the traditional politicians jockeyed for power and failed to deal with the rebellion that had exploded in the south.

Young officers led by Muhammad Ja'far Numeiri launched a coup d'état on May 25, 1969 and crushed the traditional political groups. Numeiri turned against his left-wing allies in 1971 but mollified the south by granting regional autonomy in 1972. He instituted major economic development programs in the mid-1970s, backed by his one party, Sudan Socialist Union. Economic development remained hampered by poor planning, high-level corruption, and skyrocketing oil prices. In 1977/78, Numeiri sought to widen his base of support by reconciling with the traditional and fundamentalist religious forces. That led to the gradual Islamization of the political system. Numeiri instituted Islamic criminal punishments in September 1983, which he enforced against widespread opposition by draconian emergency measures. By spring 1985, Numeiri's support was confined to the Islamic fundamentalists—northern secularists, the banned political forces, and the

Sudanese member of the Qadiriyya Sufi brotherhood. (© Chris Kutschera)

Tayba'a mosque in Jazira, Sudan. (© Chris Kutschera)

southerners (who resumed their civil war in 1983) actively sought to overthrow him.

In April 1985, a popular uprising led to a bloodless coup and the installation of a one-year Transitional Military Council. Elections were held in April 1986, but the subsequent parliamentary government proved as ineffective and unstable as the previous democratic experiments—1956 to 1958 and 1964 to 1969. The coalition governments were unable to act decisively to end the civil war or to revive the economy. On June 30, 1989, Brigadier Ahmad al-Bashir overthrew the government, with support from the fundamentalist National Islamic Front. Once again, constitutional institutions were banned. In early 1991, Bashir instituted Islamic rule. By then, his opponents had formed the National Democratic Alliance, which, from exile, sought to overthrow the government and reinstitute democracy. The continuing ethnic, religious, and regional tensions, however, did not make the prospect of forming a stable democracy likely.

Finally, the geostrategic location of Sudan contributes to its sociopolitical instability. Located astride the Nile, whose headwaters flow from Ethiopia and Uganda into Sudan and through Egypt to the Mediterranean Sea, Sudan has been the object of contention by those neighbors as well as external powers. Egypt cannot tolerate the presence of a hostile government in Khartoum, since the Egyptian economy depends on the Nile waters. In turn, Sudan and Egypt worry that Ethiopia might dam the Blue Nile and deprive them both of water. Sudan also borders the Red Sea, a major artery of international trade, which adjoins eight countries. Lacking the capacity to police its remote desert borders and its long coast along the Red Sea, the country is vulnerable to incursion. Refugees from neighboring civil wars and famines find haven in Sudan, and hostile governments support rebellious Sudanese groups. Sudanese governments have, in fact, meddled in the politics of such neighbors as Ethiopia, Chad, and Uganda, although those countries can easily undertake reprisals.

Some view Sudan as a *terra media,* lying between and linking Africa and the Arab world; others see it as lying on the fault line between the two peoples, torn between them and unable to unite.

BIBLIOGRAPHY

ABDEL RAHIM, MUDDATHIR. *Imperialism and Nationalism in the Sudan.* London, 1986.
BECHTOLD, PETER K. *Politics in the Sudan.* New York, 1976.
BESHIR, MOHAMMED OMER. *Revolution and Nationalism in the Sudan.* London, 1974.
KHALID, MANSOUR. *The Government They Deserve: The Role of the Elite in Sudan's Political Evolution.* London, 1990.
MAHMOUD, FATIMA BABIKER. *The Sudanese Bourgeoisie.* London, 1984.
VOLL, JOHN OBERT, and SARAH POTTS VOLL. *The Sudan.* Boulder, Colo., 1985.

Ann M. Lesch

Sudanese Civil Wars

Two drawn-out wars fought since the independence of Sudan in 1956.

There have been two prolonged civil wars in Sudan since independence in 1956. The first lasted from August 1955 to March 1972, and the second began in May 1983. Although both wars have been fought in the southern third of the country, their aims diverged. The first aimed at independence or at least autonomy for the south, whereas the second aims at restructuring the central political institutions.

The first civil war was triggered by the Torit mutiny (August 1955) by the Southern Defence Force and was heightened by the northern politicians' rejection of a federal system that would devolve certain powers to the regions. Under the parliamentary system (1956–1958), the south was marginalized politically. Under the military rule of General Ibrahim Abbud (1958–1964), the religious and ethnic norms that predominate in the north were imposed on the south: Arabic became the language of government and education; Islam was promoted and Christianity repressed; and increasingly harsh military means were used to quell the revolt. The return to civilian rule in late 1964 did not, in itself, end the conflict. Although the Round Table Conference of March 1965 examined southern grievances, the preponderant northern political forces continued to seek an Islamic state, which was anathema to the southerners as well as to northern secularists. Only after Muhammad Ja'far Numeiri seized power in May 1969 was an effort made to recognize the inherent ethnic and religious diversity in Sudan and negotiate with the rebels (known as Anya-Nya). The Addis Ababa Accord of February 27, 1972, which ended the first war, was implemented through the Regional Self-Government Act for the Southern Provinces (promulgated on March 3, 1972) and incorporated into the permanent constitution of 1973. The three southern provinces joined in one large region, with its own regional assembly, and elected a High Executive Council (HEC), having considerable autonomy in the social and economic fields. Religious discrimination was prohibited, and English was conceded to be the principal language in the south. Major efforts were made to reintegrate the refugees who had fled the country during the seventeen years of fighting and to absorb the Anya-Nya into the regular armed forces.

Despite the constitutional safeguards against altering the Addis Ababa Accord, Numeiri interfered continually in its operation. He dissolved the regional assembly, dismissed the HEC, tried to prevent potential oil revenue from accruing to the south, and decreed on June 5, 1983 that the south would be redivided into three provinces. That illegal action completed the dismemberment of the accord. By then, members of the absorbed Anya-Nya forces had engaged in sporadic mutinies, which culminated in the Bor and Pibor mutinies in spring 1983. When Numeiri sent troops to crush the mutineers, they fled to the bush, where they were joined by Colonel John Garang de Mabior, head of the army research center in Khartoum.

By midsummer 1983, Garang molded the Sudan Peoples Liberation Army (SPLA) and its political wing, the Sudan Peoples' Liberation Movement (SPLM). In contrast to the previous rebellion, the SPLM emphasized that Sudan must remain unified, but on a new basis: proportional sharing of power among the various peoples and regions; special attention to the socioeconomic needs of the deprived east, west, and south; and nondomination by any one religious or racial group over the others. The SPLM gained increasing support as Numeiri's policies led to economic ruin and his institution of Islamic law in September 1983 alienated a wide array of citizens. Numeiri's overthrow in April 1985 did not, however, end the rebellion. The transitional government (April 1985 to April 1986) and the elected government under Prime Minister al-Sadiq al-Mahdi (May 1986 through June 1989) failed to respond to the underlying demands of the SPLM/SPLA. They sought to modify, rather than annul, Islamic laws and tended to treat the SPLM as a southern movement only. Nonetheless, the high command of the armed forces compelled the politicians to accept bases for an accord with the SPLM, in spring 1989, that involved canceling Islamic laws until a constitutional conference could be convened that would decide on the legal basis of rule in Sudan. By then, the SPLA controlled nearly 90 percent of the countryside in the south and had made inroads into areas in the north. It then instituted a cease-fire as an expression of good faith in anticipation of holding the constitutional conference.

That effort to negotiate a solution was undermined abruptly by the coup d'état on June 30, 1989, whose leaders rejected the agreement to hold the constitutional conference and insisted that Islamic laws be retained. In fact, a comprehensive Islamic legal system was instituted in the north in early 1991 and a federal system was decreed. It retained the division of the south into three areas and kept substantial powers in the hands of the central government. After the coup d'état, the SPLM demanded not only the implementation of the agreement to convene a constitutional conference but also the prior restoration of democratic rule. The SPLM aligned with the exiled opposition National Democratic Alliance in March 1990 and gained the support of the ousted high command of the armed forces in September 1990. Thus, the SPLM became an active element in the nationalist opposition to the Islamist military government. By 1991, the SPLA controlled nearly all the south, but it still lacked the capacity to march on Khartoum. Moreover, internal tension caused a split in the SPLA in August 1991 that weakened its ability to control the government's military offensives. The prospects for a negotiated solution vanished in mid-1989, despite subsequent efforts to negotiate between the SPLM and the government, and the civil war caused increasing devastation and famine in the south. The concentration of government revenues on prosecuting the war also led to acute economic problems in the north and to the increasing dependence of the regime on such foreign funders as Libya and Iraq.

The two civil wars sought to deal with the underlying problem of Sudan—how to build unity in a multiethnic and multireligious country. The first war proposed regionalism as the means to give each community a degree of autonomy; the second war proposed restructuring power in the center so that regional autonomy could be secure. Sudanese politicians still grapple with that fundamental problem.

BIBLIOGRAPHY

ALIER, ABEL. *Southern Sudan*. Exeter, 1990.
BESHIR, MOHAMMED OMER. *The Southern Sudan*. London, 1968.
KHALID, MANSOUR, ed. *John Garang Speaks*. London, 1987.

Ann M. Lesch

Sudd

Great swamps of the Upper Nile.

Sudd is derived from the Arabic word *sadd* (barrier). It came into general use among European and Arab merchants to describe the great swamps of the Upper Nile. The Sudd is approximately the size of Belgium. Its penetration in 1841 ended the isolation of equatorial Africa.

Robert O. Collins

Suez Canal

Channel built from 1856 to 1869 by the Universal Maritime Suez Canal Company, linking the Mediterranean Sea to the Red Sea.

Several earlier rulers of Egypt constructed canals for the passage of seagoing ships, usually linking the Nile river to the Gulf of Suez. The followers of Saint-Simon, the French utopian socialist (Claude Henri de Rouvray, Comte de Saint-Simon, 1760–1825), proposed building the canal in the early nineteenth century. The entrepreneur who actually carried out this scheme was Ferdinand de Lesseps, a former French diplomat who was on friendly terms with Muhammad Sa'id Pasha. As soon as Sa'id became

Southern entrance to the Suez Canal in Egypt. (Richard Bulliet)

Egypt's viceroy in 1854, de Lesseps described to him his plan for constructing and financing this waterway, which would be the largest public-works project in Egypt since the pyramids. Sa'id consented, but it took some time for de Lesseps to secure approval from the sultan of the Ottoman Empire and the European powers (Britain was strongly opposed to a canal that might imperil its defense of India) and to raise the necessary capital.

The construction cost, estimated at more than 450 million French francs (worth about $100 million at that time), was borne mainly by Egyptian taxpayers and by thousands of unpaid or underpaid Egyptian peasants who were forced to do the manual labor as corvée labor until the European powers and the Ottoman government enjoined the Suez Canal Company to stop this practice.

When the one-hundred-mile (160 km) waterway was opened in 1869, it was thirty feet (9 m) deep and one hundred feet (30 m) wide, adequate for most oceangoing vessels at the time. It soon became a main trade route for steam-driven passenger and cargo ships because it reduced travel time between Europe and East Africa, South Asia, China, Japan, and the East Indies. The canal was supposed to be open to ships of all nations in war or peace, but, in fact, Britain made sure that it was closed to shipping for Germany and its allies in both world wars, and Egypt barred its use to Israel and to other countries' ships carrying goods for Israel until 1975. The canal was administered by the Canal Company until it was nationalized by Egypt under Gamal Abdel Nasser in 1956. Since then it has been administered by the Suez Canal Authority. It was closed from 1956 to 1967 and from 1967 to 1975 because of the Arab–Israel conflict.

The canal was enlarged from 1960 to 1964 and from 1975 to 1980 to accommodate larger oil tankers, which have become its main users; in 1992, it was 590 feet (190 m) wide at its narrowest point and had a maximum draught of 53 feet (16.15 m). Transit time now takes 15 hours, and 80 ships can transit per day. In 1966, 21,250 ships, having 275 million tons (250 million t) displacement, transited the Suez Canal; in 1990, it took 17,644 ships, having 410 million tons (370 million t) displacement. One reason for the declining number of vessels is that much petroleum is now transported by the Italian-built Sumed pipeline from Ayn Sukhna on the Red Sea to Sidi Kreir near Alexandria on the Mediterranean Sea.

BIBLIOGRAPHY

BEATTY, CHARLES. *De Lesseps of Suez*. New York, 1956.
MARLOWE, JOHN. *The Making of the Suez Canal*. London, 1964.
SCHONFIELD, HUGH J. *The Suez Canal in Peace and War*. Coral Gables, Fla., 1969.

Arthur Goldschmidt, Jr.

Suez Canal University

Public university founded in Isma'ilia, Egypt, in 1976.

Egypt's President Anwar al-Sadat (1970–1981) founded Suez Canal University as part of his plan to rebuild and symbolically reclaim the war-damaged Suez Canal cities. He had reopened the canal in 1975; it had been blocked since the June 1967 Arab–Israel war. With branch colleges in Suez and al-Arish, the university had 730 faculty members and 10,320 students in the late 1980s.

BIBLIOGRAPHY

The World of Learning 1992, 42nd ed. London, 1991.

Donald Malcolm Reid

Suez Crisis

See Arab–Israel War (1956)

Suez–Mediterranean Pipeline

Pipeline linking the Red and Mediterranean seas.

The Suez–Mediterranean Pipeline (SUMED) was opened in 1977. It consists of two pipelines 210 miles (336 km) long and 42 inches (1.07 m) in diameter. As of April 1994, the capacity was 2.4 million barrels per day. SUMED allows the Gulf

oil-producing states to bypass the Suez Canal, which cannot accommodate tankers larger than 150,000 tons. It also provides them with an alternative route if the canal is blocked, as happened in 1973.

Half of the pipeline is owned by the Egyptian General Petroleum Company. The balance is divided among PETROMIN of Saudi Arabia, the Abu Dhabi Oil Company, and the Qatar General Petroleum Company.

SUMED is designed to allow easy transshipment and dispatch to numerous destinations with minimal disruption. It can transport different grades of crude oil with minimal contamination. The terminals at Ain Sukhna, on the Red Sea, and at Sidi Kreir, near Alexandria, can accommodate both very small tankers and those over 500,000 tons.

Seventy-three percent of the oil transported by SUMED is destined for Europe. The pipeline has more than forty clients. The main ones are the major oil companies, Arabian American Oil Company, and the National Iranian Oil Company.

BIBLIOGRAPHY

ARAB PRESS SERVICE ORGANIZATION. *Middle East Economic Survey*.

Jean-François Seznec

Sufism and the Sufi Orders

Islamic theosophy and groups that emerged from it.

The common definition of Sufism as the mysticism or esotericism of Islam suggests that it was a rarefied, peripheral, or even clandestine phenomenon in the Islamic world. More accurately, Sufism should be seen as a combination of theosphical speculation, devotional zeal, and ritual transmitted by initiation that for many centuries made up the essence of religion for perhaps a majority of Muslins. On the eve of the modern age, the Sufi orders that were the vehicles of this traditional religiosity remained vigorous, both doctrinally and organizationally; they were to be found in virtually every part of the Middle East, gave rise to new branches, and produced a number of outstanding personalities.

Almost all the figures associated with the eighteenth-century revivalist movements of Islam were Sufis, and the late decades of that century as well as the early decades of the following one witnessed the emergence of several Sufi masters whose influence extended far beyond their lifetimes.

The earliest was Sayyid Ahmad al-Tijani, born in Ayn Madi (Algeria) in 1737. Originally affiliated to the Khalwati order, he established his own order on the basis of a claim to have received directly from the Prophet Muhammad his initiation into the Sufi path as well as a distinctive litany for recitation. The Tijaniyya order became widespread in Algeria and West Africa and also expanded into Egypt and the Sudan.

Contemporary with al-Tijani was Shaykh Ahmad al-Darqawi (d. 1823), who founded in Morocco a new and vigorous branch of the well-established Shadhili order. This in turn gave rise to a number of sub-branches that were influential in different parts of North Africa as well as the areas that are now Syria, Palestine, and Yemen.

The third significant figure of this period was Mawlana Khalid Baghdadi (d. 1827), a Kurd, who after his initiation to the Naqshbandiyya in India founded a new branch of the order—the Khalidiyya—in the Middle East. There, it displaced almost entirely all existing branches of the Naqshbandiyya, took the place of the Qadiriyya as the dominant order in Kurdistan, and became well established throughout parts of the Ottoman Empire that are now Syria, Iraq, and Anatolia, as well as in the Ottoman capital, Istanbul. In keeping with the traditional emphases of the Naqshbandiyya, Mawlana Khalid's aim was to promote the ascendancy of the SHARI'A (Islamic law) and strengthen the loyalty of Muslims to the Ottoman Empire, which he considered to be the ultimate guarantor of the *Shari'a*. To this end he recruited numerous high-ranking scholars and members of the Ottoman bureaucracy and sought to make of his own person the focus for a lasting organizational unity of the order. This unity did not survive his death, but the Khalidiyya continued to flourish and expand, especially in Ottoman Turkey. Among the spiritual descendants of Mawlana Khalid in late Ottoman times was Shaykh Diya al-Din al-Kumushkhanawi (Gümüşhanevi, d. 1893), a great scholar of *hadith* (the tradition of what the Prophet said or did), whose lineage has continued in Istanbul down to the present. The Khalidiyya now counts as the most vigorous of the Sufi orders still active in the Middle East.

Posthumous influence of a more diffuse kind was exercised by Ahmad ibn Idris (d. 1837). He, too, originated in North Africa, but the most important part of his career was spent in the Hijaz and the Asir region immediately to the south. Rejecting certain Sufi practices that he regarded as contrary to Islamic law, he formulated the principles of his own order with direct reference to the Qur'an (the holy book of Islam) and the *sunna* (the practice of tradition) of the Prophet. An order named after him—the Idrisiyya—came into being after his death, and it even spread across the Indian Ocean to the Malay world. More important, however, were movements founded by two of his followers.

Muhammad ibn Ali al-SANUSI (d. 1859) joined the following of Ahmad ibn Idris while in Mecca, but three years after the death of his master, he found it advisable to leave the Hijaz for the Jabal Akhdar in Cyrenaica. There he gained the loyalty of many of the nomadic tribes and established a distinctive system of multifunctional *zawiyas* (hospices or lodges) that gave the SANUSI ORDER a solid socioeconomic basis. The Sanusiyya waged a prolonged campaign of resistance to Italy's occupation of Libya, which began in 1911, and it was partly in recognition of this that the hereditary head of the order was made king of Libya after the expulsion of the Italians at the end of World War II. This marked the effective end of the Sanusiyya as a Sufi movement.

A fellow disciple of al-Sanusi was Muhammad Uthman al-Mirghani (d. 1853), the scion of a central Asian family that established itself in Mecca toward the close of the eighteenth century. He established the Mirghaniyya (also known as the Khatmiyya) after the death of Ahmad ibn Idris and propagated it with particular success in the Sudan. It found itself at odds there with the movement of the MAHDI and thus became an ally of the Anglo–Egyptian regime that replaced the Madhist state. The Mirghaniyya retains its influence in Sudan even down to the present day.

As the case of Ahmad ibn Idris and his disciples shows, the holy city of Mecca was an important crucible for new developments in Sufism. In addition, together with the sister city of Medina, it was a great center for the propagation of all the principal Sufi orders, old as well as new. Sufi shaykhs (mystical leaders) of diverse national origins, but principally Indians and Ottoman Turks, maintained hospices of their respective orders in the holy cities, where they would initiate many of the pilgrims who came to the Hijaz during the nineteenth century in increasing numbers. For numerous such pilgrims, especially those from the Malay world, initiation into a Sufi order functioned as a kind of appendage to the rituals of the *hajj* (pilgrimage), a proud souvenir of the holy cities.

Conscious of this transnational appeal of the Sufi orders, Sultan Abdülhamit II (ruled 1876–1909) established close relations with a number of Sufi shaykhs in order to bind the Arab provinces of the Ottoman Empire more closely to its capital and, more generally, to further his policy of pan-Islam—uniting Muslims across the world in loyalty to the Ottoman dynasty as the heir to the caliphate. Abdülhamit was himself the disciple of Muhammad Zafir al-Madani, leader of the Madani offshoot of the Darqawiyya, for whom he built a hospice adjacent to the Yıldız palace. Also close to the sultan were

Abd al-Huda al-Sayyadi (d. 1909), a Rifa'i shaykh from Aleppo, and several Naqshbandi shaykhs who undertook diplomatic missions on his behalf in places as far apart as Hungary and China.

Two developments in the wake of World War I severely damaged the Sufi orders of the Middle East. The first was the conquest of the Hijaz in 1924 by the Saudis, who proceeded to impose the tenets of the Wahhabi (MUWAHHIDUN) sect on the people of Mecca and Medina. The Wahhabis rejected all organized Sufism as an unacceptable innovation in religion, objecting particularly to the Sufis' sessions of *dhikr* (invocation), their offering of ritualized salutations to the soul of the Prophet, and the role they assigned the shaykh in spiritual life. An earlier Wahhabi occupation of the Hijaz, in the first decade of the nineteenth century, had resulted in the suspension of all Sufi activity; now, the great hospices of the holy cities were closed forever as their shaykhs departed for exile. The role of Mecca and Medina as unique centers for the diffusion of the orders was thus at an end. But Sufism as such has not died out in the Hijaz. Much clandestine Sufi activity persists, frequently surfacing during the hajj season when the sheer numbers of pilgrims strain the capacity of Saudi Arabia's government for censorious surveillance.

In September 1925, one year after the Saudi conquest of the Hijaz, Mustafa Kemal Atatürk banned the Sufi orders in Turkey in accordance with his program for the coercive reorientation of Turkish society. The orders were firmly entrenched in traditional Turkish culture, and they were deemed, moreover, to represent a potential source of at least passive resistance to secularism. Their hospices were therefore closed, and the performance of their rites was banned. Certain orders thereupon died out, notably the Mevleviye, which was closely tied to the sociopolitical order that was being replaced, but other orders showed capacities of adaptation and survived. The most important of these orders was the Khalidi branch of the Naqshbandi. Often credited with militant opposition to the Turkish Republic, the Khalidis have by and large contented themselves with attempting to continue their traditions of learning and spirituality—albeit in attenuated form—under the new conditions imposed on them. The sole significant exception was furnished by the uprising of Shaykh Said of Palu in 1925, an uprising that was inspired in part by Kurdish separatism. Important among Khalidi shaykhs of the republican period have been Mehmed Esad (d. 1931), Abdülhakim Arvasi (d. 1943), Mehmed Zahid Kotku (d. 1979), and Sami Ramazanoğlu (d. 1984). As for the Nucru movement, centered around the person and writings of Bediüzzaman Said NURSI (d. 1960), it contains important elements of Sufism without being structurally organized as an order.

From the 1930s onward, the standing and influence of the Sufi orders in the Arab lands were adversely affected by the rise of modernist movements that, drawing on the teachings of Wahhabism and claiming to revive the original path of Islam, criticized Sufism for alleged indebtedness to extra-Islamic sources and encouragement of passivity in the face of social and political ills. It is, however, to be noted that Hasan al-Banna (d. 1949), founder of the Muslim Brotherhood, began his religious activity in a Sufi fraternity; described his movement as being, among other things, Sufi; and prescribed for certain echelons of members many of the devotional duties of Sufism. Later leaders of the Brotherhood were less sympathetic to Sufism, and when Egypt's President Gamal Abdel Nasser began persecuting the movement, some of the Egyptian orders avenged themselves by allying themselves with his regime. (Others, by contrast, served as covers for continued Brotherhood activity). The situation in Syria was considerably different: there, a number of prominent Sufi shaykhs, most importantly Muhammad Hamid al-Hamawi of Hama (d. 1969), have cooperated closely with the Brotherhood.

The Shi'a (see SHI'ISM) Sufi orders of Iran, unlike the Sunni Sufi in Ottoman Turkey and the Arab lands, were never able to establish a harmonious, still less symbiotic, relationship with the *ulama* (Islamic scholars). They were subject even in premodern times to regular denunciation by the esoterist scholars. Thus, when the Ni'matallahi order reappeared in Persia (now Iran) at the end of the eighteenth century after a period of exile in India, it collided inevitably with the power of the Shi'a *mujtahids* (experts on Islamic law). The result was that several of its most important representatives—notably Ma'sum Ali Shah Dakkani (d. 1797), a flamboyant proselytizer—were put to death at the behest of the *ulama*. Later Ni'matallahis were more circumspect, and as the open hostility of the *ulama* declined, Ni'matallahi Sufism found its niche in Iran as a minor form of religiosity. One consequence of this relative integration into the religious milieu was that the order grew and underwent a series of internal splits, so that by the end of the nineteenth century nothing remained of its original unity. Less widespread than the Ni'matallahiyya is the Zahabi order, a Shi'a derivative of the central Asian (and therefore Sunni) Kubravi order. Although the most prominent Ni'matallahi leader now lives abroad, the Shi'a Sufi orders have continued to maintain a modest level of activity, since the advent of Iran's 1979 Islamic republic.

BIBLIOGRAPHY

ALGAR HAMID. "Der Nakṣibendi-Orden in der republikanischen Türkei." In *Islam und Politik in der Türkei,* ed. by Jochen Blaschke and Martin van Bruinessen. Berlin, 1985.

GABORIEAU, MARC, ALEXANDRE POPOVIC, and THIERRY ZARCONE, eds. *Naqshbandis: Cheminements et situation actuelle d'un ordre mystique musulman.* Istanbul, 1990.

GRAMLICH, RICHARD. *Die schiitischen derwischorden Persiens,* 3 vols. Wiesbaden, Germany, 1965–1981.

O'FAHEY, R. S. *Ahmad ibn Idris and the Idrisi Tradition.* Evanston, Ill., 1990.

POPOVIC, A., and G. VEINSTEIN, eds. *Les ordres mystiques en Islam.* Paris, 1986.

Hamid Algar

Suhaj

Egyptian governorate and city.

Located 290 miles (467 km) south of Cairo, Egypt, the governorate of Suhaj (also called Sohag) covers 597 square miles (1,546 sq. km) and had a population of 2,455,000 in 1986. The capital city of the governorate is also named Suhaj. The city of Suhaj, with a population of about 50,000 in 1987, is a major commercial center for products of agriculture. In addition, cotton-weaving factories and other textile industries are located there.

BIBLIOGRAPHY

Middle East and North Africa 1992, 38th ed. London, 1992.

David Waldner

Suissa, Albert   [1959–   ]

Israeli author.

Suissa was born in Casablanca, Morocco, and immigrated to Israel in 1963. He grew up in Jerusalem, where he studied in an Orthodox school. Later he moved to Paris and studied mime, taught theater, and performed with a mime troupe. He now lives in Paris and Jerusalem.

Bound, Suissa's only book, consists of novellas that cumulatively form a variation of a bildungsroman. The protagonist is a child of an immigrant North African family uprooted and replanted on the outskirts of Jerusalem—for that matter, on the margins of Israeli society. Rich with ornamental details, fantasy, and ethnic authenticity, the novel relates the development of a child whose disintegrating family has had its very foundations undermined by its trans-

plantation. Pitted against the slogans of Eastern European Zionism and mainstream Israeli culture, the impotence and irrelevance of the family is portrayed boldly. Both the original home and the new home seem to be driven by violence and oppression, which breed a devastating alienation. Suissa's language and the structure of the novel are arabesque in pattern and logic, baroque in style, and modern in psychological sensitivities.

Zvia Ginor

Sulayman, Abdullah

Saudi Arabia's finance minister from 1932 to 1936.

Sulayman was secretary, then paymaster for King Abd al-Aziz Al Sa'ud in the 1920s. In 1932, he was made finance minister of Saudi Arabia. During the impoverished years before the country's petroleum resources were discovered, he played a crucial role in keeping the Saudi state solvent. He bargained shrewdly in the 1932/33 oil-concession negotiations to establish what later became ARAMCO (Arabian American Oil Company) but was unable to grasp the complexities of an oil-fueled economy. He resigned in 1936.

BIBLIOGRAPHY

YOUNG, ARTHUR A. *Saudi Arabia: The Making of a Financial Giant.* New York, 1983.

Malcolm C. Peck

Sulayman, Hikmat   [1889–1946]

Iraqi government official.

Hikmat Sulayman held various senior administrative positions and ministerial posts in Iraq in the 1920s and 1930s. Associated first with Yasin al-Hashimi and Rashid Ali al-Kaylani, he fell out with them in 1935. His friendship with Bakr Sidqi led to his becoming prime minister after the latter's coup in October 1936, a post he held until Sidqi's overthrow in August 1937.

Peter Sluglett

Sulayman ibn Himyar   [1907–   ]

Paramount shaykh of the Banu Riyam tribe and leader of the Ghafiri confederation in Oman during the second quarter of the twentieth century.

Although notionally loyal to the Ibadi imamate, Sulayman consistently followed an independent policy, evidenced by his self-styled title King of the Green Mountain, courting the support of the Saudi, Musqati, British, and American governments until his overthrow (by Sultan Said ibn Taimur) and his exile in 1957.

Calvin H. Allen, Jr.

Sulaymani Sharifs

Rulers of Asir in the twelfth and thirteenth centuries.

These descendants of the Prophet Muhammad ruled Asir, the highland region in Saudi Arabia to the north of modern North Yemen, just before and during the rule of the Ayyubids and the Rasulids in Yemen in the twelfth and thirteenth centuries.

Robert D. Burrowes

Sulaymaniya

Town in northeastern Iraq, capital of Iraqi Kurdistan.

A market town in Kurdistan, Iraq, sixty miles (96.5 km) east of Kirkuk, Sulaimaniya is bounded on the east and south by Iran. Its name was linked to Süleyman Paşa, *wali* of Baghdad when the town was founded in 1781. Surrounded by mountains, the town has cold winters and mild summers. It has archeological sites (some in caves) that date to about fifty thousand years ago.

Most of the population are Kurds. Dokan Dam, thirty-seven miles (60 km) northwest of the town, has a hydroelectric station.

BIBLIOGRAPHY

Harris, George L. *Iraq: Its Society, Its Culture*. New Haven, Conn., 1958.
al-Hassani, Abdul Razzak. *The History of Modern Iraq*. Baghdad, 1980.

Nazar al-Khalaf

Suleiman, Mulay

Alawi sultan of Morocco, 1792–1822.

Heir to the badly divided government of his brother and predecessor, Mulay Yazid (ruled 1790–1792), Suleiman also faced provincial unrest and a weakened tax base. He brought much of coastal and central Mo-

rocco under *makhzan* control, although his capture and subsequent release by Berber forces in the central Atlas mountains in 1819 underscored the limits of the crown's control over large provinces of Morocco. Suleiman is also known for his bid to suppress popular Sufism and other local socioreligious activities. In the face of growing European pressures, Suleiman adopted a generally hostile and insular stance.

BIBLIOGRAPHY

Abun-Nasr, Jamil. *A History of the Maghrib*. Cambridge, U.K., 1976.
Burke, Edmund, III. *Prelude to Protectorate in Morocco*. Chicago, 1976.

Matthew S. Gordon

Süleymancu

Twentieth-century Islamic movement in Turkey.

The name Süleymancu is derived from Süleyman Hilmi Tunahan (1888–1959), the founder of the movement. The movement is also known as Süleymancılık, but its members reject this name because of its negative connotation.

The Süleymancu movement, a branch of the Naqshbandi Sufi order, is distinguished from other Naqshbandi groups by an esoteric doctrine including the belief that Tunahan was the thirty-third and final link in a spiritual genealogy (*silsila*) of saints going back to the prophet Muhammad. This belief is probably connected with specific expectations concerning the end of the world and the role that the founder of the movement will play before the apocalypse, but these expectations are among the secrets of a core group of the movement.

Tunahan studied Islamic theology and law in Constantinople (now Istanbul) between 1908 and 1920. We know little of his activities during the Kemalist reform in the 1920s and 1930s, but by the end of the 1930s he was a preacher in Istanbul. In 1943, the authorities cancelled his permission to preach because of his antisecular views. His main importance lies in the fact that he established a large network of Qur'an courses in western Anatolia and Istanbul. After his death in 1959 his work was continued by his son-in-law, Kemal Kaçar, who heads the Süleymancu movement.

Tunahan's Federation for the Establishment and Maintenance of Qur'an Courses in Turkey, which had more than nine hundred local member organizations, was an important rival of the religious education system controlled by the Turkish state. In 1971, the government decreed that all Qur'an courses would be placed under supervision of the Directorate for Religious Affairs. The Süleymancus circumvented state control by reorganizing their network, shifting attention to the housing of pupils and students. About the same time they became active in western Europe, establishing about three hundred Islamic centers for Turkish migrants.

In both Turkey and western Europe, the Süleymancus have been accused of being right-wing extremists and using religion for the political purpose of damaging the secular Turkish state. Some of its adherents supported the views of the Nationalist Movement party of Alparslan Türkeş in the 1970s. The leader of the movement, Kemal Kaçar, however, was a member of parliament for the Justice party of Süleyman Demirel. Although the Süleymancus can be regarded as one of the re-Islamization movements in present-day Turkey, they have never challenged the legitimacy of the republic or the principle of secularism on which it is based.

BIBLIOGRAPHY

GÖKALP, ALTAN. "Les fruits de l'arbre plutôt que ses racines: Le suleymanisme." In *Naqshbandis: Cheminements et situation actuelle d'un ordre mystique musulman,* ed. by M. Gaboreau, A. Popovic, and T. Zarcone. Istanbul, 1990.

Nico Landman

Süleyman Hüsnü   [1838–1892]

Ottoman military officer.

A prominent military officer, Süleyman Hüsnü was appointed by Sultan Abdülaziz to be director of the Ottoman war academy, where he was an energetic reformer of military education. He advocated constitutional as well as educational reform in several written works and was affiliated with the YOUNG OTTOMANS. In 1876, he was one of the principal officers who deposed Sultan Abdülaziz. During the Russo–Ottoman war of 1877/78, he held off a Russian advance for months in the famous siege at Shipka Pass in Bulgaria. But in January 1878, 32,000 Ottoman troops were lost when the Russians finally broke through. After the defeat, he was banished to Baghdad, where he died.

BIBLIOGRAPHY

LEWIS, BERNARD. *The Emergence of Modern Turkey.* New York, 1961.
SHAW, STANFORD J., and EZEL KURAL SHAW. *History of the Ottoman Empire and Modern Turkey,* vol. 2. New York, 1977.

Elizabeth Thompson

Süleymaniye Library

Manuscript collection in Istanbul.

Located in part of Mimar Sinan's sixteenth-century mosque complex, the library was established in 1918. It houses the old documents from religious establishments that were declared illegal by Atatürk's new republic; they were gathered and stored there by Turkey's education ministry in 1927. The library holds more than 64,000 manuscripts and some 100,000 books in Arabic, Persian, and Turkish.

BIBLIOGRAPHY

Cumhuriyet dönemi türkiye ansiklopedisi. Istanbul, 1983.

Elizabeth Thompson

Süleymaniye Mosque

Ottoman mosque.

The Süleymaniye mosque (1550–1557) in Istanbul is the central building of an important early educational complex of the Ottoman Empire, founded by and named after Sultan Süleyman I, called the Magnificent (1494–1566).

A masterpiece of the chief court architect Sinan, the Süleymaniye mosque comprises a spacious domed interior preceded by a graceful forecourt with four minarets, one at each corner.

BIBLIOGRAPHY

KURAN, APTULLAH. *Sinan: The Grand Old Master of Ottoman Architecture.* New York, 1987.

Aptullah Kuran

Süleyman Nazif   [1869–1927]

Ottoman Turkish poet and writer.

The son of a historian, Süleyman Nazif was born and educated in Diyarbekır. While employed in the civil service, he began to write for the provincial press and, in 1897, was forced into exile in Paris. While in Paris, he contributed articles to Ahmet Riza's *Meşveret.* During the Constitutional period, he joined Ebüzziya Tevfik in producing *Tasvir-i Efkar.* Süleyman Nazif's poetry, which was published in *Servet-i Fünun* under the name Ibrahim Cehdi, was strongly influenced by Namık Kemal. He published four volumes of poetry and numerous other literary and academic works.

BIBLIOGRAPHY

ÖZKIRIMLI, ATILLA. *Türk edebiyati ansiklopedist,* vol. 4. Istanbul, 1982.

David Waldner

Sulh, Riyad al-   [1894–1951]

Lebanese politician; prime minister, 1943–1945 and 1946–1951.

Riyad al-Sulh (also al-Solh) was born into a prominent Sunni family that had played a major role in the Arab nationalist movement during the last decades of the Ottoman Empire. Unlike many other aristocratic families in Beirut, whose concerns revolved around parochial issues, the Sulhs were known for their cosmopolitanism, sophistication, and wide-ranging contacts throughout the empire. His father, Rida, had served as governor (*mutasarrif*) in Salonika and in 1909 had been elected one of Beirut's two representatives in the Ottoman parliament at Constantinople.

Sulh studied law at the University of Istanbul and at St. Joseph University in Beirut. After World War I, he and his father were elected to the National Congress of Syria, which proclaimed Emir Faisal king of an independent Syria. Following the military defeat of Faisal by France in July 1920, and the establishment of Greater Lebanon two months later, he became a vocal opponent of France's mandate. Forced to flee Lebanon, he was sentenced to death in absentia and spent most of the 1920s in exile, primarily in Paris and Geneva, where he worked closely with other Arab nationalists. In 1929, Sulh was allowed to return to Lebanon after Emile EDDÉ intervened on his behalf with the government of Charles Dabbas. From then on, except for another brief period of exile in 1935, he lived in Beirut. By the early 1930s, he had become one of the most influential Arab nationalist politicians, despite France's efforts to contain his power.

In the late 1930s, Sulh was progressively converted to the concept of an independent Lebanon that would be free of France's control and separate from Syria. This position, which he adopted in part under the influence of his cousins Kazem al-SOLH and Taki al-Din al-SOLH, reflected the growing recognition among large segments of the Sunni community that their interests lay in the preservation of existing boundaries and an alliance with moderate Maronite leaders.

The outbreak of World War II made possible the Christian–Muslim alliance that Sulh had advocated. The war weakened France's influence and prestige in Lebanon and thus undermined those in the Maronite community, led by Eddé, who insisted on a Christian Lebanon closely aligned with France. By the same token, it strengthened the hand of those Maronites, led by Bishara al-KHURI and his Constitutional Bloc, who called for an independent and sovereign Lebanon based on Muslim–Christian accommodation. Taking advantage of this changing balance of power within the Maronite community and of active support for Lebanese independence by Britain and the United States, Khuri and Riyad al-Sulh formed an alliance that led the movement for an end to France's mandate.

After parliament elected him president of Lebanon in September 1943, Khuri immediately chose Sulh as his prime minister. The two quickly concluded the informal agreement known as the NATIONAL PACT, which embodied the "historical compromise" between Muslims and Christians that they had supported for some time. Because of his role in the National Pact, which became the backbone of postindependence politics in Lebanon, Sulh can be regarded as one of the founding fathers of independent Lebanon. His pragmatism and tolerance made him ideally suited to play a leading role in designing a system based on interconfessional accommodation, while his charisma, dynamism, and political skills ensured that he could deliver the support of his community. His vision of a secular, sovereign Lebanon based on a cross-confessional understanding and open to the outside world continued to inspire generations of Lebanese politicians long after his death, and despite its shortcomings, it permitted Lebanon to experience several decades of political stability, remarkable economic growth, and rapid modernization. It is important to note that Sulh appears to have been aware of the limits of the political formula embodied in the National Pact, which called for the distribution of positions in the government and the bureaucracy among the country's various sects. He saw this confessional system as only a temporary expedient that would have to be eliminated in the long run. He once described political sectarianism as "an obstacle to national progress, impeding the representation of the national will and poisoning the good relations between diverse elements of the Lebanese population."

One of the first decisions of Sulh's government was to abrogate the parts of the 1926 constitution that limited Lebanon's sovereignty to the benefit of France. The mandate authorities responded by arresting Khuri, Sulh, and all but two members of the cabinet. Strikes and widespread demonstrations and riots ensued; together with pressure by Britain and the United States on the government of Free France, they forced the latter to reverse its policy and reinstate Khuri and Sulh on November 22, 1943. This date effectively marks the emergence of independent Lebanon.

Until the beginning of Khuri's second term in 1949, Sulh maintained a close working relationship with the president. Between 1943 and 1951, he headed six cabinets for a total of some sixty-five months. For most of his tenure as prime minister, he was involved in all important decisions and was widely seen as almost an equal of Khuri, for whom he was a precious ally because of the weight his opinions carried with the Sunni masses. Following Khuri's reelection, however, strains developed between the two men, largely as a result of the president's increasing tendency to bypass the cabinet and rely instead on a group of cronies, influence peddlers, and advisers headed by his brother Salim. Sulh resigned on February 14, 1951. He was assassinated on July 16 by a member of the Parti Populaire Syrien (PPS), who killed him at the airport in Amman, Jordan, in revenge for Lebanon's 1949 execution of Antun Sa'ada, the PPS's founder and leader.

BIBLIOGRAPHY

BINDER, LEONARD, ed. *Politics in Lebanon.* New York, 1966.
GORIA, WADE R. *Sovereignty and Leadership in Lebanon, 1943–1976.* London, 1986.
HUDSON, MICHAEL C. *The Precarious Republic: Political Modernization in Lebanon.* Boulder, Colo., 1985.
JOHNSON, MICHAEL. *Class and Client in Beirut: The Sunni Muslim Community and the Lebanese State, 1840–1985.* London, 1986.

Guilain P. Denoeux

Sulh, Sami al-   [1890–1968]

Lebanese Muslim politician.

Sami al-Sulh (also al-Solh), born to a prominent Sunni Muslim family, studied in Beirut and earned a law degree from Istanbul. He went to France to obtain a doctorate in law but returned to Lebanon before completing his studies. He claimed that while in Istanbul he had joined Arab secret societies working against the government of the Ottoman Empire, but no documentation supports his claims. He is accused of having supported the Ottoman government when other educated Arabs were struggling for Arab independence. He was a judge from 1920 to 1942, and, with French support, he was appointed prime minister in 1942. He represented Beirut in the Chamber of Deputies from 1943 to 1960 and from 1964 to 1968 and was prime minister seven times between 1945 and 1958.

The most controversial aspect of al-Sulh's political career was his support for Camille Chamoun. During the 1958 civil war he refused to criticize Chamoun, opposing the tide of Muslim public opinion. Al-Sulh was seen as a weak prime minister who did not stand up to President Chamoun. Chamoun used al-Sulh as a token Muslim because al-Sulh did not object to Chamoun's pro-Western foreign policy. His close association with Chamoun earned him the wrath of the Muslim masses, and his house in Beirut was burned down. He fled Lebanon for several months, then settled in the predominantly Christian area of Beirut.

Al-Sulh surprised all those who had prematurely written his political obituary by returning to public life in 1964 after winning a parliamentary seat from Beirut. Christian support in his district of course helped make his victory possible, but within a few years he was able to win the backing of some Muslims who had declared him a traitor in 1958. He spent the rest of his life defending his position in 1958, writing two memoirs to vindicate himself. He claimed that he never opposed President Gamal Abdel Nasser of Egypt, and that he was a staunch defender of the Palestinian cause. He blamed Nasser's supporters in Lebanon for the anti-Nasser reputation that was associated with his name after 1958.

Being the oldest deputy made al-Sulh president pro tem of the parliament. Members of the Christian establishment saw al-Sulh as demonstrating how Muslim politicians should conduct themselves. His support for Chamoun was viewed by the Phalange party, which supported him, as evidence of his patriotism. He was nicknamed Abu al-Faqir (Father of the Poor) because he championed the common people.

As'ad AbuKhalil

Sullivan, William   [1922–   ]

American ambassador to Iran, 1977–1979.

After graduating from the Fletcher School of Law and Diplomacy in 1947, William Healy Sullivan joined the U.S. State Department. He served as ambassador to Iran (1977–1979). During the IRANIAN REVOLUTION of 1979, Sullivan was blamed for the failure of the United States to support the shah and other American interests in Iran. According to his own version of those events (published in 1981), Sullivan believed that American policy failed during the crisis because he had been prohibited from exerting any influence over Washington policy decisions.

BIBLIOGRAPHY

SULLIVAN, WILLIAM H. *Mission to Iran.* New York, 1981.

Neguin Yavari

Sultan

Title implying political power; a king or sovereign, especially of a Muslim state.

The title of sultan came to prominence around 1000 C.E., after the political position of the caliphate (office of the leader of Islam) had eroded around the time of the establishment of the Seljuk sultanate. Turko–Iranian dynasts used the title as an equivalent of the Eurasian steppe title khan. Later, it was used generally in Islamic lands by many states large and small. In some cases, for example, in Persia (now Iran), from 1500 on, the term was further devalued to denote a governor, not even a petty ruler.

In the Ottoman Empire, sultan, along with padishah and khan, was one of the titles of the sovereign (e.g., Sultan Süleyman Khan), as well as the other members of the ruling family. The ruler's sons and grandsons, who served as governors and thus shared political power in the steppe manner, were all styled sultan. In the case of the female members of the ruling house, the title followed the personal name of the main designation—for example, Hürrem Sultan, *valide sultan* (dowager queen), *khasseki sultan* (favorite consort), or Mihrimah Sultan, who was a princess. The sultanate of the Ottoman Empire was abolished in 1922, just before the Republic of Turkey was founded.

I. Metin Kunt

Sultan Ahmet Mosque

Ottoman mosque.

Popularly known as the Blue mosque because of the predominantly turquoise-colored faience tile panels that embellish its vast prayer hall, the mosque of Sultan Ahmet I (1590–1617) stands next to Istanbul's Hippodrome. Supporting a domed, cruciform superstructure and six slender minarets, it is the major work of the architect Sedefkar Mehmed Ağa.

BIBLIOGRAPHY

GOODWIN, GODFREY. *A History of Ottoman Architecture.* London, 1971.

Aptullah Kuran

Sultan Hasan Mosque

One of the finest examples of Arab Egyptian architecture; situated below the citadel in Cairo.

Sultan Hasan mosque was built for the Mamluk Sultan Hasan al-Nasir in 1356–1363. The ground plan of the mosque takes the form of an irregular pentagon and occupies 9,450 square yards (7800 sq. m). It boasts a 267-foot (88 m) minaret in its south corner, the tallest in Cairo, and a massive main door at the north corner that is almost eighty-five feet (26 m) high. The exterior walls echo an ancient Egyptian temple, with large expanses of stone that are relieved by blind niches and double round arched windows. Stalactitic cornices, heavily restored, crown the facades. The mausoleum, which extends from the southeast wall, carries a 180-foot-high (55m) dome of the Arab Turkish style that was almost completely rebuilt in the eighteenth century.

Raymond William Baker

Sultani Schools

Ottoman intermediate schools.

Sultani lycées were higher secondary schools funded by the sultan's personal treasury. The first and most famous of these was GALATASARAY LYCÉE (also called Mekteb-i Sultani), founded in 1868 in Istanbul and modeled on the French lycée. An 1869 educational reform law provided for one sultani lycée in each provincial capital. In an expansion of the humanist education offered at these schools, in 1908 ten former IDADI SCHOOLS, whose curriculum had partly overlapped that of the lycées, were renamed sultani schools. By 1914 there were 8,380 students, mostly from elite backgrounds, enrolled in twenty-four sultani schools across the Ottoman Empire.

BIBLIOGRAPHY

KAZAMIAS, ANDREAS M. *Education and the Quest for Modernity in Turkey.* Chicago, 1966.

Elizabeth Thompson

SUMED

See Suez–Mediterranean Pipeline

Sunay, Cevdet   [1899–1982]

Turkish military officer and politician; president of Turkey, 1966–1973.

Sunay was born in Trabzon, the son of a village effendi in the Ottoman Empire. He attended the Küleli military high school and fought in Palestine in World

War I. In the Turkish War of Independence (1921–1922), Sunay fought on the Maraş, Gaziantep, and Western fronts, finally chasing enemy armies to İzmir. He became a staff officer for the new Republic of Turkey in 1930, after completing studies at the War Academy; he was promoted to general in 1958. In 1961, he was appointed chief of staff, following the military coup, although he apparently did not play a direct role in the plot against Adnan Menderes.

Sunay resigned his office to become president of Turkey in 1966 in an alliance between the Justice party and military interests. He served as president through the 1971 coup, in which some observers said he played a key role. Sunay's presidency ended in 1973, when his bid for an extended term fell one vote short in the assembly. His term in office is associated with the continued penetration of the military into Turkish politics.

BIBLIOGRAPHY

LEWIS, GEOFFREY. *Modern Turkey.* New York, 1974.

Elizabeth Thompson

Sun Language Theory

A 1930s movement that claimed Turkish was the mother of all languages.

H. F. Kvergic is credited with inventing this theory in 1935, although numerous others contributed to its general formulation. The theory draws its name from Kvergic's initial proposition that a Turkish man was first inspired to create language while looking at the sun. Others, such as Ibrahim Necmi Dilmen, presented charts of concept groups drawn from the sun—for example, light/beauty, fire/excitement, and motion/time. Supporters of the theory held that since Turks inhabited the so-called cradle of civilization, central Asia, their language was the origin for later languages, such as those of the Hittites, Arabs, and Europeans.

Although criticized for fantastic speculations, the theory attracted interest in the mid-1930s for several reasons. Some supporters, including Atatürk, used it to stem the drastic expurgation from the modern Turkish language of foreign words by language reformers. Supporters argued that since foreign words were derived from Turkish, they should remain in use. Others found in the theory justification for radical nationalist Turkist ideologies in their vaunting of the Turks' ancient heritage. They also used its link to the Hittites to establish a long history for the Turks in Anatolia. By World War II, interest in the theory faded, although Atatürk's support of it is occasionally

evoked today by opponents of the direction of Turkish-language reform.

BIBLIOGRAPHY

LEWIS, GEOFFREY. *Modern Turkey.* New York, 1974.

Elizabeth Thompson

Sunna

An Arabic word that literally means "trodden path" and is often translated as "customary procedure" or simply "tradition."

In pre-Islamic Arabia, *sunna* usually referred to an idealized ancestral life pattern (including political, economic, religious and other social norms). By the end of the first century of the Muslim era, however, *sunna* came to denote at least three things, none of them necessarily mutually exclusive: (1) the traditions of the ancestral Arabs; (2) the customary practice of a given locale within Muslim domains; and (3) the sayings and deeds of the Prophet Muhammad as the living example of the perfect response to the commands of God. Not long after the death of its most famous exponent, Muhammad ibn Idris al-Shafi'i (d. 819 C.E.), the belief that *sunnat al-nabi* or the "Sunna of the Prophet" is the one and only *sunna* normative for the Muslim community gained widespread acceptance. The subsequent development of Muslim jurisprudence was radically influenced both by this belief and by its corollary, that the authoritative memory of the prophetic *sunna* is preserved only in the HADITH literature. As a result, Muslims have for centuries revered the prophetic *sunna* as second only to the Qur'an as a source of divine law and have esteemed the *hadith* literature as sacred scripture that provides indispensable insight into the revelation of the Qur'an.

Scott Alexander

Sunni Islam

Branch of Islam that follows the tradition of the Prophet Muhammad.

The majority of Muslims (90%) are Sunnites, those who follow the *sunna* (the sayings and reported practices of the Prophet Muhammad). The death of Muhammad in 632 deprived the Islamic community of a leadership that had binding authority in both the religious and the temporal spheres. Eager to preserve memory of the Prophet's practices on issues that the Qur'an did not address, the early community turned to his actions as precedent. The deaths of the generation of Muhammad's companions, the growing historical distance of the Muslim community from the time of its origin, and the expansion of the Islamic caliphate into the culturally different Byzantine and Sasanian empires heightened the need to preserve the early Islamic ideals. Information about the sayings of the Prophet (*hadith*) took the form of oral accounts narrated on the authority of reporters going back to the generation of companions.

The application of the advice, principle, or behavior reported in hadith required the establishment of a living body of tradition (*sunna*). *Sunna* (in Arabic, established custom or "trodden path"), however, also referred to pre-Islamic Arabian custom, much of which survived into Islam, and later, to some established provincial practices within the fledgling caliphate.

The overlapping definitions of *sunna,* coupled with the proliferation of an unrealistically large number of hadith reports, impelled scholars in the eighth century to scrutinize the sources of Islamic tradition. The religious scholar Malik ibn Anas (d. 795) pioneered the effort by emphasizing that Islamic *sunna* was best exemplified by the existing norms and practices in Medina, and he gathered the sayings of the Prophet and the early companions in a compendium called *Al-Muwatta*. A generation later, the scholar al-Shafi'i (d. 820), focusing on hadith, stressed the importance of examining the reliability of the *isnad* (chain of transmitters) in identifying authentic hadith. Once authenticated, hadith gained binding legal power second only to the Qur'an. Only in the absence of a Qur'anic or hadith statement on a legal matter, Shafi'i argued, could the community reason by analogy to other situations that the Qur'an or hadith did address. And, if analogy proved to be impossible, the community could accept the *ijma* (consensus) of its religious scholars (*ulama*).

The ninth century witnessed the codification of the hadith in six canonical compendia, the most famous of which were made by Bukhari (d. 870) and Muslim (d. 875). Sunni religious thought thereafter diversified into four major legal schools that are distributed today as follows: the Hanafi school (the Near East), the Shafi'i school (Egypt and South Asia), the Maliki school (North Africa), and the Hanbali school (Saudi Arabia). The stress on differences among these schools has declined, although popular opinion still holds that Hanafi law is more liberal, because it allows for reasoning of developing situations, and the Hanbali school stands as the most conservative, following the letter of hadith.

Despite their differences, Sunni schools all turn to a classical body of Islamic tradition that prevailed under or was relayed by the early companions. Unlike Shi'a Islam, which believes that after the Prophet's death religious knowledge was invested in Ali, the Prophet's cousin and fourth caliph, and that political succession should be through his line of descendants, Sunni Islam accepts the political succession of the first three caliphs and views Ali only as an equal of his predecessor caliphs.

BIBLIOGRAPHY

GIBB, H. A. R. *Muhammedanism*. Oxford, 1975.
GOLDZIHER, IGNAZ. *An Introduction to Islamic Theology and Law*. Princeton, N.J., 1981.
WATT, W. MONTGOMERY. *The Formative Period of Islamic Thought*. Edinburgh, 1973.

Tayeb El-Hibri

Suphi Ezgi [1869–1962]

Turkish composer and musicologist.

Suphi Ezgi was born in Istanbul and attended the Military Medical Academy. At the same time, he was studying music with Turkish masters like Dede Zekai. Between 1913 and 1920, Suphi Ezgi, along with Sadeddin Arel and Rauf Yekta Bey, created modern Turkish musicology. Suphi Ezgi was also an accomplished singer and tanbur player and composed more than seven hundred pieces. The most important of this fourteen books on musicology is the five-volume *Nazari ve ameli Türk musikisi* (Turkish Music in Theory and Practice).

BIBLIOGRAPHY

Yeni türk ansiklopedisi, vol. 3. Istanbul, 1985.

David Waldner

Supreme Muslim Council

Muslim institution in Palestine, 1921–1948.

During Ottoman rule in Palestine (1516–1917), Muslim WAQF (plural, *awqaf*) and SHARI'A courts were headed by the Shaykh al-Islam, and in the nineteenth century were administered by the Ministry of Awqaf in Constantinople (now Istanbul). The British occupation of Palestine, starting in 1917, severed all ties with Constantinople, and these Muslim institutions were placed under British officials. Palestinian Muslims were alarmed at the prospect of their religious affairs being controlled by a Christian power headed by Zionists: Sir Herbert Samuel, the first high commissioner, and Norman Bentwich, legal secretary in charge of the *awqaf* and *Shariʿa* courts. The Muslims complained of religious discrimination and demanded control over their affairs. Anxious lest the 1921 anti-Zionist disturbances recur and wanting to provide the Palestinians with autonomous institutions that the Zionists were granted, Samuel proposed that the Muslim secondary electors to the last Ottoman parliament choose a higher body that would control the affairs of the Muslim community.

Samuel issued an order in December 1921 establishing a Supreme Muslim Council (SMC) constituted for "the control and management of Moslem *awqaf* and *Shariʿa* affairs in Palestine." It was to consist of a president and four members, two of whom were to represent the district of Jerusalem and the remaining two to represent the districts of Nablus and Acre. All were to be paid from government and *awqaf* funds. In the first election, held on 9 January 1922, the mufti of Jerusalem, Hajj Amin al-Husayni, was elected president; his budget was 50,000 British pounds.

Husayni initiated an Islamic cultural revival in Palestine in the 1920s. Through the SMC, he established an orphanage, supported schools, expanded welfare and health clinics, and renovated religious buildings. The most ambitious and impressive project was the renovation of the two dilapidated mosques within the Haram al-Sharif, the third holiest shrine of Islam. The restored structures enhanced the importance of Jerusalem in the Muslim and Arab worlds and asserted Jerusalem's centrality within Palestine. By the end of the decade, the mufti had consolidated his religious power and had increased his political influence throughout Palestine. He used his enhanced political position to advocate Palestinian self-determination. After he led the PALESTINE ARAB REVOLT (1936–1939), however, the British dismissed him and dissolved the SMC in 1937.

BIBLIOGRAPHY

MATTAR, PHILIP. *The Mufti of Jerusalem: Al-Hajj Amin al-Husayni and the Palestinian National Movement,* rev. ed. New York, 1992.

PALESTINE GOVERNMENT. *A Survey of Palestine for the Information of the Anglo-American Committee of Inquiry.* Jerusalem, 1947. Reprint, Washington, D.C., 1991.

Philip Mattar

Suq

A bazaar or marketplace, typically with narrow alleys, sometimes arcaded.

The suq is a feature of Middle Eastern towns. At one time, single alleys within it were occupied by a single trade—such as tailors, saddlers, goldsmiths, coppersmiths, textile weavers, and carpetmakers—resembling the craft guilds of preindustrial Europe. In modern times, single-trade alleys are likely to be found only in the oldest sections of traditional suqs.

Jenab Tutunji

Suq al-Manakh

Kuwait's unofficial share market.

The first Gulf Arab state to develop a stock market and establish itself as a financial center, Kuwait is better known for its large speculative unofficial share market that developed in 1977 after the government imposed strict regulations on the official market. This market, known as Suq al-Manakh, collapsed in September 1982, causing major losses to many investors, unofficial estimates ranging from ten to ninety-four billion dollars. The drop in oil prices in the 1980/81 period, the ensuing liquidity shortage, and the wide use of post-dated checks by investors were the primary causes for the crash. Despite government intervention to save many of the investors, which included most businessmen as well as some members of the royal family, the Suq al-Manakh crisis haunted Kuwait for the rest of the 1980s. The collapse shook the Kuwaiti financial system and forced the government to close Suq al-Manakh in 1984, but another ten years passed before the government was able to fully resolve the crisis. Stock market speculation and investment also became subject to tightened controls and regulations.

BIBLIOGRAPHY

The Middle East and North Africa, 1991, 37th ed. London, 1991.

Emile A. Nakhleh

Suri al-Jadid, al-

An Arabic daily published in Homs, Syria.

Published under the patronage of Hashim al-Atasi, whose family, retainers, and friends dominated Homs and much of the surrounding countryside, *al-Suri al-Jadid* (the New Syria) was the only opposition organ to print manifestos and articles denouncing President Adib Shishakli. Its chief assets were the personal standing of Atasi and its courageous opposition to Shishakli.

Muhammad Muslih

Sursuq Family

Prominent Lebanese landowning business family.

One of the wealthiest Greek Orthodox families in Beirut, the Sursuqs (also Sursock or Sursok) benefited from the 1858 Ottoman land reform to acquire large tracts of fertile land in northern Palestine. They were also bankers who controlled cotton and grain trade in Acre. The family was associated with controversial land sales to Zionists before and after World War I.

Various family members were active in Beirut politics before World War I, with Albert Sursuq a leading member of the Beirut Reform Society and Michel Sursuq a member of the Ottoman parliament. After the war, the family became a target of anti-Zionist criticism when their land sales to Jews in the Jezreel valley and at Lake Huleh displaced hundreds of peasants. The family remained prominent among Beirut's Europeanized elite after World War II. In the 1960s, the family villa was turned into the Nicolas Sursuq Museum.

BIBLIOGRAPHY

ABBOUSHI, W. F. *The Unmaking of Palestine*. Brattleboro, Vt., 1990.

Elizabeth Thompson

Surur, Hail al-

Syrian politician.

Shaykh Hail al-Surur was a tribal leader from the village of Umm al-Jimal, Syria, on the Jordanian border. He led the Masa'id bedouin in the 1956 Syrian Social National party revolt and was indicted in December 1956 for his involvement.

BIBLIOGRAPHY

SEALE, PATRICK. *The Struggle for Syria*. London, 1965.

Charles U. Zenzie

Suwaydani, Ahmad   [1932–   ]

Syrian military officer.

Born in Syria, Ahmad Suwaydani received a military education and served as a major general in the Syrian army. As the director of military intelligence, he was involved in the forging of the Ba'th regime in the spring of 1963. He went on to serve as army chief of staff in 1965. He was dismissed from this post and attempted a coup against the increasingly divisive party elite and subsequently fled to Iraq.

BIBLIOGRAPHY

Who's Who in the Middle East, 1967–1968.

Charles U. Zenzie

Suwayda Province, al-

A province in the southern part of Syria, a former Druze territory.

Centered on the city of al-Suwayda, Syria, the province consists mostly of JABAL DRUZE. In the administrative divisions of 1952, the province of al-Suwayda included 119 towns and villages and 37 farms (*mazra'as*). It was then divided into two parts (*qada*): Shahba and Salkhad. In the 1982 administrative divisions, the province of al-Suwayda was divided into three subprovinces (*mintaqas*): the center of the province (Suwayda), Shahba, and Salkhad. It had 11 subdivisions (*nahiyas*), 16 cities and towns, 126 villages, and 42 farms.

In the 1980 census, the city of al-Suwayda numbered 43,414 inhabitants out of a total of 149,228 for the whole province. The province produces large quantities of fruits, especially grapes. Al-Suwayda province is also an important archeological site for Roman antiquities.

Abdul-Karim Rafeq

Suwaydi, Tawfiq al-   [c. 1889–1968]

Iraqi politician.

Tawfiq al-Suwaydi, a pro-British moderate, was born in Baghdad to an influential Sunni family. His origins trace back to Abbas, the uncle of the Prophet Muhammed, whose descendants established the Abbasid dynasty that ruled Baghdad from 750 to 1258. Suwaydi attended school in Baghdad and studied law in Istanbul and France. He was elected to parliament and served in various government capacities: minister of education (1928), ambassador to Iran (1931), minister of justice (1935), and minister of foreign affairs (1934, 1937, 1941). Suwaydi was prime minister three times (1929, 1946, 1950). During his second term he legalized previously banned political parties. In his last term, he initiated negotiations for a new oil agreement, established the Board of Development to improve economic conditions, and enacted a law permitting Iraqi Jews to leave the country, provided they gave up their citizenship and property. In the aftermath of the 1958 revolution, Suwaydi was sentenced to life imprisonment. In 1962 he was permitted to leave Iraq for Lebanon, where he died.

BIBLIOGRAPHY

KHADDURI, MAJID. *Independent Iraq, 1932–1958: A Study in Iraqi Politics.* London, 1960.

Ayad al-Qazzaz

Suwaydi Family

Iraqi family prominent in religious affairs and politics.

The Suwaydi family of al-Karth district of Baghdad traces its origins to Abbas, the uncle of the Prophet Muhammad, whose descendants founded the Abbasid dynasty that ruled Baghdad from 750 to 1258. A well-known member was Shaykh Abdullah al-Suwaydi, a Sunni jurist who took part in the famous theological conference at al-Najaf in 1773 that sought to bring about reconciliation between the Sunni and Shi'a sects.

The Suwaydi family also has played a leading role in the affairs of modern Iraq. For example, Yusuf Suwaydi (1854–1925), a *shar'i* (religious) judge, played a leading role in the Arab movement against the Ottoman Empire. He was imprisoned in 1913 and 1914 for his political activities and later released. He also was involved in the revolt against the British in 1920.

Two of Yusuf's children, Naji and Tawfiq, completed their legal training in Istanbul in the early part of the twentieth century and helped to draft Iraq's constitution. Both of them were elected deputy and senator, and both served as prime minister. Naji advocated pan-Arabism and resented British interference in Iraq. He participated in the 1941 uprising against the British. When the uprising failed, he was exiled to Rhodesia, where he died in 1945. Tawfiq was a pro-British activist. After the revolution of 1958, he was sentenced to life imprisonment but was released in 1962. Tawfiq moved to Lebanon where he died in 1968.

BIBLIOGRAPHY

KHADDURI, MAJID. *Independent Iraq, 1932–1958: A Study in Iraqi Politics.* London, 1960.
LONGRIGG, STEPHEN HEMSLEY. *Iraq, 1900 to 1950: A Political, Social , and Economic History.* London, 1953.

Ayad al-Qazzaz

Suwayhli, Ramadan al-   [?–1920]

Tripolitanian nationalist.

Member of a prominent Arab family from the eastern Tripolitanian coastal town of Misurata. They opposed the interests of the other leading family, the Muntasirs.

Suwayhli had been tried and acquitted of murdering Abd al-Qasim Muntasir shortly after the Young Turk Revolution of 1908, when Tripolitania was part of the Ottoman Empire. Suwayhli had played a vital role in supporting the Ottomans against Italian and Sanusi incursions. After the Treaty of Ouchy (1912), which ended the war between Italy and the Ottoman Empire, Suwayhli sought an independent Tripolitania. He had been instrumental in founding the short-lived Tripolitanian republic in 1917, which had not been recognized by Italy but was tolerated (even after the laws of 1919, the *Legge Fondamentale,* when alternative administrative structures were established). Its members, including Ramadan al-Suwayhli, were paid large stipends by the Italian authorities until the structure of the republic collapsed. Italy then connived in Suwayhli's death, at the hands of the Muntasir family (who still held him responsible for Abd al-Qasim's murder) and Abd al-Nabi Bilhayr, leader of the Warfalla (who had fallen out with him concerning the republic).

[See also: Muntasir Family; Tripolitania]

BIBLIOGRAPHY

ANDERSON, LISA S. "The Tripoli Republic, 1917–1922." In *Social and Economic Development of Libya,* ed. by E. G. H. Joffe and K. S. McLachlan. Cambridge, U.K., 1982.

George Joffe

Sykes, Mark   [1879–1919]

British politician and diplomat.

A Liberal member of Parliament, Sykes advised the War Cabinet on Middle Eastern affairs and was sent to the Middle East during World War I to negotiate the SYKES–PICOT AGREEMENT (1916). Associated with the Arab Bureau during the war, Sykes penned several of the public statements issued by British officials in the Middle East, among them, General Allenby's December 1917 Jerusalem Proclamation and the Anglo–French Declaration of 1918.

BIBLIOGRAPHY

ANDERSON, M. S. *The Eastern Question*. London, 1966.
SHAW, STANFORD, and EZEL KURAL SHAW. *The History of the Ottoman Empire and Modern Turkey*. New York, 1977.

Zachary Karabell

Sykes, Percy Molesworth   [1867–1945]

British soldier and administrator; historian of Iran.

In 1915, Sykes raised a Persian force for the Allies to secure southern Iran, which was overrun with German-recruited guerillas. His eight thousand South Persia Rifles fulfilled its commission and even quelled a Qashqa'i (Qashgha'i) rising against Sykes's base of Shiraz. As well as career memoirs (*Ten Thousand Miles in Persia,* 1902), Sykes wrote a two-volume *History of Persia* (1915) and a *History of Afghanistan* (1940).

BIBLIOGRAPHY

YAPP, M. E. "Two British Historians of Persia." In *Historians of the Middle East,* ed. by Bernard Lewis and P. M. Holt. Oxford, 1961.

John R. Perry

Sykes–Picot Agreement

World War I document of 1916 that would have divided the Middle East into British and French spheres.

The Sykes–Picot Agreement was one of the pivotal diplomatic documents of World War I concerning the Middle East. It was negotiated in secret at the end of 1915 by Sir Mark Sykes of Great Britain and Georges François Picot of France, with full knowledge by their respective foreign ministries. It provided for a partition of the Middle East into French and British spheres.

The French were to have direct control of Syria, Lebanon, and Cilicia plus a zone of influence extending east from Damascus and Aleppo through Mosul. The British were granted direct control of the Mesopotamian provinces (now Iraq) of Baghdad and Basra as well as a zone of influence extending from Basra to Palestine. Palestine was itself to be placed under international administration.

Under the subsequent Anglo–Russian–French Agreement of 1916, the Russians adhered to Sykes–Picot after extensive discussions between Sykes and the Russian foreign minister, Sergei Sazanov. In return for their support, the Russians were granted direct control over much of eastern Anatolia. In a successful attempt at embarrassing the coalition, the terms of the Anglo–Russian–French Agreement were made public by the Bolsheviks in the spring of 1918. The Arabs claimed that Sykes–Picot contradicted promises made to them by the HUSAYN–MCMAHON CORRESPONDENCE, and the Jews claimed that it contravened the BALFOUR DECLARATION. U.S. President Woodrow Wilson wished to annul Sykes–Picot, and even Sykes soon repudiated the agreement. Nonetheless, though the French renounced their claim to Mosul and Britain won control of Palestine, the Middle East treaties framed at the PARIS PEACE SETTLEMENTS after World War I closely mirrored the Sykes–Picot Agreement.

BIBLIOGRAPHY

ANDERSON, M. S. *The Eastern Question*. London, 1966.
FROMKIN, DAVID. *A Peace to End All Peace*. New York, 1989.
HUREWITZ, J. C., ed. *The Middle East and North Africa in World Politics*. New Haven, Conn., 1979.

Zachary Karabell

Syria

Formally, the Syrian Arab Republic (al-Jumhuriyyah al-Arabiyya al-Suriyya).

Geography. Syria's 71,500 square miles (185,185 sq. km) include a narrow plain along the Mediterranean between Turkey to the north and Lebanon to the south, that contains the ports of Latakia and Tartus; fertile highlands between the capital, DAMASCUS, and

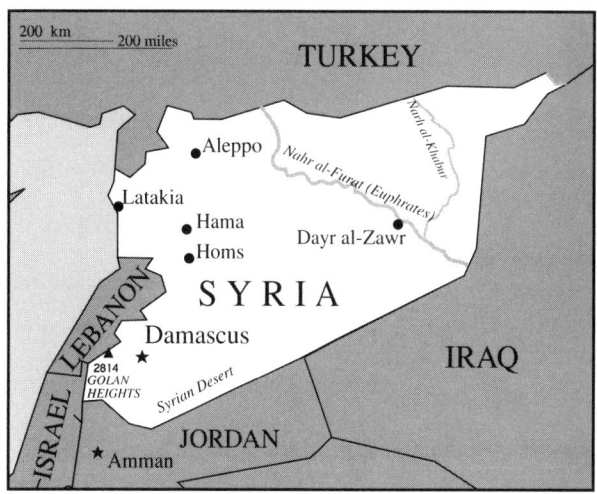

The Krak des Chevaliers, a Crusaders' castle in Syria.
(Laura Mendelson and David Rewcastle)

the border with Jordan, called the Hawran (Hauran); an extensive central plain, in which are situated the cities of Homs, Hama, and Aleppo; the Euphrates River valley, in which are the cities of al-Raqqa (Rakka) and Dayr al-Zawr; an eastern plateau bounded by Turkey to the north and Iraq to the east, whose major centers are al-Hasaka and al-Qamishli; and a large southeastern desert adjacent to Iraq and Jordan, whose oases contain the ruins of ancient fortifications and trading posts.

Syria has three major rivers. The largest, the Euphrates, enters from Turkey and is joined by the Khabur and the Balikh before crossing into Iraq southeast of Al Bu Kamal. The Euphrates system is regulated by a dam at Tabaqa, just west of al-Raqqa, which stores water for use in irrigation and power generation. Running south from mountains in the pre-1920 Syrian province of Iskenderun (now the Turkish province of Hatay), through the fertile Ghab basin and past the cities of Hama and Homs, is the Orontes river (Nahr al-Asi). The Yarmuk river, across which small irrigation dams were constructed during the 1980s, defines the border between Syria and Jordan. At current rates of use, Syria's groundwater reserves are expected to run dry by 2010, leaving the country entirely dependent upon river water.

Population. The total population, according to the 1990 census, numbered 12.5 million, with some 2.5 million living in Damascus and 1 million in Aleppo. Population growth has been very rapid, averaging 3.2 percent annually in the 1960s, 3.5 percent annually in the 1970s, and 3.6 percent annually during the 1980s. The birthrate has been quite high in recent years, whereas the death rate has plunged from

21 deaths per 1,000 in the early 1950s to 7 per 1,000 at the end of the 1980s. Several thousand Armenians moved to Syria from the Soviet Union in 1945–1946, and constitute a sizable community in Aleppo. After the establishment of the State of Israel, virtually all of the Syrian Jewish population emigrated, and about 100,000 Palestinians fleeing Israel's takeover of the Galilee in 1948 ended up in camps on the fringes of Damascus.

Muslims make up at least 85 percent of the population; 80 to 85 percent of this number are Sunnis, 13 to 15 percent are Alawis, about 1 percent are Isma'ilis, and less than 1 percent are Twelver Shi'ites. Some 3 percent of Syrians are Druze, a sect that follows a mixture of Christian and Shi'a doctrines. Isolated pockets of Yazidis exist in the hills outside Aleppo and northeast of al-Qamishli. About 10 percent of the population are Christians, divided among at least a dozen sects. The Greek Orthodox and Armenian Gregorian communities are the largest and most influential.

Administration. Syria's governmental structure is highly centralized and strictly hierarchical, concentrating power primarily in the hands of the president and secondarily with the top leadership of the BA'TH party. This system developed after March 1963, when military supporters of the Ba'th overthrew the parliamentary order that had reappeared following the dissolution of the union with Egypt in 1961. In November 1970, Gen. Hafiz al-Asad, minister of defense and head of the Ba'th party's military wing, seized power. Since then he has served as head of state, commander in chief, and secretary-general of the Regional (Syrian) Command of the Ba'th. Shortly after coming to power, the new regime appointed a representative body, the People's Assembly, to draft a

Aerial view of the Umayyad mosque in Damascus.
(Syrian Ministry of Tourism)

The ruins of the Monastery of St. Simeon in Syria. (David Rewcastle)

permanent constitution. This document, approved in March 1973, provides for a seven-year presidential term of office; it empowers the president to appoint and remove the vice presidents, the prime minister, and other cabinet ministers. In addition, it grants the president the authority to dissolve the People's Assembly and call national plebiscites to ratify legislative measures not adopted by the parliament.

Syria consists of thirteen provinces, each administered by a governor. Each governor is advised by a provincial council, one-fourth of whose members are appointed and the remainder of whom are elected by popular balloting. Since 1970, these councils have exercised little decision-making autonomy. Municipal councils provide public services, license businesses, and supervise the collection of local taxes. Each municipal council is headed by a mayor. Damascus city constituted a separate governorate until 1987, when it merged with the surrounding province of Damascus to form a single administrative unit.

Economy. Syria's economy expanded dramatically during the 1940s, due to a combination of restrictions on imports and heightened spending by British and French occupation forces. The Korean War perpetuated the boom by creating greater demand for Syrian cotton on world markets. Private enterprise provided the main impetus for economic growth until the union with Egypt in 1958, when state officials introduced an extensive program of land reform, nationalization of industry, and regulation of commercial transactions. The short-lived parliamentary regime that seceded from the union in 1961 attempted to resurrect the private sector, but the Ba'th-affiliated officers who overthrew the civilian regime in March 1963 gradually extended government control over

most sectors of the economy. State intervention peaked with the nationalization of industry, banking, and trade that began in January 1965. Under the regime of Salah Jadid (1966–1970), extensive state control accompanied the establishment of a network of production and distribution cooperatives, state farms, and Ba'th-affiliated popular-front organizations.

By the end of the 1960s, Syria's public-sector enterprises were experiencing severe financial difficulties. The government responded by relaxing restrictions on the activities of private business, particularly in construction and trade. Private enterprise quickly moved into agriculture and manufacturing as well, supported both by the return of large amounts of local capital that had fled the country during the late 1950s and by an influx of investment from the oil-producing Arab Gulf states. The economy grew at a rate of more than 9 percent per year during the 1970s, but slowed to around 2.5 percent annually from 1981 to 1983 and then declined by some 3 percent per year from 1983 to 1987.

Government spending jumped from approximately 29 percent of gross domestic product (GDP) in 1972 to around 37 percent of GDP in 1987. This rise was not matched by an increase in current revenues, resulting in yawning budget deficits. The shortfalls resulted primarily from sharp increases in military spending; by 1987, support for the armed forces accounted for 39 percent of total state outlays. Such an imbalance could be sustained only by greater reliance on Communist bloc governments and the Arab oil states.

Education. Since 1967, Syria's schools, technical institutes, and universities have been supervised by the Ministry of Education or the Ministry of Higher Education. Successive Ba'th regimes have expanded the education system, and have taken steps to reduce illiteracy by establishing adult and women's educa

Aerial view of Aleppo. (Richard Bulliet)

An Armenian beverage vendor in Damascus. (D.W. Lockhard)

tion programs. Elementary education is free and compulsory. Secondary education, which consists of three years of preparatory school and three years of high school, is free but not compulsory. The great majority of children attend public schools; several private schools in Damascus serve foreign nationals and the elite. The Ministry of Education regulates textbooks, curricula, and teacher certification.

Syria has four universities. The largest and most prestigious is the University of Damascus, founded in 1923, which has some 60,000 students. The University of Aleppo, chartered in 1958, serves around 30,000 students. Tishrin University in Latakia and al-Ba'th University in Homs offer limited curricula. The University of Aleppo operates a faculty of agriculture in Dayr al-Zawr. Technical institutes are scattered throughout the country. The language of instruction is Arabic, although English and French are required as second languages by many faculties.

History. Syria's modern history began with the end of the Egyptian occupation (1831–1840). After the reassertion of Ottoman control, European manufactured goods flooded the country, ruining the textile industry and leading urban merchants to invest in agricultural land. The trend toward private estate ownership was reinforced by the Ottoman land law of 1858, which allowed landholders to convert

nominally state-owned communal lands in the villages into private property. At the end of the nineteenth century, French enterprises won numerous concessions in exchange for loans to the Ottoman authorities. French firms invested in ports, railroads, and highways, opening the cities of the interior to the outside world. As manufacturing continued to contract, to the evident benefit of Syria's well-connected minority communities, anti-Christian and anti-European riots erupted. These drew European governments into local politics, and growing outside interference generated rising disaffection with Ottoman authority among Syria's Arab elite.

During the 1890s, clubs advocating Syrian independence formed in Aleppo, Damascus, and Beirut. These coalesced into political parties after the 1908 revolution that brought the Committee of Union and Progress (CUP) to power in Constantinople (now Istanbul). Members of an underground CUP branch in Damascus led popular demonstrations in support of the coup, prompting prominent religious notables to form an organization of their own, the Muslim Union. Candidates sympathetic to the latter won the parliamentary elections of 1909. Liberal opponents of the CUP openly de-

Arab coffee house in Syria during the 1950s. (D.W. Lockhard)

A city square in Homs, Syria. (Syrian Ministry of Tourism)

nounced the regime in Constantinople, setting the stage for new elections in 1912, which were rigged to ensure that only CUP supporters won seats in parliament.

Following the balloting, influential Syrian liberals emigrated to Cairo, where they formed the Ottoman Party of Administrative Decentralization to seek greater autonomy for the empire's Arabic-speaking provinces. The publication of its program accompanied widespread anti-CUP agitation orchestrated by secret societies including the Constantinople-based Qahtan society, the Paris-based Young Arab society, and the Iraq- and Syria-based Society of the Covenant (Jam'iyyat al-Ahd). The seeds of Arab nationalism germinated among these societies prior to World War I.

Nationalist sentiment blossomed during the war, and when FAISAL I IBN HUSAYN of the Hijaz led an Arab army into Damascus in October 1918, he was welcomed as a liberator and Damascus declared itself an autonomous Arab administration for the whole of greater Syria. Faisal attempted to consolidate popular support by calling elections in mid-1919, but CUP sympathizers won most of the seats representing Damascus. Members of the Young Arab Society dominated the rest of the assembly, and in the fall of 1919 this organization formed the Committee of National Defense to resist Faisal's alleged willingness to capitulate to French demands. Faisal responded by forming the National party, whose platform called for the establishment of a constitutional monarchy with French assistance. The assembly, led by Hashim al-Atasi of Homs, acclaimed Faisal king of an independent Syria. His acquiescence in the declaration led France to occupy Damascus in 1920, establishing

a tutelary regime that governed the country for the next quarter-century.

After independence in 1946, the armed forces became a major means of advancement for Syria's minority communities, particularly poorer Alawis and Druze, who entered the military academy in rapidly growing numbers. There they encountered radical political ideas, including those of the Ba'th and the local Communist party. Rising disaffection within the ranks prompted the military high command to champion social reform programs and solidarity with nationalists in neighboring Arab states. Popular and parliamentary discontent over Syria's defeat in Palestine persisted through the winter of 1948/49, and in March 1949 a clique of commanders led by Col. Husni al-Za'im overthrew the elected government. Za'im abrogated the 1930 constitution, suppressed all political parties, and ruled by decree. That June he was assassinated by rival officers, who restored civilian rule and called for elections to a popular assembly to frame a new constitution. The assembly fragmented along regional lines, and in December a group of junior officers led by Col. Adib SHISHAKLI seized power. Shishakli's regime adopted a revised constitution in 1950 but soon resorted to severe tactics to control the resurgent labor unions and peasant movement, and was ousted in 1954.

The new military-civilian coalition restored the 1950 constitution and held parliamentary elections, in which the Arab Ba'th Socialist party won a substantial number of seats. Leftist forces were unable to form a coalition cabinet, and the liberal People's party took over the government. This development sparked renewed militancy among workers and peasants, convincing the cabinet to implement wide-ranging agricultural and industrial

The National Museum in Damascus, Syria. (Mia Bloom)

reforms. Startled by the reforms, as well as by demands for greater change from the Ba'th and the communists, conservatives in parliament mobilized support for former President Shukri al-Quwatli, who won the presidency in 1955. By 1957, escalating tensions among pro–United States, pro–Egypt, and Syrian nationalist politicians led to a postponement of local elections while military intelligence officers uncovered an elaborate plot by agents of Iraq to undermine the government. These developments sent Chief of Staff Afif al-Bizri to Cairo to request immediate union with Egypt. In 1958, President Quwatli announced the creation of the UNITED ARAB REPUBLIC.

Efforts to unify the two countries eventually provoked widespread unrest in Syria. When the cabinet nationalized and redistributed the assets of private enterprises during the summer of 1961, largely in response to problems in Egypt, merchants and tradespeople in Syria's cities agitated for dissolution of the union. A group of military officers and civilian politicians orchestrated secession that September. Over the next two years, Syria's politics consisted of jockeying among socialists, who favored continued state control over key sectors of the economy; large landholders and rich merchants, who advocated the restoration of private property and parliamentary rule; and moderates, including a wing of the Ba'th party led by Michel Aflaq, who supported maintaining a mixed economy. In 1962, a compromise government supported by the military high command took steps to dismantle the public sector and remove doctrinaire socialists from the armed forces, moves that precipitated both resistance among Ba'th and communist officers and growing Islamist opposition. Spurred by threats to the position of radicals within the military and burgeoning popular unrest, members of the military committee of the Ba'th carried out a coup in 1963, ushering in three decades of Ba'th party–military rule.

BIBLIOGRAPHY

HADDAD, GEORGE. *Fifty Years of Modern Syria and Lebanon.* Beirut, 1950.

HINNEBUSCH, RAYMOND A. *Authoritarian Power and State Formation in Ba'thist Syria: Army, Party and Peasant.* Boulder, Colo., 1990.

KHOURY, P. *Syria and the French Mandate: The Politics of Arab Nationalism, 1920–1945.* Princeton, N.J., 1987.

———. *Urban Notables and Arab Nationalism: The Politics of Damascus, 1860–1920.* Cambridge, U.K., 1983.

LONGRIGG, STEPHEN HELMSLEY. *Syria and Lebanon under the French Mandate.* London, 1958.

SEALE, PATRICK. *The Struggle for Syria: A Study of Post-War Arab Politics, 1945–1958.* London, 1965.

TIBAWI, A. L. *A Modern History of Syria Including Lebanon and Palestine.* London, 1969.

TORREY, GORDON, H. *Syrian Politics and the Military, 1945–1958.* Columbus, Ohio, 1964.

WINDER, F. BAYLY. "Syrian Deputies and Cabinet Ministers, 1919–1959." Parts 1, 2. *Middle East Journal* 16, no. 2 (1962): 407–429; and 17, no.1 (1963): 35–54.

Fred H. Lawson

Syrian Desert

A huge stretch of mostly barren land covering parts of four countries: Syria, Iraq, Jordan, and Saudi Arabia.

Known in Arabic as *Badiyat al-Sham* after the nomadic bedouin (Badu, hence Badiya) who roam its parts in search of pasture, it is also known as the Greater Badiyat al-Sham (Badiyat al-Sham al-Kubra) because it extends between the desert of al-Nufud on the Arabian peninsula and the Euphrates river. Badiyat al-Sham covers about two-thirds—about 52,000 square miles (130,000 sq. km)—of the overall area of Syria. It is divided into two parts: the first, in the northeast, is called Badiyat al-Jazira, and the second, in the southeast, is called al-Shamiyya or Badiyat al-Sham, that is, the Syrian desert. This desert begins at the Syro–Jordanian border, skirts the frontier of settlement towards the north at a line east of Jabal Druze, al-Ghuta oasis of Damascus and its *marj* (meadow), then up along the Qalamun mountains, then east of al-Jabbul, the finally ends at Meskene on the Euphrates.

The Syrian desert, in turn, is divided into two parts, which differ in their surface structure. The first, a plateau in the southwest, is more elevated than the other part and also much drier. The part to the northeast starts at lower elevation in the south—2,208 feet (673 m)—and ends at 623 feet (190 m) in the north. This part is dry and has dry river channels (wadis) exposed to flooding. These wadis range in length from 93 to 186 miles (150–300 km) and in width from 0.3 to 0.6 miles (0.5 to 1 km). Annual precipitation in the Syrian desert does not exceed 5.85 inches (150 mm).

The few plants and animals of the Syrian desert are of the type that can withstand a subtropical climate. The nomads raise sheep and camels, and they move according to the seasons, from one region to the other across political frontiers seeking pasture. Phosphates, oil, and butane gas have been discovered in this desert, and modern network of roads and railways makes the exploitation of the desert much easier than before.

BIBLIOGRAPHY

Al-mu'jam al-jughrafi li al-qutr al-arabi al-suri (The Geographical Dictionary of Syria), vol 1. Damascus, 1990.

Abdul-Karim Rafeq

Syrian Protestant College

See American University of Beirut

Syrian Social Nationalist Party

Political party established in Lebanon in 1932 with the aim of uniting the Syrian nation.

The Syrian Social Nationalist party (SSNP) was the brainchild of Antun SA'ADA, a Greek Orthodox Lebanese who was inspired by Nazi and fascist ideologies. Originally known as the PARTI POPULAIRE SYRIEN, the party operated in secret until 1935 when the French authorities arrested Sa'ada. Three years later he left for Brazil, returning in 1947.

According to party bylaws, the SSNP is headed by a president and is composed of a high council, a dean's council, executive units, and management units. In 1959, the SSNP had twenty-five thousand members in Lebanon. During the 1975/76 civil war, the SSNP fielded two thousand fighters in Beirut and other Lebanese towns and cities.

The party's ideology, as defined by Sa'ada, centers on the goal of unifying the Syrian nation with all its components. In one of his publications, Sa'ada wrote: "[The] Syrian homeland is that geographic environment in which the Syrian nation evolved. It has natural boundaries which separate it from other countries, extending from the Taurus range in the northwest and the Zagros in the northeast to the Suez Canal and the Red Sea in the south and including the Sinai peninsula and the Gulf of Aqaba, and from the Syrian Sea (Mediterranean) in the west, including the island of Cyprus, to the arch of the Arabian desert and Persian Gulf in the east. (This region is also called the Syrian Fertile Crescent, the island of Cyprus being its star.)"

Sa'ada argued that Lebanon did not constitute a separate entity but was instead part of the Syrian nation. This philosophy led to clashes with Lebanese authorities. In 1949, Sa'ada declared an armed revolt against the government and called on his supporters to carry weapons and attack police stations. With the help of Syrian leader Husni al-Za'im, Lebanese authorities retaliated and arrested Sa'ada. He was executed in July 1949. Sa'ada's death led to the overthrow of Za'im in Syria and to increased popularity for the SSNP in the 1950s. The killing of a major Ba'th party official and the adversarial relationship between SSNP members and Arab nationalists ultimately caused the party to lose its support in Syria. In the Lebanese upheaval of 1958, the SSNP allied itself with President Camille Chamoun against the pro-Arab nationalist forces in Lebanon. At the end of 1961, the SSNP was involved in an unsuccessful coup against the Lebanese government. As a result, many of the party leaders were arrested and the other party members dispersed or left the organization.

During the civil war (1975–1976), the SSNP regained some strength but was a divided party. One faction retained Sa'ada's original ideology. Another group, led by In'am Raad, believed it possible to combine Marxist doctrine with the ideology of the SSNP. This group also considered violence a legitimate means of achieving political aims. Raad and his group split from the original SSNP and joined the Lebanese National Movement. In September 1977, a third splinter of the SSNP was formed for the purpose of unifying the party.

BIBLIOGRAPHY

SULEIMAN, MICHAEL W. *Political Parties in Lebanon.* Ithaca, N.Y., 1967.

George E. Irani

Syrkin, Nachman   [1867–1924]

Early Socialist Zionist.

Nachman (also spelled Nahman) Syrkin wrote a brochure in German, "The Jewish Problem and the Socialist Jewish State," under the pseudonym Ben Elieser, in Switzerland in 1898. The pamphlet was his considered opinion on solving the Jewish problem with Socialist Zionism. Born a Russian Jew who subsequently went to the West for an education, Syrkin drew on his experience of both Russian socialism and the misery and suffering of Russian Jewish life. He was one of the first to do so.

He attended the first Zionist Congress in 1897 and remained in the World Zionist Organization until 1905, when at the seventh Zionist Congress it was clear that the British offer of Uganda as a place for a Jewish state was impossible. He moved to the United States in 1907 to continue as an official of the Labor Zionist movement and worked as a territorialist (a member of Israel Zangwill's Jewish Territorial Organization [ITO], willing for the Jewish people to settle any unpopulated area). He also wrote and edited journals in Yiddish and Hebrew in support of his views.

Syrkin's socialism was utopian and ethical, not Marxist. At the base was his view that the common people would realize a Jewish state, not the successful or wealthy; and the state was necessary, since even a new socialist order would not integrate the Jewish minority. He reasoned that modern anti-Semitism was different from historical forms that had been unleashed in earlier eras, since it stemmed from dislocations of modernization.

BIBLIOGRAPHY

HERTZBERG, ARTHUR. *The Zionist Idea.* New York, 1984.
SYRKIN, MARIE, ed. *Nachman Syrkin: Socialist Zionist.* New York, 1960.

Donna Robinson Divine

Szold, Henrietta   [1860–1945]

Founder of Hadassah, the largest Jewish women's organization.

Szold was the daughter of a modernist rabbi from Baltimore. After visiting Palestine in 1909, she resolved to bring modern medical care and hygiene to the area and to establish a health-care system to meet the needs of the Jewish community there. Szold was the first director of the YOUTH ALIYAH.

BIBLIOGRAPHY

DASH, JOAN. *Summoned to Jerusalem: The Life of Henrietta Szold.* New York, 1979.
GELLER, L. D., ed. *The Henrietta Szold Papers in the Hadassah Archives, 1875–1965.* 1982.

Mia Bloom

Ta'arrof

Iranian form of courtesy.

Ta'arrof is a term implying an exchange of polite language, compliments, or gifts in Iran, and in the case of such an exchange between two equal partners, it may be taken as a sincere expression of regard. That ta'arrof is never used in intimate exchanges and that, in fact, its application by definition excludes intimacy, goes to show that genuine respect, affinity, and admiration lie categorically outside the domain of ta'arrof. Rather than an expression of genuine intentions, ta'arrof operates more as a code of culturally sanctioned behavior for the advancement of one's ulterior motivations. More often than not, social exchange takes place between two unequal partners, and in such cases, ta'arrof acquires added significance, as an embodiment of hierarchical norms in Iranian society. It has been called the active ritualization of differential perceptions of superiority and inferiority in interaction. Ta'arrof, in addition, serves as a vehicle for the fostering and perpetuation of traditional cultural norms; in the guise of an innocent exchange of compliments, the integrity of culturally defined roles is reinforced. It occurs in three different situations: it demands deference to superiors, it is conferred on inferiors, and it is imposed on equals, so that social order is maintained when its demands are acknowledged and observed. More importantly, failure to resort to the exigencies of ta'arrof definitively and categorically impairs social interaction in the Iranian context. Westerners, young Iranians, and westernized, secular Iranians are confronted with such crippling reactions on a day-to-day basis. It is important to note that one of the cultural ramifications of the Iranian revolution of 1979 has been the revivification of the institution of ta'arrof, the utility of which had been undermined in the Pahlavi period, when more modern and Western sociocultural codes were appropriated by the empowered middle and higher classes.

Also ta'arrof is strategically employed by Iranians to ensure domination in their interactions. It has been argued that the most effective and widely used strategic formula in the use of ta'arrof is to consciously aim for a lower relative status position and defer to another person. This can be interpreted as one's correct perception of a behavior in accordance with one's relative status. Or, when dealing with an inferior, it exudes magnanimity and thus not only reinforces one's superiority but at the same time enhances and brings to the fore the relative inferiority of the party concerned. This comes in handy, especially when the parameters of the relative hierarchy of individuals engaged in a discourse are ambiguous. If utilized astutely, ta'arrof can define the situation and allow the user to exploit the relationship for his or her own ends.

As expected, the language of ta'arrof is also distinguished from the language of intimacy. This is especially manifest in the use of the plural rather than the singular in addressing a person of import. On a more subtle level, certain verbs and nouns substitute for their most frequently used synonyms when ta'arrof is exercised.

BIBLIOGRAPHY

BEEMAN, WILLIAM O. *Language, Status, and Power in Iran.* Bloomington, Ind., 1986.

Neguin Yavari

Taba

A piece of land disputed by Egypt and Israel.

Taba is a 250-acre patch of land that juts into the Gulf of Aqaba, a dozen miles south of Eilat. When the Israeli and Egyptian governments finalized terms on January 19, 1982, for the return of the entire Sinai peninsula to Egypt, Israeli negotiators claimed that Taba should remain within Israel. They based their claim on alleged ambiguities in the physical description of Taba in the October 1, 1906, accord that demarcated the administrative border between Palestine and Egypt. Israel reinforced that claim by constructing two hotels, after spring 1982, within the Taba zone. Article 7 of the Egypt–Israel peace treaty of 1979 provided for mediation or arbitration of such differences if direct negotiations failed to resolve them. Egypt urged the formation of an international arbitration team, but the Israeli cabinet did not agree to the principle of arbitration until January 13, 1986. The membership and terms of the arbitration team were agreed upon by September 12, 1986. The three-person panel was empowered to decide on the location of the boundary pillars as of 1948, the end of the Palestine mandate, and its rulings were final and binding on both parties. On September 29, 1988, the panel ruled in favor of Egypt. Israel evacuated Taba on March 15, 1989. Egyptian sovereignty was restored over Taba and over the hotels that Israel had constructed. However, Israelis could visit the enclave without obtaining an Egyptian visa, and Israel continued to supply Taba's water and electricity from Eilat. The Taba accord was a rare example of the resolution of a contentious issue through judicial means.

BIBLIOGRAPHY

LESCH, ANN MOSELY. "The Egyptian–Israeli Accord to Submit the Dispute over Taba to International Arbitration." In *The Middle East and North Africa: Essays in Honor of J. C. Hurewitz,* ed. by Reeva S. Simon. New York, 1990.

Ann M. Lesch

Tabaqa Dam

Dam on the Euphrates river built to irrigate Syria.

Started in 1968, the dam was finished in 1973 with Soviet assistance, at a total cost of 600 million U.S. dollars. It forms Lake Asad on the Euphrates, above Rakka, Syria. It is intended to irrigate 1.5 million acres (640,000 ha) by the year 2005 and produce six hundred megawatts of electricity. By the mid-1980s, only about 187,500 acres (75,000 ha) were under irrigation and five of the eight power generators were not operating.

When all projects are completed, the dam will take seven billion cubic meters of the thirty billion cubic meters of water that once entered Iraq each year. Iraq complains of this and that the upstream irrigation projects lower Iraq's water quality by raising salinity levels. Turkey also has ambitious irrigation projects under way at Keban and Karababa, which will reduce Iraq's share to eleven billion cubic meters. Syria has protested to Turkey about excessive use of Euphrates water and tried in 1984 to block Arab oil states from making loans to Turkey for construction of the Karababa dam. No treaty exists for sharing the flow, thus this serious dispute has no foreseeable prospect of resolution.

BIBLIOGRAPHY

DRYSDALE, ALASDAIR, and GERALD H. BLAKE. *The Middle East and North Africa.* New York, 1985.

John R. Clark

Tabaqjali, Nazim al-Kami   [1913–1959]

Iraqi revolutionary and soldier.

Nazim Tabaqjali (also Tabaqchali) was one of the Free Officers behind the Iraqi revolution of July 1958. An ardent pan-Arabist, he turned against Abd al-Karim Kassem because of the latter's tolerance of the communists. In March 1959, when divisional commander at Kirkuk, he supported an unsuccessful army revolt against the Kassem government in Mosul. For this, he was tried in the "people's court" of Fazil Abbas al-Mahdawi and subsequently executed on September 20, 1959.

Peter Sluglett

Tabataba'i, Mohammad   [1841–1920]

Persian religious scholar; one of the principal leaders of the Constitutional Revolution, 1905–1909.

Born in Karbala, Persia (now Iran), in 1841 to a family with illustrious scholarly antecedents, he spent his early childhood in Hamadan in the care of Aqa Sayyed Mehdi, his paternal grandfather, before moving to Tehran, the capital, where his father, Sayyed Sadeq, was firmly established as a leading religious authority. There he studied jurisprudence with his father and other prominent scholars, philosophy with Mirza Abul-Hasan Jelve, and—most significant for his political activity in later years—ethics with Shaykh Hadi Najmabadi, many of whose opinions were regarded as subversively liberal. At the same time, he began taking an interest in the affairs of Europe, through reading newspapers and closely questioning returning travelers, an interest that was atypical for the religious scholars of his time.

In 1882, Tabataba'i set out from Tehran with the intention of making the pilgrimage to Mecca. He took a circuitous route, traveling via Russia, Anatolia, and Istanbul, meeting new scholars and men of state wherever he alighted, and he arrived in Mecca too late for the pilgrimage. Cholera was raging in the Hijaz, so he left promptly for the area that is now Iraq, where he joined the circle of the great scholar Mirza Hasan Shirazi in Samarra. He spent more than ten years with Shirazi, perfecting his command of Shi'a jurisprudence and acting as the trusted adviser of his teacher in political matters. It was no doubt in this capacity that he was addressed a letter by the celebrated Jamal al-Din Asadabadi (Afghani), then resident in London, calling on him to intensify the political use of Shirazi's prestige that had been inaugurated by the Tobacco Revolt and boycott of 1891.

Despite the oppositional tendencies that Asadabadi correctly perceived in Tabataba'i, his return to Tehran was due to an initiative of Naser al-Din Shah. The monarch wished to create in Tehran a counterweight to Mirza Hasan Ashtiani, a cleric whose prestige had grown considerably in the course of the tobacco boycott, and he accordingly suggested to Shirazi that he should send one of his prominent disciples to Tehran. Shirazi selected Tabataba'i for the purpose, and he arrived back in Tehran in the fall of 1893. His father had died almost a decade before, but Tabataba'i fell heir to his influence in the Iranian capital with little difficulty. The shah's expectations of Tabataba'i were disappointed; not only did he establish cordial relations with Mirza Hasan Ashtiani, but he also emerged as an implacable critic of the corruption and tyranny of the court. In 1911 he claimed, indeed, to have begun working for the cause of constitutional government immediately after his return from Samarra, preaching from the pulpit on the need for establishing a consultative assembly. On

another occasion, he stated frankly that he and his colleagues in the clerical class had no direct acquaintance with the concept of constitutionalism, having learned of it from those with experience of Europe. It may therefore be assumed that during the decade leading up to the constitutional revolution he deepened both his understanding of constitutional government and his contacts with secular intellectuals working for the same goal.

The beginnings of the revolution may be dated to an alliance concluded by Tabataba'i with another leading cleric of Tehran, Sayyed Abdollah Behbahani, on November 23, 1905, initially for the purpose of obtaining the dismissal of Ayn al-Dowleh, the prime minister of the day. Soon thereafter a meeting convened by the two men at the Masjed-e Shah in Tehran to protest government policies was broken up by force, and they led a migration of their colleagues and supporters to the shrine of Shah Abd al-Azim south of Tehran, where they formulated the demand for an *adalat-khaneh* (house of justice) as a condition of their return. Their demand was formally accepted, and on January 12, 1906, Tabataba'i and Behbahani returned to the capital in triumph. Ayn al-Dowleh remained in office, however, and he temporized in implementing the royal decree for convening a house of justice. The tensions that persisted between him and the constitutionalists led to a new and more significant migration of Tabataba'i, Behbahani, and their associates, this time to Qom, on July 15, 1906. They demanded the dismissal of Ayn al-Dowleh, in addition to the establishment of a consultative assembly. Their demands were accepted, and on August 18, 1906, Tabataba'i and Behbahani were able to reenter Tehran. Tabataba'i exercised great influence in the *majles* (assembly) that was convened soon thereafter, attempting to preserve the alliance of personalities and interests that had made possible the introduction of constitutional government. His success was limited, however, and the *majles* was in a state of chronic dissension when its debates were brought abruptly to an end by the royal coup of June 23, 1908. Tabataba'i was arrested and taken in chains to the garrison at Bagh-e Shah. After a spell of imprisonment, he lived in seclusion in Shemiran, north of Tehran, before being banished to Mashhad. He returned to Tehran on August 24, 1909, one month after the restoration of the constitution, but thereafter appears to have tired of direct political involvement. He spent the rest of his life in Tehran, with the exception of a journey in 1917 to the shrine cities of the area that is now Iraq. He died in 1920.

Tabataba'i stands out above all as the most prominent religious leader of his time to have fully understood and accepted the far-reaching implications of constitutionalism for Iranian society, recognizing, for example, that it required a modernization of the educational system. This broadness of outlook may have been connected to the Freemasons' affiliations he had inherited from his father, which led him also to join the Masonic Lodge Reveil de l'Iran, the first Iranian lodge officially affiliated to the Grand Orient of France.

BIBLIOGRAPHY

HAIRI, ABDUL-HADI. *Shi'ism and Constitutionalism in Iran.* Leiden, 1977.
KERMANI, NAZEM AL-ESLAM. *Tarikh-e Bidari-ye Iranian.* Ed. by Ali Akbar Sa'idi-Sirjani. Tehran, 1978.

Hamid Algar

Tabataba'i, Ziya   [c. 1889–1969]

Anglophile Iranian politician and journalist.

Born in Iran, in the southeastern city of Yazd, Tabataba'i began his public career as a journalist in Shiraz, publishing a series of newspapers—*Islam Sharq* (the East), and *Barq* (Lightning)—in which he supported the causes of constitutional government and social reform. He next moved to Tehran, where during World War I he published *Ra'd* (Thunder), a journal staunchly supporting British policy in Iran. This earned him favorable standing with the British, enabling him to act as a go-between for Iranian notables who wanted their checks cashed by the British-owned Imperial Bank of Persia, which in turn gained for him considerable influence in Tehran society. In 1919, Tabataba'i traveled to Baku (in Azerbaijan) to negotiate on behalf of Iran a political and commercial treaty with the temporarily independent states of the south Caucasus, taking advantage of the opportunity to impress other members of the delegation with his political acumen. In 1920 and 1921, he was active in the Anjoman-e Pulad (Steel Committee), a reformist political committee that was the offshoot of a similar organization established by the British in Isfahan and sought to bring together politicians and military officers to initiate change. At the same time, he maintained close links with the head of the British military mission in Iran. These relations with the British enabled him, together with Reza Khan (later Reza Shah Pahlavi), then a commander of the Iranian Cossack Brigade, to launch a coup d'état on February 21, 1921, that resulted in the appointment of Tabataba'i as prime minister.

The real significance of this coup was that it marked the first stage in the rise of Reza Khan to supreme power and the replacement of the Qajar dynasty by the Pahlavis, and the premiership of Tabataba'i did not last long. He began energetically enough, banning newspapers hostile to his government and imprisoning many of the titled landowners for whom he nurtured a lifelong enmity. He then concluded a treaty of friendship with the Soviet Union and formally abrogated the already moribund Anglo–Iranian Agreement of 1919. His intention, as he privately informed the British minister in Tehran, was to "throw dust in the eyes of the Bolsheviks and native malcontents" (*Documents on British Foreign Policy, 1919–1939,* London, 1963, vol. 13, p. 731). However, differences soon arose. Over the objections of Tabataba'i, on May 6, 1921, Reza Khan succeeded in bringing the gendarmerie under the control of the Ministry of War and then, some two weeks later, in obtaining the dismissal of the British officers who had been seconded to the Iranian army. The swift erosion of Tabataba'i's position became fully apparent on May 24, when most of the enemies he had had arrested were released without his permission; the following day he went into exile.

Tabataba'i spent the next nine years in Switzerland, moving in 1930 to Palestine, where he lived for thirteen years under the protection of the British mandate government. In the course of World War II Reza Khan was deposed by the Allies (1941), and in September 1943 Tabataba'i was able to return to Iran—in the face of strong objections from the Iranian court, the Soviet Union, and the United States, which were overcome only by the energetic representations of the British.

Embarking on the second half of his political career, Tabataba'i first aligned himself with the Patriotic Caucus (Fraksiun-e Mihan), a pro-British grouping in the Majles (Iran's legislature). Soon, however, he founded his own party, the Fatherland party (Hezb-e Vatan), which early in 1944 was reorganized along authoritarian lines and renamed the National Will party (Hezb-e Erade-ye Melli). He launched yet another newspaper, *Ra'd-e Emruz* (Today's Thunder), in which he denounced the remnants of the military dictatorship established by Reza Khan, the continued hold on national life of the landowning oligarchy, and the growing influence of the communist Tudeh party. Tabataba'i's views won him the support of many bazaar merchants and guild leaders, as well as some lesser-ranking religious scholars, but his National Will party did not contest parliamentary elections. Nonetheless, he was elected to the Majles as deputy from Yazd, under the auspices of the Patriotic Caucus. He opposed a whole series of prime ministers, including most notably Qavam al-Dowleh, who had him arrested for several months in 1946, probably to placate the Soviet Union, the patron of the Tudeh party. Despite his rooted aversion to the Tudeh party, Tabataba'i sided with it in 1948 when efforts were under way to wrest control of the army from the shah. This tactical alliance did not last long, and it was in part because of a growing dependence on the Tudeh party that Tabataba'i opposed the government of Mohammad Mossadegh from 1951 onward (his continued alignment with the British was, no doubt, a more important factor in this regard).

Tabataba'i appears to have withdrawn from active political involvement even before the royalist coup of August 1953 that restored full-fledged autocracy to Iran. He spent the remaining years of his life in the village of Sa'adatabad, dying there in 1969. Notwithstanding his earlier hostility to the Pahlavis, he is said to have become a trusted consultant of the shah during the last phase of his life, meeting with him regularly at least once a week.

BIBLIOGRAPHY

ABRAHAMIAN, ERVAND. *Iran between Two Revolutions.* Princeton, N.J., 1982.
AVERY, P. W. *Modern Iran.* London, 1965.

Hamid Algar

Tabbula

Salad made with bulgur (cracked wheat), chopped fresh parsley, scallions, mint, and tomatoes, and dressed with salt, pepper, olive oil, and lemon.

Since tabbula is always made with fresh, in-season vegetables, it is commonly served as part of MAZZA during the summer or is eaten with fresh lettuce, cabbage, or vine leaves. Although the Lebanese are credited with perfecting the most popular version of tabbula, the idea for incorporating bulgur in a salad may have originated with the Turks.

Jenab Tutunji

Tabenkin, Yitzhak   [1887–1971]

Pioneer Labor Zionist.

Yitzhak Tabenkin was born in Belorussia, went to Palestine in 1911, and died in Israel. He was among the founding members of AHDUT HA–AVODAH (1919), the Histadrut labor organization (1920), and the MAPAI political party (1930). He advocated the establishment of large collective farming (the kibbutz movement) and unity for the various socialist par-

ties; he was against the Revisionist movement in Zionism and the partition of Palestine. In 1944, he was part of the group that split from MAPAI because of David Ben-Gurion's acceptance of partition (as head of the Zionist Executive) and his weakening commitment to socialism. After Israel's conquest of the West Bank in the Arab–Israel War of 1967, Tabenkin joined the Whole Land of Israel movement, lobbying against Israel's withdrawal from this territory. In the early 1960s, Tabenkin resigned all his offices and became a teacher.

BIBLIOGRAPHY

HERTZBERG, ARTHUR. *The Zionist Idea.* New York, 1984.
SHAPIRO, YONATHAN. *The Formative Years of the Israeli Labour Party.* London, 1976.

Donna Robinson Divine

Tabet, Ayoub   [1874–1947]

Fifth president of Lebanon under the French mandate, 1943.

Born to a Maronite family in Bhamdun, where he attended school, Tabet completed his degree in medicine at the Syrian Evangelical School (which later became the American University of Beirut). In 1905, he left for New York to specialize in internal medicine.

By the beginning of World War I, he was back in Lebanon but escaped from the Ottomans by going first to Paris, then New York (while in New York, he joined the Evangelical church), where he strongly attacked Turkish rule over the Arabs. In 1918, he returned to Lebanon and called for a French mandate. He ran in the elections and won the minority seat in the Lebanese parliament.

In 1934, a few days after the election of Emile Eddé as president, Tabet was appointed secretary of state. On March 8, 1943, he became president and lost his post the same year because of reforms he wanted to introduce into the electoral laws.

BIBLIOGRAPHY

Arab Information Center, Beirut.

George E. Irani

Tabriz

Provincial capital in northwestern Iran.

Tabriz, the capital of East Azerbaijan, is one of Iran's important cities, dating back to the Parthian period.

In 1295, the Mongol ruler Ghazan Khan made Tabriz the capital of his Persian Empire. In the fourteenth century, Tamerlane conquered Tabriz. The Safavid Shah Isma'il I made it his capital in 1501, until his defeat at the hands of the Ottoman Turks in 1514. Tabriz was occupied by the Ottomans from 1585 to 1603, and again from 1724 to 1730. The Russians held Tabriz for a year in 1827. In the Qajar period, Tabriz was the seat of the crown prince, and major military headquarters against the Russian frontier. During the Constitutional Revolution (1905–1911), it was the site of antigovernment activity. It was occupied again by the Russians during World War II. Russian troops refused to withdraw from the city in 1945 and supported the Autonomous Government of Azerbaijan, a secessionist movement headed by Ja'far Pishevari. The troops of Mohammad Reza Shah Pahlavi occupied Tabriz in 1946 and put an end to Pishevari's government. As an important commercial center, Tabriz also played a prominent role in the revolution of 1979.

By the 1980s, Tabriz was the fourth largest city in Iran, with a population of more than 600,000. The Blue mosque, built in the fifteenth century, and the Rub'e Rashidi, constructed by the famous Mongol vizier Rashid al-Din Fazl Allah, are among its archeological sites.

BIBLIOGRAPHY

SA'IDIAN, ABDOLHOSEYN. *Da'erat al-ma'aref-e sarzamin va mardom-e Iran* (Encyclopedia of the Land and People of Iran), 3rd ed. Tehran, 1984.

Neguin Yavari

Tabriz University

Public university in Tabriz, Iran.

Established in 1949 as the Daneshgah-e Azarbayjan (University of Azerbaijan) in the city of Tabriz in Azerbaijan, Tabriz University had 5,187 students by 1970. It includes schools of literature, agriculture, science, and engineering, and an institute for advanced studies. The journal published by its faculty of literature and philosophy, called the *Publication of the School of Literature and Social Sciences* (or *Nashriyyeh-ye daneshkadeh-ye adabiyyat va olum-e ensani*) has attained a reputation for solid scholarship.

BIBLIOGRAPHY

LENCZOWSKI, GEORGE. *Iran under the Pahlavis*. Stanford, Calif., 1978.

Parvaneh Pourshariati

Tagger, Sioneh   [1900–1988]

Israeli artist.

Sioneh Tagger was born at the turn of the century in Jaffa to Sephardic Jews who had settled there in the nineteenth century. Her parents helped to found the modern city of Tel Aviv. She studied art at the Herzliya Gymnasium in 1919/20 with a Russian sculptor, Joseph Constant, who introduced her to cubism and European modernism. In 1921 she moved to Jerusalem to study at Bezalel on condition that she live with her grandfather's family, who were religious people. Her works from this period include drawings of elderly Jews and "Oriental types" of Jews, as well as decorative metalwork and painting of miniatures. In 1924 she went to study in Paris, where she learned to build her drawings based on simple geometric structures. Tagger was influenced by several painters from the Jewish School of Paris, as well as by André Derain and Picasso, whose influence can be seen in "Clown" (1925) and "Harlequin" (1901). Later in life, Tagger painted on plexiglass, inspired by memories of glass paintings decorating quotations from the Qur'an hanging in Arab homes in Jaffa (she, though, used Jewish themes).

Julie Zuckerman

Taghuti

Derogatory term used in Iran.

Taghuti, from *taghut* (an idol, a false god; by extension an illegitimate ruler), is a Qur'anic term popularized by Ayatollah Ruhollah Khomeini in his struggle against the Pahlavi monarchy in Iran. In the Qur'anic verse (4:60) those who have gone for judgment to the illegitimate ruler (taghut) are admonished. Since the Iranian revolution of 1979, taghuti is mostly used as a sociological category comprising all stances and phenomena akin to Western, secular, and antirevolutionary tendencies.

BIBLIOGRAPHY

ENAYAT, HAMID. *Modern Islamic Political Thought*. Austin, Tex., 1982.

Neguin Yavari

Taha, Mahmoud Muhamed   [1909–1985]

Founder of the Republican Brothers, an Islamic sect.

Mahmoud Muhamed Taha was born at Rufa, in central Sudan. He was the founder and spiritual leader of the Republican Brothers, whose central tenet is to give primacy to the Prophet Muhammad's revelation at Mecca. The sect considers the later revelations at Medina a revealed legislative adaptation to the particular social conditions of the times. This premise gave Taha freedom to modernize Islamic thinking.

His teaching emphasized the individual human being, openness to modern learning and social practice, total gender equality, and the elimination of social and political discrimination based on religious belief. As a result, the sect was seen as heretical by other Muslims. This hostility came to a head in 1984, when, under the Numeiri regime, Taha was accused and convicted of apostasy. He was executed in January 1985.

His sect has continued to face discrimination and persecution in Sudan. Today, many of its members are in exile around the world. They tend to gather in specific locations so that they can maintain their religious identity and support one another.

Paul Martin

Tahini

Sesame seed paste.

One of the basic ingredients of Middle Eastern food, tahini is an oily paste made from crushed sesame seeds. It is used in a variety of foods such as hummus and babaghanush as well as on its own as a condiment. Tahini is also popular in Israel.

BIBLIOGRAPHY

DER HAROUTUNIAN, ARTO. *Vegetarian Dishes from the Middle East.* London, 1983.

Zachary Karabell

Tahir, Kemal   [1910–1973]

Turkish novelist.

The son of a naval officer, Tahir was born Ismail Kemalettin Demir in Istanbul and attended the prestigious Galatasaray Lycée (secondary school), though he did not graduate. In 1932, he began writing for newspapers and periodicals, as well as historical novels that glorified the Ottoman past. Between 1938 and 1950, he was imprisoned, along with the poet Nazim Hikmet, by the government of Turkey because of his ideological views and political convictions. During his incarceration, Tahir collected the

observations of villagers who were in prison with him; he used these as the basis for a series of novels that authentically depicted the mentality, social structure, and mode of life in the villages of central Antolia. He was released from prison in 1950 as part of a general amnesty.

Tahir's novels and his political-cultural theories influenced many Turkish authors, known collectively as Tahiris. His influence spread beyond the realm of literature into cinema, inspiring filmmakers to create films rooted in popular Turkish culture, not Western masterpieces. One of Tahir's last novels, *Mother State,* which took as its subject the founding of the Ottoman Empire in the thirteenth century, signaled a transition in Turkish literature from portraying social realities to searching for new models for change.

BIBLIOGRAPHY

ERTOP, KONUR. "Trends and Characteristics of Contemporary Turkish Literature." In *The Transformation of Turkish Culture: The Atatürk Legacy,* ed. by Günsel Renda and C. Max Kortepeter. Princeton, N.J., 1986.
HALMAN, TALAT SAIT. *Contemporary Turkish Literature: Fiction and Poetry.* Rutherford, N.J., 1982.
UNLU, MAHIR, and ÖMER OZCAN, eds. *Yirminci Yüzyil Türk Edebiyatı.* Istanbul, 1987.

David Waldner

Tahtawi, Rifa'a al-Rafi al   [c. 1801–1873]

Egyptian writer and educator and the founder of the translation movement; precursor of modern Arab secular thought.

Rifa'a al-Rafi al-Tahtawi was born in Tanta, in upper Egypt, into a family of rural notables with a religious learning tradition, whose genealogy went back to al-Husayn ibn Fatima, grandson of the prophet Muhammad. In his early childhood, his family was exposed to pecuniary difficulties following the confiscation by Muhammad Ali of the *iltizamat* (tax farms).

He was educated in al-Azhar in the traditional range of religious and linguistic studies, but was exposed there to the influence of the unconventional Shaykh Hasan al-Attar who advocated a broader outlook to *ilm* (knowledge) than the range to which al-Azhar was confined. His career was further inspired in Paris (1826–1831), where he was attached to the first mission of students from Egypt, initially as an imam (prayer leader) but soon as the mission's only translation student. Tahtawi read in a wide range of subjects, became acquainted with French liberal tradition, established direct contacts with leading French orientalists and noted the institutionalization of Arabic studies in L'Ecole Spéciale des Langues Orientales Vivantes. He also followed closely the 1830 revolution, studied the structure of the French political system and keenly observed Parisian social life and manners. He provided in great detail the first documented Arabic account of modern encounters with Western life and society in his *Takhlis al-Ibriz fi Talkhis Bariz* (The Extraction of Gold in the Summary of Paris, 1935).

Tahtawi's institutional career thrived during the reigns of Muhammad Ali and Isma'il in two distinct and separate phases. In each phase, he held several positions, all at the same time. The first of these phases (1837–1849), started toward the end of Muhammad Ali's expansion of education and continued up to the large-scale closure of schools at the time of Abbas (1848–1854). During that phase, Tahtawi directed the newly established *Madrasat al-Alsun* (School of Languages), then founded and headed *Qalam al-Tarjama* (Translation Department) and became chief editor of *al-Waqa'i al-Misriyya* newspaper in 1842. The second phase (1863–1873), corresponds to the reign of Isma'il (1863–1879), during which new activity in translation and education was initiated. In this second phase, Tahtawi headed the reinstated Qalam al-Tarjama, participated in *Qumisyun al-Ta'lim* (a central commission for educational planning), and was chief editor of a new fortnightly (*Rawdat al-Madaris al-Misriyya*). He continued to hold these positions until his death in 1873. During the long interlude between these phases (1849–1863), a general trend of reductions in education, and hence translation, prevailed under Abbas (1848–1854) and Sa'id (1854–1863). Tahtawi, virtually exiled to the Sudan for four years (1850–1854), was kept from institutional channels of influence, notwithstanding a relatively short-lived assignment to run a new military school with wide-ranging departments from its opening in 1855 to its closure in 1860.

Tahtawi practically founded the translation movement in Egypt. Works translated by Tahtawi and his pupils into Arabic and Turkish number more than two thousand, many of them geared to a wide variety of educational and general policy requirements. As an educator, he was equipped to run an integrated syllabus of studies. When initial contractions in Muhammad Ali's military establishment forced retrenchments in education, several schools were amalgamated in 1842 into a single institute under Tahtawi's directorship. He ran in that expanded domain the first curriculum that offered a combination of Islamic studies—including law—and European studies, in an educational milieu which had been characterized by strict dualism. These orientations earned Tahtawi the

resentment of the *ulama,* whose traditional positions (i.e. as judges) were being threatened by his pupils. During the reign of Isma'il, Tahtawi cosubmitted a project (*Makatib al-Milla*) for the establishment of a new educational administration to promote and supervise an integrated syllabus in existing elementary schools of traditional learning (*Katatib*), and to sponsor the opening of a network of similarly oriented government elementary schools.

Towards the end of his life, Tahtawi articulated prescriptive reformist views on knowledge, education and the political order in *Manahij al-Albab al-Misriyya fi Mabahij al-Adab al-Asriyya* (The Paths of Egyptian Minds to the Joys of Modern Manners, 1869) and *al-Murshid al-Amin fi Tarbiyyat al-Banat wa al-Banin* (The Honest Guide in the Upbringing of Girls and Boys, 1874). Within the context of a dominating traditional heritage, Tahtawi challenged traditional notions on knowledge and education in effective support for state-managed change. He preached that any branch of learning which contributed to human welfare fell within the realm of necessary *ilm,* that civilization had a material component acquired through adoption of rational sciences from advanced sources in Europe by appropriately prepared calibers, and that education should therefore be aimed at producing new men of knowledge capable of making such adoptions. On these premises, the existing state of al-Azhar *ulama* was criticized and education reforms were advocated, including girls' education, a call that coincided with the opening of the first girls' school in Egypt at the time of Isma'il.

Tahtawi's prescriptions for political reform involved a blend of traditional Islamic and modern secular orientations. He referred to Egypt as a distinct and historically continuous entity, and perceived of the community in terms of a social and political order pertinent to a territorial nation (*watan*) whose members were bound by the common tie of nationhood and were equally entitled to freedom of belief. He recognized that the social order could be organized on the basis of a man-made law equally applied to all members in the national community (*al-jam'iyya*), that the political order involved three distinct functional organs, including a legislative organ, and that its role in binding the community made it a necessity to include basic political education in schools' syllabi. But the inherent secular and liberal orientations were constrained by traditional premises and dimensions. Religion was maintained as a determinant within the political community by the perception that a common religious law was among the binding elements for a nation and by preaching equal civil rights of non-Muslims on an appeal to tolerance and justice based on *Shari'a* (Islamic law) rather than on the implications of equality inherent in nation-hood. The absolute authority of the monarch was maintained by requiring that absolute obedience was due to him, that he was not held accountable to his subjects, and that the parliamentary organ's functions were only consultative and supportive. It is on the basis of his general exposure of the Arab mind to reform issues, rather than on the specific positions taken on each, that the origin of modern Arab secular thought is identified with Tahtawi.

His role through state-sponsored institutions, as well as the congruence and timing of specific elements of his thought with specific policy measures, prompted a perception of him as an etatiste ideologue. The mix of reformist and conservative notions in his writings is interpreted accordingly by Israel Altman. Based on this perception, Tahtawi's thought is seen to have reflected a blend of vested interests in educational reform, intellectual commitment to the cause, and self-assertion vis-à-vis the Turco–Circassian bureaucratic superiors, all characteristic of Egyptian officials who participated in state reform policies between 1830 and 1880.

The Western influence on Tahtawi is generally emphasized. However, the contention that his thought was largely a process of acculturation to the West was recently challenged, and it was shown that Tahtawi's work involved "the reestablishment of direct contact with certain elements of classical Islamic [rationalist] tradition." The genuine and indigenous elements in Tahtawi's thought, and in the Arab "renascence" in general, are accordingly highlighted and emphasized.

Tahtawi produced over thirty publications of translations and original works, including Fénelon's *Les Aventures de Télémaque* (1867), the first translation into Arabic of a work of Western literature. Among his other important original writings were two attempts made to simplify the teaching of Arabic grammar, the second of which, *al-Tuhfa al-Maktabiyya li-Taqrib al-Lughat al-Arabiyya* (The Bookshelves' [or Library's] Antique [*sic*] for the Simplification of Arabic Language, 1869) involved a departure from the prose-memorizing method applied then to the presentation of rules in a tabulated and systematic form. As chief editor of *al-Waqa'i al-Misriyya,* he introduced the newspaper article as a new genre of writing through various commentaries on current affairs. He wrote in serial form, in *Rawdat al-Madaris al-Misriyya,* the first *sira* (prophet's biography) in modern times, later published as *Nihayat al-Ijaz fi Sirat Sakin al-Hijaz* (The Ultimate Brief on the Biography of the Resident of Hijaz, 1876).

Notwithstanding the specific differences in interpreting his role and in classifying his political thought, Tahtawi's contributions to the policies and notions of cultural change, as well as his contributions to Arab secular thought, continue to be recognized. More than a century after Tahtawi's death, he remains relevant to contemporary endeavors. During Nasser's era, the widely circulating Egyptian daily *al-Ahram* used his words as epigraph for its opinion page: "Let the watan, the fatherland, be a place for our common happiness, which we build with freedom, intellect, and factories."

BIBLIOGRAPHY

ALTMAN, ISRAEL. "The Political Thought of Rifa'a Rafi' at-Tahtawi, A Nineteenth Century Egyptian Reformer." Ph.D. diss., University of California at Los Angeles, 1976.

COLE, JUAN R. "Rifa'a al-Tahtawi and the Revival of Practical Philosophy." *The Muslim World* 70 (1980): 29–46.

HEYWORTH-DUNNE, J. "Rifa'a Badawi Rafi' at-Tahtawi: The Egyptian Revivalist." *Bulletin of the School of Oriental and African Studies* 9 (1937–1939): 961–967; and 10 (1939–1942): 399–415.

AL-HUSRY, KHALDUN S. *Origins of Modern Arab Political Thought.* New York, 1980.

Abdel Aziz EzzelArab

Ta'if, al-

A highland city in Saudi Arabia.

Situated in Saudi Arabia's Hijaz region, al-Ta'if is about seventy-five miles (125 km) southeast of the holy city of Mecca. An agricultural center, it has served as a summer residence of kings and wealthy Meccans. In 1924 al-Ta'if was the first city in Hijaz to fall to the Al Sa'ud.

John E. Peterson

Ta'if, Treaty of al-

Treaty that concluded the 1933–1934 border war between Saudi Arabia and the Imamate of Yemen.

The treaty was signed in al-Ta'if (Hijaz) in May 1934. After Saudi Arabia's occupation of the port city of Hodeida, Yemen—and under pressure from Great Britain and Italy, which were wary of the extension of Saudi Arabia's power nearer their colonies (Aden and Eritrea, respectively)—King Abd al-Aziz (Ibn Sa'ud) and Imam Yahya agreed to settle the border issue. Yemen recognized Saudi Arabia's sovereignty over Asir and the towns of Najran and

Jizan and agreed to pay Saudi Arabia an indemnity of 100,000 pounds sterling in gold. In exchange, Saudi Arabia evacuated its forces from Hodeida and other areas of Yemen it had captured. The border was drawn from the Red Sea coast to just east of Najran; beyond that point it was undefined. The agreement was part of a twenty-year friendship treaty concluded by the two nations. Yemen has subsequently argued that the border demarcation must be renewed every twenty years; Saudi Arabia contends that although some elements of the treaty are subject to renewal, the border demarcation is permanent.

F. Gregory Gause, III

Ta'if Accord

Agreement ending the civil war in Lebanon, 1989.

In July 1989, the Arab Tripartite Committee (Morocco, Saudi Arabia, and Algeria) made recommendations to resolve Lebanon's civil war: expanded Lebanese sovereignty, a pullback of Syria's forces, and formalization of Syria and Lebanon's relationship with Israel. Syria promptly rejected them. In September, in the city of Ta'if, Saudi Arabia, representatives of the various Lebanese factions accepted a new National Unity charter. Under it, Syria would restrain Shi'ite groups backed by Iran in exchange for recognition of its dominance in Lebanon and the isolation of the Christian militia leader Michel Aoun; vacant parliamentary seats would be filled by the new government before holding elections; Syria was empowered to become involved in reconstituting national governmental authority; redeployment of its forces left Syria firmly in control of territory strategically important for access to Beirut; and the governments of Syria and Lebanon were permitted to conclude secret agreements.

Bryan Daves

Ta'iz

Province and largest city in the south of North Yemen.

Ta'iz province, embracing the Hujariyya region, is, with Ibb province, the heart of the Shafi'i south of North Yemen, and the city of Ta'iz is its soul. The southern uplands of Ta'iz province, at a few thousand feet, have a more temperate climate and more rainfall than do the northern highlands, and the agriculture of the province has in the past supported a larger, denser population than farther north. The city

Landscape of Ta'iz, Yemen, 1939. (D.W. Lockhard)

of Ta'iz was until recently compared only to San'a, and favorably by most southerners. But by the 1980s, it was clearly outstripped in size and political importance by San'a and in size and commercial importance by Hodeida. In the past, it was an important center of political power in Yemen, especially under the Rasulids from the mid-thirteenth to the mid-fifteenth centuries, and, more recently, when Imam Ahmad ibn Yahya Hamid al-Din insisted on residing there between 1948 and 1962.

Linked since the late nineteenth century to a growing Aden by an increasing flow of workers, merchants, and students, and then through Aden to the outside world, Ta'iz was far more a part of world commerce and in touch with the modern world and its ideas than was San'a. It remains in the 1990s a major center of business and light industry, and its links to Aden, and the latter's new economic role, may enhance the position of Ta'iz in unified Yemen. Within defining walls and highlighted by great whitewashed mosque minarets and domes, its back pressed against the cloud-topped mountain named Jabal Sabr, which towers over it, Ta'iz was a jewel of a small Arab Islamic city. The Ta'iz of today has burst its walls, and modern construction has replaced, crowded out, and hidden most of the old.

Robert D. Burrowes

Tajiks

People of central Asia; the original Iranian population of Afghanistan and Turkistan.

Tajiks form the majority of the population in the Republic of Tajikistan, newly independent since the demise of the Soviet Union in 1991. Tajiks also live in other neighboring Muslim republics, as well as in Iran and Afghanistan. Tajiki, their language, is a dialect of Persian (Farsi), which was originally written in Arabic script but, since 1940, has been written in the Russian Cyrillic script (a practice that might be changed with independence).

Since the spread of Islam into central Asia in the seventh and eighth centuries, the Tajiks have been the subjects of Arab, Turkish, Uzbek, Pakhtun, and Russian conquerors. Tajiks have, however, played prominent roles in administration, trade, and scholarship, owing to the Persian language, used historically in many of the Muslim empires.

More recently, given the visible contribution of Tajiks to the struggle against Soviet occupation in Afghanistan, Tajiks are likely to assume leadership positions in that country.

BIBLIOGRAPHY

DUPREE, LOUIS. *Afghanistan*. Princeton, N.J., 1980.

Ashraf Ghani

Tajin

Moroccan earthenware casserole pot; Tunisian stuffed omelette.

Tajin is the name of an earthenware casserole with a conical top lid used in Morocco to make a variety of stews known by the same name. Meat and vegetables are simmered for a long time until the meat is soft and the stew aromatic. Touajen (plural of tajin) are flavored with cumin, *harissa,* coriander, caraway, paprika, and other spices.

In Tunisia, a tajin is an entirely different dish, a variety of stuffed omelette similar to the Spanish (but not the Mexican) tortilla.

Clifford A. Wright

Takfir, wa al-Hijra, al-

Egyptian Islamic fundamentalist organization.

Al-Takfir wa al-Hijra is the name given by Egyptian authorities to a group that calls itself the Society of Muslims (Jama'at al-Muslimin). The group was formed in the early 1970s by Shukri Mustafa, who, influenced by Sayyid Qutb, argued that Egyptian society was corrupt, decadent, and non-Islamic (*jahiliyya*). The response of the group was to remove itself from this society and forge a new, purely Islamic

society, in the unpopulated hinterland off the Nile river valley. (Though the group did spend some time living in caves, for most of its existence, members lived in shared apartments in the poor neighborhoods of Cairo). Hence the group's popular names al-Takfir (accusation of unbelief) and al-Hijra (religiously motivated flight). When the government arrested and detained several members of the group in 1977, the organization responded by kidnapping, and ultimately murdering, the minister for religious endowments. After a large-scale shootout with the police, several hundred members of the group were arrested and tried. Shukri Mustafa and four other leaders were sentenced to death, while others received prison sentences from five to twenty-five years.

BIBLIOGRAPHY

IBRAHIM, SA'AD AL-DIN. "Anatomy of Egypt's Militant Islamic Groups." *International Journal of Middle East Studies* 12 (December, 1980): 423–453.
———. "Egypt's Islamic Activism in the 1980s." *Third World Quarterly* 10 (April, 1988): 632–657.
KEPEL, GILLES. *Muslim Extremism in Egypt: The Prophet and Pharoah.* Berkeley, Calif. 1985.

David Waldner

Takvim-i Vekayi

Ottoman newspaper.

The first official, Turkish-language Ottoman newspaper, *Takvim-i Vekayi* (Calendar of Events) was founded by order of Sultan Mahmud II. The first issue, which numbered five thousand copies, appeared on May 14, 1832. Sultan Mahmud II closely supervised the paper, at one point even ordering that it use only words and terms intelligible to the common people. The paper was divided into sections covering domestic and foreign news, military affairs, arts and sciences, religious affairs, and commerce. Originally planned as a weekly, *Takvim-i Vekayi* averaged only fifteen to twenty issues per year. Subsequent difficulties in disseminating news in a timely fashion led one government minister to remark, "As history, it is current, but as news, it is behind the times." The paper was closed down in 1879, but it resumed publication in 1891. For the next three decades it suffered periodic closures until the last issue appeared on November 4, 1922.

BIBLIOGRAPHY

EMIN, AHMED. *The Development of Modern Turkey as Measured by Its Press.* 1914. Reprint, New York, 1968.

David Waldner

Tal, Abdullah al-   [1919–1973]

Jordanian soldier who achieved fame during the Arab-Israel War of 1948 and notoriety in its aftermath.

Abdullah al-Tal came from a prominent political family of Irbid that also produced Wasfi al-Tal. An ardent Arab nationalist, al-Tal became a highly able soldier, whose relationship with Glubb Pasha—Sir John Bagot Glubb, British chief of staff of the ARAB LEGION—was based on mutual mistrust.

In early April 1948, Captain al-Tal was put in charge of convoy security on the road from Jerusalem to Gaza, an assignment he fulfilled successfully. A month later he was promoted to major and given command of the Sixth Infantry Battalion, with the duty of protecting the eastern flank of the Arab Legion. Glubb's order to withdraw all units of the Arab Legion from Palestine, including Jerusalem, before the expiration of the British mandate, May 14, 1948, troubled al-Tal.

When the Arabs invaded the new State of Israel, and the Israelis launched an offensive on Jerusalem, May 17, 1948, Jordan's King Abdullah had al-Tal rush to the rescue of the Old City. In Jerusalem, al-Tal assumed command of all the Arab forces, including the Palestinian irregulars for whom he had strong sympathy. He organized the defense of the Old City against repeated Israeli attacks and forced the surrender of the Jewish Quarter there.

On October 10, 1948, al-Tal was appointed military governor of Jerusalem with the rank of colonel. In this capacity he met his opposite number, Israeli Colonel Moshe Dayan, and on November 30, they signed an agreement for "an absolute and sincere cease-fire" covering the entire Jerusalem area. This agreement paved the way for a de facto partition of the Holy City between Jordan and Israel, which aborted the United Nations plan to internationalize it. Subsequently, al-Tal acted as an intermediary in setting up secret meetings between King Abdullah and Israeli officials, while formal armistice negotiations were being conducted under UN auspices in Rhodes. Jordan's neutrality in response to Israel's attacks on the Egyptian army persuaded al-Tal that the regime in Jordan had to be changed and that British control over the Arab Legion had to be broken. By his own admission, in December 1948, al-Tal began to hold private talks with other disaffected Jordanian officers—with Colonel Husni al-Zaʿim who captured power in Syria in March 1949 and with the Egyptian authorities—about the possibility of staging a coup d'état in Jordan. Glubb heard about these plans, and in October 1949, al-Tal escaped to Egypt, where he was welcomed as a political exile.

He played an active part in an Egyptian media campaign that denounced the Jordanian monarch as a traitor to the Arab cause, attributing the Arab defeat in Palestine to the king's collusion with Israel. Al-Tal was also accused of playing a part in the assassination of King Abdullah in July 1951. In 1965, al-Tal was allowed to return to Jordan where he settled in his home town of Irbid and became a senator. He died in Amman in 1973.

Al-Tal published an autobiography in Arabic, *The Palestine Catastrophe* (Cairo, 1959). Although it is a partisan, self-serving account, it is highly revealing about the politics of the Arab Legion, the inter-Arab rivalries, and the part they played in causing the Arab defeat in Palestine.

Avi Shlaim

Tal, Mustafa Wahbi al-   [1899–1949]

Jordan's most famous poet.

Al-Tal's use of colloquial expressions in his poetry plus mentions of geographical places helped establish a unique Jordanian literary tradition in the Arabic language. Despite numerous positions in the government of Jordan, his populist politics and anti-establishment behavior landed him in prison or exile on several occasions. He is also the father of the Jordanian politician Wasfi al-Tal.

BIBLIOGRAPHY

TAYLOR, RICHARD LORING. *Mustafa's Journey, Verse of Arar, Poet of Jordan.* Irbid, Jordan, 1988.

Michael R. Fischbach

Tal, Wasfi al-   [1920–1971]

Prime minister of Jordan (1962–1963, 1965–1967, 1970–1971).

Tal was born in Irbid, in northern Jordan. After being educated at the American University of Beirut, he served as an officer in Britain's army (1942–1945), then joined Jordan's civil service, rising to the rank of ambassador to Iraq (1961–1962). Tal was expelled from Baghdad for alleged subversive activities against the regime of Abd al-Karim Kassem; he was also channeling funds to the anti-Nasser Syrian Nationalist party in Lebanon.

Tal formed his first cabinet in January 1962 and embarked on an efficiency campaign in the civil service and attempted to promote economic development. He also launched a policy designed to show that Jordan was the true repository of Palestinian aspirations; it was a failure.

A Jordan–Saudi Arabia summit in August 1962 resulted in an agreement to coordinate foreign policy. When a coup took place in Yemen in October 1962, resulting in the proclamation of the Yemen Arab Republic, Jordan and Saudi Arabia backed the insurgents under Imam al-Badr. In November 1962, Tal supervised parliamentary elections in which political parties were banned. Ba'athist coups in Baghdad in February 1963 and in Damascus in March 1963 led Iraq and Syria to launch unity talks with Egypt. A shift in policy was required, so Tal resigned at the end of March.

In February 1965, Tal began his second term as prime minister. He helped King Hussein ibn Talal reactivate the entente with Saudi Arabia, and on 9 August 1965, a treaty was signed delimiting borders between the two countries. Jordan joined an alliance of Islamic states organized by Saudi Arabia and directed against Egypt, Syria, and Iraq.

Al-Fath raids into Israel began. Under pressure from the Arab League, Jordan agreed to set up "summer camps for military training and moral guidance" for Palestinian recruits. In June 1966, King Hussein said there could be no cooperation with the Palestine Liberation Organization (PLO), and Tal prevented elections for the PLO National Council.

Tal closed the PLO office in Amman and expelled Ahmad Shuqayri, head of the PLO. In retaliation for an operation by al-Fath guerrillas supported by Syria, Israel launched a raid against Jordan, demolishing the village of Samuwa on 13 November 1966. Residents of the West Bank and refugee camps hated Tal because of his disbanding of the National Guard, which had been stationed in frontier villages. Under the press law of 1 February 1967, instigated by Tal, all existing papers and periodicals were closed down, and newly licensed publications had to have 25 percent government ownership. Tal resigned in March 1967 and was appointed chief of the royal court, in which position he tried unsuccessfully to keep Jordan out of the Arab–Israel War of 1967.

Tal began his third term as prime minister on 26 September 1970. The following day, King Hussein and PLO chairman Yasir Arafat signed an agreement in Cairo that called for the withdrawal of Palestinian guerillas from the cities but allowed them to continue the battle against Israel from the countryside. However, Tal and the military devised a plan to drive the guerillas out of Amman, Irbid, Jerash, and Ajlun. It was all over by 18 June 1971. In revenge, during a visit to Cairo in September 1971, Tal was assassinated by the Black September.

BIBLIOGRAPHY

AMOS, JOHN W., II. *Palestinian Resistance: Organization of a Nationalist Movement.* New York, 1980.
DANN, URIEL. *King Hussein and the Challenge of Arab Radicalism: Jordan, 1955–1967.* New York, 1989.
IYAD, ABU, with Eric Rouleau. *My Home, My Land: A Narrative of the Palestinian Struggle.* Tr. by Linda Butler. New York, 1978.
LUNT, JAMES. *Hussein of Jordan: Searching for a Just and Lasting Peace.* New York, 1989.

Jenab Tutunji

Talabani, Jalal [1933–]

Kurdish leader.

Jalal was born near Koi Sanjaq, in Iraqi Kurdistan. The son of a Qadiri *murshid* (teacher), he studied law in Baghdad. In 1962, he joined General Mustafa Barzani in the armed struggle of the Kurds against the Arabs. From 1966 until 1970, Talabani led a group of government mercenaries (*jash*). Since founding the PATRIOTIC UNION OF KURDISTAN (PUK) in 1977, he has competed with Mas'ud al-Barzani for the leadership of the Iraqi Kurdish movement.

BIBLIOGRAPHY

KUTSCHERA, CHRIS. *Le mouvement national kurde.* Paris, 1979.

Chris Kutschera

Talal ibn Abdullah [1909–1972]

King of Jordan who, during his brief reign, encouraged democracy.

King Talal is the tragic figure of Jordanian politics. He sacrificed his health and happiness by assuming the duties of king at a critical period of transition in Jordan's history. When King ABDULLAH IBN HUSAYN was assassinated on July 20, 1951, a group of Jordanian royalists, who were to resemble an oligarchy over the next two years, were deeply conscious of the fact that King Abdullah had chosen his grandson, Prince Hussein ibn Talal, as his successor and had begun grooming him for the task. But Hussein was too young. Crown Prince Talal was suffering from acute depression and paranoia yet had improved considerably under medical treatment in Switzerland. He could have led an almost normal life if he were kept in an anxiety-free environment. But the only way to ensure the legitimacy of transition to Hussein was for Talal to become king. The alternatives were either to crown

Prince Na'if, the regent and Talal's half-brother, or to accede to some form of union with Iraq, in which case a member of the Iraqi branch of the Hashimite dynasty would succeed to the Jordanian throne. Neither alternative was considered palatable. From this perspective, Talal was to be an interim figure, yet he was significantly more than that.

At the time of Abdullah's assassination, Prime Minister Samir Rifa'i convened an emergency cabinet meeting. It was decided that the veteran prime minister, Tawfiq Abd al-Huda, should be entrusted with the formation of a new cabinet under the regent's commission. On September 5, 1951, the cabinet proclaimed Talal king, and the newly elected parliament confirmed Talal on the throne on receipt of a medical report by Minister of Health Jamil Tutunji. Prince Na'if, the regent, flew to Switzerland to escort his brother home.

The most notable legacy of King Talal's brief reign was to turn Jordan into what was the truest democracy in the Arab world at the time in view of the separation of powers and the ability of parliament to act as a check on the actions of government, a function that the Lebanese parliament, for instance, did not exercise. Under Talal's instructions, Abd al-Huda won a vote of confidence in parliament on September 24, 1951. This was unprecedented in the constitutional history of Jordan. A new constitution was promulgated, declaring the people the source of all power. Citizens were guaranteed individual liberty and equality before the law. The constitution was approved by the lower house on November 7, 1951, passed the upper house on December 29, and was signed by King Talal on January 1, 1952. It enshrined the freedom of opinion, the right to hold public meetings and form political parties and trade unions, the freedom of conscience and worship, compulsory free education, as well as the right to own property. It was these liberties that were to make possible the phenomenon of Sulayman al-Nabulsi a few years later.

The new constitution made the cabinet collectively and individually responsible to parliament. Ministers could be impeached. The king could dissolve parliament, but new elections had to be held within four months, otherwise the old parliament would be reinstated. According to Article 93, parliament could override the king's veto over legislation by a two-thirds majority. Parliament was empowered to ratify treaties and could assemble without being called to do so by the king.

The fly in the ointment was that, in the event of an emergency, on the decision of the cabinet, the king could declare martial law by decree.

Perhaps the biggest factor responsible for this liberal constitution was King Talal himself, though other conditions were ripe. There was a need to satisfy the Palestinians, who had more liberal traditions and who had recently been incorporated into the union, and the cabinet was wary of an authoritarian king, given the circumstances. King Talal became immensely popular.

On the foreign policy front, he invited Abd al-Huda to declare on September 18, 1951, that Jordan was not seeking union with Iraq. In December 1951, he visited Saudi Arabia and made clear his desire for good relations with the house of Sa'ud. He was skeptical of Western alliances, and in January 1952, King Talal led Jordan into acceptance of the Arab Collective Security Pact.

Yet barely within eight months of ascending the throne, the tribulations of office were having a visible effect on the king. His psychological troubles had returned and his weight had dwindled to a mere ninety pounds. He left the country in May 1952 to vacation in Europe, leaving behind a Regency Council. Within a week, the cabinet transformed that body into a Crown Council, which exercised the powers of head of state for the rest of Talal's reign. On August 11, 1952, parliament deposed him and proclaimed Prince Hussein king. King Talal accepted gracefully. The duties of king were assumed by a Regency Council until Hussein came of age, the same Regency Council the king had established earlier, headed by Ibrahim Hashim. Abd al-Huda remained in the office of prime minister. Paradoxically under the circumstances, he exercised more power than any other prime minister in the history of Jordan.

Meanwhile, the press in Israel and rival Arab countries accused the Jordanian government, in complicity with the British, of inventing the king's illness to be rid of him.

King Talal moved to Egypt for a while, then he took up residence in Turkey for the rest of his days. He was given a hero's funeral when he died twenty years later. He was the first king of Jordan to graduate from the Royal Military College at Sandhurst, an English school, and had absorbed a real taste for democracy. Sir John Bagot Glubb recalls in his memoirs, *A Soldier with the Arabs*: "The tragedy of King Talal seemed to be rendered more poignant by the fact that, apart from his insanity, he appeared so ideally fit to be king. . . . He was of acute intelligence, outstanding personal charm, faultless private morals, and inspired by a deeply conscious wish to serve his country and his people, with no selfish motives."

BIBLIOGRAPHY

ABIDI, AQIL HYDER HASAN. *Jordan: A Political Study, 1948–1957.* New Delhi, 1965.

GLUBB, JOHN BAGOT. *A Soldier with the Arabs.* New York, 1957.

MADI, MUNIB, and SULAYMAN MUSA. *Ta'rikh al-Urdun fi al-qarn al-ishrin, 1900–1959.* Amman, 1988.

Jenab Tutunji

Talat, Mehmet [1874–1921]

Turkish statesman.

Born in Edirne, Talat Bey became chief administrator of the telegraph and postal office in Salonika in the Ottoman Empire. There, he became part of the secret Committee of Union and Progress. After the Young Turk revolution, he went to Istanbul in December 1908 to assume a leading position in the Young Turk government, rising to minister of interior. After 1913 and until the Ottoman defeat in World War I, Talat Paşa, Enver Paşa, and Cemal Paça comprised the unofficial triumvirate that controlled the Ottoman Empire. While Enver was a military leader and Cemal was famous for his ruthlessness, Talat was a sophisticated diplomat and a consummate politician. In February 1917, Talat became grand vizier and held that position until October 8, 1918, just before the armistice of Mudros, which signaled the Ottoman surrender to the Allies. On November 2, three days after the armistice was signed, Talat left Istanbul on a German ship and was murdered in Berlin in 1921.

BIBLIOGRAPHY

LEWIS, BERNARD. *The Emergence of Modern Turkey.* New York, 1961.

RAMSAUR, E. E. *The Young Turks.* Princeton, N.J., 1957.

SHAW, STANFORD, and EZEL KURAL SHAW. *History of the Ottoman Empire and Modern Turkey.* Cambridge, U.K. 1977.

Zachary Karabell

Talebof, Abd al-Rahman

See Talebzadeh, Abd al-Rahman

Talebzadeh, Abd al-Rahman [1837–1910]

Persian-born playwright and scholar.

Talebzadeh lived in Tiflis (Tbilisi) in Russian Georgia. He authored translations, plays, and novels. His most notable work was *The Book of Ahmad,* in which ideas of reform and modernization are introduced through the discussions of a father and son.

Farhad Shirzad

Talfah, Adnan Khayr Allah [1940–1989]

Iraqi government official; relative of Saddam Hussein.

Talfah was Saddam Hussein's brother-in-law and a maternal cousin; Hussein is married to Talfah's sister Sajida. Talfah was born in Tikrit and combined military and political careers in Iraq. In 1977, when still a colonel, through Saddam Hussein's pressure he became a member of the Regional Leadership of the Ba'th party and of the Revolutionary Command Council, as well as minister of defense. During the Iran–Iraq War (1980–1988), he played a major role in mediating between the civilian leadership and the military. In 1988 his relations with Saddam Hussein became strained through a family dispute. In May 1989 he was killed in a helicopter crash amid rumors of foul play on the part of Hussein.

BIBLIOGRAPHY

BARAM, AMATZIA. "The Ruling Political Elite in Ba'thi Iraq, 1968–1986." *International Journal of Middle East Studies* 21 (1989): 447–493.

Amatzia Baram

Tali'a, al-

Leftist journal (the Vanguard) published in Cairo, 1945–1946 and 1965–1977.

The second of these journals, edited by Lutfi al-Khuli and part of Muhammad Hasanayn Haykal's al-Ahram empire, provided a forum for Marxist and other leftist thought. Al-Tali'a was closed following the 1977 riots, which were blamed on the left.

BIBLIOGRAPHY

BAKER, RAYMOND WILLIAM. "Making Revolution Real: The Marxists of *The Vanguard.*" In *Sadat and After: Struggles for Egypt's Political Soul.* Cambridge, Mass., 1990.

Donald Malcolm Reid

Talib, Naji [1917–]

Iraqi general and statesman.

Born in al-Nasiriya, a town in the south of Iraq, Naji Talib is the son of al-Haj Talib, who was a deputy in the Iraqi parliament. Talib graduated from the Military College of Iraq, obtained his staff rank from London, and attained the rank of general in the Military Engineering Corps of the Iraqi army. He joined the organization of Free Officers and, after the 1958 coup, became minister of social affairs, minister of industry, and minister of foreign affairs. Finally, in August 1966, he was appointed prime minister under President Abd al-Rahman Arif.

Mamoon A. Zaki

Talmud

Authoritative body of Jewish law and tradition codified in the centuries following dispersal of the Jews by the Roman Empire.

In Hebrew, *talmud* means "instruction, study." After the Hebrew Bible (the Old Testament, as it is called in Christianity), the Talmud is the most important work of religious law in Judaism. The basic texts are the Mishnah, which codified oral law, and the Gemara, the commentary on it. Two versions exist—the Babylonian Talmud and the Jerusalem Talmud.

After the Romans dispersed the Jews from their kingdoms and lands about 70 C.E., the rabbis of Yavne and later Usha in Galilee began the process of Talmudic codification; Jewish oral law had arisen from interpretations of laws in the Bible—known as written law—much coming from the answers (*responsa*) to questions sent by Jews in the Diaspora to rabbis still in the Holy Land. (Responsa have continued until today.) Rabbi Judah ha-Nasi (c. 170–c. 219 C.E.) disapproved of the way that scripture was continuously interpreted, based on new developments in Jewish life, and to counter this he ordered the Mishnah to be written definitively. Change continued, however, so the Mishnah became merely the foundation for many new interpretations and commentaries.

At the time of Rabbi ha-Nasi's death, the Roman-dominated Middle East was in disorder because of political strife within the empire; many Jews left Galilee for Persian-ruled Babylon, where they lived well and their scholars continued to codify oral law into the Talmud. The Jerusalem Talmud was finalized in about 400 C.E., and the Babylonian in about 500 C.E. The Babylonian Talmud is about four times larger, contains thirty-nine tractates (volumes), and is generally accepted as the more authoritative.

Throughout the centuries of the Diaspora (and today), young Jewish boys (and some girls) learned, read, and discussed the Talmud with their rabbis and teachers, with some of them becoming Talmud scholars in their own right and some becoming ordained rabbis. The Talmudic rulings have always regulated the private and public lives of observant Jews worldwide. A vast rabbinic literature now exists based on discussions and counterdiscussions concerning the Talmud.

The original Talmud consisted of the collected works of the Mishnah and the Gemara (from the Hebrew *gamar,* "complete"). The Gemara includes the Aggadah, a collection of legends and stories, proverbs, parables, and anecdotes. The parts of the Talmud dealing with Jewish law, ceremony, and rites are known as HALAKHAH, "the path."

BIBLIOGRAPHY

GILBERT, MARTIN, ed. *The Illustrated Atlas of Jewish Civilization: 4,000 Years of Jewish History.* New York, 1990.

Benjamin Joseph

Tal Za'tar Refugee Camp

Refugee camp in East Beirut, Lebanon.

Built in 1950 by UNRWA (United National Relief and Works Agency for Palestinian Refugees in the Near East), Tal Za'tar's Palestinian and South Lebanese population exceeded thirty thousand refugees by the early 1970s. In perhaps the bloodiest battle of the Lebanese Civil War that started in 1975, members of the Christian PHALANGE laid siege to the camp June 22, 1976. Thousands of residents are believed to have been killed during the siege and the mass killings that followed the Phalangist victory August 12. The remaining population of the camp was transferred to West Beirut. The Phalangists' intent is believed to have been the expulsion of all non-Christians, and particularly the Palestine Liberation Organization (PLO), from East Beirut. The Christian militias had largely avoided direct confrontations with the PLO until the Syrian army entered the war in Lebanon on the Christian side May 31, 1976. The PLO defended the camp for fifty-two days before it fell with the help of Syrian artillery.

BIBLIOGRAPHY

GRESH, ALAIN, and DOMINIQUE VIDAL. *A to Z of the Middle East.* Atlantic Highlands, N.J., 1990.
PETRAN, TABITHA. *The Struggle over Lebanon.* New York, 1987.
SMITH, PAMELA ANN. *Palestine and the Palestinians, 1876–1983.* London, 1984.

Elizabeth Thompson

Tamashaq

See Twareg

TAMI

Israeli political party.

TAMI (Tnu'at Masoret Yisrael, or Tradition of Israel movement) was formed in 1981 under the leadership of the Aharon Abuhatzeira primarily to increase attention to the problems of Oriental Jews, especially those from North Africa. It won three seats in the tenth Knesset of 1982, and was part of the second Begin coalition government, but fell to only one seat in 1984. Its program was Zionist and traditional, with emphasis on equality of opportunity for members of all ethnic groups. It was one of only a few essentially ethnic parties in Israeli history. In 1988, it became a faction of the Likud.

Walter F. Weiker

Tamimahs

Paramount shaykhs of larger Omani tribal groupings.

Tamimahs are selected from an elite family within the tribe, and their main functions are to resolve disputes and provide a focus of leadership among lineages within the tribe. The title implies complete or total authority to the extent that the bearer has the power to impose the death penalty on a tribesman, although this is rarely the case at the tribal level in Oman.

Calvin H. Allen, Jr.

Tamimi, Amin al-   [1892–1944]

Palestinian politician.

Born to a Muslim family in Nablus, Palestine, Tamimi studied in Istanbul, where he encountered Arab literary and political circles before World War I. After the war, he served as an adviser to the regime of the Syrian king, Faisal I, in Damascus and joined delegations to Istanbul and to Lausanne in 1922 to seek Turkish support for Arab independence. He was a leader of the Nablus MUSLIM–CHRISTIAN ASSOCIATION, and a member of the Supreme Muslim Council of the *mufti* (interpreter of the law of Islam) in Jerusalem from 1926 to 1938.

Tamimi went to Iraq in 1939 and participated in the 1941 Rashid Ali al-Kaylan revolt of pan-Arabism against Britain. The British then interned him in Rhodesia, where he died. He was proclaimed a martyr in the streets of Jerusalem. His son Adnan, an Iraqi citizen, was a UN official until 1983.

BIBLIOGRAPHY

HUREWITZ, J. C. *The Struggle for Palestine.* New York, 1950, 1976.

Elizabeth Thompson

Tamir, Shmuel   [1923–   ]

Israeli politician and attorney.

Born in Jerusalem, Shmuel Tamir was influenced by the Hebron mass killing of civilians in 1929 and, at age fifteen, joined Irgun Zva'i Le'umi. He was arrested in 1947 and deported to Kenya, where he was allowed to take his final law examinations. Returning to Israel after its statehood, he was active in the Herut movement, where he was viewed as a natural heir to Menachem Begin. In 1977 Tamir joined the Democratic Movement for Change and was appointed minister of justice under Begin. In 1981 he resigned from politics and returned to his legal practice.

BIBLIOGRAPHY

BELL, J. BOWYER. *Terror out of Zion: Irgun Zva'i Leumi, Lehi, and the Palestine Underground, 1929–1949.* New York, 1977.

Julie Zuckerman

Tammuz, Benyamin   [1919–1989]

Israeli novelist and journalist.

Benyamin Tammuz was born in Kharkov, in the Ukraine, and emigrated to Palestine in 1924. Throughout his life, he worked for various newspapers, including *Haaretz.* Tammuz was a founding member of the Canaanite movement, which advocated the creation of a Hebrew, rather than a Jewish, state in Israel. This association undoubtedly influenced his earlier works, which were republished as *Angioxyl, Terufah Nedirah* (1973; A Rare Cure, 1981). He left the movement following a stay in Europe, which brought him into close contact with European Jews. Tammuz served as cultural attaché at the Israeli embassy in London in 1971.

In his works, Tammuz criticizes Israeli society's loss of soul and its lack of normalcy. *Requiem Le-Na'aman*

(1978; Requiem for Na'aman, 1982) is considered his most forceful work. He deals with the seemingly intractable Arab–Israel conflict in his metaphorical *Ha-Pardes* (1971; The Orchard, 1984) and in *Taharut Sehiya* (1952; Swimming Race, 1953). In his *Mishlei Baqbuqim* (1975, Proverbs of Bottles), Tammuz addresses Israel's lack of spirituality, while in *Pundaqo Shel Yirmiyahu* (1984, Jeremiah's Inn), he satirizes the involvement of the ultra-orthodox in Israeli politics.

Ann Kahn

Tan

Turkish newspaper.

Tan (Dawn) was an important Istanbul daily founded in 1936 by the Iş Bankası that became a leading leftist critic of fascism and social problems during World War II. In the postwar relaxation of censorship, it became a principal forum for political dissent by Adnan Menderes and other Republican People's party discontents. But in December 1945, its presses were smashed and the paper closed down by a mob of students inspired by government-supported anti-communist sentiment.

In response, in 1946, *Tan* owner Zekeriya Sertel founded the Association for Protection of Human Rights, but he left the country after he was charged with being a communist in 1947. Although readership had fallen off, Halil Lütfü Dördüncü continued publishing *Tan* until 1956. The name *Tan* was revived in 1983 by businessman Asıl Nadır for a sensationalist magazine-type daily newspaper.

BIBLIOGRAPHY

AHMAD, FEROZ. *The Turkish Experiment in Democracy, 1950–1975*. Boulder, Colo., 1977.
KARPAT, KEMAL H. *Turkey's Politics: The Transition to a Multi-Party System*. Princeton, N.J., 1959.

Elizabeth Thompson

Tanburi Cemil   [1871–1916]

Ottoman Turkish musician and composer.

Tanburi Cemil was born in Istanbul into a family of musicians. He enrolled in the Mulukhiyya but left before finishing his studies and began to study music. By his death at the age of forty-five, he was considered the foremost Turkish virtuoso. Although he was most well known for playing the *tanbur* (guitar), an instrument he had mastered as a child, Tanburi Cemil was equally proficient on the *kemençe* (a small

three-stringed violin) and the *lavta* (lute). Tanburi Cemil's compositions, characterized by a refined sensitivity, are considered among the masterpieces of Turkish music. Among his best-known works are *Ferahfeza Saz Semaisi, Mahur Peşrevi, Muhayyer Saz Semaisi,* and *Hicazkar Saz Semaisi.*

BIBLIOGRAPHY

Yeni türk ansiklopedisi, vol. 2. Istanbul, 1985, p. 488.

David Waldner

Taner, Haldun   [1916–1986]

Turkish writer.

The son of a university professor, Taner was born in Istanbul, where he attended Galatasaray Lycée. He studied political science at Heidelberg University in 1938 and later studied literature in Istanbul. He then taught literature and art history for a number of years at the Journalism Institute and at the Ankara Language, History, and Geography School. Taner became popular in the 1950s for his short stories about the urban middle class, which have been translated from Turkish into more than a dozen languages. He worked as a journalist and in 1960 became editor-in-chief of the Istanbul daily *Tercüman.*

Taner also made his mark in the theater world, joining a young generation of playwrights in the 1950s who addressed the tensions between traditional values and the demands of modern life. He drew on the epic traditions of Turkey for his play *The Ballad of Ali from Keshan,* which was also made into a film. He won a prize with Orhan Kemal in 1957 for their screenplay *Ferhat, the Mountain Lover.* Taner also founded a private theater, the Devekusu Kabare Tiyatrosu.

BIBLIOGRAPHY

RENDA, G., and C. MAX KORTEPETER, eds. *The Transformation of Turkish Culture*. Istanbul, 1986.

Elizabeth Thompson

Tangier

Port city, provincial capital, and province in northwestern Morocco situated on a bay of the Strait of Gibraltar seventeen miles (27 km) from the southern tip of Spain.

Tangier (Arabic, Tanja; French, Tanger; Spanish, Tánger) was first established as a Phoenician trading post. It subsequently became a Carthaginian and then a Roman settlement called, at first, Tingis. It was already an international city in 42 C.E., as well as the capital of the Roman province of Mauretania. After five centuries of Roman domination it was occupied by the Vandals and then by the Byzantines. From 705 to 1471 C.E., it was ruled by successive Islamic dynasties, then by the Spanish and Portuguese until 1662. As part of the dowry of Portugal's Catherine of Braganza upon her marriage to England's Charles II, Tangier was given to the English crown, which fortified the city during the mid-seventeenth century. In the 1680s, Tangier was returned to Morocco. During the nineteenth century, Tangier emerged as Morocco's diplomatic capital, with British trade dominating the area, and it became the seat of the European consular legations.

When the rest of Morocco became French and Spanish protectorates in 1912, Tangier obtained special status; in 1923 it became an official international zone, governed by a commission composed of representatives from Great Britain, France, Spain, Portugal, Belgium, the Netherlands, Sweden, and, later, the United States. Tangier remained an international zone until October 1956, several months following Morocco's independence, when it was integrated into the Sharifian kingdom. Between the years 1940 and 1945 Tangier lost its international status, following Spain's temporary annexation of the zone. During World War II, Nazi propaganda and pro-Franco factions dominated Tangier's political scene. During the period from 1923 to 1956, the Moroccan government (*makhzan*) was represented by one of the Sultan's emissaries known as the *mandub*.

Pre-1956 Tangier had a highly heterogeneous population. In 1950 there were 40,000 Muslims, 20,000 Spanish, 12,000 Jews, 6,000 French, and 5,000 other Europeans, for a total of 83,000. Although in much of Morocco Muslims and Jews dwelled apart—the Muslims in the *madinas* and the Jews in the *mellahs*—in Tangier the communities were relatively integrated. In fact, politically, during the colonial era, the Jews of Tangier enjoyed a measure of autonomy unheard of in the rest of Morocco. They possessed rights granted by the international zone's legislative assembly and consented to by the *makhzan*. They had a community council composed of fifteen members, which included the head of the rabbinic tribunal of Tangier, who served as an adviser on matters relating to Jewish law.

Tangier still ranks among Morocco's most important cities: the others are Casablanca, Marrakech, Fez, Agadir, and Meknes. Tangier is built on the slopes of a chalky limestone hill. The old town (*madina*) is dominated by the casbah, the Moroccan king's palace (now a museum of Moroccan art), the Great mosque, and several important synagogues. European quarters, which declined after Moroccan independence in 1956, stretched to the south and west of the city. The American University was established there in 1968 and the University of North Africa in 1971. Whereas other important Moroccan trade centers, such as Essaouira, declined from the 1890s onward, Tangier remained a vital port and trade center. None of Morocco's coastal and port cities reached the prominence and importance of Beirut, Alexandria, or Constantinople, but Tangier gained some prestige.

Today, Tangier has excellent roads, rail, and international airport facilities connecting it with major Moroccan centers, such as Fez, Meknes, Rabat, and Casablanca, as well as with Europe. The port handles cereals and major imports; in addition to its role as a tourist center, Tangier has a textile industry.

Tangier province stretches southeastward from the city to the Rif mountains. It is bounded to the north and west by the Atlantic Ocean and to the east and south by Tetuan province. In 1975, there were 241,000 inhabitants in the city; in 1981, in both city and province, approximately 405,000.

BIBLIOGRAPHY

GRAHAM, STUART. *The International City of Tangier.* Berkeley and Los Angeles, 1955.
LASKIER, MICHAEL M. *The Alliance Israélite Universelle and the Jewish Communities of Morocco, 1862–1962.* Albany, N.Y., 1983.

Michael M. Laskier

Tangier, Treaty of

Franco–Moroccan agreement of September 10, 1844.

The Treaty of Tangier followed the defeat of the Moroccan army at the Battle of Isly by a French force pursuing the Algerian resistance leader ABD AL-QADIR, who had frequently sought refuge in Moroccan territory. The treaty obligated the Moroccan government to consider Abd al-Qadir an outlaw and to offer him no assistance.

BIBLIOGRAPHY

JULIEN, CHARLES-ANDRÉ. *Histoire de l'Algérie contemporaine: La conquête et les débuts de la colonisation, 1827–1871.* Paris, 1964.

Kenneth J. Perkins

Tanin

Ottoman newspaper.

Tanin (the Echo), the principal organ of the Committee of Union and Progress (CUP), began publication on 2 August 1908. The editors were Hüseyin Cahit Valçin, Hüseyin Kazım, and Tevfik Fikret. In early 1909, the offices of the paper were attacked and destroyed by a mob opposed to CUP rule. In order to escape censorship, *Tanin* often appeared under the names "Cenin," "Renin," "Senin," and "Hak." *Tanin* was opposed to the war of independence, and in 1925, it was ordered closed by the Independence courts.

BIBLIOGRAPHY

SHAW, STANFORD, and EZEL KURAL SHAW. *History of the Ottoman Empire and Modern Turkey*, vol. 2: *Reform, Revolution, and Republic: The Rise of Modern Turkey, 1808–1975*. Cambridge, U.K., 1977.

David Waldner

Tanpınar, Ahmed Hamdi   [1901–1962]

Turkish professor and author.

The son of a *qadi* (judge), Tanpınar was born in Istanbul and moved with his father to various cities of the Ottoman Empire. He graduated from the Antalya secondary school and studied at the Faculty of Literature, where he was a student of Yahya Kemal. After graduating in 1923, he taught at secondary schools, including the Fine Arts Academy, until 1939, when he was appointed professor of modern Turkish Literature at Istanbul University. He wrote a major volume on post-Tanzimat-era Turkish literature, a monograph on Tevfik Fikret, and a series of critical essays.

Tanpınar also wrote poetry, novels, and short stories. In his novels, he studied the era from the Crimean War (1854) to World War II (1939), portraying developments within Turkish society and the fate of traditional ties in a modernizing society. In 1942, Tanpınar was elected to the parliament, representing Maraş.

BIBLIOGRAPHY

ERTOP, KONUR. "Trends and Characteristics of Contemporary Turkish Literature." In *The Transformation of Turkish Culture: The Atatürk Legacy*, ed. by Günsel Renda and C. Max Kortepeter. Princeton, N.J., 1986.

David Waldner

Tanta

Egyptian city.

Located in the Nile river delta, fifty miles (80 km) north of Cairo, Tanta is the capital of the GHARBIYYA governorate. It is also a major transportation center, basing its economy on the processing and distribution of cotton and sugar. The population of Tanta was 374,000 in 1986.

BIBLIOGRAPHY

The Middle East and North Africa, 38th ed. London, 1992.

David Waldner

Tanzimat

Mid-nineteenth-century Ottoman reform movement.

The Tanzimat-i Hayriye (Auspicious Reorganization) was a series of governmental reforms between 1839 and 1876 that sought to centralize and rationalize Ottoman rule and capture more tax revenues for the military defense of the empire. The Tanzimat period is usually associated with particular personalities in the central government: the sultans Abdülmecit II and Abdülaziz, and the high-ranking bureaucrats Mustafa Reşid Paşa, Ali Paşa, and Fuad Paşa. The Tanzimat was preceded by earlier reform efforts since the eighteenth century, particularly by Abdülmecit I and Abdülaziz's father, Mahmud II, between 1808 and 1839. And it would be followed by reforms in the early reigns of Abdülhamit II and the Young Turks.

The thirty-seven years of the Tanzimat period are significant in this long process for establishing the basic principles and the governmental apparatus of reform. The bywords of the movement were justice and order, which were seen as prerequisites to effecting substantial social and economic change. The major product of the movement was a huge increase in the power of the central state. The major edicts of the Tanzimat significantly enlarged the scope of government activity by creating new fiscal, legal, and administrative instruments. For example, the edict that inaugurated the Tanzimat, the 1839 Edict of Gülhane (see HATTI ŞERIF OF GÜLHANE), proposed replacing inefficient tax farms with a centralized revenue service and establishing a new imperial council, the Meclis-i Vala, to formulate and direct reform policy. Subsequent edicts sought to promote justice and confidence in government, such as those of 1840, 1850, and 1870 to 1876 that laid out uniform codes of law for commerce, civil transactions, and criminal cases. A series of provincial reforms culminating in the 1864 Vilayet Law regularized the structure of local government and strengthened lines of authority to Constantinople (now Istanbul). And in the capital itself, government was reorganized into formal departments and specialized ministries. During the Tanzimat period, the Ottoman state also began to intervene in society in new ways. The 1839 Gülhane edict and other laws expanded military conscription. And the state established new elite secular schools. The 1869 Regulation of Public Instruction introduced an empire-wide school system intended to produce bureaucrats and military officers at every level of government equipped with the skills necessary to implement policy.

But the Tanzimat was not solely a project of administrative reform. Its goals of order and justice were often ancillary to other, more immediate goals. The 1839 Gülhane edict was issued when the Ottomans were fighting to regain territory captured by Egypt in 1832. Greece had already won its independence in 1839, and in the Crimean War (1853–1856) the Ottomans would again go to war with Russia. Hence, the 1839 edict would promise to continue the military buildup begun by Mahmud II to defend the empire from external threats. The military was reorganized in 1842 and 1869, producing a larger, more unified structure under the *serasker,* a combined chief of staff and war minister. And many other reforms were explicitly intended to raise more revenue for defense.

Tanzimat goals were further complicated by international affairs with the growing influence of France and England in the empire. The Ottomans sought European alliances for protection against Russian and Egyptian invasions. This alliance was bought at a price. For their own domestic reasons, and to further their interests in the empire, France and England pushed another set of often contradictory goals. While the Europeans advocated equal rights and democratic participation in the empire, they also acted to protect the privileges and separate status of non-Muslim millets (see MILLET SYSTEM). So, while the Gülhane edict and the 1856 HATT-I HÜMAYUN proclaimed equality of all citizens regardless of religion, and new secular courts were established to offset any prejudice in *Shari'a* (Islamic law) courts, in fact, society remained divided by religion in subcommunities with separate legal and social institutions.

Missing from the great initiatives of the Tanzimat was serious fiscal and economic reform. Roger Owen explains the neglect of economic reform thus: "Limited financial resources, the lack of competent administrators, the growing technological gap between Europe and the rest of the world, and the constraints imposed by Turkey's social structure and weakened international position all combined to set strict limits on the types of economic politics pursued" (Owen, p. 116). Restricted in their development of policy, the Ottomans were also plagued by the misfortune that they were attempting reform precisely during a period of economic boom in France and England.

The Tanzimat coincided with the first wave of industrial imperialism. France and England used their diplomatic influence in Constantinople to facilitate imperialist expansion at the expense of economic reform within the empire. For example, the 1838 Anglo–Turkish commercial convention, which preceded British support in fighting Egypt, promoted the spread of European imports in Ottoman markets. In the 1850s and 1860s, the British and French established new kinds of investment banks equipped to funnel domestic savings into overseas loans and projects. These banks played no small part in encouraging Ottoman indebtedness. The first foreign loan was taken out in 1854, for 3 million British pounds, to pay war expenses. Twenty years later, the Ottoman government would devote more than half of its budget to servicing foreign loans totalling 242 million British pounds.

The Tanzimat reforms had not yet produced a government apparatus capable of mounting an economic defense. For example, attempts to increase collection of taxes (and avoid foreign loans) faltered without trained personnel until well after 1859, when the Mekteb-i Mülkiye school to train bureaucrats was established. And although the 1858 land code sought to encourage more efficient exploitation of agriculture by promoting private land ownership, poor administration derailed it. In many areas, wealthy absentee landowners succeeded in registering large tracts of land, taking control away from the peasants who, if they had owned the land, might have found incentive to improve efficiency in cultivation. Instead, sharecropping discouraged investment in the land.

This is not to say that there was no effort at economic development, but rather that these efforts were overwhelmed by external factors. The Tanzimat period saw the first boom in building roads, ports, and other economic infrastructure that facilitated the transport of goods. But the tariff structure made the new transport more profitable to foreign traders than domestic merchants. While Ottoman exports increased nearly 500 percent between 1840 and the 1870s, these exports represented less than 10 percent of total production in the empire and were largely in the form of raw agricultural materials sent to England and France. In the meantime, the empire's terms of trade with Europe actually worsened. Ottoman industry, especially textiles, was undermined by unprecedented foreign competition. Although Ottoman officials established an industrial reform commission in the 1860s, they produced no significant industrial policy. So while Ottoman port cities boomed in this period, producing the first bloom of bourgeois culture, their wealth came from the profits of international trade, not from local production. The empire still relied overwhelmingly on an agricultural economy, and peasants remained as destitute as ever. And despite pockets of prosperity, the empire as a whole would sink so far into debt that it would declare bankruptcy in 1875.

It would be misguided, however, to conclude that the Tanzimat was the handmaiden of European imperialism. Older theories that it was primarily European pressure that forced the Tanzimat on the "sick man of Europe" have been substantially revised. Scholars like Shaw and Ortaylı have suggested that the main impetus for reform came from bureaucrats, most prominently Mustafa Reşid Paşa, author of the 1839 edict. They acted from alarm at internal corruption and weakness, as well as from the desire to advance their own interests and protect their rights against the power of the sultan. Hence the 1839 edict abolished the sultan's right to confiscate property, commonly practiced on bureaucrats. Disenchanted bureaucrats led a second reform movement, the YOUNG OTTOMANS, who in the 1860s and 1870s advocated liberalization and curtailment of the sultan's power. This led to a coup in 1876 that established a short-lived constitution and parliament.

European influence, while not a primary motive of reform, was nonetheless significant. French and British diplomats repeatedly contributed to drafts of the various Tanzimat reform edicts, particularly those issued in times of war, as in the 1839 expulsion of the Egyptians and in 1856, at the end of the Crimean War. And Ottoman reformers often turned to European institutions for inspiration, as in the 1864 restructuring of provincial administration, the 1868 Council of State, and the 1869 Education Law, all modeled on French institutions.

Finally, a motive for reform came from the peoples of the empire. Dissatisfaction with Ottoman military weakness and a growing perception of alternatives to the current regime promoted unrest. This included not only the often cited Balkan nationalist movements, but smaller intermittent outbreaks, like the 1860 riots in Mount Lebanon and in Damascus that grew out of economic upheaval. Religious leaders, too, organized protest, as in the 1859 KÜLELİ INCIDENT in Constantinople. And religious minorities agitated against the oppressive and often corrupt rule of their state-sponsored patriarchs, leading to reform of the millets in the 1860s. Provincial notables used the local councils established in 1840 as a forum for protest and as a vehicle for negotiating the path of reform.

In assessing the success of the Tanzimat, it is important to recognize that it was not a coherent, prefabricated plan; the Gülhane proclamation was not a blueprint. The Tanzimat took shape through efforts in Constantinople and in the provinces of Ottoman officials and notables to reconcile the many pressures on the empire. In Istanbul, the MECLİS-İ VALA, in concert with the grand vizier and sultan, had to weigh a variety of simultaneous and often conflicting interests, including military challengers like the Russians, Egyptians, and separatist movements in the Balkans; entrenched interests like those of landowners and the religious hierarchy; and the expanding aims of France and England. In the provinces, local representative councils and governors faced their own spectrum of interests to satisfy: landowners, *ulama* (Islamic clergy) who resented the new secular courts and schools, artisans hurt by European imports, and peasants who couldn't pay the new taxes.

Tanzimat goals were thus formulated and implemented through bargains made among opposing forces. Policy steered between the simultaneous aims of central control and provincial autonomy, between the ideal of a universal and equal Ottoman citizenry and reality of divisive religious social structures and nationalist particularisms, between the need to appease international challenges and the need to protect domestic interests, and between the efficacy of autocratic, top-down reform and the equally necessary participation of the public in effecting change.

In the end, the reform program succeeded most in its goal of order: reorganizing the central and provincial bureaucracy, restructuring the military, and building infrastructure for trade and transport. Less auspicious was its progress toward justice; while law codes were rationalized and venality in office reduced through improved salaries, economic inequalities increased and political participation remained minimal. The concentration of power in Constantinople lent itself to abuse. The Tanzimat period would conclude with a far more effective administrative and legal apparatus, but one that would be commandeered by an autocratic sultan, with the accession of Abdülhamit II in 1876. And in some ways, the Tanzimat was too little, too late. Efforts to strengthen the military and to integrate a population riven with religious and ethnic differences would not proceed quickly enough to avert the dismemberment of the Balkan provinces and the disastrous Russo–Turkish War of 1877/78.

The Tanzimat was, however, a bold and often impressive attempt to restructure the Ottoman polity; it simply did not have the time or opportunity by 1876 to effect significant social and economic change. Much of what the Tanzimat started, however, would bear fruit under Abdülhamit, who continued the Tanzimat's pursuit of order. And while Abdülhamit would leave behind other significant aspects of the Tanzimat, like justice and political participation, these would be taken up again with the rise of a new generation trained in the Tanzimat's schools and the 1908 constitutional revolution.

BIBLIOGRAPHY

DAVISON, RODERIC H. *Reform in the Ottoman Empire, 1856–1876.* Princeton, N.J. 1963.

DUMONT, PAUL. "La période des Tanzimat (1839–1878)." In *Histoire de l'empire Ottoman,* ed. by Robert Mantran. Paris, 1989, pp. 459–522.

LEWIS, BERNARD. *The Emergence of Modern Turkey.* New York, 1961.

OWEN, ROGER. *The Middle East in the World Economy, 1800–1914.* New York, 1981.

PAMUK, ŞEVKET. *The Ottoman Empire and European Capitalism, 1820–1913.* Cambridge, U.K. 1987.

SHAW, STANFORD J., and EZEL KURAL SHAW. *History of the Ottoman Empire and Modern Turkey,* vol. 2. Cambridge, U.K., 1977.

THOMPSON, ELIZABETH. "Ottoman Reform in the Provinces: The Damascus Advisory Council, 1844–1845." *International Journal of Middle East Studies* 25, no. 3 (August 1993).

Elizabeth Thompson

TAPLINE

See Trans-Arabian Pipeline

Taqbilt Language

Berber language as spoken in Kabylia.

Taqbilt, which also is used for a female Kabyle speaker and as a feminine adjective, is increasingly replaced by *tamazight* (meaning both Berber language and female Berber speaker).

Thomas G. Penchoen

Taqla, Bishara   [1852–1902]

Lebanese journalist and publisher.

Taqla was born in Kafar Shima, Lebanon. He was educated at the National school and the Batriyarqiyya school, both in Beirut. After completing high school, he taught at the Ayn Tura school. In 1875 he joined his brother Salim Taqla becoming a collaborator in his publishing and editing ventures. He traveled to Europe and Turkey, cultivating business for the newspaper *al-Ahram.* After the death of Salim in 1892, Bishara took over the paper; moved its offices from Alexandria to Cairo in 1898. Taqla enlarged *al-Ahram* and made it the most widely read paper in the Middle East. He also published *Sada al-Ahram* in Alexandria (not to be confused with the *Sada al-Ahram* that the brothers had published earlier). He also published a French version of the paper, *Pyramides.* He died in Lebanon.

As'ad AbuKhalil

Taqla, Philippe   [1915–   ]

Lebanese statesman.

Philippe Taqla was born into a well-established Greek Catholic family with strong Arab nationalist credentials and a long history of involvement in Lebanese politics. His father, Salim Taqla, was a minister under the French mandate between 1943 and 1945. A member of Bishara al-Khuri's Constitutional Bloc party, Philippe Taqla became a minister for the first time in 1946, the year his father died. In 1947, he was elected to parliament and held several ministerial positions between 1946 and 1952. Afterward, his opposition to President Camille Chamoun (1952–1958) kept him out of power for several years, although he was once again elected to parliament in 1957.

A member of the United National Front, a coalition of prominent anti-Chamoun leaders, he benefited when the opposition was able to deny President Chamoun a second term. Under presidents Fu'ad Chehab (1958–1964) and Charles Hilu (1964–1970), he was minister of foreign affairs in eight separate cabinets, for a total of some fifty-seven months, a record by Lebanese standards. From 1965 to 1966, he was head of the Bank of Lebanon. In 1967 he became the permanent representative of Lebanon to the United Nations and then ambassador to France from 1968 to 1971. During his public career, which spanned the three decades from 1946 to 1976, he belonged to more cabinets than any other Lebanese politician except Majid Arslan. As foreign minister during Lebanon's Chehabist experiment, he was instrumental in designing and implementing a carefully balanced foreign policy whereby he sought to reconcile a pro-Nasser orientation in regional politics with a pro-West position within the international system. From 1975 to 1976, he was a member of the Syrian-sponsored NATIONAL DIALOGUE COMMITTEE, which unsuccessfully sought to put an end to the civil war that had just broken out.

BIBLIOGRAPHY

GORIA, WADE R. *Sovereignty and Leadership in Lebanon, 1943–1976.* London, 1985.
SALAME, GHASSAN. "Is a Lebanese Foreign Policy Possible?" In *Toward a Viable Lebanon,* ed. by Halim Barakat. London, 1988.

Guilain P. Denoeux

Taqla, Salim   [1849–1892]

Lebanese journalist in Egypt.

Taqla was born in Kafar Shima, Lebanon. He was educated at the American School in Abay, which he left in 1860 for the National School in Beirut. He taught Arabic in the Batriyarqiyya School in Beirut, where the writer Nasif Yaziji was his colleague. Taqla went to Egypt during the rule of Khedive Isma'il; a poem praising the latter gained him a permit to publish a newspaper. In 1875 he began publishing *al-Ahram* weekly with his brother Bishara Taqla in Alexandria, and seven years later he was publishing *Sada al-Ahram* as a daily. His printing house was burned down in 1882 in the wake of the Urabi movement; his support for the khedive angered many Egyptians. Although he and his brother were pro-French, he believed Egypt should be separate from France and autonomous. The French intervened when the government of Egypt arrested Taqla because of an article that appeared in the paper. He died at Bayt Miri, Lebanon. Besides publishing the newspaper, he wrote poetry and an Arabic grammar, and translated European novels into Arabic.

As'ad AbuKhalil

Taqlid

Deference to the legal interpretations of an established school of law or master jurist.

Taqlid is the noun form of an Arabic verb that literally signifies the act of "placing something around the neck" of an animal or person. In an Islamic context, the term can be used in a general sense to refer to the investing of another with authority in matters of religion. In its more technical and most common usage, however, *taqlid* is sometimes translated as "imitation" or "emulation." According to

the standard conventions of Sunni jurisprudence, all Muslims—including highly qualified jurists—are obliged to render taqlid (i.e. deference) to the doctrine of their particular school of law (*madhhab*) as it has been articulated by the grand medieval masters of that school. Even the most learned contemporary Sunni jurists are expected to defer to established doctrine whenever possible, and thus to minimize the application of individual interpretative effort (*ijtihad*) aimed at formulating original legal judgments. By way of contrast, the conventions of Twelver Shi'a jurisprudence recognize, in every age, a small elite of the most learned jurists as being qualified and obliged to formulate their own interpretations of legal doctrine. These elite jurists bear the title of MARJA' AL-TAQLID (literally, "reference point for emulation"); the remaining Shi'a jurists and lay people are required to adhere to the rulings of at least one marja.

Scott Alexander

Tarbush

A round, stiff cap, usually of red cloth or felt, with a tassel attached to the top.

The tarbush is worn by Middle Eastern men with or without a turban. In Egypt, a *mutatarbish* is a man who wears a tarbush and is a member of the educated middle class. In Turkey and other parts of the Middle East, the tarbush is also known as the fez. Although it has persisted in many places as a traditional sign of piety, often replacing the turban as such a sign, it was abolished by Mustafa Kemal Atatürk as part of his westernizing reforms in Turkey.

Marilyn Higbee

Tarcan, Selim Sirri   [1874–1956]

Turkish athlete and educator.

Born in Yenişehir, Selim Sirri Tarcan attended school in Constantinople (now Istanbul). In 1908 he went to Sweden, where he studied physical education and gymnastics. He returned to Constantinople and became a teacher at the Teacher's College. Sirri was a pioneer in organizing Turkish sports, and in 1909 was the first athlete to represent the country on the international Olympics committee. He became a prominent organizer of the youth movement and was appointed by Enver Paşa in 1916 to head the General Youth Clubs Inspectorate. In 1935 he was elected to the National Assembly, where he served until 1946.

BIBLIOGRAPHY

Türk ansiklopedisi, vol. 30. Ankara, 1981.

Elizabeth Thompson

Tarhan, Abdülhak Hamit [1852–1937]

Turkish poet, diplomat, and politician.

Tarhan was born into a wealthy Istanbul family; his grandfather was physician to the sultan of the Ottoman Empire. He was privately tutored, then enrolled in a French school, and after a tour of Europe became one of the first Muslim students to enroll at Robert College (now part of Bosporus University). In 1871, he married into an aristocratic family and served in the empire's embassy in Paris. In 1878, his play *Nestren* was deemed subversive, and he was dismissed. In 1881, he was readmitted to the Ottoman foreign service and was posted abroad (in Paris, Bombay, London, and Belgium) until 1921. This was also his most active period of literary production. In 1922, he returned to Turkey, where he was soon elected to represent Istanbul in the new Turkish Grand National Assembly.

Tarhan was a major writer of the Tanzimat era. His participation in the *Servet-i Fünun* (Wealth of Sciences) movement, with its concern for technique and its valorization of art for its own sake, helped to prepare an environment for the flowering of modern literature in Turkey. The sheer extent of his output—the drama *Finten* is five hundred pages—is more remarkable than the quality of his prose, with its mixed meters and bombastic language. Tarhan is not widely read today.

BIBLIOGRAPHY

ERTOP, KONUR. "Trends and Characteristics of Contemporary Turkish Literature." In *The Transformation of Turkish Culture: The Atatürk Legacy,* ed. by Günsel Renda and C. Max Kortepeter. Princeton, N.J., 1986.
MITLER, LOUIS. *Ottoman Turkish Writers: A Bibliographical Dictionary of Significant Figures in Pre-Republican Turkish Literature.* New York, 1988.

David Waldner

Tarik

Ottoman newspaper.

Tarik (the Way) was one of four daily newspapers published in Istanbul in the 1890s, a time when the sheer volume of Young Turk agitation overwhelmed the ability of the censor to close down all offending newspapers. *Tarik* was owned and published by Filip Efendi. Like the papers *Sabah* and *Ikdam, Tarik* advocated the blending of Islam with elements of Western civilization.

BIBLIOGRAPHY

EMIN, AHMED. *The Development of Modern Turkey As Measured by Its Press.* 1914. Reprint, New York, 1968.

David Waldner

Tarikh Tolana

The Afghan Historical Society.

Founded in 1941 at the suggestion of Zahir Shah to promote the historical study of Afghanistan, Tarikh Tolana produced many publications, including the journals *Aryana* and *Afghanistan*. It is now part of the Afghan Academy of Science.

BIBLIOGRAPHY

ADAMEC, LUDWIG. *Historical Dictionary of Afghanistan.* Metuchen, N.J., 1991.

Grant Farr

Tariki, Abdullah [1919–]

Cofounder of OPEC.

Tariki's father, a Saudi camel owner, had hoped his son would follow his occupation. However, Abdullah, who showed high intelligence at a young age, was sent to Kuwait for schooling. He continued his studies in Cairo and at the University of Texas, becoming one of Saudi Arabia's first technocrats. In 1955 he was appointed head of the Saudi Directorate of Oil and Mining Affairs. In 1959 Tariki met with Juan Pablo Perez Alfonzo of Venezuela and representatives of Kuwait, Iran, and Iraq. They drew up a gentlemen's agreement to establish an oil consultative commission, defend the price structure, establish national companies, and reject the fifty-fifty principle that Western oil companies favored. This infant alliance later developed into the ORGANIZATION OF PETROLEUM EXPORTING COUNTRIES (OPEC). On September 14, 1960, after Western oil companies initiated a price cut without consulting with nationals of the oil countries, OPEC was officially formed.

Tariki was vehemently opposed to the methods the American oil companies employed when operating in Saudi Arabia. He supported President Gamal Abdel Nasser of Egypt and Arab nationalism; he thus became known to some as "the Red Shaykh." In 1962 he was fired from his position by King Faisal and replaced by

Shaykh Ahmad Zaki Yamani. From 1962 to 1976 Tariki was a consultant for petroleum-producing countries (including the revolutionary government of Libya, headed by Muammar al-Qaddafi, in 1970), a journalist, and a polemicist. He continually denounced Western oil companies and urged Arabs to seize full control over their natural resources.

BIBLIOGRAPHY

PETERSON, J. E. *Historical Dictionary of Saudi Arabia.* Metuchen, N.J., 1993.

YERGIN, DANIEL. *The Prize: The Epic Quest for Oil, Money and Power.* New York, 1991.

Les Ordeman

Tashilhit Language

Berber dialect spoken in the south of Morocco.

The Berber language as a whole is composed of three dialects: Tashilhit, used in the region of Agadir and Sous (southwest of Marrakech); Tamazight, widespread in the Middle Atlas and High Atlas mountains in the heart of Morocco; and Tarifit, spoken in the Rif, a region in the north of Morocco. *Tifinagh* is the name given to the writing of Tashilhit.

Rahma Bourqia

Tasvir-i Efkâr

Ottoman newspaper.

Tasvir-i Efkâr (Description of Ideas) was the second Tanzimat-era newspaper. It was established in 1862 by İbrahim Şinasi, one of the first journalists in the Ottoman Empire. When Şinasi fled to Paris, Recaizade Mahmud Ekrem became the editor.

This newspaper played a major role in the literary and intellectual life of the empire. After 1865, it was an organ for the dissemination of ideas for the Young Ottomans society. The four-page newspaper, which was published twice a week, was closed in July 1867.

BIBLIOGRAPHY

SHAW, STANFORD, J., and EZEL KURAL SHAW. *History of the Ottoman Empire and Modern Turkey.* Cambridge, U.K., 1977.

David Waldner

Tati

See Iranian Languages

Taurus Mountains

Major mountain chain of southern Turkey.

The Taurus chain is composed of several parallel limestone ranges rimming and reaching the Mediterranean, for about 930 miles (1,500 km), from Muğla in the west to Lake Van in the east. The summits often exceed 10,000 feet (3,000 m), the highest nonvolcanic peak being 12,323 feet (3,756 m)—the Aladağ—north of Adana. The average width of the range is 95 miles (150 km), and it forms a barrier to the Anatolian plateau but provides a valuable source of water for irrigation, forest products, and summer pasture. The most important pass is north of Tarsus, called the Cilician Gates. To the northeast is the extension of the range, called the Anti-Taurus.

BIBLIOGRAPHY

FISHER, SIDNEY N. *The Middle East.* New York, 1979.

John R. Clark

Tawfiq [1852–1892]

Ruler of Egypt, 1879–1892.

Tawfiq became ruler of Egypt following the deposition of his father, Isma'il, by the Ottoman sultan, who was under pressure from Egypt's European creditors. Tawfiq confronted challenges from two groups: Egyptian nationalists, led by Colonel Ahmad Urabi, and the British and French who were seeking to establish control over the Egyptian economy. Faced with revolt by Urabi in the spring of 1882, Tawfiq appealed to Britain and fled to Alexandria, where he remained until British forces had secured military control of the country. The British returned Tawfiq to the throne where he remained, subject to British approval, until his death.

BIBLIOGRAPHY

GOLDSCHMIDT, ARTHUR, JR. *Modern Egypt: The Formation of a Nation-State.* Boulder, Colo., 1988.

David Waldner

Tax Farming

Means of managing agrarian revenues, as well as of financing governmental programs.

Similar to the contemporary concept of privatization, tax farming is a poorly understood phenomenon in Middle Eastern history. It is often linked to the abuse of state power and debates on the institutional causes of the fall of premodern Islamic states. In essence, however, tax farming refers to any type of tax collection conducted by private individuals rather than salaried state personnel. These individuals acquire the right, often by auction, to collect a defined revenue for a specific period of time. From the Umayyads onward, Islamic states contracted out collection of taxes in proximate and more distant provinces. Tax farming allowed administrators a degree of flexibility and an opportunity to strike a compromise between the old and the new. Indeed, the earliest Islamic administrators of Egypt awarded contracts to Copts and women. Although the powers of tax farmers were contingent on the type of revenue collected, the status of taxpayers, and the degree of state oversight, Islamic governments found ways to curb abuse and default of contract by requiring financial guarantors and subdividing responsibilities. As this form of collection falls under the legal notions of contract, Islamic lawyers usually separate the discussion of tax farming from the actual fiscal responsibilities of Muslim and non-Muslim subjects in terms of alms (*zakat*), tithes (*ushr*), and poll taxes (*jizye*).

There are few comprehensive studies of tax farming during the period between the Abbasids and the Mongols, though Middle Eastern states contracted out to private agents many types of taxes, both those that were Islamically recognized and those that were not. More than an institutional or legal question, tax farming may be regarded as a window on the evolving structure of premodern Islamic states and its relation to society. Because most of the Islamic schools of law regarded conquered land of non-Muslim populations (*kharaj*) to be, effectively, state land, tax farming was utilized alongside the *iqta* or tax fief, a form of resident administration, as an important means of managing agrarian revenues. Pending further research, one may speculate that the alternation between military and privatized forms of tax collection preceding and after the thirteenth-century Mongol invasions was not only the result of corruption of institutions or abuse of office, as the private auction of tax fiefs during the later Mamluk period in Egypt suggests, but also a means of coping with the dislocation of agrarian populations, greater demand for cash revenues, and changing land-use patterns.

Although the forms of tax farming in the Middle East after the sixteenth century have similar legal bases, the practices coincide with new worldwide trends, namely the escalating costs of warfare and expanding global trade. In the Ottoman Empire, for example, tax farming before the sixteenth century had been largely limited to certain commercial revenues and tariffs, and many of the tax farmers were non-Muslims. But as participants in the "gunpowder revolution" and the battle for Europe and West Asia, the Ottomans required ever greater sources of cash to pay their infantries. Auctions of revenue contracts were a means of borrowing: They allowed the state to anticipate future tax receipts, albeit at a certain loss. Although the Ottoman state continued to administer many taxes directly, over the seventeenth century, many Muslim Ottoman officers and civilians bid for rights to collect taxes on the extensive crown and vizierial domains, tariffs, and manufacturing and tribal taxes, as well as to hold certain offices. A 1695 decree gave Muslim tax farmers the right to hold contracts for life (*malikâne mukataa*) and to pass these holdings on to male heirs. Although this extensive use of tax farming produced many problems, it also reinforced the loyalty of Muslim tax farmers, if only by dint of self-interest, to the state, which awarded and recognized these rights.

Since the French Revolution, social scientists have tended to regard fiscal decentralization as one of the ancien régime's greatest evils as did the Ottoman state planners who tried to restrict and then eliminate tax farming in the early decades of the nineteenth century. Despite good intentions, Middle Eastern reformers were frustrated by chronic fiscal shortfalls and lack of administrative staff. No such compunctions about modern statecraft burdened the French colonial regime in Algeria, however. Well into mid-century, French imperialists continued to adapt an older tax-farming system to new political and fiscal purposes.

BIBLIOGRAPHY

CUNO, KENNETH M. *The Pasha's Peasants: Land, Society, and Economy in Lower Egypt, 1740–1858.* Cambridge, U.K., 1992, pp. 19–27.
FRANTZ-MURPHY, GLADYS. "Land Tenure and Social Transformation in Early Islamic Egypt." In *Land Tenure and Social Transformation in the Middle East,* ed. by Tarif Khalidi. Beirut, 1984, pp. 131–140.
JOHANSEN, BABER. *The Islamic Law on Land Tax and Rent.* London, 1988.
MORONY, MICHAEL G. "Land Holding and Social Change: Lower al-Iraq in the Early Islamic Period." In *Land Tenure and Social Transformation in the Middle East,* ed. by Tarif Khalidi. Beirut, 1984, pp. 209–222.
SALZMANN, ARIEL. "An Ancien Régime Revisited: Privatization and Political Economy in the Eighteenth-Century Ottoman Empire." *Politics & Society* 21, no. 4 (1993): 393–423.

Ariel Salzmann

Taya, Maouiga Ould Sid Ahmed
[1943–]

President, prime minister, and secretary of defense of Mauritania.

Taya served in the Saharan war (1976–1978) as chief of military operations and garrison commander at Bir Mogkrein. He was minister of defense (1978–1979), commander of the national gendarmerie (1979–1980), minister in charge of national recovery (1979–1981), and army chief of staff (1980–1981, 1984) before becoming prime minister in 1984.

Mia Bloom

Tayyara, Sami

Syrian lawyer and politician.

Syrian-born and educated at Damascus University, Tayyara earned a doctorate of laws. He was a founding member of the Arab Socialist Action party under Akram al-Hawrani in January 1950. As a member of the Republican Front, he was appointed minister of health and public works in 1951. He resigned from this position upon orders of the party, breaking Khalid al-Azm's tenuous coalition. He was elected minister of education in June 1952.

BIBLIOGRAPHY

SEALE, PATRICK. *The Struggle for Syria: A Study of Post-War Arab Politics, 1945–1958.* London, 1958.

Charles U. Zenzie

Tchernichovsky, Saul [1875–1943]

Hebrew poet, translator, and physician.

Tchernichovsky (also Tsharnikhousky) was born in Mikhailovka, a village bordering on the Ukraine and Crimea. The most versatile of Hebrew poets, he was instrumental in the development, both in form and content, of Hebrew poetry. He published his first poem, *Ba-Halomi* (1892; In My Dream), at seventeen in the U.S. Hebrew paper *Ha-Pisgah.* His first book of poetry, *Hezyonot U-Manginot* (1898; Visions and Melodies), is romantic in style and deals with love and nature. From 1899 to 1906, he studied medicine in Heidelberg and Lausanne. During this period he wrote the first of his "Greek" poems—an indictment of Judaism's weakness vis-à-vis the vitality of Greek culture. The most powerful of these poems is *Lenokhah Pesel Apollo* (In the Presence of Apollo's Statue). In 1906 he returned to Russia, and until World War I, he held various positions as a doctor.

The turbulent period in Russia following the war is described in his collection *Sonnetot Krim* (Crimean Sonnets). His *Lashemesh* (To the Sun), a series of sonnets written beginning in 1919, is in stark contrast to the surrounding darkness. In 1922 he left Russia but, failing to reach Palestine, he settled in Berlin where he translated such classical writers as Goethe, Molière, Shakespeare, and Homer. In 1929 he began to publish a ten-volume jubilee edition of his poetry, short stories, plays, and translations.

In 1931, at the invitation of Dr. A. M. Masie's family, Tchernichovsky arrived in Palestine to complete and edit a medical dictionary begun by the deceased doctor. The result was a trilingual work in Latin, English, and Hebrew, *Sefer Ha-Munahim Li-Refuah U-Lemadaei Ha-Tev'a* (1934, A Book of Terminologies in Medicine and the Natural Sciences). Tchernichovsky first resided in Tel Aviv and then moved to Jerusalem, where he wrote his final works of poetry. In 1937 he published *Kol Shirei Shaul Tchernichovsky* (The Poems of Saul Tchernichovsky). In 1942 the Tel Aviv municipality established a prize in his name for translations of classics and world classical literature with Tchernichovsky as its first recipient. Once in Palestine, his poems became strongly nationalistic, and in the resettlement of Eretz Yisrael, he saw the redemption and rejuvenation of pre-exilic Judaism. He expressed all these sentiments in ballad form, such as in *Amma Dedhahaba* (1943; The Golden People). Tchernichovsky died after a long illness and was buried in Tel Aviv's old cemetery.

Ann Kahn

Tea

A drink for social occasions and after meals.

In the Middle East, tea is a popular drink brewed with the leaves and water in a kettle (tea bags are less common). Hot tea is strained into small glasses, often set in decorative metal holders, and served with various additions depending on region and personal taste. These include sugar, honey, lemon, apple flavoring, and mint. (Mint tea is also a very popular digestive drink; it is made solely from mint leaves of the genus *Mentha,* which grow throughout the Mediterranean region and Eurasia.)

Tea is imported to the Middle East from the Asian tea plantations of China, Japan, India, Sri Lanka, and islands of the East Indies. It is also cultivated along Iran's Caspian coast. Originally it came into the region by way of ancient caravan routes along the Silk Road (from China to Persia to the Black Sea and Constantinople) or ship routes into the Arabian Sea, the Indian Ocean, and the South China Sea.

BIBLIOGRAPHY

HARTEL, H., et al. *Along the Ancient Silk Routes*. London, 1982.

Clifford A. Wright

Tebu Tribe

Group of black Africans of unknown origin centered in the Tibesti mountains of the Sahara.

The Tebu are located in both southern Libya and northern Chad. Their language is part of the Nilo-Saharan family. The Tebu are Muslims, their form of Islam strongly influenced by the Libyan Sanusi movement of the nineteenth century. Their economy is a combination of pastoralism, farming, and date cultivation.

BIBLIOGRAPHY

Libya: A Country Study, 4th ed. Washington, D.C., 1989.

Stuart J. Borsch

Technion-Israel Institute of Technology

Israeli university.

The Technion-Israel Institute of Technology, located in Haifa, was founded because of the lack of opportunities for technical studies for Jews in places such as Russia. This void meant that Jews were excluded from technical professions and pushed into urban commercial occupations. While the cornerstone was laid in 1912, World War I delayed the opening. The first classes were held in 1924. Hebrew became the language of instruction only after a long "language conflict" over whether German or Hebrew should be used.

There are faculties and departments in aeronautical engineering, agricultural engineering, architecture and town planning, chemical engineering, chemistry, civil engineering, electrical engineering, food and biotechnology, general studies, industrial and management engineering, materials engineering, mathematics, mechanical engineering, mechanics, nuclear sciences, physics, and teacher training. The student population in 1992/93 was 10,600.

Miriam Simon

Technology

See Science and Technology

Tehiya

Israeli political party founded in 1979 to oppose the surrender of land as provided by the Camp David Accords.

Tehiya, a radical right-wing party, won three seats in the Knesset of 1981 and five in 1984. It did not join the 1984 National Unity Government in protest of the latter's policy limiting new settlements. In the 1988 election, Tehiya fell back to three seats, and it failed to win any in 1992. Tehiya included among its main successes the 1980 Jerusalem Law and the extension of Israeli law to the Golan Heights.

BIBLIOGRAPHY

ROLEF, SUSAN, ed. *Political Dictionary of the State of Israel*. New York, 1993.

Walter F. Weiker

Tehran

Capital of Persia from 1788 to 1935 and, since then, capital of Iran.

First mentioned by the twelfth-century traveler Yaqut, by the fourteenth and fifteenth centuries Tehran was described as a town of some importance. In the sixteenth and seventeenth centuries, it was favored by the Safavid monarchs as a temporary residence. Agha Mohammad Shah Qajar, founder of the Qajar dynasty (1796), chose it as his capital, mainly because of its proximity to the north, where his tribal followers lived.

Improvements began slowly with little change during the life of Agha Mohammad. During the reign (1797–1834) of his successor, Fath Ali Shah Qajar, new buildings were constructed, but still the city remained small and insignificant, encircled by the old walls built by the Safavids, with four gates, a moat, and a population estimated at about 50,000 in 1801.

The first expansion dates from the reign (1848–1896) of Naser al-Din Shah, the third Qajar monarch, but the first to travel to Europe; he tried to emulate some of what he had seen. The old walls were pulled down, plans for an octagonal wall on a French model were followed, and the city now had twelve gates. New grounds were added to the city compound, as well as large boulevards and imposing public and private buildings, designed with many European features. The city had a small railway leading to a place of pilgrimage in the south, and the summer resorts in the Alborz mountains in the north were developed, which became popular with richer Tehranis. In 1852, a first census and a count of all the buildings were made, which show how small the city still was—it had only 12,772 buildings, 8,697 houses, and 4,220 shops. The second census, prepared in 1869, gave the population as 150,000.

The second phase of the development of Tehran dates to the reign (1925–1941) of Reza Shah Pahlavi, founder of the Pahlavi dynasty (1925–1979). The city was expanded outside the walls of the older city, especially to the north and the northwest. A notable feature was the neoclassical-style buildings, designed mainly by European architects, especially exiled White Russians fleeing the Russian Revolution but also Iranians who had studied abroad. Houses began to be built facing outward to the street instead of inward to the courtyard, and streets were planned for the passage of motorcars. The old ornate gates, a special feature of old Tehran, were pulled down, as were many buildings of the Qajar dynasty period.

The third phase of the development of Tehran dates to the early 1950s, when a new generation of Iranian architects and technocrats, who had studied in American universities, returned to erase many of the old remaining features of the city. Tehran began to be expanded drastically, because of the petroleum industry and the oil boom of the 1960s and early 1970s. In the 1990s, the population was estimated at nearly 10 million, and the city displays all the negative features of a major metropolis.

BIBLIOGRAPHY

BAHRAMBEYGI, H. *Tehran: An Urban Analysis.* Tehran, 1977.

BEMONT, F. *Les villes de l'Iran,* 2 vols. Paris, 1969.

ETTEHADIEH, MANSOUREH. "Patterns in Urban Development: The Growth of Tehran, 1852–1903." In *Qajar Iran: Political, Social and Cultural Change, 1800–1925,* ed. by C. E. Bosworth and C. Hillenbrand. Edinburgh, 1983.

Mansoureh Ettehadieh

Tehran University

The first university in Iran, founded in 1935.

Modern higher education began in Persia in 1851, with the founding of the Dar al-Fonun by Amir Kabir, but by the early twentieth century, it had declined. In 1900, the School of Politics was founded; it was followed in 1920 by six other colleges, those of medicine, teacher training, law, agriculture, commerce, and veterinary medicine.

In 1935, the Majles (national assembly) passed a law to found the University of Tehran. Originally, it had six faculties, those of law, medicine, literature,

science, theology, and technology. A printing press and a central library were added. The university has developed and expanded in every field.

In 1943, it became independent of the ministry of education and a board of directors was organized. Elected by the faculty, the new governing body also elected the dean. This independence was undermined, however, when the election of the dean became a formality, since it had to be approved by the shah. Later the shah began to make appointments from among politicians instead of academics, further undermining the university's academic integrity.

The University of Tehran has had another political role; it became the nurturing ground for all the opposition movements against the shah's regime, including the Iranian Revolution of 1979.

The 1979 revolution and the Iran–Iraq War caused a temporary recession in the development of the University. But since peace has been established, it has continued to develop and expand. Several new faculties have been added, and in the early 1990s, the annual enrollment was about twenty-seven thousand students. The administration of the university is still based on the pattern established during the previous regime.

Many new universities have been founded in Tehran as well as in the rest of Iran, but Tehran University enjoys a privileged status gained from more than fifty years of existence.

BIBLIOGRAPHY

MAHBUBI ARDAKANI, M. *Tarikh-e tahavvol-e daneshgah-e Tehran, va mo'assesat-e ali-ye amuzeshi-ye Iran dar asr-e Pahlavi* (The History of the Development of the University of Tehran and Institutions of Higher Learning in the Reign of the Pahlavis). Tehran, 1970.

Mansoureh Ettehadieh

Tek, Vedat   [1873–1942]

Turkish architect.

Tek was born in Istanbul to a family of Ottoman aristocrats. His father was Sinan Paşa, one of the grand viziers of the Ottoman Empire; his mother was Leyla Hanım, a well-known poet and composer. He received his degree in civil engineering at the Ecole Centrale, and his degree in architecture at the Ecole Nationale des Beaux-Arts, both in Paris. Tek returned to Istanbul in 1897 and was appointed chief municipal architect in 1899. In 1908 Sultan Mehmet V Reşat appointed him chief imperial architect. After Turkey was proclaimed a republic in 1923, Tek led the National Architecture movement, which used elements of traditional Ottoman architecture, such as domes and arches, in modern architecture. His eclectic designs include the main post office building in downtown Istanbul, the ferry landing at Haydarpasha, and various residential and public buildings. He died in Istanbul.

BIBLIOGRAPHY

Büyük larousse sözlük ve ansiklopedisi, vol. 22. Istanbul, 1993.

METIN SOZEN-METE TAPAN. *Fifty Years of Turkish Architecture.* Istanbul, 1973.

Niyazi Dalyanci

Tekin Alp   [1883–1961]

Turkish intellectual.

Born Moiz Kohen in Serez, Tekin Alp became a lawyer in Salonika before joining the Law Faculty in Constantinople (now Istanbul) shortly before World War I. Associated with Turkish nationalists like Ziya Gökalp, he advanced a philosophy of social and economic revolution based on French solidarity and German ideas of a nationalist economy, contributing to the ideologies that would form KEMALISM in the early years of the republic. He published several books and journals, such as the *Iktisadiyat Mecmuası* (Economics Journal), and with Gökalp, *Yeni Mecmua* (New Journal).

Elizabeth Thompson

Tekke

Local headquarters for Sufi orders.

Tekke is the Turkish word for the local meeting and living center of a Sufi fraternity. The Persian equivalent, *khangah*, is commonly used in most non-Turkic contexts, while *zawiya* (Arabic) functions as a distinctively North African synonym.

The late tenth and eleventh centuries saw a rise in the popularity of Sufi teachings and charismatic leaders, as well as the concurrent evolution of various Sufi organizations or "fraternities." As they expanded, these fraternities began to establish special living quarters for their members, as well as space for the various ritual, scholarly, and social service activities conducted by the local chapters of what gradually grew into international Sufi orders. In different contexts, either the state or private citizens endowed a vast network of tekke and khangah complexes designed to serve as regional headquarters for the fraternities. Many of these were composed of residence cells, a large kitchen-refectory for members and guests, a Qur'an school for local youth, a library for advanced study, a tomb-shrine of a deceased spiritual master, and a mosque. Partly because the money used to endow tekkes and khangahs was often invested in local business and agriculture, a number of them throughout the late medieval and early modern Muslim world (c. 1200–1900) functioned as important economic, cultural, and political centers. In fact in some regions—particularly southern Asia, western North Africa, and the Balkans—tekkes and khangahs played a role in the Islamization of local peoples and cultures. Although the institution of the tekke generally flourished under Ottoman patronage, the stridently secularist vision of Mustafa Kemal Atatürk and his regime led to the 1925 closing of all the great Anatolian tekkes—including that of the Mevlevi Brotherhood (the famed "whirling dervishes") in Konya—and the subsequent abolishment of nearly all institutional Sufi activity in the new Turkish republic.

BIBLIOGRAPHY

TRIMINGHAM, J. S. *The Sufi Orders of Islam.* Oxford, 1973.

Scott Alexander

Tel Aviv

Coastal city founded in Ottoman Palestine in 1909; capital of Israel, 1948–1950.

Tel Aviv is a sprawling metropolis surrounded by suburbs; it was the first city to be established by Jews in the modern era. As numerous Jewish settlers arrived in Palestine in the late nineteenth century,

Nahalat Binyamon, the commercial center of Tel Aviv. (Miriam Simon)

Agam Fountain. (Miriam Simon)

Diezengoff section of Tel Aviv. (Miriam Simon)

they had increasing difficulties finding accommodations at affordable prices in the overcrowded residential areas of Jerusalem and Jaffa. In both cities, Jews began to purchase land and build new suburbs.

Jaffa is adjacent to, and today part of, Tel Aviv because Ahuzat Bayit, the building society, purchased beachfront property and underwrote the construction of Tel Aviv's first sixty houses in 1909 —initially intended as a new suburb of Jaffa. Important differences between this project and other suburbs could be immediately discerned. Architects and engineers helped design the arrangement of houses and streets; individual land grants were large; all connecting roads and streets were paved; and running water was supplied to each house. Ahuzat Bayit became the most spacious and comfortable suburb in all Palestine. The building society changed the name to Tel Aviv in 1910, marking both a biblical text (Ezekiel 3:15) where the name appears and mention in Nahum Sokolow's translation of Zionist leader Theodor Herzl's *Alteneuland* (The Old New Land). Initially planned as a residential suburb, all of Tel Aviv's

first settlers worked in Jaffa. Many of Tel Aviv's founders had private capital; they owned businesses and worked in the free professions. Jewish engineers and contractors built the city's first houses with supplies furnished by Jewish factories. Symbol of the New Yishuv (Jewish community), Tel Aviv's relatively rapid expansion paused during World War I, but resumed and intensified during the British mandate (1923–1948).

Although Zionism stressed agricultural settlement, and donated funds subsidized the cost of collective and communal settlements, most immigrants chose to live in cities and many selected Tel Aviv. By 1935, the population had grown from 2,000 to

Israeli independence day celebration in Tel Aviv. (D.W. Lockhard)

Tel Aviv beach on the Mediterranean. (Mia Bloom)

120,000 and Tel Aviv became the political, economic, and cultural center of the Jewish National Home. Factories and businesses stood alongside the Histadrut (Jewish Labor Federation) and military headquarters. Publishing firms, major newspapers, several dance and theater companies, the symphony, and an important museum were founded. Transport and roads radiated out to other cities and the countryside.

In May 1948, David Ben-Gurion proclaimed the independence of the State of Israel at a meeting held in the Tel Aviv Museum. In 1950, the commercial port city of Jaffa was incorporated with Tel Aviv, forming the twin city of Tel Aviv-Jaffa. Tel Aviv-Jaffa has benefited from Israel's rapid economic growth, today numbering more than 350,000 residents. The Histadrut headquarters no longer dominates the skyline or the city's economy. Art, music, and drama flourish in galleries and theaters, and there is an impressive array of shops, cabarets, and restaurants (both kosher and nonkosher). Much of Tel Aviv's cosmopolitan core now remains open on the Jewish Sabbath, presenting an urban profile that differs in scale and tone from that projected by Jerusalem.

BIBLIOGRAPHY

KARK, RUTH. *Jaffa: A City in Evolution, 1799–1917.* Jerusalem, 1990.

KATZ, YOSSI. "Ideology and Urban Development: Zionism and the Origins of Tel Aviv, 1906–1914." *Journal of Historical Geography* 12 (1986): 402–424.

ORNI, EFRAIM, and ELISHA EFRAT. *Geography in Israel.* Jerusalem, 1966.

Donna Robinson Divine

Tel Aviv Stock Exchange

The only recognized market for shares and bonds in Israel.

The Tel Aviv Stock Exchange (TASE) was founded as a limited company in 1953. In 1992 TASE had twenty-five members, thirteen of whom were banks (including the Bank of Israel) and twelve non-bank members. Turnover in 1992 came to 75.3 billion shekels, and the total value of the market, at the end of that year, was 166.6 billion shekels, of which 81.9 billion were shares. In 1992, 396 companies had their shares traded on the exchange, compared with 306 in 1991. The market is dominated by a small number of traders and shareholders. The shares of the largest twenty companies accounted for 53 percent of the total value of shares quoted. The 5 largest banks accounted for 60.8 percent of turnover.

The real value of shares, as measured by the general share index rose by 75.2 percent in 1992, following a 37.1 percent increase in 1991 and a 1.5 percent fall in 1990.

Paul Rivlin

Tel Aviv University

Israeli university.

In 1953 the city of Tel Aviv founded the university to meet the higher education needs of the populous, developing area.

There are programs in the arts and sciences within the nine faculties of engineering, exact sciences, humanities, law, life sciences, management, medicine, social sciences, and visual and performing arts. In 1993 the student population was approximately twenty-three thousand.

Miriam Simon

Telegraph

See Communication

Television

See Radio and Television

Tel Hai

Pioneer Jewish settlement in Palestine that became a national symbol.

A Jewish settlement founded in 1918 in Galilee, on the northern frontier of Palestine, became a national symbol of the determination of Zionists to hold on to settlements at all costs. After the British gave up responsibility for Syria and Lebanon at the end of World War I, and before the French mandate began, a hiatus in authority led to irregular warfare that endangered Jewish settlements in the undefined upper Galilee northern border area. Many Zionist leaders, among them Vladimir Ze'ev Jabotinsky, advised the small number of settlers at Tel Hai to withdraw because a reasonable defense could not be mounted. They remained, and six Jews died in the 1920 final attack, among them the military hero Yosef Trumpeldor, who had been sent to organize their defense. Since that battle, Tel Hai has been associated with the premise that Jewish national life in Palestine would require personal sacrifice.

BIBLIOGRAPHY

ZERUBAVEL, YAEL. "New Beginning, Old Past: The Collective Memory of Pioneering in Israeli Culture." In *New Perspectives on Israeli History,* ed. by Laurence J. Silberstein. New York, 1991.

Donna Robinson Divine

Tell

A mound with archeological remains; also a geographical region of North Africa.

The term *tell* (hill) was adopted by Europeans and came into English in 1864. From the concept of hill, came the concept of mound—a hill of the remains of successive human settlements that now yield archeological information about the history and prehistory of the Middle East—for example, Tell Arpachiya in Iraq (ancient Assyrian city, near Nineveh), or Tell Asmar in Iraq (ancient Eshnunna, where Sumerian artifacts indicate the presence of the Sumerians of c. 3000–2350 B.C.E.).

The Tell is also a geographical region of North Africa, stretching eastward along and near the coast from the Moroccan border to the Gulf of Tunis and Cape Bon. It consists of several series of valleys and mountain ranges; it is bisected in eastern Algeria and all of Tunisia by the Mejerda river. As an extension of the Atlas mountains, it is often called the Tell Atlas region. In Algeria, it contains the bulk of the population and the major urban centers; in Tunisia, it contains the best agricultural lands.

BIBLIOGRAPHY

Algeria: A Country Survey. Washington, D.C., 1986.
Tunisia: A Country Survey. Washington, D.C., 1988.

Matthew S. Gordon

Temple, Henry John   [1784–1865]

British statesman, diplomat, and prime minister whose aggressive policies in the Middle East curtailed Ottoman power in the mid-nineteenth century.

Henry John Temple was born at Westminster and died at Brocket Hall, England. At the death of his father, April 17, 1802, he became third Viscount Palmerston at age seventeen. Although his family had been devoted Whigs since the Glorious Revolution of 1688, Palmerston found it expedient to become a Tory when he first entered politics in 1806. In the era of the French Revolution and the Napoleonic Wars, English political life had become conservative. As the viscountcy was an Irish peerage and he was not seated in the House of Lords, Palmerston began his unbroken fifty-nine years in the House of Commons.

During his first twenty years in Commons, he did a competent job as secretary at war, but he held no cabinet rank. He was dismissed by contemporaries as brilliant but unambitious. He delayed matrimony until 1839, marrying the widow of Lord Cowper, Emily, née Lamb, sister of Prime Minister Lord Melbourne.

In 1828 he had first attained cabinet rank during the prime ministership of that arch-Tory, the Duke of Wellington. Following a quarrel with the Iron Duke in 1830, Palmerston returned to the Whigs. The Liberal party, which absorbed the Whigs in 1832, claimed his loyalty for the rest of his life.

In his distinguished career, Lord Palmerston was foreign secretary 1830–1841 and 1846–1852. He was prime minister 1855–1858 and 1859–1865. Before his death, he had become the prototype of John Bull, styled "the most English Minister."

His relationship to Queen Victoria was a stormy one, leading her to describe him as "that terrible old man." Certainly, when confronted by royal disapproval of his aggressive foreign policy, he did not hesitate to express his personal opinions in private letters, sent on his own stationery, to ambassadors abroad. Bypassing the necessity of winning royal assent to every dispatch going out of the foreign office may have been one of the more obvious expressions of Palmerston's Whig resistance to royal authority.

He had the happy fortune of living in that era of "Splendid Isolation" when Britain, secure in her island fortress, guarded by the greatest navy in the world, could remain clear of foreign alliances. Britain could afford to remain aloof until it was plain that there was a clear danger to British control of the sea, freedom of trade, or significant strategic bases.

The high points of Palmerstonian diplomacy centered on the creation of the Kingdom of Belgium, the colorful business of finding politically suitable husbands for the queens of Spain and Portugal, his conclusion of the Opium Wars with China, the Mexican expedition of 1862, the United States Civil War, warm encouragement given to Italian unification, and constant efforts to coordinate his policy with Napoléon III, precluding any chance of a renewal of the Napoleonic Wars remembered from his youth.

In the Middle East, Palmerston was equally aggressive. When Muhammad Ali, viceroy of Egypt, attempted to seize control of the entire eastern Mediterranean coast, renouncing his fealty to the Ottoman sultan, Palmerston risked war with France (1839–1841). The viceroy and his son Ibrahim Pasha had been supported by France as they concentrated Egyptian troops in Syria. In the end, the French failed to support their client. Britain bombarded Beirut and Acre, landed troops there, and gave a series of graded ultimatums to Muhammad Ali, offering him greater rewards for immediate retreat. The Egyptians, harboring false expectations of French aid, hesitated too long. The London Conference of 1840 (and its follow-up held in 1841), inspired by Palmerston, ended by depriving Muhammad Ali of Syria, Lebanon, Palestine, and the Sinai desert, leaving him only the consolatory title Hereditary Viceroy of Egypt. At those conferences, all the great powers supported Palmerston by declaring that warships, except for small vessels in diplomatic service, were barred from passing the Straits of the Bosporus and Dardanelles while the Ottoman Empire was at peace. Even France supported the London Conference of 1841.

In 1850, Palmerston risked losing office when he sent the navy to bombard Piraeus after the Greek government had been desultory in paying damages to a British subject whose property had been destroyed in a riot. He emerged enjoying the confidence of the Parliament, stronger and more popular than ever.

Even before Muhammad Ali's retreat from Syria, Palmerston had succeeded in persuading the Ottomans to allow foreign consuls to be stationed in Jerusalem and to allow foreign nationals to reside permanently in the holy city—something not previously tolerated. William Tanner Young, who opened the British consulate in 1838, had full capitulatory rights, including powers of life and death to judge British subjects in Ottoman Jerusalem that were under British law.

When Anthony Ashley Cooper, seventh earl of Shaftesbury, married Lady Palmerston's daughter by her first marriage, Palmerston found himself under personal pressure to support his stepson-in-law's evangelical Christianity. This chiefly meant giving aggressive support to English and German Protestant missions in Palestine. Jews were the largest single group at whom missionary efforts were directed. It was illegal in Turkey to convert Muslims to Christianity. Thus, by 1847, Britain was prepared to extend consular protection to Russian and other stateless Jews whose visas had expired. For a brief period, Palmerston contemplated creating a Jewish commonwealth in Palestine, under British protection, but under Ottoman suzerainty. Even after the abandonment of that idea as premature, Palmerston continued to encourage Consul James Finn in Jerusalem to grant blanket protection not only to Jews without valid passports but to such native Ottoman subjects as Druze, Samaritans, and Armenians. He

saw no contradiction between the acquisition of willing protégés and the primary British goal of saving the Ottoman Empire from partition at the hands of the French or Russians. In the Middle East, France had been the protector of Roman Catholics and Russia had been the protector of Orthodox Christianity. If England were to become the protector of Palestinian protégés, Palmerston merely regarded it as an evening of the contest.

As it happened, Palmerston was out of office in 1853, at the moment when Britain, France, and Russia blundered into the Crimean War. He did become prime minister in 1855, however, in time to participate in the negotiation of the Treaty of Paris (1857), a settlement that ensured the total removal of all fortifications and warships from the Black Sea.

Throughout his career, Palmerston did everything possible to prevent France from sponsoring the construction of a canal at Suez. He feared that it would become still another source of conflict. He did not live to see its completion—and certainly could not have predicted that by 1874 Britain would control that waterway.

By July 1860, Palmerston was sufficiently comfortable with Napoléon III that Britain became a party to a treaty, negotiated at Paris, permitting France to send 6,000 troops to Lebanon to end the endemic strife there between the religious sects of that country.

Palmerston died in office, two days short of his eighty-first birthday.

BIBLIOGRAPHY

BELL, HERBERT C. F. *Lord Palmerston*, 2 vols. Hamden, Conn., 1966.
CONWELL, BRIAN. *Regina v. Palmerston: The Correspondence between Queen Victoria and Her Foreign and Prime Minister, 1837–1865*. London, 1962.
SOUTHGATE, DONALD. *"The Most English Minister": The Policies and Politics of Palmerston*. New York, 1966.
WEBSTER, CHARLES. *The Foreign Policy of Palmerston, 1830–1841: Britain, the Liberal Movement, and the Eastern Question*, 2 vols. New York, 1969.

Arnold Blumberg

Temple Mount and Haram al-Sharif

Site of Solomon's temple in the Old City of Jerusalem and current site of numerous Jewish, Christian, and Islamic shrines.

Temple Mount in Jerusalem was expanded by Herod the Great (ruled 40–4 B.C.E.); it is known to Muslims

The Dome of the Rock with al-Aqsa mosque in the background. (Mia Bloom)

as al-Haram al-Sharif and has dozens of structures on it from various periods. Most notable is the Dome of the Rock—a sanctuary located over the ancient Jewish Temple of Solomon (founded 970 B.C.E.; destroyed by the Babylonians in 586 B.C.E.; the Second Temple rebuilt under Herod the Great during the Roman Empire, of which only the Western [Wailing] Wall still stands as a sacred Jewish site). The rock is supposedly the spot where Abraham attempted to sacrifice his son to God; in Islamic belief, it is the site where Muhammad ascended to heaven during his famous night journey. Al-Aqsa mosque is also located on the mount.

The mount is surrounded by a wall, that dates to Herod's time. Political and religious tensions have exploded into violence on the mount many times during the Arab–Israel conflict; during the 1967 Arab–Israel War, the Old City of Jerusalem and the Temple Mount were occupied and integrated with the Israeli sector.

BIBLIOGRAPHY

PETERS, F. E. *Jerusalem.* Princeton, N.J., 1985.

Benjamin Joseph

Templer, Gerald   [1898–1979]

British general.

Chief of Britain's general staff, General Sir Gerald Templer arrived in Jordan in December 1955 for discussions with the government on significantly increasing Britain's subsidy to Jordan in return for Jordan joining the BAGHDAD PACT. Nationalist feelings in Jordan, however, prevented the government from joining the pact.

BIBLIOGRAPHY

ABIDI, AQIL HYDER HASAN. *Jordan, A Political Study, 1948–1957.* New York, 1965.
EL-EDROOS, SYED ALI. *The Hashemite Arab Army, 1908–1979: An Appreciation and Analysis of Military Operations.* Amman, 1980.

Abla M. Amawi

Templers

German evangelical settlers in Palestine in the late nineteenth century.

The Temple Society (Tempelgesellschaft) was founded in the mid-nineteenth century in the Kingdom of Würtemberg. Pietistic Evangelicals, the Templers criticized the church and decided at first to settle and found colonies and, later, to improve the land in Palestine as they awaited the imminent Kingdom of Heaven. They brought modern European methods of agriculture, established the carriage trade from Jaffa to Jerusalem, exported wine, and established settlements in Jaffa, Haifa, Sarone (part of modern Tel Aviv), Jerusalem, Wilhelma, Galilen Bethlehem, and Waldheim. Individuals settled in Jerusalem and founded a German colony there that, although denied official support by the German government, numbered some twelve hundred people by 1914.

Deported as enemy aliens by the British from 1917 to 1918, as German nationals they kept a low profile during the Palestine mandate after they were permitted to return. Their religious fervor had decreased by the third generation, and, as Germans, many were receptive to National Socialism, even though there was no official advocacy of support for the Nazi party. Many sympathetic members were allowed to join the party; they also enlisted their children in Nazi Youth and disseminated Nazi propaganda.

With the outbreak of World War II, there were approximately fifteen hundred Germans of Templer origin who were interned, and afterward they were repatriated to Germany in exchange for Palestinians who had fallen into German hands. Some were deported to Australia. In 1948, their property (later to be taken into account during the reparations negotiations) was taken over by the Israeli government.

BIBLIOGRAPHY

CARMEL, ALEX. "The German Settlers in Palestine and Their Relations with the Local Arab Population and the Jewish Community, 1868–1918." In *Studies on Palestine during the Ottoman Empire,* ed. by Moshe Ma'oz. Jerusalem, 1975.

THALMANN, NAFTALI. "Introducing Modern Agriculture into Nineteenth Century Palestine: The German Templers." In *The Land That Became Israel: Studies in Historical Geography,* ed. by Ruth Kark. Jerusalem, 1990.

Reeva S. Simon

Tepeyran, Ebubekir Hazım   [1864–1947]

Ottoman Turkish novelist.

Ebubekir Hazım Tepeyran was born and educated in Niğde. A career civil servant, he was also a member of parliament in the republican period. His only novel, *Küçük Paşa,* is notable for its depiction of village life. Tepeyran also published poetry in Turkish and French. His memoirs were published in 1947.

BIBLIOGRAPHY

ÖZKIRIMLI, ATILLA. *Türk edebiyatı ansiklopedisi,* vol. 4. Istanbul, 1982.

David Waldner

Terakkı

Ottoman newspaper.

Terakkı (Progress) was a poplar name for Ottoman newspapers. One incarnation of *Terakkı* was founded by Prince Sabahettin, one of the more radical Young Turks, as an organ for disseminating ideas about reform of the empire. Between 1868 and 1870, 443 issues of *Terakkı* appeared. A second *Terakkı* was founded also in 1868 by Ali Raşit and Filip Efendi. This *Terakkı* originally was published twice a week, but with issue thirty-four began to appear five times a week. On 27 June 1868, *Terakkı* also began to publish the first Ottoman women's magazine. It appeared weekly and advocated independence and equal rights for women. *Terakkı* also spawned a humor magazine, originally named *Terakkı Eğlence;* the name was later changed to *Letaifi Asar.* A third *Terakkı* was a daily newspaper devoted to technical and scientific news that was published in 1874.

BIBLIOGRAPHY

SHAW, STANFORD, and EZEL KURAL SHAW. *History of the Ottoman Empire and Modern Turkey,* vol. 2: *Reform, Revolution, and Republic: The Rise of Modern Turkey, 1808–1975.* Cambridge, U.K., 1977.

David Waldner

Tercüman-i Ahval

Young Ottoman newspaper.

The first privately owned Turkish-language newspaper in the Ottoman Empire, *Tercüman-i Ahval* (Translator of Events) was established in 1860 by İbrahim Şinasi and Ağa Efendi. Initially a biweekly paper, within a few years, it was appearing five times a week. In addition to coverage of domestic and international news, business, and economics, it included articles on literature, culture, and politics that were designed to enlighten the common people. Relations with the government were never good, however, and *Tercüman-i Ahval* had the distinction of being the first newspaper ordered closed in May 1861. The paper resumed publication, but the last issue appeared on 11 March 1866.

BIBLIOGRAPHY

İNUĞUR, M. NURI. *Türk basınında "İz" bırakanlar.* Istanbul, 1988, pp. 4–5.

David Waldner

Tercüman-i Hakikat

Ottoman newspaper.

Tercüman-i Hakikat (Translator of the Truth) was founded in 1878 by Ahmet Midhat with the financial assistance of the sultan. Muallim Naci edited the literary section, which featured original literature and articles by Ahmad Rasim, Ahmed Cevdet, and Hüseyin Rahmi Gürpinar, as well as a regular column written by Ahmet Midhat in which he argued against liberal economic policies and in favor of synthesizing Islam and Western civilization. Midhat took care to write in a style intelligible to those with even limited education. The paper ceased publication in 1922.

BIBLIOGRAPHY

SHAW, STANFORD, and EZEL KURAL SHAW. *History of the Ottoman Empire and Modern Turkey,* vol. 2: *Reform, Revolution, and Republic: The Rise of Modern Turkey, 1808–1975.* Cambridge, U.K., 1977.

David Waldner

Ter-Petrossian, Levon   [1945–]

Armenian scholar; president of Armenia, 1991– .

Levon Ter-Petrossian was born in Aleppo, Syria. His family, which originated in Musa Dagh, emigrated to Soviet Armenia in 1946. A graduate in Oriental studies from the Department of Philology at Yerevan State University, Ter-Petrossian continued his education at the Leningrad Institute of Oriental Studies. He received his master's degree in 1971 with specializations in Armenian and Syriac philology. From 1972 to 1978, he worked as a junior scholar at the Institute of Literature of the Academy of Sciences in Armenia and from 1978 to 1985 was the academic secretary at the Matenadaran, the library of ancient manuscripts, in Yerevan. He was promoted to senior scholar at the Matenadaran in 1985 and was awarded his doctorate in philology from Leningrad University in 1987.

That same year, with the era of glasnost and perestroika in the Soviet Union declared by Mikhail Gorbachev, Armenian political activists raised the issue of unifying Armenia with the Armenian-populated enclave of Nagorno-Karabagh in Soviet Azerbaijan. By early 1988, these activities resulted in a mass movement led by a group called the KARA-BAGH Committee. Ter-Petrossian's natural skills in oratory and persuasion earned him a place on the committee, and he soon emerged as one of its most respected figures. His arrest after the December 8, 1988 earthquake in Armenia, along with the rest of the Karabagh Committee, drew the attention of human rights organizations in the West, which protested his imprisonment in Moscow. He was released on May 31, 1989, and in August of that year, he was voted a deputy to the Supreme Soviet in Armenia in an open election.

When, in November 1989, the ARMENIAN NA-TIONAL MOVEMENT (ANM) was formally organized to lead the popular movement for democracy and independence, he assumed the presidency of the ANM, and the Supreme Soviet in Armenia voted him a member of its presidium. He was returned in May 1990 to the Supreme Soviet of Armenia, and by August 1990, in a series of nationwide free elections, the ANM wrested control of the legislature in Armenia from the Communist party. On August 4, 1990, by an overwhelming majority vote, the deputies elected Ter-Petrossian president of the Armenian parliament. On August 24 the same parliament adopted a declaration on independence, charting for Armenia a new course as envisioned in the ANM program: popular democracy, free-market system, political pluralism, and a legal society guaranteeing basic freedoms. It also changed the name of the country, proclaiming it the Republic of Armenia.

Under the leadership of Ter-Petrossian, the Armenian parliament wasted no time in introducing laws on privatization. Its first, most sweeping enactment legalized private ownership of farmland and in a year's time had denationalized most of the agricultural lands in Armenia. Proceeding with the program of their August declaration, in the referendum organized for September 21, 1991, the Armenian people voted for independence, and, a month later by popular vote in an open election, Ter-Petrossian became the first president of the Republic of Armenia.

The brief years of independence have been trying. The conflict over Nagorno-Karabagh resulted in the blockade of the landlocked country by neighboring Azerbaijan. The economic impact of the blockade was devastating, especially in view of the serious reduction of energy supplies reaching Armenia. Ter-Petrossian's government has come under criticism from domestic opposition groups, but no political party has yet garnered enough support to challenge the ANM. Ter-Petrossian has earned points for conducting a foreign policy that promotes moderation and compromise in a zone rife with conflict, while his domestic policies have resulted in disaffection among sectors of the Armenian population that have been seriously affected by the energy crisis. Despite calls for halting the process of denationalization until such time as peace is established in the region, Ter-Petrossian has remained unwavering in his commitment to privatizing the economy step by step. In contrast to the other former Soviet republics and despite its economic woes, Armenia under Ter-Petrossian has proceeded furthest in the program to introduce a free-market economy. Ter-Petrossian was elected for a five-year term, which expired in 1996.

Rouben P. Adalian

Terrorism

A highly fraught term that often betrays its user's political leanings.

There is no universally agreed-upon understanding of what the word "terrorism" means in the context of the modern Middle East. Although acts of violence against civilian targets have been highly publicized since the 1960s and many people associate the region with terrorism, there is no qualitative difference between terrorism in the Middle East and that in other parts of the world. Historically, sea predation by North African Muslim principalities in the eighteenth and nineteenth centuries, called piracy by the European states except when ships from Christian countries carried out the raids, anticipated the airplane hijacking and hostage taking of the late twentieth century. The assassination of Naser al-Din Shah of Iran by a religious militant in 1896 anticipated the assassination of Anwar al-Sadat in 1981. Yet hijackings and assassinations occurred in other parts of the world as well, and there is no evidence that such violence was more frequent in the Middle East than elsewhere. Although a definition of terrorism is difficult to formulate, several distinctions can help to elucidate the phenomenon.

Terror. The Reign of Terror in the French Revolution established the modern denotation of terror as the use of frequent and seemingly capricious violence to suppress opposition to the government and the extreme fear that this violence evokes. The justification for violent acts has normally been the protection of the state from real or suspected enemies. The practice of inflicting such punishments and instilling such fear is one possible meaning of terrorism. In the Middle East, the Syrian government's annihilation of its Islamic opposition in the city of Hama in 1982, the Iranian government's campaign to exterminate the Mojahedin-e Khalq organization from 1982 onward, and the Iraqi government's destruction of the Da'wa organization fall into this category. Israel's efforts to suppress the Palestinian Intifada from 1987 onward and the efforts of the Egyptian and Algerian governments to suppress Islamic opposition groups in the 1990s less clearly fell into this category because their main instrument has been imprisonment rather than execution. The actions of one country and those of another are seen differently by different parties, however. Fear is a commonplace tool of repressive governments everywhere in the world, and denominating a particular instance of its use as terror or terrorism usually bespeaks a political motivation.

Terrorist Organizations. Another understanding of terrorism is needed for the small groups of violent militants often referred to as terrorist organizations. "Terrorism," like other isms, denotes an ideology or belief. In this respect, terrorism is the belief that a specific political goal can be attained by creating a climate of fear. The hope of the terrorist group is that dramatic violence will persuade the government—its target—to desist from certain activities or adopt policies the group favors; cause the government to institute severe repression (counterterrorism) that will alienate its citizens and cause them to sympathize with the group; or weaken and delegitimize the government because of its inability to suppress the group.

Size and military capability are factors in determining the plausibility of referring to specific groups as terrorist organizations in this sense. A large group with a well-developed military capability may adopt this ideology as part of a larger strategy of waging

guerilla war. But small groups that have no prospect of deploying other means of attaining their end are more frequently called terrorist organizations. These organizations typically choose civilian targets, such as hotels, airliners, and tourist facilities, and carry out their activities in such a fashion as to garner maximum publicity. The attack on the Israeli Olympic team in Munich in 1972 and on the Israeli town of Ma'alot the following year are examples of acts referred to as terrorist. The bombing of the U.S. embassy and marine barracks in Beirut in 1982 would also fit into this category, even though the targets were not civilian. In none of these cases was the group involved in a position to challenge Israeli or U.S. power in any other fashion. By contrast, the mass killing at Dayr Yasin in 1948, though carried out by Israeli organizations outside the regular armed forces and directed against civilians, was conducted in the course of a war that successfully secured dominion for Israel in the territories involved. The Palestine Liberation Organization, though persistently referred to by the Israeli government as terrorist until shortly before the agreement in September 1993 to start the process of reverting territory on the West Bank and in the Gaza Strip to the Palestinians, was organized as a broadly functioning national movement with a credible military force. It was not strong enough to carry out effective armed resistance against Israel, but it had a broad political and military strategy that set it apart from many smaller groups.

Terrorist organizations defined in this narrow, ideological way are typically limited in their capacity to commit violent acts. Yet the revulsion and fear generated by their acts typically give rise to a public apprehension that they constitute a powerful, secret network, capable of the most horrendous acts and endowed with unlimited resources. This apprehension is sometimes reinforced by people claiming to have expertise in the field of terrorism and is often compounded by the common belief that terrorists are psychotic sadists who act without reason or measure.

Terrorist organizations arose quite suddenly in the 1960s with the perception that a terrorist incident could gain broad news coverage not just in the print media, but in the electronic media as well. Television and instantaneous electronic communication enhanced the plausibility of terrorism as an ideology because they strongly affected the general public, prompting it to put pressure on the government. Images of hijacked airliners, sometimes filled with hostages, sitting on runways in Jordan or Uganda; of soldiers breaking from a military review to kill Sadat; or of kidnaped U.S. citizens reading propaganda statements prepared by their captors haunted the world media from the late 1960s to the 1990s. While the capacity of the media to multiply the impact of terrorist acts is universally apparent, in no part of the world has it been used to such advantage as in the Middle East. Organizations in Europe such as the Irish Republican Army, the Red Brigades, and the Baader-Meinhof Gang relied less on the news media than did the Palestinian group Black September or the Lebanese Shi'a group Hizbullah.

State Terrorism. The term "state terrorism" or "state-sponsored terrorism," like the word "terrorism," is difficult to define. Just as a group deemed terrorist by one political camp will be considered a guerilla organization or a body of freedom fighters by the opposite camp, so violent activities short of war carried out by a nation beyond its borders are sometimes thought of as terroristic, depending on the politics of the observer. The myriad Israeli raids against Palestinian and Shi'ite targets in Lebanon, whether by air or by commando team, have yielded hostages, cost lives, and induced fear. From a Palestinian viewpoint, they constitute a massive exercise in terrorism conducted by a state. From an Israeli viewpoint, they are part of a broad, legitimate counterterrorist strategy, even when they are not in response to an immediately preceding act of violence.

Many people who would exonerate Israel of the charge of state terrorism would still use the term for the support given by various governments to organizations outside their borders that engage in violent acts. Iran's support of Hizbullah and Iraq and Syria's support of Palestinian organizations are usually cited as cases in point. Yet this usage of the term is fraught with inconsistency. The United States maintains a list of terrorist states in accordance with U.S. law restricting dealings with such states, yet U.S. military and political support for religious groups fighting in Afghanistan was never termed "state terrorism" in the United States, despite the fact that after the collapse of the Soviet-supported Afghan government, some of the groups, such as that led by Golbuddin HEKMATYAR, were frequently described in the U.S. press as terrorist organizations.

Terrorism and Rhetoric. As the frequency and luridness of incidents called "terrorist" substantially increased in the Middle East from the 1960s onward, the words "terrorism," "terrorist organization," and "state terrorism" acquired definitions and connotations that served the interests of the people coining them more than they did definitional principles of consistency and precision. Since "terrorist" became a stigmatizing term comparable to "racist" or "anti-Semite," it was often used without precision for political purposes. Identifying groups or persons as "terrorists"

effectively put them outside the law and justified whatever action, including kidnapping and killing, might be taken against them. However, referring to the same groups or persons as guerillas, fighters for national independence, or fighters for the faith implied they had a higher cause and broader strategy that deserved some degree of respect. It is a characteristic of the Middle East in the post–World War II era that terminology and rhetoric play major roles in the struggle for political supremacy. Although this characteristic is sometimes attributed to how language is used by Arab leaders, all governments and politicians in or concerned about the region commonly use inflammatory words like "terrorism" for political purposes, thereby obscuring efforts at a precise, consistent definition.

BIBLIOGRAPHY

LAQUEUR, WALTER. *Terrorism.* Boston, 1977.
RUBIN, BARRY. *Terrorism and Politics.* New York, 1991.
———, ed. *Politics of Terrorism: Terror as a State and Revolutionary Strategy.* Washington, D.C., 1989.
WRIGHT, ROBIN. *Sacred Rage: The Crusade of Modern Islam.* New York, 1985.

Richard W. Bulliet

Tetuan

Provincial capital of Morocco's northern Rif region.

Tetuan, with a population of about 200,000 (1982 census), was founded (1306–1307) by the Maranid sultan to serve as a base for attacks against Ceuta. It was destroyed by Henry III of Castile in 1400, and rebuilt around 1492. Tetuan was occupied by Spain on February 6, 1860, after they had defeated the Anjar tribesmen.

As the first part of Morocco to be occupied by Europeans in two centuries, Tetuan symbolized the threat from Christian Europe. Pressure by Britain and rethinking within Spain's leadership resulted in Spain's agreement to evacuate the city (May 2, 1862) in return for a lower indemnity payment. In 1906, Spain was given responsibility for policing the port of Tetuan by a thirteen-nation conference called to maintain the balance of power between European states in Morocco, and to institute economic reforms and an open door policy. Three years later, Spain began its conquest of northern Morocco and built road links to Tetuan. It was made the capital of the Spanish protectorate in 1913, and remained so until Morocco attained independence in 1956 and Spain evacuated the area.

Bruce Maddy-Weitzman

Tevetoğlu, Fethi   [1916–1989]

Turkish nationalist politician and writer.

Born in Istanbul, Tevetoğlu earned his medical diploma in 1941 from Istanbul University. In Samsun, he published the Turkish folk magazine *Kopuz* and practiced medicine until 1947. During World War II, he was brought to trial (1944), along with other pan-Turkists who had collaborated with the Germans, but charges were dismissed.

He continued writing for nationalist and anticommunist causes while joining Turkey's new Democrat party in the 1940s but switched to the Justice party in the 1960s, serving as senator from Samsun from 1961 to 1973. In the 1970s, he joined Islamist political groups and headed several Islamic and Middle East councils. Tevetoğlu also authored several books on communism and socialism in Turkey.

BIBLIOGRAPHY

SCHICK, IRVIN C., and ERTUĞRUL AHMET TONAK, eds. *Turkey in Transition.* New York, 1987.
WEIKER, WALTER F. *The Turkish Revolution, 1960–1961.* Westport, Conn., 1963.

Elizabeth Thompson

Tevfik Fikret   [1867–1915]

Ottoman Turkish poet and editor.

Tevfik Fikret, the son of a bureaucrat in the foreign service, was born Mehmet Tevfik in Istanbul. He studied literature at the prestigious Galatasaray lycée, where his teachers included Muallim Naci and Recaizade Mahmud Ekrem. At the age of fifteen, he published his first poetry in the newspaper *Tercüman-i Hakikat* under the name Nazmi. He entered the civil service but later resigned, drawing public attention when he donated his salary to the refugee commission, saying that it was "a disgrace to accept so much money for so little work." In 1896, he became the editor of *Servet-i Fünun,* the main journal of the new literary movement. At this time, he became known as Tevfik Fikret. Under the influence of the French Parnassian school, his pre-1901 poetry emphasizes art for its own sake, preferring form and technique over content, and poetry over prose. Generally written in the *aruz* meter, Fikret's poetry draws from scenes of everyday life, as in the poems "Hasta çocuk" (The Sick Child), "Balıkçılar" (The Fishermen), and "Bir içim su" (A Drink of Water). In 1899, Fikret became professor of literature at Robert College. Following the Young Turk Revolution in 1908, he joined with Hüseyin Cahit Yalçın in establishing the newspaper *Tanin* (The Echo).

BIBLIOGRAPHY

MITLER, LOUIS. *Ottoman Turkish Writers.* New York, 1988.
SHAW, STANFORD, and EZEL KURAL SHAW. *History of the Ottoman Empire and Modern Turkey,* vol. 2: *Reform, Revolution, and Republic: The Rise of Modern Turkey, 1808–1975.* Cambridge, U.K., 1977.

David Waldner

Texaco

See Arabian American Oil Company

Textile Industry

Production of fibers, filaments, and yarns used in making woven or knitted cloth for domestic or foreign trade is widespread in the Middle East.

The oldest textile materials produced and used in the Middle East—linen and wool—go back to remote antiquity. Cotton and silk, which originated in In-

Turkish kilim weaver, 1952. (D.W. Lockhard)

Wool spinners in Mosul, Iraq, 1942. (D.W. Lockhard)

dia and China, respectively, came into the region during the Roman Empire, in the early centuries of the Christian era. By the early Middle Ages, quantities of flax (for linen) were exported to Europe, chiefly from Egypt; of raw cotton from Syria and Egypt; of silk thread from Iran, Syria, and the Bursa region (northwest Turkey); and of mohair from Turkey. Flax and silk fibers and fabrics were traded to Europe for many centuries, but flax was gradually produced in many European nations, and the silks of India, China, and Japan competed with Middle East silks and cottons as well as with cottons from the newly colonized Americas and from India. In the nineteenth century, however, the introduction of long-staple cotton made Egypt an important producer, and in the twentieth century, Egypt has been joined by Turkey, Syria, Sudan, and Israel. In the 1990s, the Middle East produces 75 percent of the world output of long-staple cotton but only about 8 percent of the total world output of all cottons.

Although the preeminence of the Middle East in the manufacture of handloomed textiles goes back to antiquity, by the late Middle Ages, European products were fine enough to be imported by the Middle East—woolens, fine silks, and linens. Until the middle of the eighteenth century, the Middle East continued to export cotton cloth and yarn to Europe, but European protective tariffs soon restricted even that trade. With the Industrial Revolution, European machine-loomed fabrics overwhelmed Middle Eastern handmade products and local markets. The number of Middle Eastern handlooms and their total output declined sharply; for example, in Bursa, output of cloth fell from 20,000 pieces in 1843 to 3,000 in 1863. In Aleppo and Damascus combined, the number of looms dropped from about 12,000 in the 1820s to some 2,500 in the 1840s. Middle Eastern weavers were able to recover by using improved looms, importing cheaper

and better European yarns, concentrating on inexpensive products, and drastically reducing wages. Handcrafted fabrics continued to form a large proportion of the textile output until after World War II. In Syria, in the 1930s, there were some 40,000 handweavers, and in Egypt in the 1940s, some 50,000. In Turkey and Iran, carpetmaking was greatly stimulated by rising foreign demand, lower freights that reduced export costs, and some foreign capital investments in the industry. Just before World War I, in 1913, Turkey exported 1,500 tons of carpets, then worth three million U.S. dollars, but the subsequent world wars devastated the industry. Persian carpet exports in 1914 were then worth five million U.S. dollars, and by the 1950s Iran's rugweaving and carpetmaking employed some 130,000 people—with exports of 5,000 tons, then worth twenty-five million U.S. dollars, the carpets accounted for 16 percent of Iran's non-oil exports.

Mills. Textile factories, or mills, were first used in the Middle East in the 1830s, in the modernizing pro-

A dye works in Fez, Morocco. (© Yto Barrada)

gram of Muhammad Ali's Egypt. The mills exported large amounts of cotton textiles, but they did not survive his death. A few small factories were also set up in Turkey in the nineteenth century, and by World War I, several textile centers had been developed in Turkey—notably in Adana, Izmir, and in the Salonica region. Egypt also had cotton-spinning mills in Alexandria and Cairo. Iran had a small spinning mill in Tehran, but other unsuccessful mills had closed. In Syria, one small mill, founded in Damascus in the 1860s, was operating, but two others, in Beirut and Antioch, had failed. Some two hundred small silk-reeling factories were set up in Lebanon, with others in Bursa, Izmir, and other silk-growing regions of Turkey. In Iran, there was a mill in Gilan.

After World War I, the textile industry wove rayon as well as cotton and wool and expanded greatly, especially after the tariff reforms. Table 1 shows the situation in the cotton industry in 1939, at the outbreak of World War II. By then, textile factories had been built in all the main towns and cities of the Middle East, and local production of cotton yarn and fabrics met 35 to 50 percent of total domestic demand within the larger countries.

During World War II, the region's textile industry expanded by about 50 percent, and the expansion continues—with several additional countries, with diversification, and with improvement in quality, especially in the finishing processes. Foreign investments have been gradually taken over, and the industry is now owned mainly by the state or local citizens. Turkey, Israel, Egypt, and Lebanon now export significant textile lots to worldwide markets. Table 2 shows the most recent figures.

TABLE 2

Middle East Textile Output in 1987

	Cotton		Wool		Silk
	Yarn[2]	Fabrics[3]	Yarn[2]	Fabrics[3]	Fabrics[3]
Egypt	251	694	19	24	5
Iran[1]	88	140	16	26	—
Israel	16	—	4	—	—
Jordan	—	2	—	—	—
Syria	39	180	2	1	—
Turkey	332	399	51	27	1
Total	726	1,415	92	78	6
World	15,091	47,360	2,223	3,484	2,248

1. 1981
2. In million metric tons
3. In million square meters

Source: United Nations. *Industrial Statistical Yearbook,* (New York, 1988).

BIBLIOGRAPHY

Food and Agricultural Organization of the United Nations. *Agricultural Statistics.* Rome, 1989.
Issawi, Charles. *An Economic History of the Middle East and North Africa.* New York, 1982.
United Nations. *Industrial Statistical Yearbook.* New York, 1988.

Charles Issawi

TABLE 1

Middle East Cotton Industry in 1939

	Spindles (thousands)	Power Looms (thousands)	Output of Yarn (thousands of metric tons)	Output of cloth (million square meters)
Egypt	250	15	24	100
Iran	188	4	—	—
Iraq	—	1	—	—
Lebanon	14	1	1	—
Palestine	12	2	1	4
Syria	10	4	1	—
Turkey	189	6	23	152
Total	663	33	50	256

Source: United Nations, *Review of Economic Conditions in the Middle East, 1951–52* (New York, 1953).

Thaalbi, Abd al-Aziz [1874–1944]

Tunisian political leader and founder of the Destour party.

Thaalbi's father was a notary whose family had emigrated to Tunis following the French occupation of Algeria in 1830. During his studies at Zaytuna University, Thaalbi became conversant with SALAFIYYA concepts. For a year following his graduation from Zaytuna in 1895, he published a religious journal called *Sabil al-Rashid* (the Proper Path). When the French authorities suspended the journal, Thaalbi left the country and traveled in Libya, Egypt, and India until 1902. Soon after his return to Tunis, he was imprisoned by a beylical tribunal for making a reformist attack on the local saints, who formed an important part of popular religious practices. In 1904, he published, in both an Arabic and a French edition, *L'Esprit Libérale du Coran* (The Liberal Spirit of the Qur'an), which criticized the religious establishment. At this time, Thaalbi established links with the Young Tunisians. He became the editor of the Arabic edition of its newspaper, *Le Tunisien,* in 1909 and participated in all of its political activities until his expulsion from Tunisia in 1912. He returned to the country at the start of World War I.

At the end of the war, Thaalbi joined a delegation of former Young Tunisians that went to Versailles to petition the Allies for a relaxation of French control. Frustrated by France's unwillingness to make concessions, Thaalbi wrote *La Tunisie Martyre* (Tunisia Martyred) in early 1920. In this book, he stressed the need for restoration of the Tunisian constitution of 1861, the creation of an elected assembly and an independent judiciary, the development of education, and the safeguarding of individual liberties. He also urged that the establishment of the protectorate had stalled Tunisian development. Thaalbi was arrested and brought back to Tunisia. Upon his release in 1921, he assumed the leadership of a group of middle-class merchants, artisans, and lower level *ulama,* many of them formerly affiliated with the Young Tunisians, that had evolved into a political party, the Destour, based on the program elaborated in *La Tunisie Martyre.*

In response to Destour demands, France introduced a series of limited reforms in 1922. Thaalbi guided Destour's rejection of these changes, arguing that they fell too far short of Tunisian requirements to merit consideration. The death in 1923 of the Tunisian ruler Nasir Bey, who had sympathized with Destour, and the growing impatience of the protectorate authorities with the party convinced Thaalbi that his political activism would not be tolerated much longer, and he fled the country in the same year.

After fourteen years of exile in Egypt, Iraq, and India, he returned in 1937, when the relative liberalism of the French Popular Front government created a more congenial atmosphere for the expression of nationalist grievances. By that time, however, the remnants of Thaalbi's Destour party had given way to the Neo-Destour, whose youthful, dynamic, and secular leaders had little use for Thaalbi or for the traditional Arab–Islamic values he stressed. Finding support among only a small segment of the population and encountering opposition from Neo-Destour militants who disrupted his public appearances, Thaalbi attempted to revive Destour but failed miserably, though the party survived in moribund form until his death in 1944.

BIBLIOGRAPHY

DABBAB, MOHAMED. *Les délégations destouriennes à Paris, ou la "question tunisienne" dans les années 1920.* Tunis, 1980.

MAHJOUBI, ALI. *Les origines du mouvement national en Tunisie, 1904–1934.* Tunis, 1982.

Kenneth J. Perkins

Thalweg Line

The principle in international law whereby the middle of a body of water is considered the boundary between nations.

In the Middle East, the thalweg principle was applied to the Shatt al-Arab between Iraq and Iran in a treaty between the two in 1975. The fall of the shah of Iran led Iraq to believe that the time was ripe to capture the Iranian side of the Shatt al-Arab, as well as the oil-rich Iranian province of Khuzistan, thus leading to the outbreak of the Iran–Iraq War in September 1980.

Julie Zuckerman

Thani Family

See under Al Thani *for specific members of the dynasty.*

Tharthar Project

Reservoir constructed in eastern Iraq to control flooding and provide irrigation.

The Wadi al-Tharthar is a vast natural depression forty-two miles (68 km) southwest of Samarra and one hundred miles (160 km) north of Baghdad between the Tigris and Euphrates rivers. The Iraqi Development Board, on the recommendation of the International Bank for Reconstruction and Development, created an enormous storage reservoir in the Wadi al-Tharthar depression to drain runoff from the Tigris and thereby protect Baghdad from flooding. Staged construction of the reservoir, the largest earthmoving project of its kind in the Middle East, began in 1952. A regulator built on the Tigris near Samarra diverted excess water into the reservoir, which was also connected by a channel with the Euphrates. By 1972, with a capacity of 110 billion cubic yards (85 billion cu. m) when filled to a height of 200 feet (60 m) above sea level, the water contained in the reservoir could be used to irrigate nearly half a million acres (200,000 ha) of land.

BIBLIOGRAPHY

SALTER, LORD. *The Development of Iraq: A Plan of Action.* London, 1955.

Albertine Jwaideh

Tharwat, Abd al-Khaliq [1873–1928]

Egyptian politician.

A graduate of the School of Law in Cairo, Tharwat was one of the first Egyptian nationalist leaders and a founder of the LIBERAL CONSTITUTIONALIST PARTY. His negotiations with Britain's high commissioner for Egypt, Edmund Allenby, led to the declaration of Egyptian independence from Britain in 1922. Tharwat supported the declaration, even though it guaranteed the maintenance of British influence in Egypt, because he believed that it made possible the drafting of a constitution and the establishment of parliamentary politics. He formed the first government following the declaration and helped to draft the post-independence constitution. Tharwat was opposed by Sultan Fu'ad, who objected to being reduced to a constitutional monarch, and by the Wafd party, which objected to the preservation of British control. Tharwat resigned as prime minister in November 1922. He formed a second ministry in April 1927, but again confronted opposition from Fu'ad—who had taken the title of king in 1922—and the Wafd. He resigned in February 1928.

BIBLIOGRAPHY

AL-SAYYID MARSOT, AFAF LUTFI. *Egypt's Liberal Experiment, 1922–1936.* Berkeley, Calif., 1977.

David Waldner

Thawb

See Dishdasha

Thawra, al- (Iraq)

Daily newspaper issued by the Ba'th party of Iraq.

Al-Thawra was preceded by a series of irregular underground party newspapers, the best known of which was *al-Ishtiraki* (the Socialist), prior to the July 1968 revolution. Between 1958 and 1968 *al-Thawra* was an independent paper with a socialist leaning. On the first days of the July 1968 revolution, *al-Thawra* was commissioned to be the mouthpiece of Gen. Abd al-Razzaq al-Nayif, an army officer and a central figure in the military junta who was later ousted by the Ba'th. Consequently, many journalists resigned from *al-Thawra* and joined *al-Jumhuriyyah,* the party organ at that time. Only in August 1968, shortly after Nayif's ouster, did *al-Thawra* become the party's daily newspaper.

Its first Ba'thi editor was Karim Shinta, a drab old-timer. In May 1969, he was replaced by a rather more capable personality with a long history in the party's underground press—Tariq Aziz. Under his editorship, the paper voiced the opinions of Saddam Hussein on several divisive issues, including the March 1970 pact with the Kurdish opposition, thus gaining Aziz a rapid promotion to the rank of minister of information in November 1974.

The Ba'th regime attached unprecedented importance to the media as a means to spread its message. The prices of all the newspapers were heavily subsidized, making them affordable to all. *al-Thawra*'s circulation in the 1970s and 1980s reached 200,000 and even 250,000 copies—an unusual number by any standard. The change, however, was in the contents. In the mid-1970s, with the victory of Saddam's line, *al-Thawra* could no longer be the stage for alternative views within the party. On orders of the ministry of information, the differences between the newspapers rapidly diminished. Since the beginning of the Iran–Iraq War in September 1980, *al-Thawra*—and the Iraqi media in general—reflected Saddam's personality cult. This included placing the president's portrait in differing shapes and sizes on the front page every day. The editors were no longer leading Ba'thi functionaries but mediocre intellectuals and drab officials of the ministry of information such as the present editor (1996), Taha al-Basri.

After the Gulf War and the ensuing embargo, *al-Thawra* suffered a severe drop in circulation, reaching a low of thirty thousand copies. The number of pages was cut from sixteen to a mere eight, due to paper shortages. In addition, the newly founded newspaper *Babil*, owned by the president's son Uday, initiated a harangue against *al-Thawra* as part of an overall critical approach toward the party. This might have influenced the readers: A recent survey carried by *Babil* showed that *al-Thawra* lost more of its readership.

Ronen Zeidel

Thawra, al- (Syria)

Syrian newspaper named after the Arabic word for revolution.

In the classical Arabic usage, the verb *thara* means to rise or to rebel, hence *thawra* as a noun means rising, rebellion, or revolution. A successful revolution usually publishes a newspaper to advocate its policies. The newspaper is very often called *al-Thawra* to emphasize and perpetuate the revolutionary character of the regime. Thus a daily newspaper called *al-Thawra* has been published in Syria since 1964 to emphasize the revolutionary nature of the Ba'th party, which came to power in 1963. Other usages of the term occur, also in a revolutionary context, as in the case of calling the dam built on the Euphrates river at the Tabaqa site in Syria al-Thawra dam, focusing attention on the dam as one of the major contributions of the Ba'th regime in Syria.

Abdul-Karim Rafeq

Theater

[This entry includes the following articles: Arab Theater; Israeli Theater; Karagöz.*]*

Arab Theater

A genre that exists in a wide variety of forms.

The premodern cultural tradition of the Middle East reveals several types of dramatic presentation, although few examples survive in text form. One is the *ta'ziya',* a passion play based on the martyrdom of the Prophet Muhammad's grandsons, al-Hasan and al-Husayn, and performed among Shi'a communities during the Islamic month of Muharram. Records also exist of performances of shadow plays (*khayal al-zill*) and puppet theater performances, usually known under the Turkish name *karagöz,* used to poke fun at officialdom in its various guises. Another type of public performance was the narration of popular collections of tales in both poetry and prose, the great sagas of heroes like the pre-Islamic poet cavalier, Antar, and Abu Zayd, champion of the Banu Hilal tribe. Given the widespread existence of such precedents, it is hardly surprising that for many modern Arab dramatists the storyteller has been a prominent Brechtian device.

If these examples represent the precedents to a popular dramatic tradition that has continued to flourish, the more elite, literary kind of drama traces its origins to the nineteenth century and to contacts with the European theatrical tradition, through educational exchanges and translations. Beginning in 1848, the Lebanese writer Marun al-Naqqash (d. 1855), mounted in his own home performances of plays based on those of Molière. Al-Naqqash also adapted tales from the famous story collection, *A Thousand and One Nights*. This process was contin-

ued in Damascus by Abu Khalil al-Qabbani (d. 1902), whose attempts to stage dramatic performances aroused the opposition of the religious establishment, a situation that provided the material for a modern play by the Syrian Sa'dallah Wannus (b. 1941). Al-Qabbani's problems became so acute in Damascus that he moved to Egypt, where artistic opportunities seemed more promising.

The Egyptian Jewish writer Ya'qub SANU (d. 1912), gathered a troupe of actors and combined his own scripts, heavily satirical of cultural stereotypes, with a generous dose of music and song to produce a series of popular productions. The repertoire of performable drama had also been expanded by the translation movement, especially Muhammad Uthman Jalal (d. 1894), who translated and Egyptianized Molière into Egyptian colloquial drama. The encouraging atmosphere that Egypt seemed to offer was also attractive to a number of Syrian troupes and writers; as a result, Egypt became the center of theatrical experimentation for many decades to come. Beginnings elsewhere in the Arab world were extremely dependent on the political situation and, very often, visits from Egypt-based troupes, such as that of Jurj Abyad. This was the case with Tunisia in 1908 and Morocco in 1923.

Accounts of theater performances at the end of the nineteenth century make clear that audiences who had been used to participating with some vigor in more popular types of public drama were bemused by the expectations of the new genre, not least because it placed women on the stage in situations that were regarded as little short of scandalous. Furthermore, if the genre was to be accepted as a contribution to the literary tradition, the issue of language had to be addressed. The colloquial language of everyday communication was not regarded as an appropriate medium for literature; on the other hand, it was difficult to expect actors to perform roles in a language that was the reserve of written literary documents—a situation that indeed encouraged some actors to indulge in considerable displays of histrionics.

It was the role of the Egyptian dramatist Tawfiq al-HAKIM (d. 1987) to address many of these problems. Returning from a period of study in France in the late 1920s, he composed a stream of dramas based on many of the great legends, stories, myths, and texts of the European and Arabic Islamic heritage: Among the most noteworthy were *Ahl al-Kahf* (The Men of the Cave, 1933), *Shahrazad* (1934), *Pygmalion* (1942), and *Al-Sultan al-Ha'ir* (1960). Many of his plays do not transfer well to the stage, leading him on many occasions to talk in terms of a "theater of ideas." During his long career, however, he undertook many experiments with drama, making use of different levels of language, as in *al-Safqa* (The Deal, 1956), and composing a number of absurdist dramas, of which *Ya Tali al-Shajara* (O Tree Climber, 1962) was the most successful.

Following the Egyptian Revolution in 1952, al-Hakim's successors were able to use the élan of the historical moment to produce what in retrospect seems the brightest moment in modern Arabic drama. Nu'man Ashur (d. 1987) wrote immensely popular dramas depicting the plight of the urban poor, for example, *al-Nas illi taht* (The Folks Downstairs, 1956), and the peasants in the countryside. Ali SALIM (b. 1936) wrote comedies that pilloried the absurdities of daily life and especially the behavior of bureaucrats. Alfred Faraj (b. 1929) produced a series of plays that made use of the tales and legends of the past to comment on the troubles of the present; the most accomplished was *Ali Janah al-Tibrizi wa-Tabi'uhu Quffa* (Ali Janah from Tibriz and His Henchman Quffa, 1968). Both Yusuf IDRIS (d. 1991) and Mikha'il Ruman (d. 1973) used their plays to explore the more sinister side of the modern state; the former's *al-Farafir* (The Farfours, 1964), a modernist nihilistic farce, was a notable success. Najib Surur (d. 1978) and Shawqi Abd al-Hakim (b. 1930s) found their inspiration in popular Arabic folktales. This thriving tradition was just one of many cultural victims of the Arab–Israel War of 1967 (also called the Six-Day War).

Elsewhere in the Arab world, the development of a tradition of modern drama has varied in chronology and scope in accordance with cultural circumstances and the nature of governmental control. Thus, in Lebanon the theater managed to operate in a relatively open social and political environment, at least until the onset of the civil war in 1975. Isam Mahfuz (b. 1939) and Roger Assaf are among its most notable practitioners. In Syria and Iraq, governmental supervision of drama has been extremely tight, but Sa'dallah Wannus, Walid IKHLASSI (b. 1935), and Yusuf al-ANI (b. 1927)—to cite just a few of the more prominent names—have managed to transcend more local issues to assume a more general significance. Theater has flourished in some of the countries of the Maghrib region, in particular, Tunisia and Morocco. In the former, Izz al-Din al-Madani (b. 1938) has written a series of plays that pursue the topic of popular revolution, including *Thawrat Sahib al-Himar* (Donkey-Owner's Revolt, 1971) and *Diwan al-Zanj* (The Zanj Collection, 1974). In Morocco, both Ahmad al-Ilj (b. 1928) and al-Tayyib al-Siddiqi (b. 1938) have made creative adaptations of works from other genres and cultures to the modern stage. Finally, we should mention Palestine where, under the watchful eye of the Israeli

armed forces, theater troupes like the Balalin and Hakawati have been producing highly experimental dramas that comment on the plight of their fellow countrymen.

BIBLIOGRAPHY

BADAWI, M. M. *Early Arabic Drama.* Cambridge, 1988.
———. *Modern Arabic Drama in Egypt.* Cambridge, 1987.
JAYYUSI, SALMA, and ROGER ALLEN, eds. *Modern Arabic Drama.* Bloomington, Ind., 1995.
AL-KHOZAI, MOHAMED A. *The Development of Early Arabic Drama, 1847–1900.* London, 1984.
LANDAU, JACOB M. *Studies in the Arab Theater and Cinema.* Philadelphia, 1969.
MANZALAOUI, MAHMOUD, ed. *Arabic Writing Today: The Drama.* Cairo, 1977.
MOREH, SHMUEL. *Live Theatre and Dramatic Literature in the Medieval Arabic World.* Edinburgh, 1992.
WAHAB, FAROUK ABDEL, ed. *Modern Egyptian Drama.* Minneapolis, Minn., 1974.

Roger Allen

Israeli Theater

A central aspect of cultural life in Israeli society.

Popular across the board, Israeli theater enjoys one of the world's highest ratios of attendance per capita. In 1993, when the country's total population over age five was 5,196,000, theater attendance reached 1,801,000 (not including special festival performances), about one-third of whom were children and young adults. The statistics are particularly impressive since certain segments of the population, such as ultraorthodox Jews and recently arrived immigrants, avoid the theater because of religious prohibitions or linguistic barriers. Because the Israeli theater performs mostly in Hebrew and offers only a few musical extravaganzas, it rarely attracts tourists and remains essentially native. Currently, Israel has about twenty regular theater companies ranging from large-scale national and municipal companies, such as Habima, Israel's national theater, the Cameri Theater of Tel Aviv, and the Haifa and Beersheba municipal theaters, to smaller, publicly owned theaters, fringe groups, children's theaters, and non-Hebrew (Arabic, Russian, and Yiddish) companies. All these companies receive financial subsidies from state or municipal authorities.

The Hebrew theater began in the late nineteenth century but actually came into being only in the 1920s. Unlike the Yiddish-language Jewish theater, Hebrew theater did not grow out of a popular folk tradition. Rather, its formation was part and parcel of the Zionist revolution, which aspired to create a new national culture in Hebrew, the recently revived language that was considered the chief instrument of the national renaissance.

The first modern Hebrew-language performance was staged in 1890 by the students of the Laemel Secondary School in Jerusalem. The play was a Hebrew translation from the Yiddish of *Zerubabel* (The Return to Zion) by Moses Leib Lilienblum. This was most probably the first theatrical production, in any language, in the history of the modern Jewish settlement in Palestine. Other schools and amateur groups followed suit, but the establishment of a professional theater remained a far-fetched dream for the next quarter century.

The first step toward the formation of a Hebrew-language art theater took place in Moscow in 1914 when Nahum Zemach organized a small group of amateurs who wished to perform in Hebrew. The group, which in 1917 named itself Habima, became affiliated with Konstantin Stanislavsky's studio. Directed by Evgeny Vakhtangov, one of the most brilliant young Russian directors of the time, Habima staged in 1924 a world-renowned production of *The Dybbuk* by S. Anski, translated into Hebrew by Hayyim Nahman BIALIK, the Hebrew poet laureate. The production, which made theater history, was done in an expressionist style that Vakhtangov called theatrical realism. It was characterized by stylized mise-en-scène, sharp visual contrast, exaggerated, often grotesque movement, masklike makeup, and a profusion of music and dance. The production became one of the gems of the modern stage and was part of Habima's repertoire until the early 1960s. Habima left Moscow in 1926 and successfully toured Europe and the United States. It first went to Palestine in 1928, and, in 1931, it settled permanently in Tel Aviv. For years, Habima was considered the exemplary Hebrew art theater. In 1968, it was officially proclaimed Israel's national public theater.

In the 1920s, while Habima was active in Europe, a new quasi-professional theater, the Hebrew Theater of Palestine, was established in Tel Aviv. Some of the actors who wished to further their theatrical training went to Berlin, where they established the TAI (Teatron Eretz Israeli), a company that specialized in modern interpretation of biblical drama. It premiered in Berlin in 1924 with a Hebrew version of *Belshazzar* by Henie Rochetand, a production enthusiastically received by Berlin critics. The TAI's return to Palestine in 1925 marked the beginning of a new era of a professional theater with highly trained actors. Other theaters followed: Ha-Ohel, a workers' theater, was established in Tel Aviv in 1925; and Ha-Kumkum, a satirical cabaret, was established in 1927 and replaced by the long-lived Ha-Matateh in 1928.

In the mid-1940s, a new generation of native Hebrew-speaking actors became dissatisfied with the theatrical pathos and Russian accent of the Habima actors. They organized in 1944, in Tel Aviv, in a group that would develop within a few years into the Cameri Theater, led by the director Josef Millo. The new sabra theater was strongly influenced by Brechtian concepts and wished to present, in native Hebrew, current material in a chamberlike atmosphere. The Cameri made history on May 31, 1948, with its production of Moshe Shamir's original Hebrew play *He Went through the Fields,* the first drama to focus on current events and present a native kibbutz sabra who fights in the War of Independence as protagonist.

In the mid-1950s, small avant-garde theaters that produced plays by modern writers such as Jean-Paul Sartre and Samuel Beckett emerged. Theater proliferated in the 1960s and 1970s. While the Hebrew theater had suffered for years from a paucity of native drama, the situation changed drastically with the emergence of a new generation of native Hebrew playwrights in the 1970s. Most notable among them were Nissim Aloni, Hanoch LEVIN, Yehoshua SOBOL, Avraham B. YEHOSHUA, and Hillel Mitelpunkt. In 1993, 48 percent of the 171 plays produced by Israeli theaters were written by native playwrights.

BIBLIOGRAPHY

ABRAMSON, GLENDA. *Modern Hebrew Drama.* New York, 1979.
KOHANSKY, MENDEL. *The Hebrew Theatre.* New York, 1969.
TAUB, MICHAEL, ed. *Modern Israeli Drama in Translation.* Portsmouth, N.H. 1993.

Edna Nahshon

Karagöz

The name of the Ottoman shadow theater and of its lead character.

An urban entertainment, Karagöz was performed privately during circumcision and other festivities and publicly in coffeehouses during Ramadan. Against minimal scenery, its colorful, two-dimensional figures (traditionally made of camel hide, and manipulated on rods from behind the screen onto which their shadows were projected) represented plants, animals, supernatural beings (such as witches and jinns), and a cross section of the Ottoman human scene. The puppeteer sang, recited poetry, and spoke the dialogue, giving the appropriate timbre and accent to the voice of each character. There was considerable improvisation, even of well-known plots, and commentary (often satirical) on the philosophy of life, human foibles, and, not infrequently, politics. Karagöz was a "man of the people": uneducated, rough and ready, frequently in financial straits, and quarreling with his wife, but always resilient. The other main character, Hacivat (Hajivat), representative of refinement, was his foil; their comic verbal clashes usually led to blows.

Nineteenth-century censorship, the development of modern theater, and changing cultural tastes dealt Karagöz a severe blow. The last great puppeteer died in 1974, and although efforts have been made to preserve the tradition, the shadow theater now barely survives—these days it is only seen on children's television programs.

[*See also:* Ortaoyunu].

BIBLIOGRAPHY

Encyclopaedia of Islam, vol. 4. Leiden, 1975.
METIN, AND. *Karagöz: Turkish Shadow Theatre.* Istanbul, 1975.

Kathleen R. F. Burrill

Thesiger, Wilfred   [1910–   ]

British explorer.

Wilfred Thesiger was born in Addis Ababa, Ethiopia, where his father served as British minister plenipotentiary. Thesiger was educated in England at Eton and Oxford. After employment in the Sudan by Britain's Political Service and the Defence Force and after military service in Ethiopia, Egypt, Libya, and Syria during World War II, he gained fame as an explorer of Rub al-Khali (the Empty Quarter) in southeastern Arabia.

BIBLIOGRAPHY

THESIGER, WILFRED. *Arabian Sands.* London, 1959.

Benjamin Braude

Thessaloniki

See Salonika

Thiers, Adolphe   [1797–1877]

French statesman.

Thiers was French foreign minister and then premier (1839–1840) during the second Muhammad Ali crisis. In spite of advice to the contrary by both Gen. Horace Sebastiani and François Guizot, Thiers sup-

ported Muhammad Ali and refused to negotiate with Lord Palmerston in the mistaken belief that England would not act against Egypt without French support. Egypt was defeated, and Thiers was forced to resign in October of 1840. He later became the first president of France's Third Republic (1871).

BIBLIOGRAPHY

AL-SAYYID MARSOT, AFAF LUTFI. *Egypt in the Reign of Muhammad Ali.* New York, 1984.

Zachary Karabell

Third International Theory

Governing philosophy of Libya's Qaddafi.

The Third International Theory comprises the utopian theoretical underpinnings of the JAMAHIRIYA, established in Libya in March 1977. Understood by its author, Libyan ruler Muammar al-Qaddafi, as an alternative to (and improvement upon) both capitalism and communism, the Third International Theory is contained in the GREEN BOOK.

Lisa Anderson

Thomas, Bertram   [1892–1950]

British explorer.

A political officer in Mesopotamia (now Iraq) during World War I, Thomas was transferred to Transjordan in 1922 as one of the British advisers to Emir Abdullah ibn Husayn. In 1924, he became the financial adviser to the sultan of Musqat. From Oman, he journeyed into the Rub al-Khali (Empty Quarter) of the southern Arabian peninsula and became famous as the first European ever to cross it. *Arabia Felix,* his account of the adventure, was published in 1932.

BIBLIOGRAPHY

BRENT, PETER. *Far Arabia.* London, 1977.

Zachary Karabell

Thrace

Southeastern part of the Balkan peninsula, shared by Greece, Bulgaria, and Turkey.

Inhabited by Thracians in ancient times (akin to Illyrians), it became a Roman province (69–79 C.E.)

and, as part of the Eastern Roman Empire, fell to the Ottoman Turks by 1453. In 1878, the northern part separated to become Eastern RUMELIA. Today, Thrace is the southern part of the ancient region, divided by the Maritsa river into Greek Western Thrace and Turkish Eastern Thrace.

Thrace was the site of the Battle of Lüleburgaz in the first Balkan War. After the second Balkan War, part went to Bulgaria. By the treaties of 1919 and 1920, nearly all Thrace went to Greece (1920–1923). European Turkey is the southeastern corner, comprising about 3 percent of Turkey's land, including the European part of Istanbul.

BIBLIOGRAPHY

SHAW, STANFORD J., and EZEL KURAL SHAW. *History of the Ottoman Empire and Modern Turkey*, 2 vols. Cambridge, U.K., 1977.

John R. Clark

Thuwayni ibn Sa'id   [?–1866]

Sultan of Oman (1856–1866).

Sayyid Thuwayni ruled part of a hitherto powerful domain embracing both Zanzibar and Oman that was sundered by a British-brokered partition. Resulting political crises were exacerbated by the concurrent collapse of Oman's maritime economy. Thuwayni's troubled reign ended when he was murdered by his son.

BIBLIOGRAPHY

LANDEN, ROBERT G. *Oman since 1856: Disruptive Modernization in a Traditional Arab Society*. Princeton, N.J. 1967.

Robert G. Landen

Tiberias

Town located on the eastern shore of Lake Tiberias (also referred to as the Sea of Galilee or Kinneret) in northern Israel.

The town of Tiberias was founded by Herod Antipas and named for the Roman emperor Tiberius. It is a favorite tourist site because of the freshwater lake and the relatively warm climate in winter. In the 1948 Arab–Israel War, fighting broke out in March with an Arab attack on Jews in the older sections of the town. Jewish fighters were able to push out their Arab adversaries, and eventually the Arab inhabitants fled to Jordan.

Bryan Daves

Tiberias, Lake

See Galilee, Sea of

Tigris and Euphrates Rivers

River systems that join to drain into the Persian/Arabian Gulf.

The Tigris (Arabic, *Shatt Dijla;* Hebrew, *Hiddekel;* Turkish, *Dicle*) rises in a lake in the mountains north of Diyarbakir, in southeastern Turkey. It picks up major tributaries, the Zab rivers, downstream from Mosul, then the Diyala, just past Baghdad—flowing some 1,180 miles (1,900 km). It ends at the confluence of the Euphrates, in southeast Iraq, to form the Shatt al-Arab, which empties into the Gulf. With its short tributaries flowing directly from the mountains, it floods in April, about one month before the Euphrates, and with about 50 percent greater flow.

The Tigris waters originate as rain and snow in Turkey and Iran; since both countries lack large irrigable areas in their watersheds, neither will drain the Tigris (as Syria and Turkey will the Euphrates). Consequently, most of Iraq's future irrigation schemes rely on Tigris water.

The Euphrates (Arabic, *Furat;* Hebrew, *Perath;* Turkish, *Fırat*) also originates in Turkey, from a spring in the Taurus mountains. It flows for 1,740 miles (2,800 km), passing through northern Syria and

Baghdad waterfront on the Tigris river, circa 1925. (Richard Bulliet)

Yemeni village on the Tihama coastal plain. (Richard Bulliet)

Bridge over the Euphrates river at Dayr al-Zawr, Syria. (Syrian Ministry of Tourism)

providing that country with an important water source. In 1973, Syria completed construction of the large Euphrates Dam. From Syria, the Euphrates flows into Iraq, where it joins the Tigris.

Since the Sumerian era (3500 B.C.E.), canals have connected tributaries to the Tigris–Euphrates confluence area, although the lower course was farther west at that time. The capitals of great empires—Ashur, Nineveh, Seleucia, Ctesiphon, and Baghdad—were built on or near its banks.

BIBLIOGRAPHY

The Oxford Regional Economic Atlas: The Middle East and North Africa. Oxford, 1960.

John R. Clark

Tihama

Coastal desert region of North Yemen.

The long, narrow, and flat coastal desert between the Red Sea and the foothills of Yemen's abruptly rising mountains, the Tihama is twenty to forty miles (30 to 60 km) wide and runs from well north of the present border of Yemen south to Bab al-Mandab. The Tihama constitutes a distinct region of Yemen, one distinguished by its hot, humid, almost rainless climate near sea level and a variant of Yemeni culture and society greatly influenced by nearby black Africa. Hodeida (al-Hudayda) and all of the other ports of north Yemen back on the Tihama, and the region depends heavily upon fishing, shipping, and other port activities. Although most of the Tihama is uninhabitable, vast mountain-fed aquifers and surface runoff from the mountains during the rainy season make the Tihama the area of greatest agricultural potential in Yemen. The highlands of Yemen have usually dominated the Tihama over the centuries, and the highlanders have tended to look down upon the Tihamis (mixed Arab and African), in part, it seems, on racial grounds.

Robert D. Burrowes

Euphrates river gorge just south of Kemaliye, Turkey, 1952. (D.W. Lockhard)

Tikrit

Iraqi city on the Tigris river northwest of Baghdad, on the main road to Mosul.

Tikrit (also Takrit) is located in north-central Iraq, some one hundred miles (160 km) north-northwest of Baghdad. The fortress around which the city was built was constructed by a Sassanid Persian king as a border post against the Byzantines. The first dwellers

Tikrit before modernization. (D.W. Lockhard)

Tikriti, Hardan al-   [1925–1971]

Iraqi government official of the Ba'th party.

Born in Tikrit, Iraq, to the family of a Sunni Arab policeman, al-Tikriti graduated from both flight and staff academies, joining the Ba'th party in 1961. After the Ramadan Revolution, from February to November 1963, he commanded the air force. After the second Ba'th coup of July 1968, he served as deputy commander in chief of the armed forces, deputy prime minister, minister of defense, and member of the Revolutionary Command Council. In 1970, after a power struggle with his two distant relatives President Ahmad Hasan al-Bakr and Saddam Hussein, he was dismissed from his posts and promoted to the ceremonial position of vice president; he was then formally dismissed and exiled. He was killed in Kuwait in 1971 by Saddam Hussein's agents.

BIBLIOGRAPHY

BATATU, HANNA. *The Old Social Classes and the Revolutionary Movements of Iraq.* Princeton, N.J., 1978.

Amatzia Baram

Tikriti Family

Iraqi family prominent in the Ba'th party.

The Tikriti family takes its name from Tikrit, a town one hundred miles north of Baghdad. Tikrit, a Sunni Muslim community, has produced many influential figures in Iraq's modern history. Mawlud Mukhlis, a Tikriti born in Mosul, was a confidant and a close adviser of King Faisal I. He held several cabinet positions and was appointed senator several times. Using his authority, Mukhlis helped his family and friends join the armed forces and other government services. Many played important roles in Iraq's affairs in the second half of the twentieth century.

After the Ba'th coup of July 31, 1968, the Tikriti role became more dominant in the Ba'th party. The most influential Ba'thist Tikriti to date is Saddam Hussein. Born at Tikrit in 1937 to a landless peasant family, he became president of Iraq in 1979. During his presidency, Iraq experienced the Iran–Iraq War (1980–1988) and the Gulf crisis of 1991. Both devastated the country and claimed thousands of lives. Other Tikritis have played major roles in Iraq's recent regimes, including key positions in the Revolutionary Command Council, the Ba'th party, military and security agencies, and the cabinet: Ahmad Hasan al-Bakr, president (1969–1979); Hardan al-Tikriti, defense minister (1968); Hammad Shihab, defense

of the city belonged to the Banu Iyad tribe of Christian Arabs, and its name is believed to have honored the tribal chief's daughter. It was conquered by Muslims in the mid-600s C.E. Today, Tikrit's population is mainly Sunni Arab, with some Kurds. The Kurdish Muslim hero Salah al-Din al-Ayyubi (Saladin, 1137–1193) was born in Tikrit.

With the decline in sales of *kalaks* (rafts of inflated skins), for which the city was noted, many people moved to Baghdad during the nineteenth century. Under the monarchy, some entered the military academy with the help of an influential Tikriti. Then, after the Ramadan Revolution and 1968 takeover by the Ba'th party, Tikritis became the single most powerful group in Iraq's senior officers' corps and in the civilian flank of the party. Both Ahmad Hasan al-Bakr and Saddam Hussein were from Tikrit, so they invested large sums in modernizing the city. In 1990, its population numbered between 100,000 and 120,000.

BIBLIOGRAPHY

BATATU, HANNA. *The Old Social Classes and the Revolutionary Movements of Iraq.* Princeton, N.J., 1978.

Amatzia Baram

minister (1970–1973); Adnan Khairallah, defense minister (1977–1989); and Sa'di Mehdi Saleh, member of the Regional Command (since 1982). In 1976, the government banned the use of family names in public documents in order to disguise the disproportional influence of Tikritis in the government.

BIBLIOGRAPHY

BATATU, HANNA. *The Old Social Classes and the Revolutionary Movements of Iraq.* Princeton, N.J., 1978.
HENDERSON, SIMON. *Instant Empire.* San Francisco, 1991.
METZ, HELEN CHAPIN. *Iraq: A Country Study.* Washington, D.C., 1990.

Ayad al-Qazzaz

Timar

Land rights earned in exchange for service to the Ottoman state.

The timar system began under Murad I (1359–1389), who granted land rights as payment to his military officers. In the fifteenth and sixteenth centuries, timars became the primary means of financing the Ottoman military. The typical timar holder was a provincial cavalry officer who contributed troops and supplies when called up for battle. He financed these through his timar, a state grant of nonhereditary rights over land, usually in the village where he lived. The officer kept a set amount of the tax revenue as his salary and delivered the remainder to the central state. He also ensured that the legal status of the land was maintained and that it was properly cultivated. Timars, found throughout the Ottoman provinces, were less often granted to nonmilitary Ottoman bureaucrats for their livelihood.

With economic and technological change in the late sixteenth and seventeenth centuries, timars were gradually supplanted by tax farms. The state confiscated timars from officers who died or could no longer afford to send troops and assigned them to a notable who would contract to collect taxes for monetary compensation, without the requirement of performing other services for the state. These provincial officers were gradually replaced with salaried troops in the new Janissary Corps, which was trained in newer forms of battle, substituting firearms for swords. Although they contributed less and less to imperial tax revenues, timars continued to exist on a small scale through the nineteenth century.

BIBLIOGRAPHY

KARPAT, KEMAL H. "The Land Regime, Social Structure, and Modernization in the Ottoman Empire." In *The Beginnings of Modernization in the Middle East: The Nineteenth Century,* ed. by William R. Polk and Richard L. Chambers. Chicago, 1966.
KEYDER, ÇAĞLAR, and FARUK TABAK, eds. *Landholding and Commercial Agriculture in the Middle East.* Albany, N.Y., 1991.

Elizabeth Thompson

Tiran, Strait of

Strait connecting the Gulf of Aqaba and the Red Sea.

The strait of Tiran is barely 2.5 miles (4 km) wide at its narrowest. It is the only access from Israel's port of Eilat through the Gulf of Aqaba to the Red Sea, and it is easily blocked as Egypt did in the early 1950s. From 1954 to 1956, and again in 1967, the Egyptians denied passage to Israeli shipping, contributing to the Arab–Israel wars of 1956 and 1967.

BIBLIOGRAPHY

SHIMONI, YAACOV, ed. *Political Dictionary of the Middle East in the Twentieth Century.* New York, 1974.

Zachary Karabell

Tishrin

Arabic word referring to the tenth month of the Gregorian calendar.

In its political context, especially in Syria, and also in Egypt, where the English equivalent "October" is also used, *Tishrin* refers to the calendar month in which the 1973 Arab–Israel War occurred. The month actually was *Tishrin al-Awwal,* that is, October. In 1974, to commemorate its victory, Syria issued a daily newspaper named *Tishrin.* It is one of the three major dailies in Syria, alongside *al-Ba'th* and *al-Thawra,* which predate it. The third Syrian university, established in the city of Latakia in 1971, had its name changed from Latakia University to Tishrin University to commemorate the war.

Abdul-Karim Rafeq

Tiwizi

Community agricultural aid to families short of manpower in Berber society.

Tiwizi is mandated and organized by the DJEMA'A and is an obligation for those who can provide such aid (usually of plowing or harvesting). It thus enables families to survive difficult periods.

Thomas G. Penchoen

Tlas, Mustafa [1932–   ]

Syrian military officer and politician.

Born in al-Rastan, near Homs, Mustafa Abd al-Qadir Tlas (Tallas) attended Syria's military academy in Homs (1952–1954). Commissioned in the tank corps, he served in Egypt (1959–1961) during the period of the United Arab Republic.

Tlas joined the Ba'th party in 1947. The Ba'thist military committee that overthrew Syria's government in 1963 brought him into its ranks after the coup. Tlas was granted important positions through which he proved his loyalty to the party and the military committee. He was elected to the Regional Council of the Ba'th party in 1965 and headed courts trying persons accused of plotting against the regime, including one established following the 1964 anti-Ba'thist violence in Hama. As commander of the garrison at Homs in 1965, Tlas was associated with the "radical" faction of the Ba'th during the period of growing intra-Ba'thist friction. Removed from his post in December 1965, after trying to dismiss officers loyal to President Amin al-Hafiz, Tlas returned to the military after Salah Jadid's "radical Ba'th" coup in 1966.

Tlas's importance in Syrian history lies, however, in his long-standing and loyal association with the powerful Ba'thist Hafiz al-Asad. Tlas and al-Asad studied together in the military academy and came from similar backgrounds. Although Tlas is a Sunni Muslim and Asad an Alawi, both are of humble village origins and supported the secular, pan-Arab socialist ideology of the Ba'th. As Asad's confidant, Tlas quickly rose to high positions in the military and the regime. While defense minister, Asad appointed Tlas chief of staff and deputy defense minister (1968). When Ba'thist rivals tried to depose the two in 1970, Asad seized power; he appointed Tlas defense minister in 1972. Tlas has been Syria's defense minister since then, overseeing a tremendous growth in the size and technological sophistication of the nation's military through Soviet assistance. He also has remained a key member of the Asad regime, having been elected to the Ba'th central committee in 1980.

Tlas is known as an outspoken hard-liner in Syria's frosty relationship with the Palestine Liberation Organization (PLO) and its chairman, Yasir Arafat, since the mid-1970s. Tlas and Syria's military had assisted guerillas from Arafat's Fath movement in the 1960s and during the PLO's conflict with Jordan in 1970. He became increasingly hostile to Arafat following Syria's intervention against the PLO in Lebanon's civil war in 1976 and the bitter Syria–PLO relations that followed.

Tlas runs a publishing house in Damascus, Dar al-Tlas, and has written numerous books on military science, literature, and other topics.

BIBLIOGRAPHY

SEALE, PATRICK. *Asad: The Struggle for the Middle East.* Berkeley, Calif., 1988.

Michael R. Fischbach

Tlemcen

City near the Moroccan border in eastern Algeria.

Situated on a high ridge of the Little Atlas mountains thirty miles (50 km) inland from the Mediterranean Sea, Tlemcen has a population of 150,000. The Almoravids founded Tlemcen in the eleventh century, on an ancient Berber, Phoenician, and Roman site. It was an important trade and political center in the Middle Ages, as capital of the Arab sultanate, and was Abd al-Qadir's capital from 1837 to 1842, when it came under French colonial rule. Tlemcen had received many of the Moors expelled from Spain after 1492. The city came under the Ottoman Empire in 1555 and was attached to Algeria in 1942.

Laurence Michalak

The lands around Tlemcen seen from the forested slopes of the Atlas mountains. (Richard Bulliet)

Tlili, Mustafa [1937–   ]

Tunisian novelist.

Tlili was born in Fériana, Tunisia. He attended the *madrasa* (traditional school) in his native city and later received a bilingual education, studying at the Sorbonne, where he received a *diplôme d'études supérieurs de philosophie.* He also studied at the UN Institute for Training and Research, and worked for almost thirteen years at the UN offices in New York. He moved to France in 1980. He was made a Knight of the French Order of Arts and Letters.

Tlili has published four novels, all written in French. Each reflects, in its own way, the writer's preoccupation with life's meaning. In spite of this global outlook, he remains strongly linked to the Maghrib. He appears bent on denouncing corruption, especially among the aristocracy, whether in the Arabian peninsula, as revealed in *Gloire des Sables* (Glory of the Sands, Paris, 1982); in Paris, as described in *La Rage aux Tripes* (Visceral Anger, Paris, 1975); or in New York, as can be observed in *Le Bruit Dort* (The Noise Sleeps, Paris, 1978). The fourth novel, *La Montagne du Lion* (Lion Mountain, Paris, 1988), centers on corruption in Tunisia.

Tlili's language reflects a playful anger and humorous cynicism toward certain classes of society. His multilingual and multicultural background enhances the quality of his novels and reflects a new trend among the Maghribi writers who write in French. Instead of being confined to the limits of two cultures—Arabic and French—like their predecessors, they are expanding their horizons. With Tlili it is possible to speak of the beginning of the cultural liberation of the French-educated Maghribi writers.

BIBLIOGRAPHY

FONTAINE, JEAN. *La littérature tunisienne contemporaine.* Paris, 1990.

MEMMI, ALBERT. *Ecrivains francophones du Maghreb: Anthologie.* Paris, 1985.

Aida A. Bamia

Tobacco Revolt

A popular rebellion (1891–1893) in Persia that defeated tobacco concessions granted to Britain.

Persia witnessed a period of uncertainty and turmoil in the late nineteenth century. The country, at the brink of modernity, faced growing demands from the imperialist powers, whose leaders promised the Qajar kings political, financial, and technical support in exchange for a major share of Persia's riches. The riches were exploited through a series of concessions granted by the government to foreign subjects. One of the most controversial of these concessions was granted to a Major Talbot of Britain and was registered simultaneously at the British legation and the Ministry of Foreign Affairs at Tehran (March 8, 1890). The commodity in question was tobacco, highly profitable and popular in the Middle East. All rights to the production, purchasing, and sales of Persian tobacco were to be transferred to Major Talbot and his company, the Imperial Tobacco Corporation of Persia, for a price of 25,000 pounds, with an annual payment of 15,000 pounds to the Imperial Treasury. This payment was also to be accompanied by a 25 percent share of the net profits after the deduction of a 5 percent shareholder's dividend. This arrangement between Major Talbot and the Persian government was to be maintained for a period of fifty years. In the previous years, a similar agreement had been drawn between Turkey and Great Britain; yet the terms of the Turkish regime were markedly more favorable than those obtained by the Qajar government. The Turks received a per-annum payment of 650,000 pounds and were allowed to maintain their rights over the exports of tobacco. In addition, the duration of their concession was for thirty instead of fifty years.

In Iran, the population, especially the tobacco merchants, felt increasingly alienated from Naser al-Din Shah and the Qajar administration. Under the conditions accepted by the Qajar king, the local population would be forced to purchase its tobacco from the British company, which controlled all rights to both the importing and the exporting of the product. It was popularly believed that the British company would purchase the tobacco in cash from the local farmers at a very cheap price and would proceed to sell it to merchants and manufacturers at a high price, thereby securing great profits. Meanwhile the local merchants, who had previously been responsible for exporting tobacco outside of Persia, were prohibited from doing so at a time when the three different kinds of domestically grown tobacco were in high demand by neighboring countries. These kinds of tobacco were *tumbak,* used for smoking in water pipes and cultivated in southern Fars and in parts of Isfahan; *tutun,* also used exclusively for pipe smoking and sown in Kurdistan and Kermanshah; and cigarette tobacco, grown mostly in Gilan.

The unacceptable terms evoked nationalistic fervor among the Persian population, the majority of whom consumed some form of tobacco on a daily basis, and they looked for someone to represent their grievances vis-à-vis the government. The void in leadership prompted the politicization of the intellectuals and the clergy, two politically inactive sectors of Persian society. As the events of 1890 and 1891 unfolded, it became clear that the *ulama* (the clergy), who were involved in the everyday lives of the Persian people and had extensive knowledge of Islamic law, could successfully mobilize the crowds against the government and the existing policies. Under the supervision of the leading *ulama,* unrest soon grew in Shiraz, Tabriz, Mashhad, and throughout the rest of the country. In Isfahan, two leading *ulama,* Aqa Najafi and his brother Shaykh Muhammad Ali, pronounced the use of tobacco unclean as their followers took to the streets and broke all visible water pipes in the bazaars. Following this incident, a fatwa (legal opinion) that is believed to have been issued by the most prominent *mujtahid* (expert on Islamic law) of the times, Mirza Muhammad Hasan SHIRAZI, was enforced. It demanded that all forms of smoking be abandoned until the tobacco concession was abolished.

The *ulama* had established a separate form of authority and had undermined the power of the king. Shops throughout the bazaars were closed and smoking was completely abandoned, even by the shah's own harem. The value of the shares of the Imperial Bank was reduced by 50 percent. On Christmas Day placards were hung throughout the bazaars threatening the Europeans with a possible holy war and making foreigners targets of violence. Three days later, the shah announced the conditional withdrawal of the tobacco concession and requested that the population resume smoking. The apprehensive crowds awaited the final approval of the mujtahids before breaking the fatwa. Meanwhile, Mirza Hasan Shirazi expressed positive sentiments toward the shah, congratulating him on a wise decision, yet not articulating a firm decision to remove the prohibition. By this time, the agitated shah had sent a personal letter to mujtahid Mirza Hasan Ashtiyani demanding that he immediately resume smoking or face possible exile from Tehran. Ashtiyani defied the king's order and continued to abstain from smoking while remaining in Tehran. As the news of the shah's message spread through the capital, the enraged crowds, prodded by the *ulama,* occupied the streets surrounding the shah's palace. Fearing for the safety of the shah, the troops opened fire on the rioters, killing seven people, including the sayyid who had originally led the crowds. With the help of the merchants, the *ulama* sent a strong message to Naser al-Din Shah and his prime minister, Amin al-Soltan. Naser al-Din Shah, feeling the severity of the situation, abolished the concession completely a few days later and the joyous crowds resumed smoking.

BIBLIOGRAPHY

BROWNE, E. G. *The Persian Revolution of 1905–1909.* London, 1966.

KAZEMZADEH, F. *Russia and Britain in Persia, 1864–1914.* New Haven, Conn., 1968.

KEDDIE, N. *Religion and Rebellion in Iran: The Tobacco Protest of 1891–1892.* London, 1966.

———. *Sayyid Jamal ad-Din al-Afghani.* Berkeley, Calif., 1972.

LAMBTON, A. K. S. *Qajar Persia.* London, 1987.

Roshanak Malek

Tobruk

Small Libyan seaport west of the Egyptian border; scene of fierce fighting during World War II.

Tobruk had been occupied by General Erwin Rommel's Afrika Korps but fell to British forces under General Archibald Wavell on January 22, 1941 during World War II. In April 1941, Rommel's counteroffensive left Tobruk under siege until December, when it was retaken by the British. Rommel's drive into Egypt in May 1942 led to the surrender of twenty-five thousand troops at Tobruk on June 21, after a one-day assault. Tobruk remained in German hands until liberated by General Bernard Law Montgomery's Eighth Army, after Britain's successful conclusion to the battle of al-Alamayn in November 1942.

BIBLIOGRAPHY

PITT, BARRIE. *The Crucible of War: Year of Alamein, 1942.* London, 1982.

Daniel E. Spector

Toman

A Persian gold coin worth ten silver krans or ten thousand dinars.

The toman was introduced around 1600 and continued in use until 1927, when it fell victim to the depreciation of Middle Eastern coinage that had begun in the late nineteenth century. The word *toman* is of Tatar origin and originally meant a military division of ten thousand men.

Marilyn Higbee

Topkapı Palace

Governmental seat of the Ottoman Empire.

The New Palace (Saray-Cedid), now known as the Topkapı Palace (in reference to the eighteenth-century royal summer residence next to the seaside Cannon Gate), occupied the site of Byzantium's ancient acropolis in what was then the city of Constantinople (now Istanbul). Enclosed by protective walls, the Topkapı Palace stood in the middle of a vast woodland to serve, for a period close to four centuries, as the principal center of governance for the entire Ottoman Empire.

The administrative functions of the government were located in the outer (*birun*) court of the fortress-palace, while the inner (*enderun*) court included space for the royal pavilions and the palace school. The quarters for the sultan's pages surrounded the inner court; the harem quarters were behind its northern wall, overlooking the section of Istanbul known as the Golden Horn. The harem, originally very small, began to grow in size during the late sixteenth-century reign of Murad III.

The Topkapı Palace lost its importance when the court moved to the Dolmabahçe Palace in 1854. After that date, aside from certain ceremonial occasions involving the holy relics of Islam (kept in the privy chamber), it was hardly ever used. Since its renovation in the 1930s, the Topkapı Palace has been a museum.

BIBLIOGRAPHY

NECIPOĞLU, GÜLRÜ. *Architecture, Ceremonial and Power.* New York, 1991.

Aptullah Kuran

A diwan in the interior of Topkapı Palace in Istanbul, Turkey. (Mia Bloom)

Torah

See Bible

Touareg

See Twareg

Toubi, Tawfiq   [1922–1994]

Israeli Palestinian politician.

Born in Haifa, Tawfiq Toubi was educated at the Mt. Zion school in Jerusalem. He joined the Communist party in 1941 and later was one of the founders of the League for National Liberation, which originally opposed partition of Palestine but later came to accept it, after the Soviet Union indicated that it would support partition. After the state of Israel was proclaimed (1948), he became a member of the Knesset on the Maki list and a member of the Central Committee. In 1976, he was elected secretary general of the Hadash political faction. He was also the editor of *al-Ittihad.*

BIBLIOGRAPHY

ROLEF, S. H., ed. *Political Dictionary of the State of Israel.* New York, 1987.

Bryan Daves

Tourism

Service industry in the Middle East that promotes geological, archeological, historical, recreational, and cultural features to travelers.

Tourism is important to the economic and cultural life of the Middle East, and it is likely to grow. The benefits and pitfalls of tourism as a producer of revenue cause much debate, and government attitudes range from hostility to enthusiasm. Middle Eastern tourism remains on a relatively small scale as compared with some other parts of the world. It includes both international sightseeing as well as the travels of local residents for mountain and coastal recreation. Certain countries are favorably located to attract tourists from Western Europe—a potentially large source. Morocco, Tunisia, Egypt, Cyprus, and Turkey have the advantage of good communications with Europe; they also have the Mediterranean environment that first attracted independent tourists and package tours.

Lebanon and Syria also have long been destinations for tours. While the countries on the Mediterranean have generally encouraged tourism, less desire exists for such activity in the Arabian peninsula, but this might change in the smaller Gulf states when long-term economic diversification is sought.

The scale of international tourism in the region grew markedly during the 1980s, but numbers fluctuated in response to political events, especially to violence or the risk of violence. International boundaries are sometimes closed when relations between neighboring states deteriorate; war stops tourism altogether. This was demonstrated by the collapse of Lebanon's once–thriving tourism in the face of its long-standing civil war, and the Gulf War of 1990/91, which reduced Iraq's two million annual visitors to a trickle. Likewise, Israel's tourist earnings declined markedly during the INTIFADA (uprising). With the Oslo Agreement in 1995 marking the potential beginning for Israeli–Palestinian peace, tourism earnings began to recover as travelers again visited Israel to see its many biblical sites and historical features. But as the series of terrorist bombings in early 1996 illustrate, Israel's tourist industry remains volatile to political violence. Clearly, two of the preconditions for developing tourism must be peace and political stability; being able to make reservations by telephone or fax and to cross international boundaries is also crucial to the tourist.

Problems of data collection and definition make numerical comparisons of tourist arrivals potentially misleading. Muslims making the HAJJ (pilgrimage) to Saudi Arabia, for example, should not be classified as tourists; in recent years pilgrims from abroad have exceeded one million. Some national statistics include day visitors from cruise ships, while others do not. Bahrain even shows some one million visitors crossing the causeway from Saudi Arabia by car. Nevertheless, certain features of the statistical record are clear: Three states—Tunisia, Jordan, and Turkey—receive more than three million tourists each; two states—Egypt and Morocco—receive more than two million each; and four receive more than one million each—Cyprus, Israel, Syria, and Bahrain.

Turkey's annual visitors now number some eight million, and it remains the country with the region's greatest tourist potential. Egypt had hoped to increase tourist numbers to five million by the mid-1990s, a goal that was not reached because extremist Islamist groups targeted Egypt's tourist industry as a means of expressing their grievances toward the government, setting off a series of bombs near tourist sites from 1992 to 1996. Iran was eager to encourage tourism in the past, but has received relatively few since the Islamic Revolution of 1979. The annual number of international tourists to the Middle East now exceeds twenty million, approximately 5 percent of the world's international travelers. (Several European states, however, each receive substantially larger numbers than the whole of the Middle East and North Africa.) In some countries, tourist earnings represent an important contribution to the gross national product, notably in Cyprus, Tunisia, Morocco, Egypt, and Israel; they are also a vital source of foreign exchange. Locally, tourism may also provide development and employment where alternative economic activities are limited; Algeria developed hotels in certain Saharan oases for this purpose. Several Mediterranean ports, such as Tangiers, Alexandria, Haifa, and Istanbul, are popular with cruise ships and benefit from passenger spending.

Tourism is thus part of the development strategy of several Middle Eastern states, especially those on the European fringe. Such countries often have ministries of tourism and advertise widely in Europe, Japan, and the Americas. Israel's ministry of tourism oversees the region's most carefully planned and marketed industry, making good use of the attraction of biblical sites, Roman sites, water sports, and urban nightlife. Like the other Mediterranean countries, Israel has abundant sunshine, magnificent land- and seascapes, extensive historical and archeological sites and museums, and a richly diverse cultural environment expressed in local-style foods, music, costume, and folklore. It has a special lure for those interested in Judaism and Jewish history, but Christians and Muslims consider it the core area for their religions as well.

Actually, almost any part of the Middle East has potential for increased tourism. Libya, Jordan, Syria, and Iraq—which are not the most popular tourist destinations—each possess historic remains of world significance. Even oases and deserts provide a certain fascination, as do the flora and fauna and the special sunsets. The Red Sea is famous for its tropical marine life; the Dead Sea is famous for its mineral salts, which soothe and heal in mud and water that have provided medicinal bathing since ancient times. In winter and spring, the highest mountain ranges have snow, and ski resorts in Morocco, Algeria, and Lebanon reflect the leisure habits of the modern well-to-do Middle Easterner. Given the range of attractions, some areas are clearly underdeveloped—notably in Syria, Yemen, Algeria, and Afghanistan—and could become destinations for climbing and adventure holidays of the kind now popular in Nepal, if peace and security existed. In general, large-scale investment is needed in roads and hotels; and regional cooperation needs to be developed to facilitate border crossings.

Some argue against further tourist activity in the region, for religious and nationalistic reasons, and in favor of keeping out intrusive non-Islamic influences. Others have economic and environmental arguments against large-scale tourism, which tends to degrade sites and the local environment and causes commercialism, overcrowding, and pollution. Parts of Tunisia, Cyprus, and Israel already experience such environmental stresses, and the most famous sites in Jerusalem, Cairo, Istanbul, and elsewhere have already received dangerously high numbers of tourists.

BIBLIOGRAPHY

BLAKE, G. H., J. C. DEWDNEY, and J. K. MITCHELL. *The Cambridge Atlas of the Middle East and North Africa.* Cambridge, U.K. 1987.

WORLD TOURISM ORGANISATION. *World Travel and Tourism Statistics.* Madrid, 1990.

Gerald Blake

Townshend, Charles   [1861–1924]

British general.

After serving in India, Egypt, and the Sudan, during World War I, Townshend was second in command of Sir John Nixon's Indian Expeditionary Force, which invaded Mesopotamia (now Iraq) in the fall of 1914. By November 1915, Townshend had advanced up the Tigris river almost to Baghdad, but in the face of stiff resistance from Ottoman Empire troops, he had no choice but to retreat south to KUT AL-AMARA. Beseiged there by the Turks until April 1916, Sir Charles was finally forced to surrender his army. He was taken prisoner to Istanbul and remained captive until October 1918.

BIBLIOGRAPHY

SLUGLETT, PETER. *Britain in Iraq.* London, 1976.

Zachary Karabell

Trabzon

Turkish port city on the Black Sea.

The city is located between the Riza and Trabzon mountains in northeast Turkey. Its 1980 population was 108,403. Trabzon (also Trebizond) is home to a naval base and a seaport, which was a principal Black Sea trade depot during the Ottoman Empire.

The countryside around Trabzon on the Black Sea, 1952. (D.W. Lockhard)

In the medieval era, the city was the seat of a thirteenth-century empire, an important point on the trade route to Persia. It was founded in the eighth century B.C.E. by Greek colonists and was called Trapezus in ancient times.

BIBLIOGRAPHY

Chambers World Gazetteer. New York, 1988.

Elizabeth Thompson

Trachoma

Eye infection caused by the microorganism Chlamydia trachomatis.

The *Chlamydia* microorganism grows in the conjunctiva, the tissue that lines the inside of the eyelids. The conjunctiva becomes reddened and thickened, and the eye is clouded with secretions. In severe cases, inflammation spreads to the cornea, resulting in scarring and eventual blindness. The microorganism is spread directly by the secretions or indirectly by common use of a contaminated towel. Trachoma is prevalent in hot, dry climates with poor sanitary conditions and water shortages.

Trachoma can be treated with tetracycline; surgery is necessary to repair damaged eyelids and scarred corneas. Its prevention requires early treatment of the disease in children, expansion of the water supply, and improvements in public and personal hygiene. Although the incidence of trachoma has been reduced, the disease remains endemic to many of the countries of the Middle East and North Africa.

Stuart J. Borsch

Trad, Petro [1876–1947]

Lebanese politician.

Trad was born to a Greek Orthodox family in Beirut and received a law degree from the University of Paris. Known for his eloquent presentations, he was one of a handful of wealthy lawyers who monopolized law practice in Beirut. Trad was also involved in politics; he was one of six signatories to a petition presented to the French Foreign Ministry in 1913 on behalf of Christian sects in Beirut, that demanded an end to Ottoman control of Syria (including Palestine and Lebanon) and called for a separate entity run by "French specialists." This petition so angered CEMAL PAÇA against Arabs in general and Christians in particular that he asked the War Council in Alay to execute the six signatories. They fled Lebanon.

After the World War I, Trad returned to Beirut as an ally of the French and founded the League of Christian Sects, which comprised the elite of Beirut society and demanded a French mandate over Syria and Lebanon. His law firm attained fame throughout the region, partly because he would defend poor persons who could not afford his fees. He was elected deputy from Beirut in 1925, with both Arab and French support. Trad served in the parliament for much of the 1920s and 1930s, either elected or appointed by the French authorities. He was a member of the parliamentary committee that worked on the French–Lebanese treaty of 1936. The French rewarded his support by appointing him speaker of parliament in 1937, a post he held until September 1939.

Trad could not stay neutral in the political feud between the staunchly pro-French Emile EDDÉ and the moderately pro-French Bishara al-KHURI. In his memoirs al-Khuri accuses Trad of supporting Eddé. In fact, Trad believed that both al-Khuri and Eddé were incapable of winning the presidency. He promoted himself as a consensus candidate.

Trad became president by default. He was briefly appointed by the French government, to oversee the election of a new president by members of an appointed parliament. The election of al-Khuri made it clear to him that his chances of winning the presidency were nil. He died in Beirut.

As'ad AbuKhalil

Trade

The geographical position of the Middle East has made the region part of far-flung trade networks as both market and supplier since antiquity.

Since antiquity, the Middle East has engaged in a regional trade; since before the early Middle Ages, in interregional trade. Its large population, early civilizations, agricultural and herding base, cities, seaports, and traditional crafts constituted first a large internal market and then a market both for the export of local goods and the import of foreign goods.

With the rise of Islam in the seventh century C.E. and its subsequent dominance throughout the region, the prevalence of a common legal system (*Shari'a*) with the widespread use of Arabic facilitated trade. The central position of the Middle East—between Europe, Asia, and Africa—and its access by land or sea further contributed to the emergence of a far-flung trade network. To Europe and Africa, the Middle East exported mainly high-quality manufactured products and generally earned a surplus in its balance of trade. To Asia, trade was more diversified, since both manufactures and raw materials were exported and imported; but here the Middle East showed a deficit in its balance of trade.

For a long time, the Indian Ocean area was the main market and supplier. A variety of spices was imported for Middle Eastern consumption as well as for reexport. Teak and other tropical woods were imported from India; porcelain and silk from China. After smuggling silk worms out of China in the sixth century C.E., the Middle East became a large producer of silk cloth and an exporter to Europe and elsewhere. Arab and Persian shipping dominated the Indian Ocean, as far as the Straits of Malacca, where Chinese junks took over, sailing to Guangzhou (Canton) and other Chinese ports; there, Middle Eastern exports were sold—rugs; linens, cottons, and wool fabrics; metal work; iron ore; pearls, and ivory.

An active overland trade also existed with the Baltic region—by way of the Volga and other Russian rivers. Along the route, the Middle East exported various manufactured goods; imports were furs, wax, amber, and slaves. The ancient sea trade with East Africa greatly expanded with the spread of Islam and the immigration of Arabs and Persians down the East African coast. Exports to Africa consisted of cloth, glassware, weapons, and trinkets; imports were of wood, ivory, palm oil, and gold. Slaves were also imported to the Middle East in large numbers. Most remained in the countries bordering the Red Sea and Persian/Arab Gulf, but some were sent on to India and China. The trans-Sahara trade was also greatly expanded by the introduction of caravans between Egypt, the North African ports, and tropical Africa. Imports to the Middle East consisted of gold, ivory, pepper, and slaves; exports were of salt, weapons, copper, textiles, glassware, and trinkets.

Eventually, trade with Europe was to overshadow all others, but for centuries it remained small. Early and medieval imports from Europe consisted of wood, iron, furs, and other raw materials, as well as raw labor itself in the form of slaves. In return, the Middle East sent the high-quality manufactures for which it was famous since antiquity—glassware, metal goods, and linens. Before Europe's Industrial Revolution, new products were added based on crops or processes learned from Asia—silk and cotton textiles, sugar, and paper. Muslim ships and merchants seldom went to Europe; much trade passed through Jewish intermediaries—merchants, traders, peddlers—in the 1700s. European ships came into Muslim ports but piracy and the corsairs in the Mediterranean harassed them. By the late 1700s and early 1800s British, French, and American navies were attacking and winning both peace and trade agreements, some of which led to colonialism.

By the nineteenth century, a slow but increasing reversal in the trade pattern occurred as Europe began to supply improved goods to the Middle East that had originated there. Sugar, grown in Sicily, Spain, the Azores—and especially the New World—was refined in Europe to supply most of the Middle East's consumption. The same thing occurred, a little later, with coffee. Fine paper and glass were also made in Europe for export. Gradually, the same process occurred in textiles, as superior European silks and woolens were exported to the Middle East, putting many artisans out of business. Europe also exported technological goods: clocks, spectacles, and weapons. Middle East cotton and yarn exports to Europe continued, however, until close to the end of the eighteenth century. Nevertheless, a reversal in trade position continued. By the Industrial Revolution in Europe, the Middle East increasingly imported manufactured goods and exported primary goods—wool, cotton, grain, and hides. The region had become peripheral to the European industrial core.

In the course of the nineteenth century and until World War I, total world trade rose from some 1.7 billion in 1800 to 42 billion U.S. dollars in 1913. The Middle East's share fell from about 3 percent to 1.5 percent, probably the lowest figure in its long history. The trade increase took place almost solely with Europe, where people had an insatiable appetite for Middle Eastern foodstuffs and raw materials, and where machine-made goods still flooded the marketplaces, accounting for some 80 to 90 percent of Middle Eastern commerce. The main trading countries were England, followed by France and Austria and—by the end of the century—Germany and Italy. The composition of Middle Eastern trade also changed. Exports of manufactured goods almost disappeared and each country gradually concentrated on a few or even just one raw material: cotton in Egypt; tobacco, dried fruits, and cotton in Turkey; silk and opium in Iran; wheat, barley, and dates in Syria and Iraq; silk in Lebanon; oranges in Palestine;

and coffee in Yemen. Imports of European milled textiles and other manufactured goods greatly increased, with devastating effects on local handicrafts. In general, Middle East exports lagged behind imports, so it paid out large amounts of bullion accumulated in previous generations. The large trade expansion of the nineteenth century was facilitated by such changes as the introduction of mechanical transport to the Middle East, the investment of large amounts of European capital, the abolition of monopolies and other local administrative obstacles, and the adoption of low uniform tariffs on imports.

After World War I, the Middle East followed economic world trends. Recovery in the 1920s was followed by a collapse in the 1930s, when the price of agricultural products fell sharply, exports shrank, and the import surplus increased, with disastrous consequences for the regional economy. During World War II, the volume of trade greatly declined, owing to blockades and the dangers of shipping. Since the end of the war, however, there has been an almost uninterrupted period of petroleum production and sale, as well as an OPEC-dominated oil inflation (see ORGANIZATION OF PETROLEUM EXPORTING COUNTRIES). Table 1 shows the growth of trade since 1938. It also shows that the Middle East's share in world trade steadily increased, until the 1980s fall in oil prices. Table 1 clearly demonstrates the shift in economic position among the countries of the region. Until 1948, Egypt and Turkey accounted for the majority of Middle Eastern trade. After that, the oil-producing countries moved ahead and now represent an enormous proportion of the total, especially on the export side. Saudi Arabia has consistently occupied first place in oil exports but the others have been affected by political crises, such as the Arab–Israel Wars, the Iranian Revolution, the Iran–Iraq War, and the Iraqi invasion of Kuwait that resulted in the Gulf Crisis of 1990/91. Since its establishment in 1948, Israel has also been economically hampered by the ARAB BOYCOTT.

As regards the balance of trade, in the oil-producing nations revenues have covered, and usually more than covered, imports of goods and services. In the others—Egypt, Israel, Jordan, Syria, Turkey, and Yemen—the huge import surplus has been met by foreign aid and loans, and these countries have large foreign debts. In the rest of the nations, the composition of exports has changed. Traditional exports, such as cotton and grain, have declined, owing to greater consumption or processing at home. A small but growing export trade has been built in manufactured goods, such as textiles, especially in Israel, Turkey, Egypt, and Lebanon. On the import side, there has been a large increase in foodstuffs, durable consumer goods, industrial and

TABLE 1

Foreign Trade of Some Middle East Countries*

	1938	1948	1963	1977	1984
Egypt					
Imports	190	700	900	4,800	10,300
Exports	150	600	500	1,700	3,200
Israel					
Imports	56	300	700	4,700	8,400
Exports	29	40	300	3,000	4,900
Turkey					
Imports	120	300	700	5,700	10,800
Exports	115	200	400	1,800	7,100
Iran					
Imports	—	200	500	13,800	11,500
Exports	—	500	900	24,200	13,200
Iraq					
Imports	50	—	300	3,900	19,900
Exports	—	—	800	9,700	9,800
Kuwait					
Imports	—	—	300	4,500	8,300
Exports	—	—	1,100	9,800	10,600
Saudi Arabia					
Imports	—	—	—	14,700	39,200
Exports	—	300	1,100	43,500	46,900
United Arab Emirates					
Imports	—	—	—	4,600	9,400
Exports	—	—	—	9,500	14,400
Total					
Imports	400	1,500	4,300	58,500	123,400
Exports	400	1,500	5,700	106,000	119,700
Middle East as percentage of the world					
Imports	1.6	2.4	2.6	5.2	6.2
Exports	1.7	2.6	3.7	9.4	6.3

*In millions of U. S. dollars, rounded.

Source: United Nations, *Statistical Yearbook* (New York, 1986).

transport machinery, and raw materials to feed growing industrial production.

In the 1990s, the direction of trade has shown relatively little change. As in the past, Western Europe constitutes the main market for raw materials, foodstuffs, and petroleum, which is also exported in large amounts to Japan and other parts of Asia and Africa. The main suppliers to the Middle East remain Western Europe, Japan, and the United States—the latter largely because of the large outlays of monetary aid to the region. Trade with the Soviet Union, Eastern Europe, and China was small before 1989, and the new post-1989 polities have yet to change the pattern. Intraregional trade is very small because of political tensions between the various countries but also because they all tend to produce the same kinds of agricultural and industrial goods. Attempts to form an Arab Common Market have, so far, been largely unsuccessful.

BIBLIOGRAPHY

ISSAWI, CHARLES. *An Economic History of the Middle East and North Africa.* New York, 1982.
PAMUK, ŞEVKET. *The Ottoman Empire and European Capitalism.* New York and London, 1987.
RICHARDS, D. S., ed. *Islam and the Trade of Asia.* London, 1970.

Charles Issawi

Trans-Arabian Pipeline

Pipeline transporting crude oil from Saudi Arabia to the Mediterranean.

The Trans-Arabian Pipeline (Tapline) was constructed by ARAMCO to carry crude oil from Abqaiq, Saudi Arabia, to the Mediterranean coast. As originally conceived during World War II, the line was to follow a great circle route, running northwest through Saudi Arabia and Jordan, that would have located the Mediterranean terminus at Haifa, then part of the British mandate of Palestine. The postwar conflict over the disposition of Palestine ended in the Arab–Israel War (1948) that put Haifa in the new state of Israel. Tapline's route, more than one thousand miles (1,600 km) long, was altered to run through Syria and site its western terminus a few miles south of Sidon, Lebanon.

The construction of Tapline was hastened by the end of the RED LINE AGREEMENT, which brought a new infusion of capital into ARAMCO as the result of the removal of the restriction preventing Standard Oil of New Jersey (now Exxon) and Socony Vacuum (now Mobil) from joining the partnership then composed of SOCAL (now Chevron) and Texaco. Capital was not the only requirement in short supply. Steel was also scarce following the end of World War II, and its allocation was controlled by the U.S. government. A second important factor speeding the construction of Tapline was support from the administration of U.S. President Harry S. Truman, which regarded Middle Eastern oil as crucial to the success of the Marshall Plan.

When Tapline was built, it was the world's largest privately financed construction project. At the peak of construction, it employed more than sixteen thousand men. Towns were constructed at Qaisumah, Rafha, Badana, and Turaif, where the four main pumping stations in Saudi Arabia were located. Initial capacity was 320,000 barrels per day (b/d). In 1957, auxiliary pumping stations were installed that raised capacity to 450,000 b/d. Tapline's capacity in 1990 was 500,000 b/d.

Tapline increased ARAMCO's capacity to export crude oil and reduced its oil transport expenses. This prompted the government of Saudi Arabia to demand 50 percent of Tapline's profits under the fifty-fifty profit-sharing agreement that governed oil production. ARAMCO argued that transport was not covered under the profit-sharing agreement and claimed that Tapline was not an affiliate of ARAMCO but a separate company. After years of negotiations, the company agreed in 1963 to pay Saudi Arabia half the difference, after costs were deducted, between the price of petroleum at Ra's Tanura and the price at Sidon. The agreement, retroactive to 1953, netted the government $93 million in arrears.

Tapline and other pipelines in the region not only reduce transport cost and increase oil export capacity but also provide alternatives to shipping from the Persian Gulf and/or through the Suez Canal. However, pipelines have security problems. Syria halted the passage of oil through Tapline for twenty-four hours in October 1956, during the Arab–Israel War, and in Syria a tractor ruptured Tapline in May 1970, just as Libya was restricting the production of OCCIDENTAL PETROLEUM during the early days of the "squeeze." This blocked the transit of 500,000 barrels of crude from Saudi Arabia to the Mediterranean, and triggered an immediate threefold rise in oil tanker rates. The vulnerability of Tapline was highlighted by several incidents of sabotage in 1973, including an armed attack on the Sidon terminal and attacks on the pipeline itself in Syria and in Saudi Arabia.

In order to counter some of the strategic liabilities of relying so heavily on Tapline for pipeline transport, Saudi Arabia constructed a twelve-hundred-kilometer (720-mi.) crude oil pipeline, Petroline, from the eastern oil fields to Yanbu, on the Red Sea, during the Iran–Iraq War (1980–1988). A parallel line, connected to a spur running from Iraq's southern oil fields, was constructed to enable Iraq to continue to export oil at a time when its shipping was a primary target of Iran's military activity. This line was closed under UN sanctions against Iraq following its invasion of Kuwait. Petroline is located entirely within Saudi Arabia. Its maximum capacity as of 1994 was over five million barrels per day, about half of Saudi Arabia's production capacity. Like Tapline, it increases the kingdom's export flexibility and demonstrates its commitment to a secure supply.

BIBLIOGRAPHY

NAWWAB, ISMAIL I., PETER C. SPEERS, and PAUL F. HOYE, eds. *Aramco and Its World: Arabia and the Middle East.* Dhahran, Saudi Arabia, 1980.
YERGIN, DANIEL. *The Prize: The Epic Quest for Oil, Money and Power.* New York, 1991.

Mary Ann Tétreault

Transcaucasian Republic

Region between the Black and Caspian seas.

After the Bolshevik revolution in November 1917, the ethnic groups of the CAUCASUS banded together and created the Transcaucasian Republic in December. However, war and then negotiations with the Ottoman leader Enver Paşa led to internal divisions that proved fatal to the republic. In the spring of 1918, the people of Georgia and Azerbaijan seceded. The Armenians soon followed suit.

BIBLIOGRAPHY

LENCZOWSKI, GEORGE. *The Middle East in World Affairs,* 4th ed. Ithaca, N.Y., 1980.

Zachary Karabell

Trans-Iranian Railway

North–south railroad completed in 1938, which links Caspian ports in the north to Tehran and Persian/Arabian Gulf ports in the south.

The Trans-Iranian railway, one of the great engineering feats of the twentieth century, was commissioned by Reza Shah Pahlavi after his consolidation of power in Iran in 1925. Preliminary planning and construction efforts were contracted with KAMPSAX, a Scandinavian syndicate, in 1933. With the hub at Tehran, single tracklines were laid north and south through mountain and desert terrain to newly constructed ports on the Caspian Sea and Persian/Arabian Gulf coasts. The 865-mile (1,392-km) railroad became operational in 1938, with 190 tunnels, totaling 47 miles (76 km), and traversing mountain passess higher than 7,000 feet (2,135 m).

The railway symbolized the new regime's goals of nationalism, independence, and modernization. To avoid foreign exploitation, particularly from English and Russian interests, it was financed by taxes on the popular subsistence items of tea and sugar. Ironically, during World War II, the railroad was commandeered by the Allies as a major supply route to the Soviet Union.

BIBLIOGRAPHY

MILLSPAUGH, ARTHUR C. *Americans in Persia*. Washington, D.C. 1946.

Jack Bubon

Transjordan

See Jordan

Transjordan Frontier Force

Military group established to defend Palestine and Transjordan (1926–1948).

The Transjordan Frontier Force (TJFF) was organized by the high commissioner for Palestine to fulfill Britain's responsibility under terms of the mandate treaty. The TJFF should not be confused with the ARAB LEGION, from which it was entirely separate.

Confusion arose out of the TJFF's having a name identifying it with Transjordan but being a part of the imperial forces in Palestine and thus a Palestinian responsibility. In the end, the British treasury agreed to have Palestine pay five-sixths of the cost of the TJFF and Transjordan pay one-sixth, following the line of reasoning that security in Transjordan contributed to security in Palestine.

Further disagreement arose over the need for a force to undertake responsibilities many believed could be handled by the Arab Legion. The high commissioner for Palestine, Lord Plumer, considered that the frontiers with Syria and Saudi Arabia were vulnerable. The latter frontier was regarded as particularly open to the possibility of expansion efforts by ABD AL-AZIZ IBN SA'UD AL SAUD, who had proclaimed himself king of the Hijaz in January 1926 and conceivably would seek to expand into areas controlled by the Hashimites, particularly Transjordan. The TJFF proved incapable of patrolling the desert of Transjordan and retired across the Jordan river to Palestine in 1930 when John Bagot Glubb created the DESERT MOBILE FORCE, which became the nucleus of the Arab Legion, and took over responsibility for the frontiers.

When the TJFF was formed, its recruits came from the disbanded Palestine gendarmeries, including noncommissioned officers and enlisted men who had had five years of experience. Some 70 percent of the recruits were Arabs from Palestine, mainly literate fellahin from the villages. In addition, there was a camel company of Sudanese enlisted men; it was replaced in 1933 by a mechanized unit. Some Jews and town Arabs served in administrative and technical services. Before 1935, about 25 percent of the force were Circassians.

The TJFF was under direct control of the high commissioner in Jerusalem, and above him the War Office in London. Non-British officers were not to attain command positions that gave them seniority over British personnel. Therefore, the officer corps and squadron commanders (majors or above) were British. Troop commanders (captains) and below included Palestinians, Syrians, Sudanese, Circassians, and a few Jews.

Initially the TJFF had three squadrons of two companies each, plus one camel company. In 1930, a mechanized company was added, bringing the total to eight companies. After the camel corps was replaced by a mechanized company, the TJFF consisted of three squadrons and two mechanized companies until the TJFF was disbanded.

All in all, there were some one thousand officers and men in the TJFF. Command headquarters, al-Zarqa, near Amman, was headed by a British lieutenant colonel. By 1935, there were twenty-four British officers in command of the TJFF: the commanding officer, seven majors, and sixteen captains. This complement remained more or less constant.

BIBLIOGRAPHY

DANN, URIEL. *Studies in the History of Transjordan, 1920–1949: The Making of a State*. Boulder, Colo., 1984.
VATIKIOTIS, P. J. *Politics and the Military in Jordan: A Study of the Arab Legion, 1921–1957*. New York, 1967.

Jenab Tutunji

Transport

Ships, caravans, railroads, and pipelines carry Middle Eastern goods to market.

Until the twentieth century (and in many places, until mid-century), people, animals, and water were the primary modes of transport in the Middle East.

Shipping. Waterways are few and not always navigable, but coastal navigation has always been important.

Of the various river systems, only two were basically navigable—the Nile river and the Tigris and Euphrates rivers. All were used for irrigation as well as transport, and canal systems were built to extend their benefits. The Nile runs north through East Africa, emptying across a broad delta into the eastern Mediterranean Sea. As the longest river in the world, it flows from Lake Victoria through the countries of Uganda, Sudan, and Egypt. Since the prevailing winds blow in a northerly direction, unmotorized boats can sail upstream and float downstream. The Tigris and Euphrates rivers are less suited to navigation, since their currents are swifter, their levels vary, and they often change course before merging into the SHATT AL-ARAB, which drains into the Persian/Arabian GULF. Because of these accessways to the sea, both areas transported bulk goods by water and built seaports that accommodated goods from other coastal trading areas, such as Turkey and Syria. Since antiquity, the coastal people of the Mediterranean traded, traveled, and warred among themselves—often coveting the riches of one another's lands.

Caravans. For the local movement of goods, the movement of goods to rivers or seaports, and even long-distance overland journeys, caravans were relied on—caravans of mules and, especially, camels, which took over from wheeled traffic at the end of the Roman era. Camel loads vary, generally ranging from 550 to 660 pounds (250–300 kg); the speed of a caravan is 2.5 to 3 miles (4–5 km) per hour; the usual daily stage is 15 to 20 miles (25–30 km). Caravans differed greatly in size, depending on the need and the availability of people and animals: In 1820, before the Suez Canal was built, the Suez caravan had about 500 camels; in 1847, the Baghdad–Damascus caravan had some 1,500 to 2,000 camels; and the Damascus–Baghdad some 800–1,200. In the 1870s, some 15,000 pack animals made three round-trips a year on the Tabriz–Trabzon route (Azerbaijan to Turkey), the carrying equivalent of seven or eight sailing ships each way. Boats and pack animals were adequate for a relatively small volume of traffic under traditional conditions, before the advent of the Industrial Revolution and the expansion of European trade and imperialism into the Middle East.

Steamships. In the nineteenth century, transport was revolutionized. In the 1820s and 1830s, regular steamer lines linked the Middle East with Europe across the Mediterranean, with Russia and Austria across the Black Sea, and with India through the Red Sea. Later, services were established in the Caspian Sea and the Gulf. By the closing decades of that century, the bulk of the region's foreign trade was carried on steamships, and freight costs were drastically reduced. Starting in the 1830s, steam tugs and steamboats were used on the Nile and on the Euphrates, soon carrying a large portion of domestic trade. Since no port improvements had occurred since Roman times, the steamers loaded and unloaded by lighters. The first modern port facilities were installed in Alexandria in 1818 (followed by later improvements), at Suez in 1866, İzmir in 1875, Aden in 1888, Beirut in 1895, and Istanbul in 1902. Except for Alexandria and Suez, all these harbors were built with European capital. The opening of the Suez Canal in 1869 by a French company was a major advance for world navigation.

Railroads. The first railway in the Middle East was begun in 1851, at British insistence, to link Alexandria with Cairo and Suez, speeding transport on the Mediterranean–India route. Like all Egypt's main lines, it was financed by the government. Soon after, British capital built two lines from İzmir in Turkey to the countryside. The Ottoman Empire, however, wanted a railroad that linked Istanbul with their provinces of Anatolia, Syria, and Iraq; following the completion of the Vienna–Istanbul line in 1888 (which became the Orient Express), it gave a concession to a German company for an Istanbul–Ankara line, later extended to Basra. This so-called BERLIN–BAGHDAD RAILWAY aroused much international controversy, which was settled just before the outbreak of World War I. When the war ended in 1918, the

TABLE 1						
Length of Rail in Service (in kilometers)						
	1870	*1890*	*1914*	*1939*	*1948*	*1975*
Egypt	1,400	1,797	4,314	5,606	6,092	4,856
Iran	—	—	—	1,700	3,180	4,944
Iraq	—	—	132	1,304	1,555	2,203
Jordan	—	1,650	—	332	332	420
Lebanon	—	—	—	232	423	417
Palestine/ Israel (as of 1948	—	—	—	1,188	1,225	902
Saudi Arabia	—	—	800	—	—	612
Sudan	—	—	2,396	3,206	3,242	4,556
Syria	—	—	—	854	867	1,761
Turkey	230	1,443	3,400	7,324	7,634	8,138
Total	1,630	4,890	11,042	21,746	24,550	28,809

line reached Aleppo in northern Syria, and a small stretch had been built in Iraq. Other foreign-owned short lines were built in Palestine, Lebanon, and Syria. The HIJAZ RAILROAD (1903–1908), linking Damascus, in Syria, to Medina, in western Saudi Arabia (near Mecca), was financed by contributions from Muslims throughout the world.

During World War I, the British army built extensive rail lines in Iraq and Palestine and put the Arabian section of the Hijaz railroad out of service. In Iran, the Russians built a line to Tabriz in Azerbaijan. After the war, Turkey doubled its mileage and Iran built a railroad between the Caspian Sea and the Persian/Arabian Gulf. Since then, important lines have been built in Iran, Saudi Arabia, and Syria. Table 1 (p. 1783) shows the length of rail service built from 1870 to 1975. Rail service reduced both the time and costs of transport. On the Ankara–Istanbul route, the rate per ton-mile fell from 10 cents to 1 cent; on the Damascus–Beirut line, from 4.5 cents to 1.5 cents; the journey from Damascus to Cairo was reduced from 25 days to 18 hours. In some areas telegraph lines accompanied, or preceded, the railroads.

Modern Services. As of the mid-1900s, the Middle East was served by an extensive network of telegraph and telephone lines, which extend to all cities, towns, and almost all villages. Computer, electronic mail, internet, and photofacsimile (fax) services exist in main centers as well.

Modern roadways were first built in the late nineteenth century; except for those in northern Iran and Lebanon, they played no significant role in the transport system. After World War I, and then again after World War II, they were greatly expanded and improved. Motor vehicles, which came to the Middle East before World War I, carry the bulk of inland transport. Air transport has a similar history: every country has its own airline and the region has become a hub of air traffic, connecting North America and Europe with Africa, India, and Asia.

Because of the Suez Canal, the Middle East plays an important part in world navigation. Just before Egypt nationalized the canal in 1956, it saw 13 percent of world shipping, but 20 percent of oil tankers. The canal has been repeatedly enlarged and deepened, to accommodate increasingly larger tankers and supertankers. In the 1990s, most petroleum producers maintain a large fleet of tankers, and oil-refining and consumer nations have sizeable merchant and tanker fleets; still, the share of the Middle East in world shipping is only 1 percent, and in world tankers only 3 percent. Nationalization of all transport facilities has been a fact of the Middle East, beginning with Turkey's railways in the 1920s.

TABLE 2

Modern Means of Transport, as of 1987

	Railway Tracks (thousands of km, 1985)	Paved Roads (thousands of km, 1987)	Passenger Motor Vehicles (thousands, 1987)	Commercial Motor Vehicles (thousands, 1985)	Ships (thousands of tons, 1987)*	Airlines (millions of passengers/km, 1987)*
Egypt	4.3	16.2	941	293	1,074	4,467
Iran	4.6	—	72	53	3,977	1,931
Iraq	1.7	—	258	273	1,002	—
Israel	0.6	13.0	613	115	515	7,284
Jordan	0.6	4.1	152	56	—	3,485
Kuwait	0	3.8	417	119	2,088	3,771
Lebanon	0.4	—	—	—	461	642
Saudi Arabia	0.6	—	—	—	2,692	10,342
Sudan	4.8	3.3	88	6	97	407
Syria	1.7	6.0	120	109	63	776
Turkey	8.4	—	983	381	3,336	2,351
United Arab Emirates	—	—	—	—	732	2,209

*Ships and airlines refer to vessels under the national flag and national airlines.

Sources: United Nations, *Statistical Yearbook* (New York, 1985); *The Statesman's Yearbook* (London, 1987).

Oil has brought another form of transport to the region: pipelines. The first, opened in 1934, carried Iraq's oil to the Mediterranean. Since then, far longer and larger pipelines were built to transport the oil of Saudi Arabia and Iraq through Syria to the Mediterranean, as well as Iraq's oil through Turkey and Saudi Arabia. Many no longer operate due to various political conflicts.

BIBLIOGRAPHY

EARLE, EDWARD. *Turkey, the Great Powers and the Baghdad Railway.* New York, 1923.
ELEFTERIADES, ELEUTHÈRE. *Les chemins de fer en Syrie et au Liban.* Beirut, 1944.
INTERNATIONAL AIR TRANSPORT ASSOCIATION. *World Air Transport Statistics.* Montreal, 1991.
———. *World Motor Vehicles Data.* Detroit, 1989.
ISSAWI, CHARLES. *An Economic History of the Middle East and North Africa.* New York, 1982.
UNITED NATIONS. *Statesman's Yearbook.* New York, 1989.
———. *Statistical Yearbook.* New York, 1989.
WIENER, LIONEL. *L'Egypte et ses chemins de fer.* Brussels, 1932.

Charles Issawi

Trans-Turkey Pipeline

Oil pipeline connecting fields in Iraq and Turkey.

The Iraq–Turkey pipeline connects the rich oil fields around Kirkuk, Iraq, to the Mediterranean port of Yumurtalık in Turkey. It consists of two parallel pipes, 941 kilometers long (641 km in Turkey), with a total capacity of fourteen million barrels of crude oil. The first line was opened in 1977; the second, in 1987. It is operated jointly by the national oil companies of Iraq and Turkey. Oil flows through the pipeline ceased in 1991, in accordance with UN sanctions against Iraq after its invasion of Kuwait.

Niyazi Dalyanci

Travel Diary of Abraham Beg

The first Iranian novel, published anonymously in Cairo in 1896.

In this novel, *Siyahatnameh-ye Ibrahim Beg,* an Azerbaijani merchant abroad comments on the comparatively sorry state of Iran. Although banned, it was widely read and was influential in the CONSTITUTIONAL REVOLUTION. Subsequent volumes published in Calcutta (1905) and Tehran (1909) revealed the author to be Zayn al-Abedin of Maragheh.

Farhad Shirzad

Treaty between the United States and the Ottoman Empire

Agreement clarifying commercial procedures between the United States and the Ottoman Empire, 1830.

As the United States became more involved in commerce with the Ottoman Empire, it became necessary to establish clear rules and regulations regarding tariffs, consulates, and other essential elements. In addition to these clauses, the treaty, signed May 7, 1830, included a secret article, which provided for the sale of American warships to the Ottomans, who had severe naval losses in the war for Greek independence.

BIBLIOGRAPHY

HUREWITZ, J. C., ed. *The Middle East and North Africa in World Politics.* New Haven, Conn., 1975.

Zachary Karabell

Treaty of 1815

U.S.–Algiers pact ending piracy against U.S. shipping.

At the end of the Napoleonic Wars, the United States was unable to pay its annual tribute to the Algerian CORSAIRS. The *dey* of Algiers lifted its protection of American shipping in the Mediterranean Sea. The Americans dispatched a naval squadron to Algiers in May 1815. The expedition was extremely successful for the Americans, as the treaty concluded on June 30, 1815, abolished the annual tribute and granted the United States the ability to trade with Algiers.

BIBLIOGRAPHY

HUREWITZ, J. C., ed. *The Middle East and North Africa in World Politics.* New Haven, Conn., 1975.

Zachary Karabell

Treaty of Peace (1912)

Treaties that ended the Tripolitanian War between Italy and the Ottoman Empire over Libya.

The treaty of peace is actually two treaties: The Treaty of Ouchy was signed on October 15 and the Treaty of Lausanne on October 18, 1912. Italy was confirmed in possessing the Libyan provinces of Tripoli and Cyrenaica and agreed to respect the rights of Muslims in these territories. Italy was also ceded the Dodecanese islands, which had been seized during the war. The Ottoman sultan never renounced his claims on these territories, but World War I changed the entire situation, since the Ottoman Empire was an ally of the losing Central powers and much of the Ottoman territory was divided among the winners. Italy thus maintained control of Libya, albeit against great local opposition; tens of thousands of Italians colonized the country, contributing to agricultural and industrial development, while the military command attempted to subdue the opposition throughout the 1920s and 1930s.

BIBLIOGRAPHY

HUREWITZ, J. C., ed. *The Middle East and North Africa in World Politics*. New Haven, Conn., 1975.

Zachary Karabell

Treaty of Protection

British treaty made with south Arabian rulers.

This formal treaty of friendship and protection between Britain and the rulers of Qishn and Socotra in 1886 was followed by similar treaties with the rulers of the other states along the southern coast of the Arabian peninsula and with the major tribal shaykhs of the interior that were deemed crucial to the security and commerce of Aden. Designed to end growing threats posed by the Ottoman Turks in North Yemen and by other European imperial powers, these treaties were a major step toward the creation of the Aden Protectorates and the binding of Aden to the interior territories in modern times. The local rulers traded control of foreign policy for British protection and modest subsidies. Between 1886 and 1895, Britain signed treaties with the Aqrabis, Lower Aulaqis, Fadhlis, Hawshabis, Alawis, Lower Yafais, and some of the Wahidis.

Robert D. Burrowes

Treaty of

See under specific place names.

Trebizond

See Trabzon

Tribalism

Yemeni tribes, rather than being mere vestiges of the past, are vital forces that continue to play determinant roles in the political, social, and cultural spheres.

Despite the tendency to characterize the highlands of Northern Yemen as "tribal" and southern Yemen as "peasant," tribes and tribalism are part of the cultural, social, and political landscape of nearly all regions of Yemen, even the Tihama coast and Wadi Hadramawt. For centuries, however, what has distinguished the northern highlands from the other regions of the country is the importance of the tribe as a unit of identification and action and the great extent to which tribes can be mobilized and organized into larger confederations when the interests of the tribe or tribal system are at stake. Although many residents of the southern uplands and the Hadramawt claim a tribal lineage, this often seems to be less important as a basis of personal identity than place of origin—a village, valley, or region—or some other attribute. By contrast, many men of the highlands define themselves primarily in terms of their tribes, and many of these northern highland tribes with their present names were in existence at least a thousand years ago.

The majority of tribesmen in most parts of Yemen are sedentary farmers who grow sorghum, but the sparsely populated arid land on the edge of the Rub al-Khali (Empty Quarter) and the Ramlat al-Sabatayn is home to nomadic tribes principally engaged in animal husbandry. These bedouin populations have declined in recent years, in part because they were forced to give up their traditional roles as guardians and pillagers of the old trade routes, and now constitute a tiny portion of the total population of unified Yemen.

Robert D. Burrowes

Tribes, Arabian Peninsula

In the peninsula, a tribe is a group defined by perceived descent from a common male ancestor.

The word *qabila* (tribe) refers not only to a kinship group but also to a status category: *qabili* families claim descent from one of two eponymous Arab ancestors, Adnan or Qahtan, and feel themselves to be distinct from and superior to the nontribal *khadiri*, freeborn people who cannot claim such descent. The khadiri included most of the tradesmen, artisans, merchants, and scholars of pre-oil Arabia.

People of qabili status divide themselves into superior and inferior tribes, with the former able to claim purity in blood and origin (*asl*). The most prominent of the superior tribes of Arabia are the ANAZA, SHAMMAR, Harb, Mustair, AJMAN, Dhafir, Banu Khalid, Banu Hajir, al-MURRAH, Qahtan, UTAYBA, DAWASIR, Sahul, Manasir, BANU YAS, Sebei, Qawasim, Banu Yam, Za'ab, and Banu Tamim. The main tribes considered inferior are the Awazim, Rashaida, Hutaim, Aqail, and Sulubba. The Sulubba, who traveled the desert as tinkers and metalworkers in service to the more affluent bedouin, were at the bottom of the tribal social scale.

Marriage between individuals of qabila and khadiri status, and between individuals of superior and inferior tribes, is frowned upon. Since the qabili claim to status is dependent upon purity of descent through the paternal line, the children of such a marriage would suffer the taint of mixed blood and reflect on the status of the tribe as a whole. These status barriers to marriage are beginning to break down in contemporary Saudi Arabia as success to education and economic advantage have created new status categories, which are beginning to compete with tribal affiliation and are undermining its importance in the social hierarchy.

The proportion of the population of Saudi Arabia that claims a tribal affiliation is unknown. Nearly all nomadic people are organized in tribal associations, and in 1950 Saudi Arabia's nomadic population was estimated at 50 percent. Since, historically, branches of tribal groups have lived in agricultural settlements at least part of the year or were permanently settled in towns, an estimate (according to a study done in the late 1970s) that the proportion of the population who claim a tribal affiliation could be as high as 80 percent would seem reasonable. A more recent study, however, suggests that the bulk of the settled population in NAJD were nontribal khadiri, many of whom intermarried with the *abd,* or black slaves. Since the major cities of the HIJAZ—Jidda and Mecca—and the towns of the Persian/Arabian Gulf have long attracted foreigners, it is likely that the proportion of the contemporary Saudi population claiming a tribal affiliation is far smaller.

Structurally, nomadic tribal groups are organized by patrilineal descent, which unites individuals in increasingly larger segments. The smallest functional unit is the *hamula* (lineage), which consists of three to seven generations of one family related through the paternal line. Since lineage members are patrilineal cousins, the hamula is also referred to as one's *ibn amm* (father's brother's son), or *ahl* (people). The residential unit within the lineage is the *bayt* (house or tent), usually consisting of members of a nuclear family, including wife or wives and children.

Members of a single lineage usually camp close to one another and herd their animals as a unit. The lineage shares joint responsibility for avenging wrongs suffered by its members and pays compensation for any caused by its members. Although tribes may differ in status, all lineages within a given tribe are considered equals. Water wells, aside from the newer deep wells drilled by the government, are held

in common by lineages. Among nomads, lineage membership is the basis of summer camps, and all animals, though they are owned by individual households, bear the lineage's brand. In terms of social relationships, access to government bureaucracy, and economic well-being, connection with the lineage is the most important relationship for the individual member of a tribe.

Above the level of lineage there are larger segments that together make up the tribe. The *fakhd* (thigh) consists of a number of lineages that together control pasture and wells in the tribal area, while the *ashira* (pl. *asha'ir*) consisting of numerous fakhds, is the largest segment below the tribe. While the system allows lineages to locate themselves genealogically relative to other groups in the same tribe, in general the larger the tribal segment, the smaller its function in the daily life of the individual.

In eastern Arabia, there is a recognized division among tribal groups based on perceived origin: the Yamani (or Qahtani) who predominate in Oman are believed to have emigrated in ancient times from Yemen in the south, while the Adnani (or Nizari) tribes—settled in northern Oman, the Trucial coast, Bahrain, and Qatar—are believed to have come from the north and are considered racially less "pure" than those from the south. Most of the tribal groups in Qatar, despite their common origin, are also located throughout eastern Arabia. The ruling family of the State of Qatar are the AL THANI, originally part of the Banu Tamim tribe of central Arabia who arrived in Qatar in the early seventeenth century. The Manasir, one of the most widespread tribes of eastern Arabia, are mostly bedouin and range from the al-Buraymi oasis, across the United Arab Eminates to Qatar and al-Hasa in the west, with some residing in Sharja and Ra's al-Khayma, and in the al-Shafra and al-Liwa oases in western Abu Dhabi. Some sections of the formerly powerful al-Na'im tribe of Oman reside in Qatar as well as in the rest of eastern Arabia. The Quabysat section of the Banu Yas Tribe tried unsuccessfully in the early twentieth century to settle at Khawar al-Udayd, a marshy inlet at the eastern base of the Qatar peninsula.

In Saudi Arabia, a new national consciousness to compete with tribal identities is starting to emerge as the centralized state undercuts tribal autonomy, sedentariazation undermines the economic benefits of tribal organization, and children are exposed to a common government-imposed school curriculum. However, tribal affiliation, especially for nomadic people, plays a pivotal role in relations between individuals and the central government. Since the mid-1980s, the central government has assumed the right to officially designate tribal leaders who may act as representatives on behalf of tribal members' interests.

These leaders are expected to work through district amirs and governors and to deal with such issues as education, agricultural development, assistance in legal matters, transportation and communication improvement, welfare and social assistance, and in helping to attain citizenship privileges.

For many tribal groups such as the al-Murrah, the National Guard has institutionalized tribal solidarity and strengthened tribal ties to the central government. Membership in individual National Guard units is based on tribal affiliation, and leadership of each tribal unit can be synonymous with traditional tribal leadership. Through the National Guard, former nomads receive training and the potential for higher level careers, instruction in military sciences, housing, and health and social services for dependents and families.

For those tribal people who continue to live as bedouins, the government also provides water taps; market areas in cities, towns, and villages that are used in marketing livestock; veterinary services; subsidized fodder; and buildings for storage. It has been estimated that only 5 percent of the Saudi population today remain wholly nomadic.

Most tribes are affiliated with the House of Sa'ud through marriage ties as the product of Ibn Sa'ud's deliberate policy of cementing ties between himself and the tribal groups. Today the political alliance between tribe and state is being reinforced through marriage between tribal women and government officials as well as Saudi princes. Among the al-Saar bedouin in southern Arabia, for example, these marriages are encouraged by tribal leaders as a means of ensuring ongoing access to governmental leaders.

BIBLIOGRAPHY

ANTHONY, JOHN DUKE. *Historical and Cultural Dictionary of the Sultanate of Oman and the Emirates of Eastern Arabia.* Metuchen, N.J., 1976.

COLE, DONALD, and SOROYA ALTORKI. "Was Arabia Tribal? A Reinterpretation of the Pre-Oil Society." Unpublished paper delivered at MESA, 1990.

DAHLAN, AHMED MASSAN, ed. *Politics, Administration and Development in Saudi Arabia, Amana, 1990.*

DICKSON, HAROLD. *The Arab of the Desert.*

DOUGHTY, CHARLES. *Travels in Arabia Deserta.* Reprint, New York, 1980.

HOPKINS, NICHOLAS. "Class and State in Rural Arab Communities." In *Beyond Coercion,* ed. by Adeed Dawisha and I. Zartman. London, 1980.

KINGDOM OF SAUDI ARABIA. *Fifth Plan.* N.d.

MANA, AISHA. "Economic Development and Its Impact on the Status of Women in Saudi Arabia." Ph.D. diss., 1981.

Eleanor Abdella Doumato

Tripartite Declaration

See Lebanon

Tripartite Treaty of Alliance

See Anglo–Russo–Persian Treaty of Alliance

Triple Alliance

See World War I

Triple Entente

See World War I

Tripoli

City on the Mediterranean coast of northwest Libya.

Tripoli is the capital, largest city, and chief seaport of Libya. The city was founded by the Phoenicians on a small, rocky promontory. Known by the Romans as Oea, it formed (with Sabrata and Leptis Magna) the *tripolis* (Greek, three towns) from which its modern name derives. (In Arabic Tripoli is known as *Tarablus al-Gharb*—Tripoli of the West—to distinguish it from Lebanon's Tripoli.) Tripoli owed its preeminence to a fair harbor on the short sea route to Malta, Sicily, and Italy; to good water supplies and a moderately productive oasis and hinterland; and to domination of the northern ends of the shortest trade routes from the Mediterranean to central Africa via FEZZAN.

After a history of foreign and local rule, prosperity declined by the end of the nineteenth century with the demise of Barbary Pirates and Mediterranean corsairing as well as the collapse of the trans-Saharan trade system. In 1911, the population was estimated at some 20,000, when Tripoli was the prime objective of the Italian invasion. It remained in Italian hands throughout the varying fortunes of Italy's presence in Libya. Under Italian rule, and especially during the post-1922 Fascist era, Tripoli was developed outside the walled Old City and acquired modern municipal services and the appearance of an Italian provincial town. In 1934, it became the capital of the colony of Libya, combining Tripolitania and

Cyrenaica. During World War II, Tripoli fell, with little damage, to the invading British Eighth Army in January 1943 and became the seat of the British military administration that ruled Tripolitania until Libya's UN-supervised independence in 1951. On independence, Tripoli became joint capital of the Libyan federal kingdom, with BENGHAZI.

The oil boom of the 1950s and 1960s brought commercial expansion and increased population, with development into the outlying villages of the oasis. Shantytowns—which housed migrants from the countryside—proliferated on the outskirts. The United States had a large air base at Wheelus (al-Mallaha) to the east of the city, and the international airport was developed at the Royal Air Force base at Idris, near Gasr ben Gashir to the south. After the 1969 revolution, Tripoli became the sole capital of the Libya and, following expulsion of its remaining Italian and Jewish communities, took on a more overtly Arab and Muslim character. Shanty towns were cleared and large public-housing schemes and commercial developments spread in a six-to-ten-mile (10–15 km) radius from the city center. The population doubled between 1973 and 1984.

Attempts by the royalist regime to create a new capital at Baida and move the central administration to the central Libyan oases did little to diminish Tripoli's political, commercial, and social preeminence. It dominates one of Libya's main agricultural and industrial regions, and its port, airport, and roads to Tunisia, Fezzan, and Cyrenaica make it a key communications and transshipment center.

BIBLIOGRAPHY

ROSSI, ETTORE. *Storia di Tripoli e della Tripolitania dalla conquista araba al 1911* (History of Tripoli and Tripolitania from the Arab Conquest to 1911). Rome, 1968.
WRIGHT, JOHN. *Libya.* London and New York, 1969.

John L. Wright

Tripoli Conference

Conference of Arab leaders in Tripoli, Libya.

The Tripoli Conference was convened December 2, 1977, in response to Egyptian President Anwar Sadat's trip to Jerusalem the previous month. It established the Steadfastness and Confrontation Front to oppose Sadat's peace initiative toward Israel. The front was joined by all of the attending heads of state, from Libya, Syria, Algeria, and South Yemen, and by leaders of Palestine Liberation Organization (PLO) factions.

Iraq, which sent a minor delegate, refused to join. On December 5, Sadat broke diplomatic relations with all countries that attended the conference. A second result of the conference was the brief reunion of feuding PLO factions under Syria's sponsorship.

BIBLIOGRAPHY

COBBAN, HELENA. *The Palestinian Liberation Organization.* New York, 1984.

Elizabeth Thompson

Tripoli Programme

Document representing the first comprehensive endeavor to define an identity and direction for independent Algeria.

At the end of the Algerian War of Independence, the Tripoli Programme, one of the most important documents in modern Algerian history, was introduced, the product of the meeting in Libya of Algeria's Front de Libération Nationale (National Liberation Front, FLN). This occasion in June 1962 marked the last time the wartime FLN convened before the intra-elite conflict of that summer, which established the new government under Ahmed Ben Bella.

The program proposed a "socialist option" for Algeria's development. According to its chief authors, Redha Malek, Mohamed Bedjaoui, and Mohamed Benyahia, the quest for democracy necessitated class conflict and economic transformation. It projected the nationalization of foreign interests, the establishment of an industrial economy, and the inauguration of agricultural cooperatives. Stridently anticolonial, the program viewed the recently signed Evian agreements with France as neocolonialist. The Tripoli Programme was complemented in April 1964 by the ALGIERS CHARTER and by Algeria's National Charter (1976; 1986).

BIBLIOGRAPHY

CUBERTAFOND, BERNARD. *La république algérienne démocratique et populaire.* Limoges, 1979.

Phillip C. Naylor

Tripolitania

Former province of northwest Libya.

Tripolitania, also called Tarablus, bordered the Mediterranean, Tunisia, Algeria, and the former Libyan provinces of CYRENAICA and FEZZAN. In the twentieth century, Tripolitania's administrative areas have been changed. The main cities in this region today are Tripoli (the capital of Libya and its main port) and Misurata.

John L. Wright

Tripolitania–Cyrenaica Defense Committee

Libyan exile organization opposed to Italian rule.

Established in Damascus, the committee was headed by Bashir al-Sidawi, a member of the 1922 Tripolitan delegation to the Sanusi leader, Muhammad Idris. It was one of several Libyan émigré groups formed during the Italian occupation.

Stuart J. Borsch

Tripolitanian War

See Turkish–Italian War

Trucial Coast

Colonial precursor of the United Arab Emirates.

The Trucial Coast was known to Europeans as the Pirate Coast in the late eighteenth and early nineteenth centuries, when the powerful federation of the Qawasim, operating primarily from the port of Ra's al-Khayma, ravaged shipping in the lower Persian/Arabian Gulf. The government of British India sent several expeditions against them, finally subduing them in 1819. In the following year, Britain through the General Treaty of Peace, imposed a truce that condemned piracy and implied Britain's obligation to maintain peace in the Gulf. Subsequent treaties (truces) made the agreements more explicit, and the territories ruled by the shaykhs who were signatories to them became, in European usage, the Trucial Coast. The terms "Trucial States" and, confusingly, "Trucial Oman" were also used.

Fear of European rivals led Britain to establish "exclusive agreements" with these shaykhs in 1892. These engagements made Great Britain, through the colonial government in Delhi, responsible for the foreign relations of these shaykhdoms and, by implication, for their protection. The British, interested primarily in the security of the Gulf, kept their involvement on land to a minimum. Their intervention however, tended to freeze political relationships. This situation remained essentially unaltered until the interwar period, when the British government forced the rulers to deal only with prospecting oil companies of which it approved. Britain's simultaneous establishment of an air route across the Gulf began to open the area to the outside world, especially SHARJA, where an Imperial Airways airfield was established. Moreover, oil concession agreements created the need for the novel concept of fixed borders, which the British began to establish.

After World War II, Britain was much more fully involved in the affairs of the Trucial States. After 1947, with India's independence, the states became the responsibility of the Foreign Office in London. Britain's representative in the Trucial States was a permanent political officer assigned to Sharja in 1948 (upgraded to political agent in 1953), and several state institutions were established. In 1951 the Trucial Oman Levies, a small force with British officers, was created to keep order in the Trucial States. Expanded and renamed the Trucial Oman Scouts in the mid-1950s, it became the nucleus of the United Arab Emirates, armed forces in 1971. In 1952 the Trucial States Council was created; though limited to a consultative role, it provided the first forum in which the rulers of the seven shaykhdoms could discuss common concerns. From 1965 until independence a Development Office, operating under the aegis of the Council, carried out infrastructure projects financed through a development fund to which Britain, Kuwait, Bahrain, Qatar, and Abu Dhabi contributed; Abu Dhabi carried the lion's share as its oil income expanded from the mid-1960s.

In December 1968, Britain's Labor government, beset by a balance-of-payments crisis, decided to withdraw military forces and relinquish responsibilities in the Gulf by the end of 1971. Though some of the rulers viewed Britain's withdrawal with alarm, Shaykh Zayid of Abu Dhabi and Shaykh Rashid of Dubai, the wealthiest of the seven Trucial States, agreed, as early as February 1968, to form a federation that would include Bahrain and Qatar. Despite British encouragement of this venture, it had foundered by early 1971. On December 2, 1971, a few months after Bahrain and Qatar had become separately independent, Sharja, Umm al-Qaywayn, Ajman, and Fujayra joined Abu Dhabi and Dubai in the federation of the UNITED ARAB EMIRATES. In February 1972, Ra's al-Khayma belatedly joined the United Arab Emirates.

BIBLIOGRAPHY

ANTHONY, JOHN DUKE. *Arab States of the Lower Gulf: People, Politics, Petroleum.* Washington, D.C., 1975.

HEARD-BEY, FRAUKE. *From Trucial States to United Arab Emirates.* New York, 1982.

PECK, MALCOLM C. *The United Arab Emirates: A Venture in Unity.* Boulder, Colo., 1986.

Malcolm C. Peck

True Path Party

Turkish political party.

Formed in the aftermath of the 1980 military coup, the True Path party became the prime inheritor of the political legacy of the pre-1980 JUSTICE PARTY. This is symbolized by the leadership of Süleyman DEMIREL, although he was not legally permitted to assume control of the party until 1987. Its name may be intended to appeal to religious propensities of the electorate, since it evokes the Qur'anic concept of the "straight path." Its program is ideologically liberal or center-right, supporting individual rights, secular democracy, and free expression of the popular will.

In the 1987 parliamentary election, the first in which it was able to compete, it polled 19 percent of the vote and won 59 of 450 seats, placing third. In 1991, it vaulted to first place with 27 percent of the vote and 178 seats. Its leader then became prime minister at the head of a coalition cabinet in which the SOCIAL DEMOCRATIC POPULIST PARTY was the junior partner. In May 1993, True Path party leader Demirel was elected president of the republic.

BIBLIOGRAPHY

LANDAU, J. M. "Turkey." In *Political Parties in the Middle East and North Africa,* ed. by F. Tachau. Westport, Conn., 1994.

Frank Tachau

Truman, Harry S.   [1884–1972]

American president.

Born in Missouri, Truman was elected to the U.S. Senate in 1934. He became vice president in 1944 and then president in May 1945. In May 1947, he presented the Truman Doctrine after Great Britain had announced that it was unable to continue its aid to Greece and Turkey. The former was in the midst of a civil war; the latter was under pressure from Josef Stalin to concede control of the Turkish straits to the USSR. Believing that without support both countries would fall under Soviet control, Truman and Under Secretary of State Dean ACHESON decided to give economic and military assistance to these two

nations. The Truman Doctrine was soon extended to include any other country endangered by communism. Truman was also pivotal in the creation of Israel, and he supported the November 1947 United Nations Partition Plan. Under his initiative, the United States was the first country to recognize the new state of Israel, but he also cosponsored the 1950 Tripartite Declaration, which placed restrictions on the sale of arms to any of the combatants in the Middle East. At the end of his second administration, in 1952, Truman attempted to create a Middle East equivalent of NATO, known as MEDO (MIDDLE EAST DEFENSE ORGANIZATION).

BIBLIOGRAPHY

DECONDE, ALEXANDER, ed. *Encyclopedia of American Foreign Policy.* New York, 1978.

SPIEGEL, STEVEN. *The Other Arab–Israeli Conflict.* Chicago, 1985.

Zachary Karabell

Trumpeldor, Yosef   [1880–1920]

Zionist leader and military organizer in Palestine.

Born in the northern Caucasus in Russia, Trumpeldor served in the czar's army during the Russo–Japanese War (1904–1905). He was wounded and lost an arm but returned to combat, which earned him decorations and promotion as the first Jewish officer in the Russian army.

Ardent about Zionism and an advocate of agricultural settlements, he organized Jewish self-defense groups in Russia (for immigration) and later in Ottoman Palestine, where he immigrated. During World War I, he lobbied for the creation of a British-backed JEWISH LEGION, serving as second-in-command in what became the Zion Mule Corps. After the war, he was affiliated with HE-HALUTZ (the agricultural pioneers) and encouraged Russian Jewish youth to go to Palestine to create agricultural and industrial settlements. Just before the British and French mandates took effect in the Middle East, he was sent to organize the defenses of TEL HAI, a pioneer Jewish settlement in northern Galilee. He died defending it on March 1, 1920. Tel Hai is now a national monument.

BIBLIOGRAPHY

ZERUBAVEL, YAEL. "The Politics of Interpretation: Tel Hai in Israel's Collective Memory." *American Jewish Studies Review* 16 (1991): 133–160.

Donna Robinson Divine

Tudeh Party

The main orthodox Communist organization in contemporary Iran.

The Tudeh party (Hezb-e Tudeh-ye Iran; the Party of the Iranian Masses) was formed in 1941 in Iran by members of the famous Fifty-three, who had been arrested in 1937 but released immediately on the British–Soviet occupation of Iran during World War II. The Fifty-three were predominantly young university-educated Marxist intellectuals from middle-class and Persian-speaking families. The Tudeh party quickly grew to become the organization of the masses in reality as well as in name. It did so in part because its labor unions mobilized a significant portion of the wage-earning population; in part because it attracted many civil servants, professionals, and intellectuals; and in part because it successfully portrayed itself as the champion of patriotism and constitutional liberties against foreign imperialism and the threat of royal dictatorship. By 1945, the list of Tudeh sympathizers read like a *Who's Who* of Iran's intelligentsia.

After 1945, however, the Tudeh suffered a series of setbacks. Its patriotic credentials were undermined when it supported the Soviet-sponsored revolt in Azerbaijan, echoed the demands of the Soviet Union's Josef Stalin for an oil concession, and failed to give full backing to Mohammad Mossadegh's campaign to nationalize the petroleum industry. Its constitutional and democratic credentials were brought into question once it declared itself a Marxist–Leninist party and became a formal member of the Soviet-led Communist movement. Moreover, its ability to function was drastically curtailed—first in 1949, when the party was banned after an attempt was made on the life of Mohammad Reza Pahlavi; second, after the 1953 coup, when SAVAK, the secret police, helped by the U.S. Central Intelligence Agency (CIA), vigorously unearthed its underground network. Over forty Tudeh members were executed in the 1950s.

The Tudeh was further weakened by two major internal disputes. In the aftermath of the Azerbaijan revolt, a number of intellectuals left the party and in later years joined Mosaddegh's National Front (Jebhe-ye Melli). In the 1960s, at the height of the Sino–Soviet dispute, a number of younger activists, denouncing the Tudeh leadership as reformist and revisionist, formed their own pro-Chinese Sazman-e Engelab-e Hezb-e Tudeh-ye Iran (Revolutionary Organization of the Tudeh Party of Iran).

By the time of the Iranian Revolution (1978/79), little remained of the Tudeh within Iran. Despite this, the party tried a comeback; it instructed its cad-

res to return and elected as its first secretary Nur al-Din Kianuri, the proponent of an alliance with Ayatollah Ruhollah Khomeini. The previous first secretary, Iraj Iskandari, had favored the secular liberals, especially the National Front. From 1978 until 1983, the Tudeh supported the Islamic Republic of Iran, even when much of the Left denounced the regime as a medieval theocracy.

This support ended abruptly in 1983, in the midst of the Iran–Iraq War, when Khomeini ordered Iranian troops to cross the border into Iraq. As soon as the Tudeh criticized this action most of the party's leaders and cadres were arrested and tortured into confessing that they were "spies and traitors plotting to overthrow the Islamic Republic." The most extensive recantation came from Ehsan Tabari, a member of the Fifty-three and the most important intellectual in the Tudeh leadership. Tabari died in prison from heart failure, but 163 of his colleagues were killed—some under torture, others by hanging. A few party leaders escaped to Western Europe, where they continue to produce the organization's main publication, a weekly named *Nameh-ye Mardom* (the People's Newsletter). The party also broadcasts on a clandestine radio station.

BIBLIOGRAPHY

ABRAHAMIAN, ERVAND. *Iran between Two Revolutions.* Princeton, N.J., 1982.

RAFFAT, DONNE. *The Prison Papers of Bozorg Alavi.* Syracuse, N.Y., 1985.

ZABIH, SEPEHR. *The Communist Movement in Iran.* Berkeley, Calif., 1966.

Ervand Abrahamian

Tuhami al-Glawi   [1879–1956]

Pasha of Marrakech under the French protectorate in Morocco, 1912–1956.

The younger brother of Madani al-GLAWI, who established the power of the family, Tuhami ibn Muhammad al-Mazwari al-Glawi first served as pasha of Marrakech under Morocco's Sultan Abd al-Hafid from 1908 to 1911. He then benefited from Madani's alliance with the protectorate government of France in 1912, and following Madani's death in 1918 Tuhami was named pasha of Marrakech. A staunch supporter of the French protectorate and a wily politician, he accumulated enormous wealth and power as viceroy of southern Morocco and gained a reputation of being greedy and oppressive.

His leadership of the movement to depose Sultan Muhammad V (1953), part of a pro-French effort to prevent the collapse of the protectorate, gained him much notoriety among Moroccan nationalists. He died in 1956, after the independence of Morocco.

BIBLIOGRAPHY

PASCON, PAUL. *Capitalism and Agriculture in the Haouz of Marrakech*. London, 1986.

Edmund Burke III

Tuman Bey   [1473–1517]

The last independent Mamluk sultan of Egypt.

After the death of Qansuh al-Ghuri al-Ashrafi in the battle of Marj Dabiq near Aleppo (August 1516), the Mamluks selected his viceroy, Tuman Bey, to continue the struggle against the invasion of Sultan Selim the Grim.

Superior Ottoman tactics and weaponry forced the Egyptian ruler to hurriedly manufacture cannons and raise an infantry corps that used muskets similar to those used by the janissaries. He rejected an offer to submit to Ottoman suzerainty in exchange for being allowed to remain governor of Egypt. The two armies met in Raydaniyya, near Cairo, on January 22, 1517. The Mamluk cavalry again suffered defeat, and Selim entered the capital in triumph. On January 28, Tuman Bey launched a surprise night attack against the Ottomans in Bulaq. The battle raged for four days, with both sides displaying extreme ferocity, but the Mamluks finally withdrew to the haven of Upper Egypt. There, Tuman Bey raised an army composed of a combination of Arab bedouins and Mamluks, and he returned, on April 2/3, to attack Selim near Giza. After another defeat, Tuman Bey escaped north to a village near Damanhur, where he was captured by Ottoman troops. He was hanged a fortnight later in Cairo.

BIBLIOGRAPHY

GLUBB, JOHN. *Soldiers of Fortune: The Story of the Mamlukes*. New York, 1973.

Bassam Namani

Tunb Islands

Islands in the Strait of Hormuz.

The Greater and Lesser Tunbs are two small, strategically placed islands in the lower Persian/Arabian Gulf. They had been the possessions of the Qawasim rulers of Ra's al-Khayma for about a century when,

in 1971, the British gave independence to that emirate and the other Trucial States. On November 30, the day before the British treaty of protection was due to expire, Iran, largely motivated by the perceived need to act forcefully after relinquishing its claims to Bahrain the year before, seized the islands. Britain, anxious not to jeopardize its important relations with Iran, did not act. Local demonstrations of anger erupted briefly against Iran and Britain, Iraq broke diplomatic relations with Britain, and Libya nationalized British Petroleum's assets on its soil.

Iran has continued to hold the islands. In the spring of 1992 it renewed pressure on the United Arab Emirates by violating the agreement it had reached with Sharja, at the time the Tunbs were occupied, to share the island of ABU MUSA. The issue of the islands has thus become a source of renewed tension between Iran and the emirates.

BIBLIOGRAPHY

PECK, MALCOLM C. *The United Arab Emirates: A Venture in Unity*. Boulder, Colo., 1986.

Malcolm C. Peck

Tunis

Capital of the Republic of Tunisia.

Tunis, the largest city in Tunisia, has a population (est. 1991) of between 597,000 and 1 million, the latter figure including the suburbs. Greater Tunis contains one-eighth of the country's total population of 8,450,000.

In 1160, Tunis became the provincial capital of the Moroccon-based Almohad dynasty. The Almohads built the *qasba* (citadel) that remained the seat of political power in the city until France's protectorate (1881). In the thirteenth century, under the Hafsid dynasty, Tunis became the national capital, a distinction it has retained ever since.

A city square in Tunis. (Mia Bloom)

Tunis rooftop with floral tiles and pottery. (Mia Bloom)

Tunis had only one congregational mosque, that of al-Zaytuna, until 1252, when the mosque of al-Tawfiq was constructed. Subsequently congregational mosques were built throughout the city. Following their seizure of Tunis in 1574, the Ottomans converted the mosques of the qasba and al-Qasr to follow the Hanafi usage, the school of Islamic law to which they adhered. In the seventeenth and eighteenth centuries, the Tunis skyline was altered by construction of new mosques, including those of Yusuf Dey (1612), Hammuda Pasha (1655), and Sidi Mahriz (1692), and the New Mosque of Husayn (1726).

Corsair wealth of the deys and beys transformed Tunis into a cosmopolitan complex dominated by mosques, madrasas (Islamic secondary schools), *zawiya*s (Islamic mystic centers), palaces, and elegant homes. The Turks also constructed a *maristan* (hospital) in the seventeenth century.

Prior to 1858, Tunis was organized into a quarter system centered on major mosques. The gates between quarters were locked at night and whenever public disturbances occurred. Each quarter was self-sufficient, with its own bread ovens, markets, bathhouses, wells, cisterns, Qur'anic schools (*kuttab*), and prayer mosques (*masjid*). Daytime security was provided by the *dawlatli* (a position directly descended from the dey). The *shaykh al-madina* (chief guild leader, akin to city mayor) controlled night-time security patrols.

This loose administration ended in 1858, when Muhammad Bey established the City Council (*al-majlis al-baladi*). He appointed the shaykh al-madina to head this council of fifteen members. Today the shaykh al-madina is president of the City Council and is appointed by the country's president.

France's protectorate (1881–1956) brought changes to Tunis. A deep-water channel was constructed that made it possible for oceangoing vessels to dock in the port of Tunis, near the modern city's downtown area. A causeway beside this channel connects Tunis and its suburbs of La Goulette (now Halq al-Wadi), Carthage, Sidi Bou Said, and La Marsa. France also drained the swamp that separated the walled old city from the Lake of Tunis and built there a new European-style city with parks, broad avenues, cathedrals, an embassy, and modern housing.

In the twentieth century, Tunis has become the major destination of rural-to-urban migration because of its being the political, social, educational, economic, and entertainment center of Tunisia. It is the seat of the national government and the national headquarters of the government party, the CONSTITUTIONAL DEMOCRATIC RALLY (Ralliement Constitutionel Démocratique; RCD), and the site of the national university.

BIBLIOGRAPHY

ABDELKAFI, JELLAL. *La medina de Tunis.* Paris, 1989.
DAOULATLI, ABDELAZIZ. *Tunis sous les Hafsides: Evolution urbaine et activité architecturale.* Tunis, 1976.
REVAULT, JACQUES. *Palais et demeures de Tunis (XVIIIe et XIXe siècles).* Paris, 1971.
ZBISS, SLIMANE-MOSTAFA. *La medina de Tunis.* Tunis, 1981.

Larry A. Barrie

Tunisi, Bayram al-   [1893–1961]

Egyptian poet.

Born into a small merchant family in a popular quarter of Alexandria, Bayram al-Tunisi studied at religious schools but learned the form of poetry called *zajal* by memorizing oral poetry. In 1919, he began to publish poetry critical of Egypt's monarchy and of the British occupation, in the journal *Issues,* leading to a long period of exile in France and Tunisia. After his return to Egypt in 1938, al-Tunisi published poetry in various Egyptian newspapers.

David Waldner

Tunisia

Arab republic in central North Africa.

Tunisia is bordered by Algeria on the west, the Mediterranean on the north and east, and Libya on the southeast. It includes the Kerkenna Islands off the east coast and the island of Djerba in the southeast. In 1993, Algeria and Tunisia settled a border dispute that had been under negotiation since 1983.

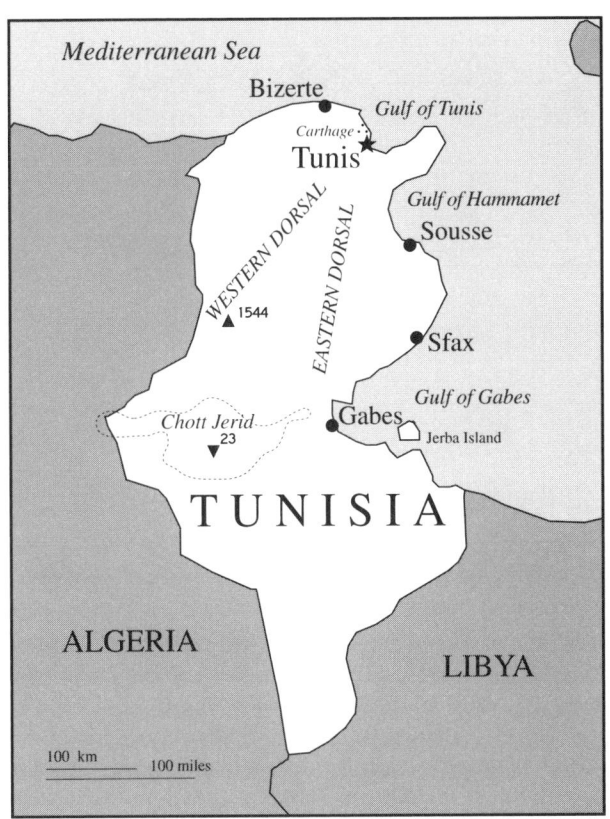

Geography and Climate. Tunisia's landmass comprises 59,984 square miles (155,360 sq. km); the total area is 63,170 square miles (163,610 sq. km). The country has three distinct regions: the northern Tell or high plains; the central steppes; and the arid south, characterized by date palm oases and numerous *shatts* (salt marshes), the largest of which is the Shatt al-Jarid.

The Dorsale massif, an extension of the Atlas mountains, limits rainfall on the central steppes. The highest point in the chain is Mount Chambi (1,544 meters; 5,066 feet). The mountains enter Tunisia northwest of Fernana and veer northeast across Cape Bon before plummeting into the Mediterranean near El Haouaria.

One of Tunisia's few perennial rivers, the Medjerda, rises in Algeria, crosses northern Tunisia, and empties into the Gulf of Tunis. Most other Tunisian streams, except the Miliana, dry up during the summer. Since antiquity the Medjerda valley has contained Tunisia's richest farmland.

The central steppes are high near the border with Algeria and low near the coast, then merge into the Sahel (coast), an area lying between Hammamet (near Cape Bon) and Sfax. Farther south lies the Sahara.

The north and the Sahel are the most urbanized and most densely populated regions of Tunisia. TUNIS is the largest city and the national capital. The second largest city, SFAX, has half as many inhabitants as

Tunis proper (600,000–1,000,000). Other important cities are QAIRAWAN (an important religious center and the first Arab town in the country, founded in 670 C.E.), SOUSSE, Gafsa, and BIZERTE.

Tunisia's natural resources include phosphate mines near Gafsa and a developing natural gas and petroleum industry. Foreign companies compete for oil concessions and continue to explore for new fields. Tunisia also produces small quantities of iron ore, lead, zinc, and salt. The Sahel region is a rich olive-growing area, and the southern oases contain extensive date-palm groves.

Northern Tunisia has a Mediterranean climate with cool, damp winters and warm, humid summers. Precipitation declines south of the Dorsale along the coast and is minimal in the interior steppes and Sahara, where winter days are mild but nights can be bitterly cold. Summer daytime temperatures in the interior steppes and southern desert can be very high. Temperatures at Tunis range from 6°C (43°F) to 33°C (91°F). Precipitation averages sixty inches in the north and eight inches in the Sahara.

The People, the Language, and Religion. Tunisia's 8.4 million people are concentrated in the north, in the Sahel, and in regional urban centers such as Qairawan and Gafsa. More than half the population lives in the northern Tell and the Sahel, on about 20 percent of Tunisia's total land surface. About 53 percent (4,452,000) of Tunisians live in cities. Population density is 133 persons per square mile. Family planning programs in the 1970s and 1980s managed to lower the population growth rate from over 3 percent to about 2.1 percent by 1992; 38 percent of Tunisians were under age fifteen in that year. Many Tunisians engage in agricultural pursuits, but a growing number are in the tourist industry, humanities and professions, commercial sector, and government.

Tunisia's ethnic base is primarily mixed Arab-BERBER or arabized Berber. There are a few Berber speakers in isolated regions of the south. A tiny Jewish minority still exists; most Tunisian Jews left the country after 1957. Some European Christians live in Tunisia, primarily in the capital.

Tunisia's national language is Arabic (the first language of at least 98 percent of the people); French is the major second language as well as the dominant language of commerce and education. Although the print and audiovisual media use standard Arabic, most Tunisians speak their own dialect, which has three variations: an urban dialect, a rural village and small town dialect, and a Bedouin dialect. Knowledge of the Egyptian dialect has been increasing since the 1970s because of Egypt's domination of the Arab cinema and television soap operas.

Roman ruins at Carthage. (Mia Bloom)

Islam is the official state religion. At least 98 percent of the population are SUNNI Muslims. The island of Djerba harbors many Khariji Muslims. In the 1980s the Islamic Tendency Movement (Mouvement de Tendance Islamique; MTI) was formed, with Rached Ghannushi and Abdelfattah Mourou as its ideological leaders.

Observance of Islamic rituals increased considerably in Tunisia during the 1980s and early 1990s. In recognition of this fact, and to thwart the designs of Islamists, the government sought to control all mosque appointments and to encourage moderation in religion. The government has grown more outwardly Islamic, following such traditional practices as waiting for the new moon before announcing the start of the Ramadan fast, and the firing of cannon to herald the first and last days of Ramadan.

The Economy. Tunisia's economy has improved due to good harvests (since 1990), economic restructuring, a growing manufacturing industry, a developing

City center of Sidi Bou Saïd. (Mia Bloom)

Sky-blue shutters and wrought iron characterize the homes of Sidi Bou Saïd. (Mia Bloom)

oil and gas sector, remittances from expatriates (an estimated 400,000 Tunisians work overseas), and a healthy tourist trade. Economic growth since 1988 has averaged about 4.2 percent, peaking at 8.6 percent in 1992. Unemployment ranges from the official 15 percent to a high of 20 to 50 percent in informal sectors of the economy. High rural unemployment has caused many young people to migrate to urban centers in search of work, causing deterioration of public services and the taxing of city resources, especially in Tunis.

Tunisia's gross domestic product is about 10 billion U.S. dollars, and per capita income is about 1,235 dollars. Agriculture comprises some 16 percent of the gross domestic product, and industry accounts for about 38 percent. The work force is estimated at 2,250,000, with 34 percent in industry, 26 percent in agriculture, and 40 percent in services. Women make up just under 25 percent of the work force (probably a much higher percentage of the rural "informal" sector). Labor unions have organized between 11 and 20 percent of the working class. The General

Union of Tunisian Workers (UNION GÉNÉRALE DES TRAVAILLEURS TUNISIENS; UGTT), headed by Ismail Sahbani, collaborates closely with the government and the Tunisian Union of Industrialists, Businessmen, and Artisans (UNION TUNISIENNE DES INDUSTRIALISTES, COMPAGNIES, ET ARTISANS; UTICA).

History. Tunisia's geographic openness has made its history one of periodic invasions. Berber peoples settled the country in the fifth and fourth millennia B.C.E. The first outside civilization to make an impact came from Phoenicia, when émigrés from Tyre founded Carthage in 814 B.C.E. Carthage developed a maritime empire in the western Mediterranean and in the third century B.C.E. confronted Rome for control of the western Mediterranean. Three conflicts ensued that came to be known collectively as the Punic Wars. In the final battle of the Second Punic War (Zama, 202 B.C.E.), Rome's Scipio Africanus defeated Carthage's Hannibal. Rome now supplanted Carthage as mistress of the Mediterranean and dominated North Africa until the Vandal invasion of 429 C.E. Following the Vandals, the Byzantines in 533 extended their hegemony over Tunisia.

The most enduring historical legacy for Tunisia derives from the Arab invasions of the late seventh century. From 643 until 698, the Arabs struggled to

Countryside near Nabeul on Cap Bon peninsula. (Richard Bulliet)

defeat the Berbers and impose the Arabic language and Islam upon them. Qairawan was the capital for most medieval Tunisian dynasties. Founded in 670, it survived for centuries as the main garrison town and political and religious center.

The Aghlabid dynasty (800–909) ruled from Qairawan. The Shi'a Fatimids (909–969) moved their capital to Mahdiya, then Egypt, founding a new imperial capital at Cairo. They left their lieutenants, the Zirids, in charge of North Africa. In 1049 the Zirids broke with the Fatimids who, in retaliation, unleashed the Banu Hilal nomads. They disrupted the countryside, intensified the renomadization of the steppes, and introduced a new dialect. Their defeat at Haidaran in 1052 and the sack of Qairawan in 1057 led the Zirids to move to Mahdiya.

The Almoravids, a Tuareg puritanical religious group, swept out of the western Sahara in the eleventh century. In the middle of the twelfth century,

Zaytuna mosque in Tunis. (Richard Bulliet)

Irrigation of date groves in the oasis of Tozeur. (Richard Bulliet)

the Berber Almohads came down from the High Atlas and extended their domains into Tunisia.

By 1250, Almohad power had waned to such a degree that a successor dynasty, the Hafsids, emerged in Tunisia to rule for the next three centuries with Tunis as their capital. In 1574, an Ottoman Turkish fleet under Sinan Pasha landed forces at La Goulette (now Halq al-Wadi). Following a brief siege, those forces seized Tunis and laid the foundations for Ottoman control that continued until the imposition of a protectorate by France in 1881. To collect taxes and to maintain security, the Ottomans established a rudimentary administration. Initially an Ottoman *bulukbash* (commander) was placed in charge of the janissary garrison (*ocak*). In 1590, rebel janissaries formed a government dominated by the deys, who ran the country through the *diwan* (council). After 1640, an important tax-collecting official, the bey, emerged, and the powerful Muradid family exercised considerable control over the government. During a civil war from 1702 to 1705, Ibrahim al-Sharif seized power. In 1705 an associate of al-Sharif, Husayn ibn Ali Turki, proclaimed himself bey of Tunis. In 1710 the Ottoman sultan officially recognized Husayn and legitimized his rule. The Husaynid dynasty ruled the country independently until 1881, and thereafter under France's control until 1956.

In the nineteenth century, the Husaynids accepted the suzerainty of the Ottoman Empire while pursuing their own reform agendas and independent foreign policies vis-à-vis Europe. Misguided military reforms in the 1840s, financial mismanagement in the 1860s, and increasing pressures from Europe in the 1870s culminated in France's protectorate based on the treaty of BARDO (1881) and the LA MARSA CONVENTION (1883).

The protectorate authorities speeded up the economic development of Tunisia, built a physical infrastructure, reformed the educational system, and imposed a political administration while retaining the bey as figurehead ruler. Simultaneously they heeded settler demands for land, sweeping aside informal tribal and village ownership agreements. Arabs were excluded from participation in politics. French settlers dominated the political structures, the courts, and the media.

Although there had been armed resistance to the French occupation from southern tribal elements, most of it was crushed by the end of 1883. The first stage of Tunisian nationalism was an intellectual elitist movement known as the Young Tunisians, which aimed to assimilate to the civilization of France so they could eventually rule their own country. They agitated for equal treatment because of their accomplishments, but the French did not take them seriously. A more serious stage in protonationalist agitation occurred just before and just after World War I in a movement led by Abd al-Aziz THAALBI. The third stage came in the 1930s when a young lawyer, Habib BOURGUIBA, broke with the DESTOUR PARTY and proclaimed the Neo-Destour.

World War II slowed the development of nationalism in Tunisia. After the war, however, Bourguiba followed a staged process, arguing that its cumulative effect would result in political independence. By late 1955, Algeria violently challenged France's rule through a war of national liberation. France therefore agreed to Tunisia's autonomy in 1955 and to its independence in March 1956. In 1957 the Republic of Tunisia proclaimed Bourguiba its first president.

In Tunisia's first decades of independence, continued dominance of the Neo-Destour, which became the Socialist Destour in 1964, and the government's antireligious attitude tarnished the nation's image. Police intimidated those who sought to chant the Qur'an in public, often beating and imprisoning them. In protest, pious intellectuals organized the Society for the Preservation of the Qur'an and, in the early 1980s, created the MTI.

Bourguiba's anti-Islam policies led to Zayn al-Abidine BEN ALI's palace coup of 7 November 1987. Ben Ali tried to co-opt the Islamists for the promised elections of 1989. To demonstrate his piety, he appeared on television participating in Ramadan rites at al-Zaytuna mosque in Tunis. In the spring of 1989, however, Ben Ali hedged on his promise to recognize the MTI if they removed religious terminology from their name. As the April elections approached and MTI changed its name to the Renaissance party, the government refused to recognize it.

Ben Ali's regime considers the Islamists to be the major challenge to its survival, equating them with terrorists. Ben Ali announced in late 1993 that national elections would be held in March 1994. He promised that seats would be set aside for minority party candidates. Ben Ali then announced his candidacy for a second presidential term.

Tunisia's "regime of change" has tamed the Islamist movement for the moment, has modestly improved its human rights and democratic credentials, and has continued economic restructuring and privatization. The economy is functioning reasonably well, harvests continue to be good, tourism has rebounded dramatically, and the immediate prospects for the future appear good.

BIBLIOGRAPHY

ABUN-NASR, JAMIL. "The Beylicate in Seventeenth Century Tunisia." *International Journal of Middle East Studies* 6 (1975): 70–93.

ANDERSON, LISA. *The State and Social Transformation in Tunisia and Libya, 1830–1980*. Princeton, N.J., 1986.

BARRIE, LARRY A. "Tunisia: The Era of Reformism, 1837–1877." Master's thesis, Harvard University, 1966.

ENTELIS, JOHN P. *Comparative Politics of North Africa: Algeria, Morocco, and Tunisia*. Syracuse, N.Y., 1980.

PERKINS, KENNETH J. *Tunisia: Crossroads of the Islamic and European Worlds*. Boulder, Colo., 1986.

VALENSI, LUCETTE. *On the Eve of Colonialism: North Africa before the French Conquest*. New York, 1977.

ZARTMAN, I. WILLIAM, ed. *Tunisia: The Political Economy of Reform*. Boulder, Colo., 1991.

ZUSSMAN, MIRA. *Development and Disenchantment in Rural Tunisia: The Bourguiba Years*. Boulder, Colo., 1992.

Larry A. Barrie

Tunisia, Political Parties in

Tunisia has ten active political parties.

There are seven legal political parties in Tunisia, including the government party. There are also three parties that have not been authorized: the Popular Unity Movement (MOUVEMENT DE L'UNITÉ POPULAIRE; MUP), a socialist party founded by Ahmed Ben Salah, former planning minister who fled Tunisia in 1973; the Tunisian Communist Workers party (Parti Ouvrier Communiste Tunisien; POCT), a Maoist group; and the RENAISSANCE PARTY (Hizb al-Nahda in Arabic), the party of Islamists, under the leadership of Rashid Ghannushi and Abdelfattah Mourou. The seven legal parties are the CONSTITUTIONAL DEMOCRATIC RALLY (Ralliement Constitutionnel Démocratique; RCD), the Movement of Socialist Democrats (Mouvement des Démocrates Socialistes; MDS), the Popular Unity party (PARTI D'UNITÉ POPULAIRE; PUP), the MOVEMENT OF RENEWAL (Harakat al-Tajdid), the Socialist Progressive Rally (Ralliement Socialiste Progressiste; RSP), the Unionist Democratic Union (Union Democratique Unioniste; UDU), and the Socialist Liberal party (Parti Socialiste Liberale; PSL).

RCD. The RCD has dominated all governmental institutions since Tunisia's independence in 1956. The party was founded by Habib Bourguiba and others in 1934 as the Neo-Destour. They broke away from the DESTOUR (Constitution) party, established by Abd al-Aziz Thaalbi in 1920. Bourguiba's group felt that the Destour had become too elitist, confined to the Tunis upper middle class. Bourguiba sought to build a grassroots party that could appeal to the rural and small-town folk that the Destour failed to represent. By 1956, Bourguiba and the Neo-Destour dominated Tunisia's political scene and continued to do so after independence. In 1964, the party congress agreed to change the party's name to Socialist Destour party (Parti Socialist Destourien; PSD). The party's final name change occurred in 1988, when the party congress adopted the name Constitutional Democratic Rally. This expressed the new direction of the government party following a coup that replaced Bourguiba with Zayn al-Abidine Ben Ali. Moderate and pragmatic, the RCD has opened up the political system to multiple parties and has attempted to refashion a market economy out of the rubble of its earlier centralized socialist planning system. President Ben Ali is party president, and Chedli Neffati occupies the post of secretary-general. The party claims over 1.5 million members, distributed in thousands of cells nationwide. It controls the national parliament (Chamber of Deputies).

MDS. Ahmad MESTIRI, formerly a member of the ruling party, founded the MDS in 1978 and welded the new party into the largest opposition to the RCD. With its forty thousand members, the MDS offers almost the same program as the RCD, except that it is more Arab nationalist and socialist. Mohamed Mouaada is secretary-general.

PUP. Popular Unity party membership is over twelve thousand. Headed by Mohamed Belhaj Amor, the PUP offers a nationalist and socialist program. It splintered off from the MUP in 1981 due to the MUP leadership's refusal to participate in the political process.

Movement of Renewal. Secretary-General Mohamed Harmel is a longtime Communist party activist. Movement of Renewal adopted the name Mouvement Ettajdid (Arabic, Harakat al-Tajdid) in 1993, dropping the name Tunisian Communist party (Parti Communiste Tunisien; PCT). It now follows a leftist, non-Marxist ideology that offers an alternative for leftists and intellectuals. It remains a small party whose membership numbers somewhere in the low thousands. Many defections occurred because of the change to a noncommunist status.

RSP. Nejib Chebbi, a lawyer, heads the Socialist Progressive Rally (RSP), which has a nationalist and socialist emphasis. RSP leaders are willing to accommodate all nonviolent political viewpoints in national elections. The RSP seeks a broader role for Tunisia in Arab politics.

UDU. Abderrahmane Tlili founded the Unionist Democratic Union (UDU). It has close ties with the

UNION GÉNÉRALE DES TRAVAILLEURS TUNISIENS (UGTT), the country's largest labor union. A high concentration of union members make up UDU's constituency. UDU espouses both Arab nationalism and Israel–PLO peace talks. It also leans toward involvement in labor issues.

PSL. In 1993 the Social Party for Progress (PSP) became the Socialist Liberal Party (PSL). Led by Mounir Beji, a lawyer, PSL supports liberalism, economic privatization, and American foreign policy interests in the region. Probably the weakest legal party, the size of its membership is unknown but presumed to be very small.

Elections held on March 20, 1994, increased the membership of the Chamber of Deputies from 144 to 163 seats, through the 19 seats promised to opposition candidates by the revised electoral law of 1993. Opposition seats were allocated according to a complicated mathematical formula based on the greatest voter support for opponents who lost to ruling-party candidates. RCD and MDS candidates contested seats in all of Tunisia's twenty-five electoral regions; smaller parties contested votes in eighteen or fewer regions.

BIBLIOGRAPHY

NELSON, HAROLD D., ed. *Tunisia: A Country Study,* 3rd ed. Washington, D.C., 1986.
PERKINS, KENNETH J. *Historical Dictionary of Tunisia.* Metuchen, N.J., 1989.
ZARTMAN, I. WILLIAM, ed. *Tunisia: The Political Economy of Reform.* Boulder, Colo., 1991.

Larry A. Barrie

Tuqan, Fadwa   [1917–   ]

Palestinian poet.

Fadwa Tuqan is a well-known Palestinian poet who developed sensual themes in modern Arabic verse and poetry that inspires nationalism. Israeli General Moshe Dayan praised her work, equating the power of one of her poems to that of ten Palestinian commandos. Among her works are "Alone with the Days," "Give Us Love," and "The Freedom Fighter and the Land."

BIBLIOGRAPHY

TUQAN, FADWA. *A Mountainous Journey: An Autobiography.* Tr. by Olive Kenny (text) and Naomi Shihab Nye (poetry); ed. by Salma Khadra Jayyusi. St. Paul, Minn., 1990.

Abla M. Amawi

Tuqan Family

Prominent Palestinian family from Nablus.

Descended from an ancient Arabian tribe, the Tuqans settled in Nablus (in the West Bank) in the twelfth century. Through the nineteenth century, they were associated with other Qaysi tribes in rivalry with the local Yemeni federation. By the 1800s they had amassed great wealth, owning an imposing palace as well as a number of villas in Nablus. They shared the post of governor with the Abd al-Hadi family and used their land and tax-farm wealth to build up Nablus's famed soap and olive oil industries. Their political dominance in Nablus lasted through the 1970s as various family members gained posts under the rule of Jordan.

Prominent family members include Hafiz Tuqan, a late nineteenth-century banker; Ahmad Tuqan, an Oxford University graduate who was prominent in education under the British mandate and Jordanian rule; Sulayman Tuqan, mayor of Nablus in the 1930s and a leader of resistance to Zionism; and Fadwa and Ibrahim Tuqan, brother and sister who became noted poets. Ahmad, Sulayman, Jamal, Qadri, and Beha'eddine Tuqan were ministers in the Jordanian government in the 1950s through 1970s.

BIBLIOGRAPHY

MUSLIH, MUHAMMAD Y. *The Origins of Palestinian Nationalism.* New York, 1988.

Elizabeth Thompson

Turabi, Hasan al-

Fundamentalist Islamic thinker.

Hasan al-Turabi earned his doctorate in constitutional law from the Sorbonne in Paris. Formerly dean of the University of Khartoum Law School, he is leader of the Sudanese branch of the Muslim Brotherhood, which was transformed into the National Islamic Front (NIF) in 1985 under his leadership. He is widely viewed as the power behind the al-Bashir military regime in Sudan.

Turabi is viewed as a fundamentalist Islamic thinker because he views Islam as superseding the state. Yet he does not advocate a return to earlier Islamic practices; instead he advocates a progressive Islamic revival. He argues that the state's only purpose is to set rules to enable society to conduct its affairs, and it must allow society, the primary institution in Islam, to freely pursue its interests. The SHARI'A and the Islamist jurists ensure that the role of the state remains limited. Since any society has the right to exercise *shura* (consultation) and *ijma* (consensus), and since this requires producing *ijtihad* (opinions), pluralism is necessary to enable society to identify which policies best serve its interests. As such, Turabi argues, democracy is simply a Western term describing practices identical to Islam's shura and ijma. Although ultimate sovereignty belongs to God, practical and political sovereignty belong to the people. Society, therefore, always remains free to choose its rulers and representatives.

Turabi distinguishes the conditions of contemporary life from those present during the rise of Islam in the seventh century. Since Muslims are living in a world much different from the one that Islamic jurisprudence legislated, they must look toward radical social and political reforms in order to bring about the necessary Islamic revival. The historical development of Islamic jurisprudence must be rejected in favor of a process that depends on free thinking, and the state must establish a new circle of *ulama* (Islamic clergy) while continuing to derive its jurisprudence from the people. Any democratic developments in Islam must extend to the institutions of society and the family, each segment of which must work to further Islamic revival in both public and private life. Political freedom is an original part of creed and nature because freedom is what distinguishes man from animal. This includes the freedom of expression, which is stipulated in the *Shari'a*.

As for the individual, Turabi notes that man is not forced to worship God but chooses to do so. Individual freedom is essential and cannot be taken away by the state, institutions, or society. This freedom, he argues, must be embodied in a constitution to ensure that the strength of any political leader may be checked by representative councils. Since institutionalization of freedom inevitably leads to its destruction, individual freedoms are bound and protected by Islam.

Turabi's views and writings on Islam would seem to place him in the category of moderate Islamist thinkers, but the practice of his authority in Sudan suggests otherwise. Although he has called for freedom of association and multiparty representative bodies, the current Sudanese government has systematically destroyed most civic associations and remains one of the most oppressive regimes and egregious human rights violators in the Middle East.

BIBLIOGRAPHY

ESPOSITO, JOHN. *Voices of Resurgent Islam.* Oxford, 1983.
MOUSSALLI, AHMAD. "Modern Islamic Fundamentalist Discourses on Civil Society." In *Civil Society in the Middle East,* vol. 1, ed. by A. R. Norton. Leiden, 1994.
AL-TURABI, HASAN. "Islam, Democracy, the State and the West: Summary of a Lecture and Roundtable Discussion with Hasan al-Turabi," prepared by Louis Cantori and Arthur Lowrie. *Middle East Policy* 1, no. 3 (1992): 52–54.

Jillian Schwedler

Turban

A traditional Middle Eastern headdress that usually distinguishes Muslims.

The turban (Arabic, *imama*; Persian, *dastar*) consists of a stiff, round cap with a long piece of cloth wrapped around it. The modern turban is a synthesis of Arab and Persian styles; the many ways of tying the cloth reveal social distinctions and individual personality. Different colors of the cloth have at different times indicated religious status: descendants of the Prophet wrapped with a green cloth, Egyptian Copts with a blue cloth, and so on. In the Middle Ages the turban was known as the badge of Islam, but today it is worn almost exclusively by members of the religious scholarly elite.

Marilyn Higbee

Turkey

Modern republic formed from the central regions of the Ottoman Empire.

The Republic of Turkey (*Türkiye Cumhuriyeti*) was established on October 29, 1923. The government of Turkey was an authoritarian dictatorship until 1946, when the first competitive elections were held. In subsequent decades, there have been three military coups, but each time the military regime has stepped down and permitted the resumption of democratic politics.

According to the census of October 21, 1990, the population of Turkey was 56,473,035 people living in an area of 300,948 square miles (779,456 sq. km). The Asian portion of Turkey, Anatolia (historically Asia Minor), comprises 291,773 square miles (755,693 sq. km), or about 97 percent of the total; the section located on the European continent is 9,175 square miles (23,763 sq. km). The European portion of Turkey is separated from the Asian by the Sea of Marmara, which is in turn connected to two larger bodies of water by two narrow straits. In the northwest, the Bosporus strait connects the Sea of Marmara to the Black Sea, while in the southeast, the Dardanelles strait connects it to the Aegean Sea.

Turkey is bordered on the west by the Aegean Sea and Greece, on the northwest by Bulgaria, on the north by the Black Sea, on the northeast by Georgia, on the east by Armenia, on the southeast by Iran and Iraq, and on the south by Syria and the Mediterranean Sea.

The capital of Turkey, ANKARA, is located in the central Anatolian plains; no more than a village in 1923, Ankara today is home to more than 2.6 million people. The largest city, ISTANBUL, straddles the European and Asian sides of Turkey and has a population of 6.6 million people. An important historical city, Istanbul (formally Constantinople) was first the capital of the Byzantine Empire and later the capital of the Ottoman Empire. Today, it is the cultural and business capital of Turkey. The third largest city is IZMIR (historically Smyrna), a major industrial center with a population of just under one million people.

Geographically, Turkey consists of a ring of mountains that enclose a series of plateaus that lie between 2,625 and 6,560 feet (800 and 2,000 m) above sea level. The highest mountains are in the east, with Mount Ararat reaching 16,945 feet (5,165 m), while in the west, the highest mountain, Mount Erciyas, reaches 12,800 feet (3,900 m). The coastal regions on the south, east, and north are extremely narrow. Most of the coastal regions receive adequate rainfall; as much as 100 inches (254 cm) fall annually on the eastern Black Sea coast, and almost as much on the Aegean coast. The central plateau, on the other hand, is sheltered by its ring of mountains and receives little rainfall, generally under 10 inches (250 mm) annually. There are extensive expanses of arid steppe and even

desert. Turkey's two major rivers, the Tigris and Euphrates, are both in the east. There are many lakes, both salt and freshwater; the largest is Lake Van, which covers 1,100 square miles (2,850 sq. km). Climate in the central plain ranges from severe winters with temperatures often dropping to minus 22 degrees Fahrenheit (minus 30 degrees Celsius) to hot and dry summers, with temperatures ranging from highs of 85 to 110 degrees F (30 to 43 degrees C) in the southeast. In the western region, winters are relatively mild, hovering around freezing, and summers are hot. The Aegean coast is mild in winter and temperate in summer.

Administratively, Turkey is divided into seventy-three provinces, each administered by a governor. According to the 1982 constitution, legislative power is vested in a unicameral Grand National Assembly composed of four hundred deputies elected by universal adult suffrage and serving five-year terms. In 1987, the number of deputies was raised to 450. Executive power is vested in the office of the prime minister and in the office of the president, who is elected to a seven-year term by the assembly. While the prime minister heads the government, the president has the power to appoint a prime minister, senior civil servants, and senior members of the judiciary; submit constitutional amendments for popular referenda; challenge the constitutionality of laws by submitting them to the constitutional court; call for new elections; declare martial law; and order the armed forces into action domestically or internationally. In addition, the National Security Council—composed of the president; prime minister; chief of

Anti-Taurus mountains in the Nemrut region of Turkey. (Laura Mendelson)

The blue waters of the Bosporus, with Europe in the foreground and Asia in the background, 1957. (D.W. Lockhard)

staff; heads of the army, navy, air force and police; and ministers of interior, foreign affairs, and defense—has the power to present compulsory orders to the government in matters of national security.

There are no official census data on the ethnic, religious, and linguistic composition of the population of Turkey. The majority of Turks are native Turkish speakers. Ethnically, they trace their roots back to central Asia, although many Turks are Caucasians, particularly Circassians and Georgians. There is also a significant population of Kurds, a people of Indo-European descent that speak Kurdish, whose estimated numbers range between eight and fifteen million people. Kurds are concentrated in the east and southeast and along the Syrian and Iraqi borders, but significant numbers have migrated to major cities. A large number of Arabs inhabit the region of Hatay, a small territory formerly part of Syria but ceded by the French to Turkey in 1939. What had been in the nineteenth century large populations of Greeks and Armenians were reduced by war and deportations to relatively small numbers living in Istanbul: roughly six thousand Greeks and sixty thousand Armenians. The vast majority of Turkish citizens are Muslim. The Kurds and most Turks are Sunni Muslim, but there are also an estimated ten to twenty million Shi'a Muslims. There are also small numbers of Jews (22,000), Greek Orthodox, Armenian Orthodox, and Assyrian Christians.

Turkey's major agricultural products are cereals, cotton, tobacco, grapes, figs, olives, hazelnuts, oilseeds, and tea. Until 1980, agricultural products, particularly cotton, provided the bulk of exports. Despite continued government attention to raising agricultural output, growth has been slow, limited by the lack of irrigated land and the low rainfall on the central plateau. Only about one-third of all land is cultivated, mostly on family-size plots, with larger farms in the coastal regions. Today, agriculture provides about 20 percent of the gross national product.

The Turkish government initiated a strategy of state-led industrialization in the 1930s when a series of public enterprises were established. After 1950, in-

A yacht plying the waters of the Bosporus. (Mia Bloom)

creasing support was given to the private sector, so that by 1970, private sector industrial output and investment was almost equal to that of the public sector. In 1980, the government launched a program of liberalization, designed to diminish state economic intervention and increase the role of market forces. Beginning in 1987, the government began to privatize some of the state economic enterprises, though progress on this front has been slow. The largest industry is textiles, providing about one-third of output and export earnings. Turkey's production and export of iron and steel have increased rapidly, as have production of cement and paper products. Motor vehicle production began in the 1950s but consists mostly of assembly industries; because production has been spread out over a large number of small plants, production costs are high and exports have been negligible. Turkey's petrochemical industry produces fertilizers and a range of industrial inputs. Other manufacturing industries include tobacco, chemicals, pharmaceuticals, glassware, and engineering.

Turkey has a large mining industry, mostly in the public sector, employing over 200,000 workers. Important mineral resources include bauxite, borax,

The Valide Sultan mosque on the bank of the Golden Horn in Istanbul. (Mia Bloom)

The waterfront at Büyük Ada in the Princess Islands. (Mia Bloom)

Ruins at Nemrut Daği. (Laura Mendelson)

Herdsman in early spring overlooking Hasan Dağ, 1952. (D.W. Lockhard)

Road near Gümüşane, 1952. (D.W. Lockhard)

The village of Tunceli, 1952. (D.W. Lockhard)

Gök Medrese, Sivas. (Richard Bulliet)

Camel caravan moves along a winding road through Anatolia during the 1940s. (D.W. Lockhard)

A village near Ulukışla in the hills of south-central Anatolia, 1955. (D.W. Lockhard)

Antalya–Anamur road along the Mediterranean coast. (D.W. Lockhard)

The main square in Yozgat, 1955. (D.W. Lockhard)

chromium, copper, iron ore, manganese and sulfur. The center of coal mining is at Zonguldak, on the Black Sea coast. Oil was first discovered in 1950 in the southeast, but production is limited, accounting for about 10 percent of domestic consumption; the remainder is imported. In 1990, petroleum products accounted for about 15 percent of all imports. Of Turkey's natural resources, only borates and petroleum products are exported in small quantities.

Urban culture in Asia Minor dates to the second millennium B.C.E. In 330 C.E., the Roman Emperor Constantine founded the city of Constantinople (now Istanbul), which became the capital of the Eastern Roman, or Byzantine, Empire. In the eleventh century, Ghuzz Turks who had established the Seljuk empire in the area that is today Iran and Iraq began to migrate into Anatolia, conquering territory from the Byzantine Empire. By the thirteenth century, independent princedoms were established in Anatolia, including the principality of the House of Osman, or Othman, in the northwest. Over the next

View of Istanbul's Golden Horn. (Robin Bhatty)

A side street of Istanbul with Süleymaniye mosque in the background. (Richard Bulliet)

several centuries, the Ottoman (from Othman) Empire conquered all of the Byzantine Empire, capturing Constantinople in 1453, as well as much of eastern Europe and the Middle East.

By the year 1800, however, several European states as well as the Russian Empire had become stronger than the Ottoman Empire. The 1800s would be a century of reform, with efforts to strengthen the Ottoman military, government, political organization, and economy in order to meet the competition presented by rivals. By 1830, the traditional infantry, the Janissary Corps, had been abolished and a new military established; military modernization continued throughout the century. In 1839, Sultan Abdülmecit I initiated a series of reforms of state and society known collectively as the TANZIMAT. Important episodes in the Tanzimat reforms include HATT-I ŞERIF OF GÜLHANE (the Imperial Rescript of Gülhane; 1839), which reinterpreted the responsibilities of the state to include the protection of life and security of property and the provision of equal justice for all citizens, regardless of religion;

the LAND CODE of 1858, which provided the legal basis for private ownership of land while attempting to rationalize the system of tax collection; and the adoption of a constitution in 1876. Under the reign of Abdülhamit II, however, the constitution was abolished and autocratic rule was reestablished.

In the course of the nineteenth century, a middle class emerged in the Ottoman Empire. Educated in the new schools of the empire, members of the middle class had a vision of a liberal society ruled by a constitutional government and formed movements to achieve their goal, such as the Young Ottomans and later the Young Turks. These groups were alternately supported by reformist governments or suppressed by autocratic governments. In 1908, the Committee of Union and Progress (CUP) overthrew Abdülhamit II and restored the constitution. The CUP government initially enjoyed widespread popular support. But subsequent opposition to its modernizing reforms, combined with foreign wars, led the CUP to establish its own dictatorship. In 1914, the CUP formed an alliance with the Central powers and entered World War I. After four years of fighting a bitter defensive war against the Allies on many fronts, the empire was defeated; Allied armies had captured the Middle Eastern territories of Palestine, Syria, and Iraq; and Allied forces occupied Istanbul. On October 30, 1918, the Turks signed an armistice at Mudros.

On May 15, 1919, Greek forces invaded western Turkey, triggering the formation of a new Turkish army that would defeat the Greeks and then establish the modern Turkish republic. The leader of the Turkish war of liberation was Mustafa Kemal, later given the name ATATÜRK (father of the Turks). On July 23, 1919, Kemal convened a nationalist congress in the city of Erzurum, delegates to which later is-

Traditional Turkish costume. (D.W. Lockhard)

Beşiktaş mosque, with the Bosporus in the background. (D.W. Lockhard)

sued the National Pact (Mithaq al-Watani), a declaration calling for the dissolution of the empire and control over non-Turkish provinces, the end of foreign occupation, and the independence of all areas inhabited by Turks. Pulling together an army, the independence movement succeeded in defeating the Greek army and negotiating a withdrawal of Allied forces. The Treaty of Mudanya recognizing Turkish sovereignty was signed on July 24, 1923. On October 29, 1923, Turkey was declared a republic with Kemal as its first president and Ankara as its capital.

The next two decades were years of reform, as Kemal and his associates attempted to complete the now 100-year-old project of modernizing Turkey. The 1924 constitution created an elected parliament, which was the sole repository of sovereignty, and a presidency exercising executive power. In practice, however, Kemal's government was a dictatorship. A single party, the Republican People's party (RPP), was formed as the agent of central government rule and control. In 1924, the caliphate, the highest religious office, was abolished, while in 1928, Turkey was declared a secular state. The old legal codes were annulled and replaced with civil and criminal codes adopted from Europe. The fez, the trademark Otto-

Tile-makers on the Ordu–Samsun road. (D.W. Lockhard)

man headgear adopted in the nineteenth century, was considered a symbol of the old order and was declared illegal, while the Arabic alphabet was replaced with a Roman one.

In 1929, with the onset of the Great Depression and the lapsing of the Treaty of Lausanne, which had imposed a laissez-faire trade policy on Turkey, Kemal launched a program of state-led economic development. Influenced by the Soviet experiment with five-year development plans, in 1934 the government formulated its own five-year plan for industrial investment. Completed in 1939, the plan introduced heavy industry into Turkey while allowing the country to weather the depression with a trade surplus.

In addition, during the 1930s, Kemal transformed the RPP on the model of European fascist parties. The distinction between party members and government officials was blurred, as all public officials were expected to work to implement the new ideology of the party. This ideology, officially adopted in 1931 and known as KEMALISM, emphasized six themes: republicanism, nationalism, populism, statism, secularism, and a sixth theme, *devrimçilik,* which was interpreted by moderates as reformism, and by radicals, as revolutionism. In 1938, Kemal Atatürk died and was replaced as president by his lieutenant, İsmet İNÖNÜ. Although İnönü kept Turkey neutral during World War II, a number of government policies on resource mobilization created widespread economic austerity, alienating large sectors of the population including those businessmen who opposed the policy of state-led economic development.

The post–World War II period was a new era for the Turkish republic. Responding to the dissatisfaction of wartime economic policies and feeling the need to win American support against Soviet en-

croachments, İnönü announced the resumption of multiparty politics and competitive elections. There had been two experiments with a second party in the 1920s, but in both cases, the opposition party was closed down after a short life. This time, the commitment to democracy was greater, and in the general elections of May 1950, the chief opposition party, the Democrat party (DP), won an overwhelming victory. The DP had campaigned on a platform of economic and cultural liberalism and increased political freedoms. Their new economic policies, based on import-substituting industrialization and the encouragement of agriculture, increased the standard of living of wide sectors of the population, particularly peasants, and they permitted more freedom of religion than the Kemalists, who were militantly hostile to religion. But the DP increased the role of the state in the economy instead of reducing it; as the 1950s passed, the party showed signs of becoming dictatorial. A combination of incipient economic crisis and antidemocratic measures prompted a military coup on May 27, 1960.

The new military rulers formed themselves into a thirty-seven-member NATIONAL UNITY COMMITTEE (NUC) and convened a constitutional convention, dominated by supporters of the RPP, which promulgated a new constitution in 1961. The new constitution included several liberal provisions, including the creation of a constitutional court empowered to review legislation; provisions guaranteeing freedom of thought, expression, association, and publication; and a commitment that the state would plan economic development in a way that would achieve social justice without infringing on the right of the individual to own and inherit property or to work. Finally, the constitution gave workers the right to form unions and strike.

In 1961, the NUC allowed political parties to resume their activities. The two principle parties were the RPP, still led by İsmet İnönü, and the Justice party (JP), the successor to the DP. A series of short-lived coalition governments were formed, first between the JP and the RPP, and later between the RPP and several smaller parties, and then the JP with smaller parties. In October 1965, the JP, led by Süleyman DEMIREL, won a majority. The Turkish economy, now supervised by the State Planning Organization, which issued five-year development plans, grew at a rapid rate during the 1960s. But political instability came from two sources. First, there were numerous defections of members from existing parties and the proliferation of smaller parties, rendering difficult the formation of a stable government. Of particular significance, in 1970, Necmeddin Erbakan formed the National Order party, which called for the establishment of an Islamic state. Second, beginning in 1968, political unrest began to erupt into street violence as radical students and organizations on the left clashed with extremist students and organizations on the right. On March 12, 1971, the military leadership accused the government of allowing the country to slip into anarchy and called for the creation of a stable government. Later that day, the Demirel government resigned. Six weeks later, martial law was declared.

After martial law was finally lifted in September 1973, Turkey was ruled by a series of weak coalition governments as economic conditions deteriorated. Following a military coup in Cyprus in July of 1974, the Turkish army intervened to protect the Turkish minority on the island. Since that time, Cyprus has been divided into Turkish and Greek sectors. By the end of the decade, the economy was in critical condition, and beginning in 1978, political violence once again erupted on the streets.

In January 1980, a JP government announced a new economic strategy designed to liberalize the Turkish economy and encourage exports. Increasing political violence, however, convinced many people that the economy could only be repaired if the political situation was stabilized. Consequently, on September 12, 1980, the military intervened for the third time in two decades. All existing political parties were banned, their members prohibited from engaging in politics. A new constitution, promulgated in 1982, reversed some of the liberal measures of the 1961 constitution by enhancing the authority of the president and the cabinet vis-à-vis parliament and placing restrictions on political activity. In 1983, elections were held between three new parties. The winning party was the Motherland party (Anavatan Partisi; ANAP), led by Turgut Ozal, a technocrat who had designed the January 1980 measures. Ozal formed a new government and accelerated the strategy of economic liberalization and encouraging exports. Despite some success at economic liberalization, persistent government deficits resulted in high inflation and eroded popular support for the government. New parties emerged to rival ANAP: the True Path party (TPP; Doğru Yol Partisi), a continuation of the Justice party, led by Süleyman Demirel after 1987; the Social Democratic Populist party (Sosyal Demokrat Halkçı Parti; SHP), a continuation of the RPP under the leadership of Erdal İNÖNÜ, the son of İsmet İnönü; and the Welfare party, the continuation of the National Salvation party. In 1989, Ozal was elected president. In the 1991 elections, ANAP, now led by Mesut Yılmaz, came in third, and the top two parties, the TPP and the SHP, formed a coalition government. On April

17, 1993, Ozal died, and Demirel replaced him as president. On June 13, 1993, Tansu Çiller, an American-trained economist and former professor at Bosporus University, became the new head of the TPP and prime minister. Çiller was the first woman to serve as prime minister of Turkey.

BIBLIOGRAPHY

A good source for data on Turkish society, economy, and polity is the annually updated *Middle East and North Africa* (London). For detailed but technical descriptions of the geography, geology, and climate of Turkey, see the relevant chapters of W. B. FISHER's *The Middle East: A Physical, Social, and Regional Geography,* 7th ed. (London, 1978). Two classic accounts of modern Turkish history are BERNARD LEWIS's *The Emergence of Modern Turkey,* 2nd ed. (Leiden, 1966), and STANFORD J. SHAW and EZEL KURAL SHAW's *History of the Ottoman Empire and Modern Turkey,* vol. 2: *Reform, Revolution, and Republic* (New York, 1977). For a detailed treatment of the Young Turk period, see FEROZ AHMAD's *The Young Turks: The Committee of Union and Progress in Turkish Politics, 1908–1914* (Oxford, 1969). AHMAD has also written an excellent history of the democratic period, *The Turkish Experiment in Democracy, 1950–1975* (London, 1977). An important interpretation of modern Turkish political development is METIN HEPER's *The State Tradition in Turkey* (London, 1985). For a general overview of Turkish modernization, see WILLIAM HALE's *The Political and Economic Development of Modern Turkey* (New York, 1981).

David Waldner

Türkeş, Alparslan   [1917–   ]

Turkish soldier and politician.

Born in Cyprus, Alparslan Türkeş, moved with his family to Istanbul at age fifteen and embarked on a military career after completing his studies at the military academy in 1938. He was involved in plots preceding the military intervention of May 27, 1960. He was the most prominent of those who favored long-term retention of power by the military. He and thirteen of these colleagues were purged from the ruling National Unity Committee in November of 1960 and sent into virtual exile. After his return in 1963, he joined the Republican Peasants' Nation party and became its leader in August 1965; he changed its name to Nationalist Action party (NAP) in 1969 and gave it a stridently nationalist tone leaning toward pan-Turkism. Parliamentary arithmetic propelled Türkeş, into an important position in coalition cabinets of the 1970s. The 1980 military junta prosecuted him on a number of serious charges, including instigation of violence, the murder of hundreds of persons, and attempting to infiltrate the military. Although he was not executed, he remained in detention for some time. He benefited from the political amnesty approved in a popular referendum in September 1987 and assumed leadership of the Nationalist Work party, a rejuvenation of the old NAP. In 1991, he served briefly as interim speaker of the Grand National Assembly (parliament) because he was the oldest member elected in that year.

BIBLIOGRAPHY

DODD, C. H. *The Crisis of Turkish Democracy,* 2nd ed. 1990.
LANDAU, J. M. *Radical Politics in Modern Turkey.* 1974.

Frank Tachau

Turki, Fawaz   [1940–   ]

Palestinian writer.

Fawaz was born near Haifa, Palestine. He has taught in Europe and in Australia, and has traveled widely in India, the Middle East, and the United States. In the mid-1990s he was living in Paris, where he was teaching and writing. His best-known book, *The Disinherited: Journal of a Palestinian in Exile* (1972), expresses the longing for a national identity experienced by Palestinians of his generation.

Jenab Tutunji

Turkish–Afghan Treaty

Agreement between Turkey and Afghanistan designed to secure their independence from Soviet and British influence.

The Turkish–Afghan treaty, signed May 28, 1928, was the third in a series of bilateral agreements between Turkey and Afghanistan, non-Arab Muslim states bordering the Soviet Union. While the treaty did not include a mutual defense pact, it did proclaim peaceful relations between the two countries, barred either party from entering into a hostile alliance against the other, and called for mutual consultations in the event of threat of aggression from third parties.

BIBLIOGRAPHY

HUREWITZ, J. C. *The Middle East and North Africa in World Politics: A Documentary Record.* 2 vols, 2nd ed. New Haven, Conn., 1975–1979.

David Waldner

Turkish Grand National Assembly

The legislative body of Turkey, also known as TGNA.

Turkish experience with a multiparty national legislature dates back to 1908, but the Turkish Grand National Assembly (*Turkiye Büyük Millet Meclisi*) was founded on April 23, 1920, at the outset of the Turkish War of Independence; the republic was then proclaimed on October 29, 1923. The assembly functioned as a legislature with one party until 1946, with a transition to multiparty politics initiated by the original party, the Republican People's party. This transition did not demand new laws, and the constitution of 1924 remained in force. According to this basic law, the assembly was a symbol of national will. Its function, according to Article 26, was to legislate, supervise the executive via the budget, and elect the head of state.

From 1950 to 1960 the assembly was headed by the Democrat party, the new opposition party; it represented a legislature of elites in dissent on the fundamental features and rule of Turkey's political regime. In 1950, about 80 percent of the seats had new occupants. The majority system favored disciplined Democrat party voting during the 1950s, so the assembly evolved into a submissive body. Financial and economic crises and the electoral losses of the Democrat party in 1957 led to the adoption of authoritarian policies and laws aimed at the dissolution of the opposition parties. These measures brought about the military coup of 1960; the activities of the assembly were then suspended for a year; all the deputies and cabinet members of the Democrat party were prosecuted, and it dissolved.

The constituent assembly, which then drafted the 1961 constitution, submitted to a referendum with 62 percent approval and aimed at installing numerous checks and balances to control arbitrary executive rule and excessively fast legislation. A lower house was formed, the National Assembly (*Millet Meclisi*), with 450 members elected to four-year terms. The upper house, the Republican Senate (*Cumhuriyet Senatosu*), consisted of 150 members elected to six-year terms—with fifteen contingent senators appointed by the president of the republic, on the basis of merit, and a varying number of ex-officio life members who belonged to the National Unity Committee of the interim of 1960/61, along with former presidents of the republic. The legislative powers of the Senate remained limited and subordinate to the National Assembly. Joint sessions of the two assemblies constituted the new Turkish Grand National Assembly (TGNA). After 1980, the Senate was abolished.

Since none of the dissolved Democrat party members could participate in the new constitution of 1960/61, the successor party, the Justice party, declared the new constitution unfit. Hence, the TGNA, from 1961 to 1980 was an arena of discord. Civil liberties guaranteed by the 1961 constitution and proportional representation enabled what had been covert religious and socialist tendencies to become expressed openly. Therefore the TGNA of the 1970s witnessed almost unceasing legislative battles. By March 1971, tensions led to limited military intervention, but the legislature was not suspended. Rather, the resignation of the Justice party government was demanded, and constitutional amendments were imposed that curtailed the autonomy of the universities and media.

After a return to democratic life in 1973, following the general elections, the TGNA and its legislative agenda were influenced by opposition parties. Tension not only nurtured unruly legislative behavior but finally led to complete paralysis of the legislative process by 1980. The final crisis had to do with the inability to realize the election of the head of state. Again, the military intervened—for the third time in twenty years. On September 12, 1980, the legislature was dissolved and all political parties banned. The interim regime lasted two years, and an appointed consultative assembly prepared a new constitution.

Approved in a referendum on November 7, 1987, the new constitution defines Turkey as a democratic secular state in which legislative power is vested in a unicameral assembly, elected by universal adult suffrage (of those aged twenty-one and over) for a maximum of five years. Article 96 forbids reelection of deputies who switch parties, but this provision has been circumvented by the stratagem of funding new parties and then dissolving them prior to mergers with other parties. Executive power is exercised by a president and a council of ministers, headed by a prime minister appointed by the president. When a president's term ends, the legislature must elect a successor within thirty days. If it fails to do so by the fourth ballot, it must dissolve itself.

Prior to the 1987 elections, a referendum gave a narrow majority that lifted a ten-year ban (enshrined in the 1982 constitution) on more than 100 politicians who had been prominent before the 1980 military coup. The 1987 elections enlarged the membership of the TGNA from 400 to 450, although a stipulation required at least 10 percent of the valid votes for representation to restrict the number of parties obtaining seats to three. Such a proportional system favors large parties. In 1987, it enabled the Motherland party to win with 36.3 percent of the vote but 64 percent of the seats; while the Social Democratic Populist party got 24.8 percent of the votes and 20 percent of the seats; the True Path party got 19.3 percent of the vote and only 13 percent of the seats.

The main functions of the TGNA are defined in Article 87 of the constitution: "enactment, amendment and repeals of laws; supervision of the Council of Ministers; the authorization of the Council of Ministers to issue governmental decrees having force of law, the approval of the budget, the power to decide on printing currency, declaring war; the ratification of international agreements, the proclamation of amnesties and pardon, the confirmation of death sentences passed by courts."

BIBLIOGRAPHY

BODURGIL, A., ed. *Turkey, Politics and Government: A Bibliography, 1938–1975.* Washington, D.C., 1978.

Nermin Abadan-Unat

Turkish Hearth Association

Group formed to promote Turkish nationalism.

Toward the end of the Ottoman Empire, Ziya GÖKALP and other Turkish intellectuals founded the Turkish Hearth Association (Türk Ocağı) in 1911 to promote nationalism, especially Gökalp's synthesis of Turkism, Islamism, and modernism. The association provided the Union and Progress political party with ideological direction. With government support, this private association sponsored nationalistic publications, speeches, sports, health, and economic development projects. By 1930, the association had 254 branches in cities and towns across Turkey. In 1931/32, the Republican People's party dissolved the association, took over its property, and established the PEOPLE'S HOUSES (*Halk Evleri*) in its place.

BIBLIOGRAPHY

LEWIS, BERNARD. *The Emergence of Modern Turkey.* London, 1961.

Paul J. Magnarella

Turkish Historical Society

Academy dedicated to the study of Turkish history.

The forerunner to this society was the Turkish Historical Committee of the Turkish Hearth (Türk Ocağı Türk Tarih Heyeti) formed on June 4, 1930.

This committee was reorganized as the Society for the Study of Turkish History (Türk Tarihi Tetkik Cemiyeti) on April 12, 1931 (officially recognized on April 15, 1931), and renamed the Turkish Historical Society (Türk Tarih Kurumu) on October 3, 1935. On November 7, 1982, the society was made subordinate to the Atatürk Kültür, Dil ve Tarih Yüksek Kurumu that now oversees the cultural, linguistic, and historical societies. The society has convened historical congresses (the first one, held July 2–10, 1932), publishes the journal *Belleten*, as well as monograph series devoted to all periods of the history of Turkey from the civilizations of ancient Anatolia to the modern day. It also serves as an academy for historical sciences honoring Turkish and foreign scholars.

BIBLIOGRAPHY

COKER, FAHRI. *Türk Tarih Kurumu: Kuruluş amacı ve çalışmaları* (The Turkish Historical Society: The Goals of Its Foundation and Its Activities). Ankara, 1983.

Uli Schamiloglu

Turkish–Italian War

War launched by Italy in Libya, 1911–1912.

The Turkish–Italian War (September 29, 1911–October 18, 1912) was launched by Italy in Libya as a step toward becoming a modern empire. Viewing the Roman Empire as its natural expansion ground, Italy realized that due to the international power structure, Libya was among the few areas still open for its occupation. The diplomatic ground for this move was prepared by reaching secret bilateral agreements with Britain, France, Germany, Austria-Hungary, and Russia, which gave Italy a free hand in Libya in exchange for reciprocity elsewhere. This was in violation of the Congress and Treaty of Berlin (1878), in which the European powers guaranteed the sovereignty and territorial integrity of the Ottoman Empire. Once Italy invaded Libya, the powers suggested that the Ottoman government accept the fact.

Since peaceful penetration through economic and cultural means did not bring Libya under Italian rule, Italy sent an ultimatum to the Ottoman government on September 26, 1911, declaring that it was occupying Libya to protect the security of its citizens and their property, and to advance the region. It was left for the Ottoman government to accept the ultimatum within twenty-four hours. Meanwhile, Italian military and naval units were readied for the invasion. When its demands were not met, Italy declared a state of war to exist with the Ottoman Empire

(September 29), placed a blockade on the Libyan coast, and started its landing in Tripoli (October 4). The conquest of the coastal towns was swift—Tripoli (October 12), Derna (October 18), Benghazi and Khoms (October 21), and the smaller towns soon after.

The Ottoman military force in Libya was small and much below the standard; its arms were old and the additional weapons that reached Tripoli on September 25 were regarded by Italy as a *casus belli*. There were few fortifications and old, stationary guns, mainly around Tripoli, whose range was shorter than that of the Italian naval guns. Military conscription of the Libyan population started only in the summer of 1911 with the mobilization of several hundred troops and the establishment of a reserve force. Meanwhile, nonmobilized tribal forces were accustomed to fight under the leadership of their chiefs, and were often well equipped with an unknown amount of diverse arms. This military situation resulted from financial constraints and the greater need of army units and weapons elsewhere. When the war broke out, the Ottomans could not forward military support to Libya due to the Italian sea blockade and the decision of Britain and France to prevent the passage of military reinforcements to the belligerents through Egypt and Tunisia.

As a result of these conditions, the Ottoman authorities in Istanbul allowed volunteers to infiltrate into Libya (among them were Enver Paşa, who later became the minister of war, and Mustafa Kemal Atatürk, the founder of the Turkish republic). They left the actual direction of the war to the Ottoman military command in Libya—which decided to retreat from the coast—where the Italians had a clear military advantage owing to the size and quality of their forces—and prepare for defense in the hinterland in cooperation with tribal fighters. An Ottoman–Libyan force was established, composed of tribal soldiers, Ottoman professionals, and a mixed Ottoman-tribal command, which in Cyrenaica was strongly connected with the Sanusi leadership and network of *zawiya*s (religious compounds). Ottomans were at the top, but fighting units had a mixed command, and all received arms, ammunition, equipment, and salaries from the Ottomans.

The large and modern Italian invading forces were innovative in being the first to make military use of airplanes (for reconnaissance and bombing). They made no meaningful gains after their initial conquests because they attempted to fight a trench war against the resistance, which engaged in guerilla warfare and took advantage of the hilly or desert terrain and the support of the population. Only later did the Italians develop combined means—military, political, and economic—to occupy Libya, a process that took some twenty years.

Failing to advance into the hinterland, the Italians widened the scope of the war to the eastern Mediterranean to put more pressure on the Ottomans. During April and May 1912, Italy occupied the Dodecanese, tried to force the Dardanelles, and bombarded some Ottoman ports, including Beirut. These operations caused the Ottomans heavy damage, aroused strong apprehension among the European powers, and resulted in growing international efforts to solve the crisis. In the summer of 1912, unrest increased in the Balkans, resulting in the outbreak of the first Balkan War (October 8, 1912). The inability of the Ottomans to fight on two major fronts, and the fact that the Balkans were more important to the empire than Libya, persuaded the Ottoman government to end the war in Libya. The Treaty of Peace was reached on October 15, 1912, in Lausanne, and it was approved in nearby Ouchy three days later. Ottoman forces were to leave Libya, but Muslim religious representation was to be sent there by the Ottomans. This was to be followed by an Italian evacuation of the Dodecanese. The issue of sovereignty was not clearly stated, and while Italy regarded Libya as part of the Italian homeland following its declaration on the extension of Italian law over Libya (November 5, 1911), the Ottomans told the local population that they were granted autonomy under Ottoman rule. Most of the Ottoman forces left Tripolitania, but many remained in Cyrenaica, and reinforcements were also sent later, especially during World War I. Until then, Italy managed to occupy most of Tripolitania, preventing the functioning of the Ottoman-chosen religious representation.

BIBLIOGRAPHY

CHILDS, T. W. *Italo–Turkish Diplomacy and the War over Libya, 1911–1912.* Leiden, Neth., 1990.

EVANS-PRITCHARD, E. E. *The Sanusi of Cyrenaica.* Oxford, 1949.

MALGERI, F. *La guerra libica (1911–1912).* Rome, 1970.

SIMON, R. *Libya between Ottomanism and Nationalism: Ottoman Involvement in Libya during the War with Italy, 1911–1919.* Berlin, 1987.

Rachel Simon

Turkish Language

Türkçe, official language of the Republic of Turkey.

In 1990, Turkish was spoken by 57 million people within the borders of Turkey and 2 million in Europe, with the greatest concentration in Germany. An estimated 1.5 million additional speakers live in the Balkans and on Cyprus. After Arabic, Turkish is the most widely spoken language in the Middle East.

Turkish is one of the Turkic languages of the Altaic language family, one of the major language families of the world. Turkic, Mongolian, and Manchu-Tungus constitute the Altaic language family, which was originally spoken around the Altai mountain ranges in central Asia, straddling Mongolia, China, and Russia. Altaic languages are usually grouped with the Uralic languages, for example, Samoyed, Finnish, and Hungarian. Debates continue about whether the admitted typological and lexical similarities between the two signal a common ancestor language or prolonged contact.

The Turkic language group includes most of the languages and dialects spoken along a wide Eurasian belt that goes from Eastern Siberia to Eastern Europe and the Balkans. The major representative Turkic languages are (starting in the east) Yakut, Altai, Khakas, Kazak, Kirgiz, Uygur, Uzbek, Azeri, Turkish, Turkmen, and further to the west, Bashkir, Tatar, and Chuvash. With the exception of Turkish, all of these languages are spoken in the republics and territories of the former Soviet Union and in northwestern China.

Turkish, Azeri (also referred to as Azerbaijani Turkish), and Turkmen are the major members of the southwestern, or Oghuz, branch of the Turkic languages. In demographic terms, this branch is the most important Turkic group—there are today, by conservative estimates, 85 million speakers of the southwestern branch. Azeri is spoken in the Republic of Azerbaijan and in the province of Azerbaijan of northwestern Iran. Turkmen is spoken in the Republic of Turkmenistan and in the adjoining territories in northern Iran and Afghanistan, as well as in Iraq. Lesser-known members of the southwestern branch are Gagauz, spoken in Balkan states of Bulgaria and Moldavia, and Qashqai, spoken by nomadic tribes in southwestern Iran. The languages of this branch are closely related and have a relatively high degree of mutual intelligibility. Interfering with complete comprehension of written material is mainly the vocabulary as developed or acquired by each language while functioning in different historical and cultural spheres. In oral communication, differences in pronunciation slow down comprehension.

Turkish was introduced to the Middle East with the westward migration of various Turkish tribes from the western regions of central Asia, which had early converted to Islam. By the end of the eleventh century, these Muslim Turks had conquered Asia Minor, and the Turkish language began to be established in what is today the Turkish heartland, Anatolia. As the official administrative language of the Ottoman Turks, Turkish spread further with the continuing Ottoman conquests, into the Balkans and central Europe to the north, and into the Arab lands and North Africa to the south. Turkish became the lingua franca in many of these regions, and the impact of Turkish on the indigenous languages after centuries of contact is clearly discernible today.

The earliest written Anatolian Turkish materials are in Arabic script and date from the thirteenth century. Earlier materials exist, most notably in the monumental treatise, written in 1073 by Mahmut Kashgari, on Turks and their languages. Three basic periods are recognized for the historical development of the Turkish language, based on written data: (1) Old Anatolian Turkish for the thirteenth through fifteenth centuries; (2) Ottoman Turkish for the fifteenth through the early twentieth centuries; (3) Modern Turkish for the twentieth century. The linguistic base remained remarkably stable, particularly for the spoken language, so that some poetry, including early hymns of Sufism written in the fourteenth century, can be understood and appreciated by a general audience today. However, in the process of adapting to Islam and the Arab–Persian culture, Turkish gradually acquired many words and some syntactic elements from Arabic and Persian. As the Ottoman Turks became the standard-bearers for the Islamic world, borrowing from both Arabic and Persian accelerated to such an extent that, by the nineteenth century, an official or literary Ottoman Turkish text could be understood only by an educated elite conversant in Turkish, Persian, and Arabic.

By the start of the twentieth century—and hastened by the post–World War I disintegration of the Ottoman Empire—nationalistic notions about a distinct Turkish identity inspired moves to rid the language of excessive foreign elements. The Alphabet Reform of 1928, which abandoned Arabic script and mandated a phonetic writing system for Turkish based on the Latin alphabet, was a crucial factor in the emergence of Modern Turkish. The new writing system was tailored exclusively to the vowel-rich Turkish sound system, eventually setting up a well-defined modern national standard for Turkish based on the dialect of Istanbul, the old capital of the Ottoman Empire and the educational, cultural, and intellectual center of the country.

The Turkish language shares a core vocabulary with the other Turkic languages and exhibits characteristic common features: vowel harmony, agglutination, and, on the syntactic level, left-branching. Turkish has eight vowels, four pairs with corresponding front/back [e, i, ö, ü/a, ı, o, u], high/low [i, ı, ü, u/e, a, ö, o], and rounded/unrounded [o, ö,

u, ü/a, e, ı, i] sounds, which form the basis for vowel harmony. According to vowel harmony rules, vowels of suffixes must have the same properties as the vowel in the last syllable: either front/back: *ev-lerimiz/kapı-larımız* or rounded/unrounded: *onuncu/beşinci.* There are 21 letters representing consonants: b, c, ç, d, f, g, ğ, h, j, k, l, m, n, p, r, s, ş, t, v, y, z; all except for ğ are universal sounds. Agglutination in Turkish takes the form of suffixes attached to the end of a word, whether noun or verb. Suffixes add to the word's meaning and/or mark its grammatical function. Thus, *ev-ler-imiz-den* 'from our houses' has 'house' [*ev*] + plural [*ler*] + 'our' [*imiz*] + 'from' [*den*]. English *pre*position concepts are *post*positions in Turkish: *annem gibi* 'like my mother' is 'mother' [*anne*] + 'my' [*m*] + 'like' [*gibi*]. Turkish does not have a definite article, nor is it gender marked. *O* indicates 'he' or 'she' as well as 'it'; *evi* can be 'her house' as well as 'his house.' At the sentence level, Turkish follows the subject-object-verb pattern: *Babam evi gördü;* My father saw the house. As a left-branching language, all qualifying or modifying information precedes the element modified:

{*en güzel*} *ev* = {the most beautiful} house
{*dün gördüğüm*} {*en güzel*} *ev* =
   {the most beautiful} house {I saw yesterday}

Turkish sentences, unlike English, work on the principle of syntactical *co*ordination instead of *sub*ordination. This allows for a lot of information to be strung together in a Turkish sentence, affecting written and formal discourse. One Turkish sentence will usually produce several sentences in English.

A lexical inventory of today's Modern Turkish clearly shows that the Turkish language has enriched itself by borrowing freely from other languages and continues to do so. In the transition to today's Modern Turkish, the lexical base of the language has had fifty years of tampering by the language-reform policies that were initiated in 1931 by the Turkish Linguistic Society. The goals were to eliminate diglossia (two forms), thus making the language accessible to all, while rejuvenating the language so that the communicative needs of a modernizing nation could be met. The effective result has been that Arabic and Persian borrowings not fully assimilated into the language were almost immediately eliminated, with neologisms or borrowings from Western languages replacing needed words.

BIBLIOGRAPHY

BOESCHOTEN, HENDRIK, and LUDO VERHOEVEN, eds. *Turkish Linguistics Today.* Leiden, 1991.
DENY, JEAN. *Grammaire de la langue turque.* Paris, 1921.
HAZAI, GYÖRGY, ed. *Handbuch der türkischen Sprachwissenschaft.* Wiesbaden, 1990.

HEYD, URIEL. *Language Reform in Modern Turkey*. Jerusalem, 1954.

KOWALSKI, T. "Ottoman Turkish Dialects." In *Encyclopaedia of Islam,* vol. 4.

LEWIS, GEOFFREY L. *Turkish Grammar*. Oxford, 1967.

SLOBIN, DAN I., and KARL ZIMMER, eds. *Studies in Turkish Linguistics*. Amsterdam, 1986.

Erika Gilson

Turkish Linguistic Society

Organization devoted to the study of Turkish and the Turkic languages.

The Society for the Study of the Turkish Language (Türk Dili Tetkik Cemiyeti) was founded on July 12, 1932, on the model of a similar society that already existed for the study of Turkish history. In 1934, its name was updated to the Türk Dili Araştırma Kurumu reflecting the society's interest in purging the TURKISH LANGUAGE of its numerous borrowed Arabic and Persian words. In 1936, the name was changed again to the Turkish Linguistic Society (Türk Dil Kurumu). On November 7, 1982, the society was made subordinate to the Atatürk Kültür, Dil ve Tarih Yüksek Kurumu that now oversees the cultural, linguistic, and historical societies. The society has convened linguistic congresses (the first congress opened in 1932), publishes the journal *Türk Dili*, and publishes dictionaries and other works related to Turkish and all the other Turkic languages. In contrast to other such societies in Turkey, the activities of the Turkish Linguistic Society have not been led by scholars of the Turkish language, and one result has been that the society's activities have assumed a populist character. The society has also been at the center of recurring and intense national debates over language reform, most recently over the degree to which vast numbers of neologisms (new words or word forms adopted from foreign words) should be introduced into the Turkish language (often over the objections of many politicians and scholars).

BIBLIOGRAPHY

HEYD, URIEL. *Language Reform in Modern Turkey*. Jerusalem, 1954.

Uli Schamiloglu

Turkish National Pact

A resolution that stated the goal of political independence for Turkey.

This resolution adopted by the Ottoman parliament in Istanbul on February 17, 1920, declared support for the demands of the nationalist movement led by Mustafa Kemal Pasha (Atatürk). It included: the integrity of all territories inhabited by "an Ottoman Islamic majority"; popular plebiscites to determine the future of territories whose status was in doubt (Kars, Ardahan, and Batum in the Caucasus; western Thrace; and areas with Arab majorities); "protection" of the city of Istanbul and the Sea of Marmara and negotiation regarding trade and commerce in the Bosporus and the Dardanelles; recognition of minority rights provided reciprocal rights were extended to Muslim minorities in other countries; and recognition of full independence and sovereignty for "the country." This was essentially the program implemented in the wake of the defeat of the Greek army in western Anatolia and the withdrawal of British power from Istanbul and its environment in 1922. Functionally, the national pact served as a declaration of independence by nationalist Turkey.

BIBLIOGRAPHY

SHAW, S. J., and E. K. SHAW. *History of the Ottoman Empire and Modern Turkey,* vol. 2. Cambridge, U.K. 1977.

Frank Tachau

Turkish News Agency

A leading information cooperative, 1950–1987.

Founded in 1950 as a privately owned news cooperative, the Turkish News Agency (Türk Haberler Ajansi, THA) published a daily three-page bulletin. In 1968, Kadri Kayabal turned it into Turkey's nationwide news and photo agency with bureaus in fourteen cities, employing more than one hundred correspondents. The THA also distributed Reuters (London) and UPI (U.S.) news stories. In 1982, it was bought by Güçlü Yayimcilik A. S. (which publishes the *Güneş* newspaper), but ceased operations in 1987.

BIBLIOGRAPHY

KURIAN, G. E. *World Press Encyclopedia*. New York, 1982.

Elizabeth Thompson

Turkish Unity Party

See Unity Party

Turkish University Women's Association

Organization of Turkish female university graduates, established in 1949.

Membership in the association (Türk Üniversiteli Kadınlar Derneği) is restricted to female graduates of universities or other institutions of higher education. Its purposes are ties of friendship and solidarity between female university graduates in Turkey; exchanging cultural, professional, and scientific information; doing research and publishing on women's questions in Turkey; and combating illiteracy. The association has about one thousand members.

Niyazi Dalyanci

Turkish Workers Party

Turkish political party, 1961–1971.

This first avowedly socialist group to make a significant impact on the Turkish party system was founded in February of 1961. Its emergence signified the relative liberalism of the political order in the wake of the military intervention of May 27, 1960. The party competed successfully in the elections of 1965 and 1969, polling about 3 percent of the vote and gaining fifteen seats in the former and two in the latter election (the difference is attributable to changes in the electoral law). Its presence on the scene may have pulled the centrist Republican People's party (RPP) to the left. The party was subject to official and mob harassment, including violent attacks on its facilities and members. It was dissolved by order of the constitutional court in July 1971 on grounds that its leaders had encouraged communism and ethnic divisiveness (specifically, Kurdish separatism).

BIBLIOGRAPHY

AHMAD, F. *The Turkish Experiment in Democracy, 1950–1975.* Boulder, Colo., 1977.

Frank Tachau

Turkism

Political and cultural movement that emerged in the late nineteenth century and helped to form the new Turkish republic.

A movement of many tendencies, Turkism evolved largely in response to European nationalism and to the perceived failure of Ottomanism, as the empire

was rocked by minority nationalist movements in the Balkans and Armenia. Sentiments of Turkish nationalist feeling can be traced to historical writings of the mid-nineteenth century, such as those of AHMET VEFIK Paşa (1823–1891). The first Ottoman Turcologist was Necib Asim (1861–1935). Politically, Turkism was most prominently expressed by the Young Turk movement, first in exile in the 1890s in Europe and Egypt and later in Anatolia after the 1908 Young Turk revolution. Competing tendencies included Anatolian nationalism, which traced Turkish roots in the territory to ancient times, and pan-Turkism, espoused especially by Turkish refugees from Russia and central Asia. The political manifesto of pan-Turkism is considered Russian-born Yusuf Akçura's 1904 essay, "Üç Tarz-i Siyaset" (Three Kinds of Policy), which rejected Ottomanism and Islam as bases of national identity and policy.

A major Turkish literary movement appeared in the early twentieth century, with groups like the GENÇ KALEMLER (Young Pens) founded in 1911 in Salonika and the Türk Deneği (Turkish Society) founded in 1908 in Constantinople (now Istanbul). These and other groups were devoted to reviving Turkish folklore, studying the roots and branches of the various Turkic languages, and purifying the Ottoman language of non-Turkish words. The most important ideologue of the Young Turk era was the pan-Turkist writer and sociologist, Ziya GÖKALP (1876–1924), who developed a populist vision of the rebirth of Turkish society. Eventually, Anatolian-based Turkism would prevail, with Mustafa Kemal's revolution and war of independence, beginning in 1919.

BIBLIOGRAPHY

LEWIS, BERNARD. *The Emergence of Modern Turkey.* New York, 1961.

SHAW, STANFORD J., and EZEL KURAL SHAW. *History of the Ottoman Empire and Modern Turkey,* vol 2. Cambridge, U.K., 1977.

Elizabeth Thompson

Turkmanchai, Treaty of

Russo–Iranian treaty giving land and rights to Russia, 1828.

In this treaty, signed in the village of Turkmanchai (Torkaman) in Azerbaijan after a two-year war, Iran conceded the provinces of Yerevan (Erevan) and Nakhjavan (Nakhichevan) to czarist Russia. In addition, Russia was granted naval rights on the Caspian Sea, a permanent mission, and extraterritorial rights for her citizens in Iran.

Farhad Shirzad

Turkmen

Central Asian Turkish tribal people of Iran, Turkmenistan, and Afghanistan.

Located east of the Caspian Sea and west of the Amu Darya river, these central Asian Turks numbered more than four million in the 1990s. Sizable numbers of diaspora Turkmen also reside in Iraq, Syria, and Turkey. They speak western Oghuz Turkic and follow Sunni Islam. Almost all Turkmen were nomadic pastoralists until the twentieth century; by the 1990s, most no longer followed nomadism but were settled and practiced a mixed pastoral-agricultural economy.

BIBLIOGRAPHY

IRONS, WILLIAM. *The Yomut Turkmen: A Study of Social Organization among a Central Asian Turkic-Speaking Population.* Museum of Anthropology Anthropological Paper, no. 58. Ann Arbor, Mich., 1975.

Lois Beck

Türk Ocaği

See Turkish Hearth Association

Turkology

The academic study of the languages and civilization of the Turkic peoples with a traditional emphasis on sources written in Turkic languages.

The modern Turkic languages include Turkish, Uzbek, Kazakh, Azeri, Kazan Tatar, Turkmen, Kirghiz, Chuvash, Bashkir, Karakalpak, Yakut, Kumik, Crimean Tatar, Uighur, Tuvan, Gagauz, Karachay, Balkar, Xakas, Noghay, Altay, Shor, Dolgan, Karaim, and Tofalar. Native scholars have been writing descriptions of the Turkic dialects since the eleventh century. In the West, the earliest works on Turkey appeared in the fifteenth and sixteenth centuries, and the first descriptions of the Turkish language were published in the seventeenth century. The formal study of Turkish and other Turkic languages was introduced in Europe in the eighteenth century, and by the end of the nineteenth century, there were prominent centers of Turkology at universities in Paris, Moscow, Saint Petersburg, Kazan, Budapest, and Vienna. Today Turkology is widely taught in modern political units representing individual Turkic peoples: the Turkish republic, the Turkic republics of the former USSR, and the Uighur Autonomous Region in the People's Republic of China, where it is synonymous with the study of the local national culture. Turkology is also offered at major universities in Europe and North America, though the study of the language and civilization of the Turkish republic is far better represented than the study of the Turkic peoples as a whole.

BIBLIOGRAPHY

MENGES, KARL H. *The Turkic Languages and Peoples: An Introduction to Turkic Studies.* Wiesbaden, 1968.
POPPE, NICHOLAS. *Introduction to Altaic Linguistics.* Wiesbaden, 1965.

Uli Schamiloglu

Turko–Persian War

The final war between the Qajar Persians and the Ottoman Turks.

This conflict began in 1821 when the Persian governor of Erzerum gave protection to tribes fleeing Azerbaijan. Actually, the conflict was instigated by Russia, which was anxious to weaken the Ottoman position in the Greek Revolution. The Russians induced Abbas Mirza, son of Fath Ali Shah Qajar, to invade Ottoman Turkey. He did, occupying Kurdistan and all the districts adjacent to Azerbaijan. As a counter move, the Ottoman viceroy of Baghdad invaded Persia but was defeated and chased back to Baghdad. In retaliation, Fath Ali Shah Qajar's oldest son, Mohammad Ali Mirza, laid siege to that city; his illness, and later death, lifted the siege, and the action shifted to the north. In the battle of Erzurum (1821) Abbas Mirza's army of 30,000 men defeated an Ottoman army of over 50,000. An epidemic of cholera precluded further action in the south, and the two powers ended hostilities with the Treaty of Erzurum on July 28, 1823. This treaty involved no change in territorial borders, but it did guarantee Persia access to the holy places in Iraq and Arabia; Ottoman suppression of Kurdish raids on Persian territory; release of the possessions of Persian merchants in Turkey; and an exchange of ambassadors.

BIBLIOGRAPHY

SYKES, PERCY. *A History of Persia.* New York, 1969.

Daniel E. Spector

Turks

National, cultural, or political term variously applied in the Middle East.

Turkey's government regards all of its citizens as Turks, regardless of their mother tongue or their expressions of separate identity. However, since the nationalist ideology regards Turkishness as a quality primarily of language and folkways, many Turkish citizens, notably those whose native tongue is Kurdish, reject this identity. Of the numerous other peoples who speak Turkic languages, most identify themselves as Uzbek, Kazakh, or Tatar. In Azerbaijan, the people who speak a Turkic language are generally called Torks (speakers of Torki).

The term "Turk" has also been used pejoratively and/or politically. Ottoman usage called nomads Turks, reserving the term "Osmanli" for more urbane and educated people. European usage, for many centuries, equated Turks with Ottomans, despite the multiethnic makeup of the Ottoman Empire, or even with Muslims in general. These pejorative senses have continued in the Serbian designation of the Muslims of Bosnia as Turks despite their linguistic and ethnic affinities with the Serbs.

Richard W. Bulliet

Türk Tarih Kurumu

See Turkish Historical Society

Türk Yurdu

Young Turk magazine.

Türk Yurdu (The Turkish Homeland) was the organ of the Turkish Homeland Society. Yusuf Akçura and Ahmet Agaoğlu began to publish *Türk Yurdu* on 31 August 1911 in order to disseminate their messages of Turkish nationalism, populism, and the need to develop a Muslim bourgeoisie. Ziya GÖKALP was a regular contributor. As part of an effort to establish new contacts with the masses, the magazine placed special emphasis on popular poetry, folklore, and myth, all written in a simple language.

BIBLIOGRAPHY

SHAW, STANFORD, and EZEL KURAL SHAW. *History of the Ottoman Empire and Modern Turkey*, vol 2: *Reform, Revolution, and Republic: The Rise of Modern Turkey, 1808–1975.* Cambridge, U.K., 1977.

David Waldner

Tutunji, Jamil   [1896–1981]

Jordanian doctor and diplomat.

Born in İzmir of Turkish extraction, Tutunji was orphaned when young. He studied medicine at the American University of Beirut but graduated from Istanbul University. In the Arab Legion, he was director of medical services and was private physician to Jordan's Abdullah ibn Husayn and Prince Talal ibn Abdullah. He was director of public health and minister of health between 1950 and 1962, frequently combining these posts with the portfolio for social welfare. His testimony to parliament on Talal's health was instrumental in the prince's accession to the throne and later abdication. In 1964 he was Jordan's first ambassador to the USSR.

BIBLIOGRAPHY

ABIDI, AQIL HYDER HASAN. *Jordan: A Political Study, 1948–1957.* New Delhi, 1965.
BAKHIT, MUHAMMAD ADNAN. "Introduction to the Memories of Dr. Jamil Fa'iq Tutunji," *Dirasat* 12 (October 1985).

Jenab Tutunji

Twareg

Berber-speaking people of the Sahara, mostly in Algeria.

Twareg is an apparently non-Berber plural; the singular is *targui* or *targi*. Twareg call themselves, according to the region, *amahagh, amaiagh,* or *amashagh,* all reflexes of *amazigh,* the term more widely used for Berber in the rest of North Africa. It is estimated that there are 400,000 to 500,000 Twareg-language/

Two Twareg boys in traditional dress. (Richard Bulliet)

dialect speakers. Most are fair-skinned Europids, although many are descendants of or mixed with negroid populations (of whom most were slaves). Twareg traditionally distinguish socially between the "noble" clans, camel nomads who in the past could range far and wide, wage war, and claim a share of the resources of groups they dominated (and whose protection they assured), and "vassal" clans, also nomadic but essentially herdsmen (mainly goats, but also camels belonging to the nobles, and cattle in some places), subjects of the noble clans. Other groups often are counted as Twareg, notably sedentary former slave populations (now primarily agriculturalists in the oases and artisans).

The requirements of modern states—fixed borders, schooling of children, control of territory and citizens—and the industrial exploitation of resources have placed extreme pressures on the nomadic existence and traditions dear to the Twareg. They nonetheless maintain such traditional cultural traits as a strong matrilineal principle (in much of their inheritance of property, succession to chieftainship, rights and obligations toward vassal groups, etc.) and the strict veiling of men (women, however, typically are not veiled).

Thomas G. Penchoen

Twayni, Ghassan [1926–]

Lebanon's best-known journalist and publisher; former minister, ambassador, and representative from Lebanon to the United Nations.

A Greek Orthodox born in Beirut, Ghassan Twayni (also Tueni) has been one of the most influential figures in post–World War II Lebanon. His impressive and successful multifaceted career as academic, journalist, businessman, politician, diplomat, and man of letters has made him a prime shaper of public opinion in his country and one of the most respected commentators on Lebanese and Arab affairs throughout the United States and Europe.

He received a bachelor of arts degree in philosophy from the American University of Beirut (AUB) in 1945 and a master of arts degree in political science from Harvard University in 1947. After a year as lecturer in political science at AUB (1947–1948), he became editor in chief of the *al-Nahar* daily newspaper in 1948, a position he still occupied in the early 1990s. Indeed, he never gave up journalism and publishing and has been active as founder and chairman (1960 onwards) of Press Cooperative S.A.L. publishing group, editor-publisher of the *al-Nahar* S.C.P.A. Publishing Company after 1963, publisher and editor in chief of the French-language dailies *Le Jour* (1965) and *L'Orient–Le Jour* (1970–1991), and chairman of the board of Société Générale de la Presse et d'Edition (1985–1991).

In 1951, embarking on a political career, Twayni won a parliamentary seat after running successfully in Mount Lebanon as a candidate of the Socialist National Front, a loose coalition of politicians, headed by Camille Chamoun and Kamal Jumblatt, calling for the resignation of President Khuri, whose second term in office had become tainted with charges of nepotism, administrative corruption, and heavy-handed tactics. Twayni was reelected in 1953 and 1957, both times as a representative for Beirut, and was deputy-speaker of parliament between 1953 and 1957. By then, he had established himself as one of the most prominent and competent members of a new generation of young, well-educated, reform-minded professionals who had become active in politics in an effort to modernize the Lebanese state. It was this reputation that led to his appointment in October 1970 as deputy prime minister and minister of information and education in President Sulayman Franjiyya's first cabinet (the so-called Youth Cabinet, headed by Sa'id Salam and composed predominantly of young technocrats recruited from outside parliament). Twayni resigned in January 1971, however, in protest against the president's and the prime minister's unwillingness to support the educational reforms he had proposed. He was subsequently appointed minister of labor and social affairs, tourism, and industry and oil in a cabinet headed by Rashid Karame (July 1975 to December 1976).

After the 1960s, Ghassan Twayni frequently represented his country abroad, both in official and unofficial positions. Following the 1967 Arab–Israel War, he was ambassador-at-large and personal representative of President Charles Hilu on a special mission to the United States. In December 1976, he was President Ilyas Sarkis's special emissary to Washington, D.C. His diplomatic skills and achievements eventually led to his appointment in September 1977 as ambassador and permanent representative of Lebanon to the United Nations, a position he held until September 1982. Between 1982 and 1988, he served as special adviser to President Amin Jumayyil. His responsibilities during this period included coordinating negotiations for the withdrawal of foreign forces from Lebanon. Since July 1990, he has acted as President of Balamand University and continues to shuttle back and forth between Lebanon, Europe, and the United States.

BIBLIOGRAPHY

HUDSON, MICHAEL C. *The Precarious Republic: Political Modernization in Lebanon.* Boulder, Colo., 1985.
PETRAN, TABITHA. *The Struggle over Lebanon.* New York, 1987.

Guilain P. Denoeux

Twin Pillars Policy

Policy that made Iran and Saudi Arabia the two foundations of U.S. policy in the Middle East.

Developed in conjunction with the Nixon Doctrine (1969), the Twin Pillars Policy gave Iran and Saudi Arabia massive military assistance. U.S. President Richard Nixon hoped that doing so would prevent Soviet influence and ensure continued Western access to oil. The policy kept those nations in the U.S. orbit but did not prevent them from pursuing policies at odds with U.S. interests, particularly during the 1973–1974 Organization of Petroleum Exporting Countries (OPEC) oil embargo. The policy collapsed with the fall of Mohammad Reza Shah Pahlavi in 1979.

BIBLIOGRAPHY

RUBIN, BARRY. *Paved with Good Intentions.* New York, 1980.
SPIEGEL, STEVEN. *The Other Arab–Israeli Conflict.* Chicago, 1985.

Zachary Karabell

Tyre

Historic coastal city in south Lebanon on the Mediterranean Sea.

Throughout its history, Tyre (now Sur), which is located fifty-two miles (83 km) from Beirut, has known several invasions and occupations. In the eighth century B.C.E., Tyre rebelled against the Assyrians, and in the sixth century B.C.E., the population of Tyre organized a revolt against the Chaldeans. In 333 B.C.E., following his defeat of the Persians, Alexander the Great was welcomed by all Phoenician cities with the exception of Tyre.

Tyre has also had a golden age (especially under the Romans) because of its flourishing glass and purple dye manufacturing. It was under the Romans that Christianity reached Tyre in the person of Saint Paul, who visited the city and stayed for ten days. In 638 C.E., Tyre fell under the control of the Fatimids, where it remained until 1124. In that year Tyre was besieged by the Crusaders and was incorporated in the kingdom of Jerusalem, as a part of which it grew prosperous. The city was recaptured and destroyed by the Mamluks in 1291.

Oranges, citrus, bananas, and sugar cane are the major fruits and vegetables produced in Tyre. Some of the inhabitants of the city and the surrounding region also make their living as fishermen. The old Phoenician city today has a large number of banks and financial institutions, several educational and humanitarian institutions, and hospitals and health centers. In a city that also has an active sport life, soccer clubs are especially popular.

George E. Irani

Tzomet

Right-wing Israeli political party.

Tzomet was formed for the 1992 election in which it won eight seats. The basis of its appeal was a hard line on the Palestinian issue but populist positions on many quality-of-life issues. Its most prominent personality is the former chief of staff of the Israel Defense Forces, Rafael Eitan.

Walter F. Weiker

U

Ubayd, al-

Capital of Kordofan province in the Republic of Sudan.

Al-Ubayd (Al-Ubayyid, El Obeid), which lies west of Khartoum, had a population of approximately 140,000 in 1983. It has grown in recent years through the influx of persons displaced by the drought of the 1980s and of southern Sudanese uprooted by civil war. Al-Ubayd is the world's leading market for gum arabic and a center for trade in sesame and peanuts. As the provincial capital it is the hub of the KORDOFAN road system, and is served by a branch line of Sudan Railways and an airport. Here the Baqqara Arabs from southern Kordofan sell their cattle, and the Hamar and Rizayqat sell goats, sheep, and camels. There is a large community of Fallata, West Africans mostly from northern Nigeria, who are petty traders. Outside the town is Fula, a natural lake that provides the town with water. The Qubba al-Wali Isma'il, the domed tomb of a prominent holy man and grandfather of Isma'il Azhari (the first president of the Republic of Sudan) is the most famous monument and place of pilgrimage in the town.

Robert O. Collins

Ubayd, Hamad

Syrian politician.

Hamad Ubayd was a Druze officer and head of the Paramilitary National Guard at the time of the Ba'th party coup in Syria in 1963. He subsequently broke with the regime and, with other Druze officers opposed to Alawite dominance of the Ba'th, took as hostage Salah Jadid, leader of the Alawi faction. Defense Minister Hafiz al-Asad threatened to bomb the Druze center of al-Suwayda province, and Ubayd fled to Jordan. He returned to become minister in 1965 and was arrested after a coup on February 23, 1966.

BIBLIOGRAPHY

HINNEBUSCH, RAYMOND A. *Authoritarian Power and State Formation in Ba'thist Syria: Army, Party and Peasant.* Boulder, Colo., 1990.

Charles U. Zenzie

Ubaydat, Ahmad   [1938–   ]

Jordanian politician.

Born in Irbid, Ubaydat began his public career in the Jordanian security forces in 1961. He moved on to the intelligence service, serving as director from 1974 to 1982. He also has served as minister of interior (1982–1984), prime minister and minister of defense (1984–1985), and senator (since 1985). He was perceived as an honest politician during the 1980s, a period of corruption in government.

BIBLIOGRAPHY

ABU GHIDA, RASHID. *Man Huwa?* (Who's Who?). Amman, 1988.
Who's Who in the Arab World, 9th ed. Beirut, 1988/89.

Michael R. Fischbach

UDMA

See Union Démocratique du Manifeste Algérien

Uganda Project

A proposal for a Jewish state in British territory in East Africa.

Against pressure from many Zionists to support colonization by Jews without official authorization, World Zionist Organization (WZO) president Theodor Herzl insisted on international recognition as a precondition to the resettlement of Jews in Palestine (which was, during the end of the nineteenth century, ruled by the Ottoman Empire). Repeatedly failing to produce tangible results, Herzl seized on the possibility of establishing some sort of national entity within Britain's empire—first in the Sinai peninsula and, when this idea failed, in British territory in Africa—in what became known as the Uganda Project (also Uganda Plan).

Following reports of atrocities and casualties from a pogrom in Kishinev (Russia) in April 1903, Herzl was desperate to help the Jewish refugees from Russia. He recommended that the Zionist Congress authorize sending an exploratory expedition to Uganda to investigate the prospects for Jewish colonization and settlement. Herzl was able to secure passage of the proposal at the sixth Zionist Congress but at the cost of deeply dividing the Zionist movement. Many delegates upheld the idea of Palestine as the only site for a Jewish homeland; some insisted on a "peopleless" territory; and others were willing to accept any territory suitable for Jewish colonization.

The Uganda Plan was finally rejected by the seventh Zionist Congress in 1905, a year after the death of Herzl. Several Zionists led by Israel Zangwill, the British author, left the WZO to establish the Jewish Territorial Organization (ITO).

BIBLIOGRAPHY

VITAL, DAVID. *The Origins of Zionism.* Oxford, 1975.

Donna Robinson Divine

Ujayli, Abd al-Salam al-

Syrian physician and novelist.

Dr. Abd al-Salam al-Ujayli was born in the town of Raqqa on the Euphrates river. He served as a parliamentary deputy in 1948 and was one of two deputies to fight in the Arab–Israel War (1948)—the other was Akram al-Hawrani. Ujayli was known in later life for his political novels, among them *Al-Maghmarun* (The Submerged; 1977), a story about refugee displacement, and *Al-Nahr Sultan* (King River), an allegory about Ba'th party water politics on the Euphrates river.

BIBLIOGRAPHY

SEALE, PATRICK. *Asad: The Struggle for the Middle East.* Los Angeles, 1988.

Charles U. Zenzie

Ulama

Muslim male religious scholars.

The term *ulama* literally means those who possess knowledge (*ilm*), most particularly of Islam. The *ulama* emerged as the first interpreters of the Qur'an and transmitters of Hadith, the words and deeds of the Prophet Muhammad. These scholars also became the first to outline and elaborate the basic principles of Islamic law (SHARI'A). The *ulama* were central to Islamic education in the premodern Middle East. They regulated instruction at all levels and were instrumental in the process of training Islamic scholars in *madrasas,* residential colleges, which were established by the eleventh century. These medieval institutions developed a rigorous curriculum centered around instruction in the law and trained future jurists, theologians, and state functionaries. This system of higher education was the first in a series of successful attempts to link the *ulama* to political authority in the Islamic world. Members of the *ulama* might also participate in Islamic mysticism as members, even leaders, of organized Sufi fraternities.

The *ulama* are often defined as a class, when in fact the socioeconomic status of their membership remained quite varied. Lawyers and judges were key members of the *ulama;* their legal skills were critical to the regulation of Islamic society in social and commercial matters such as wills, marriage, and trade. The *ulama* also included theologians, prayer leaders, and teachers, many of whom continued to participate in the economy as traders or artisans. Until the mid-nineteenth century, state bureaucracies in the Middle East employed members of the *ulama* as tax collectors, scribes, secretaries, and market inspectors. The *ulama* formed a cultural elite and retained the admiration and respect of the Muslim masses because the *ulama,* not the rulers, were perceived as the true guardians and interpreters of the Islamic faith. As long as the *ulama* remained independent of state control, they continued to represent a base of potential support or opposition to ruling elites.

The advent of secularism and nationalism in the Middle East aroused the resistance of the *ulama,* who, increasingly, were perceived as obstacles to modernism and reform. The traditional power of the Sunni *ulama* over law, education, and bureaucracy was stripped away in the nineteenth century throughout the Ottoman Empire and in Egypt. Confiscation of WAQF properties, the traditional means of economic support for the *ulama,* increased their reliance on government authority for economic maintenance and served to compromise the group's independent religious and political influence. In the late nineteenth century, individual members of the *ulama,* such as Muhammad Abduh, directed their influence in educational and religious reform through Egypt's famed Sunni theological center al-Azhar. More recent twentieth century Islamic political movements in Egypt, such as the MUSLIM BROTHERHOOD, successfully circumvented what was perceived as the compromised model of the traditional *ulama.*

An exception to the pattern of the *ulama*'s modern decline may be found in Shi'a Iran since the Iranian Revolution of 1979. Under the weak Safavid and Qajar dynasties the strength of the *ulama* had increased. Beginning in 1925, despite the Pahlavi regime's attempts at secular government and bringing the *ulama* under state control, the *ulama* remained a potentially potent source of opposition. The *ulama* assumed a position of leadership in the organized resistance to the shah, which culminated in the 1979 revolution and the formation of the Islamic Republic of Iran. The Shi'a *ulama* in Iran successfully utilized their religious prestige as the only legitimate interpreters of Islam as a revolutionary weapon against a modern secular government.

BIBLIOGRAPHY

KERR, MALCOM H. *Islamic Reform: The Political and Legal Theories of Muhammad Abduh and Rashid Rida.* Berkeley, Calif., 1966.
MITCHELL, RICHARD P. *The Society of the Muslim Brothers.* London, 1969.
MOTTAHEDEH, ROY P. *The Mantle of the Prophet: Religion and Politics in Iran.* New York, 1985.

Denise A. Spellberg

Ülkü

Official journal of Turkey's Republican People's party (RPP).

Ülkü (Ideal) was first published in 1933 as the institutional journal of the RPP's PEOPLE'S HOUSES—cultural centers set up throughout Turkey the previous year to advance adult literacy and understanding of Atatürk's reforms. The journal gained twenty thousand readers by 1933; it was published until 1950, when the Democrat party (the new opposition party) came to power.

Editorial content was controlled by the RPP, which used *Ülkü* to counter a rival Kemalist ideology of those years, the Marxist-influenced *Kadro* journal. *Ülkü* contained articles on literature, history, arts, economics, sports, agriculture, health, and other subjects. It was associated in the 1940s with Prime Minister Recep Peker's hard-line reformism.

BIBLIOGRAPHY

ROBINSON, RICHARD D. *The First Turkish Republic.* Cambridge, Mass., 1965.

Elizabeth Thompson

ULPAN

Language-instruction method used with new immigrants to Israel.

Located in Jerusalem and founded in 1949, Ulpan Etzion was the first ULPAN school. The technique entails immersing the students in Hebrew by using it as the language as well as the subject of instruction. Ulpanim are used in Israel to facilitate the transition of immigrants into their new society.

Bryan Daves

Ulus

Official daily newspaper of the Turkish Republican People's party.

Named *National Sovereignty* when Mustafa Kemal Atatürk founded it in Ankara in 1920, he changed the paper's name in 1934 to make it sound more Turkish. The paper became the prime target of repression in the 1950s under Democrat party rule (the new opposition party).

Despite two closures and 232 lawsuits, *Ulus* (Nation) continued to publish through the 1970s, until the party's demise after the 1980 coup. Over the years, its masthead carried an illustrious list of editors including Salıh Rifki Atay, Yakup Kadri Karaosmanoğlu, and Bülent Ecevit.

BIBLIOGRAPHY

LEWIS, GEOFFREY. *Modern Turkey.* New York, 1974.

Elizabeth Thompson

Ulusu, Bülent

Prime minister of Turkey, 1980–1983.

A retired navy commander (August 1980), Ulusu was a compromise choice for prime minister in the government formed after the military intervention of September 12, 1980. The cabinet he headed was composed of nonparty technocrats and military officers. Ulusu and his cabinet were overshadowed by the National Security Council, consisting of the top military officers who had assumed control of the government. He was also politically outranked by Turgut OZAL, deputy prime minister in charge of the economy, who had initially been appointed by Prime Minister Süleyman Demirel late in 1979 and was retained by the military junta. Ulusu remained in office until after the November 1983 election, which brought Ozal to power as prime minister.

BIBLIOGRAPHY

Dodd, C. H. *The Crisis of Turkish Democracy,* 2nd ed. 1990.

Frank Tachau

Umari, Arshad al-   [1888–?]

Iraqi prime minister in 1946 and in 1954.

Arshad al-Umari was born in Mosul in what is today northern Iraq. Having precipitated the fall of the "liberal" cabinet of Tawfiq al-Suwaydi in 1946, he inaugurated a period of considerable repression, most notoriously the shooting of strikers at the Iraq Petroleum Company in Kirkuk that July. He was a close associate and political ally of Nuri al-Sa'id.

Peter Sluglett

Umari, Mustafa al-   [1898–?]

Iraqi government official.

Mustafa al-Umari, prime minister of Iraq between July and November 1952 and a substantial landowner, was born into a wealthy family in Mosul. In June 1941, after the fall of Rashid Ali al-Kaylani, he became minister of interior, a position he held again later in the 1940s. His premiership in 1952 came at a time of acute tension between the government and opposition forces.

Peter Sluglett

Umar Pasha   [1806–?]

Ottoman ruler in Lebanon.

Umar Pasha, orginally named Michael Latas, was born to a Christian family in Croatia, then part of the Ottoman Empire. He later converted to Islam and was nicknamed "the Austrian" (al-Namsawi). In 1842 he was appointed ruler of Mount Lebanon in the wake of Druze (Muslim)–Maronite (Christian) confrontations that made the prospects for cooperation between the two groups almost impossible. Although the Druze accepted the administrative change that was intended to end the separate emirate status of Mount Lebanon, the Christians insisted on preservation of the emirate. Umar Pasha's major task was to dash any hope for the return of the Chehabi rule to Lebanon. To gain the support of the anti-Chehabi forces, he restored some lands to both Druze and Maronite landlords. He also appointed members of prominent families in both sects as his personal advisers. He used intimidation and forgery to create an image of popular support for his rule. When the Druze turned against him, he resorted to force but could not save his position. He was dismissed in December 1842, in the wake of intensified Druze rebellions.

As'ad AbuKhalil

Umayyad Mosque

Mosque established in Damascus by the Umayyad Caliph Walid ibn Abd al-Malik (705–715).

To construct and decorate the mosque, Walid employed the best craftsmen from Constantinople (now Istanbul) and from the Umayyad Empire. The design included a large open courtyard, a covered area on

Umayyad mosque in Damascus, Syria. (Mia Bloom)

Detail of a mosaic on the Umayyad mosque. (Mia Bloom)

the side closest to the *qibla* (the direction of Mecca), and walls covered with elaborate mosaics. The mosque was one of the spectacular results of the building program of the Umayyads, who made Damascus the capital of their empire. The Umayyad mosque is one of the most monumental artistic structures in modern Syria.

Muhammad Muslih

Umma

Qur'anic term designating the community of all Muslims.

Although originally composed of Arabs from western Arabia (the Hijaz), the *umma*'s inherent flexibility and universality have kept it a meaningful term today. Although *umma* signifies the spiritual fraternity and unity of hundreds of millions of Sunni and Shi'a Muslims worldwide, the term does not have a specific political connotation.

Richard W. Bulliet

Umm al-Qaywayn

One of the United Arab Emirates.

Umm al-Qaywayn (in local usage the "q" is pronounced like a "g") is bordered by the emirates of Sharja and Ra's al-Khayma. It possesses the second smallest territory, approximately 300 square miles (777 sq. km.), and has the smallest population, about 20,000. The capital town of the same name, which contains most of its population, was established on a sand spit for physical security. Only Abu Dhabi shares

Umm al-Qaywayn's advantage of being located in a single contiguous territory.

Along with Ajman and Fujayra, Umm al-Qaywayn is one of the poorest of the United Arab Emirates and is heavily dependent on the largess of Abu Dhabi for its economic development. It has very modest gas production, and much of its population engages in the traditional pursuits of fishing and shipbuilding.

The ruling family is the Mualla, sometimes referred to as the Al Ali. The current emir, Shaykh Rashid ibn Ahmad, has ruled since 1981, when he succeeded his father, Shaykh Ahmad ibn Rashid al-Mualla, whose rule had begun in 1929.

BIBLIOGRAPHY

PECK, MALCOLM C. *The United Arab Emirates: A Venture in Unity.* Boulder, Colo., 1993.

Malcolm C. Peck

Umm al-Qura University

Saudi Arabian university.

King Abd al-Aziz University was founded in Jidda in 1967 as a private college. Later taken over by the Saudi state, it opened branches in Mecca and Medina; the former became independent as Umm al-Qura University in 1979. It opened a second campus at al-Ta'if in 1981, which had 2,000 students by 1992. The library in Mecca possesses more than 370,000 volumes, while that at al-Ta'if has 50,000. In 1992, King Abd al-Aziz University employed 1,147 faculty and taught 20,077 students, while possessing a library of 435,000 volumes.

Khalid Y. Blankinship

Umma Party

Political party in Sudan founded by Abd al-Rahman al-Mahdi in 1945.

Sayyid ABD AL-RAHMAN AL-MAHDI, the posthumous son of the Mahdi, used his wealth (acquired through his loyalty to the British during World War I) and religious influence to enhance his political ambition by launching a newspaper, *al-Umma*, then established the Umma party in February 1945. The name was chosen to appeal to the community of Islam. Its political platform was intended to embrace all who favored "the Sudan for the Sudanese," a continuation of the policies of the MAHDIST STATE, which was hostile to any imperial ambitions of Egypt. The founding members included all the most prominent Mahdists. Abd al-Rahman publicly remained aloof, but in fact he provided the funds and spiritual guidance for the party. Everyone knew that the Umma was his political party, a fact that alienated many non-Mahdists, who were alarmed at his monarchical tendencies, and drove them into the rival political party, the Ashiqqa, led by Isma'il Azhari, which advocated union with Egypt.

Because union with Egypt was anathema to the British, the Umma acquired the stigma of a British government creation, which it did not fully deserve. Though its goal, "the Sudan for the Sudanese," represented the feelings of virtually every British official in the Sudan, the party's patron was not a British puppet and his ambition to become king of the Sudan were antithetical to Britain's goal of a democratic Sudan. The more Abd al-Rahman sought British support for the Umma, the more the British realized the party was more of a liability than an asset in the continuing contest with Egypt over the future of the Sudan. Frequent attempts to reconcile the Unionists with Egypt and the Umma "secessionists" only hardened the position of each party.

Following independence in 1956, the Umma continued in parliament and even under the military regimes of General Ibrahim Abbud and Muhammad Ja'far Numeiri, when political parties were officially proscribed. It sustained an often intense rivalry with the Democratic Unionist party (DUP), whose patrons, the Mirghani family of the Khatmiyya *tariqa*, played a role similar to that of the descendants of the Mahdi, who dominated the Umma. Like the DUP, however, the Umma party was not without its internal rivalries, particularly among the more conservative Ansar, led by Imam al-Hadi until he was killed in the suppression of the Ansar by Numeiri in 1970. Since then Sadiq al-Mahdi, the great grandson of the Mahdi, has led the Umma party. He served as prime minister in all the coalition governments between 1986 and 1989, after which he was placed under house arrest by the government of Lt. Gen. Umar Hasan Ahmad al-Bashir, which seized control of the government of Sudan in a coup d'état on June 30, 1989. During his detention Sadiq has continued to lead the Umma party in opposition to the Bashir government.

Robert O. Collins

Umm Kulthum   [c.1904–1975]

The most famous Arab singer of the twentieth century.

Umm Kulthum performed for more than fifty years, beginning in the villages and towns of the Egyptian delta in the early twentieth century and continuing until her final illness in 1973. In the course of her long career, Umm Kulthum recorded over three hundred songs and appeared in six films. She performed throughout the Arab world and is often considered the most accomplished singer of her time.

She was born in the Egyptian village of Tammay al-Zahayra in the province of Daqhaliya to Shaykh Ibrahim al-Sayyid al-Baltaji (died 1932), the imam of the village mosque, and his wife, Fatma al-Maliji (died 1947). Her father augmented his income by singing religious songs for local celebrations. Umm Kulthum learned the songs while listening to him train her brother Khalid as his accompanist. Impressed with the power of his young daughter's voice, Shaykh Ibrahim eventually included her along with Khalid and their cousin Sabr in his performances.

The young girl with the very strong voice became the family's star attraction. To protect her reputation, the father had her wear a boy's coat and head covering, and he conducted all business on her behalf. By 1917, the family began to consider a serious singing career for Umm Kulthum and in about 1922 they moved to Cairo to launch her in the commercial music business.

In Cairo, Umm Kulthum was not an immediate success. Compared with the women already established as successful performers and recording stars, including Munira al-Mahdiyya and Fathiyya Ahmad, she was viewed as unsophisticated and countrified. She engaged music teachers and endeavored to copy the manners of the elite women in whose homes she sang. Like other aspiring performers, she was aided and schooled by a number of mentors, including singer Shaykh Abu al-Ila Muhammad, poet Ahmad Rami, and the amateur musician Amin al-Mahdi. By 1928, she surpassed the popularity of her competitors and remained at the top of musical society for the remainder of her career.

Umm Kulthum began to make commercial recordings in 1924. Although recording companies were usually conservative and disinclined to take a chance on an unknown singer, they vied with each other for the largest possible share of the market; as a result the relatively unknown Umm Kulthum was recruited by Odeon Records and recorded fourteen songs in 1924 and 1925. These were immediately successful, for, as she later explained, her long years of performing in the delta provided her with a larger audience outside Cairo than most other singers.

This experience awakened Umm Kulthum to the nature of her potential audience. During the late 1920s and the 1930s she began her lifelong involvement with the mass media: commercial recording (1924), radio (1934), film (1934), and television

(1960). Commercial recordings had been circulating in Egypt since about 1904 and, despite the relatively high cost of phonograph players and records, were widely accessible. They were installed in public places, such as coffee houses, where even those who could not afford the equipment could hear the records. (Later, radios, televisions, and cassette players were similarly shared.) From 1937 until her final illness, her concerts on the first Thursday of each month were broadcast live to an ever growing audience. These concerts were certainly her best-known professional activity and allowed Umm Kulthum to count among her audience millions of listeners beyond the ticket-buying audience in Cairo.

She started with a repertoire of traditional, predominantly religious songs as a child; in the late 1920s and 1930s, she began to sing new virtuosic songs, often composed for her by Muhammad al-Qasabji on the romantic poetry then in vogue by Ahmad Rami. During her golden age in the 1940s and 1950s, she sang colloquial songs of populist expression written by Zakariyya Ahmad and Bayram al-Tunsi and serious neoclassical songs by Riyadh al-Sunbati and Ahmad Shawqi; these have become her best known. In the late 1950s and 1960s, she commissioned new love songs by younger poets and composers and finally collaborated with her colleague and rival, Muhammad Abd al-Wahhab; they produced ten songs, which retain great popularity to the present day.

In her later years, she was recognized as an important public figure, in general, and a symbol of authentically Egyptian and Arab culture and art. She served seven terms as president of the musicians' union and as a member of the selection committee for radio and of several national commissions on the arts. After the Egyptian defeat in the Arab–Israel War (1967), she initiated a series of benefit concerts in Egypt and throughout the Arab world designed to replenish the Egyptian treasury. She appeared in Morocco, Libya, Sudan, Lebanon, Abu Dhabi, and Tunisia, and her trips to these countries took on the character of diplomatic visits.

Health problems that had plagued Umm Kulthum for much of her life worsened as she aged, and she spent most of the last year of her life under medical treatment. She died on February 3, 1975.

BIBLIOGRAPHY

Awad, Mahmud. *Umm Kulthum: Allati la ya'rifuha ahad* (The Umm Kulthum Nobody Knows). In *Middle Eastern Muslim Women Speak,* ed. and tr. by Elizabeth Warnock Fernea and Basima Qattan Bezirgan. Austin, Tex., 1977.
Danielson, Virginia. "Shaping Tradition in Arab Song: The Career and Repertory of Umm Kulthum." Ph.D. diss., University of Illinois, 1991.
Fu'ad, Ni'mat Ahmad. *Umm Kulthum wa-asr min al-fann* (Umm Kulthum and an Era of Art). Cairo, 1976.
Shushah, Muhammad al-Sayyid. *Umm Kulthum: Hayat nagham* (Umm Kulthum: Life of a Song). Cairo, 1976.

Virginia Danielson

Umm Na'san

Second largest of the thirty-three islands in the archipelago that constitutes the State of Bahrain.

Umm Na'san occupies some 8.5 square miles (22 sq. km) and lies approximately 2.5 miles (4 km) off the western coast of the main island of Bahrain, the largest in the archipelago. It is reserved for the private use of the ruler. Several small springs provide water for a limited pastureland, and date palm gardens grow along its western shore, gardens planted and stocked with deer and gazelle by Shaykh Hamad ibn Isa al-Khalifa during the 1930s. Ruins dot the surface of the island, lending credence to local legends that it was the seat of the ancient rulers. The causeway from Saudi Arabia to the main island, Bahrain, passes through Umm Na'san.

BIBLIOGRAPHY

Cottrell, Alvin J., ed. *The Persian Gulf States: A General Survey.* Baltimore, 1980.

Fred H. Lawson

Umm Sa'id

Qatar's major industrial center and oil terminal.

Umm Sa'id, known locally as Musayid, boasts state-of-the-art technology and export facilities; it symbolizes Qatar's policies of progress and modernization. As the site of Qatar's petroleum refinery, Musayid has been connected by pipeline to Doha and the Doha International Airport. Musayid has become the major center of all oil-related industry in Qatar.

BIBLIOGRAPHY

Nyrop, Richard, ed. *Persian Gulf States: Country Studies.* Washington, D.C., 1985.

Emile A. Nakhleh

Umran, Muhammad [1922–]

Syrian military officer.

Of Alawite descent, Muhammad Umran was a pro-Ba'th party junior officer in the 1954 rebellion against Adib Shishakli. He became a member of a secret military committee in the early 1960s that ultimately took control of Ba'th leadership. Umran commanded the Seventieth Brigade at Qatana at the time of the 1963 Ba'th takeover. A supporter of Michel Aflaq, he eventually lost his standing in the party, in subsequent intraparty rivalries that shifted power to radicals led by Salah Jadid. He became ambassador to Spain in late 1964, was recalled to become minister of defense in January 1966, and was arrested in the 1966 coup.

BIBLIOGRAPHY

HINNEBUSCH, RAYMOND A. *Authoritarian Power and State Formation in Ba'thist Syria: Army, Party and Peasant.* Boulder, Colo., 1990.

Charles U. Zenzie

UN

See under United Nations

UNEF

See United Nations Emergency Force

UNESCO

See United Nations and the Middle East

Uniate Churches

See Christians in the Middle East

UNIFIL

United Nations Interim Force in Lebanon established in 1978.

During Israel's invasion of Lebanon in March 1978, twenty thousand troops entered Lebanon's territory to clear the way for the expansion of a zone in south Lebanon controlled by Israel's client, Major Sa'd Haddad. When the government of Lebanon proved unable to defend its territory from constant encroachments by Israel and to separate Israel's forces in south Lebanon from the Palestine Liberation Organization forces and the Lebanese National Movement, the United Nations dispatched six thousand troops to maintain order and peace in south Lebanon and northern Israel.

The presence of the force, however, did not stop the combatants from continued attacks and shelling. UNIFIL, which became largely dedicated to the provision of services and humanitarian relief to the inhabitants of the area under its control, was largely ignored by the heavily armed groups in southern Lebanon and by Israel. Furthermore, the government of Israel resisted efforts to extend the mandate of the force into what it calls "the security zone," an area in southern Lebanon under Israel's control. In June 1982, Israel ignored the presence of UNIFIL when it invaded Lebanon. Many UNIFIL members were killed in the line of duty.

As'ad AbuKhalil

Union and Progress Society

See Committee of Union and Progress

Union Démocratique du Manifeste Algérien

A moderate Algerian organization whose goals changed from autonomy within the colonial system to full independence.

The Union Démocratique du Manifeste Algérien (UDMA; Democratic Union of the Algerian Manifesto) was founded by Ferhat ABBAS during the spring of 1946 and ceased to exist in April 1956 when Abbas, in Cairo, announced his alliance with the Front de Libération Nationale (FLN; National Liberation Front). It grew out of the moderate wing of the Algerian political spectrum, which in the 1930s had sought reform within the colonial system. When the colons refused such reform, it moved in the 1940s toward Algerian autonomy.

Winning eleven of the thirteen Algerian seats in the second French Constituent Assembly in 1946, Abbas proposed an autonomous Algeria within the framework of the French Union. When this program failed to carry, the party was diminished considerably in influence. Representing mainly educated, middle-class levels of society, the party had some three thousand members by 1950 and participated actively in the Algerian Assembly established by the Organic Law in 1947.

After joining the FLN, Abbas and other UDMA leaders served in the Conseil National de la Révolution Algérienne (CNRA; National Council of the Algerian Revolution) and subsequently in the Provisional Government of the Algerian Republic (Gouvernement Provisoire de la République Algérienne; GPRA).

BIBLIOGRAPHY

QUANDT, WILLIAM B. *Revolution and Political Leadership: Algeria, 1954–1958.* Cambridge, Mass., 1969.

John Ruedy

Union Générale des Travailleurs Marocains (UGTM)

Moroccan labor union.

The Istiqlal party founded the General Union of Moroccan Workers (UGTM) in 1959 to compete with the socialist Moroccan Labor Union (Union Marocaine du Travail; UMT). Although UGTM cooperates at times with UMT, it competes with and opposes the mililtant Democratic Confederation of Labor (Confédération Démocratique du Travail; CDT). It primarily organizes teachers, hotel and food-service workers, railroad workers, and urban civil servants. The union represents the labor branch of the Istiqlal party, which emphasizes nationalistic, pro-Islamic, and pan-Arab policies. One of its prominent leaders, Driss Laghnimi, was imprisoned by the government. At a May Day rally in 1993, UGTM leader Abderazzak Afilal called for Laghnimi's release and for greater democracy and human rights in Morocco. As a result, on 12 July 1993 Laghnimi was released by order of King Hassan II.

Labor in Morocco has seen a worsening of conditions since 1991. High inflation rates, drought, and decline of real wages have combined to lower the living standards of workers. Grievances exist, and the unions, including the UGTM, have been calling for strikes to increase pressure on the government to address labor issues and negotiate fair wage increases and other union demands.

BIBLIOGRAPHY

NELSON, HAROLD D., ed. *Morocco: A Country Study*, 5th ed. Washington, D.C., 1986.

Larry A. Barrie

Union Générale des Travailleurs Tunisiens (UGTT)

Tunisian labor union.

The General Union of Tunisian Workers (al-Ittihad al-Amm al-Tunisi li al-Shughl in Arabic) is the strongest labor union in Tunisia, currently representing about 16 to 20 percent (500,000) of the Tunisian work force (estimated at about 2.4 million). Founded in 1946 by Ferhat HACHED, the union was the first indigenous attempt to organize Tunisia's workers. Hached broke with the French communist-led General Confederation of Workers (Confédération Générale des Travailleurs; CGT). The new union worked closely with the nationalist movement in Tunisia. Consequently, members of the French resistance organization Red Hand assassinated Hached in 1952.

From 1952 until 1969, the union was under the influence of Ahmed Ben Salah and his socialist economic policies. The fall of Ben Salah in 1970 led to its reorganization and reemergence in 1976 under the leadership of Habib Achour, who dominated the UGTT until 1989. The UGTT tended to oppose economic liberalization because this would lessen its control of the labor movement and adversely affect workers. Achour signed the Social Contract of 1977, which stipulated that the union would control labor unrest. Deteriorating economic conditions, however, caused Achour to break this compact. A wildcat work stoppage at Qsar Hellal in October 1977 led to a confrontation between the army and striking workers, the first time the government had used the army to suppress labor. In early January 1978, the UGTT issued a resolution extremely critical of the economic policies of Habib Bourguiba's regime. On January 26, 1978, dubbed "Black Thursday," a bloody clash left 150 people dead. The government declared a state of emergency and arrested UGTT leaders. Achour was tried for sedition and sentenced to ten years in jail. The regime imposed a new executive bureau on the union and weakened it as a force for opposition to the government's economic policies.

Pardoned in 1981, Achour returned to the post of UGTT president, with leftist Taieb Baccouche as secretary-general. By 1985, the UGTT had again run afoul of the government by threatening to strike if the decline in workers' real wages was not reversed. In December, the government again disbanded the union and jailed its leadership on various charges. The 1987 palace coup of Zayn al-Abidine BEN ALI led to improved relations between the government and the UGTT.

In 1989, Achour was replaced by Ismail Sahbani and Ali Romdhane. In late December 1993, Sahbani consolidated his position and expelled his chief opponents—Romdhane, Tahar Chaieb, Kamel Saad, and Abdennour Madahi—from the UGTT's executive bureau. A similar occasion in the early 1980s had led union dissidents to form the National Union of Tunisian Workers (Union Nationale des Travailleurs

Tunisiens; UNTT). New members of the 1993 UGTT executive bureau—Noureddine Fathalli, Moncef Yacoubi, Abid Briki, Salem Abdelmajid, and Neji Messaoud—are Sahbani loyalists. The importance the government accords the UGTT and its closeness to the regime were made obvious by the fact that President Ben Ali opened the 1993 congress.

BIBLIOGRAPHY

NELSON, HAROLD D., ed. *Tunisia: A Country Study,* 3rd ed. Washington, D.C., 1988.

OUAJAH, LOTFI. "Sahbani-Romdhane: La rupture." *Réalités/Haqa'iq* no. 429 (24–30 December 1993): 5–6.

———. "Le vote et les hommes." *Réalités/Haqa'iq* no. 429 (24–30 December 1993): 7–9.

Larry A. Barrie

Union Marocaine du Travail (UMT)

Morocco's oldest and largest trade union.

The Moroccan Labor Union (Union Marocaine du Travail, UMT) was formed in 1955 with the help of the nationalist Istiqlal party; it had a membership of over 600,000 in the early 1960s and remains the nation's largest labor organization, controlling an estimated 60 percent of the labor force. While affiliated briefly with the Union Nationale des Forces Populaires (National Union of Popular Forces, UNFP) from 1959 to 1962, the UMT has maintained its autonomy from political parties. Despite its non-confrontational stance toward the government and peaceful negotiation of salaries and benefits, UMT has frequently been repressed by the government of Morocco and now faces serious competition from other large trade unions. It has occasionally clashed with the Progressive Socialist party, escalating into a violent confrontation in May 1993 south of Casablanca. The UMT gained five seats in the Chamber of Representatives in the 1984 indirect elections.

Mahjoub Ben Seddiq has been its general secretary since 1955. Its leading bodies are a seven-member national bureau, an administrative commission, and a new union council. The UMT draws its strongest support from workers in basic industries. The policies of the union are relatively moderate, stressing job creation, wage increases, and avoidance of strikes or radical actions that would damage the bargaining power it maintains with the government.

BIBLIOGRAPHY

CLEMENT, JEAN-FRANÇOIS, and JIM PAUL. "Trade Unions and Moroccan Politics." *Merip Reports* 127 (October 1984): 19–24.

Bradford Dillman

Union Nationale des Etudiants Marocains (UNEM)

Left-wing opposition group in Morocco, supported by teachers and high school students.

The UNEM was involved in extralegal and radical activities against the monarchy and its governments during the 1960s and 1970s. Its agenda encompassed political, social, economic, and educational grievances. In July 1963, Hamid Berrada, secretary-general of the UNEM, was charged with plotting against the state. He fled the country and, with Mehdi Ben Barka and Muhammad al-Basri, initiated a campaign to denounce the monarchy. Between 1963 and 1973, UNEM leaders were repeatedly arrested and imprisoned for organizing strikes and engaging in subversion. The peak of the government's crackdown came in April 1972, with a mass trial of eighty-one student leaders on charges of treason. Twenty-eight received long jail sentences.

The UNEM was dissolved in 1973 and reauthorized in 1978. The new leadership initiated a number of demonstrations between 1979 and 1981, resulting in further clashes with the authorities, but in general the political calm in Morocco during the 1980s was reflected in the UNEM's relatively low profile. In 1991, clashes on university campuses between leftists and Islamists were related, in part, to their respective attempts to gain control of the UNEM.

Bruce Maddy-Weitzman

Union Nationale des Forces Populaires (UNFP)

One of Morocco's leading leftist political parties.

The National Union of Popular Forces (Union Nationale des Forces Populaires, UNFP) was founded in 1959, when radical leaders of the Istiqlal party, the main nationalist party of Morocco, split from it. Members of the Moroccan Labor Union (Union Marocaine du Travail, UMT) threw their support behind it. The principal leaders at the time of its founding were Mehdi Ben Barka, an Istiqlal organizer; Abdullah Ibrahim, the prime minister from 1959 to 1960; Mahjoub Ben Seddiq, secretary general of the UMT; and Muhammed al-Basri and Abderrahim Bouabid, young members of the Istiqlal. The policy of the UNFP was socialist, calling for a transformation of the social structure, nationalization of the means of production, greater rewards for workers, and land reform. It consistently opposed the leadership of Morocco's King Hassan II and called for the creation of a representative democracy. In its foreign policy, the UNFP supported Arab democracy and Arab unity within a socialist framework, favored third-world revolutionary movements, and opposed Western involvement in the economy.

Ben Barka served as the UNFP's general secretary until his assassination in France in 1965. The party's principle leadership structures were a central committee, an administrative commission, and an office of the general secretary. In 1967, the UNFP created a political bureau composed of Bouabid, Ibrahim, and Ben Seddiq, which the party's administrative commission dissolved in 1972. The leadership of the UNFP was often divided throughout the party's existence. The party held its second and last national congress in 1963. The UMT provided most of the party's infrastructure at the local level.

After briefly heading the government in 1959 and 1960, the UNFP fell, becoming the opposition. At the height of its power in the early 1960s, it won 414 out of 765 seats in the 1960 local elections and 28 out of 144 seats in the 1963 parliamentary elections. Severe repression by the king after 1962 and a split with the UMT caused it to lose much of its strength in the late 1960s.

Following two coup attempts in 1971 and 1972, the government arrested many UNFP members and placed them on trial. This led to severe divisions within the party, causing the UNFP section in the city of Rabat to split from the party and found a new party, the UNION SOCIALISTE DES FORCES POPULAIRES (National Union of Socialist Forces, USFP), in 1974. Because most of the UNFP's members joined the USFP, the remnant UNFP headed by Ibrahim became an insignificant party under the guidance of the UMT. It failed to participate in the 1977 and the 1984 elections.

The UNFP had a diverse membership united more by a commonality of interests than a common group ideology. Second-generation nationalists of the Istiqlal with modest family backgrounds and French educations held top positions. Professionals, teachers, and government workers composed much of the party's middle-level hierarchy. Rank and file members were largely trade-union adherents and students. Wealthy members of the UNFP provided most of its financing. It had a diverse constituency, attracting its greatest support from workers living in Atlantic coast cities and from government cadres, students, and traders in the Sousse region.

BIBLIOGRAPHY

PALAZZOLI, CLAUDE, ed. Le Maroc politique de l'indépendance à 1973. Paris, 1974.
WATERBURY, JOHN. The Commander of the Faithful: The Moroccan Political Elite—A Study of Segmented Politics. New York, 1970.

Bradford Dillman

Union Socialiste des Forces Populaires (USFP)

One of Morocco's leading socialist opposition parties.

The Socialist Union of Popular Forces (Union Socialiste des Forces Populaires, USFP) was formed in 1974 by a large breakaway faction of the National Union of Popular Forces (UNION NATIONALE DES FORCES POPULAIRES, UNFP) led by Abderrahim Bouabid. Its policies are moderately socialist, calling for greater democratization and some nationalization of private companies. It strongly supports Morocco's retention of the Western Sahara.

Bouabid was the party's first secretary until his death in 1992. Abderrahman Youssoufi has replaced him. The party's main leadership structures are a political bureau and an administrative commission. Most of its members—primarily teachers, students, and government workers—come from urban middle-class backgrounds. It has a strong constituency among students, workers, and the unemployed. The USFP is closely allied with the Democratic Labor Confederation, one of Morocco's leading trade unions. Although harshly repressed in 1981 and 1982, it has held a number of seats in the Chamber of Representatives since 1984.

BIBLIOGRAPHY

SEHIMI, MUSTAPHA. "Les élections législatives au Maroc." Maghreb-Machrek 107 (January–March 1985): 23–51.

Bradford Dillman

Union Tunisienne des Industrialistes, Compagnies, Artisans (UTICA)

Tunisian employers' organization.

Under President Hedi Jilani, the Tunisian Union of Industrialists, Businessmen, and Artisans (UTICA) is the management portion of a group that includes the government and the UNION GÉNÉRALE DES TRAVAILLEURS TUNISIENS (General Union of Tunisian Workers; UGTT). They regularly negotiate wages and working conditions. Based on these negotiations, the government sets annual wages for the labor force. The 1966 labor code guarantees a minimum wage, provides for arbitration to settle disputes, authorizes union membership, sets workweek and other labor standards, and provides for social security and disability insurance payments. The government also seeks to ensure that wages do not lag behind inflation. As long as the union maintains the social peace, the government is committed to maintaining the wage structure and reining in the employers' desires to increase their profits at the expense of their workers.

Since 1986, Tunisia's economic restructuring program has led to the privatization of a number of public conglomerates, the reduction of food subsidies, and a general liberalization of the economy. The promised decline in the state's bureaucratic impediments to business has not been sufficiently dramatic thus far. Tunisia continues to depend on financial support from the International Monetary Fund and the World Bank.

UTICA supports a technology park that was scheduled to open near the Tunis-Carthage International Airport in May 1994. It views the transfer of technology and automation to Tunisia as a key to the country's economic diversification. It believes the park will attract more foreign investment and export businesses to Tunisia. The park could serve as a model for other cities in Tunisia and as a regional economic magnet for the Maghrib.

BIBLIOGRAPHY

NELSON, HAROLD D., ed. *Tunisia: A Country Study,* 3rd ed. Washington, D.C., 1988.

Larry A. Barrie

United Arab Emirates

Federation of seven shaykhdoms at the southern end of the Persian/Arabian Gulf.

Land and People. The United Arab Emirates (U.A.E.) borders Qatar, Saudi Arabia, and Oman. It has an area of just over 32,000 square miles (82,880 sq. km), about the size of the state of Maine. ABU DHABI occupies nearly 87 percent of the total; DUBAI, less than 5 percent; and SHARJA, just over 3 percent. The emir-

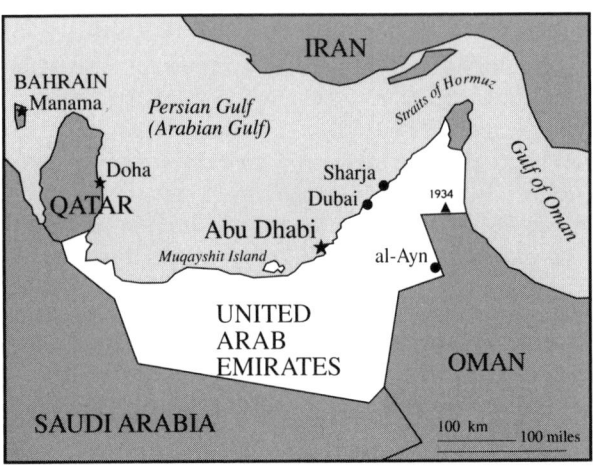

ates of RA'S AL-KHAYMA, FUJAYRA, UMM AL-QAYWAYN, and Ajman occupy the remainder. The U.A.E. is the only country to border both the Persian/Arabian Gulf and the Gulf of Oman, thus forming a land bridge south of the strategic Strait of Hormuz. Its topography is varied: a flat coastal plain; an interior desert, part of the Empty Quarter (RUB AL-KHALI); an elevated plateau; and the Hajar mountains, shared with Oman. Rainfall is scanty and fluctuating. Summer temperatures often reach 115°F (46°C) on the humid coast, and higher in the dry interior. From October to March the weather is mild and pleasant.

The U.A.E.'s population has risen from about 180,000 in 1968 to approximately 2 million in 1993; the influx of expatriate workers and their dependents accounting for most of the growth and some 80 percent of the total population. The U.A.E. is overwhelmingly urban, with the cities of Abu Dhabi and Dubai each having over 500,000 inhabitants, and Sharja more than 250,000. All the indigenous population and most expatriates are Muslims; significant exceptions include Indians and Filipinos. Sunnis account for 85 percent of all Muslims. Tribal affiliation remains very important in all the emirates, whose rulers are drawn from the leading families of the dominant tribe.

History. Most of the current ruling families were established when Great Britain imposed a truce in 1820 to end piracy in the lower Gulf. Subsequent treaties tended to freeze the formerly fluid power relationships among the tribally organized shaykhdoms, though Dubai became independent of Abu Dhabi in 1833, Ra's al-Khayma seceded from Sharja in 1869, and Fujayra gained independence from Sharja in 1952. From the 1930s, exploration for oil necessitated the establishment of exact borders and precisely delimited territorial states, a concept new to Arabia.

Independence came in 1971, because financial difficulties led Britain to cut its remaining imperial responsibilities east of Suez. Britain encouraged a federation of nine, to include Bahrain and Qatar, with which it had similar treaty arrangements. The failure of this scheme led the rulers of Abu Dhabi and Dubai, Shaykh Zayid ibn Sultan al-Nahayyan and Shaykh Rashid ibn Sa'id al-Maktum, to establish the seven-member federation, becoming its president and vice president, respectively. At its inception Abu Dhabi's dispute with Saudi Arabia and Oman over the Buraymi (al-Ayn) Oasis remained unresolved; traditional rivalries among the seven emirs threatened the federation's viability; and Iran coerced Sharja into a joint occupation of Abu Musa island (which contributed to a coup attempt that took the

Dubai creek, an inlet of the Persian/Arabian Gulf. (Richard Bulliet)

life of Sharja's ruler, Shaykh Khalid ibn Muhammad), and forcibly seized the Tunb Islands from Ra's al-Khayma. Zayid's patient diplomacy led to a border settlement, and his strong commitment to the federation enabled it to survive as the only successful union of Arab states until the two Yemens merged in 1990. The issue of the islands, however, continued to strain relations between Iran and the U.A.E. in the mid-1990s.

Economy. The U.A.E.'s oil reserves of about 100 billion barrels, a tenth of the world's total, are mostly in Abu Dhabi. Dubai possesses 4 billion barrels; Sharja, 1.4 billion; and Ra's al-Khayma, 400 million. Abu Dhabi also has the bulk of the country's natural gas reserves. The gap in economic development between Abu Dhabi, Dubai, and Sharja, on the one hand, and the rest of the emirates is considerable, though it is moderated by federal government spending on infrastructure, with most of the funding from Abu Dhabi. Dubai, long the major trading center of the lower Gulf, is the region's leading entrepôt with the most extensive port facilities. Its Jabal Ali free zone has helped expand the U.A.E.'s nonoil sector to 60 percent of total GDP. Promotion of traditional economic activities, including agriculture and fishing, has created employment opportunities in the poorer emirates and achieved significant import substitution. Despite the collapse of the Bank of Credit and Commerce International, whose principal backer was Shaykh Zayid, and reduced oil prices in the early 1990s, the U.A.E. economy remains sound, even though it experienced a balance-of-payments deficit for the first time in 1992.

Government and Politics. The U.A.E.'s constitution provides for federal legislative, executive, and judi-

cial institutions. The political system is a mix of presidential and parliamentary features, with the greatest power in the executive Federal Supreme Council, whose members are the rulers of the seven member states. Zayid has been president since independence, and Rashid served as both prime minister and vice president, posts assumed by his son Maktum in 1986, following Rashid's incapacitation. The legislature, called the Federal National Council, has only consultative powers, despite being given a somewhat greater role in the 1990s. Its forty members are appointed by the rulers: eight each from Abu Dhabi and Dubai, six each from Sharja and Ra's al-Khayma, and four apiece from the remaining emirates. Real legislative authority resides in the Council of Ministers, which initiates most laws, oversees implementation of federal laws, and prepares the federal budget.

Considerable powers are left to the individual emirates, each governed in an essentially traditional manner by a hereditary ruler. Even in foreign affairs, defense, and finance, theoretically federal concerns under the constitution, the individual emirates act autonomously. In 1976 a federal defense command was created, but it has not yet been meaningfully implemented. Each emirate has pursued its own oil policy. Dubai and Sharja maintained business as usual with Iran while the federal government tilted toward Iraq during the Iran–Iraq War (1980–1988). Zayid has championed a centralized U.A.E., whereas others, especially his former rival, Rashid, have favored the loose federal arrangement that seems destined to persist.

Foreign Relations. The U.A.E. maintains generally friendly relations with its neighbors, although these can be complicated by the independent actions of various emirates. It has played an active role in the

Building a dhow in an Abu Dhabi shipyard. (Richard Bulliet)

Gulf Cooperation Council (GCC), which promotes economic and security ties to the other five conservative Gulf Arab states. Zayid has assumed a major role in the Arab world as a force for moderation, as in his efforts to promote Egypt's reintegration into the Arab League. Relations with the United States have been friendly, though sometimes strained because of what is seen as a one-sided American policy toward the Arab–Israel conflict. The United States, Japan, and the United Kingdom are the U.A.E.'s major trading partners. During the Gulf crisis the U.A.E. cooperated closely with the anti-Iraq coalition, and is expected to join Kuwait, Bahrain, and Qatar in signing a defense pact with the United States. It has joined the other GCC states in supporting the Israel–PLO "Gaza-Jericho plan" of September 1993 as the first step toward an Arab–Israel settlement.

[See also: Buraymi Oasis Dispute; Trucial Coast]

BIBLIOGRAPHY

ANTHONY, JOHN DUKE. Arab States of the Lower Gulf: People, Politics, Petroleum. Washington, D.C., 1975.
HEARD-BEY, FRAUKE. From Trucial States to United Arab Emirates. New York, 1982.
PECK, MALCOLM C. The United Arab Emirates: A Venture in Unity. Boulder, Colo., 1986.
TARYAM, A. O. The Establishment of the United Arab Emirates, 1950–1985. New York, 1987.

Malcolm C. Peck

United Arab Republic

Union of Syria and Egypt, 1958–1961.

By the late 1950s, Egypt was the most powerful Arab state. Many Arabs were enamored of President Gamal Abdel Nasser's advocacy of pan-Arab unity under Egypt's leadership. Syria, which shared Egypt's anti-Western stance, was considerably weaker, facing both external threats and an unstable internal political situation. For some Syrians, particularly members of the Ba'th party, union with Egypt offered hope for resolving a host of problems. As early as November 1957, Syria's National Assembly called for union with Egypt. Nasser agreed, but only on his terms: full union (not a federation) under his leadership. On 1 February 1958, he joined Syria's president, Shukri al-Quwatli, in announcing the formation of the United Arab Republic (UAR). A referendum on union and Nasser's presidency was approved on 21 February.

New governmental institutions were created in March 1958. Four vice presidents were appointed: two Egyptians (Abd al-Hakim Amir and Abd al-Latif al-Baghdadi) and two Syrians (Akram al-Hawrani and Sabri al-Asali). Amir also was commander of the joint UAR military. A regional council of ministers was established for each province, as was a unified cabinet (whose members were appointed in October). In March 1960, a new National Assembly was created. Nasser appointed its delegates—a higher proportion of whom were Egyptians—who first met that July. He also imposed Egypt's one-party system on Syria. Only the National Union, established in Egypt in May 1957, was allowed to function.

Formation of the UAR threatened the West with the prospect of Arab unity under Nasser's leadership. The fact that the UAR immediately tried to draw in other states furthered this perception. In March 1958, the United Arab States was forged with Yemen and would last until December 1961. More significantly, cooperation talks were held between the UAR and the government that came to power during the July 1958 revolution in Iraq. Although the two never unified, Britain and the United States were unsettled by the prospect. Formation of the UAR, the civil war in pro-Western Lebanon, and the revolution in Iraq, formerly the West's leading Arab client, prompted the dispatch of U.S. troops to Lebanon and British troops to Jordan in July 1958, to bolster anti-UAR Arab governments.

Syria soon became disappointed with the UAR. Ba'thists were angered at being barred from power in a union that some Syrians felt more closely approached Egypt's occupation of Syria. By late 1959, major Ba'thists had been dismissed from the government. The powerful Syrian bourgeoisie was alienated by Nasser's state-managed economic policies, especially limits on landholdings and the 1961 socialist decrees. In August 1961, Nasser strengthened his centralized control by abolishing the two councils of ministers and the cabinet, and adding three new vice presidents, for a total of seven (only two of whom were Syrians).

Postage stamps from the United Arab Republic. (Richard Bulliet)

Syria's units of the UAR army in Damascus launched a secessionist coup on 28 September 1961. Following limited fighting, Nasser decided against enforcing union militarily. The breakup of the UAR was a tremendous blow to Nasser's prestige and the dream of pan-Arab unity. Egypt used the name United Arab Republic until 1971, when it became the Arab Republic of Egypt.

Michael R. Fischbach

United Jewish Appeal

The main organization through which U.S. Jews support Jews abroad.

In 1939 the United Palestine Appeal joined with the American Jewish Joint Distribution Committee and the National Refugee Service to form the United Jewish Appeal (UJA). Most of what it raises goes to what is now called the United Israel Appeal, which operates through the JEWISH AGENCY in Israel. The UJA operates through two hundred federations and welfare funds in the United States.

BIBLIOGRAPHY

AMERICAN JEWISH COMMITTEE AND PUBLICATION SOCIETY. *American Jewish Yearbook, 1989.* Scranton, Pa., 1989.

Paul Rivlin

United National Front

See Jabha al-Wataniyya, al-

United Nations and the Middle East

The United Nations has played a prominent role in the Middle East through partitions, resolutions, and negotiations.

The problem of Palestine was brought before the United Nations in April 1947. In May 1947 the General Assembly set up the UNITED NATIONS SPECIAL COMMITTEE ON PALESTINE (UNSCOP). In its report, dated 31 August 1947, the majority of the members of UNSCOP recommended a plan of partition. On 29 November 1947, the General Assembly adopted the partition plan and decided that the British mandate over Palestine should be terminated not later than 1 August 1948. The JEWISH AGENCY accepted the plan, but the ARAB HIGHER COMMITTEE and all Arab states rejected it.

First Arab–Israel War. On 14 May 1948 the British mandate over Palestine expired. The Jewish Agency proclaimed the State of Israel on the territory allotted to the Jewish community under the partition plan. On the following day, the Arab states instituted armed action in Palestine. On 21 May Count Folke Bernadotte of Sweden was appointed the UN mediator for Palestine to promote a peaceful adjustment of the situation.

The ARAB–ISRAEL WAR (1948) ended in June with a truce. The military observer mission set up at that time, the United Nations Truce Supervision Organization (UNTSO), was the first UN peacekeeping operation. At the end of hostilities, Count Bernadotte began his mediation efforts, but he was assassinated in Jerusalem on 17 September 1948 by the Stern Gang. His work was immediately resumed by Ralph BUNCHE of the United States. On 11 November 1948, the General Assembly set up the UN Conciliation Commission on Palestine (France, Turkey, and the United States).

In 1949, armistice agreements were concluded between Israel and Egypt, Jordan, Lebanon, and Syria under Bunche's auspices. They gave temporary control of the Gaza Strip to Egypt; of the West Bank, including East Jerusalem, to Jordan; and of the remaining parts of Palestine to Israel. During the armistice negotiations, Israel was admitted to the United Nations on 11 May, 1949.

In December 1949, the General Assembly established the UNITED NATIONS RELIEF AND WORKS AGENCY to provide assistance to Palestinian refugees. The Trusteeship Council drafted a statute for the internationalization of Jerusalem in April 1950; it was rejected by Israel and Jordan.

After the conclusion of the armistice agreements, the responsibility for promoting a final settlement of the Palestine problem fell on the Conciliation Commission, but no progress was achieved. Despite the efforts of UNTSO, the situation along the armistice demarcation lines remained tense, Palestinian fida-'iyyun (freedom fighters) carried out frequent raids against Israel, which were invariably followed by harsh retaliation by Israel's armed forces.

Suez Crisis. Tension in the region rose to a critical level in 1956 when the government of Egypt nationalized the Suez Canal Company, which was controlled by British and French interests, and closed the Suez Canal to Israel's shipping. While UN Secretary-General Dag Hammarskjöld endeavored to work out a compromise solution, Israel's troops invaded Egypt on 28 October 1956 and within a few days occupied the Gaza Strip and most of the Sinai peninsula, while an Anglo–French force landed in

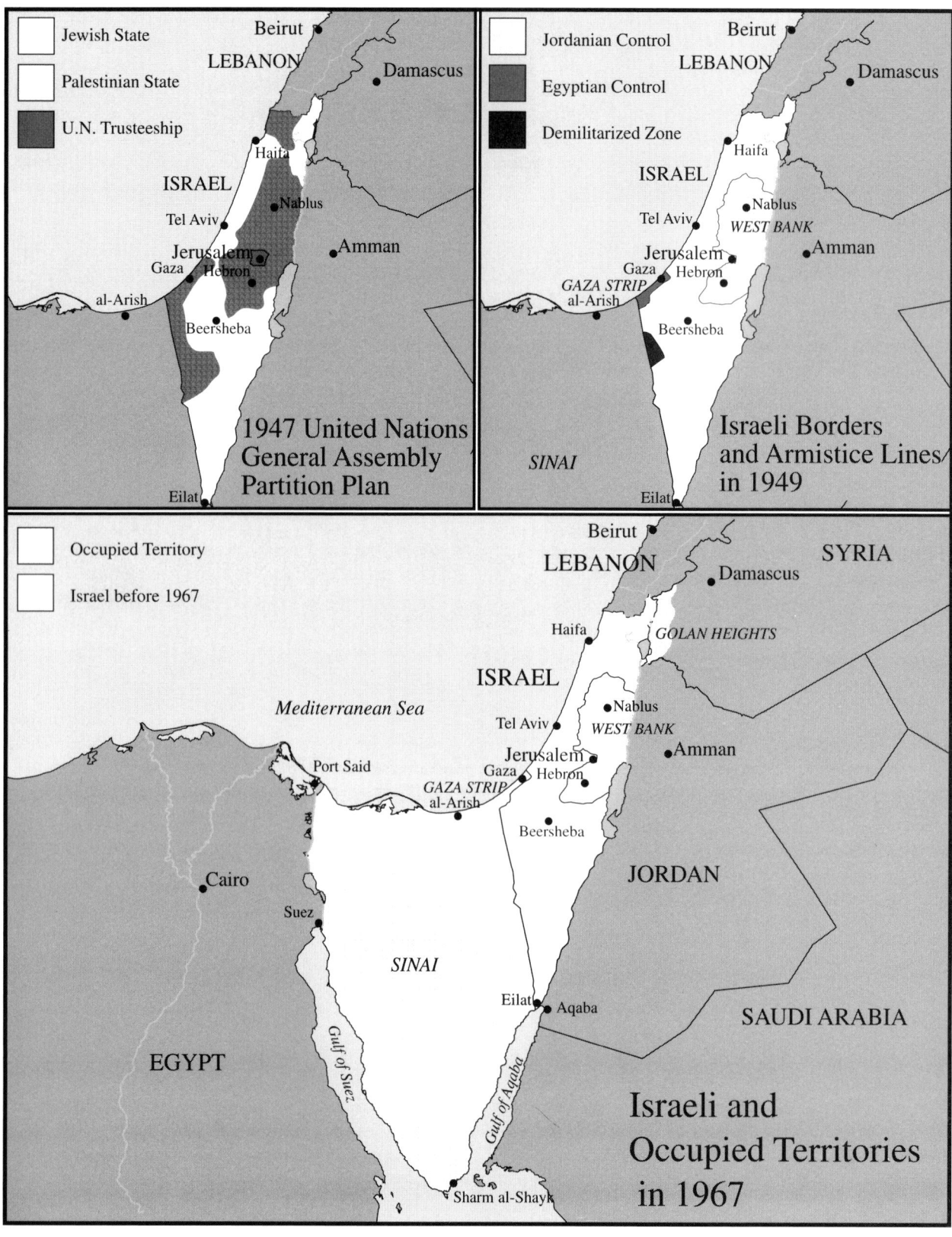

Map 1 (top left): Legend
- Jewish State
- Palestinian State
- U.N. Trusteeship

Beirut
LEBANON
Damascus
Haifa
ISRAEL
Nablus
Tel Aviv
Jerusalem
Gaza   Hebron
al-Arish
Beersheba
Amman
Eilat

1947 United Nations General Assembly Partition Plan

Map 2 (top right): Legend
- Jordanian Control
- Egyptian Control
- Demilitarized Zone

Beirut
LEBANON
Damascus
Haifa
ISRAEL
Nablus
WEST BANK
Tel Aviv
Jerusalem
Gaza   Hebron
GAZA STRIP
al-Arish
Beersheba
Amman
SINAI
Eilat

Israeli Borders and Armistice Lines in 1949

Map 3 (bottom): Legend
- Occupied Territory
- Israel before 1967

Beirut
LEBANON
SYRIA
Damascus
Haifa
GOLAN HEIGHTS
ISRAEL
Mediterranean Sea
Nablus
Tel Aviv
WEST BANK
Port Said
Jerusalem
Gaza   Hebron
GAZA STRIP
al-Arish
Beersheba
Amman
Cairo
Suez
JORDAN
SINAI
Eilat   Aqaba
SAUDI ARABIA
Gulf of Suez
EGYPT
Gulf of Aqaba
Sharm al-Shaykh

Israeli and Occupied Territories in 1967

the Suez Canal zone. To help resolve the crisis, the United Nations established the UNITED NATIONS EMERGENCY FORCE (UNEF) in the Sinai.

Six-Day War. On 18 May 1967 UNEF was withdrawn at the request of Egypt. Three weeks later, war broke out again. Hostilities started on the Egyptian front on 5 June and soon thereafter spread to the Jordanian and Syrian fronts. The war ended on 10 June with a cease-fire. By that time, Israel had taken Sinai and the Gaza Strip from Egypt, the West Bank (including East Jerusalem) from Jordan, and the Golan Heights from Syria.

On 22 November 1967, the Security Council unanimously adopted Resolution 242, known as the "land for peace" resolution. It called on the parties to seek a comprehensive settlement in the Middle East and stipulated that the establishment of a just and lasting peace should be based on the withdrawal of Israel's armed forces from territories occupied in June 1967 and the recognition of the right of all states in the region to live in peace within secure boundaries. Gunnar Jarring of Sweden, special representative of the secretary-general, began his mediation mission in December 1967, but little progress was made. The mission ceased in early 1973.

October 1973 War. War broke out on 6 October 1973 when Egypt's and Syria's forces launched simultaneous attacks against Israel's posts in the Suez Canal zone and on the Golan Heights in order to liberate their occupied territories. As fighting intensified, especially on the Egyptian front, the Security Council met on 22 October and adopted Resolution 338, which called on the belligerent parties to cease all fighting and to begin negotiations for establishing a just and durable peace on the basis of Resolution 242.

But the fighting continued. At the request of President Anwar al-Sadat of Egypt, the Soviet Union agreed to send troops to the area, a move the United States strongly opposed. On 25 October 1973 the Security Council ordered an immediate cease-fire and established the second UN Emergency Force (UNEF II) to supervise it.

A peace conference convened in Geneva under U.S.–Soviet sponsorship in December 1973. Chaired by Secretary-General Kurt Waldheim, it was attended by Egypt, Israel, and Jordan. Syria refused to participate, and the Palestine Liberation Organization (PLO) was not invited. The conference lasted only two days, but it paved the way for mediation by the United States, which led to the conclusion of military disengagement agreements between Israel and Egypt and Syria.

The Camp David Accords and the Egypt–Israel Peace Treaty. The peace process was partially revived in November 1977 when President Sadat visited Jerusalem. His visit was followed by direct negotiations between Egypt and Israel under the auspices of the United States, negotiations that led to the conclusion of the Camp David Accords in September 1978 and the signing of the peace treaty between Egypt and Israel in March 1979.

It was the clear intention of the parties to the peace treaty to use UNEF II and UNTSO military observers for peacekeeping along the border. But the Soviet Union, which strongly opposed the peace treaty, made it clear that it would veto a further extension of UNEF II past July 1979. The Security Council therefore decided to let the mandate of the UNEF II lapse. The United States later organized the Multinational Force and Observers (MFO) to carry out the functions of UNEF II.

Invasion of Lebanon. Although relations between Egypt and Israel had been normalized with the peace treaty, the other aspects of the Arab–Israel conflict deteriorated further with Israel's invasion of Lebanon in March 1978. The invasion was launched after a terrorist raid against Israel by PLO fighters based in southern Lebanon. On 19 March the Security Council called on Israel to withdraw from Lebanon's territory and established the UN Interim Force in Lebanon (UNIFIL) to confirm the withdrawal process. UNIFIL was unable to fulfill its mandate, however. In 1982, Israel again invaded Lebanon. In 1985, Israel's forces withdrew from most of the occupied territory but continued to hold a border area known as the "security zone."

Resumption of the Peace Process. The Madrid Peace Conference on the Middle East was convened in November 1991 by the United States and the Soviet Union to promote a comprehensive settlement of the Arab–Israel conflict on the basis of Security Council Resolutions 242 and 338. On 13 September 1993 Israel and the PLO signed the Declaration of Principles for interim self-government for the Gaza Strip and Jericho. The United Nations played only a marginal role in the peace process, but it has been active in international assistance supporting the implementation of the declaration of principles.

The United Nations maintains three peacekeeping operations in the area: the UN Disengagement Observer Force (UNDOF) on the Golan Heights, UNIFIL, and UNTSO. UNRWA assists about 3.2 million Palestinian refugees in Gaza, the West Bank, and in neighboring Arab states.

The 1958 Rebellion in Lebanon. In May 1958 a rebellion by armed Muslims broke out in Lebanon when President Camille Chamoun, a Christian Maronite announced his intention to seek an amendment to the Constitution that would enable him to stand for a second term. Lebanon's government brought the matter before the Security Council, charging that the United Arab Republic (formed by the union of Egypt and Syria under President Gamal Abdel Nasser) was supporting the rebellion.

By Resolution 128 of 11 June 1958, the Security Council decided to dispatch an observation group to Lebanon. The UN Observation Group in Lebanon (UNOGIL), composed of Galo Plaza Lasso of Ecuador, Rajaswar Dayal of India, and Major General Odd Bull of Norway was assisted by 591 UN military observers.

By August 1958 General Fu'ad Chehab, the Maronite commander of the army, had been elected president of Lebanon, effectively removing the question of a second term for Chamoun. In November 1958, Lebanon's government informed the Security Council that cordial and close relations had been reestablished between Lebanon and the United Arab Republic. UNOGIL was terminated the following month.

Yemen. In September 1962, a rebellion led by the army overthrew Imam Muhammad al-Badr and proclaimed the Yemen Arab Republic. Following his overthrow, the imam rallied the tribes in the northern part of the country and, with financial and material support from Saudi Arabia, the royalists fought a fierce guerrilla war against the republican forces. At the beginning of October 1962, large numbers of troops were dispatched from Egypt to Yemen, at the request of the revolutionary government. After the 1962 session of the General Assembly, Secretary-General U Thant undertook a peace initiative. In April 1963, he submitted to Egypt, Saudi Arabia, and the Yemen Arab Republic a disengagement plan, which all three accepted. Saudi Arabia would terminate all support to the Yemeni royalists, and Egypt would withdraw its troops from Yemen. A demilitarized zone would be established on each side of the border between Saudi Arabia and Yemen, and impartial observers would monitor the disengagement.

The UN Observation Mission in Yemen (UNYOM) began operations in July 1963. Following the conference of Arab heads of state at Cairo in mid-January 1964, the relations between Egypt and Saudi Arabia improved markedly. UNYOM was withdrawn from Yemen on 4 September 1964, after Egypt and Saudi Arabia, which shared its cost, ended their financial support.

Cyprus. Following the outbreak of fighting between the Greek and Turkish communities on Cyprus in December 1963, the matter was brought before the Security Council. By Resolution 186 of 4 March 1964, the council established the UN Peacekeeping Force in Cyprus (UNFICYP) to prevent a recurrence of fighting and to return normal conditions to the island. UNFICYP became operational on 13 March. After August 1964 quiet was restored and lasted until July 1974.

On 20 July 1974, after supporters of enosis (union of Cyprus with Greece) had staged a coup d'état against the Cyprus government, Turkey launched an extensive military operation on the island. The fighting ended in August 1974. By that time, Turkey's army controlled about 38 percent of Cyprus, in the northern part. To prevent a recurrence of fighting, UNFICYP established a zone across the island between the Cyprus National Guard to the south and the Turkish and Turkish Cypriot forces to the north.

Resolution 186 also asked the secretary-general to appoint a mediator to promote a peaceful settlement of the Cyprus problem. The mediator, Galo Plaza Lasso, reported in April 1965 that a settlement could best be achieved on the basis of a unitary government with adequate protection and guarantees for individual and minority rights. His report was rejected by the Turkish side and Plaza resigned in December 1965. Intercommunal talks began in 1968 under the auspices of the secretary-general, but they made little progress.

After Turkey's military intervention, the Turkish Cypriot leadership in February 1975 announced the establishment of the Turkish Federated State of Cyprus in the northern part of the island. On 12 March, the Security Council affirmed that this unilateral move did not prejudice a final political settlement. This led to new rounds of intercommunal talks, which continue intermittently. UNFICYP, whose mandate has been repeatedly extended, now has a total strength of about 1,250 military personnel.

Bahrain. Bahrain, which until 1970 had "special treaty relations" with Britain, was claimed by Iran because the island had been under its sovereign jurisdiction before 1783. Britain announced its intention to withdraw its armed forces from east of Suez in 1968, and in early 1969, Iran and Britain asked Secretary-General U Thant to help resolve the problem. Following nearly one year of negotiations, an agreement was reached under which U Thant would appoint a personal representative to ascertain the wishes of the people of Bahrain.

On 28 March 1970 U Thant appointed Vittorio Winspeare Guicciardi of Italy as his personal representative and the head of the UN Good Offices

Mission in Bahrain. The mission visited Bahrain from 29 March until 18 April 1970. Its report of 30 April 1970 affirmed that the overwhelming majority of the people of Bahrain wished it to be a fully independent and sovereign state. On 11 May 1970 the Security Council endorsed the findings. Shortly thereafter, Bahrain gained its independence. It became a member of the United Nations in September 1971.

Afghanistan. On 27 December 1979 the Soviet Union entered Afghanistan to assist the communist-led government in its fight against insurgent movements. It was soon embroiled in a brutal guerilla war with the fighters of the Afghan resistance, known as mojahedin, who received substantial financial and material support from Pakistan and the United States. During the hostilities, some three million refugees fled to Pakistan and about two million to Iran.

On 14 January 1980 the General Assembly adopted a resolution that called for the withdrawal of all foreign troops from Afghanistan. In February 1981 Secretary-General Kurt Waldheim appointed Javier Pérez de Cuéllar of Peru as his personal representative to deal with the situation. When Pérez de Cuéllar succeeded Waldheim as secretary-general in January 1982, the mission was taken over by Diego Cordovez of Ecuador.

On the basis of a peace plan put forward by Pérez de Cuéllar, Afghanistan and Pakistan agreed in 1982 to engage in indirect negotiations, with Cordovez as an intermediary. Those negotiations led to the conclusion in April 1988 in Geneva of the Agreements on the Settlement of the Situation relating to Afghanistan. Under the agreements, Afghanistan and Pakistan each undertook not to interfere in the internal affairs of the other, and the Soviet Union and the United States undertook not to interfere in the internal affairs of Afghanistan and Pakistan. The agreements also provided for a phased withdrawal of the Soviet Union's forces from Afghanistan by 15 February 1989 and for the establishment of the UN Good Offices Mission in Afghanistan and Pakistan (UNGOMAP) to monitor its implementation.

UNGOMAP, set up at the end of April 1988, was headed by the personal representative of the secretary-general. Besides monitoring the withdrawal of the Soviet Union, it assisted in the voluntary return of refugees to Afghanistan. The final withdrawal of the Soviet Union's 100,300 troops was completed on 12 February 1989. UNGOMAP was terminated in March 1990.

The civil war continued after the withdrawal of the Soviet Union, and the two superpowers continued to send large quantities of weapons until January 1991. In May 1991 the secretary-general proposed a peace plan that called for free and fair elections leading to the establishment of a broad-based government. In April 1992 the Communist regime collapsed with the defeat of the government forces, but this did not stop the civil war; fighting has continued between rival mojahedin factions.

Iran–Iraq War. On 22 September 1980 the armed forces of Iraq invaded Iran and soon occupied a sizable portion of its territory. By Resolution 479 of 28 September 1980, the Council called upon Iran and Iraq to refrain from further use of force and to settle their dispute by peaceful means, but Iran rejected the resolution as one-sided. On 11 November Secretary-General Kurt Waldheim appointed Olof Palme, former prime minister of Sweden, as his special representative to promote a peace settlement. Palme made some initial progress over the freeing of merchant ships stranded in the Shatt al-Arab and the exchange of limited numbers of prisoners of war, but a peace settlement remained elusive.

During the initial phase of the war, Iraq's forces had advanced inside Iran to a depth of 80 to 120 kilometers (48–72 mi.). In December 1980, however, the Iranian forces stopped their advance and, by late 1982 had pushed them back in some areas beyond the international border. Then fighting settled down into a stalemate with entrenched front lines along or near the international border. Both parties engaged in frequent air attacks against military and oil installations and civilian cities. In June 1984 Secretary-General Javier Pérez de Cuéllar appealed to both sides to refrain from attacks on civilian population centers.

On 20 July 1987 the Security Council adopted Resolution 598, which demanded that Iran and Iraq observe an immediate cease-fire and withdraw their forces to the international border. The adoption of Resolution 598 was followed by intensive diplomatic negotiations that lasted until 8 August 1988, when both parties formally accepted the cease-fire arrangements.

In accordance with those arrangements, on 9 August 1988 the Security Council established the UN Iran–Iraq Military Observer Group (UNIIMOG) to supervise the cease-fire and the withdrawal process. The mission began operations in mid-August with 400 military observers from 26 countries and about 500 military support personnel. Both parties generally complied with the cease-fire and withdrew their forces to the international border. After the cessation of hostilities, Iran and Iraq began direct talks to settle outstanding issues. On 15 August 1990, shortly after its invasion of Kuwait, Iraq lifted its claim over the Shatt al-Arab, thus removing a major cause of conflict with Iran. UNIIMOG was terminated on 28 February 1991.

Following the war, Pérez de Cuéllar used the close relationship he had developed with Iran's leaders to obtain the release of hostages in Beirut. After securing Iran's cooperation in 1989, he asked Giandomenico Picco of Italy to deal with this matter in a one-man secret mission. There followed a long series of negotiations with kidnap groups in Beirut and with representatives of the governments of the United States, Britain, Israel, and Syria. The Picco mission, which lasted from 1989 until 17 June 1992, resulted in the release of all eleven Western hostages detained in Beirut at the time and of ninety-one Lebanese held by the kidnap groups.

Gulf Crisis. On 2 August 1990 Iraq invaded Kuwait, quickly occupied the country, and annexed it. On the same day, the Security Council condemned the invasion and demanded the immediate withdrawal of Iraq's forces. When Iraq failed to comply, the council met again on 6 August and imposed economic sanctions. On 29 November the council adopted Resolution 678, which authorized member states cooperating with Kuwait to use all necessary measures to implement its resolutions if Iraq failed to do so by 15 January 1991.

Between the adoption of Resolution 678 and the deadline of 15 January 1991, the United States and other countries cooperating with Kuwait dispatched large numbers of armed forces to the region. On 16 January 1991 the coalition forces led by the United States launched military operations against Iraq. The United Nations was not involved in the conduct of the Gulf war, but it played a key role again after the military operations were suspended on 28 February. At that time, the coalition forces had driven Iraq's troops from Kuwait and had occupied part of southern Iraq.

On 2 March 1991 the Security Council demanded that Iraq implement all its resolutions and specified the measures to be taken to end the hostilities. The next day, an informal cease-fire was signed by military commanders in the field, after Iraq had agreed to fulfill the obligations set by the council. On 3 April 1991 the Security Council adopted Resolution 687, which laid down in detail the specific terms that Iraq must accept to obtain a formal cease-fire. After receiving Iraq's official acceptance, the Security Council established the UN Iraq–Kuwait Observation Mission (UNIKOM) to supervise the cease-fire and to monitor a demilitarized zone between Iraq and Kuwait.

In the aftermath of the Gulf War, the Kurdish population in northern Iraq and the Shi'ites in the south rebelled against the government, which took harsh action to suppress the rebellions. By Resolution 688 of 5 April 1991, the Security Council demanded that Iraq immediately end the repression and give international humanitarian organizations access to all those in need of assistance within its territory. A UN humanitarian operation to provide food and essential relief supplies in all parts of Iraq, especially in the northern Kurdish area, was launched.

The lifting of the sanctions will be decided by the Security Council in the light of Iraq's compliance with its resolutions. So far, the conditions for lifting such sanctions have not been fully met.

Western Sahara. In 1985 Secretary-General Pérez de Cuéllar and the chairman of the Organization of African Unity sought to promote a peaceful settlement of the conflict between Morocco and POLISARIO (Frente Popular para la Liberacion de Saguia al-Hamra y de Rio de Oro) over Western Sahara. In August 1988 the two warring parties accepted the settlement proposals in principle. Those proposals envisaged a cease-fire followed by a referendum that would enable the people of Western Sahara to choose between independence and continued union with Morocco.

In April 1991 the secretary-general submitted to the Security Council a detailed plan for implementing the settlement proposals. It provided for the establishment of the UN Mission for the Referendum in Western Sahara (MINURSO) and contained a tentative timetable for the operation, according to which the referendum would be held twenty weeks after the cease-fire. On 29 April 1991 the Security Council approved the implementation plan and established MINURSO, and on 24 May the secretary-general announced that the cease-fire would enter into effect on 6 September 1991. It did so, and, as an interim measure, military observers were sent to Western Sahara to monitor the cease-fire.

So far the key outstanding issue, which relates to the identification and registration of voters, has remained unresolved. Boutros Boutros-Ghali, who succeeded Pérez de Cuéllar in January 1992, and his special representative have continued to seek a compromise solution acceptable to both parties. Meanwhile, the situation in Western Sahara has been generally quiet.

[*See also:* Arab–Israel War (1967); Arab–Israel War (1973); Cairo Conference; Gulf Crisis; Iran–Iraq War; Mandate System; Pakistan and the Middle East; Partition Plans (Palestine); Security Council Resolutions 242 and 338; Western Sahara War; Yemen Civil War]

BIBLIOGRAPHY

Annual Report of the Secretary-General on the Work of the Organization, 1988–1989, 1989–1990, 1990–1991. New York, 1989, 1990, 1991.

The Blue Helmets: A Review of United Nations Peace-keeping. New York. 1990.

FORSYTHE, DAVID P. *United Nations Peacemaking: The Conciliation Commission for Palestine.* Baltimore, 1972.

HIGGINS, ROSALYN. *United Nations Peacekeeping, 1946–1967,* vol. 1. London, 1970.

United Nations Yearbook. New York, 1947–1996.

URQUHART, BRIAN. *Hammarskjold.* New York, 1972.

———. *Ralph Bunche: An American Life.* New York, 1993.

F. T. Liu

United Nations Economic Survey Mission

UN research group instructed to survey the Israel–Palestine area for a major economic redevelopment project that would benefit the people and help reintegrate refugees into the economy of the region.

In August 1949 the UN Conciliation Commission for Palestine established the UN Economic Survey Mission, instructing it to survey the situation throughout the area and then recommend ways to promote a major economic development program, which could help reintegrate the Palestinian refugees into the economic life of the Middle East, resolve the Palestinian refugee problem, and promote Middle East peace. Finding itself faced by insurmountable political and emotional obstacles in carrying out its task, the mission recommended that the UN General Assembly establish an agency, the UN Relief and Works Agency (UNRWA), and provide it with enough funds and authority to carry out both sustained relief efforts and also a small works program for an eighteen-month period. In December 1949 the General Assembly passed a resolution to implement this recommendation and the UN Economic Survey Mission ceased to exist.

BIBLIOGRAPHY

UNITED NATIONS CONCILIATION COMMISSION FOR PALESTINE. *Final Report of the United Nations Economic Survey Mission for the Middle East.* New York, 1949.

Fred J. Khouri

United Nations Emergency Force

Peacekeeping operation established during the Suez crisis.

The Suez crisis, during which Israel, France, and Britain invaded Egypt and occupied sizable portions of its territory, was brought before the UN General Assembly in early November 1956. Secretary General Dag Hammarskjöld submitted a plan for setting up an emergency UN force to supervise the cessation of hostilities on November 5. The General Assembly then authorized the establishment of the United Nations Emergency Force (UNEF), the first UN peacekeeping force.

UNEF was composed of contingents provided by member states. Troops from the five permanent members of the Security Council and any countries that might have a special interest in the conflict were excluded. UNEF's establishment in the conflict area required the consent of all parties concerned. Its soldiers had light defensive weapons but were not authorized to use force except in self-defense.

UNEF, operational by mid-November 1956, initially had about six thousand troops from Brazil, Canada, Colombia, Denmark, Finland, India, Indonesia, Norway, Sweden, and Yugoslavia. Its first commander was Maj. Gen. E. L. M. Burns of Canada. As the troops were deployed to supervise the cease-fire, negotiations were being carried out for the withdrawal of the occupation forces. A phased withdrawal began under the supervision and with the assistance of UNEF. The withdrawal of Britain's and France's forces was completed by December 22, 1956, and that of Israel's forces in March 1957.

After the withdrawal, UNEF was deployed along the Egypt–Israel border and maintained a post at Sharm al-Shaykh, which controlled access to the Gulf of Aqaba. By 1967 UNEF had been reduced to about thirty-four hundred troops.

In May 1967, as tension arose again to a critical level in the Middle East and, despite Secretary General U Thant's appeal, President Gamal Abdel Nasser of Egypt requested the withdrawal of UNEF. UNEF therefore discontinued its operations on May 18, 1956. Three weeks later there was a new war in the Middle East.

[*See also:* Arab–Israel War (1956)]

BIBLIOGRAPHY

BURNS, E.L.M. *Between Arab and Israeli.* Toronto, 1962.

THANT, U. *A View from the UN.* New York, 1977.

F. T. Liu

United Nations Palestine Conciliation Commission

UN commission appointed in 1949 to deal with problems facing dislocated Palestinians and to help reach a peace settlement at the conclusion of the 1948 Arab–Israel War.

The UN General Assembly resolution of December 11, 1949, established the Conciliation Commission for Palestine, instructing it "to take steps to assist the parties concerned to achieve a final comprehensive peace settlement of all questions outstanding between them" and to facilitate the repatriation or resettlement with compensation of the Palestinian refugees. The commission was composed of representatives from France, Turkey, and the United States. At a Paris peace conference in September 1951, the commission sought but failed to achieve any agreement on a peace settlement. The UN General Assembly continued to pass resolutions urging the commission to continue its efforts to secure the implementation of earlier resolutions on the Palestine problem. Nevertheless, the commission, convinced that the parties were not yet prepared to make peace, largely confined its efforts to dealing with the Palestinian refugee problem. Even then, it was able to make only limited progress, largely confined to technical aspects of this problem. Despite the lack of any progress, the General Assembly still continues to pass annual resolutions calling on the commission to continue its efforts to carry out its original mandate.

BIBLIOGRAPHY

FORSYTHE, DAVID P. *United Nations Peacemaking: The Conciliation Commission for Palestine.* Baltimore, 1972.
HAMZEH, FUAD SAID. *United Nations Conciliation Commission for Palestine.* Beirut, 1968.

Fred J. Khouri

United Nations Relief and Works Agency for Palestine Refugees in the Near East

Organization that aids Palestine refugees.

The United Nations Relief and Works Agency for Palestine Refugees in the Near East (UNRWA) was created by UN General Assembly Resolution 302 (IV) on December 8, 1949, with the mandate to provide humanitarian assistance and emergency relief to Palestine refugees who had lost their homes and livelihood as a result of the 1948 Arab–Israel War. Palestine refugees within the purview of UNRWA are persons whose normal residences were in Palestine for a minimum of two years before the 1948 war, and their descendants. In 1949, UNRWA extended asistance to some 750,000 refugees, practically all of them Palestinian Arabs.

UNRWA's humanitarian activities have centered on three major programs: an educational program that ran some 650 elementary and preparatory schools and vocational centers with over 400,000 students in 1993; a health program with a network of units and medical staff that registered over 6 million patient vis-

its in 1993; and a relief and social services program to assist disadvantaged groups. UNRWA also has set up special programs to improve the living conditions in refugee camps, especially housing and environmental sanitation, and to respond to emergencies.

UNRWA has often had to carry out its mission in the midst of civil strife and military conflict. During the 1967 Arab–Israel War, more than 500,000 Arabs fled from the territories seized by Israel; these included 200,000 refugees from the 1948 war, who were displaced for a second time. Later, the 1970 fighting between Jordan's army and the armed elements of the Palestine Liberation Organization stationed in Jordan, another Arab–Israel war in October 1973, the Lebanese civil war that started in 1975, Israel's invasions of Lebanon in 1978 and in 1982, the Palestinian uprising (Intifada) and Israel's response to it from 1987 on, and more recently, Iraq's invasion of Kuwait and the Gulf war all had serious effects on the conditions of Palestine refugees and the work of UNRWA.

As of February 1996 UNRWA was providing assistance to about 3.2 million Palestine refugees— about 1.2 million in the Gaza Strip and the West Bank, and the remainder in Jordan, Lebanon, and Syria. Its budget for 1995 amounted to about 350 million U.S. dollars, funded almost entirely by voluntary contributions.

[*See also:* Refugees, Palestinian]

BIBLIOGRAPHY

VIORST, MILTON. *Reaching for the Olive Branch: UNRWA and Peace in the Middle East.* Washington, D.C., 1989.

F. T. Liu

United Nations Special Committee on Palestine

Committee created in 1947 to deal with all matters relating to Palestine.

The United Nations Special Committee on Palestine (UNSCOP), set up by the General Assembly on May 15, 1947, consisted of the representatives of Australia, Canada, Czechoslovakia, Guatemala, India, Iran, the Netherlands, Peru, Sweden, Uruguay, and Yugoslavia. It was mandated to investigate all matters relevant to the problem of Palestine and to submit a report to the General Assembly not later than September 1, 1947, containing its proposals for the solution of the problem.

UNSCOP submitted its report on August 31, 1947. It unanimously recommended the termination of the British mandate over Palestine no later than August 1, 1948; independence for Palestine after a transitional period, during which the country would be administered by the United Nations; and the preservation of all holy places. Canada, Czechoslovakia, Guatemala, the Netherlands, Peru, Sweden, and Uruguay supported a partition plan, known as the Majority Plan, under which Palestine would be divided into an Arab state, a Jewish state, and the city of Jerusalem as a separate body under a special international regime, the three entities to be linked by an economic union. India, Iran, and Yugoslavia supported a federal state plan, known as the Minority Plan, which would give Palestine a federal system of government with two federated states, one Arab and one Jewish, with Jerusalem as the federal capital. The representative of Australia abstained from voting on either plan.

On November 29, 1947, the General Assembly adopted a resolution based on the Majority Plan.

[See also: Mandate System; Palestine]

BIBLIOGRAPHY

LOUIS, WILLIAM ROGER. The British Empire in the Middle East, 1945–1951. Oxford, 1984.
WILSON, EVAN. Decision on Palestine. Stanford, Calif., 1979.

F. T. Liu

United Nations Truce Supervision Organization

UN peacekeeping operation.

The United Nations Truce Supervision Organization (UNTSO) was created through several UN resolutions to oversee the truce agreement between Israel and the Arab states, which was called for in the Security Council and went into effect on June 11, 1948. Unarmed UN military observers were first sent to Cairo and throughout Palestine. As hostilities continued in Palestine, UNTSO was expanded and charged with overseeing the signatories' application of the four 1949 armistice agreements. Its observers were stationed along armistice lines between Israel and Egypt, Syria, Lebanon, and Jordan. Observers remained in the region through the 1956 Suez crisis and were supported by the new and more broadly empowered UN Emergency Force. In June 1967, UNTSO demarcated the cease-fire lines between Israel and Syria, supervised the cease-fire, and oversaw renegotiations for observers along the Suez Canal. UNTSO observers assist other armed peacekeeping operations in the Middle East, such as the UN Interim Force in Lebanon. As of 30 June 1990, UNTSO had 291 observers; its maximum strength was 572 observers in 1948; and 28 have died in service since 1948. UNTSO is headquartered in Jerusalem.

BIBLIOGRAPHY

UNITED NATIONS. The Blue Helmets: A Review of United Nations Peacekeeping. New York, 1990.

Charles U. Zenzie

United States of America and the Middle East

The Middle East has been an area of vital interest to the United States since World War II.

Although American interest in the Middle East can be traced to the early years of the republic, the region has only been a principal focus of U.S. foreign policy since World War II. Oil investments and the special relationship with Israel were the chief reasons for U.S. involvement in that area of confrontation between the United States and the Soviet Union during the Cold War.

American contacts with the Middle East started about 1800 in North Africa. United States naval forces defeated the Barbary pirates in 1816, but most American contacts in the nineteenth century were educational and commercial in nature. Protestant missionaries established several schools, medical facilities, and colleges in Egypt, Turkey, Syria, and Lebanon.

In 1919, President Woodrow Wilson sent the KING–CRANE COMMISSION to inquire into the wishes of the Syrian and Palestinian people as to their political future. In the 1920s and 1930s, American oil companies invested heavily in Iran, Iraq, Bahrain, Saudi Arabia, and Kuwait. During World War II, the United States participated in the Allied battles for North Africa and established the Persian Gulf Command to transport Lend-Lease materials from the Gulf, through Iran, to the Soviet Union. By 1945, several American air bases, supply depots, and transportation facilities were operating throughout the Middle East.

From the end of World War II until the collapse of the USSR in the early 1990s, the major objective of United States foreign policy was to prevent Soviet penetration of the Middle East. When British political and military commitments in the area diminished, several Middle Eastern countries signed agreements with the United States and the region became the recipient of the greatest portion of American military and economic aid.

Responding to feared Soviet encroachments in Greece, Turkey, and Iran, the United States, under the Truman Doctrine of 1947, sent four hundred million dollars in aid to Greece and Turkey, and helped modernize Turkey's armed forces. U.S. advisers were also sent to Iran. Soviet pressure on Turkey and Iran marked the beginning of the Cold War, and the Truman Doctrine represented one of the first efforts in the new "containment" policy to halt Soviet expansion.

Founded in 1948 with American support and, by the 1960s, viewed as an important strategic asset, Israel became the largest single recipient of U.S. economic and military assistance. Close ties with Israel were reenforced by humanitarian impulses inspired by knowledge of the Holocaust. The assistance to Israel rendered it difficult for the United States to establish closer ties with the surrounding Arab nations. During the 1950s, Egypt refused to join a Middle East defense organization proposed by the United States, Great Britain, and France. Instead, the Northern Tier or Baghdad Pact, based on a military alliance between Turkey, Iraq, Iran, and Pakistan, was devised. The pact was linked with other containment alliances through Turkey's membership in the North Atlantic Treaty Organization in the west and Pakistan's affiliation with the Southeast Asia Treaty Organization in the east.

Efforts by Western countries to keep Soviet influence out of the Middle East were undermined by the Arab–Israel War of 1956 and the events leading up to it. The attempts of the United States to cultivate better relations with Egypt were subverted when the United States refused to provide Egypt with the aid to construct the Aswan High Dam; as a consequence, President Gamal Abdel Nasser nationalized the Suez Canal in 1956. Despite the strain in relations between the two countries, the Eisenhower administration strongly opposed the invasion of Egypt by Britain, France, and Israel in October 1956 and joined the Soviet Union in condemning the attack.

Following the war, unrest throughout the Middle East and the spread of nationalist doctrines that the U.S. government perceived as leftist led, in January 1957, to the Eisenhower Doctrine, whereby military and economic assistance was dispensed to the Middle East and the use of U.S. forces was provided to protect countries in the region "against overt aggression from any nation controlled by international Communism." The doctrine was tested in April 1957 when the U.S. Sixth Fleet was sent to the eastern Mediterranean to support Jordan's King Hussein. After the 1958 revolution in Iraq,

Lebanon's President Camille Chamoun also called on the United States for assistance to protect his regime from revolutionary forces, and President Eisenhower responded by sending fourteen thousand marines. They were withdrawn a few weeks after a truce was arranged, through intervention of the United States, between the various conflicting Lebanese parties. The United States' efforts to resolve the Arab–Israel dispute during the Eisenhower administration centered on the Arab refugee problem and projects intended to achieve the economic reconstruction of the Middle East through cooperative development of the region's water resources. However, Eric Johnston, Eisenhower's special representative, failed to obtain agreement for proposals to resettle the refugees.

The Kennedy administration sought to promote good relations with "progressive" Middle Eastern countries concerning containment. Kennedy also approved the first sale by the United States of a major weapons system to Israel.

After the Arab–Israel War of 1967 between Israel and Egypt, Syria, and Jordan, UN SECURITY COUNCIL RESOLUTION 242, drafted with U.S. help, became the basis for American policy in the Arab–Israel conflict. Its requirement that Israeli forces withdraw from territories occupied during the war hinged on the achievement of a comprehensive peace settlement. The Nixon administration's Rogers Plan, which was based on Resolution 242, called for Israel to withdraw with minor exceptions, to its pre-June 1967 borders. After the 1967 war, Egypt and Syria were rearmed by the Soviet Union, with whom they signed defensive alliances. In 1968, when the British announced their planned withdrawal from the Persian Gulf, the United States decided to build up the military forces of Saudi Arabia and Iran (see TWIN PILLARS POLICY).

During the 1973 October War between Israel and Egypt and Syria, U.S.–Soviet relations worsened. Moscow and Washington provided their respective clients with billions of dollars in arms; the threat by the USSR to send troops to assist Egypt and the nuclear alert by the United States brought the two countries to the brink of war. After the outbreak of the war in late October, the Arab oil-producing nations imposed an oil embargo that created an energy crisis in the United States and Western Europe. A peace conference at Geneva in December 1973 broke up after two days without settling the conflict, but Secretary of State Henry Kissinger subsequently initiated step-by-step negotiations that resulted in disengagement agreements between Israel, Syria, and Egypt and provided for Israel's withdrawal from parts of Sinai and the Golan area.

Relations between Egypt and the United States improved after 1973 as Egypt's President Anwar al-Sadat shifted from relying on Soviet aid to being receptive to American influence. Hoping to capitalize on the improved diplomatic climate, President Jimmy Carter attempted to reconvene the Geneva Peace Conference in 1977, but Sadat flew to Jerusalem in November to start direct negotiations with Israel. Sadat's dramatic initiative began a new peace process based on direct bilateral contacts between Egypt and Israel. When bitter disagreements between the two adversaries threatened to disrupt negotiations, however, Carter intervened. He invited Sadat and Israel's Prime Minister Menachem Begin to Camp David, where two frameworks for peace were hammered out—one dealing with Egyptian–Israeli relations and the other with the Palestinian issue. Under Carter's guidance, the CAMP DAVID ACCORDS were shaped into the Egyptian–Israeli peace treaty that was signed in Washington during March 1979.

Elsewhere in the Middle East, Carter's policy of containing Soviet influence in the Persian Gulf was undermined when his close ally, the shah of Iran, was overthrown in 1979. The president's efforts to obtain the release of American hostages held by the new revolutionary government in Tehran took over a year to resolve successfully, and this delay was a factor in his loss of the 1980 presidential election.

Presidents Ronald Reagan and George Bush continued the containment policies of their predecessors and also became deeply involved in the Arab–Israel conflict. During the Lebanese war in 1982, Reagan sent the Sixth Fleet and the U.S. Marines to Beirut as part of a multinational peacekeeping force. Lebanese militias attacked the marines, inflicting heavy casualties, and the marines were withdrawn soon after. The Reagan Plan for Middle East peace envisioned "self-government by the Palestinians . . . in association with Jordan" as the "best chance for a durable, just and lasting peace." Bush's attempts to continue negotiations based on the Reagan Plan and Resolution 242 were stymied until 1991, when the MADRID CONFERENCE convened. Sponsored by the United States and Russia, the new peace process provided for bilateral talks between Israel and Syria, Lebanon, and joint Jordanian-Palestinian delegations. It also included a series of multilateral meetings on such substantive issues as security, environment, economic development, water, and refugees.

President Bush involved the United States in its largest foreign military operation since Vietnam when he sent American forces to drive Iraq from Kuwait (see GULF CRISIS). From a military perspective, the operation was a success since the United States and the allied forces sustained only minor ca-

sualties. Bush was sharply criticized, however, because Iraq's President Saddam Hussein remained in power despite his defeat on the battlefield.

When the Soviet Union collapsed in 1991, a new phase of American foreign policy began; containment was no longer the principal objective. Instead, Russia and the United States cooperated in regard to the Middle East. As Soviet influence in the region declined, the United States became the dominant power and its influence was paramount. This situation greatly facilitated Washington's goal of maintaining the political status quo through its support of friendly regimes. It also made it easier to intervene when American concerns such as assured access to oil and the security of Israel appeared to be threatened.

BIBLIOGRAPHY

CARTER, JIMMY. *The Blood of Abraham*. Toronto, 1982.
DOWTY, ALAN. *Middle East Crisis: U.S. Decision-making in 1958, 1970, and 1973*. Berkeley, Calif., 1984.
QUANDT, WILLIAM B. *Decade of Decisions: American Policy toward the Arab-Israeli Conflict, 1967–1976*. Berkeley, Calif., 1977.
SICK, GARY. *All Fall Down: America's Tragic Encounter with Iran*. New York, 1985.
SPIEGEL, STEVEN. *The Other Arab–Israeli Conflict: Making America's Middle East Policy, from Truman to Reagan*. Chicago, 1985.
TANTER, RAYMOND. *Who's at the Helm? Lessons of Lebanon*. Boulder, Colo., and Oxford, 1990.

Don Peretz

Unity Party

Turkish political party, active in the 1960s and 1970s.

The Unity party came to be identified with the Shi'a Alevi minority community. It changed its name to the Turkish Unity party in November of 1971, perhaps to overcome this image. With the outlawing of the TURKISH WORKERS PARTY, eight of its former members were allowed to run as independents on the Unity party's election list in 1973, giving it a distinct leftist inclination. It polled only 1 percent of the vote and gained only one seat, however, compared to nearly 3 percent and eight seats in 1969. In 1977 it did even less well, failing to win any seats at all.

BIBLIOGRAPHY

WEIKER, W. F. *The Modernization of Turkey*. New York, 1981.

Frank Tachau

University of Jordan

The oldest of four public universities in Jordan.

The University of Jordan was established in 1962 on a picturesque hillside on the outskirts of Amman that used to be the site of an agricultural research station. The university contains faculties of arts, sciences, economics and commerce, *Shariʿa* (Islamic law), medical sciences (including general medicine, nursing, and pharmacy), education, agriculture, engineering and technology, law, and physical education. The university also has a teaching hospital. As with all public universities in Jordan, students pay nominal tuition and are able to buy books and materials at subsidized prices. In the 1989/90 academic year, the university graduated 4,273 men and women with bachelor's degrees, 236 with teaching diplomas, 660 with master's degrees, and 17 with doctoral degrees.

BIBLIOGRAPHY

GUBSER, PETER. *Jordan: Crossroads of Middle Eastern Events.* Boulder, Colo., 1983.

Jenab Tutunji

UNRWA

See United Nations Relief and Works Agency for Palestine Refugees in the Near East

UNSCOP

See United Nations Special Committee on Palestine

Uqayli, Abd al-Aziz al-   [1920–1982]

Iraqi government official.

Uqayli was born in Mosul to a working-class family. He graduated from the military academy, staff college, and Baghdad Law College. Before the July 1958 Republican Revolution, he served as a brigade commander and joined the clandestine Free Officers group of Abd al-Salam Arif and Abd al-Karim Kassem. After the revolution, he was appointed commander of the First Division, but in February 1959, dismissed for pan-Arab leanings. Later that year, he was tried for supporting the pan-Arabist anti-Kassem revolt of Abd al-Wahhab al-Shawwaf in March 1959 but was acquitted.

After the Ramadan Revolution of 1963, under President Abd al-Salam Arif, Uqayli became minister of defense (1965/66); following Arif's death, Uqayli competed unsuccessfully for the presidency with Abd al-Rahman Arif. From then on, he led a group of officers (mostly from Mosul) who demanded concentration on internal Iraqi unity before turning to unity with Gamal Abdel Nasser's Egypt. In 1968, he was arrested by the Baʿth party; he remained in jail where he was killed in 1982—probably because of Saddam Hussein's fear that he might become a focus of opposition of disgruntled officers.

BIBLIOGRAPHY

BATATU, HANNA. *The Old Social Classes and the Revolutionary Movements of Iraq.* Princeton, N.J., 1978.

Amatzia Baram

Uqayr Conference

Conference that fixed the borders of Iraq and Kuwait with Saudi Arabia.

At the conference, arranged by Britain in November 1922, Sir Percy Cox, Britain's high commissioner in Iraq, presided and dictated the borders that still exist (except for two neutral zones, later divided). The first fixed frontiers ever created in northeast Arabia gave Iraq territory that Ibn Saʿud claimed and compensated him at Kuwait's expense.

BIBLIOGRAPHY

HOLDEN, DAVID, and RICHARD JOHNS. *The House of Saud: The Rise and Rule of the Most Powerful Dynasty in the Arab World.* New York, 1981.
McLOUGHLIN, LESLIE. *Ibn Saud: Founder of a Kingdom.* New York, 1993.

Malcolm C. Peck

Uqbi, Tayyib al-   [1888–1960]

Prominent member of the Algerian Association of Reformist Ulama.

Born near Biskra in Algeria, Tayyib al-Uqbi (also Tayeb el-Okbi) studied in Medina and was influenced by the MUWAHHIDUN movement of Islam. He was known as an eloquent and controversial Islamic scholar. In 1936 al-Uqbi was accused of planning the murder of the mufti (canon lawyer) of Algiers but was acquitted in 1939. Al-Uqbi criticized Shaykh Abd al-Hamid Ben Badis's political involvements and left the association in 1938; he preferred discussion of religious and spiritual questions as disclosed by his journal, *al-Islah.*

BIBLIOGRAPHY

NAYLOR, PHILLIP C., and ALF HEGGOY. *Historical Dictionary of Algeria*, 2nd ed. Metuchen, N.J., 1994.

Phillip C. Naylor

Urabi, Ahmad   [1841–1911]

Egyptian nationalist leader and army officer.

Ahmad Urabi, the son of a village shaykh of Iraqi Arab origin, studied for two years at al-Azhar in Cairo and then entered the Cairo military academy at the behest of Viceroy Sa'id in 1854/55 and soon earned his commission. After the deposition of Khedive Isma'il in 1879, he is said to have supported the emerging National Party of Egypt, but his first proven act was to represent a group of discontented ethnic Egyptian officers who were protesting against the favoritism shown to Turkish and Circassian officers by War Minister Uthman Rifqi. Khedive Tawfiq and Prime Minister Riyad intended to dismiss Urabi and his group for insubordination, but other Egyptian officers seized control of the war office and rescued Urabi in February 1881. Subsequently, the khedive agreed to replace Rifqi with Mahmud Sami al-Barudi as war minister. On September 9, fearing a khedival counterplot, the Egyptian officers surrounded Abdin Palace, confronted Tawfiq, and obliged him to set up a constitutionalist government with Muhammad Sharif as prime minister and to increase the size of the Egyptian army.

As Britain and especially France—concerned about the safety of the Suez Canal, their investments, and their citizens in Egypt—became increasingly hostile to the Urabist movement, the Nationalists replaced Premier Sharif with Mahmud Sami al-Barudi in February 1882, and Urabi became war minister. The Nationalists continued to fear a khedival counterplot and took steps to weaken the Turks and Circassians within the officer corps, also stirring up popular feeling against the European powers. Riots broke out in Alexandria in June 1882, and many European residents fled. Britain and France threatened military intervention to support the khedive (whose relationship with the Nationalists seems to have been ambivalent) and to protect their citizens. They demanded that the Egyptian army remove all fortifications from Alexandria, and, when Urabi did not comply quickly enough, British ships began bombarding them, leading to the outbreak of fires in Alexandria. British troops (unaided by France, which had withdrawn because of a ministerial crisis) landed at Alexandria and later at Isma'ilia to restore order. Urabi and the Egyptian army continued to resist the

British, even after the khedive had gone over to their side, until their crushing defeat at al-Tall al-Kabir on September 13, 1882. Once the British entered Cairo, Urabi surrendered, was put on trial for treason against the khedive, but was not executed. He was exiled to Ceylon—until he was allowed by Khedive Abbas Hilmi II to return in 1901. He played no part in the later National party of Mustafa Kamil, died in obscurity, and was generally scorned by educated Egyptians until the 1952 revolution. Since then he has been rehabilitated by Gamal Abdel Nasser and his fellow officers—whose occupational and class backgrounds paralleled his own. Now he is generally considered a patriot who resisted the British, the khedive, and the aristocracy in favor of constitutional government and the welfare of Egypt's common people.

His writings include *Kashf al-Sitar an Sirr al-Asrar*, published in two volumes (Cairo, 1925).

BIBLIOGRAPHY

BARING, EVELYN. *Modern Egypt*. London, 1908.
BLUNT, WILFRID S. *Secret History of the English Occupation of Egypt*. London, 1907.
ISA, SALAH. *Al-Thawra al-urabiyya*. Beirut, 1972.
MANAF, ABD AL-AZIM, ed. *Al-Thawra al-urabiyya, mi'at am, 1881–1981*. Cairo, 1981.
MAYER, THOMAS. *The Changing Past: Egyptian Historiography of the Urabi Revolt, 1882–1983*. Gainesville, Fla., 1988.
AL-RAFI'I, ABD AL-RAHMAN. *Al-Thawra al-urabiyya wa al-ihtilal al-injilizi*. Cairo, 1938.
SCHÖLCH, ALEXANDER. *Egypt for the Egyptians!* London, 1981.

Arthur Goldschmidt, Jr.

Urbanization

The process of transforming a region's population from rural to urban with the attendant changes in class and occupational structures.

The first cities developed along the Tigris and Euphrates rivers in southern Mesopotamia (now in Iraq) about 3500 B.C.E. These formed the nuclei of the Sumerian civilization, the world's oldest. These cities' populations were small, seldom exceeding twenty thousand. Soon after, by 3000 B.C.E., cities also grew up along the Nile in Egypt. From these centers, urban life eventually spread throughout the Old World.

Until 1800 C.E., cities that had more than 100,000 inhabitants, such as Babylon, Alexandria, Ctesiphon, Constantinople (now Istanbul), Baghdad, and Cairo, had access to water transport (river and/or sea) and

A street in Baghdad, circa 1925, in an early stage of urbanization. (Richard Bulliet)

A residential street in the Old City quarter in San'a, Yemen. (Brad Glasser)

were also the capitals of empires. Those that developed without an imperial tax base, and were dependent on overland transport for provisioning, could seldom support a population of more than fifty thousand. Until the modern period, cities served first as foci of political and economic exploitation of their rural hinterlands; commerce was secondary. Cities dependent on industry and commerce were unusual: principally the Phoenician cities (Tyre, Sidon, Beirut, and Carthage), the Greek cities of western Anatolia, and some in Iran and Arabia (Tabriz, Palmyra, and Mecca) that depended on the caravan trade. Some were important as religious centers—Jerusalem and Bambyce (now Membij in Syria) before the Islamic conquest that began in the seventh century C.E.—and Mecca, Medina, Karbala, Qom, and Mashhad after it. The proportion of the total population living in cities in what became known as the Middle East seldom exceeded 15 percent before the nineteenth century.

This situation changed with European penetration of the Middle East after 1800. Europeans built roads and railroads to connect ports (Smyrna/Izmir, Mersin, Tripoli, Beirut, Jaffa, Alexandria, Algiers, and Rabat) with the interior. These generally became dual cities with modern colonial quarters tacked onto existing towns. The European districts acquired boulevards, streetcar lines, and electric lights, while the majority of the local people lived in densely settled traditional quarters. As trade became reoriented to these port cities, they grew rapidly. At

TABLE 1

Urban Growth, 1945–1982

City	Population	
	1945	1982
Cairo*	1,900,000	9,300,000
Tehran*	600,000	5,700,000
Istanbul	860,000	4,800,000
Baghdad*	350,000	3,700,000
Alexandria	900,000	2,300,000
Algiers*	250,000	2,200,000
Ankara*	227,000	2,050,000
Casablanca	480,000	1,650,000
Damascus*	250,000	1,200,000
Tel Aviv–Jaffa	300,000	1,000,000
Beirut*	170,000	800,000
Riyadh*	40,000	800,000
Jerusalem*	170,000	410,000

* National capital.

Aerial view of Nishapur, Iran, in 1956, showing modern streets and a traffic circle cutting through older roads, walls, and horizontally above the main crossing, the curving bazaar with its covered section. (Richard Bulliet)

the same time, local handicrafts declined in the interior cities (Bursa, Ankara, Isfahan, Tabriz, Baghdad, and Damascus) because of the influx of European trade goods. Instead, these cities became centers for the purchase and shipment of raw materials (tobacco, cotton, grains) destined for Europe.

Following World War I and the fall of the Ottoman Empire, nationalist regimes were established, first in Iran and Turkey, later in Iraq, Jordan and Syria. These focused development inward. East of Libya, the capitals of the large countries are all inland (Ankara, Cairo, Damascus, Baghdad, Riyadh, San'a, Tehran) and since their development policies were statist, these cities expanded. After World War II, rail and road networks that centered on the capitals were

extended, which facilitated migration to them. At the same time, rapid rural population growth and the mechanization of agriculture, largely implemented after 1945, pushed farmers from the land. The result was the explosive growth of the kind shown in Table 1 (p. 1848). The fastest growth was in fact among capital cities located inland.

Israel was established in 1948 and was the only Middle Eastern country to receive large numbers of permanent immigrants, most of whom were European and Middle Eastern Jews. They mainly settled directly into urban life, principally in the coastal cities of Tel Aviv and Haifa. The growth of the capital, Jerusalem, was restricted before the Arab–Israel War (1967). The establishment of the Jewish state had

View of the modern city of Casablanca. (Center for Middle East Studies, University of Texas, Austin)

caused the departure of many urban Arabs who had lived in British mandated Palestine. These, as refugees, contributed to urban growth in other countries—notably Lebanon (Tyre, Sidon, and Beirut), Jordan (Amman), and Kuwait—as well as the West Bank and the Gaza Strip.

Oil boom towns (Dhahran, Kuwait City, Abu Dhabi), grew rapidly for short periods, but they never became as large as thě major political and commercial centers. In the larger countries (Morocco, Algeria, Egypt, Turkey, Iran) close to 50 percent of the population was urban by the mid-1980s. In some of the smaller countries, Israel, Lebanon, Kuwait, the United Arab Emirates, the proportion is as high as 90 percent.

The traditional quarters remained in most of these cities of the modern Middle East, accompanied by newly constructed neighborhoods that accommodated political and economic elites. Thus, dual cities

Modern highway interchange in Bahrain. (Center for Middle East Studies, University of Texas, Austin)

resembling the colonial pattern developed in such places as Ankara and Tehran, where no colonizing power had ever ruled. The industrial districts that fueled the growth of European cities have not materialized in most Middle Eastern cities. Thus jobs are scarce and often entail menial work in the service sector at low wages. Rural migrants, already poor, generally remain so. They settle in the large tracts of *bidonvilles* (Morocco), *sarifa* (Iraq), or *gecekondu* (Turkey)—unplanned occupant-built housing often put on land not owned by the builder—that have grown up around every large Middle Eastern city. These have come to house more than 50 percent of the population of most big cities. Both the stresses of poverty and the breakdown of rural social structures have made these neighborhoods sources of unrest—supplying the manpower of the Arab "street" or the vast crowds that erupted into the squares of Tehran in 1978/79, which put the exiled Ayatollah Ruhollah Khomeini in power.

BIBLIOGRAPHY

BROWN, L. CARL, ed. *From Medina to Metropolis.* Princeton, N.J., 1973.
SAQQAF, ABDULAZIZ Y., ed. *The Middle East City.* New York, 1987.

John R. Clark

Urban Planning

City organization and layout have been affected by colonialism and petroleum wealth.

Urban planning has a long history in the Middle East. The first "city plan" for Çatal Hüyük, Turkey, dates back eight thousand years. Melville Branch bases this claim on the ordering and placement of eighty dwellings that were delineated on the wall of a cave. Examples of city planning in ancient times and the Middle Ages abound in Iran, Egypt, Mesopotamia (present Iraq), and other Middle Eastern countries. In the modern Middle East there have been two major influences on contemporary urban planning: colonialism and petroleum.

These two influences, among a host of other minor factors, have shaped the contemporary Middle Eastern urban landscape and can be divided into three periods: the colonial period (c. 1800–1940), a transitional period between the colonial period and the oil-boom era (c. 1940–1972), and the oil-boom era (post-1972).

Within these three stages, urban planning has shifted its emphasis from being a profession primarily involved in physical planning and urban design, to integrating socioeconomic and physical planning. The colonial period was dominated by the use of physical planning. In the period of transition, attempts were made to include economic, social, and demographic factors in urban planning, but planning remained in the shadow of independence politics. Today, the concept of integrating physical and socioeconomic planning is commonplace, though not always successful. Recent trends suggest that urban planners are increasingly emphasizing the anticipatory-preventive approach.

The Colonial Period. Although not all countries in the Middle East were colonized at the same time or in the same pattern, a common thread connects the urban-planning process in most countries. Europeans used urban planning successfully to establish and maintain the colonial extractive system. Physical segregation was the main tool used in implementing this policy.

Urban planning in this period was dominated by physical land-use planning and urban design, planning that chiefly concerned the arrangement of urban infrastructure and land use. The colonial use of physical planning established and maintained a trading network and facilitated a suitable living environment for European colonial administrators, workers, and their households.

To successfully carry out their mercantilist trade policies, Europeans had to orient the economy of the Middle East toward Europe by establishing a new structure of urban locations and hierarchies. To do this, the European colonialists had to do three things: build port cities to collect and ship goods (for example Aden, Casablanca, Tunis, Suez, Hormuz, and Port Said); build interior towns to serve as military establishments, local administrative capitals, or collection points for regional resources; and build infrastructure, such as roads and railways, to connect interior cities to ports. This trade-related settlement system then became the new colonial urban hierarchy that is still common all over the Middle East.

Urban planning then played its second major role in this period in maintaining and servicing the influx of European military personnel, administrators, businessmen, settlers, and fortune seekers. Planning was utilized to build the segregated city, in which a European, upper-class quarter was separated from the rest of the city.

French Morocco is the most vivid example of this kind of city planning. Marshal Louis-Hubert Gonzalve Lyautey, the resident general, imposed three rules for all new towns or existing urban centers that were to be remodeled. European quarters were to be built separate from the old Medinas, important cultural urban sites of the Moroccan urban cities were to be preserved, and the European part of the city was to utilize the latest and most up-to-date urban-planning techniques. Similar rules and laws existed in Algeria, Tunisia, Libya, and Egypt. These urban-planning rules segregated Europeans, along with some local resident minority groups (Coptic Christians and Jews) and a small community of the native rich, from the rest of the indigenous population—resulting in a dual city. A parallel but noninstitutionalized movement in Palestine saw Tel Aviv develop as a Jewish city alongside Arab Jaffa.

This dual city allowed a disproportionate share of the revenue of the city and state to be spent on the European quarters, despite the fact that taxes were raised mostly from the native quarters. As a result, the European quarters had large residential plots, low densities of population, and broad tree-lined roads and streets. They were also better connected to urban amenities like water, electricity, and sewage. These low-density residential quarters, with their superior sanitation facilities and other urban benefits, provided a healthier living environment for their residents. In addition, these facilities provided the Europeans with a culturally familiar environment, making them more interested in working in colonies and thus maintaining the colonial system.

In countries where local rulers had more autonomy or colonialism was not officially present, notably Iran and pre-1882 Egypt, the rulers tried to copy European styles of design and urban planning. In Egypt, Khedive Isma'il (1863–1879), influenced by his visit to Paris, tried to "Haussmannize" Cairo, following the physical urban plans implemented in Paris by Baron Haussmann. In Tehran, Reza Shah (1925–1941) promoted a grid-city design and constructed wide avenues through the old quarters of the city, and a "modern" city, designed along the lines of a European city, was built in northern Tehran where the rich began to reside. The primary reason for this kind of planning was the belief that copying Western urban form would lead to "modernization," but the end result was the growth of dual cities in semicolonized countries similar to those that developed in colonized cities. Indeed, the internal structure of most Middle Eastern cities can still be traced back to colonial practice.

The Transitional Period. The term "transitional period" underscores the uncertain or undefined role that urban planning assumed in the Middle East during this politically active period (1945–1972). Since most of the countries in this region had either just become politically independent or were in the process of becoming so, urban planning played a less important role, compared to existing political struggles and social movements.

The immediate postcolonial period witnessed a spontaneous population movement within some major Middle Eastern cities. In particular, the space formerly occupied by Europeans was taken over by local residents. In some countries, such as Morocco and Tunisia, this transition occurred in a peaceful and orderly fashion: the indigenous elite moved in to occupy the old European quarters. In a few countries, most notably Algeria, on the other hand, the rapid exodus of foreign settlers resulted in more diverse economic classes taking over the quarters formerly occupied by colonialists. Notwithstanding this, most Middle Eastern cities maintained their dual-sector or segregated character.

Urban planning was used to solve urban problems as they developed. The major concerns for urban planners were to provide housing for new immigrants from rural areas and to bridge the gap between the former European and traditional quarters. During this period, urban planning was also used as an appeasement tool. To consolidate power, new rulers provided various social groups with land, housing, and urban amenities in return for their political support.

In Israel in the 1950s, temporary housing was provided for immigrants arriving from postwar Europe and for Middle Eastern Jews from the adjacent countries. Immigrants were later settled in new urban neighborhoods and in newly established development towns in less populated areas of the country.

Urban planning began to develop in a new direction, emphasizing company-town building, master plan technique, and economic development. This development was particularly rapid in the Persian Gulf states of Iran, Iraq, Saudi Arabia, Kuwait, United Arab Emirates (U.A.E.), and Qatar where oil was increasingly discovered. The growth of oil revenue led governments to devise five-year economic development plans or to invest in industrial projects implemented in urban centers. This had a major impact on the development of urban planning into an integrated physical-economic approach.

American and British oil companies established company towns for their engineers and workers. The Arabian-American Oil Company (ARAMCO), using Western planners and engineers, laid out company towns such as Dhahran and Abqaiq using a system of blocks with a gridiron pattern. Similarly in Iran, British planners established the city of Abadan, modeled on the landscape of suburban England.

Middle Eastern countries depended on the West for qualified planners and consultants to carry out urban planning. Consequently, a technique of planning common in the West at that time—known as the master plan—was imported to the Middle East

and soon became ubiquitous throughout the region. Most plans were end-state master plans, in that the ultimate state of what the city would look like in the future was already predetermined. Most of the plans were also unclear about the process of city planning or procedures for implementation. Additionally, the plans were usually static and design-oriented with little consideration for the social and economic needs of the majority.

Very few master plans were actually implemented for numerous reasons, including a lack of legislative machinery in many cities and the archaic system of building control inherited from the colonial period. When specific laws existed, they were ignored. Master plans were also often inimical to the aspirations of the decision makers. When the local elite moved into the European city, they stood to lose if the new master plans were rigorously implemented. These problems notwithstanding, urban planning in this period experienced a positive development, namely, the attempt to incorporate economic considerations into the largely physical master plans.

The Oil-Boom Era. After the 1970s, the role of urban planning underwent a rapid transformation in the Middle East, particularly in the so-called oil-producing countries. With the rise in oil revenues, governments embarked on a variety of grandiose urban-based projects and the building of new towns. The major issue was the idea of comprehensive planning. Before this time, national planning was considered limited as it did not include the private sector and ignored spatial development concerns.

There were primarily three major reasons for building new towns in the 1970s. The first was to relieve the population pressures on the major cities by drawing migrants away from already overcrowded cities and/or accommodating the increasing population, as in the new towns that were built around Cairo, Ankara, Istanbul, and Tehran. New towns were also built to act as counterweights to the primary cities of the region. For example, Umm Said in Qatar, Karaj City in Iran, and Sadat City in Egypt were built and expanded to act as counterbalances to Doha, Tehran, and Cairo, respectively.

The second reason for building new towns was to accommodate the growing population of industrial workers and to facilitate industrialization. The towns of Sidi Ammar (Algeria), Jabal Ali (UAE), Jubail (Saudi Arabia), and Fulad Shahr (Iran) are examples of towns centered around a few heavy industrial plants. New towns were also built as military bases throughout the region.

The planning of these new towns, especially those in oil rich countries, has been done by Western firms. Although there has been an effort to incorporate aspects of indigenous culture into the design of these towns, such efforts have not been fully successful, and it is easy to see the influence of Western planning in their design. Most of these towns have made use of zoning to isolate human activities, as opposed to the mixed-use tradition in the region, and their layouts are designed for the use of the automobile.

With the economic growth of the Persian Gulf countries, because of oil wealth, the rejection of end-state master plans soon became common all over the Middle East. There was a common concern that the new master plans give more consideration to social and economic factors. In addition, these plans were integrated into broader regional and national planning strategies. Examples can be seen in the reorganization of countries such as Saudi Arabia, Morocco, Egypt, and Iran into planning regions based on large urban centers.

The new dynamic style of planning is seen in the use of Integrated Urban Development Projects (IUDPs) among local planners and planning consultants. The emphasis of IUDPs is on the sectoral and the spatial integration of projects, operating alongside, although often effectively replacing, comprehensive master planning. The five elements of IUDPs as put forward by planning consultants Miles and Arthur are ". . . a structure plan, a group of related, time-bound action programs and projects, the financial management plan for the executing agencies, the institutional development plans (including staff training) for these agencies, and specific cost-recovery plans associated with the action projects."

For example the Integrated Capital Development Plan (ICDP) for Baghdad consisted of three integrated plans for central Iraq, greater Baghdad, and Baghdad the city. Three models—urban corridors, growth poles, and dispersed settlements—were used to develop comprehensive alternative strategies based on future scenarios. After evaluating the scenarios, a hybrid of all three models applicable to Iraq's needs was used.

Unfortunately, while the focus of making plans had changed, the tools for implementing them still remained inadequate in most Middle Eastern countries because of a lack of cooperation among decision makers, a lack of enforcement legislation, and the conflict between the beautification and modernization of the city and the meeting of basic needs of the inhabitants. Although not at a standstill, urban planning is still grappling with numerous problems in the Middle East.

A major issue urban planning is facing is how to allocate resources between immigrants and the native population. These immigrants, often from other Middle Eastern countries, are not granted citizenship or the right to own property, placing a heavy burden on the rental markets. In addition, a new form of segregation is taking place in these oil-rich countries. Housing enclaves are planned so as to minimize contact between immigrants and the indigenous population. In the new towns of Jubail (Saudi Arabia) and Umm Said (Qatar), dormitory-style housing for single expatriate workers secludes them from the local population.

Perhaps the most important issue is rapid population growth and urbanization. At approximately 3 percent per annum, the region's population growth rate is higher than the figure for any world region with the exception of subsaharan Africa. The urbanization rate, at over 4.5 percent for most countries in the Middle East, is also among the fastest in the developing world. Most large cities of the region suffer from overcrowding; squatter settlements; housing shortage; poverty; unemployment; lack of adequate urban infrastructure, services and amenities; and increasing environmental decadence, including sometimes unbearable pollution. These and other so-called urban problems are placing increasing stress on the budgets, resources, and planning capacities of Middle Eastern governments, forcing planners and policy makers increasingly to seek new ways of managing urban growth. In fact, this has often led to planning being used as a tool to anticipate future problems and manage current ones, rather than solving them. A more preventive approach to urban planning seems to be taking root in place of the existing curative approach.

[*See also:* Architecture; Colonialism]

BIBLIOGRAPHY

ABU-LUGHOD, JANET L. "Moroccan Urbanization: Some New Questions." In *Development of Urban Systems in Africa*, ed. by R. A. Obudho and Salah El-Shakhs. New York, 1979.

AMIRAHMADI, HOOSHANG. "Regional Planning in Iran: A Survey of Problems and Policies." *Journal of Developing Areas.* 20, no. 4 (1987): 501–530.

———. *Revolution and Economic Transition: The Iranian Experience.* Albany, New York, 1990.

AMIRAHMADI, HOOSHANG, and SALAH S. EL-SHAKHS, eds. *Urban Development in the Muslim World.* New Brunswick, N.J., 1993.

BRANCH, MELVILLE C. *Continuous City Planning: Integrating Municipal Management and City Planning.* New York, 1981.

BROWN, KENNETH, MICHELE JOLE, PETER SLUGLETT, and SAMI ZUBAIDA, eds. *Middle Eastern Cities in Comparative Perspective.* London, 1986.

DENITHER, JEAN. "Evolution of Concepts of Housing, Urbanism and Country Planning in a Developing Country: Morocco, 1900–1972." In *From Madina to Metropolis: Heritage and Change in the Near Eastern City*, ed. by L. Carl Brown. Princeton, N.J., 1973.

ZAIM, SABAHADDIN. "Urbanization Trends in Turkey." In *The Middle East City: Ancient Traditions Confront a Modern World*, ed. by Abdulaziz Y. Saqqaf. New York, 1987.

Hooshang Amirahmadi

Urf

Arabic term for tribal or customary law.

Urf can be elaborate and codified, but it is usually unwritten and local, as opposed to codes such as *Shariʿa* (Islamic law), which are broader in application and usually written. "Urf" originally referred to the customary practices of Mecca and its environs but later came to refer to any system of local practices in any part of the Islamic world.

Laurence Michalak

Urwa al-Wuthqa, al-

Anti-British Muslim newspaper.

Edited from Paris by Jamal al-Din al-AFGHANI and Muhammad ABDUH, *al-Urwa al-Wuthqa* was published between March and October 1884. The title, meaning "the firmest bond," alludes to the Qurʾan; it had been used by Afghani in 1883 to refer to the pan-Islamic caliphate of the Ottoman sultan. After eighteen issues had appeared in 1884, the paper suddenly ceased publication, probably owing to lack of funds. (The closing is usually atributed to the British banning the paper from entering India and Egypt, but since it was distributed free throughout the Muslim world, this measure should not have stopped it.) The financing of *al-Urwa al-Wuthqa* is unclear, although documents suggest that a Tunisian general, probably Wilfrid Blunt, and possibly the former Egyptian Khedive Ismaʿil were involved. Subsidization afforded wide distribution, which helped to enhance the reputation of the paper and its editors.

Most of the political articles in the paper championed the struggle against British imperialism in Muslim lands. The more theoretical articles were mainly devoted to an activist reinterpretation of Islamic ideas and to a call for unity among Muslims. *Al-Urwa al-Wuthqa*, which contributed to the fame of its editors in the Muslim world, was the first forum in which Afghani stressed Muslim unity, or pan-Islam, the ideology with which he is most associated.

Nikki Keddie

Uşaklığıl, Halit Ziya   [c. 1866–1945]

Turkish novelist, journalist, and poet.

Uşaklığıl was born in Istanbul, the son of a businessman from a prestigious İzmir family. When he was fourteen years old, the family returned to İzmir, where in 1884 he published the city's first daily newspaper, *Nevruz*. He started up other İzmir newspapers while working in Istanbul as a French teacher and bank employee. In the 1890s, he became active in the Servet-i Fünun (Wealth of Knowledge) literary movement and began writing novels. In 1909, he became a professor of literary history and aesthetics at Istanbul University.

Uşaklığıl is considered a top Turkish novelist who bridged the nineteenth-century Tanzimat (reform) and twentieth-century republican periods, combining the complex storylines and heightened rhetoric of the former period with the cosmopolitan tastes and psychological realism of the later one. In the 1920s, he turned from novels to other forms, particularly short stories, and published about two hundred. He also published poetry, several plays, literary studies, and memoirs.

BIBLIOGRAPHY

MITLER, LOUIS. *Ottoman Turkish Writers*. New York, 1988.

Elizabeth Thompson

Üsküdar

The oldest and largest district of Asian Istanbul.

Situated across the Bosporus from the walled city of Constantinople, Üsküdar was called Chrysopolis in ancient times and Scutari in the Byzantine era. In the period of Ottoman rule, Üsküdar became more integrated into the life of the capital city, as it became the center of several dervish orders and TEKKES, military barracks, and, in the nineteenth century, textile and other factories. In the 1860s, it was formally incorporated into the municipal government of Constantinople (now Istanbul). It was in Üsküdar that Florence Nightingale set up her famed hospital during the Crimean War (1853–1856). And in the late nineteenth century, Russian Turks established the first center of Turkic studies in the empire in an Üsküdar *tekke*. The district, known for its fine gardens, in recent years has become a large residential quarter of the city with a population over 200,000.

BIBLIOGRAPHY

Encyclopedia of Islam, vol. 4. 1934.

SHAW, STANFORD J., and EZEL KURAL SHAW. *History of the Ottoman Empire and Modern Turkey,* vol. 2. Cambridge, U.K., 1977.

Elizabeth Thompson

Ussishkin, Menahem   [1863–1941]

Pioneer Zionist.

Menahem Ussishkin studied engineering in Moscow, where he was raised, and died in Palestine. As a member of Hibbat Zion, Ussishkin recommended the creation of a Zionist Jewish educational system in the Diaspora. After meeting Theodor Herzl, president of the World Zionist Organization (WZO), he was willing to urge affiliation with it but opposed Herzl's political Zionism. He was active in Hebrew educational work in Russia, encouraged Jewish settlement activity in Palestine through his leadership of the Odessa Committee, led the WZO's Zionist Commission in 1919 after Chaim Weizmann left Palestine, and directed the Jewish National Fund until his death.

BIBLIOGRAPHY

LUZ, EHUD. *Parallels Meet Religion and Nationalism in the Early Zionist Movement (1882–1904).* Philadelphia, 1988.

Donna Robinson Divine

USSR

See Russia and the Middle East

Ustadh

Title signifying a teacher or master.

Ustadh (also Ostad) is principally an academic title, but it is also a common form of address for intellectuals or educated people, such as lawyers, journalists, officials, and writers.

Marilyn Higbee

Usuli

Philosophy of Islamic law.

The Usuli school of Shi'a jurisprudence, developed in contrast to the AKHBARI (traditionalist) school, argues for the primacy of the *ulama* (Islamic clergy) as interpreters of Islamic law and prophetic and imami traditions. The Usulis favor the legitimacy of reasoning (*aql*) and interpretation of traditions of the Prophet and the imams (*ijtihad*) as sources for the derivation of Islamic law. Thus, they allow for the emulation of prominent Shi'a *ulama* by the believers, since they themselves are incapable of interpreting the Qur'an, or the teachings of the Prophet and the imams. In addition, the Usulis believe in critical readings of the contents of major Shi'a compilations of Prophetic and imami traditions. They also prohibit the emulation of past masters of religion, so that the centrality of living *ulama* as interpreters of Shi'a jurisprudence is preserved. Rivalry between the two schools heightened in the Safavid period, with the Usulis emerging as the ultimate victors by the eighteenth century.

Shi'a *ulama* were able to play a prominent role in the constitutional movement of Iran, from 1905 to 1911, drawing on elements of Usuli thought to justify both the ratification of the constitution, as well as the participation of clergymen in political affairs.

BIBLIOGRAPHY

ENAYAT, HAMID. *Modern Islamic Political Thought.* Austin, Tex., 1982.

HAIRI, ABDOLHADI. *Shi'ism and Constitutionalism in Iran.* Leiden, Neth., 1977.

Neguin Yavari

Utayba Tribe

The most powerful tribe in central Arabia.

The Utayba (also Otayba) were wealthy in camels and horses, which were sold on the international market, and strong in arms. In nobility, the Utayba were second only to the Anaza tribe of the Al Sa'ud, and they ranged from the eastern Hijaz to central Najd. In the nineteenth century, there were settled villages of Utayba as well as large, fully nomadic confederations. The Utayba joined the Ikhwan in the early years of the twentieth century, with some sections of the tribe settling in Artawiya and Ghatghat, the most fervent of the Muwahhidun religious settlements. The religious zealot who led the attempt to seize the Grand mosque at Mecca in 1979 was a member of the Utayba.

Eleanor Abdella Doumato

Utaybi, Juhaiman al-   [c.1940–1980]

Saudi ideologue and leader of the Ka'ba insurrection, 1979.

Utaybi was born in a bedouin settlement at Qasim in central Saudi Arabia. It is unclear whether he received any formal education. Utaybi served in the National Guards for some eighteen years, and toward the end of this period studied at the Islamic University in Medina.

The year 1974 seems to have marked Utaybi's break with formal state institutions. The circumstances under which he left the National Guards are unclear; his departure from the university resulted from his disagreement with his teachers' applied interpretation of Islamic law in relation to the Saudi regime. He began a period of self-education and preaching, drawing a circle of followers. His first *risala* (treatise), *Al-imara wa al-bay'a wa al-ta'a* (Rulership, Allegiance, and Obedience), appeared in 1974. Utaybi was arrested with ninety-eight others in 1978; all were released without trial.

At least eleven risalas by Utaybi were printed between 1974 and 1979. His writings combined a strict application of the Wahhabi (MUWAHHIDUN) doctrine with widely accepted traditions having a messianic dimension. He accused the Saudi rulers of doctrinal deviation, greed, and corruption. He also accused the religious establishment of complicity and preached that it was the duty of Muslims to combat the evils of the regime.

Utaybi anticipated that the regime would pursue and persecute its puritan opponents, whose sole and ultimate refuge would be the Ka'ba (the holy shrine at Mecca). There, the mahdi's (the messiah's) appearance would be established, armed resistance would start, and the Muslims would be led to victories in the Arabian peninsula and beyond. On 22 November 1979, Utaybi led a heavily armed group, estimated at between five hundred and two thousand, who seized the Ka'ba. They were ousted two weeks later. Utaybi and sixty-two others were beheaded on 9 January 1980.

BIBLIOGRAPHY

BUCHAN, J. "The Return of the Ikhwan, 1979." *The House of Sa'ud*, ed. by David Holden and Richard Johns. London, 1981.

EzzelArab, Abdel Aziz. "Politics as Metaphysics? Juhayman al-'Utaybi and the Seizure of al-Ka'ba: The Significance of the Doctrine for Action." *JUSUR* 9 (1993).

Kechichian, Joseph. "Islamic Revivalism and Change in Saudi Arabia: Juhayman al-Utaybi's 'Letters' to the Saudi People." *Muslim World* 80, no. 1 (1990): 1–16.

Abdel Aziz EzzelArab

Uthman, Muhammad Ali   [?–1973]

North Yemen political leader.

Uthman was a traditional Shafi'i leader with much influence in the North Yemen countryside around the city of Ta'iz. A loyal republican, he was a member of the plural executive created just after the 1967 overthrow of the regime of Abdullah al-Sallal until he was assassinated in May 1973. Uthman's killing, the result of a local dispute, was attributed wrongly to leftist dissidents supported by the People's Democratic Republic of Yemen. This contributed to the rapid worsening of inter-Yemeni relations after the 1972 border war. A modern school in Ta'iz is named in his honor.

Robert D. Burrowes

Uthman, Uthman Ahmad   [1916–   ]

Egyptian civil engineer, construction magnate, and cabinet minister.

Born in Isma'ilia and educated at Cairo University, Uthman founded a civil engineering company soon after graduation instead of entering government service. But he quickly discovered that the booming oil industry in Saudi Arabia offered him better opportunities for advancement than did Egypt. His construction firm, Arab Contractors, founded in 1949, expanded until it was able to bid on multimillion dollar projects in the United Arab Emirates (then called Trucial Oman), Iraq, Kuwait, and Libya. Although his company was sequestered by Gamal Abdel Nasser in 1961, Uthman remained in control and played a major role in constructing the Aswan High Dam.

He became highly visible in Egyptian public life during the *infitah* policy of Anwar al-Sadat, building a new bridge across the Nile river and various traffic flyways in downtown Cairo. His firm also deepened the Suez Canal and built the Dhahran International Airport, the Kuwait Municipality, the Benghazi (Libya) sewer system, the Kirkuk (Iraq) feeder canal, and a first-class hotel in Khartoum (Sudan). He became minister for reconstruction in 1973, adding housing to his portfolio in 1974. His son married one of Sadat's daughters. During the Sadat era, Uthman accumulated power and wealth in ways that aroused widespread suspicion, in part by being both a minister who could issue tenders on contracts and a contractor who could bid on them. Under Husni Mubarak he remains powerful but has fewer chances to abuse his powers. He is a strong advocate of the work ethic and of free-enterprise capitalism.

BIBLIOGRAPHY

BAKER, RAYMOND WILLIAM. *Sadat and After: Struggle for Egypt's Political Soul*. Cambridge, Mass., 1990.
HEIKAL, MOHAMED. *Autumn of Fury: The Assassination of Sadat*. New York, 1983.

Arthur Goldschmidt, Jr.

Utub, al-

Ancestors of the ruling families of Bahrain and Kuwait.

The Utub is composed of Arab families and tribes that were said to have migrated from central Arabia, in the Najd area, to the north coast of the Persian/Arabian Gulf in the early part of the eighteenth century as a result of a major drought. While there is controversy about the origins of the name, the word derives from the Arabic root *ataba,* which means "to roam or to travel." The adjective is *utbi.* Both the Al Sabah of Kuwait, the al-Khalifa of Bahrain, and the al Thani of Qatar all derive from the Utub clan, which in turn comes from the Anaza tribal confederation of north-central Arabia.

BIBLIOGRAPHY

ABU-HAKIMA, AHMAD. *A Modern History of Kuwait*. London, 1983.

Emile A. Nakhleh

Uzbeks

Some 19.5 million Uzbeki speakers live in Central Asia

In the 1920s and 1930s, before the Soviet Union implemented language and nationalities policies, the Uzbek language, an eastern Turkic language of the Altaic family generally known as Turki (Chaghatai), was written in Arabic script and was the principal literary language for all Turkic-speaking central Asians. When they were forced to adopt Cyrillic script (i.e., the Russian and Slavic alphabet), Uzbeks and other central Asian Turks were denied easy access to their rich literary heritage, which dates to the fifteenth century.

Uzbeks practice Islam; they are Sunni Hanafi Muslims. Originally pastoral nomads, by the early part of the twentieth century they were predominantly sedentary subsistence farmers, herders, or inhabitants of small towns engaged in producing and marketing crafts. Until the mid-nineteenth century, the Uzbeks were politically the preeminent force in the region. From the 1860s to 1991, the Uzbeks and other central Asian Muslims suffered colonial occupation of their lands by czarist Russia and its successor, the Soviet Union. In the mid-1990s, Uzbeks constitute more than 70 percent of the population of the independent state of Uzbekistan; they are also one of the larger ethnic minority groups in neighboring Tajikistan and in the northern part of the Islamic State of Afghanistan.

BIBLIOGRAPHY

ALLWORTH, EDWARD A. *The Modern Uzbeks from the Fourteenth Century to the Present: A Cultural History*. Stamford, Conn., 1990.

M. Nazif Shahrani

Uzi

Lightweight submachine gun used by the Israeli military.

Also used by other armed forces and the police, the Uzi was invented by Israel Defense Forces' Major Uziel Gal, after whom it was named, following the first Arab-Israel War (1948–1949). It is manufactured in Israel and sold internationally.

BIBLIOGRAPHY

THOMPSON, JIM. *Machine Guns: A Pictorial, Tactical & Practical History*. Boulder, Colo., 1989.

Bryan Daves

V

Va'ad Le'umi

National council of the Jews of Eretz Yisrael (Palestine).

Va'ad Le'umi (VL) was the supreme executive authority and representative organ of the Palestinian Jewish community (*Yishuv*) between 1920 and 1948. Functioning much like a cabinet, each Va'ad Le'umi was composed of members of an Assefat ha-Nivharim (Elected Assembly), and its day-to-day operations were largely in the hands of a chairman and a smaller executive committee. The first Assefat ha-Nivharim, which convened in October 1920, consisted of 314 elected members and produced a VL of 36 members, from which an executive committee of 14 members was formed. The first VL was headed by a praesidium of Yizhak Ben-Zvi, Yaakov Thon, and David Yellin; after 1925, the leadership of the VL continued to alternate among these three local leaders and, for short periods, also involved Pinchas Rutenberg and David Remez.

For much of its existence, the VL found itself beset by organizational difficulties and problems in establishing its authority. There were frequent squabbles between the VL, the Palestine Zionist Executive, and the Jewish Agency Executive over their proper spheres of jurisdiction and divisions of labor. The lines of authority and responsibility were easily blurred between (a) promoting international Zionist efforts devoted to building the Jewish national home and (b) representing the (largely local) concerns of the Jews actually resident in Palestine, who also saw themselves as the embodiment and vanguard of world Zionism. Most matters of high policy were decided by Zionist leaders and organs in Palestine and abroad, while the VL was often left (sometimes resentful) to implement the details of policies determined elsewhere.

The VL was able to exercise its autonomy mainly in education and in local communal affairs. One of its main functions was to act as official representative for Palestine Jewry, a task that required internal consensus building and the integration into one political organization of the widely heterogeneous, highly politicized subcommunities that made up the Yishuv. The VL was often the public forum for debating the divergent viewpoints and conflicting interests of religious versus secular Jews; farmers and employers versus organized labor; and native versus newly arrived immigrant groups having differing traditions (e.g., Sephardim versus Ashkenazim). The Palestine Royal Commission Report (1937) credited the VL and its local educational system with counteracting these divisive forces by the forging of a "national self-consciousness of unusual intensity."

After May 14, 1948, the functions and departments of Va'ad Le'umi and those of certain departments of the Jewish Agency came under the authority of a Provisional State Council of the State of Israel.

BIBLIOGRAPHY

ATTIAS, MOSHE, ed. *Sefer ha-te'udot shel ha-Va'ad ha-Le'umi le-knesset Israel be-Eretz-Israel* (Book of Documents of the Va'ad Le'umi), 2nd enl. ed. Jerusalem, 1963.

BURSTEIN, MOSHE. *Self-Government of the Jews in Palestine since 1900.* Tel Aviv, 1934.

CAPLAN, NEIL. *Palestine Jewry and the Arab Question, 1917–1925.* London, 1978.

Neil Caplan

Vaka-i Hayriye

Turkish for "the beneficial event"; the end of the Janissary Corps in 1826.

The term *Vaka-i Hayriye* has been commonly used by Ottoman and Turkish historians to describe the government-ordered destruction of the Ottoman Empire's military unit called the janissaries (June 15, 1826). This momentous event resulted in considerable bloodshed (6,000 dead, according to the conservative estimate of Cevdet) and was received with dismay and mixed emotions by large segments of the populace. In an attempt to gain public approval, Mahmud II's regime, using the services of the *ulama* (body of Islamic scholars), presented the incident as unavoidable and necessary to protect the very survival of Islam and the Ottoman Empire.

Immediately following the destruction of the Janissary Corps, Mahmud II ordered the court chronicler (*vak'anüvis*), Mehmet Esad Efendi (c. 1789–1848), to record the official version of events. Esad's account, a book entitled *Üss-i Zafer* (The Foundation of Victory) was first printed in Istanbul in 1828, and a second edition was published in 1876. The book served as the main source for every other Ottoman account of this period and was also translated into French, Greek, and Russian.

BIBLIOGRAPHY

LEVY, AVIGDOR. "The Ottoman Ulama and the Military Reforms of Sultan Mahmud II." *Asian and African Studies* 7 (1971): 13–39.

Avigdor Levy

Valensi, Alfred [1878–1944]

Tunisian Zionist.

Valensi, a member of the Sephardic elite, was one of the founders and leaders of the Tunisian Zionist Federation. While still a law student in France, he became a disciple of Max NORDAU. Valensi was a contributor to major European journals.

A brilliant theoretician and organizer, he represented Tunisian Zionists at international gatherings in London and Carlsbad with his associate Rabbi Joseph Brami. In 1926, he settled in Paris, where he was later arrested and transported by the Nazis in 1944 to his death.

BIBLIOGRAPHY

STILLMAN, NORMAN A. *The Jews of Arab Lands in Modern Times.* Philadelphia, 1991.

Norman Stillman

Vali

Provincial governor in the Ottoman Empire.

The Ottomans used *vali*—from the Arabic word *wali,* meaning "protector" or "benefactor"—variously as a term of endearment for close relatives, in religion to denote a kind of saint, and, most commonly since the sixteenth century, in government for provincial governors. From the sixteenth through the eighteenth centuries, valis, who bore the title pasha (Turkish, paşa), gradually attained a great measure of autonomy with command of local armies and control of local revenues. With the nineteenth-century reforms, valis were increasingly brought under central control and, in cases like those of Cevdet Paşa and Midhat Paşa, became the principal agents of centralizing reforms.

BIBLIOGRAPHY

Encyclopaedia of Islam, vol. 4. 1934.

SHAW, STANFORD J., and EZEL KURAL SHAW. *History of the Ottoman Empire and Modern Turkey,* vol. 2. Cambridge, U.K., 1977.

Elizabeth Thompson

Van, Lake

Salt lake in eastern Turkey.

Lake Van is the largest lake in Turkey, some 5,600 feet (1,600 m) above sea level, with a surface area of 1,400 square miles (3,700 sq. km). Having no outlet, its waters evaporate and concentrate salts, including carbonates and sulphates of soda; the resulting blue-green color creates a startling, austere beauty. Lake Van is stocked with *darek,* a herring-like fish consumed locally.

BIBLIOGRAPHY

FISHER, SIDNEY N. *The Middle East.* New York, 1979.

John R. Clark

Vance, Cyrus [1917–]

American lawyer and government official.

Vance, born in Clarksburg, West Virginia, received a bachelor of arts from Yale University in 1939 and a law degree in 1942. After practicing law, he served in a number of government positions, including general counsel for the Department of Defense (1961–1962), secretary of the army (1962–1963), deputy secretary of defense (1964–1967), and secretary of state (1977–1980). In 1967, as President Lyndon Johnson's special representative on Cyprus, Vance helped to ensure that Greece and Turkey would not be drawn into war by their conflicting claims to the island. His most prominent role in the Middle East was as secretary of state, when he was instrumental in orchestrating the CAMP DAVID ACCORDS. This required him to hold extensive consultations with Prime Minister Menachem Begin of Israel and President Anwar al-Sadat of Egypt. They led to talks with U.S. President Jimmy Carter at Camp David, Maryland, and an agreement signed by Israel and Egypt in September 1978. Vance resigned over Carter's 1980 decision to forcibly rescue the hostages held in the U.S. embassy in Tehran.

BIBLIOGRAPHY

QUANDT, WILLIAM B. *Camp David: Peacemaking and Politics.* Washington, D.C., 1986

Daniel E. Spector

Vanunu Affair

A controversy over divulgence of Israeli nuclear information to a British newspaper.

In October 1986, Mordechai Vanunu, a former employee of the Dimona nuclear reactor in Israel, provided the *Sunday Times* of London with information and photographs of the plant, claiming Israel was producing nuclear arms and that it had stockpiled one to two hundred nuclear weapons. Israel denied the charges and stated its policy that it does not possess nuclear weapons and that it will not be the first Middle Eastern country to introduce nuclear arms in the region. Vanunu was captured in Italy by the Mossad and brought back to Israel, where he was tried in secret proceedings for treason and espionage against the state. Vanunu was widely portrayed in the Israeli press as a traitor and as a mentally deranged person. His prison sentence has at times included solitary confinement, and his cause has been taken up by human rights and disarmament groups.

BIBLIOGRAPHY

GAFFNEY, MARK. *Dimona, the Third Temple? The Story behind the Vanunu Revelation.* Brattleboro, Vt., 1989.
Israel's First Bomb Victim: The Case of Mordechai Vanunu. Nottingham, U.K., 1988.

Julie Zuckerman

Varlık Vergisi

Capital tax levied in Turkey during World War II.

Adopted in November 1942 to finance Turkey's emergency military expenditures during World War II, the Varlık Vergisi was heavily criticized as confiscatory and discriminatory. It was abolished in March 1944.

Justified as a social equalization measure against those who profiteered during the war, up to 75 percent of net profits were collected as tax from trade companies. Istanbul merchants and non-Muslims were taxed far more heavily than Muslims and farmers. The tax produced long-term political effects in the fear of government as a threat to private property and in highlighting the dangers of one-party rule.

BIBLIOGRAPHY

LEWIS, BERNARD. *The Emergence of Modern Turkey.* New York, 1969.

Elizabeth Thompson

Vatan

Turkish newspaper.

Vatan (Fatherland) was an Istanbul newspaper founded by Ahmet Emin Yalman in 1923. As a consequence of several articles defending freedom of the press and criticizing the promulgation of the Restoration of Law order, the paper was ordered closed on 12 August 1925.

BIBLIOGRAPHY

SHAW, STANFORD, and EZEL KURAL SHAW. *History of the Ottoman Empire and Modern Turkey.* Vol. 2, *Reform, Revolution, and Republic: The Rise of Modern Turkey, 1808–1975.* Cambridge, U.K., 1977.

David Waldner

Vatican and the Middle East

The Roman Catholic church struggles to maintain its presence in the Middle East.

The presence of the Roman Catholic church in the Middle East goes back to the Roman and Byzantine empires, to the Crusades, and to European imperialism and colonialism. Following the Second Vatican Council (1962–1965), Vatican diplomacy in the Middle East focused on three goals: preserving Christianity and a Christian presence in what Christians term the Holy Land, fostering peace with justice between Israel and the Palestinians, and maintaining Lebanon as an example of coexistence between Christians and Muslims.

The Vatican is facing the problem of demographic changes, especially in Jerusalem and the West Bank, where Christian Arabs are leaving because of their minority status, the resurgence of Islamic and Jewish fundamentalisms, and the unstable economic and political situation. The relationship between the Vatican and Israel can be defined as a mixture of theological prejudice and political pragmatism. In recent years, however, the Holy See has established diplomatic relations with Israel (December 1993) and with the Kingdom of Jordan (April 1994) despite the fact that there are still no resolutions to the Palestinian question and the status of Jerusalem and none are expected soon.

The Lebanese Civil War (1975–1989) was a major challenge to the papacy. Several mediation missions were dispatched by both Pope Paul VI and Pope John Paul II, and in 1995 the latter convened in Rome a synod of Roman Catholic bishops, with Muslim and Orthodox Christian observers, for the express purpose of addressing the Lebanese situation. It is clear that if Lebanon were to fail as an example of coexistence, the Vatican's position in the region would be weakened.

BIBLIOGRAPHY

IRANI, GEORGE E. *The Papacy and the Middle East.* South Bend, Ind., 1989.

George E. Irani

Vatican Hospice in East Jerusalem. (Mia Bloom)

Vazhapetian, Nerses [1837–1884]

Armenian patriarch of Istanbul, 1873–1884.

Born in Istanbul, Nerses Vazhapetian spent his entire life in or near the Ottoman capital. Although deprived of a formal education at the age of fifteen after the death of his father, Vazhapetian became a teacher and joined the clergy of the Armenian Apostolic Church. Anointed a celibate priest in 1858, he was a bishop by 1862. Active in the administrative affairs of the ARMENIAN MILLET, Vazhapetian had a hand in drafting the so-called Armenian national constitution by which the Armenian Church and *millet* were regulated in the Ottoman Empire. In 1873, at age thirty-seven, he was elected Armenian partiarch of Istanbul.

The Russo–Ottoman War of 1877–1878, partly waged over the Armenian-populated provinces of eastern Anatolia, brought the issue of the Armenians to the fore of the diplomatic contest for influence in the Ottoman Empire. When the extent of the Kurdish predations over the Armenian communities became known, Vazhapetian, who had issued an encyclical supporting the Ottoman war effort, was authorized by the Armenian national assembly to appeal to Grand Duke Nicholas at San Stefano for consideration of local self-government in the areas of Armenian concentration. In the formal Treaty of SAN STEFANO, signed on March 3, 1878, by the Ottomans and Russians, Article 16 provided for reforms and security under Russian trusteeship in the so-called Armenian provinces.

While Russian withdrawal from these areas was conditional on implementation of the reforms, the

Congress of Berlin revised the terms of the treaty. The Armenian delegation sent by Vazhapetian to Berlin received no hearing, and Article 61 of the Treaty of Berlin, signed July 13, 1878, provided only for reforms as those territories were returned to the Ottomans. Still Armenians expected an international treaty to prove more binding on the Ottomans than mere promises. The failure of the European powers to require Sultan Abdülhamit II to proceed with reforms became the source of disillusionment. By the time of Vazhapetian's death in Istanbul, small groups of provincial Armenians had began to resort to self-defense in the face of continued insecurity in what became known as the Armenian Revolutionary Movement.

BIBLIOGRAPHY

NALBANDIAN, LOUISE. *The Armenian Revolutionary Movement*. Berkeley, Calif., 1963.
WALKER, CHRISTOPHER J. *Armenia: The Survival of a Nation*. New York, 1980.

Rouben P. Adalian

Vazir Afkham, Soltan Ali Khan
[1867–1918]

Iranian courtier of the Qajar period.

Soltan Ali Khan was in the service of Mozaffar al-Din Qajar from the time the latter became crown prince in Tabriz. Upon the shah's ascension to power, Soltan Ali Khan was first appointed head of the Royal Correspondence Office and then minister of revenues, and in 1901 he received the title Vazir Afkham. In 1907, he was made prime minister and minister of interior under Mohammad Ali Qajar and headed the first Iranian cabinet after the Constitutional Revolution. Opposed by the Constitutionalists, he was deposed in 1909 and died in 1918, the same year his oldest son was killed in a romantic feud.

Neguin Yavari

Vaziri, Qamar al-Moluk   [1905–1959]

Considered the first professional female singer in Iran.

Qamar al-Moluk Vaziri was born to a middle-class family in the city of Kashan, Iran, in 1905. Raised by her grandmother, a religiously inclined woman who performed as a eulogist in women's gatherings, Qamar accompanied her to these events, where she herself also performed eulogies. She later studied under masters of Persian classical music and acquired

fame as a singer. Numerous recordings were made of her songs. The singer died in 1959 from heart disease and was buried in Dhahir al-Dowleh cemetery in northern Tehran.

Parvaneh Pourshariati

Vecihi   [1869–1904]

Ottoman Turkish novelist.

The son of a member of the council of state, Vecihi was born in Istanbul and educated in the army school of engineering. Beginning in 1894, his novels were serialized in the newspaper *İkdam*, and he achieved commercial success at the age of twenty-six with his novel *Mehcure* (The Abandoned Girl). By the age of twenty-nine, he had published thirteen books, typically dealing with orphans, cruel stepmothers, and unrequited love. Vecihi suffered from alcoholism; his condition was not helped by his publishers' practice of paying him with drink. He died in his thirties in an alcoholic coma.

BIBLIOGRAPHY

MITLER, LOUIS. *Ottoman Turkish Writers: A Bibliographical Dictionary of Significant Figures in Pre-Republican Turkish Literature*. New York, 1988.

David Waldner

Velayat-e Faqih

Theory of governance in Shi'a Islam.

From the Arabic term for "the authority, or governance, of the jurist," this doctrine was associated particularly with Ayatollah Khomeini. It holds that those scholars of Shi'a Islam most qualified in terms of piety and erudition are to exercise the governmental functions of the Twelfth Imam during his major occultation (absence from the terrestrial plane), which began in 939 C.E. and still continues. Even before the occultation, the imams would delegate certain of their functions, particularly in the judicial sphere, to qualified members of the Shi'a Islam community as a matter of practical necessity. It was therefore natural that after the beginning of the occultation, other executive functions of the imam should also be assigned to the Shi'a jurists, including, for example, the collection and disbursement of religiously mandated taxes (*zakat* and *khoms*) but not the waging of offensive jihad (holy war) or (according to some jurists) the holding of Friday prayers. This led to the crystallization of the theory of the *niyabat-e amma* (general deputyship) of the jurists, a process that was complete by the middle of the sixteenth century. Already in the Safavid period the general deputyship was occasionally interpreted to include all the prerogatives of rule that had in principle belonged to the imams, but no special emphasis was placed on this. Similarly, although velayat-e faqih began to be discussed as a distinct legal topic in the nineteenth century, against a background of enhanced social authority for the Shi'a jurists, no concrete political conclusions were drawn from the concept.

It was left to Ayatollah Khomeini of Iran to claim, in typically radical and comprehensive fashion, the right or even duty of the leading Shi'a scholars to rule. He did this in his first published work (*Kashf al-Asrar*, 1944), then in a technical work on Shi'a jurisprudence, and most fully and importantly, in a series of lectures delivered in 1970 during his exile in Iraq that were later published under the title *Hokumat-e Eslami* (Islamic Government).

Khomeini's arguments in the lectures are both scriptural and rational, traditional and revolutionary. Asserting that Islamic government differs from all other forms of rule by being based on the implementation of divine law, Khomeini attributes the disarray of the Islamic world in general and Iran in particular to the prevalence of arbitrary rule and its concomitant man-made laws. He then demonstrates the centrality of government to the Islamic worldview and ridicules the opinion that the validity of the laws contained in the Qur'an (the holy book of Islam) and other sources should have been restricted to the first few centuries of the Islamic era. Next he reviews in great detail the Qur'anic verses and traditions of the Prophet Muhammad and the imams, which, in his estimation, support the thesis of velayat-e faqih; cites the opinions of previous, mostly recent, Shi'a scholars on the subject; and reaches the conclusion that "the same governance that was exercised by the Most Noble Messenger and by the Imams is also the prerogative of the jurists."

In the last of the lectures, Khomeini laments the prevalence of the "pseudo-saintly" in the religious institution, and it was indeed several years before a sizable number of Khomeini's colleagues came to accept his thesis. It was the repressive policies of the shah of Iran, Mohammad Reza Pahlavi (ruled 1941–1979), that impelled the religious scholars to conceive of broad and radical aims and enabled them to gain a favorable response from many of the Iranian people. Nonetheless, although by the autumn of 1978 a clear majority of the Iranian people had come to favor the institution of an Islamic government under the leadership of Khomeini, it cannot be said

that velayat-e faqih was a prominent slogan of the Iranian Revolution; Khomeini himself made no mention of it in the proclamations he issued during the revolution.

Not until the constitution of the Islamic Republic of Iran was elaborated by the Assembly of Experts that convened in the fall of 1979 did velayat-e faqih emerge as the pillar of the new order. It was enshrined in the preamble to the constitution, in Article Five ("During the Occultation of the Lord of the Age [that is, the Hidden Imam], the governance and leadership of the nation devolve upon the pious and just jurist who is acquainted with the circumstances of his age; courageous, resourceful, and possessed of administrative ability; and recognized and accepted as leader by the majority of the people") and in Articles 107 to 112, which specify the procedure for selecting the leader and list his constitutional functions.

Khomeini's own view was that these provisions did not do justice to velayat-e faqih, and in February 1988 he propounded the theory of *velayat-e motlaqa-ye faqih* ("the absolute authority of the jurist"). He declared obedience to the ruling jurist to be as incumbent on the believer as the performance of prayer, and his powers to extend even to the temporary suspension of such essential rites of Islam as the hajj (pilgrimage to Mecca). Although this formulation of the theory might appear to be an ideal prescription for theocratic absolutism, Khomeini was, in fact, seeking not to extend his control of Iranian affairs (which in any event was far less absolute than is often supposed) but to provide theoretical justification for government attempts to break the stalemate on controversial items of social and economic legislation.

The actual implementation of velayat-e faqih was, moreover, destined to change in a quite different direction. When Ayatollah Montazeri was compelled in March 1989 to resign from the successorship to Khomeini, none of the other senior religious scholars seemed qualified for the position. When Khomeini died on June 4 of the same year, it was therefore Hojjat al-Islam Khamene'i—a relatively junior figure in the religious hierarchy, despite his political prominence—who was chosen as leader of the Islamic Republic. This necessitated the modification of Article 109 of the constitution to remove scholarly seniority from the qualifications of the leader, a change that was approved in a referendum held in August 1989. It has been credibly argued that the resulting disjunction of political leadership from seniority in the learned hierarchy of Iranian Shi'ism effectively brings the implementation of velayat-e faqih to an end. If this be the case, velayat-e faqih must be designated as a theory that was, to a degree, workable only because of the unique qualities and appeal of Khomeini, and that falls short of being a permanent solution to the problem of governance in a Shi'a Muslim society.

BIBLIOGRAPHY

IMAM KHOMEINI. *Islam and Revolution.* Tr. by Hamid Algar. Berkeley, Calif., 1981.
SACHEDINA, ABDULAZIZ ABDULHUSSEIN. *The Just Ruler in Shi'ite Islam.* Oxford, 1988.

Hamid Algar

Venizélos, Eleuthérios   [1864–1936]

Greek statesman and prime minister.

Born in the village of Mournies on the island of Crete, Venizélos studied law and began his political career by taking part, from 1897 to 1910, in the struggle to unite Ottoman-ruled Crete with Greece. In 1910, he became prime minister for the first time, and during his first term he created a liberal political party, introduced a series of policies that modernized the economy, and democratized Greek political life. He also led Greece into the 1912/13 Balkan Wars, which resulted in considerable territorial gains for Greece. Venizélos was forced to resign in 1915 because his intention of involving Greece in World War I was opposed by King Constantine. Their conflict shaped Greek politics, which, until World War II, was dominated by the Venizélists and the royalists. (Venizélos was prime minister four more times: 1917–1920, 1924, 1928–1932, and 1933.)

Venizélos established his reputation as an internationally respected statesman after leading the Greek delegation at the Paris Peace Conference and achieving favorable settlements for Greece, which, however, were squandered when Greece was defeated in the war with Turkey (1922). Although out of the country in self-imposed exile following his electoral defeat in 1920, Venizélos agreed to represent Greece at the signing of the Treaty of LAUSANNE (1923), where he is generally considered to have been able to mitigate the consequences of Greece's defeat.

BIBLIOGRAPHY

ALASTOS, DOROS. *Venizelos: Patriot, Statesman, Revolutionary.* London, 1942.
MAKRAKI, LILI. *Eleftherios Venizelos, 1864–1910.* Athens, 1992. In Greek.

Alexander Kitroeff

Versailles, Treaty of

Treaty ending World War I; it established the mandate system for the governance and eventual independence of the Central powers' former colonies.

The armistices of October and November 1918 ending hostilities in World War I were followed by the Conference of Paris at which World War I victors and associated powers determined the terms for dealing with Germany and her allies during the war. The conference, which officially began on January 18, 1919, resulted in five treaties. The Treaty of Versailles, signed on June 28 at Versailles, France, and ratified on January 20, 1920, addressed the terms of peace with Germany. The treaties of SÈVRES, Neuilly, St. Germain, and Trianon dealt with the Ottoman Empire, Bulgaria, Austria, and Hungary respectively. Besides setting forth the terms for dealing with Germany after World War I, the Treaty of Versailles established the League of Nations and the mandate system for governing territories surrendered by Germany. This treaty included the Covenant of the League of Nations as Part I, with Article 22 giving the League the power to supervise mandated territories consisting of former German colonies. The other treaties included the covenant in their texts.

The armistice with Germany and the Conference of Paris were both predicated on U.S. President Woodrow Wilson's Fourteen Points for peace enunciated in his address to Congress on January 8, 1918. In addition to his vision of a League of Nations, these included an adjustment of all colonial claims giving equal weight to the interests of colonial populations and to those of countries with colonial claims. This led many to believe that the peace conference would lead to the independence of the Arab portions of the Ottoman Empire. Based on this, Prince Faisal I ibn Husayn arrived in Paris in January 1919 as head of the Hijaz delegation and with the objective of securing an independent Arab state. At first the French opposed recognition of the Hijaz delegation based on the fact that the Hijaz was not one of the Allied belligerent states. The British, however, intervened, and the Hijaz delegation was recognized. On January 29 Faisal submitted a statement to the conference defining Arab claims. He requested recognition as "independent sovereign peoples" for those Arab-speaking peoples of Asia from the Alexandretta–Diyarbekır line south to the Indian Ocean. Essentially, this included what is now Syria, Lebanon, Israel, Jordan, and Iraq. Faisal exempted the Hijaz as already independent, as well as British Aden. The prince addressed the conference on February 6, stressing the principle of the consent of the governed. He then proposed a commission to visit Syria and Palestine and ascertain the wishes of the populace. The French were not inclined to support this, but pressure by Wilson resulted, on March 25, in the approval of a commission, later known as the KING–CRANE COMMISSION.

Despite the sincere desires of Wilson to forge a new world in which all peoples would be the ultimate determiners of their national destinies and the eloquent arguments of Faisal and others on behalf of the Arabs, the Conference of Paris yielded to the imperial interests of Britain and France and, to a lesser extent, to those of Italy and Japan. The colonial territories of Germany and the Arab portions of the Ottoman Empire were assigned to members of the League of Nations under the mandate system established in the covenant. In the case of the Middle East, agreements made during World War I played a large role in distribution of mandates. The secret Anglo–Franco–Russian agreement of May 16, 1916, commonly known as the SYKES–PICOT AGREEMENT, divided the Arab dominions of the Ottoman Empire between Britain and France. Britain received the areas that are now Iraq, Jordan, and Israel; France got what is now Syria and Lebanon. The BALFOUR DECLARATION of November 2, 1917, also played a role in the disposition of Arab territories by the Conference of Paris. This was a letter from Lord Balfour, British foreign secretary, to Lord (Edmond de) Rothschild, a prominent British Zionist, that supported the establishment of a national home for the Jewish people in Palestine. These two documents, more than anything else, shaped the fate of the Middle East in the post–World War I era. The SAN REMO CONFERENCE of April 1920 awarded Syria, including Lebanon, as a Class A mandate to France; Iraq and Palestine, including Transjordan, became Class A mandates under British supervision. The mandate for Palestine endorsed the provisions of the Balfour Declaration. In 1921 Britain separated Transjordan from Palestine, exempting it from the provisions of the Balfour Declaration. As Class A mandates, all three were to be given independence when it was determined that they were able to stand on their own. In the case of Iraq and Transjordan, Arab dignitaries were given royal status in preparation for the eventual independence of these areas. Prince Faisal became the king of Iraq, and Prince Abdullah ibn Husayn became the emir of Transjordan. The League of Nations confirmed these mandates in 1922, some of which outlived the international organization under which they were formed. The first mandate to obtain independence was Iraq, in 1932, followed by Syria and Lebanon in 1941. Transjordan, now Jordan, gained its independence in 1946. Palestine, much of which is now Israel, gained independence in 1948.

BIBLIOGRAPHY

ANTONIUS, GEORGE. *The Arab Awakening: The Story of the Arab National Movement.* New York, 1946.
SONTAG, RAYMOND J. *A Broken World, 1919–1939.* New York, 1971.

Daniel E. Spector

Via Dolorosa

A Jerusalem street of religious significance to Christians.

Located in Jerusalem, the Via Dolorosa, or Street of Sorrows, is believed to be the route taken by Jesus as he carried his cross on the way to his crucifixion. It is today one of the holiest spots of Christian worship; pilgrims walk the Via Dolorosa and observe the fourteen stations of the cross (the stages of Christ's Passion), the last of which are located in the Church of the Holy Sepulchre.

BIBLIOGRAPHY

LEV, MARTIN. *A Traveler's Key to Jerusalem.* New York, 1989.

Zachary Karabell

Victoria College

Private English secondary boys' school in Alexandria, Egypt.

Victoria College was founded on the joint initiative of Lord Cromer (Evelyn Baring), British agent and consul general, and local English cotton merchants in 1905. Along with all other foreign schools, it was nationalized by Gamal Abdel Nasser in the wake of the Suez War in 1956 and now still survives as a pale reflection of its former self under the new label of Victory College. For more than half a century, Victoria College played an important role in providing a first-rate European education along British public school lines to successive generations of well-born Egyptians, both Muslim and Copt, as well as foreign residents in Egypt, whatever their race, color or creed, or financial circumstances. Its prestige extended well beyond Egypt to attract the scions of the English-speaking ruling elite in the rest of the region: thus, King Hussein of Jordan and his brother, Crown Prince Hassan; the last Hashimite king of Iraq, Faisal II, and his uncle, the regent Abd al-Ilah; the former sultan of Zanzibar; and the king of Albania were students at Victoria. First located in downtown Alexandria (where George Antonius was among the first five Levantine students to graduate), the school soon moved to a more rustic location at the edge of the city's suburbs. There its stately buildings and spacious playing fields stood out as an Alexandrian landmark and the envy of other less privileged schools. As part of the war effort, the school was converted to a military hospital in both world wars, the educational facilities then transferred for the duration to the even more elegant San Stefano casino. Victoria College's most notable contribution to Anglo–Egyptian relations during the heyday of British dominance in the region was to create, largely through the efforts of its most outstanding headmaster, R. W. G. Reed of Wadham College, Oxford, a genuine bond of friendship between the ruling class of pashas and their British overlords.

BIBLIOGRAPHY

HEYWORTH-DUNNE, J. *An Introduction to the History of Education in Modern Egypt.* London, 1938.
MANSFIELD, PETER. *The British in Egypt.* New York, 1971.

Alain Silvera

Vilayet

Administrative unit used in the Ottoman Empire.

Derived from an Arabic root meaning "to have authority," *vilayet* had an early meaning of the appointment and certificate of appointment of an official. It later came to refer to the area of jurisdiction of a *wali* (governor). In Mamluk Syria and Egypt, it referred to the smallest administrative unit; in Persia (now Iran), it was the largest provincial administrative unit. After the sixteenth century in the Ottoman Empire, a *vilayet* was the largest administrative unit and became the standard term for province.

BIBLIOGRAPHY

Encyclopaedia of Islam. Leiden, 1934.
SHAW, STANFORD J., and EZEL KURAL SHAW. *History of the Ottoman Empire and Modern Turkey.* Cambridge, U.K., 1977.

David Waldner

Village Institutes

Turkish institutes for training primary-school teachers.

The Village Institutes (Köy Enstitüleri) of Turkey represented a short-lived (1940–1950) but highly innovative experiment in primary-school teacher training. In the 1930s, over 75 percent of Turkey's people lived in some 35,000 villages, and over 80 percent of these villagers were illiterate. Only a small proportion of villages had primary schools, and most of their urban-born teachers had difficulty coping with rural conditions. After the dissolution of the Ottoman Empire and the establishment of the Republic of Turkey in 1923, Mustafa Kemal (Atatürk) and his ruling Republican People's Party (RPP) planned to design a national system of compulsory secular education to enculturate a new generation of Turks in the principles of modern science and Turkish nationalism. Educational reform and a cadre of new, secular teachers were to spread Kemalism and lift the masses from the depths of poverty and ignorance. While impressive educational gains were achieved in the cities, most villages remained without schools.

Ismail Hakki Tonguç, the director general of primary education, and his colleagues designed a plan they hoped would produce teachers capable of living in the villages and able to make a comprehensive impact on them. The plan called for creating special teacher-training institutes, recruiting village students to them, teaching these students general subjects plus useful village technology, and then sending them back to the villages to teach in five-year primary schools.

Shortly after the Turkish Grand National Assembly passed the necessary legislation in 1940, fourteen Village Institutes opened their doors to eager recruits. Actually, many of the institutes' facilities were incomplete, so teachers and students worked side by side building classrooms, dining halls, and dormitories. In the process, students acquired useful carpentry, masonry, and other construction skills.

The ministry of education intentionally located the institutes in rural areas, so that students could practice farming, plant orchards, develop water and sanitation systems, and generally confront typical village problems with modern skills and science. Youths of both sexes, between the ages of twelve and sixteen, who were graduated by a five-year village primary school, qualified for admission to a village institute. The government offered this education free to students who pledged to teach in an assigned village for twenty years after graduation.

Twenty-five percent of the Institute's five-year curriculum was devoted to agriculture (crop production, zootechnology, apiculture [beekeeping], and silkworm culture); 25 percent was devoted to technology (carpentry, construction, blacksmithing, health, and childcare for female students); and 50 percent dealt with general education (the Turkish language, history, literature, geography, math, biology, and civics). In 1950, the curriculum was expanded to six years. As village teachers, institute graduates were expected to teach general education subjects to children, adult-literacy classes, scientific farming and animal husbandry, and handicrafts; they were obligated to play a central role in the community and generally awaken the civic conscience of the rural population.

The institutes provided some of the most idealistic and dedicated rural teachers in Turkey's history. These young men and women inspired many villagers to continue their educations beyond primary school; some even went to the university. A number of village teachers, such as Mahmut Makal (author of *Bizim Köy,* translated as *A Village in Anatolia*), became famous writers who pioneered a new literary genre that focused on peasant life.

From their inception, however, the Village Institutes were subject to controversy. Political opponents described them as indoctrination agencies of the ruling party. Some educators claimed they failed to prepare students adequately for their exhaustive duties as rural teachers. Very conservative villagers complained that institute graduates preached revolutionary and antireligious ideas in their villages. More extreme opponents accused the institutes of teaching communism.

When the new opposition party, the Democrat party (DP), came to power in 1950, they removed institute supporters from the ministry of education and abolished the twenty-one existing institutes by transforming them into ordinary teacher-training schools. Before their demise, the institutes had graduated 15,767 men and 1,395 women.

BIBLIOGRAPHY

STONE, FRANK A. "Rural Revitalization and the Village Institutes in Turkey: Sponsors and Critics." *Comparative Education Review* 18 (1974): 419–429.

VEXLIARD, ALEXANDRE, and KEMAL AYTAC. "The Village Institutes in Turkey." *Comparative Education Review* 8 (1964): 41–47.

Paul J. Magnarella

Vizier

Title of government ministers or dignitaries, especially in the Ottoman Empire.

The first Ottoman vizier was Ala al-Din, brother of the second sultan in the fourteenth century. Under Sultan Mehmet II, the office came to denote a pasha of three tails, one step above a vali, or pasha of two tails. Since then, it has referred to the highest military and administrative rank, below that of grand vizier (*vezir-i azam*) and sultan. The term was officially

dropped in the 1830s and replaced by *vekil*, literally minister, and *baş vekil*, prime minister. But the term *vezir* continued in common usage.

BIBLIOGRAPHY

SHAW, STANFORD J., and EZEL KURAL SHAW. *History of the Ottoman Empire and Modern Turkey,* vol. 2. Cambridge, U.K., 1977.

Elizabeth Thompson

Voice of Lebanon

Independent radio station in Lebanon.

Voice of Lebanon is the first major independent radio station in Lebanon that is not run by the government. It began operation as soon as the Lebanese civil war started in early 1975 and was part of the propaganda department of the Phalange party. It played an important role in the civil war because its transmission was more powerful than the official radio station and because its news bulletins provided listeners with up-to-date information on developing stories. In April 1994, the government of Lebanon ordered all private radio and television stations to cease broadcasting news and assumed the sole power to deliver news to the Lebanese people.

As'ad AbuKhalil

Voice of Palestine

Name of a Palestinian student magazine and of a radio service.

Voice of Palestine was first used as the title for a magazine distributed in the 1950s by Yasir Arafat's Palestinian Student Union in Gaza, Jordan, Syria, Iraq, Lebanon, and elsewhere. Voice of Palestine (VOP) is also the name of a Palestine Liberation Organization (PLO) radio service, launched in 1965 in Cairo, with the help of the Egyptian government.

Voice of Palestine programs were broadcast in many Arab cities, and separate VOP services were established in Amman and Baghdad in 1966, and later in Algiers and Damascus. Egyptian President Anwar Sadat shut down the main Cairo broadcasting house in November 1977, after his peace trip to Jerusalem.

BIBLIOGRAPHY

BRAND, LAURIE A. *Palestinians in the Arab World.* New York, 1988.

Elizabeth Thompson

Volpi, Giuseppe

Governor of Libya from 1922 to 1925, after a short period as governor of Tripolitania.

Volpi abandoned the policy of trying to govern Libya through Libyan representatives in the aftermath of the first Italo–Sanusi War. This had involved recognizing a Sanusi emir in Cyrenaica or trying to use the leaders of the Tripolitanian republic in Tripolitania.

Instead, Volpi gave a free hand to the military commanders on the spot, Rodolfo Graziani and Pietro Badoglio. His new policy was enthusiastically endorsed by the Fascists when they came to power in October 1922. It had been signaled the previous April, when he sanctioned an attack on Misurata, and achieved its fullest expression with the outbreak of the second Italo–Sanusi War in early 1923.

Volpi's three-year tenure as governor also marked the introduction of an intensive colonization scheme. He sought to increase the amount of state funds made available for it, alienated to the state all uncultivated land and all rebel-held land, once it was conquered, and provided tax-relief schemes to attract investment funding. By doing this, he prepared the way for the legislation introduced by Emilio de Bono, who actually began the process of large-scale Italian peasant migration into Libya.

BIBLIOGRAPHY

LOMBARDI, P. "Italian Agrarian Policy during the Fascist Period." In *Social and Economic Development of Libya,* ed. by E. G. H. Joffe and K. S. McLachlan. Wisbech, U.K., 1982.

George Joffe

Vozuq al-Dowleh, Mirza Hasan Khan
[1873–1950]

Iranian politician.

Mirza Hasan Khan was the nephew of Mirza Ali Khan Amin al-Dowleh, the famous prime minister under Mozaffar al-Din Qajar, and he was also the brother of Ahmad Qavam al-Saltaneh. In 1892, he replaced his father as tax collector of Azerbaijan, and four years later he was granted the title Vozuq al-Dowleh. He was elected to the first parliament from Tehran (1906), and, after holding several ministerial posts, he was appointed prime minister and minister of foreign affairs (1916). In 1918, he was reappointed prime minister for the purpose of forming a cabinet, and he headed the ministry of interior. It was during his tenure as premier that the infamous Anglo-Persian

Agreement of 1919, transforming Iran into a British protectorate, was ratified. Following the conclusion of the agreement, Vozuq al-Dowleh received 60,000 pounds from the British government, but he was forced to return the sum to the Iranian government after Reza Shah Pahlavi took office. In 1921, Vozuq al-Dowleh was appointed minister of finance by the prime minister. After Reza Shah was forced by the Allied powers to abdicate in 1941, Vozuq al-Dowleh returned to private life as a land speculator.

Neguin Yavari

Vratsian, Simon [1882–1969]

Armenian political activist and leader.

Simon Vratsian was born at Great Sala, near New Nakhichevan, in southern Russia. He received his primary education locally at Russian and Armenian schools and graduated from the Gevorgian Academy at Echmiadzin in Russian Armenia. He joined the Armenian Revolutionary Federation (ARF) in 1898 and remained one of its most active figures for the rest of his life. Regarded a leader of the left wing of the party, he was a delegate at the 1907 Vienna congress of the ARF when the party formally adopted socialism. Fleeing Russia during the Stolypin reaction, he went to Erzurum, where, before the outbreak of World War I, he was involved in discussions initiated by the Young Turk government for ARF support in the impending war and the intended invasion of Russian Transcaucasia. Although elected to the party's governing bureau, he escaped to Russia and became a member of the Armenian National Council in 1917.

With the establishment of Armenian independence in 1918, Vratsian was sent to negotiate for military support from the Volunteer Army in Russia. In 1919, he was elected to the Armenian parliament and reelected to the ARF bureau. In 1920, he was appointed minister of labor and agriculture. With the fall of the Armenian government in the prelude to sovietization, Vratsian briefly held the office of prime minister from November 24 to December 2, 1920, and handed power over to the Red Army.

After going into hiding, he reemerged at the head of the Committee for the Salvation of the Fatherland when an uprising against the Bolsheviks broke out in Armenia in February 1921. He fled through Iran, spent the years 1927 through 1933 in Paris as editor of *Droshak,* the ARF party organ, and wrote the primary historical narrative on the short-lived independent Armenian state, *Hayastani Hanrapetutiun* (The Republic of Armenia), which was published in 1928. He eventually settled in Beirut, Lebanon, where he passed away after many years as the principal of the Nshan Palanjian Academy, the foremost educational institution in the Armenian diaspora.

BIBLIOGRAPHY

HOVANNISIAN, RICHARD. *The Republic of Armenia: The First Year, 1918–1919.* Berkeley, Calif., 1971.

―――. *The Republic of Armenia: From Versailles to London, 1919–1920.* Berkeley, Calif., 1982.

―――. "Simon Vratzian and Armenian Nationalism." *Middle East Studies* 5 (October 1969): 192–220.

WALKER, CHRISTOPHER J. *Armenia: The Survival of a Nation.* New York, 1980.

Rouben P. Adalian

W

Wadi

Arabic term for valley or riverbed.

In the Middle East, a wadi is usually a valley or dry riverbed, which may or may not fill with water for part of the year. In the desert, place names are often derived from the nearest wadi. For instance, Wadi Halfa is a town in northern Sudan.

Zachary Karabell

Wadi al-Araba

See Aravah Valley

Wadi al-Hasa

Jordanian river valley.

The biblical valley of Zered, Wadi al-Hasa lies 12 miles (20 km) south of al-Karak and flows into the Dead Sea. Forming the natural southern boundary of the al-Balqa region, Wadi al-Hasa is an important site for the mining of phosphates. Plans have been made to build a dam in the valley at Tannur.

BIBLIOGRAPHY

GREAT BRITAIN. NAVAL INTELLIGENCE DIVISION. *Palestine and Transjordan*. Geographical Handbook Series B.R. 514. London, 1943.

Abla M. Amawi

Wadi al-Mawjib

Deep gorge and riverbed in west-central Jordan.

From the mountains of central Jordan, Wadi al-Mawjib leads into the Dead Sea. The waters do not flow perennially, but bedouin and local peasants forage sheep and goats in the region and cultivate some crops. The wadi's bed drops some 3,300 feet (1,000 m)—from 2,300 feet above sea level to 1,300 feet below sea level (+700 to −395 m)—at the Dead Sea. The gorge through which it flows is about 2 miles (3 km) deep. Wadi al-Haydan joins Wadi al-Mawjib and the two are confluent for about 1.5 miles (2.5 km) before reaching the Dead Sea.

BIBLIOGRAPHY

BRAWER, MOSHE. *Atlas of the Middle East*. New York, 1988.

Abla M. Amawi

Wadi Hadramawt

Great valley in eastern Yemen.

Wadi Hadramawt is a 400-mile-long (640 km), well-watered valley east of Aden that constitutes one of the most agriculturally rich areas in Yemen. It produces millet, cotton, wheat, qat, and a variety of fruits and vegetables. The wadi dissects and drains the high plateau of eastern Yemen and is at the center of the HADRAMAWT, a distinctive geographic and sociopolitical region that was a famous trading state in ancient, pre-Islamic times.

Robert D. Burrowes

Wadi Natrun

Site of many monasteries in western Egypt.

As many as five hundred monasteries have been built over the years in the western desert of Egypt, housing as many as fifty thousand monks. The most famous are those located in Wadi Natrun. In recent

View of a Coptic monastery in Wadi Natrun. (Mia Bloom)

Fresco ceiling in a Coptic monastery at Wadi Natrun. (Mia Bloom)

years, Wadi Natrun assumed a renewed importance as the site of the enforced exile of Pope Shenouda III by President Sadat.

Raymond William Baker

Wafd

Major Egyptian nationalist party organized in 1919.

The party took its name from the delegation (Arabic, *wafd*) composed of Sa'd ZAGHLUL and other notables, who called for the complete independence (*istiqlal tamm*) of Egypt from the British immediately after World War I. When Britain refused to negotiate with the Wafd and exiled its leaders, Egypt launched a full-scale rebellion in 1919. A sophisticated network of organizers in key cities and villages allowed the Wafd to dominate the political scene.

The Wafd did not become a formal political party until 1924, six years after its inception. The party was organized along hierarchical lines with an executive council. Although the party enjoyed the support of a cross section of the Egyptian populace, its leaders were predominantly urban, upper and middle class, modern, and secular. The highly charismatic Zaghlul served as its president until his death in 1927. The Wafdist leadership also included both Muslims and Copts, notably Makram Ubayd. Women, particularly Zaghlul's wife, Safiyya, and Huda al-Sha'arawi, became active leaders in the struggle for voting rights, believing that the struggle against imperialism had to be accompanied with a similar struggle for gender equality.

Between the two world wars, the Wafd engaged in a three-way struggle with the British and the Egyptian monarchy. Seeking to undercut Egypt's demands for independence, Britain unilaterally declared Egypt independent in 1922 and promulgated a constitutional monarchy in 1923. As the only party to enjoy widespread popular support for its anti-British stand, the Wafd won the 1924 elections and all subsequent elections that were not manipulated or rigged by King Ahmad Fu'ad or his son Farouk.

Following Zaghlul's death, Mustafa al-NAHHAS became president of the party and continued its struggle against the British. In 1936, he signed the Anglo–Egyptian Treaty that formalized Egyptian and British relations but permitted both the continuation of a British military presence along the Suez Canal zone and British control over the Sudan.

This failure to secure complete independence, coupled with allegations of nepotism and corruption within the party, undermined some of its popular support. In the 1930s, many Egyptian youths joined various fascist and radical groups, and the Wafd countered by creating the Blue Shirts, a paramilitary youth organization. In 1941, fearing a pro-Nazi Egyptian government, Britain's Ambassador Miles Lampson (later Lord Killearn) forced King Farouk to accept Nahhas as prime minister. Nahhas's willingness to work with the British throughout World War II further undercut the Wafd's credibility as a nationalist and anti-imperialist party.

Following the 1952 military coup, which deposed Farouk, the Wafd was formally disbanded (1953); some of its leaders were then tried for corruption and crimes against the state. In 1976, when Anwar al-Sadat announced the return to a multiparty system, the Wafd was revived under the leadership of Siraj al-Din. The new Wafd called for a parliamentary, multiparty system and the dismantling of socialist measures that had been enacted under Egypt's former president, Gamal Abdel Nasser. In a short time, the Wafd gathered a notable degree of support, particularly in the richer urban areas. The Wafd voted to disband in reaction to Sadat's political crackdown of 1978. After Sadat's assassination by Islamists, the Wafd again was revived and it remains a minority party in Egypt.

BIBLIOGRAPHY

Debb, Marius. *Party Politics in Egypt: The Wafd and Its Rivals, 1919–1939*. London, 1979.
Terry, Janice J. *The Wafd, 1919–1952: Cornerstone of Egyptian Power*. London, 1982.

Janice J. Terry

Wahda Party

Political party in Iraq.

Wahda, the National Union party, was founded by Abd al-Fattah IBRAHIM in 1946 and banned by the government of Salih Jabr in 1947. Marxist in orientation, the party, whose aim was "the unity of the democratic forces of the country," attracted some five hundred members from various religious and sectarian backgrounds, including the poet Muhammad Mahdi al-Jawahiri and lawyers from Baghdad, al-Najaf, and Mosul.

Peter Sluglett

Wahhab, Abd al-Raqib Abd al-   [?–1969]

Soldier of North Yemen.

This young Shafi'i commando was leader and hero of the siege of San'a. He led the San'a mutiny in the fall of 1968 against the conservatives led by Gen. Hassan al-Amri who were about to purge the armed forces of Shafi'i leftists with connections to the National Liberation Front (NLF) in South Yemen. Abd

al-Wahhab was sent into exile and was then killed in San'a in an attempted coup in early 1969. These events were part of North Yemen's drift toward a more conservative outlook and Zaydism, which dominated in the late 1960s.

Robert D. Burrowes

Wahhabi

See Muwahhidun

Wahrhaftig, Zerah   [1906–   ]

Israeli political leader.

Born in Russia, Zerha Wahrhaftig was educated at Yestivot in Poland and the University of Warsaw. He practiced law in Warsaw and was active in the Torah ve-Avoda and Mizrachi movements and the World Jewish Congress. During World War II, he fled to Lithuania and then to Japan and New York, where he held leadership positions in the World Jewish Congress and Hapo'el Ha-Mizrahi of America.

After World War II, Wahrhaftig moved to Palestine. He became a leader of the National Religious party, and in 1949 he was elected to the Knesset and served in a number of government positions, including that of minister of religious affairs. He was a member of the Va'ad Le'umi and, after the State of Israel was proclaimed, the provisional Council of State.

BIBLIOGRAPHY

Schiff, Gary S. *Tradition and Politics: The Religious Parties of Israel*. Detroit, 1977.

Bryan Daves

Wailing Wall

See Western Wall

Wailing Wall Disturbances

A September 1928 dispute over Jewish religious rights at the Western Wall that led to political violence in August 1929.

The Wailing, or WESTERN, WALL has been holy to Muslims because it is the western part of the TEMPLE MOUNT AND HARAM AL-SHARIF where, Muslims believe, the prophet Muhammad tethered his "fabulous steed,'' al-Buraq, while on a nocturnal journey to heaven. The wall is also the holiest shrine of Judaism because it is the remnant of the western exterior of the Temple of Herod, built on the site of Solomon's temple. Jews placed a screen at the wall to separate men and women on September 23, 1928, the eve of the Day of Atonement. The Palestinians protested that the screen violated the status quo ante; the British authorities agreed and forcibly removed it. The incident was politicized by both communities over the next few months, a response that led to tensions and events such as a Revisionist Zionist demonstration on August 15, 1929, and a Palestinian counterdemonstration the following day.

Violence began in Jerusalem on August 23 when Palestinians attacked Jews in Meah She'arim. The rioters attacked the largely non-Zionist religious communities of Hebron and Safed, killing sixty-four and twenty-six people, respectively. Jewish rioters in turn killed Palestinians in a number of cities, but most were shot—some of them indiscriminately—by British troops and police suppressing the disturbances. The violence took the lives of 133 Jews and at least 116 Palestinians.

The SHAW COMMISSION, which investigated the disturbances, determined that the immediate cause of the riots was the Jewish and Arab demonstrations of August 15 and 16 and that the ultimate cause was Palestinian fear that Jewish immigration and land purchase would lead to Jewish domination.

BIBLIOGRAPHY

MATTAR, PHILIP. "The Role of the Mufti of Jerusalem in the Political Struggle over the Western Wall, 1928–1929." *Middle Eastern Studies* 19, no. 1 (January 1983): 104–118.
PALESTINE GOVERNMENT. *A Survey of Palestine for the Information of the Anglo–American Committee of Inquiry*, 2 vols. Jerusalem, 1946. Reprint, Washington, D.C., 1991.

Philip Mattar

Waite, Terry   [1939–   ]

Anglican church official who helped secure the release of several Western hostages in Iran, Libya, and Lebanon during the 1980s and was himself held hostage in Lebanon between January 1987 and November 1991.

Terry Waite was born in Styal, Cheshire, in northwestern England. Driven by a passion for traveling and dedicated to helping others, he became involved in church and relief activities in Africa in the late 1960s and early 1970s. In 1980, he went to work for the Anglican Archbishop of Canterbury, Dr. Robert Runcie, as the liaison person for the church's overseas affiliates. Although he has worked for the Anglican church for much of his professional life, he has never been ordained. As special envoy of Archbishop Runcie, he was instrumental in securing the release, in January 1981, of three British Anglican missionaries and four Iranian Anglicans who had been taken hostage by Iranian revolutionaries in 1980 (see HOSTAGE CRISES). In the time period from 1984 to 1985, he also played a leading role in convincing Libya's President Muammar al-Qaddafi to free four British citizens who had been held in Tripoli.

In late 1985, he joined in efforts to free Americans held by radical Shi'a groups in Lebanon. He was credited with helping to secure the release of Rev. Lawrence M. Jenco and David P. Jacobsen in 1986, although it is likely that the freeing of these two hostages owed more to secret U.S. arms sales to Iran than to his diplomatic skills. Willingly or not, Waite became involved in the Reagan administration's arms-for-hostages scheme. As rumors of his being tied to the American government surfaced in late 1986, his credibility and trustworthiness were compromised, and he was himself abducted in Beirut on January 20, 1987, while on a last-ditch mission to free the remaining kidnap victims there. He was released on November 18, 1991. He has written a personal account of his nearly five years of captivity, which was published in 1993.

BIBLIOGRAPHY

HIRO, DILIP. *Lebanon: Fire and Embers*. New York, 1992.
WAITE, TERRY. *Taken on Trust*. New York, 1993.

Guilain P. Denoeux

Wallach, Yona   [1944–1985]

Israeli poet.

Yona Wallach was born in Kiryiat Uno, near Tel Aviv, to a veteran pioneer family. Her father was killed in the War of Independence when she was four, a trauma that haunted Wallach throughout her short life. Her widowed mother owned the only local cinema, where the impressionable Wallach absorbed the new-wave films that later echoed in her writing. A misfit in her small town and a high school dropout, Wallach, who wrote her first poem when she was seven, studied art, joined the Tel Aviv Circle of Poets, and published in their avant-garde periodicals.

Seeking relief from her emotional unrest, she turned to mental institutions and drugs, diving uninhibitedly into intense experiences. Life and writing became one, and when her first book, *Devarim* (Words, or Things, 1966), appeared, it shook the Israeli literary world with its inner demons, imaginary and absurd situations, surreal connections, bold depictions of sexuality, and fluid, violent, and seemingly unstructured diction.

In the five books that followed, Wallach took on the feminine revolution in Hebrew writing. She subverted religious and national preconceptions unprecedentedly and often used sexual encounters as the arena for examining issues of social injustice. Her poems blur boundaries between female and male, conscious and subconscious, horror and beauty, sensuality and spirituality. The self is shattered, and its components become separate entities.

Wallach, a precursor of postmodernism, led Israeli literature to unchartered lands. She died of cancer at the age of forty-one.

BIBLIOGRAPHY

KUVOVI, MIRI. "Violence in Wallach's Poetry." *Proceedings of the Eleventh World Congress of Jewish Studies,* Division C, vol. 3. Jerusalem, 1994.

SARNA, YIGAL. *Yona Wallach: Biography.* Jerusalem, 1993.

SILBERMAN, DORIT. *Hebrew Is a Bathing Woman: On Yona Wallach's Poetry.* Tel Aviv, 1990.

Nili Gold

Waqf

An Islamic charitable trust created by an owner to assure that private property generates a permanent source of income for the public good and the donor's family.

A *waqf* (Arabic plural, *awqaf*) may be composed of either arable land or urban property, whose income provides support for such communal necessities as mosques, hospitals, schools, and water fountains. In the nineteenth century, the administration of waqf properties by religious authorities (*ulama*) began to be curtailed, reformed, or abolished throughout the Islamic Middle East. With the demise of the Ottoman Empire in the early twentieth century, secular governments in predominantly Sunni Muslim nation-states found that the reorganization of waqf properties could function as a modernizing mechanism to sever the critical link between the *ulama,* who administered and derived income from these trusts, and their economic base of support. In twentieth century Iran, where Shi'a clerics continued to maintain an effective religious infrastructure throughout the regime of Reza Shah Pahlavi and his

son, the shah's land reforms of the 1960s were perceived as a secular assault against Islamic authority.

The origin of these pious foundations may be seen as an extension of the charitable ideals that are central to Islam. While such philanthropy perpetuated family honor and served critical communal needs, the waqf system also insured that the donor's family retained access to part of the trust's income in perpetuity. The system often maintained a family's inheritance through generations, legally, without the fragmentation usually produced by Islamic inheritance laws.

BIBLIOGRAPHY

MARCUS, ABRAHAM. *The Middle East on the Eve of Modernity: Aleppo in the Eighteenth Century.* New York, 1989.

Denise A. Spellberg

Wardak

Afghan province.

Wardak is a province in east-central Afghanistan with about 350,000 inhabitants. The provincial capital is Maidanshahr. The people of Wardak are mostly farmers, and they belong to either the Ghilzai or Durrani Pushtun tribes; there are also Hazara in the north. The main highway passes through Wardak.

BIBLIOGRAPHY

ADAMEC, LUDWIG. *Historical Dictionary of Afghanistan.* Metuchen, N.J., 1991.

Grant Farr

Warnier Law

Law passed by France's National Assembly in 1873 to establish individual titles on previously undivided lands held by families and tribes in Algeria.

The Warnier Law greatly facilitated land purchases by European settlers and appropriations by the state domain. It also hastened the appearance of small and dispersed properties insufficient to support the indigenous rural population.

BIBLIOGRAPHY

AGERON, CHARLES-ROBERT. *Les Algériens musulmans et la France (1871–1919),* 2 vols. Paris, 1968.

Peter von Sivers

War of Attrition

Attempt by Egypt to cause Israel to withdraw from the Suez Canal, 1968–1970.

The aftermath of the Arab–Israel war (1967) was characterized by fighting along the borders of the new territories acquired by Israel, particularly along the Suez Canal from mid-1968 to mid-1970. In June 1969, Egypt's President Gamal Abdel Nasser announced that though his country was incapable of regaining the Sinai peninsula by force, it could and would wear Israel out—in the hope that this would bring about an eventual Israeli withdrawal from the Suez Canal. Israel responded to the hostilities by building a system of strongholds along the canal, known as the BAR-LEV LINE, after then Chief of Staff Chaim Bar-Lev.

On October 31, 1968, Israel had destroyed a power station at Naj Hamadi in Upper Egypt, but it was not until July 1969 that it began aerial attacks, which devastated Egyptian cities along the canal and turned their residents into refugees. In early 1970, Egypt received substantial amounts of Soviet military aid, but after a number of aerial confrontations between Israeli planes and Russian-flown MIG fighters, pressures increased for a cease-fire, which went into effect on August 7, 1970.

BIBLIOGRAPHY

ROLEF, S. H., ed. *Political Dictionary of the State of Israel.* New York, 1987.

Benjamin Joseph

Water

Because of its scarcity, water plays a central role in Middle Eastern politics and society.

In this naturally arid region, human settlement is found only where some source of water prevails. For example, nearly sixty million Egyptians live on only 3 percent of their nation's territory, that portion within reach of the waters of the Nile river.

Precipitation, in the form of rain but sometimes as mountain snows, is the major source of water in the Middle East. Much of this immediately evaporates. Some of it flows in thin sheets down valley slopes and ends up in shallow, ephemeral lakes that evaporate, leaving behind salt flats (*shatts* or *playas*) such as the Dasht-e Lut (Lot's Desert, i.e., "Desert of Salt" in Iran). The remainder forms streams and rivers that either end in interior basins (e.g., the Jordan river; the Helmand river in Afghanistan) or reach the sea.

Of those that enter the sea, the largest and most famous in this region are the Nile and the Tigris and Euphrates rivers.

Small streams in the Middle East and North Africa are intermittent, flowing only seasonally or when rare rainstorms occur. The large rivers are usually termed *exotic streams,* that is, those that rise in well-watered areas but pass through arid regions before reaching their final destinations. The Nile river, for example, receives no additional water downstream of the Blue Nile and Atbara rivers, which come from Ethiopia and join the White Nile near the city of Khartoum.

Exotic streams are often either transboundary or international rivers. Transboundary rivers cross national borders at an angle and are shared by two or more countries; among these are the Nile and the Euphrates, which pass through several nations along their courses. International streams, such as the Shatt al-Arab (the combined flow of the Tigris and Euphrates rivers that enter the Persian/Arabian Gulf), form boundaries between nations.

Less common are those streams that increase in size as they flow to the sea. Most of these are located in Turkey and include the Menderes (the ancient

Man drinking from an ibriq in Syria during the 1940s. (D.W. Lockhard)

Irrigated fields along a road between Ankara and Kayseri in Turkey. (D.W. Lockhard)

Meander), the Kızıl Irmak, the Sakarya, and the Yeşil Irmak.

Freshwater lakes, as distinguished from reservoirs, are a rarity. These include Lake Tana, the Ethiopian source of the Blue Nile; Lake Tiberius (also called the Sea of Galilee/Lake Kinneret) in the Jordan valley; and lakes Beyşehir, Eğridir, and İznik in Turkey. The Sudd, a papyrus swamp of great extent through which the White Nile flows, is found inland in southern Sudan.

Saline lakes form in interior basins when evaporation balances or is in excess of the stream flow that sustains them. Lake VAN and Lake Tuz in Turkey, Lake Urmia (Persian, Urumiyeh) in Iran, and the DEAD SEA between Jordan and Israel are the largest of these.

Exotic streams can be thought of as linear oases, but the term *oasis* usually applies to isolated springs

Close-up of Jonglei Canal construction in Sudan, 1982. (© Chris Kutschera)

with vegetation surrounded by desert. Called point oases, they occur when either underlying geologic structures or topological depressions in the land's surface allow water from deep aquifers to reach the surface. This water sometimes rises to the surface under natural pressure in the form of artesian springs. Traditionally, shallow wells with primitive lifts were used to raise nonartesian water. Oases support intensive agriculture and/or groves of date palms. Among famous oases in the region are Jalo and Kufra in Libya, Siwa and Kharga in Egypt, and Hufuf in Saudi Arabia. The sources of water in these oases are termed *aquifers,* water-filled strata deep beneath the surface. These supplies usually consist of fossil water, that is, water that infiltrated and was stored during more humid periods in the geologic past; once mined, this water will not be replaced.

Human use of these water sources began in ancient times. Water was lifted from shallow wells with buckets attached to counterweight poles (*shadoof*). For raising water from one ditch to another, the

Building the Jonglei Canal in Sudan, 1982. (© Chris Kutschera)

A water wheel in Hama, Syria, in the Orontes valley, circa 1940. (© Chris Kutschera)

Archimedes screw (Egyptian, *tunbur*), a tube containing a hand-operated spiral gear, was sometimes used, while giant water wheels (*noria*) were employed in Syria on the larger streams. The ancient Nabateans, in what is now southern Jordan, harvested scarce rainwater by clearing hillsides and carefully channeling the runoff into underground cisterns. Elsewhere, fresh water trapped in alluvial fans at the foot of desert mountains was led by gravity through gently sloping tunnels to lower valley surfaces. These hand-dug *qanats* or *foggaras* are still used in Iran and the Arabian peninsula. More recently, barrages, or simple diversionary dams, were built across streams and rivers to lead water to the fields. Large modern dams such as the ASWAN HIGH DAM on the Nile and the Atatürk Dam on the Euphrates in Turkey impound huge quantities of water to generate hydroelectric power or to release it gradually to even out the highly variable seasonal flow of the rivers for year-round agriculture. Aquifers deep beneath the surface are now tapped by tube wells and submersible pumps, which provide water for fields using central pivot sprinklers. Saudi Arabia in the last decade has become self-sufficient in wheat and dairy products through the use of such systems, although

the nonrenewable nature of these sources makes the duration of such projects questionable.

In those areas without surface streams or sufficient supplies of underground water, seawater is desalinized using various methods. Many cities in Saudi Arabia and elsewhere on the Arabian Peninsula now depend on this source for their municipal supplies. As aquifers become exhausted, and as growing populations increase the demand for water, DESALINIZATION will become more and more important. In the face of growing demands, the finite quantity of water from all sources in the Middle East presents a serious problem. Population increases, urbanization, modernization, agriculture, and the search for agricultural self-sufficiency all contribute to the water-scarcity crisis.

The annual discharge of the Nile from 1870 to 1959 was 121.1 billion cubic yards (92.6 billion cu. m). Of this amount, Egypt by treaty with Sudan receives 72.7 million cubic yards (55.6 million cu. m) per year and Sudan 24.2 million cubic yards (18.5 million cu. m) per year. By 1990, Egypt was using in excess of its share. In view of the population increase in Egypt—an additional one million people every nine months—an absolute water shortage is predicted for Egypt by the year 2000.

The Euphrates river, which rises in Turkey and directly and indirectly receives 98 percent of its 43.2-billion-cubic-yard (33 billion cu. m) flow from that country, is becoming the focus of international water competition. Turkey at present uses an estimated 2.6 billion cubic yards (2 billion cu. m) per year, Syria another 2.6 billion (2 billion cu. m), and Iraq perhaps as much as 19.6 billion cubic yards (15 billion cu. m) per year. Both Turkey and Syria have undertaken large development projects using Euphrates

A water wheel in Saqiya, Egypt, in the Nile delta, 1952. (D.W. Lockhard)

waters. The Southeast Anatolia Development Project (Turkish acronym: GAP) is scheduled to irrigate as much as 2.5 million acres (1 million ha) with water from the Atatürk reservoir. Water from Lake Asad behind the Tabqa EUPHRATES DAM in Syria may reach an additional 803,000 acres (325,000 ha).

Depletions from Turkish and Syrian irrigation, evaporation off reservoir surfaces, and wastage may reduce the flow of the river by 50 percent in the next 20 years. Return flow from fields will also contain dissolved salts and other pollutants, which may add to downstream problems for Syria and Iraq. Diplomatic efforts to resolve the use of these waters among the three countries are as yet at an inconclusive stage.

The sharing of the Jordan river and its tributaries among Syria, Jordan, Israel, the people of the West Bank, and Lebanon creates another major diplomatic puzzle. Jordan depends upon the river's major tributary, the Yarmuk, for much of its sparse supply of water. Israel pumps 654 million cubic yards (500 million cu. m) per year from Lake Kinneret into its national water carrier, which distributes water throughout the nation. Meanwhile, Palestinians of the West Bank contend that Israel is using more than its share of the aquifers that lead from the West Bank down into Israel proper, although this is denied by Israel. The Litani river, which flows entirely within Lebanon, is also eyed thirstily by Lebanon's neighbors.

These are just a few facets of the Middle East's water crisis as it was developing in the early 1990s. Experts, however, disagree as to the long-term nature of the situation. Some insist that the perceived shortages could be met by using less water for agriculture, since that activity takes 70 to 80 percent of all the water used in the region. Others cite conservation and education as ways to curtail the excessive use of water, although no permanent solution can be found until peace is assured, population growth is stabilized, or desalination is perfected. In any event, water will remain a key issue in the Middle East for the foreseeable future.

BIBLIOGRAPHY

ABU RIZAIZA, OMAR S., and MOHAMED N. ALLAM. "Water Requirements versus Water Availability in Saudi Arabia." *Journal of Water Resources Planning and Management* 115, no. 1 (1989): 64–74.

KOLARS, JOHN. "The Course of Water in the Arab Middle East." *American–Arab Affairs* 33 (1990): 57–68.

NAFF, THOMAS, and RUTH C. MATSON. *Water in the Middle East: Conflict or Cooperation?* Boulder, Colo., 1984.

John F. Kolars

Wattar, al-Taher [1935–   ]

Algerian novelist and short story writer.

Wattar was born on 15 August 1935 in Sedrata, eastern Algeria. His writings present a panorama of Algeria's postindependence history, with a look back at the Algerian War of Independence. Although his short stories in the collection *Dukhkhan min Qalbi* (Smoke from My Heart) indicated a primary interest in the emotional problems of Algerian youth and an effort to reconcile modernity and tradition, he soon abandoned this path for a nationalistic literature. He undertook to defend his socialist ideology and the role played by the communists in the Algerian War of Independence. His novel *L'As* (The Genius [Algiers, 1974]), in particular, revealed the communists' involvement in the fighting and was used by him as a first step to indict the political power for its many failures.

Wattar pursues this course in his fiction, concentrating on the disappointments of the people with the political agenda of independent Algeria. He portrays the situation in the symbolic novel *Al-Hauwat wa al-Qasr* (The Fisherman and the Palace [Constantine, 1980]). Another thorny subject Wattar raises is the abuses of the opportunists who benefited from both war and peace. His novels *Al-Zilzal* (The Earthquake [Beirut, 1974]) and *Urs Baghl* (The Wedding of a Mule [Beirut, 1978]) illustrate a situation that preoccupied his contemporary, Abdelhamid BEN HADOUGA. It is Wattar, however, who most dramatically portrayed the national betrayal of the memory of the martyrs of the War of Independence, in his collection of short stories *Al-Shuhada Ya'udun Hatha al-Usbu'a* (The Martyrs Are Returning This Week).

Wattar experienced great optimism during the rule of President Houari Boumédienne, as described in his novel *Al-Ishq wa al-Mawt fi al-Zaman al-Harrashi* (Love and Death in the Harrashi Time [Beirut, 1980]). But the changes on the political scene ended his dreams, as he laments in his latest novel, *Tajribatun fi al-Ishq* (An Experience in Passion [Algiers, 1994]). It is the cry of a disappointed man.

Wattar also wrote a play and ventured into poetry, but he soon abandoned these genres for fiction, where he established himself as one of Algeria's foremost writers in Arabic. He is the best-known Algerian writer in the rest of the Arab world.

[*See also*: Literature, Arabic, North African]

BIBLIOGRAPHY

ALLEN, ROGER, ed. *Modern Arabic Literature.* New York, 1987.

BAMIA, AIDA A. "Wattar, al-Taher." In *Encyclopedia of World Literature in the Twentieth Century,* vol. 5. New York, 1993.

Aida A. Bamia

Wauchope, Arthur   [1874–1947]

British high commissioner of Palestine and Transjordan, 1931–1938.

Wauchope played a crucial role in negotiating between colonial authorities and the Arab Higher Committee during the PALESTINE ARAB REVOLT, which began in 1936. However, under his authority, Jewish immigration to Palestine soared, and the Arabs became increasingly disenchanted with British policy. When clashes between British forces and Arab rebels intensified, Wauchope recommended that the Colonial Office use force to quell disorder. He retired in February 1938, before completing his second five-year term.

Karen A. Thornsvard

Wavell, Archibald Percival   [1883–1950]

Commander in chief of British forces in the Middle East; British general in World War II; Viceroy of India, 1943–1947.

Wavell was born in Colchester, England, and graduated from Sandhurst, the British military academy. He served under General Edmund Allenby in Palestine in World War I. In 1937 he was again sent to Palestine to deal with the unrest between the Arabs and Jews. He successfully quelled the PALESTINE ARAB REVOLT and returned to Britain in 1938. In 1939, he became commander in chief for all British forces in the Middle East, where he defeated the Italian forces in North and East Africa (1940–1941). He was not successful in preventing the fall of Greece and Crete, and when he succumbed to General Erwin Rommel's Afrika Korps in 1941, he was reassigned to Southeast Asia. Wavell concluded his career as viceroy of India (1943–1947), the last viceroy before Lord Mountbatten, who helped ease India into independence from the British Empire.

BIBLIOGRAPHY

COLLINS, ROBERT J. *Lord Wavell.* London, 1947.

Daniel E. Spector

Wazir, Khalil al-   [1935–1988]

A founder and leading member of the contemporary Palestinian national movement.

Khalil Ibrahim al-Wazir was born October 10, 1935, to a Palestinian Sunni Muslim shopkeeper in Ramla in Mandatory Palestine. When its inhabitants were summarily expelled by Israeli forces in July 1948, al-Wazir made his way to Gaza City, where he resumed his education at a United Nations Relief and Works Agency (UNRWA) school.

Al-Wazir (also called Abu Jihad) first became politically active in 1953, covertly receiving military training in the Egyptian-administered Gaza Strip. Probably affiliated with the Muslim Brotherhood at this time, he formed his own commando unit, whose activities led to his brief imprisonment by the Egyptian authorities in 1954. In 1954 he also first met the future Palestine Liberation Organization (PLO) chairman, Yasir Arafat, beginning a lifelong partnership and friendship, which, in association with future PLO deputy chairman Salah Khalaf (Abu Iyad), was to form the resilient core leadership of the contemporary Palestinian national movement.

After completing his studies in Cairo, where he had moved in September 1956, al-Wazir left in 1957 for Kuwait as a schoolteacher. His meeting there with Arafat that fall, a meeting of minds regarding the need to establish an independent, armed Palestinian movement, sowed the seeds for the formation of the Palestine National Liberation Movement (al-FATH) in 1959. Al-Wazir would serve on its Central Committee and the subsequently established Revolutionary Council for the rest of his life.

Among al-Fath's founders, al-Wazir alone had prior experience in forming a guerilla organization and played a leading role in its development. In 1963 he went to Algiers to open al-Fath's first diplomatic mission and organize military training for its recruits. He used this post to establish relations with China (al-Fath's first non-Arab source of arms), North Korea, and Vietnam; meet guerilla theoretician Che Guevara; and participate in the 1964 Palestine National Council, which founded the PLO. During this period he also remained, with Arafat, the leading advocate within al-Fath's Central Committee for an immediate start to military operations. When the debate was resolved in late 1964, al-Wazir was appointed deputy commander in chief of al-Fath's military wing, al-Asifa (The Storm).

After the PLO came under the control of al-Fath and other guerilla organizations in 1968/69, al-Wazir additionally assumed the post of deputy commander in chief of PLO military forces. Although this position gave him only limited authority over non-Fath forces, al-Fath's preponderance within the PLO ensured that he played a central role in PLO military affairs until his death. He firmly believed armed struggle was legitimate and consistently sought to escalate it. He also did not hesitate to attack or retaliate against civilian targets when he thought this necessary but opposed the use of violence outside the region.

Al-Wazir, who furthermore directed al-Fath's Department of the Occupied Homeland, was also among the first of his colleagues to grasp the importance of complementing armed struggle in Gaza and the West Bank with political mobilization. Particularly after the PLO's evacuation from Beirut in 1982, he worked hard to develop al-Fath's political infrastructure in the West Bank and Gaza Strip, thus helping prepare the ground for the popular uprising, or INTIFADA, which erupted in December 1987. It was primarily on account of his leading role in assisting the uprising's clandestine leadership and channeling support to the West Bank and Gaza that he was assassinated by an Israeli commando squad (which filmed the event) in Tunis on April 16, 1988. His death precipitated the most serious disturbances the West Bank and Gaza Strip had witnessed since 1967, and his funeral in Damascus was attended by hundreds of thousands, including representatives from all Palestinian factions. He is survived by his wife, prominent Fath militant Intisar al-Wazir, and four of their five children.

Along with Khalaf, al-Wazir was the most important PLO and Fath leader after Arafat and, in internal debates, consistently Arafat's closest ally. The achievements and failures of these organizations and of the Palestinian people generally during his time are therefore equally his.

A straightforward nationalist whose mind was attuned to practical action and organizational matters, al-Wazir was among Palestinians respected in life and venerated in death. Though denounced as a reactionary by more radical elements during the 1970s for his conservative positions, he enjoyed extensive contacts among other factions and later emerged as a prominent mediator. As with all Palestinian nationalist leaders during his lifetime, he was viewed by Israel as a terrorist, and Israel rejected his support of a negotiated settlement.

Neither an intellectual nor an orator, al-Wazir does not have any writings to his name and gave fewer press statements than his colleagues.

BIBLIOGRAPHY

COBBAN, HELENA. *The Palestinian Liberation Organization: People, Power, and Politics.* Cambridge, U.K., 1984.
HART, ALAN. *Arafat: Terrorist or Peacemaker?* London, 1984.

SAYID, YEZID. "Death of the 'Quiet Man.'" *Middle East International* 324 (30 April 1988): 9.

Mouin Rabbani

Wazzani, Muhammad Hassan al-
[1910–   ]

Moroccan nationalist.

In the early 1930s, Wazzani, a native of Fez, was a leader of the Comité d'Action Marocaine (CAM). He was elected secretary-general of the Bloc d'Action Nationale in October 1936, but the following year founded the PARTI DÉMOCRATIQUE CONSTITUTIONEL (PDC). Wazzani was imprisoned for nine years (1937–1946) on political charges. Periodically, he cooperated with the Istiqlal, and from 1953 to 1954, he and his followers joined the National Front. Wazzani was named minister of state without portfolio in King Hassan's 1961 coalition government. He was among those wounded in 1971 in the attempted coup against the king.

Bruce Maddy-Weitzman

Webb, Sidney   [1859–1947]

British colonial secretary.

Under Webb's authority, the British government issued a statement of policy (white paper) on Palestine October 21, 1930. The white paper sought to balance the obligations of Britain's mandate in Palestine to both Arabs and Jews. It pointed to economic as well as geographic limits to the country's capacity to absorb population. It suggested immigration restrictions on Jews as one of the available remedies, drawing vehement opposition and criticism from supporters of Zionism.

Benjamin Joseph

Weizman, Ezer   [1924–   ]

Israeli politician and soldier; president since 1993.

Born and educated in Haifa, Ezer Weizman is the nephew of Chaim WEIZMANN, one of the early Jewish political leaders of Palestine who later became Israel's first president. In 1942, at the age of eighteen, Weizman joined the Royal Air Force and served in Rhodesia, Egypt, and India. In 1946 and 1947, he studied aeronautics in Britain.

Weizman is often credited with being one of the fathers of the Israeli Air Force (IAF). Following the vote in the United Nations in favor of partitioning Palestine, he worked to acquire aircraft for the new military force, and during the Arab–Israel War (1948) he commanded one of the IAF squadrons and flew many missions. In July 1950, he was appointed chief of operations of the air force; in 1956, he became commander. After the Arab–Israel War of 1956, he continued to work to build up the air force, and in 1967 he became chief of the General Staff.

In 1969, Weizman resigned from the Israel Defense Forces and entered politics. He served as leader of the Gahal party and was minister of transportation in the Government of National Unity (1969). Although he resigned from the government in 1970 and went into private business, he continued to serve on the Executive Committee of the Herut party. In 1977, when it won its first national election, Weizman was campaign manager for the Likud party (formed from the merger of Herut, Gahal, and other right-of-center parties).

Having been appointed minister of defense by the newly elected prime minister, Menachem Begin, Weizman, in that capacity, supervised the invasion of Lebanon in 1978 and, at the same time, was one of the moderating influences in the Camp David peace talks in September 1978. Although he had been perceived as a hawk when he joined the Begin government, Weizman increasingly argued for a more moderate approach as time went on, and this change led to increasing conflicts between Weizman and other members of the Likud government. In May 1980 he resigned from his post, and six months later he voted against the government on a nonconfidence vote; he charged that Begin was intentionally frustrating the peace process.

In 1984, Weizman formed a new political party, Yahad, which continued to move to the left as he led it into a merger with the Labor party. Weizman was appointed minister of science following the 1984 elections, which produced a National Unity government. In 1987, he was the first member of the Labor party in the Knesset to publicly call for negotiations with the Palestine Liberation Organization (PLO). In January 1990, he was charged with privately undertaking secret meetings with PLO officials (such meetings were illegal at the time), but the charges were never filed because of lack of evidence. He resigned his seat as a Labor member of the Knesset before the 1992 election, and in March 1993 the Labor party nominated him to be its candidate for president. He became the seventh president of Israel on May 14, 1993.

BIBLIOGRAPHY

SACHAR, HOWARD M. *A History of Israel: From the Rise of Zionism to Our Time.* New York, 1981.
WEIZMAN, EZER. *Our Eagles' Wings.* New York, 1976.

Gregory S. Mahler

Weizmann, Chaim [1874–1952]

World-renowned Russian-born chemist; university professor; Zionist leader; first president of Israel, 1948–1952.

Weizmann was born and raised in the Jewish community of Motol, near the city of Pinsk, in Belorussia, which was in Russia's Pale of Settlement, the region assigned to Jews during the Russian Empire. His father was a timber merchant and had enough wealth to educate his twelve children in the modern

Chaim Weizmann and David Ben-Gurion (center and right, respectively). (Israel Office of Information)

style. Among the eldest and brightest, Chaim went to a Russian secondary school in Pinsk, studied in Germany, and earned his doctorate in chemistry in Geneva in 1899. From 1900 to 1904, he taught at the University of Geneva and contributed to the chemistry of dyes; in 1916 he discovered the means of mass-producing acetone, a chemical used in the manufacture of gun powder.

As a university student in Germany and thereafter, Weizmann was interested in Zionism. Committed to the promotion of *Haskala* (secular modern Hebrew literature and culture), he encouraged a group of young Zionists, called the Democratic Faction, to challenge the cautious policies of established Zionist leadership. Their initial project, the creation of a secular Jewish university, widened the rift between secular and Orthodox Jewish Zionists, threatening both the coalition fashioned by Theodor Herzl and the unity of the World Zionist Organization.

In 1904 Weizmann took a position at the University of Manchester in England. There he contributed to several major discoveries applied to the manufacture of synthetic rubber. He continued to participate in Zionist activities and concentrate his efforts on the establishment of a Jewish university.

World War I (1914–1918) dislocated the World Zionist Organization as well as the international balance of power. Weizmann's position in the English Zionist Federation and in the academy brought him into contact with a wide array of influential politicians and industrialists. He accepted a government appointment to supervise the synthetic production of acetone. As the war progressed, Weizmann's professional and social standing grew. Without the formal authorization of any official Zionist agency, Weizmann was instrumental in convincing British politicians to support Zionist aims—to enhance British strategic interests in the Middle East and secure their lines of communication to India. The Balfour Declaration was written on November 2, 1917, promising British support for the establishment in Palestine of a Jewish National Home. It marked Weizmann's wartime triumph and was a turning point in modern Jewish history.

Weizmann served as chair of the Zionist Commission, which guided the British military administration in Palestine in the implementation of the Balfour Declaration. He led the Zionist delegation to the World War I peace conference at Versailles in 1919. Elected president of the World Zionist Organization in 1920, Weizmann championed policies that would not antagonize the British but would strengthen the status of Zionism among Jews. Aware that Zionism's success depended on convincing millions of Jews to live and work in Palestine, Weizmann opposed deploying stringent financial criteria as the basis for investments. He concentrated his initial postwar activities on mobilizing funds to enable those who immigrated to Palestine to find work and to have a decent standard of living. Although not a socialist, he promoted the pioneer agricultural communities as a reasonable way of attracting Jews to Palestine. Increasingly concerned with the need to encourage all Jews to support the Zionist enterprise, Weizmann backed the proposal to include leaders of non-Zionist organizations in the Jewish Agency (which was the official liaison with British mandate authorities in Palestine). After a bitter debate, in 1929 the World Zionist Organization enlarged the Jewish Agency.

Increasing violence in Palestine between Arabs and Jews and Weizmann's concern for maintaining harmony created furor in the aftermath of the Arab riots of 1929. This led to his resignation in 1930, but in 1935, he resumed the presidency of the World Zionist Organization. Shifts in the world balance of power and British disenchantment with the policy of supporting the Jewish National Home then weakened Weizmann's authority and diminished his stature. By the end of World War II (1939–1945), his paramount influence with the British and within Zionist circles was all but spent. Weizmann's tenure as president of the World Zionist Organization ended in 1946. With the independence of the State of Israel in 1948, he served, in a largely ceremonial position, as the first president until his death on November 9, 1952.

BIBLIOGRAPHY

BERLIN, ISAIAH. *Personal Impressions.* New York, 1981.
HALPERN, BEN. *A Clash of Heroes.* New York, 1987.
REINHARZ, JEHUDA. *Chaim Weizmann: The Making of a Zionist Leader.* New York, 1985.

Donna Robinson Divine

Weizmann Institute of Science

A center of scientific research and graduate study in Israel.

Founded in 1934, the Weizmann Institute of Science is located in Rehovot, Israel. Dr. Chaim Weizmann, a world-renowned chemist, was the first president of the institute and later became Israel's first president. He organized the institute to pursue "pure" science while also dealing with practical problems facing the country and its economy. In the 1930s, Weizmann started work on projects relating to the citrus industry, dairy farming, and medicine. The institute was formally dedicated November 2, 1949.

The Weizmann Institute has eighteen departments grouped into five faculties: biology, biophysics-biochemistry, chemistry, mathematics, and physics. The student population in 1992/93 was 730.

Miriam Simon

West Bank

That part of Palestinian territory west of the Jordan river captured and occupied by Israel during the June 1967 war.

The West Bank occupies a place in the international consciousness far larger than its geography would suggest. Today it forms the last battleground of the twentieth-century struggle between Israel and the Palestinians over the disposition of the British mandate territories established in the wake of the destruction of the Ottoman Empire after World War I.

The West Bank is situated between Jordanian and Israeli territory. The area, about 2,270 square miles (5,880 sq. km), is defined in the east by the cease-fire line established between Israel and Jordan as a consequence of the 1967 ARAB–ISRAEL WAR. This line follows the path of the Jordan river to the Dead Sea. The term West Bank is derived from the fact that the area is on the left bank of the Jordan river—in that sense, it has always been the "west bank." However, the term only acquired political significance and only came into common usage after the 1967 Six-Day War, when the area was separated from the rest of the Kingdom of Jordan (the East Bank). Israel uses the terms Judea and Samaria (Hebrew, Judah v'Shomron) to describe this region.

The West Bank was originally allocated by the UN partition resolution of November 1947 to the then-to-be created Palestinian state. Palestinian opposition to the resolution and its call for the creation of a Jewish state led to the Arab–Israel War (1948) and Jordan's occupation of northeastern Palestine; the issue of Palestinian independence became moot.

The southern, western, and northern limits of the West Bank are defined by the 1949 armistice border between Israel and Jordan that followed the war. Jordan annexed the area in 1950, when King Abdullah assembled West Bank notables in Jericho to pledge their allegiance both to him and to Jordan; on April 24, Abdullah declared Eastern Palestine's annexation to Jordan. Only Great Britain and Pakistan, however, recognized this move.

After June 1967, the West Bank was administered by Israel as a belligerent occupant according to international law. On June 7, 1967, Israel's area commander for the West Bank issued a military proclamation declaring the assumption by the Israel Defense Forces (IDF) area commander of all "governmental, legislative, appointive, and administrative power" over the region and its inhabitants. Palestinian inhabitants of the West Bank continued until 1995 to be ruled under this system of military government. Municipal governments and village councils administered local services. During Israeli rule, Israel both permitted and canceled scheduled elections for local governments and appointed and dismissed elected and appointed Palestinians as officials.

Israeli settlers were subject to a separate system of laws and justice and political representation as practiced within Israel.

On June 27, 1967, Israeli law, jurisdiction, and public administration were extended over a 28 square mile (73 sq. km) area of the West Bank, including the 2.3 square miles (6 sq. km) that had constituted the municipal boundaries of East Jerusalem under Jordanian rule. This de facto annexation placed East Jerusalem and its Palestinian inhabitants under Israeli sovereignty.

East Jerusalem is considered today by Israel an indivisible part of its capital city. Palestinians view East Jerusalem as their presumptive capital. Other cities in the West Bank include Hebron, Bethlehem, Ramallah, Nablus, Jenin, and Jericho. In 1992, the Israeli settlement of Ma'ale Adumim, with a population of 15,000, became the first Israeli city in the West Bank. Total population in the early 1990s included 1 million Palestinians in the West Bank and 150,000 Palestinians in East Jerusalem; and 130,000 Israeli settlers in the West Bank and 170,000 Israeli settlers in East Jerusalem.

The West Bank and Gaza Strip were the scene of the Palestinian INTIFADA (uprising) that began in December 1987 and continued into the 1990s. In September 1993 the signing of the OSLO AGREEMENT marked the beginning of a transition to Palestinian self-rule.

BIBLIOGRAPHY

ARONSON, GEOFFREY. *Israel, Palestinians, and the Intifada: Creating Facts in the West Bank.* London, 1989.

———, ed. *Report on Israeli Settlement in the Occupied Territories.* Washington, D.C.

BENVENISTI, MERON. *The West Bank Data Project.* Washington, D.C., 1984.

BENVENISTI, MERON, and SHLOMO KHAYAT. *The West Bank and Gaza Atlas.* Jerusalem, 1988.

SHEHADEH, RAJA. *Occupiers Law.* Washington, D.C., 1985.

SHEHADEH, RAJA, and JONATHAN KUTTAB. *The West Bank and the Rule of Law.* Geneva, 1980.

Geoffrey Aronson

West Bank Data Project

Collective research initiative.

The project was begun in the early 1980s by former Jerusalem deputy mayor Meron Benvenisti. He said its goal was to "demystify the treatment of this highly contentious subject" by providing statistical information on the changing daily lives of both Jewish and Arab residents of the West Bank. The project has published several books and pamphlets on economic, demographic, and structural change in the area. Benvenisti concluded by 1984 that Israeli annexation and settlement of the territories was an irreversible process.

BIBLIOGRAPHY

BENVENISTI, MERON. *The West Bank Data Project: A Survey of Israel's Politics.* Washington, D.C., 1984.
———. *The West Bank Handbook: A Political Lexicon.* Jerusalem, 1986.

Elizabeth Thompson

Westernization

Changes in Middle Eastern institutions that followed European models after about 1800; a secularization of many cultural and social institutions.

The term *westernization* is usually equated with modernization, but it is used inaccurately to denote all the changes that took place in the Middle East since the late eighteenth century. Thus, for example, the so-called Tanzimat (reform) programs of 1839 to 1876 often are considered only as expressions of the westernization of the Ottoman Empire. Similarly, the programs of Muhammad Ali Pasha in Egypt or Ahmad Bey in Tunisia appear to some historians as regional manifestations of efforts to replicate Western institutions, customs, and manners. These historians consider anything short of full and complete westernization a failure; thus, they see discrepancies between the Middle Eastern copy and the Western original as shortcomings and inadequacies.

This view is only partially correct—there can be no doubt that the growing importance of the West in the Middle East did have a profound impact on every aspect of Ottoman, Egyptian, and Tunisian life. Western models did guide the evolution of Middle Eastern military, political, educational, social, and cultural institutions and practices; however, local populations and their leaders had their own agendas, which determined the nature, extent, and final shape of their borrowing. The resulting hybrid was not a failure of westernization because it did not fully re-

semble its source of inspiration; rather, the new form blended local ways with foreign borrowings to meet emergent needs. When the European models were unsuitable, they were either rejected or modified. Further, many economic and political changes had indigenous Middle Eastern origins quite independent of the West. The evolution of the later nineteenth-century Ottoman state may be traced to internal developments that date to the sixteenth century. Similarly, capitalism in Egypt emerged from indigenous developments in Islam during the eighteenth century. The argument that the Middle East simply copied from the West as the explanation for all nineteenth-century changes needs to be reassessed and revised.

BIBLIOGRAPHY

GRAN, PETER. *Islamic Roots of Capitalism: Egypt, 1760–1840.* Austin, Tex., 1970.
EL-HAJ, RIF'AT ALI ABOU. *Formation of the Ottoman State: The Ottoman Empire, Sixteenth to Eighteenth Centuries.* Albany, N.Y., 1991.
LEWIS, BERNARD. *The Emergence of Modern Turkey.* London, 1961.

Donald Quataert

Western Sahara

Former Spanish colony in northwest Africa; also called Spanish Sahara.

This area of some 102,700 square miles (266,000 sq. km) is bordered by Morocco, Algeria, Mauritania, and the Atlantic Ocean. It is the subject of a dispute involving the POLISARIO independence movement, Morocco, Algeria, Mauritania, and Libya. Following Namibia's independence in 1989, Western Sahara was the last colonial territory on the African continent whose political status had not been definitively determined and legitimized by the international community. (Recently, a war of independence against Ethiopia resulted in independence for Eritrea.) To rectify this, the United Nations has been attempting since 1986, when the WESTERN SAHARA WAR was still raging, to negotiate and implement a referendum among the inhabitants.

The territory is part of the Sahara desert and consists of *hammada* (mostly barren rocky plateaus), coarse gravel, and sandy plains. It is extremely arid, receiving an average of less than two inches (5.1 cm) of rainfall annually. It is sparsely populated—Spain's census of 1974 counted 73,497 persons (probably an underestimation); a U.S. Central Intelligence Agency (CIA) publication placed the population in 1991 at 196,737, including, presumably, the tens of thousands of Moroccans who have settled there since 1976. The annual growth rate was put at 2.6 percent. The capital is al-Aiun.

The indigenous Sahrawi population is a mixture of Berber tribes (whose presence in the region dates from the first century B.C.E.) and thirteenth-century Arab migrants from southern Arabia. Social organization was tribal, along the lines of confederations, factions, and subfactions. Linguistically, the Hassaniya dialect of Arabic, brought by the Arabian tribes, gradually supplanted Berber dialects. Economically and socially, the tribes were entirely nomadic until the mid-twentieth century. Calling themselves the "sons of the clouds," the Sahrawis roamed constantly in search of grazing land and water for their herds, traded with neighboring sedentary groups, engaged in livestock raiding from one another, and participated in the trans-Saharan caravan trade. Since the nineteenth century, the Reguibat have been the largest tribal grouping.

The nomadic way of life did not fit comfortably with European-introduced notions of fixed territorial delimitations. When coupled with twentieth century events—prolonged droughts, fighting against French and Spanish colonialism, gradual sedentarization, economic change, and, finally, the outbreak of war following Spain's departure—probably as many Sahrawis came to live in neighboring countries (whose boundaries were themselves of twentieth-century origin) as within Western Sahara.

The political status of the area was rarely defined, since it belonged to what is known in Moroccan history as *bilad al-siba,* the lands of dissidence, as opposed to *bilad al-makhzan,* the areas of central, sultanic authority. (Ironically, the Almoravid Empire, the first dynasty to unite Morocco during the eleventh century, originated in Western Sahara and Mauritania.) Political linkages and affiliations with Moroccan sultans in the north varied, depending on the relative strength of the sultan and the various tribes, the relations between individual tribes and the government in the north, and relations among the tribes themselves.

Spain proclaimed a protectorate over part of the region in 1884. The Moroccan nationalist movement, which first emerged in the 1930s, claimed the area as part of its natural patrimony (which included Mauritania and parts of Algeria and Mali as well). The area's status was changed by Spain in 1958 from colony to overseas province. From the late 1950s, the leadership of the newly emerging state of Mauritania also claimed it, partly to deflect Morocco's threat against Mauritania itself. POLISARIO's emergence in 1973 linked for the first time the notions of decolonization and independence for the territory, setting the stage for conflict. Spain agreed to relinquish the area in 1975, and it was divided between the two neighboring claimants, Mauritania and Morocco. Mauritania gave up its claim in 1979. Morocco has occupied the bulk of the territory since then.

BIBLIOGRAPHY

DAMIS, JOHN. *Conflict in Northwest Africa: The Western Sahara Dispute.* Palo Alto, Cal., 1983.
HODGES, TONY. *Historical Dictionary of Western Sahara.* Metuchen, N.J., 1982.
———. *Western Sahara: The Roots of a Desert War.* Westport, Conn., 1983.

Bruce Maddy-Weitzman

Western Sahara War

Conflict over control of Western Sahara, a former Spanish colony in northwest Africa.

Contention over the control of Western Sahara began on the eve of Spain's withdrawal in February 1976. The main protagonists were Morocco, which claimed the territory as an integral part of its historical patrimony, and the Algerian-backed POLISARIO independence movement. Algeria's patronage of POLISARIO was rooted in its larger geopolitical and ideological clash with Morocco. The dispute poisoned their bilateral relations and for a time held out the specter of Algerian–Moroccan fighting. Libya's initial backing for POLISARIO, which continued until the early 1980s, stemmed from Libyan leader Muammar al-Qaddafi's promotion of revolutionary upheaval. Mauritania, the weakest of the states bordering Western Sahara, initially occupied part of the territory as well but was forced to disengage and then maintain a vulnerable neutrality.

Internationally, both the United States and France had strong strategic, political, and economic interests in North Africa. To their relief, the conflict did not become another arena for Cold War competition, as the Soviet Union adopted a low, pragmatic profile. The Organization of African Unity (OAU) was actively involved in attempting to mediate the dispute between 1976 and 1981 but then became an additional arena for it, resulting in temporary organizational paralysis. The United Nations, particularly the Secretariat-General, developed a special organizational and political interest of its own in promoting a settlement.

The parameters of the conflict took shape in the fall of 1975. Following an ambiguous advisory ruling by the International Court of Justice regarding the legal status of the territory, Morocco's King Hassan II seized the initiative by dispatching some 100,000 to 350,000 unarmed Moroccans in a great spectacle of nationalist and religious fervor across the Moroccan–Spanish Sahara frontier. This Green March catalyzed the transfer of Spanish control of the territory to Morocco and Mauritania, enshrined in the tripartite Madrid Accords of November 14, 1975. Spain's formal termination of control came on February 26, 1976. Moroccan troops immediately completed their takeover of the northern two-thirds of Western Sahara, and Mauritania the southern third.

Meanwhile, fighting had already begun between Moroccan forces and POLISARIO units. On one occasion, Algerian forces assisting POLISARIO clashed with Moroccan troops. Concurrently, there was a large-scale civilian exodus (between 35 and 65 percent of the population) to camps in the Tindouf region of Algeria.

Militarily, POLISARIO's small units could not hope to block Morocco's advance. POLISARIO thus redirected its military efforts to focus on Mauritania, the weaker of its adversaries. Between 1976 and 1979, POLISARIO attacks helped destabilize the regime of President Mokhtar Ould Daddah, who was overthrown in July 1978. After renewed pressure, the new Mauritanian military junta agreed in August 1979 to cede their portion of Western Sahara, Tiris al-Gharbia, to POLISARIO. However, the Moroccan army immediately preempted POLISARIO and took control itself.

The next few years witnessed fierce fighting. Morocco was on the defensive against highly motivated and tactically superior POLISARIO mobile units. POLISARIO's strategy was to conduct a war of attrition against Moroccan forces within Western Sahara and southern Morocco, thus rendering the economic and political cost too great for Morocco to bear. Morocco responded by tripling the size of its armed forces to approximately 150,000, stationing more than half of them in Western Sahara, and conducting large-scale sweeps of its own. It also threatened to invoke, but never implemented, the right of hot pursuit against POLISARIO sanctuaries situated in both Algeria and Mauritania.

In the fall of 1980, Morocco began constructing a system of defensive sand walls, studded with fortified positions, observation points, and early warning equipment. The first wall enclosed the so-called useful triangle, one-sixth of the territory encompassing the population centers of al-Aiun and Smara, and the Bou-Craa phosphate mines. Initially, the system was ridiculed as a costly, overly static, and ultimately ineffective strategy. But by 1987, the sixth wall was completed, the network ran over two thousand miles (3,218 km) in length, and POLISARIO had been effectively closed off from 80 percent of the territory. No longer could its Land Rovers traverse the trackless territory from Algeria to the Atlantic; POLISARIO was increasingly limited to sporadic raids along the wall. Concurrently, Morocco poured hundreds of millions of dollars into the region, building schools, hospitals, and telecommunications facilities, staffed by tens of thousands of Moroccan civilians. Morocco's consolidation of its presence was made possible by generous military and civilian aid from France, the United States, and Saudi Arabia.

Whereas POLISARIO's military fortunes declined by the mid-1980s, politically it had achieved a number of successes: diplomatic recognition from over seventy countries for its government in exile, Saharan Arab Democratic Republic (SADR), and full membership in the OAU. The overall result by the late 1980s was a stalemated conflict, with neither side able to impose its will. Consequently, the situation was ripe for a new mediation effort, spearheaded by the UN secretary-general. Discussions on organizing a UN-monitored referendum began in 1986 and continued intermittently.

Increasingly, however, POLISARIO lost diplomatic ground as well. Not only had its military capabilities been severely constrained, but its main patron, Algeria, increasingly distanced itself from the conflict. One indication of this was Algeria's 1988 restoration of diplomatic relations with Morocco. More importantly, the outbreak of violent unrest in October 1988 plunged Algeria into its worst crisis since achieving independence. Although some elements of the ruling circles in Algeria continued to support POLISARIO, and even to assist it in launching occasional attacks against Moroccan positions, Algeria gradually reduced its aid to POLISARIO and retired to a mere supporting role for the UN secretary-general's diplomatic efforts. By the beginning of 1990, POLISARIO was almost completely dependent on the UN-sponsored process.

During the first years of the conflict, POLISARIO had believed that time was on its side, and thus refused to countenance any solution that fell short of full independence. King Hassan, for his part, had staked his throne on the issue, making it the glue by which he consolidated and reinforced his political authority at home. Strategically, he never wavered in his goal to incorporate Western Sahara into his kingdom. Tactically, he showed great flexibility and skill. For example, in 1981, operating from a position of relative weakness, he demonstratively accepted the principle of a referendum among the Sahrawi population during an OAU summit at Nairobi and thus bought much-needed time. By 1990, while still negotiating the details of the referendum, Morocco was operating from a position of strength, as regional and international constellations had shifted in its favor.

In April 1991, the UN Security Council authorized the establishment of a combined military and civilian force, the United Nations Mission for the Referendum in the Western Sahara (MINURSO), to organize and implement a referendum process between September 1991 and January 1992. Eligible Sahrawis were to choose between independence for the territory, necessitating immediate Moroccan withdrawal, and union with Morocco, necessitating the disbanding of POLISARIO.

Despite both sides' agreement in principle to the plan, they continued to disagree on vital aspects, the most important of which was the question of eligibility. The Spanish census of 1974 served as the basis for the voter registration list, numbering just over 70,000, prepared by UN officials. Morocco, however, insisted on major changes, so as to include up to 120,000 persons, who it said belonged to Western Saharan tribes but had migrated north during previous decades for economic or political reasons. POLISARIO wanted small-scale modifications to include more of its supporters. The September 6, 1991, cease-fire called for in the UN plan came into effect, but the timetable for full deployment of MINURSO and implementation of the referendum was repeatedly delayed. At the end of December 1991, the outgoing UN secretary-general, Javier Pérez de Cuéllar, agreed to modify eligibility criteria to include between ten thousand and thirty thousand new persons. The Moroccans expressed satisfaction; POLISARIO, dismay. The maneuvering of both parties continued, and the referendum process remained stalled.

The Western Sahara issue, while still kept alive by UN mediators, has been relegated to the sidelines of an increasingly crowded international agenda. SADR's political successes internationally had not paved the way to independence, marking a major departure from prevailing patterns of decolonization in the Third World. Morocco still desired de jure legitimation of its incorporation of Western Sahara, but its de facto rule there seemed to be accepted as unalterable by a large portion of the international community.

BIBLIOGRAPHY

DAMIS, JOHN. *Conflict in Northwest Africa: The Western Sahara Dispute.* Palo Alto, Calif., 1983.
———. "Morocco and the Western Sahara." *Current History* 89 (April 1990).
HODGES, TONY. *Historical Dictionary of Western Sahara.* Metuchen, N.J., 1982.
———. *Western Sahara: The Roots of a Desert War.* Westport, Conn., 1983.
MADDY-WEITZMAN, BRUCE. "Conflict and Conflict Management in the Western Sahara: Is the Endgame Near?" *Middle East Journal* 45 (Autumn 1991).
———. "Conflict Resolution in the New World Order: The UN and the Western Sahara." *Asian and African Studies* 26, no. 2 (July 1992).
———. "Inter-Arab Relations," annual chapters. *Middle East Contemporary Survey.* Boulder, Colo., annual.
ZARTMAN, I. WILLIAM. *Ripe for Resolution: Conflict and Intervention in Africa,* 2d ed. New York, 1987.

Bruce Maddy-Weitzman

Western Wall

The extant part of the retaining wall surrounding the Temple of Solomon; a Jerusalem landmark and a holy prayer site for Jews.

The Hebrew Ha-Kotel refers to the western retaining wall surrounding Jerusalem's Temple Mount. Sometimes called the "Wailing Wall," since Jews pray and cry near it, it is built of large limestones hewn for the Second Temple, which was enlarged during the reign of Herod (37–4 B.C.E.), king of Judea. It was destroyed by the Romans in 70 C.E.

Since then, the remaining wall has stood as a reminder and symbol of lost glory and the redemption to come; Jews turn toward it when they pray. By tradition, notes to heaven are placed in its cracks. During the British mandate, Jews had limited access in bringing religious appurtenances, which had to adhere to certain rules (e.g., using a curtain to separate men and women) or else were banned. During Jordanian rule, Jews' access to the wall was denied. After the reunification of Jerusalem in 1967, the area was excavated and became again a place of public prayer and assembly. The surrounding plaza is also the site of many national assemblies and civil religious events.

BIBLIOGRAPHY

DRUCK, MOSHE AKIVA, ed. *Western Wall.* Jerusalem, 1979.
HEILMAN, S. *A Walker in Jerusalem.* Philadelphia, 1995.
MEIR, BEN DOV, et al. *The Western Wall.* Tel Aviv, 1983.

Samuel C. Heilman

West German Reparations Agreement

Accord with Israel following World War II.

In September 1945, Chaim Weizmann, on behalf of the Jewish Agency, asked the governments of the United States, the Soviet Union, the United Kingdom, and France, which occupied Germany at the end of World War II, to secure compensation for the Jewish people.

On September 10, 1952, the government of the Federal Republic of Germany agreed to pay 3.45 billion German marks ($845 million) in the form of goods to Israel, in installments between 1953 and 1966. The Conference on Jewish Material Claims against Germany was to allocate 450 million marks ($110 million). Thirty percent of the funds were allocated for the purchase of oil in the UK and 70 percent for goods bought directly by the Israeli government. These funds played an important role in the development of Israel's economy in the 1950s.

This agreement was the result of an Israeli claim for 1 billion U.S. dollars in compensation from West Germany (and a claim for $500 million from East Germany, which was never submitted) to cover the cost of absorbing 500,000 victims of Nazi persecution, estimated at 3,000 U.S. dollars each.

BIBLIOGRAPHY

MINISTRY OF FOREIGN AFFAIRS. *Documents Relating to the Agreement between the Government of Israel and the Federal German Republic, Signed on 10 September 1952 at Luxembourg.* Jerusalem, 1953.

Paul Rivlin

Wheelus Air Force Base

U.S. Air Force base located near Tripoli, Libya.

Wheelus was established as an American military installation in 1954. In return for base rights, the regime of King Idris received military assistance grants and the right to purchase excess stocks of U.S. weapons.

In 1964, Arab nationalism and anti-Western sentiment forced King Idris to call for a withdrawal of Britain's and America's forces. Following the overthrow of Idris in 1969, the United States completed its planned withdrawal and turned the facility over to Libya on June 11, 1970. Libyan pilots subsequently trained there under the guidance of French instructors. Since 1970, June 11 has been a national holiday in Libya.

BIBLIOGRAPHY

Libya: A Country Study, 4th ed. Washington, D.C., 1989.

Stuart J. Borsch

Whirling Dervishes

See Mevlevi Brotherhood

White Flag League

Sudanese nationalist movement founded in 1924.

Ali Abd al-Latif founded the White Flag League when the Sudan was governed by the Anglo–Egyptian CONDOMINIUM AGREEMENT. The group consisted of about 150 minor officials and junior officers in the Egyptian army. Representing an alliance of Sudanese and Egyptian nationalists, it advocated the union of the entire Nile valley under the Egyptian crown.

The White Flag League was largely responsible for the 1924 revolt against the British. Events reached a crisis following the assassination of Sir Lee Stack in Cairo; Britain's Field Marshal Edmund Allenby demanded the immediate withdrawal of Egyptian units from the Sudan. Refusing to obey the order to evacuate, the Egyptian and Sudanese league troops mutinied in Khartoum. When Egypt ordered its units to withdraw, however, they complied. The Sudanese were left to confront the British on their own; their defeat marked the end of the revolt and also that of the White Flag League.

Kenneth S. Mayers

White Papers on Palestine

British policy statements about mandated Palestine issued from 1922 to 1939.

The British government, which ruled Palestine from 1918 to 1948 (under a League of Nations mandate granted in 1922, effective 1923), issued periodic policy statements, called white papers, relating to the tensions and recurring violence between the Arab and Jewish communities there.

The PALIN COMMISSION REPORT (July 1, 1920) was submitted to London as the first document of this type, but it was never made public. Instead of acting on its findings, which advocated the need to reassure the Arab residents that their rights would be maintained and that Zionist organizations in Palestine would be restricted, a civilian administration was established by the British government that reinforced the legal standing of the Palestinian Zionist organizations.

When violence recurred in May 1921, London appointed another commission of inquiry, under Chief Justice Sir Thomas Haycraft. The Haycraft Report (Command 1540), published on October 21, 1921, concluded that the Arabs' feelings "of discontent with, and hostility to, the Jews was due to political and economic causes, and connected with Jewish immigration and with their conception of Zionist policy" as leading to a Jewish state, in which Arabs would be subjugated. The British government came under contradictory pressure from the Zionist organization and the Palestine Arab Executive, which sent a delegation to London from July 1921 until August 1922. The Zionist movement sought firm implementation of the Jewish national home policy, as promised in the Balfour Declaration of November 2, 1917, with the implication that a Jewish state could be formed in Palestine once Jewish immigrants and land settlement permitted. In contrast, the Arab Executive sought explicit annulment of the Balfour Declaration and demanded rapid steps to gain independence under an Arab-majority government.

The CHURCHILL WHITE PAPER of June 1922 (Command 1700) attempted to placate both communities by emphasizing that the Jewish national home existed by right, not by sufferance, but also by stressing that the Arab community should not be subordinated to the Jewish community, much less disappear. The white paper stated that all Palestinians were equal before the law and described the Jewish national home as simply "a center in which the Jewish people as a whole may take, on grounds of religion and race, an interest and a pride." The white paper stated that Jews would have the right to immigrate to Palestine but, in practice, that immigration must not exceed "the economic capacity of the country at the time to absorb new arrivals." Moreover, it stated that London aimed to establish full self-government in Palestine in "gradual stages and not suddenly" and would hold elections soon for a legislative council with twelve elected members and ten officials. (The order-in-council of August 10, 1922, specified that the elected members would comprise eight Muslims, two Christians, and two Jews.) The Churchill White Paper thus tried to reassure the Arabs that they could work toward a degree of self-rule and that limitations would be placed on Jewish immigration. Nonetheless, the Arab Executive objected to the reaffirmation of even a modified version of the Balfour Declaration and rejected the legislative council as an insufficient guarantee of their rights. The Zionist Organization also criticized the white paper for attempting to limit the right of immigration and proposing a legislative council, which its officials hoped could be postponed until the Jewish population was more substantial. In practice, the legislative council was never established, since the Arab community boycotted the elections.

The next white paper (Command 3229) was issued in a declaration in Parliament, by the colonial secretary, on November 19, 1928, as Muslim–Jewish tension escalated over mutual rights in Jerusalem, at the Western (Wailing) Wall. The white paper affirmed that no benches or screens could be brought to the wall by Jews, since they had not been allowed during Ottoman rule. Tension continued to escalate, leading to Arab attacks against Jews at the wall, as well as in several other towns in August 1929. Religious tension compounded growing Arab fears of physical displacement. Four white papers were issued in 1930, which tried to defuse the conflict. The Shaw Commission of Inquiry report (Command 3530), issued March 30, 1930, found that Jewish immigration and land purchases were immediate causes of "Arab apprehension. . . . [And] the Arab feeling of disappointment of their political and national aspirations and fear for their economic future" were the underlying causes of the violence. The report argued that the government must issue clear statements safeguarding Arab rights and regulating Jewish immigration and land purchase. The government's white paper (Command 3682) of May 27, 1930, reaffirmed the findings of the Shaw Commission, welcomed the appointment of an international commission to investigate conflicting claims to the Western Wall, and recommended the appointment of a special commission to assess the problems facing landless Arab peasants and the prospects for expanded agricultural cultivation. Sir John Hope-Simpson's report on the land, issued August 30, 1930 (Command 3686), was published simultaneously with the Passfield White Paper (Command 3692) of October 21, 1930. Hope-Simpson recommended a drastic reduction in the volume of Jewish immigration on the grounds of insufficient cultivable Arab land and widespread Arab unemployment. He specifically criticized the Jewish National Fund, the Zionist Organization's land-purchasing agent, for forbidding the resale of land by Jews to Arabs and for banning Arab laborers on Jewish farms. The white paper accepted those findings and agreed that stricter controls should be placed on Jewish immigration and land purchase. Moreover, it asserted—for the first time—that the British government had obligations "of equal weight" to both communities and that it must renew the effort to establish a legislative council, as proposed in the Churchill White Paper of 1922.

The Arab Executive was pleased with the British policy statements during 1930, since they documented the Arabs' concerns. But Chaim Weizmann, head of the Jewish Agency, threatened to resign and precipitate a crisis if the Passfield White Paper was issued. When he carried out his threat, the British government rapidly backtracked. Zionist officials drafted a letter, signed by Prime Minister Ramsay MacDonald, to Weizmann on February 14, 1931, which expunged all potentially damaging aspects of the Passfield White Paper and upheld the primacy of the government's promises to the Jewish community. Mollified, Weizmann withdrew his resignation, but this infuriated the Arab community.

The white paper of May 17, 1939 (Command 6019), followed three years of Arab rebellion. The Peel Commission had recommended on July 7, 1937, that territorial partition and the establishment of separate Arab and Jewish states were the only solution, since Arab and Jewish aspirations were irreconcilable. Nonetheless, the Woodhead Partition Commission had concluded on November 8, 1938, that partition was not feasible. In early 1939, the British government convened the London Conference, which brought together representatives of the Jewish Agency, several Arab governments, and Palestinian Arabs in lengthy but fruitless discussions. London then issued a unilateral white paper that repudiated the concept of partition and proposed that, over a period of ten years, self-governing institutions would be developed. The eventual independent state would not be dominated by either Arabs or Jews. The white paper also limited Jewish immigration to seventy-five thousand over five years; subsequent immigration would require Arab approval. Moreover, the purchase of land by Jews would be limited in some parts of Palestine and forbidden in others. The white paper thus limited the expansion of the Jewish community and its territorial holdings.

Jewish and Palestinian Arab nationalisms were too intense and too antagonistic for a plan of one nation to succeed. The Jewish community had viewed the Balfour Declaration as a pledge to fulfill their national aspirations. Their concern that the white papers of 1922, 1928, and 1930 had restricted those aspirations gave way to relief when the Peel Commission in 1937 offered an independent state. When the white paper of 1939 withdrew that offer, their reaction was strongly hostile. Their feelings were intensified by the impact of restricting immigration just as thousands of Jews sought to flee Nazi persecution in Europe. In contrast, the Arab community felt relief that London had set aside the idea of partition and promised to restrict Jewish immigration and land purchase. Nonetheless, they were skeptical that the British would fulfill their pledges, since Zionist pressure had undermined earlier white papers; they also feared that independence would not be gained after ten years. In practice, then, the restrictions on Jewish immigration were the only aspects of the white paper of 1939 that were implemented.

BIBLIOGRAPHY

GOVERNMENT OF PALESTINE. *A Survey of Palestine*, vol. 1. Jerusalem, 1946.
INGRAMS, DOREEN. *Palestine Papers, 1917–1922: Seeds of Conflict*. New York, 1973.
LESCH, ANN MOSELY. *Arab Politics in Palestine, 1917–1939*. Ithaca, N.Y., 1979.
STEIN, KENNETH W. *The Land Question in Palestine, 1917–1939*. Chapel Hill, N.C., 1984.

Ann M. Lesch

White Revolution

Period of widespread reform in Iran, 1961–1963.

On May 9, 1961, Mohammad Reza Shah Pahlavi dismissed both the Iranian Majles and the Iranian senate for a period of twenty-nine months. His sudden rule by decree came on the heels of his attempts to implement a reform program, which had previously been undermined by the parliamentary system. The measure proved crucial, for on January 6, 1963, a new law was passed by plebiscite enforcing the Six-Point Reform Program of the White Revolution. Five and half million Iranians voted for the Six-Point Program, thereby launching a reform campaign that drastically changed the social and economic conditions of the entire country. The original items addressed by the shah on January 9, 1963, and endorsed on January 26, consisted of land reforms, nationalization of forests, sales of shares in government-owned industries, worker and employer regulations, voting rights for women, and the formation of a Literacy Corps. The program was augmented through the addition of six other points: the creation of the Health Corps, the start of the Reconstruction and Development Corps, the establishment of various courts of law called the House of Equity, nationalization of water resources, the commitment to urban and rural reconstruction, and the decentralization of administration branches and the modernization of the educational system.

The revolutionary nature of the land reforms unsettled the land aristocracy, who formed 1 percent of the population in control of 56 percent of the land. The most important part of the White Revolution, the land reforms were divided into three stages designed to dismantle the semifeudal system that had prevailed throughout Iran for centuries. In the first stage, no landowner could declare ownership of more than one village. The peasants cultivating the land were given the opportunity to buy the remainder of the villages through government loans, repayable over a fifteen-year period. In the second stage, the landowners who did not take a personal, active role in cultivating the land were to sell or rent these lands to the peasants. In the third stage, landowners who had previously rented their land had to either share their income from the fruits of the land or sell the rented area. The expensive task of financing these reforms was assigned to the public sector in the form of shares of government-owned industries sold to private citizens.

Prior to the reforms, most of the Iranian land tenure system had been based on *métayage,* or sharecropping. In sharecropping, the crop was distributed between the landowner and peasant according to how much each had contributed to the cultivation of the land. Unfortunately, the system did not live up to that principle, and the exploitation of the peasants by landowners was blatant. The peasants received minimal compensation for their work whereas the owner (the state, the religious institutions, the landlords, or the tribal khans), received the bulk of the profits. The proprietors of the large tracts were consequently resentful of the shah and his land reforms and modernization program. Resentment also grew among the clergy, whose charitable WAQF lands did not escape the reach of land reforms. Waqf lands were to be made accessible to the peasants who had cultivated them. After legislation had been passed to allow the peasants to lease these lands for a period of nine years, the *ulama* became increasingly alienated, and they reentered the political sphere. The extensive riots that broke out in Tehran in 1963 were inspired by the *ulama*'s attacks on the shah and his White Revolution. The demonstrations introduced to the Iranian political arena Ruhollah Khomeini, who acquired the title of ayatollah after leading the riots. In many respects, the events of 1963 could be regarded as a prelude to the 1979 Islamic Revolution, and the clergy frequently blamed the reforms of the White Revolution for what they perceived to be the corruption, the decadence, and the erosion of family values in the Pahlavi era. They were also disturbed by the new demands for women's rights, which were continuously reinforced through such agencies as the Women's Organization of Iran and the Family Planning Association of Iran. Women were placed in vocational training programs; they were provided with assistance in matters concerning marriage, divorce, child custody, and working conditions; and they were granted the right to vote. Many of these liberated women were volunteers in the literacy, health, and development corps, which constituted a crucial experiment in the social and economic reconstruction of the rural areas.

Roshanak Malek

Wieseltier, Meir   [1941–   ]

Israeli poet, literary editor, and translator.

Wieseltier, who was born in the Soviet Union, came to Israel in 1949 after spending two years in Poland, Germany, and France. He studied English literature, philosophy, and history at the Hebrew University in Jerusalem. Besides writing poetry, Wieseltier founded and edited several literary publications.

Wieseltier's collections of poetry, such as *100 Poems* (1969) and *Interior and Exterior* (1977) (both in Hebrew), have made him an important voice in Israeli literature since the 1960s. Against the emotional restraint and ambiguous political stance that marked Israeli poetry during the 1950s, Wieseltier wrote forcefully about a wide range of topics. In his poems, he presents exterior reality as a prelude to his interference with it—either by involving himself in it, or by taking a decisive stance in relation to it. Wieseltier does not confine the subjects of his poems to his contemporary world but extends them to include historical figures and events, which he personalizes and manipulates. Precisely because he is aware of life's fundamental ambiguity and the opportunities for vacillation it provides, Wieseltier takes decisive stances in his poems. His answers to the precariousness of the human condition and the brevity of humanity's existence take the shape of definitive ideological choices, which he promotes vigorously. Although Wieseltier recognizes that his very choices are desperate, theatrical gestures of defiance that mean very little, he does not relinquish his right to make them. Knowing the limitation of his choices, he resists what he considers the debilitating influence of compromise.

Yarom Peleg

Wifaq, al-

An organization formed in Morocco to cultivate Muslim–Jewish relations.

Al-Wifaq (French, Entente) was an organization founded under the aegis of the Istiqlal party in Rabat in January 1956 to promote Muslim–Jewish rapprochement on the eve of Moroccan independence. The organizers included a number of Moroccan Jewish political activists, among them Marc Sabah, a protégé of Mehdi Ben Barka, and Albert Aflalo, Sabah's nephew and an employee of the U.S. embassy.

The movement enjoyed little success because of the indifference of the Muslim elite, the apprehensions of the Jewish community at large, and increased tensions caused by events in the Middle East.

BIBLIOGRAPHY

STILLMAN, NORMAN A. *The Jews of Arab Lands in Modern Times.* Philadelphia, 1991.

Norman Stillman

Wilaya

See Vilayet

William Foxwell Albright Institute for Archeological Research in Jerusalem

Institution in East Jerusalem, founded 1900.

The institute, founded by a leading American biblical archeologist and Middle Eastern scholar, is supported by the American School of Oriental Research in Baltimore. Researchers there focus on areas including archeological, biblical, historical, anthropological, and geographical studies related to all periods in the ancient Near East.

BIBLIOGRAPHY

ALBRIGHT, WILLIAM F. *The Archaeology of Palestine and the Bible.* 1932–1935.

Mia Bloom

Wilson, Arnold T.   [1884–1940]

British soldier, explorer, colonial administrator, oil company executive, author, and politician.

Sir Arnold Talbot Wilson spent the first part of his career in the Persian/Arabian Gulf and Mesopotamia (now Iraq), transferring from the Indian Army to the Indian Political Department in 1909. He was British consul in various parts of southwest Persia (now Iran) between 1907 and 1914 and carried out the earliest cartographic surveys of the area (*South-West Persia: A Political Officer's Diary,* 1940). He was also a member of the commission to delineate the frontier between the Ottoman Empire and Persia in 1913/14.

For most of the next six years, Wilson was an administrator in Mesopotamia, first as deputy chief political officer to the Indian Expeditionary Force, then as deputy civil commissioner, serving under Sir Percy Cox in both capacities. In Cox's absence in Tehran between 1918 and October 1920, Wilson was appointed acting civil commissioner in Mesopotamia and the crown's political resident in the Gulf. Comparatively young for such responsibilities, Wilson proved an energetic and tireless admininstrator and inspired intense loyalty in his subordinates (although not in the Civil Commission's oriental secretary, Gertrude Bell). However, a combination of temperament and political inclinations made it difficult for him to accept that Britain could not continue to exercise direct colonial control over Iraq as part of any postwar settlement. His refusal to make any concessions to nationalist sentiment was an important, though by no means the only, factor in precipitating the Iraqi revolution against British rule in the summer and autumn of 1920.

Wilson resigned from his post in Baghdad just before Cox's return to the city in October 1920 and spent the next twelve years working for the Anglo-Persian Oil Company, first in Persia and then in London. He was elected to Parliament as a Conservative in 1933 and 1935 and chaired several parliamentary committees. He published two books about his experiences in Iraq (*Loyalties: Mesopotamia, 1914–1917* and *Mesopotamia, 1917–1920: A Clash of Loyalties*) in 1930 and 1931. They were colored by his anger at what he saw as the failings of British policy and perhaps as the betrayal of his own ideals.

In addition to these and other studies of the Middle East (*The Persian Gulf,* 1928; *The Suez Canal*), Wilson also interested himself in technical social questions. He was joint author of *Industrial Assurance* (1937) and a two-volume study, *Workmen's Compensation* (1940, 1941), whose findings were largely incorporated into British public health and social security legislation after 1945.

In the mid-1930s, Wilson visited Germany, Italy, and Spain. He was evidently "not impressed" by developments there. He voted against sanctions against Italy over Abyssinia and supported Britain's Prime Minister Neville Chamberlain's appeasement of Hitler. On the outbreak of war, however, he realized that he had been mistaken, and in spite of both his age and the exemptions available to members of Parliament, he volunteered, at age fifty-five, for active service as a rear gunner in the Royal Air Force in September 1939. He was killed in action on a bombing raid over Germany in 1940.

BIBLIOGRAPHY

MARLOWE, JOHN. *Late Victorian: The Life of Sir Arnold Talbot Wilson.* 1967.

Peter Sluglett

Wilson, Woodrow   [1856–1924]

U.S. president, 1913–1921.

As president, Wilson attempted to redefine post–World War I politics on the basis of his Fourteen Points (of January 1918), which called for the self-determination of ethnic nations within the spheres of empire lost by the Central powers. The peoples of the Middle East hoped to benefit by this policy, especially the Zionists and the Hashimite leaders of the Arab revolt, since Britain had promised them nationhood in return for their military support against the Central powers.

Wilson led the U.S. delegation at the Paris Peace Conference in 1919, and he was instrumental in forming the League of Nations (although the United States was never a member). He was sympathetic to the Arab cause, but Wilson's program and European imperial realities diverged at the conference. Wilson dispatched the King–Crane Commission to the Middle East in 1919 to evaluate the political aspirations of the peoples there. Its report was not given consideration by the League of Nations, which in 1922 awarded both Britain and France mandates in the Middle East that lasted until after World War II (allowing them control of the development of the petroleum industry, trade, and other commercial interests).

BIBLIOGRAPHY

LANGER, WILLIAM L., ed. *An Encyclopedia of World History.* Boston, 1948.

SHIMONI, YAACOV, ed. *Political Dictionary of the Middle East in the Twentieth Century.* New York, 1974.

Zachary Karabell

Wingate, Charles Orde   [1903–1944]

British military officer who supported Zionism.

A Scot fluent in Arabic, Charles Orde Wingate was sent to Palestine in 1936 as an intelligence officer in the British army, where he translated his Protestant millenarian sentiments into support for Zionism. Ordered by the commander of British forces in Palestine, General Sir Archibald Wavell, to train mixed British and Zionist units in night fighting and guerilla tactics during the Arab revolt (1936–1939), Wingate implemented the doctrine of "active defense." His "special night squads" were organized to protect the Iraq Petroleum Company pipeline. They inflicted casualties on the mufti's rebels and attacked guerilla villages in Syria and Lebanon.

Heroic to the Zionists and ruthless to the Arabs, Wingate's actions appeared to cement a British–Zionist alliance. Wingate was removed from Palestine in 1939 by the British, who considered his Zionist sympathies an embarrassment. During World War II he served as a brigadier in Ethiopia and Burma. He died in an airplane crash in Burma.

BIBLIOGRAPHY

ROYLE, TREVOR. *Orde Wingate: Irregular Soldier.* London, 1995.

Reeva S. Simon

Wingate, Reginald   [1861–1953]

Sirdar (commander in chief) and governor-general of the Sudan, 1899–1916; high commissioner in Egypt, 1916–1919.

Sir Francis Reginald Wingate was educated at the Royal Military Academy, Woolwich, England, and attained the rank of general in the British army. He served in India and participated as director of military intelligence in the campaign led by Lord Kitchener to conquer the Sudan (1896–1898).

During his seventeen-year term as governor-general of the Sudan, Wingate, who spoke Arabic and had detailed knowledge of the country, earned a reputation for competence and hard work. He was an ardent supporter of the ARAB REVOLT (1916) during World War I and consistently urged additional British monetary and military aid for the effort. In 1916, he was appointed high commissioner in Egypt.

With his extensive knowledge of the country, Wingate recognized the rise of Egyptian nationalism, caused in part by increased British military presence and controls during the war. Even before it ended, he advised the British Foreign Office and the British government to make some conciliatory gestures toward Egyptian nationalist feelings. After meeting with the nationalist delegation (Arabic, *wafd*), in November 1918, Wingate recommended that WAFD members be allowed to travel to London for direct negotiations; but Wingate lacked sufficient influence, and his recommendations were curtly rebuffed.

In the face of mounting violence and nationalist demonstrations in Egypt, Wingate was hastily removed from office while vacationing in Britain in 1919; he was replaced by the popular war hero Field Marshal Viscount Edmund Allenby.

BIBLIOGRAPHY

WINGATE, RONALD. *Wingate of the Sudan: The Life and Times of General Sir Reginald Wingate, Maker of the Anglo-Egyptian Sudan.* London, 1955.

Janice J. Terry

Wise, Stephen S.   [1874–1949]

American rabbi and Zionist leader.

Born in Budapest, Wise was brought to the United States as an infant. He graduated from Columbia University at eighteen and was ordained in 1893, serving as the rabbi of Congregation B'nai Jeshurun in New York. He met Theodor Herzl at the second Zionist Congress (1898) and agreed to serve as the American secretary of the Zionist movement. In 1902 Wise received his Ph.D. from Columbia University. In 1907 he founded the Free Synagogue of New York, which was based on freedom of the pulpit and free pews to all. In 1922 he established the Jewish Institute of Religion, which trained rabbis from all branches of Judaism. Later he was instrumental in formulating the text of the Balfour Declaration. In 1936 Wise organized the World Jewish Congress and served as its president until 1949. Wise's views are published in *Free Synagogue Pulpit: Sermons and Addresses* (1908–1932), *Child versus Parent* (1922), *As I See It* (1944), and *Challenging Years* (1949).

BIBLIOGRAPHY

Voss, C. H. *Rabbi and Minister: The Friendship of Stephen S. Wise and John Haynes Holmes.* Buffalo, N.Y., 1980.

Mia Bloom

WIZO

Organization founded to address the needs of women immigrants in Palestine; acronym for Women's International Zionist Organization.

Established in London on July 11, 1920, by the Federation of Women Zionists of the United Kingdom, WIZO focused on agricultural training for women immigrants in Palestine, and on these women's role as citizens and as primary providers of education to children. The founders and leaders of the movement were Vera Weizmann, Edith Eder, Romana Goodman, Henrietta Irwell, and Rebecca Sieff, who served as the first president of WIZO until her death in 1966.

Initially headquartered in London, the organization established a network of federations throughout the world (except in the United States and the USSR). A member of both the World Zionist Organization and the World Jewish Congress, WIZO is now based in Israel, where it supports numerous institutions, such as baby homes for children of preschool age, youth clubs, summer camps and kindergartens for schoolchildren, secondary and agricultural schools, and community centers in border settlements and development towns.

BIBLIOGRAPHY

MARDER, LUCY, and YOSSI AVNER. *Speaking for Women.* Tel Aviv, 1990.

Shimon Avish

WOJAC

See World Organization of Jews from Arab Countries

Wolff, Henry Drummond   [1830–1908]

British mission head who gained economic concessions from Iran.

Sir Henry Drummond Wolff was the head of a special British mission sent to Iran (then Persia) after 1881, when, under a conservative government, the British started actively to support concessions. He was instrumental in obtaining important economic and financial concessions from the Persian government and was sent to Persia in 1888 as British envoy. As a result of Wolff's pressure, the Qajar dynasty monarch, Naser al-Din Shah, opened Persia's only navigable river, the Karun, to international navigation. Wolff, with Baron Julius de Reuter's son, was instrumental in settling claims to the REUTER CONCESSION obtained in 1872. One concession granted by Persia was the right to establish a national bank, the Imperial Bank of Persia, which gave the concessionaires exclusive rights to issue bank notes and other negotiable papers. In 1890, Wolff obtained from the shah for British financiers a monopoly over the production, sale, and export of Iranian tobacco. This concession triggered one of the first successful mass demonstrations in the modern history of Iran, the TOBACCO REVOLT, and so the concession was abandoned.

BIBLIOGRAPHY

KEDDIE, N. *Roots of Revolution: An Interpretive History of Modern Iran.* New Haven, Conn., 1981.

Parvaneh Pourshariati

Wolffsohn, David   [1856–1914]

Second president of the World Zionist Organization.

Born in Lithuania, Wolffsohn received a traditional Jewish education and eventually settled in Cologne, Germany. He was a close friend and adviser to Theodor Herzl and succeeded him as president of the World Zionist Organization (1905–1911). In 1899 Wolffsohn founded the Jewish Colonial Trust, the financial instrument of the World Zionist Organization, and was its head until his death.

BIBLIOGRAPHY

HERTZBERG, ARTHUR. *The Zionist Idea.* New York, 1979.

Martin Malin

Women

Traditionally women had a subordinate role to men in the mostly patriarchal Middle East.

The study of women in the modern Middle East has changed dramatically since the 1960s. Before 1970, few scholars studied women or wrote about them except to mention them incidentally or to evoke stereotypical images. In the mid-1970s, newly published edited collections of studies on women helped to inspire further work. Many monographs devoted to the study of women in specific places and historical periods followed. Just as earlier studies of Middle Eastern society neglect the presence and impact of women, many of these new studies fail to indicate how women fit into the broader societies in which they live. By the early 1990s, writers in increasing numbers have attempted to integrate the study of women into mainstream scholarship, so that, for example, a study of the emergence of Palestinian nationalism would by necessity include accounts of the political ideologies and activities of women as well as men. As another example, studies of an increasingly politicized Islamic fundamentalism are more likely now than in the past to include a serious discussion of women's attitudes and actions. The study of Middle Eastern women, however, still has a long way to go before being fully acknowledged and accepted by the majority of the area's specialists. In addition, negative and distorted images of women continue to mar the work of many Western journalists.

Significant trends in the Middle East in the past two hundred years affecting women (and the rest of society) include colonialism, imperialism, expansion of capitalism, loss of or decrease in local control, modernization, westernization, the rise of nationalism, and the politicization of religious institutions and ideologies. Women have both gained and lost rights and opportunities as a result of these processes. It is not possible here to summarize the many changes that have occurred for them during this long period, for their situations have been diverse and complex. It is possible to note, however, that as outside—especially Western—influence and control have increased, and as members of Middle Eastern societies have been decreasingly able to control their own political and economic affairs, control by men over women *has* apparently increased in many parts of the region. For many men, the home and family have become the sole remaining area of life where they can exert power and authority. Societal institutions and cultural norms support this asymmetry.

Women demonstrating in Oran, Algeria, 1992. (© Susan Slyomovics)

Women wearing traditional dress in Turkey, 1952.
(D.W. Lockhard)

In the 1990s—as in the past—women and girls made up 51 percent of the population of the Middle East, a large area of great political, economic, social, and cultural complexity. Accordingly, no single pattern could possibly characterize their lives, either in the present or the past. They represent the full range of political, economic, educational, occupational, and social positions found in society and are subject to the same pressures exerted by rapid economic and social change that affect society as a whole. In some countries, the statuses and roles of many women have changed dramatically in the twentieth century, especially since the 1950s. In all countries, some women in the 1990s follow the same social patterns generations of women before them had followed.

In some countries, changes have resulted because of new legislation favoring women's greater rights. In other countries, new legislation has upheld women's customary statuses and roles or has increased restrictions on their rights. Key legislation affecting women includes introducing or facilitating voting rights, raising the legal age for marriage, banning or restricting a husband's right to take additional wives, and increasing women's rights in divorce, child custody, property ownership, and inheritance. Legal re-

formers can work within the framework of religious law to provide women with greater rights; the notion that women's rights and Islam, for example, are incompatible is proven false in many areas. Enacting legal rights and effffectively implementing new laws at the local level are separate processes, however, as the case of twentieth-century Turkey and other states indicate. Muslim men who ignore state laws prohibiting or restricting polygamy (more precisely, polygyny), for example, are aware that children born from nonlegal polygynous unions will be subsequently and routinely legitimized by state decree.

Although studies of Middle Eastern women fall into many different categories, several general orientations can be detected. Some authors, focusing on the hierarchical and patriarchal nature of society and on male domination, examine the patterns and negative effects of the subordination and suppression of women. Other authors, perhaps also acknowledging hierarchy and patriarchy, choose to focus instead on women's creative strategies and coping devices and the lives they actively form for themselves. While perhaps not occupying positions in society "equal" to men's, women are depicted as finding social support and emotional satisfaction for themselves.

To assess the status of women in specific communities, it is necessary to examine many factors, including their family's socioeconomic position in the wider society, the degree of their participation in the division of household labor, their rights to control the products they produce and the services they offer, their rights to make decisions for themselves and their children, their degree of formal education and the ways they apply it, and their participation in political, economic, religious, and social activities outside the family and household.

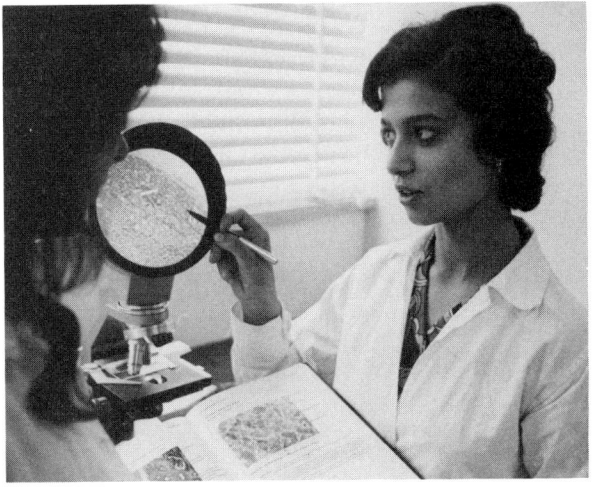

A young woman at the University of Jordan training to be a nurse. (UNRWA)

A modern woman sits with her traditionally dressed grandmother in Iran during the 1970s. (Sandra Batmangelich and the University of Chicago)

Some women in all Middle Eastern states are playing a role in improving their status and enhancing their position in society as a whole. In some states, such as Yemen and Afghanistan, only a small number of women are involved. In others, such as Turkey, Egypt, Jordan, and Morocco, many women are active in different kinds of political, religious, and social movements. In Pakistan, the Sudan, and some other states, women organize political parties to effect legal and other changes. In postrevolutionary Iran, women work through local religious institutions to improve conditions for themselves, their families, and the wider society. Women have played important roles in revolutionary struggles in Algeria, Iran, the Sudan, and Eritrea and in the Palestinian nationalist movement, and they are active in secularist movements and both Islamic fundamentalist and Islamic reform movements. As women gain literacy and increase their knowledge of Islamic and state law, they are better able to defend their rights and to interpret religious and civil law in ways that are beneficial to them.

State and local political institutions in Israel support and facilitate the participation of many women in society as a whole, particularly in education, occupations, politics, and the military. Many Jewish women have the same range of roles and statuses as those found in Europe and the United States today. Jewish women who emigrated from different parts of the Middle East, such as Yemen and Morocco, have varying patterns, some common to the Middle East. The statuses and roles of Arab Muslim, Christian, and Druze women in Israel and the territories occupied by Israel in 1967 tend to be similar to those among their coreligionists in the surrounding states. National-minority status and military occupa-

tion are additional burdens to their already difficult lives.

Many observers note that friendships among women in the Middle East are intense and enduring and that women's primary relationships, other than with their children, are with other women. The visiting patterns of kinswomen and female neighbors and coreligionists are an important part of local and community-wide social life. Women share information and assist one another in times of need.

Some observers who recognize differences between the lives of men and women in the Middle East suggest the existence of separate men's ("public" and formal) and women's ("private," domestic, and nonformal) worlds. As information about Middle Eastern women accumulates, however, many observers retreat from such possibly misleading analytical distinctions. Women's political activities, visiting patterns, and participation in religious and ritual activities demonstrate that women often act outside the home and immediate neighborhood. In many areas, also, women earn income through economic transactions and perform wage or salaried work in public arenas.

Middle Eastern women, as with women around the world, face ideological constraints affecting their behavior. Notions of propriety for women are important for them as well as for their kinsmen, and many women say they feel constrained by societal pressures if they engage in any uncommon or non-traditional activities. Many women, for example, have found it difficult to continue with formal education beyond the primary level or to work outside the home for pay because of concerns about their modesty and safety. With rapid economic change and the disappearance of many traditional home-based income-producing activities, financial necessity sometimes overrides customary ideological and social constraints. National and international labor migration, involving millions of Middle Eastern men, also places additional pressures on women to find ways to support themselves and their families during men's absences. The strategies developed by women often involve their greater participation in society as a whole.

The religious beliefs and practices of observant Muslim women are often quite different from men's. In some places women are restricted from the mosque, while in others they are relegated to a secluded section of it. Some girls receive a religious Qur'an-based education, but many others do not. For many Muslim women, their main religious activities occur outside the mosque, often in homes, and they create a religious life for themselves through local pilgrimages, attendance at shrines, contact with local religious practitioners (often women), Qur'an readings, vows, and amulets. Women in some areas, particularly North Africa and Pakistan, participate in Sufi organizations, often alongside men. A minority of Middle Eastern women are members of other faiths, including Christianity and Judaism.

The quintessential symbol of the Middle Eastern woman is the veil, and undue attention has been given to it, often at the expense of many other factors that are actually more determinative of her status and role. Veiling needs to be viewed within a wide context, for it is only one of many factors in the position of women. As an example, many middle-class, formally educated Egyptian women, whose mothers and grandmothers may never have veiled, adopt what is considered modest dress and hence are able to work at salaried jobs outside the home, among strangers, because of the symbolic protection provided by this attire. Veiling can also symbolize social and economic status, ethnic and national identity, religiosity, political affiliation, and, in the case of Iran between 1978 and 1980, revolutionary fervor.

Virtually no Middle Eastern women, if they are veiled at all, wear the Hollywood version of the veil, a small diaphanous cloth draped across only the nose and mouth. Veiling for Middle Easterners means a range of possibilities, from only a small headscarf covering part of the head and hair to a totally head- and body-enveloping opaque cloth with an embroidered lattice for the wearer's eyes. Some women cover their faces, except for their eyes, while most others do not. In some places, girls are dressed modestly when they reach school-age, while in others, modest dress comes at or just before puberty. Clothing restrictions often loosen when women move past their childbearing years. Elderly women in many settings are freed from clothing and other social restrictions. Respect for their opinions and decisions often increases with their age.

In growing numbers, Middle Eastern women are expressing through poetry, fiction, autobiography, and social analysis their own notions of their place in society and culture. Having been viewed negatively for so long by so many outsiders, especially Westerners, some of these women oppose further efforts by outsiders to comment on their lives, and they assert the importance of assuming that task for themselves.

Middle-class women are often seen as the major agents of change in the Middle East. They play pivotal roles as both secularists and Islamists. Upper-class women form a small proportion of the region and often play a negligible role in wider societal concerns. Lower-class women, a large proportion of the region, undergo severe economic constraints and are often occupied by issues of their own and their families' survival. As the middle class expands, its women will play increasingly important roles in society as a whole.

Although Benazir Bhutto is a unique example and a member of the upper class, her reelection in 1993 as prime minister of Pakistan demonstrates what a determined and politically savvy woman can do and the widespread impact she can have. By dressing modestly, her hair always partially covered in public, and by framing her behavior to conform with the ideals held by the majority of this Muslim population, she has managed to overcome many of the general societal restrictions that affect her gender.

[See also: Marriage and Family]

BIBLIOGRAPHY

ABU-LUGHOD, LILA. *Veiled Sentiments: Honor and Poetry in a Bedouin Society*. Berkeley, Calif., 1986.

BECK, LOIS, and NIKKI KEDDIE, eds. *Women in the Muslim World*. Cambridge and London, 1978.

FERNEA, ELIZABETH, ed. *Women and the Family in the Middle East: New Voices of Change*. Austin, Tex., 1985.

FERNEA, ELIZABETH, and BASIMA BEZIRGAN, eds. *Middle Eastern Muslim Women Speak*. Austin, Tex., 1977.

MILANI, FARZANEH. *Veils and Words: The Emerging Voices of Iranian Women Writers*. Syracuse, N.Y., 1992.

MOGHADAM, VALENTINE. *Modernizing Women: Gender and Social Change in the Middle East*. Boulder, Colo., 1993.

EL-SAADAWI, NAWAL. *The Hidden Face of Eve: Women in the Arab World*. Boston, 1982.

TUCKER, JUDITH. *Women in Nineteenth Century Egypt*. Cambridge, U.K., 1985.

Lois Beck

Women's Services

Services available to women in Turkey.

The Turkish parliament's confirmation of the United Nations convention against discrimination based on sex in October 1980 formed the legal basis for the government's providing services to women. It started with the establishment of a Women's Unit within the State Planning Organization in 1985. It was followed by the creation of the General Directorate of Women's Affairs (Kadının Statüsü ve Sorunları Genel Müdürlüğü) within the Ministry of Labor and Social Security in 1990. This directorate was to collect data concerning the status of women in Turkey and their major problems. It was transferred in 1991 to the office of the prime minister.

In 1993, an independent undersecretary for women's affairs and social services (Başbakanlık Kadın ve Sosyal Hizmetler Müsteşarlığı) was created within the office of the prime minister, and the general directorate came under the supervision of this undersecretary. In 1991, the directorate had a staff of five; in 1994, the staff had grown to forty-two. The provincial network has not yet been established. In 1994, its budget was about 0.002 percent of the national budget.

Special women's units have been set up in the ministries of Health, Labor and Social Security, and National Education. In 1993 the State Statistical Institute created a data bank for women's issues.

Several Turkish universities have established women's studies centers that offer graduate courses and M.A. degrees:

1. Istanbul University Women's Studies Center (Istanbul Üniversitesi Kadın Sorunları Araştırma ve Uygulama Merkezi), in 1990
2. Marmara University Women's Labor Force and Employment Center (Marmara Üniversitesi Kadın İşgücü İstihdamı Araştırma ve Uygulama Merkezi), in 1990
3. Ankara University Women's Studies Center (Ankara Üniversitesi Kadın Sorunları Araştırma ve Uygulama Merkezi), in 1993
4. The Middle East Technical University Women's Studies Graduate Program (ODTÜ Kadın Çalışmaları Yüksek Lisans Programı), in 1994

In 1980 local governments started to sponsor literacy courses, legal advice centers, and occupational orientation services for women. However, these programs remained confined to municipalities in the metropolitan areas. In 1993 labor unions began to establish women's commissions in order to acquaint female workers with their legal rights. Almost all major political parties also have women's commissions as well.

Nongovernment organizations concerned with women's issues number 211. Their major endeavors have been to increase women's visibility on the national level and create favorable public opinion regarding legislative and administrative initiatives that benefit women. They are instrumental in raising consciousness and establishing various types of platforms, particularly combating sexual harassment and violence in the family. The Women's Library and Data Bank (Kadın Eserleri Kütüphanesi ve Bilgi Merkezi Vakfı), which is supported by a foundation and the city of Istanbul, has been active in collecting oral histories of women leaders and artists and creating an archive for historical records.

Nermin Abadan-Unat

Woodhead Commission

British commission sent to Palestine in 1938.

The commission was led by Sir John Woodhead and charged with attempting a partition plan. It was to recommend boundaries for two self-sufficient states, proposed by the Peel Commission, as an alternative to the British mandate territory, which was becoming unworkable because of tensions between Arabs and Zionists.

In its October 1938 report, the Woodhead Commission concluded that an inevitable consequence of partition would be injustice to both parties; it was therefore unable to recommend specific boundaries for two self-supporting states.

BIBLIOGRAPHY

ROLEF, S. H., ed. *Political Dictionary of the State of Israel.* New York, 1987.

Benjamin Joseph

World Bank

International financial institution that supports developing countries.

The World Bank is an international organization based in Washington, D.C. It includes the International Bank for Reconstruction and Development (IBRD), along with the International Development Agency (IDA). IBRD has two affiliates, the International Finance Corporation (IFC) and the Multilateral Guarantee Agency (MIGA).

IBRD was established in 1945 and is owned by

TABLE 1

Relative Voting Strength on the World Bank Board

Members on the Executive Board	% Votes in IBRD	% Votes in IDA
Algeria	3.41	2.24
Saudi Arabia	3.15	3.47
Kuwait	2.94	2.5
Total	9.5	8.21

Source: World Bank Annual Report, 1994 (The World Bank, Washington, D.C.)

TABLE 2

Statement of Subscriptions to the Capital Stock and Voting Power of Middle Eastern Countries

Country	Capital Subscribed*	Capital Paid*	% of Vote
Algeria	1,116.00	67.10	0.65
Bahrain	133.00	5.70	0.09
Egypt	857.00	50.90	0.51
Iran	2,857.00	175.80	1.65
Iraq	339.00	27.10	0.21
Israel	573.00	33.20	0.34
Jordan	167.00	7.80	0.11
Kuwait	1,602.00	97.40	0.93
Lebanon	41.00	1.10	0.04
Libya	946.00	57.00	0.56
Morocco	337.00	26.90	0.21
Oman	188.00	9.10	0.12
Qatar	132.00	9.00	0.09
Saudi Arabia	5,404.00	335.00	3.15
Syria	149.00	10.50	0.10
U.A.E.	288.00	22.60	0.18
Total	15,129.00	936.20	8.89

*In millions of dollars.

Source: World Bank Annual Report, 1994 (The World Bank, Washington, D.C.).

TABLE 3

Loans to Middle East Countries by the World Bank in 1994

Country	IBRD Loans	IBRD Loan Amounts*	IDA Loan Amounts*
Algeria	2	140.00	
Egypt	2	54.00	67.00
Jordan	2	100.00	
Lebanon	2	77.10	
Morocco	5	412.00	
Tunisia	3	267.50	
Yemen			33.00
Total	16	1,050.60	100.00

*In millions of dollars.

Source: World Bank Annual Report, 1994 (The World Bank, Washington, D.C.).

152 countries. The bank resources come from its capital, retained earnings, and very large loans from the world financial markets (8.9 billion U.S. dollars in 1994). Its high creditworthiness allows it to borrow at the most competitive rates. IBRD lends to the more advanced developing countries on creditworthy and productive projects. Pricing is based on the cost of funds to the bank. Loans are made to governments or are guaranteed by governments. Total IBRD loans made in 1994 totaled 20,836 million U.S. dollars. IFC, established in 1956, and MIGA, established in 1984, deal with the private sectors of the developing countries. MIGA is mandated to encourage private equity investments by providing noncommercial risk guarantees.

IDA lends interest free to the very poor countries with an annual per capital GNP of 650 U.S. dollars or less per year. The loans have very long maturities and up to ten years grace period. Loans made by IDA in 1994 amounted to 6,592.1 million U.S. dollars.

The World Bank's executive board is responsible for the general operations of the bank. The board approves projects, funding programs and general management of both the IBRD and the IDA. The board is composed of twenty-four members. Each member represents and votes for his country as per its percentage contribution to the capital of either IBRD or IDA. Certain countries will also represent blocks of smaller members and vote on their behalf. The largest vote belongs to the United States with 17.42 percent of the IBRD and 15.67 percent of the IDA.

Saudi Arabia has the largest single Arab state representation on the World Bank board with 3.15 percent of the votes of the IBRD and 3.45 percent in IDA. Although Algeria appears to have numerically greater voting power, it represents seven countries, including Iran and Morocco. Kuwait represents Bahrain, Egypt, Jordan, Libya, Syria, United Arab Emirates, and Yemen.

In the Middle East, the World Bank's stated goals are "to emphasize sustained commitment to operations and analytical work, to promote employment-led growth, to foster human resources development, and to improve natural resource management." The bank provides support to countries that agree to implement stabilization and structural reform. These conditions imply substantial efforts to reduce budget deficits, cut subsidies, allow currencies to reach their market levels, and privatize the economy. Accordingly Morocco has been a major recipient of World Bank money with 2.4 billion U.S. dollars committed to it between 1990 and 1994, for a total committed to the region of 7.9 billion U.S. dollars. In the same period, Egypt received commitments of 1.3 billion U.S. dollars and Algeria 1.5 billion U.S. dollars.

Jean-François Seznec

World Federation of Sephardi Communities

Organization to support Sephardic settlement in Palestine/Israel.

A conference of Sephardic communities was held in Vienna in 1925. It created Sephardic settlements at Kfar Hittim, Zur Moshe, and Beit Hannan. In 1947 a new Sephardic organization, under A. Elyashar, was set up in Israel. The Sephardi World Congress was convened in Paris in 1951, and A. Ben-Roy was elected president. Its activities in Israel have been concentrated primarily in education and in helping the economically underprivileged Sephardic communities. It also coordinates activities with the Diaspora Sephardic community.

BIBLIOGRAPHY

Judaica Decennial Book, 1973–1982.

Mia Bloom

World Organization of Jews from Arab Countries (WOJAC)

International organization created during the late 1960s.

WOJAC's charter states that Jews from Arab lands can and should form a bridge of understanding between the Arab countries and Israel. Its leaders stress that UN Resolution 242, which spells out "the necessity for a just settlement of the refugee problem," refers to all refugees, Jews and Arabs alike; thus the legitimate rights of post-1948 Jewish refugees from Arab countries will be acknowledged.

WOJAC supports Israel's and the Jewish Agency's position that the property Jews of Arab lands left behind, and the compensation to which they may be entitled, should be taken into account. WOJAC has called upon Syria to permit all Jews who wished to emigrate to do so, in accordance with the promise made by Syria's President Hafiz al-Asad to former U.S. President Jimmy Carter at Geneva in 1977.

BIBLIOGRAPHY

"Resolutions of the Third International Conference: WOJAC—The World Organization of Jews from Arab Countries." Washington, D.C., October 28, 1987. Unpublished document.

"The Third National Convention of WOJAC—World Organization of Jews from Arab Countries." Herzliyya, Israel, April 5, 1990. Unpublished document.

Michael M. Laskier

World War I

War involving the Central powers (Germany, Austria-Hungary, Bulgaria, and the Ottoman Empire) against the Allies (Britain, France, Russia, Belgium, Greece, Romania, Italy, Portugal, Serbia, Montenegro, Japan, and the United States).

World War I (then called the Great War) began on July 28, 1914, when Austria declared war on Serbia (ostensibly because a Serbian nationalist assassinated the heir to the throne, Austrian Archduke Franz Ferdinand, and his wife on June 28); on August 1, Germany declared war on Russia; on August 3, Germany declared war on France; on August 4, Germany invaded Belgium.

In retaliation and to aid an ally, Britain declared war on Germany on August 4. The Russians crossed their western border at the Ukraine to enter Austro-Hungarian Galicia and pressed on to battle Germany, losing the Battle of Tannenberg (August 26–30), on what came to be called the Eastern Front. Germany marched on France in late August but was stopped in the First Battle of the Marne (September 6–10) on what came to be called the Western Front; here trench warfare ensued until March 1918.

In the Middle East, the leadership of the Ottoman Empire was divided among those who desired neutrality, those who wanted to join the Allies, and those who preferred to join the Central powers. The last group, led by Minister of War Enver Paşa prevailed. The Ottoman cabinet signed a secret alliance with Germany on August 2. The next week the Ottomans purchased the German cruisers *Goeben* and *Breslau*, replacing two Turkish ships (being built by Britain but confiscated by Britain at the outbreak of war). Renamed *Sultan Selim Yavuz* and *Midilli*, they shelled Sevastopol and Odessa, Russian cities on the Black Sea, October 28, bringing the Ottoman Empire into the war; Russia declared war on the Ottomans November 4; Britain and France declared war on them November 5. Germany dominated Ottoman military actions, with General Otto Liman von Sanders directing the army and Admiral Wilhelm Souchon, the navy.

In November 1914, a British naval contingent bombarded the entrance to the Dardanelles, and in

January 1915 the British organized to break through the Turkish Straits (from the Mediterranean into the Black Sea at the Bosporus and Dardanelles). Britain's First Lord of the Admiralty Winston Churchill convinced the war cabinet that an amphibious attack could accomplish this, thereby taking the Ottomans out of the war and opening a supply route to Russia. Britain's War Secretary Lord Kitchener sabotaged the plan by refusing to send the necessary land troops. Britain's navy unsuccessfully attacked in February and March; in April an Anglo–French army landed on the Gallipoli peninsula, where the Ottoman Turks caused heavy casualties to the Allies, which by then included Italian forces. The British–French–Italian forces almost broke through twice, but the lack of cooperation by the Russians at the Bosporus end of the Straits, faulty intelligence and, most of all, skillful tactics by the Turks and Germans led to a stalemate. The Allies withdrew from the Straits in January 1916.

Another area of major Middle Eastern hostilities was Egypt, under British protection since December 18, 1914. Khedive Abbas Hilmi was deposed, and the British appointed Sharif Husayn ibn Ali to be sultan of Egypt. Cemal Paça, Ottoman minister of marine, took over the Fourth Ottoman army—thereby controlling Syria, including Palestine. He sent his forces to make a surprise attack on the Suez Canal in February 1915; they crossed the Negev desert without detection. The Turkish forces could not hold the eastern bank of the canal and retired to the Sinai desert, maintaining bases in Maan, Beersheba, and Gaza. Jemal continued to raid the Suez Canal by air, forcing the British to keep a large force there, but in the end the British prevailed. A second assault on the canal was delayed until the summer of 1916 and failed totally. The Turco–German forces were on the defensive there until the end of the war, although in March and April 1917 they withstood a heavy British attack at Gaza, and moved to the offensive in the Yilderim Operation commanded by General Erich von Falkenhayn. But the Turko–German forces were defeated by a combination of factors, including the troops of British General Edmund Allenby (commander of the Egyptian Expeditionary Force), failure of some of their transport, and sabotage.

Major battles were fought in Russia, where in late 1914 the Turks attempted to take Kars and Batum. In the battles of 1915 and 1916 the Russians took Erzerum, Van, Trabzon, and Erzinjan. They were aided by Armenians—revolutionaries and irregulars. In 1916, Mustafa Kemal (Atatürk), commander of the Second Ottoman Army, joined the Third Army on the Caucasus front, but little was accomplished

due to scarce ammunition, impossible conditions for transportation, and rampant disease. The two revolutions in Russia also affected the Caucasus front, as the Russian troops (except the Armenian and Georgian divisions) withdrew and went home to attend to domestic affairs in 1917. The Turks then occupied Kars, Ardahan, and Batum, but Georgian and German forces retook Batum. A Bolshevik–Armenian coup in Baku and the killing of ten thousand Turks there produced a Turkish drive to recapture the city in September 1918 and to kill many Armenians. At the end of the war, the Caucasus became the Allies' problem.

Iraq was the scene for the major hostilities of the Mesopotamia Campaign. British forces from India seized Basra before Turkey declared war. Traveling up to the confluence of the Tigris and Euphrates rivers, the Anglo–Indian forces under General Sir Charles Townshend took Kut al-Amara in 1915. In November, his army was defeated south of Baghdad and surrendered to the Sixth Turkish Army at Kut al-Amara in April 1916. Halil Pasha erred in allowing the Anglo–Indian forces to remain in the south, for they reestablished their hold there, built a railroad, and under Britain's General Sir Frederick Stanley Maude, retook Kut al-Amara in March 1917. Baghdad fell immediately after, and the Anglo–Indian forces headed north to Mosul (on the west bank of the Tigris), which they failed to reach by the time of the MUDROS ARMISTICE (October 30, 1918).

Two national groups within the Ottoman Empire openly aided the enemy during the war: the Arabs and the Armenians. The Armenians followed the orders of the head of the Armenian Orthodox Church (who lived in Yerevan in the Caucasus) that the Russian czar was the protector of all Armenians. Some Armenians rebelled; in the region of Van and Erzurum, Armenians openly battled the Turks proclaiming an Armenian government in Van, April 1915—which touched off the Armenian deportations and the massive killing of Armenian civilians by the Turks in 1915/16.

Cemal Paça's actions in Syria—in arresting and hanging about thirty Arabs in Beirut and Damascus 1915/16, many from prominent families, as well as his refusal to share grain with the starving Lebanese in 1916—pushed many Arabs to desire independence from Ottoman Turkey. This desire was furthered by the proclamation of Arab independence by Sharif Husayn ibn Ali of the Hijaz in June 1916. Husayn's action was part of the outcome of the secret HUSAYN–MCMAHON CORRESPONDENCE.

Another secret negotiation over the division of the Arab Middle East was the SYKES–PICOT AGREEMENT between France, Britain, and Russia. An open negotiation between the Zionists and the British had led to the issuance of the November 1917 pro-Zionist Balfour Declaration, concerning a "Jewish national home" in Palestine.

The failure of the German–Turkish campaigns led to the buildup of British troops in Egypt and their move into Palestine. General Allenby led his Egyptian Expeditionary Forces west of the Jordan river, and Jerusalem fell to them in December 1917. Joined by French military detachments, he moved north to take Lebanon, while Hijazi forces, aided by Colonel T. E. Lawrence (of Arabia), Colonel C. C. Wilson, and Sir Reginald Wingate, paralleled Allenby's actions east of the Jordan. Damascus fell in October 1918—and although Mustafa Kemal (Atatürk) and the Seventh Turkish Army held Aleppo, the armistice at Mudros ended all fighting, October 30, 1918.

Four years of war had devastated Ottoman Turkey, and the old order died. A new period for the Middle East began with the peace treaties, the rise to power in Turkey of Mustafa Kemal, the fall of empires, and the creation of new nation-states and spheres of influence.

BIBLIOGRAPHY

BARKER, A. J. *The Bastard War: The Mesopotamian Campaign of 1914–1918.* New York, 1967.

FISHER, S. N. *The Middle East: A History.* New York, 1966.

KEDOURIE, ELIE. *England and the Middle East: The Destruction of the Ottoman Empire, 1914–1921.* London, 1978.

LEWIS, BERNARD. *The Emergence of Modern Turkey.* London, 1968.

Sara Reguer

World War II

War involving the Axis (Germany, Italy, Japan, Hungary, Romania, and Bulgaria) against the Allies (Britain, France, the United States, the Soviet Union, Australia, Belgium, Brazil, Canada, China, Denmark, Greece, the Netherlands, New Zealand, Norway, Poland, South Africa, and Yugoslavia).

When World War II began on September 1, 1939, the Middle East consisted of independent, semi-independent, and colonial states. From east to west they included the following: Iran and Turkey were independent, with Iran under Reza Shah Pahlavi and Turkey a republic. Syria and Lebanon were republics but under French control. Transjordan and

Iraq were monarchies but under British control. Palestine was a League of Nations mandate under British control. The Arabian peninsula consisted of Saudi Arabia and Yemen, both independent, and Oman and a variety of Persian/Arabian Gulf states within the British sphere of influence. Egypt (with the strategic Suez Canal) and the Sudan were nominally independent but really under British control. Libya was an Italian colony. The French effectively controlled the rest of North Africa—Tunisia, Algeria, and Morocco—except for the western regions under Spanish rule.

In World War II, Britain and France were allied against Germany and Italy. All except Germany had significant imperial holdings and interests in the Middle East. Germany wanted not only the defeat of Britain and France, but German gains in this region. As the war began, the Axis powers controlled only a small part of the Middle East—Libya and some other Italian territory taken during the Ethiopian annexation in 1935. The fall of France to Germany in May 1940 and the establishment of the quasi-independent Vichy republic in June 1940 dramatically altered the balance of power: In addition to Italy's territories being in their sphere of influence, the Axis powers had acquired France's territories.

The British initiated their first military action in the Middle East by an attack on French naval vessels at Oran, Algeria, July 3, 1940—which crippled the French fleet there (and resulted in 1,300 French dead). This was part of an effort to ensure that the Axis powers could not use the French fleet; the French squadron at Alexandria was disarmed while two French submarines in British ports joined the Free French forces fighting with the British. The next day, Italian forces from Ethiopia occupied border towns in the Sudan and within six weeks penetrated British Kenya and seized British Somaliland. On September 13, Italian forces under Rodolfo Graziani invaded Egypt, penetrated some sixty miles (90 km) within a week, and dug in along a fifty-mile (80 km) front from the coast to Sidi Barrani.

Since the threat to the Suez Canal was of primary importance, the British countered first against Graziani's army of 200,000. General Sir Archibald Wavell launched a surprise attack with an army of 63,000 on December 6 and drove through the Italian lines at Sidi Barrani, capturing 40,000 Italian troops by December 12. The campaign continued for two months, ending with Italian surrender at Benghazi, Libya, on February 7, 1941. With advance units at al-Agheila, the British had advanced about five hundred miles (800 km), captured 130,000 Italian soldiers, and taken four hundred tanks and one thousand guns.

On January 15, 1941, the British launched an attack against Italian forces in East Africa, from the Sudan. Mogadiscio, capital of Italian Somaliland, fell on February 26, followed by Neguelli in southern Ethiopia on March 22; the capital, Addis Ababa, fell on April 6.

These British successes were soon to be reversed. Germany had not yet committed her forces to Operation Barbarossa, the invasion of Russia (June 22, 1941), and in February and March was able to reinforce the Italians in western Libya with two divisions under General Erwin Rommel. In the meantime, the British had turned their attention to the defense of Greece, diverting troops from North Africa.

Rommel opened his attack on April 3, and the British retreated from their recent gains in Libya. The Axis forces drove the British back to the Egyptian frontier by May 29. The tables then turned when Germany diverted troops from North Africa for the invasion of Russia. The British launched an offensive on December 11 and were able to drive into Libya as far as Benghazi by December 25. A reinforced Rommel was able to begin a drive on Egypt on May 22, 1942, that did not end until checked at al-Alamayn (El Alamein) just eighty miles (127 km) from Alexandria. General Montgomery's offensive from al-Alamayn began on October 23, resulting in expulsion of Axis forces from Egypt by November 12 and the end of the threat to Egypt and the Suez Canal.

At about the same time, on November 8, a British–American force under U.S. General Dwight D. Eisenhower began Operation Torch, the invasion of North Africa. Allied forces disembarking in French Morocco and Algeria faced some opposition from Vichy forces. By November 11, the two sides had reached an armistice. Pressed by Montgomery's Eighth Army in Libya and the new threat from the west, Rommel concentrated the Axis forces in Tunisia. Into 1943, bitter fighting continued, particularly at the Kasserine pass, but by May 12 all German and Italian resistance had ended. The Axis powers had 950,000 men dead or captured and had lost 8,000 aircraft and 2.4 million tons of shipping.

While the significant fighting of World War II in the Middle East was in Africa, the British still faced serious threats in Southwest Asia. The regimes in both Iran and Iraq flirted with support of the Axis powers as a means of diminishing British influence over their affairs. On May 2, 1941, pro-Axis sympathizers in Iraq tried to seize power. British forces intervened and put down all resistance by May 31. Fearing that Reza Shah Pahlavi might take Iran into the German camp in the summer of 1941, British and Soviet forces entered Iran in late August and forced him to abdicate in favor of his son, Muhammad Reza Pahlavi, on September 16. These actions effectively secured Iraq and Iran for the Allies.

The fall of France in June 1940 threatened to bring Syria and Lebanon into the Axis sphere of influence. Quick action by the British and Free French forces prevented this. On June 8, these forces occupied Syria and Lebanon. On September 16, Syria was proclaimed an independent nation, as was Lebanon on November 26. Both remained loyal to the Allies during World War II, but soon after the end of hostilities they were able to assert their independence and obtain the withdrawal of allied forces from their territory.

World War I had led to the disintegration of the Ottoman Empire and the creation of the Turkish republic under Kemal Atatürk. Turkey then faced pressure from both sides and from within as World War II loomed on the horizon. Atatürk and his successor, İsmet İnönü, favored the British as the power they believed would ultimately win. Other Turks feared Britain's ally, the Soviet Union, as a traditional enemy and realized that by June 1941 German troops were within one hundred miles (160 km) of Istanbul. Still others remembered the disastrous decision of October 1914, when the Ottomans joined the Central powers in World War I.

Shortly after the beginning of World War II, on October 19, 1939, Britain and France concluded a fifteen-year mutual assistance pact with Turkey. German success in 1940 and the invasion of Russia in 1941, however, led many Turkish leaders to favor the Axis. Thus, on November 1, 1940, İnönü declared it to be Turkish policy to remain a nonbelligerent in the war, while maintaining friendly ties with both Britain and the Soviet Union. The Allies, of course, continued to pressure Turkey for support, and on December 3, 1941, just before the United States declared war, the American Lend-Lease program was extended to Turkey. İnönü still pursued a neutral course but by 1943 realized that the Axis would lose. In August 1944, Turkey broke diplomatic relations with Germany and on February 23, 1945, formally declared war to comply with requirements for participation in the UN conference to be held in San Francisco in April.

The Jewish and Arab populations of Palestine greeted World War II with mixed emotions. Neither was content with British rule. The Arabs resented the rule of their country by a European power pledged to uphold the Balfour Declaration (sanctioning Palestine as a haven for persecuted Jews from all parts of the world). The Jewish population, the *Yishuv,* suspected British commitment to the Balfour Declaration, especially since the British banned Jewish immigration to Palestine after 1939.

In light of the anti-Semitism of Nazi Germany and its extermination of European Jewry as a matter of state policy, the Yishuv had little recourse but to support the Allies. The resources of the Jewish community in Palestine were put at the disposal of the British, and efforts (often resisted by British authorities) were made to raise Jewish military units to support the war effort. Early in the war the Yishuv devised the Carmel Plan, to create a Jewish enclave on the Palestine coast, near Haifa, to resist a German landing and occupation. Fortunately, this never became necessary.

A small minority of Jews did continue to resist British control of Palestine. The LEHI (Stern Gang), under Abraham Stern, urged rebellion against the British and even approached the German representatives in Vichy-controlled Syria with an offer of support against the British in Palestine. Even after this offer was rejected and Stern killed in confrontation with British authorities in early 1942, this splinter group continued to resist the British; other Jewish groups then began to oppose the British as the war progressed, since British support of the Zionist cause seemed less than enthusiastic.

Some Arabs viewed Germany as an instrument to rid themselves of British rule. The mufti of Jerusalem, Hajj Amin al-Husayni, lent his support to the Nazi cause, and when fleeing from Jerusalem in 1937 and from Beirut in October 1939 to Baghdad, he established contact with the German ambassador to Turkey, Franz von Papen, offering Arab support. After an anti-British revolt in 1941, the British reestablished control of Iraq in May 1941. Hajj Amin, who participated in the revolt, left for Turkey and later for Rome and Berlin to support the Axis powers after they promised to free the Arab world and support its independence and unity. He was able to generate some support for the Axis among the Arabs, but the defeat of the Italians and Germans in North Africa prevented this from becoming a factor in the war.

World War II ended with British and French control of most of the Middle East. The war did, however, shatter the aura of the invincibility of their arms. Consequently, rapid changes occurred in the region—Arab states asserted their independence, and the Jewish population of Palestine declared the State of Israel in 1948. Iran and Turkey insisted on full partnership in the international community. The European powers would no longer have undisputed control over the fates of the peoples in this region.

With the end of the war the United States emerged the premier Western power, but the challenge of the Cold War with the Soviet Union would soon have its own impact on the oil-rich Middle East.

BIBLIOGRAPHY

HOURANI, ALBERT. *A History of the Arab Peoples.* Cambridge, Mass., 1991.
KEEGAN, JOHN. *The Second World War.* New York, 1990.
LEWIS, BERNARD. *The Emergence of Modern Turkey.* London, 1961.
PERETZ, DON. *The Middle East Today*, 3rd ed. New York, 1978.
SACHAR, HOWARD M. *A History of Israel: From the Rise of Zionism to Our Time.* New York, 1988.
TIME-LIFE BOOKS. *WW II: Time-Life Books History of the Second World War.* New York, 1989.

Daniel E. Spector

World Zionist Organization (WZO)

Organization that transformed the Zionist idea of establishing a Jewish homeland into reality.

Founded in 1897 by Theodor HERZL at the first Zionist Congress in Basel, Switzerland, the Zionist Organization, as it was originally known, was created to serve as the organizational framework for the Zionist movement and was to be composed of "all Jews who accept the Zionist program and pay the shekel."

The Zionist Congress is the supreme governing body of the WZO. Herzl, the first president of the WZO, chaired its first five congresses. Under the aegis of the WZO, the JEWISH COLONIAL TRUST was formed (at the second Zionist Congress) to serve as the financial body of the Zionist movement, and the JEWISH NATIONAL FUND (at the fifth Zionist Congress) to act as land-purchasing agent for the Jewish people. Once the State of Israel was founded in 1948, the chief task of the congresses became that of defining the relationship of the Zionist organization to the government of Israel. Before 1948, congresses were held in many European cities; thereafter, beginning with the twenty-third congress in 1951, all congresses were held in Jerusalem. Whereas they were at first held every one or two years, congresses are now regularly convened every four years.

Membership in the World Zionist Organization was initially organized on a regional basis, but as ideological differences emerged, the membership structure bifurcated along both regional and ideological lines. In 1960, the WZO adopted a new constitution under which individuals were denied eligibility for membership, which was thereafter reserved for organizations.

Article 4 of the British mandate for Palestine provided for the establishment of a JEWISH AGENCY, which "shall be recognized as a public body for the purpose of advising and cooperating with the administration of Palestine in such economic, social and other matters as may affect the establishment of the Jewish national home and the interests of the Jewish population in Palestine." During the period of the YISHUV, the WZO acted as this Jewish Agency: It represented the Yishuv to foreign governments and promoted settlement efforts in Palestine. After the founding of Israel, many of the WZO's functions were assumed by the new government, but the Jewish Agency was not dismantled. In 1952, moreover, the Law of the Status of the WZO-Jewish Agency was promulgated whereby primary responsibility was assigned to the Jewish Agency for the development and settlement of the land and for the absorption of immigrants. In 1971, the Jewish Agency was reconstituted and detached from the WZO to allow for greater representation in it of Jewish organizations that were not members of the WZO.

BIBLIOGRAPHY

ELAZAR, DANIEL J., and ALYSA M. DOTORT. *Understanding the Jewish Agency: A Handbook.* Jerusalem, 1985.

Shimon Avish

Y

Ya'acobi, Gad   [1945–   ]

Israeli politician.

Born in Kfar Vitkin, Israel, Gad Ya'acobi earned his master's degree in economics from Tel Aviv University and first became a member of the Knesset in 1969 on the Labor list. He has held a number of government posts, including that of deputy minister of transportation (1969–1974), minister of transportation (1974–1977) and chair of the Knesset's Economic Committee (1977–1984). During the National Unity government, formed after that election, he served as minister of economics and planning. Since 1993, he has been the deputy defense minister.

BIBLIOGRAPHY

Who's Who in Israel, 1992–1993.

Bryan Daves

Ya'ari, Me'ir   (1897–1987)

Israeli political leader.

Born in Galicia, Me'ir Ya'ari was educated at the Vienna Academy of Agriculture and the University of Vienna. During World War I, he served as an officer in the Austro-Hungarian army. In Vienna, he was a leader of the ha-Shomer Ha-Tza'ir youth movement before emigrating to Palestine in 1919. Founder of the first kibbutz of ha-Shomer Ha-Tza'ir and the Histadrut, Ya'ari was also an early leader of the Kibbutz Arzi of the ha-Shomer Ha-Tza'ir movement in Israel and abroad. He was elected to the first Israeli Knesset, in which he remained until 1973, and served as general secretary of MAPAM. A prolific writer on Zionist ideology, Ya'ari was a principal intellectual force in the MAPAM movement.

Bryan Daves

Yacine, Kateb   [1929–1989]

Algerian novelist, essayist, and playwright.

Kateb Yacine was born in Constantine, Algeria, on August 6, 1929. His father was an educated man, a judiciary *wakil;* his mother introduced him at an early age to poetry and the theater. Yacine first attended a Qur'anic school, then a French school. His parents feared the impact of French culture on his thinking.

Yacine wrote in French, except for five plays produced in colloquial Algerian: *Muhammad Prend Ta Valise* (Muhammad, Take Your Suitcase); *La Guerre de 2000 Ans* (The 2000 Years' War); *La Voix des Femmes* (Women's Voices); *Palestine Trahie* (Palestine Betrayed); and *Le Roi de l'Ouest* (The King of the West). His two other plays, *Le Cercle des Représailles* (The Circle of Reprisals; Paris, 1959) and *L'Homme aux Sandales de Caoutchouc.* (The Man with the Rubber Sandals; Paris, 1970), were written in French.

Yacine's two novels, *Nedjma* (a proper name meaning "star"; Paris, 1956) and *Le Polygone Étoilé* (The Star-Studded Polygon; Paris, 1966) adroitly mix history, the social problems of the Algerians during the years of French colonialism, and an important amount of autobiographical information. The events of the two books move circularly in a mazelike world of words. Described as a man of a single theme, Yacine returns incessantly to the same subject: French colonialism and its efforts to achieve the cultural dispossession of his country.

Yacine's unpublished works were collected by Jacqueline Arnaud and published under the title *L'Œuvre en Fragments* (The Work in Fragments; Paris, 1986). In 1987, Yacine received the French Grand Prix National des Arts et des Lettres.

His writings are characterized by the absence of boundaries between genres and subjects. History is closely intertwined with fiction and autobiographical information. Almost all his works are concerned with the affirmation of the Algerian entity and the rich history of his people, interrupted and distorted by French colonialism. Yacine was highly critical of the postindependence government and the religious institutions. He stressed and defended his Berber heritage.

BIBLIOGRAPHY

BONN, CHARLES. *Anthologie de la littérature algérienne (1950–1987)*. Paris, 1990.
———. *Nedjma de Kateb Yacine*. Paris, 1990.
DÉJEUX, JEAN. *Littérature maghrébine de langue française*. Ottawa, 1973.
MORTIMER, MILDRED. *The Algerian Novel in French*. Ann Arbor, Mich., 1972.

Aida A. Bamia

Yadin, Yigal   [1917–1984]

Israeli archeologist, general, and politician.

Born in Jerusalem, the son of the archeologist E. L. Sukenik, Yadin studied archeology and Semitic languages at Hebrew University (1935–1945). He joined the Haganah and adopted the personal code name Yadin, which later became his surname. Yadin was chief operations officer in the War of Independence (1947–1948), and later chief of staff (1949–1952). He joined the Hebrew University faculty in 1953 and was appointed professor of archeology in 1963. From 1977 to 1981 he was a member of the Knesset and deputy prime minister, after which he returned to Hebrew University. Yadin followed his father in studying the Dead Sea Scrolls. With

N. Avigad, he published *Genesis Apocryphon* (1956), *Ben Sira from Masada* (1965), and *Temple Scroll* (1977). His most important archeological achievements were the large-scale excavations at Hazor, the Cave of Letters in the Judaean desert, Masada, Megiddo, and Beth Shean. They yielded important finds, including documents from the time of Bar Kochba in the Cave of Letters.

BIBLIOGRAPHY

ASTOR, D., R. D. BARNETT, J. KANE, and G. VERMES. "The Yigael Yadin Memorial Lecture." *Bulletin of the Anglo–Israel Archaeological Society* (1984–1985): 9–23.
GREENFIELD, J. "Bibliography of Yigal Yadin." *Journal of Jewish Studies* 33 (1982): 11–16.

Mia Bloom

Yad Mordekhai

Kibbutz that was the site of an important battle in the Arab–Israel War (1948).

Yad Mordekhai, named for Mordekhai Anilewitz, commander of the Warsaw uprising, is located between Gaza and Ashqelon on the road to Tel Aviv. The kibbutz was attacked by Egypt's army on May 19, 1948. It held out for four days without relief; on the fifth day, the survivors broke through Egypt's lines to the settlement of Gvar Am. The attackers suffered three hundred casualties.

BIBLIOGRAPHY

ALLON, YIGAL. *The Shield of David*. Jerusalem, 1970.

Jon Jucovy

Yad Vashem

Site in Israel dedicated to commemorating the Jewish victims of Nazi persecution and extermination.

Established on the authority of the 1945 London Zionist Congress, Yad Vashem (from Isaiah 56:5) includes a museum of the Holocaust, facilities for conferences and memorial gatherings (Holocaust Remembrance Day ceremonies are held there on 27 Nisan), and a research institute. Yad Vashem is a feature of foreign dignitaries' official visits to Israel.

BIBLIOGRAPHY

YOUNG, JAMES EDWARD. *The Texture of Memory: Holocaust Memorials and Memory*. New Haven, Conn., 1993.

Jon Jucovy

Yafi, Abd Allah   [1901–1985]

Lebanese Sunni Muslim politician.

Yafi was born in Beirut and educated at the Jesuit St. Joseph University. Later he earned a doctorate in law in Paris. He was admitted to the Beirut Bar in 1926. He was minister of justice on several occasions and was considered one of the most skillful lawyers in Lebanon. He amassed a fortune from representing wealthy Persian Gulf princes, especially when Arab money was heavily invested in Lebanon before the civil war. Yafi was a member of the Lebanese delegation to the preparatory conference for founding the LEAGUE OF ARAB STATES in 1944, and of the Lebanese delegation to the founding conference of the United Nations in San Francisco in 1945. He served as prime minister in 1954 and 1956 and was in private practice between 1956 and 1966. He also served as prime minister in 1966, and in 1968 to 1969. He was elected to parliament in 1937, 1943, 1947, 1951, 1953, and 1968. He failed to win a seat in the 1972 election, although a member of his parliamentary list, Uthman al-Dana, won a seat. His dispute with Sa'ib SALAM lessened his chances of success.

Yafi never entered the close circle of top politicians in Lebanon because his approach to politics was too lawyerly and intellectual. He found it hard to compete in a game that often required thuggery—especially on the local electoral level—and he was too impatient with the procedures of Lebanese political life. He frequently lost his temper in parliamentary debates and was seen as a weak prime minister. In fact, he won the prime ministership as a result of a protracted political crisis in the country. He was the consensus candidate who did not pose a threat to the vested interests of the key politicians in the Sunni establishment.

Yafi's main rival was Sa'ib Salam. Yafi was marginalized during the civil war of 1958 because he lacked an armed organization that could satisfy his supporters' desire for combat. Salam rose to prominence in the 1958 war because he was willing to take to the streets with his toughs and engage security forces. Yafi refrained from street politics in the belief that ideas are what count. He also considered it necessary to represent the new educated Sunni middle class, whereas Salam allied himself with traditional families in Beirut.

After his defeat in 1972, Yafi seemed to lose interest in politics, although he did participate in dialogue committees (1975–1976) and was a member of the Islamic Grouping, to which all the major Sunni politicians in Lebanon belonged. In contrast to most political families in Lebanon, Yafi's sons did not follow their father's career.

As'ad AbuKhalil

Yafirids

See Yemen Dynasties

Yahiaoui, Mohmed Saleh

Algerian Front de Libératiom Nationale (FLN) party coordinator.

A veteran of the Algerian War of Independence (1954–1962), Yahiaoui became party coordinator and was identified as leader of the left wing of the FRONT DE LIBÉRATION NATIONALE (FLN; National Liberation Front). He vied unsuccessfully for Algeria's presidency after the death of Houari Boumédienne in 1978. President Chadli Benjedid included Yahiaoui in the new Political Bureau, but in 1980 he was replaced as FLN party coordinator by Mohammad Cherif Messaadia. Yahiaoui was also eased out of the Political Bureau. He resurfaced as a member of the anti-Benjedid faction of the FLN.

BIBLIOGRAPHY

ENTELIS, JOHN. *Algeria: The Revolution Institutionalized.* Boulder, Colo., 1986.

Phillip C. Naylor

Yahya, Tahir   [1918–1986]

Iraqi military officer and prime minister.

Born in the town of Tikrit, Iraq, of humble origin, Tahir Yahya, also known as al-Tikriti, was a teacher of physical education before he joined the army and attained the rank of staff colonel. During the latter period of the royal regime, he was dismissed from the army and joined the secret organization of the Free Officers. After the 1958 coup, he became chief of the police of Iraq, chief of the military staff, and minister of defense. During the presidencies of the two Arif brothers, Yahya assumed the position of prime minister more than once. He died in Baghdad.

Mamoon A. Zaki

Yahya ibn Muhammad Hamid al-Din

[1867–1948]

Imam of Yemen, 1904–1948; king of Yemen, 1918–1948.

Yahya took the patronymic al-Mutawakkil ala Allah on becoming imam in 1904. He succeeded to the imamate upon the death of his father Muhammad ibn Yahya, who had inaugurated a new period of rebellion against the rule of the Ottoman Empire in the highlands of Yemen in 1891.

Although Yahya was sometimes amenable to concessions and negotiations with the Ottoman authorities, he approved of the desire of the Zaydi people to be free of Ottoman rule. When Yahya received the bay‘a (oath of allegiance), he immediately called for a full-scale revolt against the Ottomans; his major motivation appears to have been the May 1904 boundary agreement about Yemen's southern borders, signed between the Ottomans and British, since he considered himself to be the legitimate ruler of both "north" Yemen and the territories held by the British in "south" Yemen.

Imam Yahya continued to lead the revolt against the Ottomans throughout the period before World War I. His political shrewdness as well as his ability to wage irregular war against the Ottoman state forced it to negotiate with him, most importantly in the Treaty of Da‘an in 1919, which granted most of his demands and gave him an almost free hand in matters of taxation, religious affairs, and judicial appointments.

During World War I, however, the imam sided with the Ottomans as fellow Muslims—the only Arab regime to do so. At the end of the war, the Ottomans departed Yemen and officially recognized Yahya as ruler there. For Imam Yahya, however, this was only the first step in creating the Yemen he perceived to be the patrimony of the Zaydi imams.

Yahya's primary policy objectives in the postwar period appear to have been: (1) to bring all of Yemen under his direct control; (2) to make Yemen completely independent of the influence and/or control of other states (to have complete autarky); (3) to weaken the cohesion and power of the tribes (to prevent them from developing a common front against the central government and resisting its policy objectives); and (4) to establish the ascendancy of Islamic law (Shari‘a) throughout Yemen.

The methods Yahya employed to bring about his goals were diverse, and some were, in today's light, brutal. At first he paid subsidies and bribes to various tribal elements; later, when the treasury could clearly not support the demands of these payments, he sent military units to quell uprisings against his decisions, and also employed a traditional Yemeni technique—he took hostages from the tribes, typically the sons of the tribal Shaykhs. These hostages were kept in the imam's fortresses (where they were also educated) to guarantee the good behavior of their own tribes or tribal alliances. Yahya was assassinated in 1948.

BIBLIOGRAPHY

Encyclopaedia Britannica. Chicago, 1989.
FISHER, SIDNEY N. *The Middle East.* New York, 1979.

Manfred W. Wenner

Yamani, Ahmad Zaki   [1930–   ]

A prominent Saudi Arabian oil economist.

Having studied law in the United States and Egypt, Yamani embarked on a public career that included serving as legal adviser to the Saudi government (1958–1960) and as minister of oil and natural resources (1962–1986). Involved with the Organization of Petroleum Exporting Countries (OPEC) from its inception, Yamani was its secretary-general (1968–1969) and is generally held responsible for the steep rises in world oil prices in 1973 and 1979. He was dismissed as minister in October 1986, after the increases in oil production that he had recommended for OPEC were thought to have led to the collapse of oil prices and to decreased oil revenues for Saudi Arabia.

Shimon Avish

Yanbu

A port on Saudi Arabia's Red Sea coast.

Located in the Hijaz region of Saudi Arabia, Yanbu has traditionally served the city of Medina. Originally, Yanbu consisted of the port itself, Yanbu al-Bahr, and the inland agricultural settlement Yanbu al-Nakhl. In the 1970s, it became the focus, along with al-Jubayl on the Gulf, of a massive industrial development scheme, encompassing oil refining, petrochemical industries, and heavy manufacturing complexes based on hydrocarbon fuels. Yanbu was conceived as the smaller of the two sites, with two petroleum refineries, a natural-gas processing plant, a petrochemical complex, other light industries, an industrial port, and a new city of 100,000 inhabitants. Energy for these projects was to be supplied via oil and gas pipelines from the eastern province, al-Hasa;

the terminus of the Iraqi pipeline across Saudi Arabia (IPSA) was located nearby. The pipeline was closed after Iraq's invasion of Kuwait in 1990.

John E. Peterson

YAR

See Yemen Arab Republic

Yariv, Aharon   [1920–1994]

Israeli military leader, intelligence and defense strategist, and cabinet minister.

Born in Russia in 1920, Aharon Yariv moved to Palestine at the age of fifteen and joined the Haganah in 1939. During World War II, Yariv fought in the British army, helping to liberate concentration camps. He was the first Israeli to attend the French Military Command and Staff School.

Yariv served in many positions in the Israel Defense Forces (IDF), including commander of the IDF Command and Staff School (1954), head of Central Command (1956–1957), commander of the Golani Brigade (1960–1961), and most significantly as chief of the Intelligence branch (Aman) (1964–1973) during which he provided the intelligence information responsible for the Israeli victory in 1967. From 1957 to 1960, he served as military attaché in Washington, D.C. Yariv left the Intelligence branch shortly before the Arab–Israel War (1973), although he served as head of the Israeli delegation during the Kilometer 101 disengagement talks.

Elected to the eighth knesset on the Labor Alignment ticket, Yariv became minister of transport under Golda Meir and later minister of information under Yitzhak Rabin. Together with another minister, Yariv authored a formula for peace negotiations that recommended Israel carry out negotiations with any Palestinian faction that would recognize Israel's right to exist and that would not engage in terrorism. Yariv founded the Center for Strategic Studies at Tel Aviv University in 1977 and served as its head until his death.

Julie Zuckerman

Yarmuk River

Tributary of the Jordan river.

The Yarmuk river forms boundaries between Jordan, Syria, and Israel, all of which have contested its use as a water source. About fifty miles (80 km) long, the Yarmuk rises in southern Syria and flows westward through a deep gorge along the Jordanian border of the Golan Heights region of Syria annexed by Israel in 1981. It empties into the Jordan river four miles (6.4 km) south of the Sea of Galilee. Although much smaller than the Euphrates (in Turkey, north Syria, and Iraq) or even the Litani (in Lebanon), the Yarmuk supplies up to 50 percent of the water flow in the lower Jordan river.

The Yarmuk shares a long and storied past with the Jordan river valley, as recounted in archeological evidence, holy scripture and medieval chronicles. A Roman fortress town was built at the junction of the two rivers, and ruins of Roman- and Byzantine-era synagogues have been found nearby. In the early seventh century, it was through the Yarmuk gorge that Arab armies invaded the Jordan valley.

The Yarmuk's strategic importance has continued into the modern era. Today, it is the only undeveloped tributary of the Jordan river, in a region that now exploits the maximum capacity of existing water sources. Its only significant exploitation has been Jordan's East Ghor Canal, built in 1964 to irrigate thirty thousand acres (12,150 ha) of farmland east of the Jordan river. Jordan plans to extend the nearly 50-mile (80-km) canal and build a 328-foot (100-m) dam at Maqarin to store the Yarmuk's waters for agriculture and for the cities of Irbid and Amman. Syria plans a series of small dams on the upper Yarmuk to benefit agriculture in the Hauran region.

But these plans require agreement from all parties enjoying riparian rights to the river—not just Syria and Jordan, but also Israel. Israeli interest in the Yarmuk began shortly after World War I, when Chaim Weizmann, later Israel's first president, proposed borders for Palestine that would include the river. In 1932, the Palestine Electric Corporation (now the Israel Electric Corporation) built a hydroelectric generating plant at the junction of the Yarmuk and Jordan rivers. It was destroyed by the Arab Legion in the 1948 war, but Israel has continued to claim the water rights to the Yarmuk granted by the British mandate.

Since 1948, the contest for the Yarmuk has at times been violent. Efforts in the 1950s to coordinate joint use of the Jordan river basin, like the 1953 Johnston Plan, failed to gain agreement from all sides. While Jordan pursued its unilateral East Ghor Canal, Israel, between 1953 and 1964, built its National Water Carrier, which diverts the Jordan's water from north of the Sea of Galilee to Tel Aviv and the Negev desert. In response, the Arab League in 1960 coordinated a plan to develop the Yarmuk for the benefit of Jordan, Syria, and Lebanon. The project, begun in 1964, was to divert the Jordan's northern headwaters to the Yarmuk, where a dam on the Syrian–Jordanian border would also be built. In 1965 and 1966 Israel attacked bulldozers and facilities at construction sites in Syria. Israel's 1967 occupation of the Golan Heights put a final halt to the project. In 1969 Israeli raids destroyed part of Jordan's East Ghor Canal, which was subsequently repaired.

After years of opposition, in 1987 Syria finally agreed to allow Jordan to begin construction of the Maqarin dam.

BIBLIOGRAPHY

FARID, ABDEL MAJID, and HUSSEIN SIRRIYEH, eds. *Israel and Arab Water*. London, 1985.
KHOURI, FRED J. *The Arab-Israeli Dilemma*. Syracuse, N.Y., 1968, 1976.
STARR, JOYCE R., and DANIEL STOLL, eds. *The Politics of Scarcity*. Boulder, Colo., 1988.

Elizabeth Thompson

Yarmuk University

A public university in Jordan.

Established in 1976 on the outskirts of Irbid in northwest Jordan, Yarmuk University was the kingdom's second public university, opened in response to the rapidly increasing demands for higher education. The main campus of the university was built over a fifteen-year period and includes faculties of engineering, medicine, agriculture and veterinary sciences, as well as the usual faculties of arts and sciences. At its inception, Yarmuk University pioneered new departments or programs, including a center for Jordanian studies, a department of communications and journalism, a department of continuing education, a school for public health, and a department of computer science. As with all public universities in Jordan, students pay nominal tuition and are able to buy books and materials at subsidized prices. It has about half the number of students enrolled as the University of Jordan. In the 1989/90 academic year, 2,746 men and women graduated from Yarmuk with a bachelor's degree, 132 with teaching diplomas, and 225 with master's degrees.

BIBLIOGRAPHY

GUBSER, PETER. *Jordan: Crossroads of Middle Eastern Events*. Boulder, Colo., 1983.

Jenab Tutunji

Yarmulke

Skullcap worn by Jewish males in observance of religious custom.

Through the centuries of the Diaspora, Jewish men wore yarmulkes for study and prayer—the most studious wearing them constantly and the most acculturated wearing them only in synagogue. The head covering symbolized a consciousness of human subservience to a higher power. Some suggest that yarmulke is an acronym, a contraction of the Hebrew phrase *Yarey M'Elokim,* "one who is in awe of the Lord."

In Israel, a crocheted yarmulke (Hebrew, *kippah*) has become a sign of those who share a religious perspective on Zionism, while a black velvet one is associated with the ultra-orthodox, who do not. Generally, the more observant the Jew, the larger the size of the yarmulke and the more consistently it is worn. Other headgear may be worn over yarmulkes, such as hats that define Jewish sects.

BIBLIOGRAPHY

DAVIS, E. *Hats and Caps of the Jews*. Masada, Israel, 1983.
HEILMAN, S. *Synagogue Life*. Chicago, 1976.

Samuel C. Heilman

Yaşar Kemal [1922–]

An internationally renowned Turkish novelist, short-story writer, and essayist.

Born in Gökçeli village in the foothills of the Taurus mountains, Yaşar Kemal (a pseudonym for Kemal Sadik Gökçeli) received minimal schooling but persistently sought self-education, reading widely in world literature. He includes American novelist William Faulkner among those who influenced him. Interested in folklore at a young age and active in folk singing, Kemal's earliest publications were folk-style poems and collections of folklore material.

He first found odd-job employment locally, but in 1951 he moved to Istanbul, working until 1963 as a successful journalist. He published a political journal (1967–1971), was active with the Turkish Labor party and the writers' union, but spent considerable time abroad.

In Kemal's first novel, *İnci Memed* (1955), the protagonist Slim Memed is a young villager driven to outlawry in the Taurus. With two subsequent volumes (1969, 1984) and another trilogy published in 1960, 1963, and 1968, as well as short stories (which he had started to write in 1947), his work drew attention to issues such as the poverty-stricken, harassed lives of Turkish villagers, nomads pressured into sedentary life, and the problems involved in replacing feudalism with a capitalist system. Other short stories and novels focused on urban or fishing communities, all making Yaşar Kemal a significant voice for sociopolitical reform and linking him to the social realism of the village literature movement.

Above all, however, Kemal is a superb narrator of stories, interweaving them with epic and myth, strengthened sometimes by techniques such as stream of consciousness. His fictional style is infused with the spirit of folk literature (and some of his later works are based on his own versions—or inventions—of folk tales). His language is lyrical, his descriptions of nature vivid, his character portrayal sometimes romantic but always filled with deep understanding of the physical, psychological, and spiritual needs of ordinary, and especially, underprivileged men and women, resulting in works that have great international appeal.

Edebiyat, the journal of Middle Eastern literature published in English by the Middle East Center, University of Pennsylvania, devoted a special issue to Kemal, edited by Ahmet Ö. Evin. This includes an interview with Yaşar Kemal and is the best source for further details.

BIBLIOGRAPHY

For English translations see the bibliography in *Edebiyat* 5 (January-February 1980): 221–234.

Kathleen R. F. Burrill

Yashmak

Face veil and headdress traditionally worn in public by Muslim women of the Ottoman Empire.

The yashmak consists of two pieces of fine, transparent white material. One piece, oblong in shape, covers the hair and forehead down to the eyebrows. The second piece is a square, folded diagonally and placed so that the widest part covers the face from directly below the eyes to below the chin. Both pieces are gathered and tied at the back of the head. The custom of wearing a yashmak in public spread from Turkey to Iraq, Syria, Palestine, Lebanon, the Hijaz, and Yemen. Today, it is worn only by those who adhere strictly to Muslim dress codes.

Jenab Tutunji

Yasin, Isma'il   [1912–1972]

A popular Egyptian comedian.

Yasin's movies were a staple of cultural life for more than three decades. Reruns of his movies can be seen in all Arab countries, and the availability of his films on videotape has revived interest in his unique style of clowning.

As'ad AbuKhalil

Yata, Ali   [1920–   ]

Moroccan journalist and left-wing politician.

Yata was the first Muslim secretary-general of the Moroccan Communist party. He served until it was banned in 1959. Later he established the party of Liberty and Socialism (1968) and the party of Progress and Socialism (1974 as its secretary-general). He also founded the newspaper *al-Bayane.* Yata was elected deputy in the 1977 elections saying that democratic progress had begun, but he demanded annulment of the 1983 local elections alleging fraud. He participated in the 1984 legislative elections. Yata supported Moroccan claims to the Sahara in the 1960s and to the Western Sahara in the 1970s and 1980s.

BIBLIOGRAPHY

BENSEDDIK, FOUAD. *Syndicalisme et politique au Maroc.* Paris, 1990.

C. R. Pennell

Yazdi, Ibrahim   [1931–   ]

Iranian politician.

Born in Qazvin to a father who made his living as a retailer, Ibrahim Yazdi received his doctorate in pharmacology in the United States and returned to Iran in the late 1940s. He coedited two journals, *Forugh-e Elm* and *Ganj-e Shayegan,* and was also employed at the Workers' Social Security Organization. Politically, he supported the Liberation Movement of Iran, the more religious-minded faction of the National Front. In 1960, Yazdi returned to America, where he was a founding member of the Islamic Students Association. In 1978, he frequented Ayatollah Khomeini's headquarters in France. When he returned to Iran in 1979, he was appointed deputy prime minister, and in 1980 he became foreign minister in the cabinet of Mehdi Bazargan. He was one of the group of friends of Bazargan who constituted the nonclerical, moderate figures in the Islamic movement and who cooperated closely with the Revolutionary Guards. He also headed the nationalized Kayhan Publishing Group, which produced a newspaper daily whose circulation rate exceeded that of all the other Tehran dailies. In addition, he was elected to the Islamic parliament as a deputy from Tehran (1980–1984). In the falling-out between the moderates and the more radical Islamic Republican party affiliates (1979–1981), the latter won. Abolhasan Bani Sadr was ousted from the presidency (1981) and Sadeq Qotbzadeh was executed (1982). It is believed that after these events Yazdi refrained from any further political activity and left the country. He wrote several books, including *The Endless War, U.S. Is Preparing for Other Vietnams,* and *The Last Efforts in Final Days.*

BIBLIOGRAPHY

BAKHASH, SHAUL. *The Reign of the Ayatollahs.* New York, 1984.
CHEHABI, H. E. *Iranian Politics and Religious Modernism: The Liberation Movement of Iran under the Shah and Khomeini.* Ithaca, N.Y., 1990.

Neguin Yavari

Yazidis

Kurdish tribe.

A Kurdish tribal group of nomadic clans numbering 60,000 to 70,000 persons indigenous to the area of northern Iraq (Mosul) and eastern Turkey (Diyarbekır), they practice a heterodox religion consisting of Islamic, Christian, Jewish, and pagan elements. These include baptism, dualism, the prohibition of certain foods, circumcision, fasting, pilgrimage, interpretation of dreams, and transmigration of souls. Though they possess two sacred books—*Kitab al-Jilwa* (Book of Revelation) and *Mashaf Rash* (Black Book)—written in Arabic, they are not accorded the status of Ahl al-Kitab (protected minority status).

The Yazidis (the name does not seem to be related to *Yazid* but probably the Persian word *ized* or angel) refer to themselves as Dasin or Dawasin (possibly from the name of an old Nestorian diocese). They believe themselves to be a unique people; not, for instance, descended directly from Adam and Eve like the rest of humanity. They practice a form of dualism between God and the peacock angel, with whom Shaykh Adi (to whose tomb annual devotional pilgrimages are made) was united through transmigration. Figures of peacocks made of bronze or iron are ritual devotional objects. There is a hierarchy of cleric, tribal shaykhs, and lesser priests, headed by a religious chief shaykh and a lay leader, Mirza Beg.

Pejoratively labeled as "devil worshipers" or associated with the Caliph Yazid, they were branded as heretics, and numerous unsuccessful attempts by Turks and Kurds were made to convert or completely annihilate them.

BIBLIOGRAPHY

Encyclopaedia of Islam.
HELD, COLBERT C. *Middle East Patterns.* Boulder, Colo., 1994.

Reeva S. Simon

Yaziji, Ibrahim   [1847–1906]

A leading figure in the Arabic literary revival of the nineteenth century.

Ibrahim Yaziji was a Greek Catholic poet, grammarian, and man of letters from Mount Lebanon. Following in the footsteps of his father, Nasif, who had done pioneer work in rediscovering the Arabic literary heritage, he made a significant contribution to the Arab cultural and political awakening of the late nineteenth century. Like his father, he maintained a close relationship with the American and British Protestant missionaries in Beirut and played an important role in the revitalization of Arabic as a literary language. A member of the Syrian Scientific Society, an early secret society made up of Arab intellectuals and military officers who agitated for Arab independence from the Ottoman Empire, Yaziji is best remembered for an ode, first recited at a secret meeting of the society, which called upon Arabs to remember their past greatness and shake off Turkish rule. This ode and several other poems of his were memorized by a generation of Arab nationalists and inspired the incipient political movement for Arab independence (see ARAB NATIONALISM).

BIBLIOGRAPHY

ANTONIUS, GEORGE. *The Arab Awakening: The Story of the Arab National Movement.* London, 1938.
SALIBI, KAMAL. *A House of Many Mansions: The History of Lebanon Reconsidered.* London, 1988.

Guilain P. Denoeux

Yaziji, Nasif   [1800–1871]

Lebanese Christian scholar and author.

Yaziji played a significant role in revitalizing Arabic literary traditions. He was employed by Bashir Chehab, the emir of Lebanon, and moved to Beirut in 1840 to help U.S. missionaries prepare Arabic textbooks for use in Christian mission schools. Yaziji appreciated classical Arabic literature and campaigned to eliminate the corruptions that had been absorbed into the language. His writings helped revive practices of classical scholarship and made classical literature important in contemporary Arab culture.

BIBLIOGRAPHY

Encyclopaedia Britannica. Chicago, 1989.

Mark Mechler

Yehoshua, Avraham B.   [1936–]

Israeli novelist, playwright, and professor of literature.

Yehoshua was born in Jerusalem to an old Jerusalemite family. He is one of Israel's most famous writers and many of his works have been translated into English. An adamant social critic, his works often reflect what he considers the low points of Israeli society. While his early works are allegorical, his later ones tend to be more, although not unequivocally, realistic as seen in his novel *Gerushim Me'uharim* (1982; A Late Divorce, 1984). This work ostensibly deals with complex family relationships, but it can also be interpreted as a representation of Israeli life and conditions. Among some of his earlier writings are *Shetiqah Holekhet Ve-Nimshekhet Shel Meshorer* (1966; The Continuing Silence of a Poet, 1970) and *Tehillat Qayitz 1970* (1973; Early in the Summer of 1970). His highly acclaimed book, *Ha-Me'ahev* (1977; The Lover, 1978), takes place during the Arab–Israel War of 1973 and deals with a man's search for a lover for his wife. *Molkho* (1987; Five Seasons, 1988) traces five seasons, autumn to autumn, in the life of an average, middle-aged man named Molkho from the time his wife dies of cancer. Each season finds him in a different place with a different woman as he tries to adjust to his loss and to his new freedom.

Ann Kahn

Yeki Bud Yeki Nabud

Earliest collection of modern Persian short stories.

Yeki Bud Yeki Nabud (There was one, there wasn't one—i.e., once upon a time) appeared in Berlin in early 1932. Written by expatriate Mohammad Ali Jamalzadeh (b. 1892), the book featured a preface that served as a manifesto for modernist Persian literature

and six anecdotal stories treating events of the 1910s in Persia (now Iran) with unprecedented realism, local color, and humor. The most famous story is "Persian Is (as Sweet as) Sugar," which treats the failure of a group of Iranians to understand one another and resolve a mutual problem, owing to their different origins, educational backgrounds, and class affiliations.

BIBLIOGRAPHY

A translation of the preface appears in *The Literary Review* 18 (1974); *Once upon a Time (Yeki bud yeki nabud)* was translated by Paul Sprachman and Heshmat Moayyad (1985).

Michael C. Hillmann

Yellin-Mor, Natan   [1913–]

Israeli political activist.

Born in Grodno, Poland, Natan Yellin-Mor became active in the revisionist movement Betar while studying engineering in Warsaw, and he pursued this rightist cause through his support of the Irgun Zva'i Le'umi. After arriving in Palestine in the early part of World War II, he joined Abraham Stern's faction, then known as the Stern Gang and later as Lehi. He tried to negotiate with the Nazis for a mass release of Jews from Nazi-controlled Europe in exchange for cooperation in fighting the British. Tried but acquitted in the assassination of UN emissary Count Folke Bernadotte, Yellin-Mor served in the first Knesset and shortly thereafter eschewed his earlier Zionist views and advocated a single-state solution in the conflict over Palestine between the Arabs and the Jews.

Bryan Daves

Yemen

A relatively new state on the southwestern corner of the Arabian peninsula.

The Republic of Yemen was created in May 1990 as a result of the merger of the two previous states that used the name Yemen: the Yemen Arab Republic (YAR; often called North Yemen) and the People's Democratic Republic of Yemen (PDRY; often called South Yemen).

Political Systems. The merger brought together two very disparate political systems: the North had been governed by a military/tribal elite that had supported

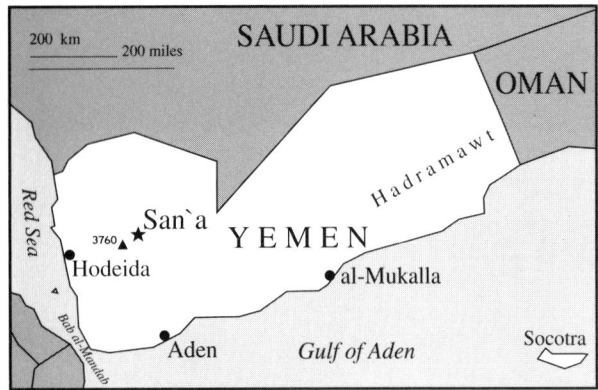

a free market economy, while the South had been governed by a Marxist-Leninist political elite that had introduced one of the most thoroughgoing centrally directed economies in the modern world. The compromise that was effected called for a transition period of thirty months, after which free elections would determine the membership of a parliament, which would in turn be responsible for policymaking, and of course, executive leadership. As expected, the president of the North, Ali Abdallah SALIH, was made president of the new unified state.

Population. A recent census of the new state has been undertaken by the Dutch government, but figures are not yet available. In 1986, the North claimed a population of 9,274,173, not counting 1,168,199 Yemenis abroad (employed primarily in Arabian peninsula states). In 1985, the population of South Yemen was estimated at 2.12 million, not counting approximately 85,000 employed abroad. Preliminary estimates of the 1995 Dutch census suggested an in-country total of around 16 million, due in large part to the return of many Yemenis as a result of the Gulf War of 1990/91.

Area and Borders. As Yemen is one of the few states in the modern world without completely demarcated borders, it is not possible to give a precise figure for its total area. In the north, east, and southeast, there has never been an internationally (or even locally) accepted border. This has led to border disputes and even wars with Saudi Arabia on the part of both of the previously existing Yemens on numerous occasions since the 1920s. The border with Saudi Arabia was demarcated as far as the Najran oasis after the Saudi–Yemeni War of 1934; this conflict also gave control of the region of Asir to the Saudi state through a treaty renewed every twenty years, creating continued difficulties in the relations between the two states. In the northwest, the generally recognized end of Yemeni sovereignty lies east of

Ma'rib; with the discovery of valuable oil and gas deposits, however, new conflicts over the border between the two states arose in this area in the late 1980s and early 1990s. To the south, Yemen lies on the Gulf of Aden; the old border between the North and South, created by the Ottoman and the British empires in the early years of the twentieth century and technically abolished as a result of the union of 1990, continues to be of some relevance. In the east, the border between Yemen and Oman was finalized in an agreement signed October 1, 1992.

Major Cities. SAN'A is the most important, largest, and possibly the oldest city in Yemen—it is mentioned in the Bible under its old name, Uzal. By the early 1990s, its population was estimated in excess of one million. It has been the capital city of Yemen for most of the past two millenia (with the exception, recently, of the reign of Imam Ahmad, 1948–1962) and became the official administrative (political) capital of the new republic after unification. Its Old City has been placed on the list of World Heritage Sites because of its unique architecture and historical importance (many of the buildings are more than eight hundred years old).

ADEN, the capital city of the former PDRY, has the best port on the Arabian peninsula. For more than a century, it was a major British military and commercial possession. After unification, it was made the economic and commercial capital of the country.

HODEIDA (al-Hudayda) is the major port of the former North Yemen. Its facilities were extensively modernized by the Soviet Union in the 1960s. Consequently it grew rapidly from a sleepy Red Sea fishing port handling primarily local trade to a major metropolitan area.

TA'IZ, the major city of the southern highlands of the old North Yemen, is located in one of the richest agricultural areas. Its population, predominantly of the Islamic Shafi'i sect, had the longest and best-developed contacts with the outside world during the reigns of imams Yahya and Ahmad in the twentieth century.

Although the country has a few other smaller cities (e.g., Ibb, Dhamar, Sa'da, and Zabid), the vast majority of the population lives in small villages each with an average population of fewer than two hundred people. Yemen has the most decentralized population of any contemporary state.

Geography and Climate. Yemen's location, combined with its geographical characteristics, gives it the most favorable climate and agricultural resources of any country on the Arabian peninsula. The country may be divided into a number of relatively clear zones:

Residential architecture of San'a, the capital of the Republic of Yemen. (Brad Glasser)

the first of these, along the Red Sea and the Arabian Sea coasts, is hot and humid; thereafter, the land slopes upward into the first range of hills and low mountains, in which the climate is considerably more temperate; eventually, after a series of high plains, the central massif is reached, the peaks of which are between 11,000 and 13,000 feet (3,355–3,965 m). These mountains have been terraced from time immemorial, and a vast array of fruits, vegetables, and grains may be raised in the many microclimates that are created by this geography. In the central mountains, the humidity is low and the temperatures quite moderate, though in the winter it is not unusual to find below-freezing temperatures and the occasional snow or ice storm. Over the centuries, the Yemenis have developed strains of various plants to occupy the many microclimates. On the other side of the central massif (and away from the monsoons, which deliver the rain that makes extensive agriculture possible on the westward side), the land slopes away into the great central desert of Arabia, the Rub al-Khali, broken only by the great HADRAMAWT valley, the home of numerous towns that exploit the limited water resources to be found there. The rainfall that the various mountain ranges wring out of the prevailing winds varies widely—from less than three inches per year in the deserts and northern reaches of the country to about thirty-eight inches per year in some of the areas around Ta'iz (about the same as Seattle, New York, or Chicago).

Political Subdivisions. Administratively the two pre-unification Yemeni states varied considerably. The units into which the two states were organized were frequently modified, sometimes as the result of political expediency and at other times due to the nature of the personnel available for major administrative duties.

For example, in the South the first administrative reorganization sought to get rid of the old tribally organized political entities. Later, the state undertook to re-create some of these entities under new names to regain popular support. In the North, after the revolution, the number of administrative units (governorates) rose with the growth in the population as well as the increasing number and variety of demands for governmental services. In the immediate aftermath of reunification, the number and characteristics of the administrative subunits within the two separate entities were retained.

The Economy. The natural resource base of Yemen has only recently begun to be developed, largely because it was not until the 1960s that either the North or the South had the opportunity to assess that base or attempt its development. The most important contemporary resources are oil and gas deposits, which were discovered in both North and South Yemen prior to unification (and which contributed significantly to the push for unification). The vast majority of the population of Yemen continues to be employed in the agricultural sector, though productivity is not adequate to the requirements of the pop-

San'a, nestled in the mountains. (Brad Glasser)

Minaret in the Old City of San'a. (© Mark Dennis)

ulation. The multiplicity of microclimates mentioned above makes it possible to grow just about any fruit or vegetable, from the citrus fruits, bananas, and cotton of the hot coastal plain; though the coffee, grains, and QAT (a small tree valued for its alkaloids) of the middle highlands; to the pears, grapes, and nuts of the high mountains.

Although industrial development has been a priority since independence in both North and South Yemen, it has not reached the stage where it is a significant factor in the economy of either region. In fact, Yemen operates a monumental deficit in its current accounts because it has very few exportable resources to offer. Until 1991, the most important positive element in its balance of payments was the remittances of its very large workforce in the various Gulf states and other countries. Following the 1991 Gulf War, however, the majority of Yemenis abroad were forced to return home.

Culture. The population of Yemen is ethnically Arab, although of different origin: the majority is descended from the ancient south Arabian peoples, and the remainder immigrated from the Fertile Crescent area more than a thousand years ago.

Arabic is the official language. Although everyone speaks it, there are substantial dialectical differences between different regions of the country. In some of the more remote areas of the island of Socotra, Mahri is still spoken.

The overwhelming majority of Yemenis are Muslims. They are, however, divided into different sects: in the northern areas, the Zaydis, a branch of Shi-'ism, predominate; in the southern areas, the Shafi'is, who follow a branch of Sunni Islam, are in the majority. There are, in addition, Isma'ilis, members of another branch of Shi'ism, in the northern mountains, as well as a small community of Jews who continue to live in and around Sa'da.

The educational infrastructure is still in the process of development. Until the revolution of 1962, an insignificant number of people received any formal education. Today, the number of schools continues to grow as well as the percentage of boys and girls receiving education. There are several universities in San'a, Ta'iz, and Aden that have a large number of colleges for specialized training.

The Government. Yemen is governed under a constitution, which was approved by the parliaments of the two Yemens in 1990 and by popular referendum in 1991. This constitution declares Yemen to be a parliamentary democracy, with an executive appointed by and responsible to the parliament. Elections to the new parliament were held in April 1993 with some eight parties as well as a sizable number of independents taking seats. Three parties dominated: the General People's Congress, formerly dominant in the North; the Islah party, a coalition of tribal and Is-

Town of Rada'a in Yemen. (Brad Glasser)

Yemeni mountain village. (© Mark Dennis)

lamic interests; and the Yemeni Socialist party, formerly dominant in the South.

The current president is Ali Abdallah Salih, formerly the president of North Yemen. In fact, although the parliament has been able to wield some influence, the military, which is led by Salih, is the primary political force in the country.

History. The contemporary state of Yemen was created by two states with very different historical experiences during the past two centuries. Although occasionally united in the past, they had not been so since 1728. Developments in the nineteenth century, however, are most important to an understanding of the events that led to the reunification of North and South Yemen in 1990.

In 1839, the British took the city of Aden in South Yemen in order to have a major port in the western Indian Ocean as well as to forestall further expansion by other parties in the Arabian peninsula. Over the years, British interests continued to grow, and they eventually established extensive links with the multitude of principalities located in Aden's (Yemeni) hinterland.

Meanwhile, the Ottoman Empire, which had occupied Yemen for a variety of strategic and economic interests, but which had departed in the early seventeenth century, decided to return. The motive for doing so was, as in the past, to play a role in the Red Sea trade (although there were other factors that came into play); this goal increased in importance with the completion of the Suez Canal in 1869. Eventually, British and Ottoman interests in southwestern Arabia clashed; the two powers decided to negotiate a frontier between their zones of influence and interest. Beginning in 1902, they agreed to demarcate a border between them; the agreement that was eventually signed in 1914 created the frontier between the Ottoman possession that became the Kingdom of Yemen (North Yemen) after World War I and the British Aden protectorates.

Under the reigns of imams Yahya and Ahmad (1918–1962), North Yemen remained largely cut off from the rest of the world, while Aden and the protectorates in the south received British subsidies and Aden developed into one of the world's busiest ports. Nevertheless, both states had political movements that sought change. In 1962, a revolution broke out in North Yemen, seeking to create a republic and removing the conservative Zaydi imams from power. After an eight-year civil war, the two major factions compromised and created the Yemen Arab Republic (Imam Muhammad al-Badr fled to Saudi Arabia). Shortly after the revolution in North Yemen broke out, various groups in South Yemen (as it became known) began to work for independence from Great Britain. After a lengthy and often violent civil conflict, the British agreed to withdraw from Aden and its protectorates in 1967, thus creating the People's Republic of South Yemen (later the People's Democratic Republic of Yemen).

Although both Yemens spoke of the goal of reunification, relations between them were often extraor-

Yemeni children at play. (Brad Glasser)

Wadi Do'an Hadramawt. (D.W. Lockhard)

dinarily poor, due largely to their very different economic and political systems. The North was governed by a military elite, which permitted an almost unrestricted though underdeveloped capitalist economy to operate and which was tied to the Western bloc; in the South, on the other hand, a Marxist-Leninist political elite took over the reigns of power and tied the country to the Communist bloc of states. Relations between the two states deteriorated into two separate wars—in 1972 and 1979.

In the late 1980s oil (and later, gas) was discovered in both Yemens; more importantly, it was found in the disputed border area between them. The effort to develop these deposits without wasting further resources in fruitless wars largely overlapped the decline in the power and influence of the USSR (and some of its satellites that were important in providing assistance in various forms to South Yemen). As a result, the potential benefits of a unified effort to develop their oil and gas deposits overcame the mutual suspicions and frictions that had characterized

Village in coastal Yemen. (Richard Bulliet)

the previous twenty-five years, leading to the unity agreement of 1990.

Disputes within the General People's Congress and the Yemeni Socialist party coalition government led to a civil war from May through July 1994, which resulted in the exile of the latter's leaders and the ascent of the Islah party as the new partner in the coalition government.

BIBLIOGRAPHY

BURROWES, ROBERT. *The Yemen Arab Republic.* Boulder, Colo., 1987.
DRESCH, PAUL. *Tribes, Government, and History in Yemen.* Oxford, 1989.
HALLIDAY, FRED. *Revolution and Foreign Policy.* Cambridge, U.K., 1990.
ISMAEL, TARIQ, and JACQUELINE ISMAEL. *PDR Yemen.* Boulder, Colo., 1986.
NYROP, RICHARD, ed. *The Yemens.* Washington, D.C., 1986.
PETERSON, J. E. *Yemen.* London, 1982.
STOOKEY, ROBERT. *South Yemen.* Boulder, Colo., 1982.
VOGEL, DIETER, ed. *Yemen.* Singapore, 1990.
WENNER, MANFRED. *Modern Yemen, 1918–1966.* Baltimore, 1967.
———. *The Yemen Arab Republic: Development and Change in an Ancient Land.* Boulder, Colo., 1991.

Manfred W. Wenner

Yemen Arab Republic

The official name of North Yemen from 1962 until its 1990 merger with South Yemen.

The emergence of North Yemen as a single political unit in modern times was largely a function of both the reoccupation of the country by the Ottomans in 1849 and the Yemeni resistance to this presence that coalesced around the imamate near the turn of the century. Defeat in World War I forced the Ottomans to withdraw in 1918, and a resurgent imamate state seized the opportunity.

From 1918 until 1962, YAHYA IBN MUHAMMAD HAMID AL-DIN and his son AHMAD IBN YAHYA HAMID AL-DIN acted to forge a monarchy much as the kings of England and France had done centuries earlier. The two imams strengthened the state, thereby securing Yemen's borders and pacifying the interior to degrees rarely known over the past millennium.

The imams used the strengthened imamate to revive North Yemen's traditional Islamic culture and society, this at a time when traditional societies around the world were crumbling under the weight

Unique architecture of San'a, the capital of the republic. (© Mark Dennis)

of modernity backed by imperial power. They were aided in their efforts to insulate Yemen by the degree to which its agricultural economy was self-contained and self-sufficient. The result was a "backward" Yemen, though a small but increasing number of Yemenis exposed to the modern world wanted change and blamed the imamate for its absence. This produced a fateful chain of events: the birth of the FREE YEMENI movement in the mid-1940s; the aborted 1948 revolution that left Imam Yahya dead; the failed 1955 coup against Imam Ahmad; and, finally, the 1962 revolution that yielded the Yemen Arab Republic (YAR).

In retrospect, the history of the YAR can best be divided into three periods. (1) The Sallal era (1962–1967), the wrenching first five years under President Abdullah al-Sallal, was marked by the revolution that began it, the long civil war and Egyptian intervention that quickly followed, and—above all—the rapid and irreversible opening of the country to the modern world. (2) A ten-year transition period (1967–1977) was marked by the end of the civil war, the republican-royalist reconciliation under President Abd al-Rahman al-Iryani, and the attempt by President Ibrahim al-Hamdi to strengthen the state and restructure politics. (3) The Salih era (1978–1990) is identified with both the long tenure of President Ali Abdallah Salih and the change from political weakness and economic uncertainty at the outset to relative political stability, the discovery of oil, and the prospect of oil-based development and prosperity in more recent years.

Of the many important changes that took place in the YAR since its birth in 1962, most of the positive ones have been compressed into the years since its fifteenth anniversary in 1977. Nevertheless, the previous decade was important, a transition in which much-needed time was bought by a few modest but pivotal acts and, most important, by economic good fortune. Global and regional economic events over which the YAR had no control facilitated a huge flow of funds into the country in the form of both foreign aid and remittances from Yemenis working abroad. This period of transition was necessary because the changes that had buffeted Yemen in the five years following the 1962 revolution had left it both unable to retreat into the past and ill-equipped to go forward. The ability to advance rapidly in the 1980s seems very much the result of the possibility afforded for a breather in the 1970s.

Given the isolation and the decentralized nature of North Yemeni society, much of the YAR's first quarter-century was taken up with the effort to establish sovereignty over the land and people. The Yemenis who made the revolution in 1962 were preoccupied from the outset with the need to create a state with the capacity to maintain public security and provide services. The long civil war that came on the heels of the revolution both increased this need and interfered with meeting it. Yemeni state-building was more hindered than helped by the fact that the new state was largely built and staffed by Egyptians and by the fact that Egyptian forces did most of the fighting on behalf of the Yemenis.

The balance of power between the tribal periphery and the state at the center tipped back toward the tribes during the civil war. As a result, the reach of the YAR extended little beyond the triangle in the southern half of the country that was traced by the roads linking the cites of San'a, Ta'iz, and Hodeida (al-Hudayda).

The YAR created in 1962 lacked modern political organization. A major theme of its first twenty-five years consisted of attempts to fashion the ideas and

A village in northern Yemen. (© Mark Dennis)

organization needed to channel support and demands from society to the regime and, conversely, to channel information, appeals, and directives from the regime to society. The civil war strained and even deformed the new republic, deferring any major effort at political construction under President al-Sallal. Egypt's heavy-handed tutelage left little room for Yemeni national politics and politicians to develop.

As with other late-developing countries, the tasks of state-building in the new YAR went beyond the maintenance of order and security to include the creation of a capacity to influence, if not control, the rate and direction of socioeconomic change. The wrenching effects of the sudden end of isolation and of virtual self-sufficiency made it obvious that state-building in all of its aspects was desperately needed. No less than the viability and survival of Yemen in its new external environment depended upon it, just as the civil war and the political weakness of the YAR made it unlikely.

The Egyptian exodus in 1967 led to the quick overthrow of President al-Sallal and the republican-royalist reconciliation that finally ended the civil war in 1970. Some state-building of importance was achieved thereafter by the regime headed by President al-Iryani. A modern constitution was adopted in 1970, and some of the ministries and other agencies erected after the revolution were strengthened. Economic needs as well as political constraints caused Yemeni leaders during the al-Iryani era to focus on financial and economic institutions; only halting first steps were taken toward reform of the civil service and the armed forces, matters of great political sensitivity. President al-Hamdi, who forced President al-Iryani into exile in 1974, believed in the modern state and worked to realize it. He promoted efforts to build institutions at the center, initiated the first major reform and upgrading of the armed forces, and fostered the idea of exchanging the benefits of state-sponsored development for allegiance to the state.

The results of efforts by the Iryani and Hamdi regimes at political construction were modest. The price of the reconciliation was the first-time granting of office and influence in the state to leading tribal shaykhs and the expulsion of the modernist Left from the body politic—prices that weakened the position of all advocates of a strong state. The result was the narrowly based center-right republican regime, which, with changes, persisted from the late 1960s until at least the early 1980s. The chief institutional focus of politics during the Iryani era was the Consultative Council, which first convened after elections in early 1971. However, political parties were banned and, in the absence of explicit organizational and ideological ties, the council functioned as an assembly of local notables, especially the shaykhs.

President al-Hamdi was unable to strengthen his position by translating his great popularity into political organization. Indeed, his major political achievement actually narrowed the political base of his regime and shortened the reach of the state. Aware that the shaykhs were using their new positions to protect the tribal system, al-Hamdi moved swiftly to drive them from the Consultative Council and from other state offices. To this end, he dissolved the council and suspended the 1970 constitution. The tribes responded with virtual rebellion. Al-Hamdi's efforts to make up for this loss of support by reincorporating the modernist Left were hesitant. In addition to maintaining ties to old leftist friends, he launched both the Local Development Association (LDA) movement and the Correction movement. Despite their initial promise, al-Hamdi seems to have had second thoughts and to have pulled back from efforts to use these two initiatives as bases for a broad, popular political movement. His subsequent plans for a general people's congress ended with his assassination in 1977. Frustrated by his failure to grant them reentry into the polity, several leftist groups in 1976 created the National Democratic Front (NDF), which a few years later became the basis of the rebellion that challenged the Salih regime.

The civil war finally behind it, the YAR in the 1970s did undergo significant socioeconomic development based upon the rapid creation of a modest capacity to absorb generous amounts of economic and technical assistance from abroad and, most important, from the massive inflow of workers' remittances that fostered unprecedented consumption and prosperity. Whereas the remittances largely flowed through the private sector, the modest strengthening of state institutions and the increase in their capacities were the critical factors in Yemen's ability to absorb significantly increased foreign aid. By the late 1970s, work on a broad array of state-sponsored, foreign-assisted infrastructure, agricultural, and human resource development projects existed side by side with high levels of remittance-fueled consumption and economic activity in the private sector.

President Salih's long term in office, beginning in 1978, was witness to major gains in state-building. After a shaky start, the Salih regime slowly increased the capacity of the state in the provinces as well as in the cities, for the first time making the republican state more than just a nominal presence in the countryside. The armed forces were upgraded again in 1979 and, more recently, in 1986 and 1988. Modest efforts were made to improve the functioning of the civil service, ministries, and other agencies.

The Salih regime increased its dominance over lands controlled by the tribes, especially the large area that fans out north and east from San'a, the capital. However, the best evidence of the growing ability of the YAR to exercise power within its own borders was the political-military defeat of the NDF. With its origins in the expulsion of the Left from the republic in 1968, the NDF rebellion had finally burst into flame over a wide area by early 1980. This uprising was extinguished in 1982, and the state was able at last to establish a real presence in lands bordering South Yemen.

In 1979, the Salih regime had little political support outside the armed forces. After the failure of ad hoc efforts to change this, the regime put in place an impressive program of political construction during the first half of the 1980s. This phased, sequential program began in early 1980 with the drafting of the National Pact. The pact then became the subject of a long national dialogue and local plebiscites orchestrated by the National Dialogue Committee. Elections to the General People's Congress (GPC), and its several-day session, were held in mid-1982 to review and then to adopt the National Pact. This done, the GPC declared itself a permanent political organization, which would be selected every four years, meet biennially and be led by a seventy-five-member Standing Committee headed by President Salih.

The key to the success of the Salih regime's political effort lay in the flexible, step-by-step process by which it moved the Yemeni polity from where it was in 1979 to the holding of the GPC in 1982. By design and a bit of luck, moreover, this sustained initiative also provided a political process largely managed by the regime into which elements of the Yemeni left could be safely incorporated when, in 1982, the NDF rebellion was quelled. Two dialogues, the one between the regime and the NDF as well as the more public one between the regime and the rest of the nation, converged in a structure that facilitated a second national reconciliation.

Although President Salih insisted that the GPC was not a political party, its activities were clearly aimed at consensus-building, guidance, and control—typical functions of a party. In fact, the GPC did become an umbrella party, a loose organization of organizations in a society that was not well organized politically for many of the tasks of the modern world.

The Salih regime was also buttressed by constitutional change during the 1980s. The 1970 constitution, suspended by al-Hamdi in 1974, had been reinstated confusingly in 1978 without its centerpiece, the Consultative Council, and with an amendment that formally created the presidency. Clarity and closure on a number of issues were not achieved until July 1988 when a new Consultative Council was finally chosen in accordance with the constitution. The council elections, the first since 1971, were hotly contested and relatively fair and open; despite the ban on parties, much partisanship was in evidence. In mid-July, the new council elected President Salih to a new term and then gave approval to the composition and program of the new government. As a result, for the first time since the Iryani regime was ousted in 1974, the head of state and the government were selected in accordance with the 1970 constitution, that is, by a properly chosen Consultative Council.

The modest prosperity that the YAR enjoyed after the mid-1970s was paralleled by the modern sector's increasing vulnerability to negative economic and political forces, domestic and external. Political uncertainty early in the Salih era threatened the limited capacity of the state to foster and manage development, and this was followed by the fall in oil prices and worldwide recession that led to sharp drops in aid and remittances to Yemen. Faced with economic crises, the regime in the early 1980s adopted austerity measures, and these had some success in forcing the country to live within more modest means in a less generous world.

The YAR's long-term development prospects improved abruptly when oil was discovered in commercial quantities in 1984. This event also placed severe demands on the still very limited capacities of the state. With the oil find, the twin tasks facing the Salih regime were to maintain the new discipline and austerity of the past few years and to gear up to absorb efficiently the oil revenues that were expected to start flowing in late 1987. Despite the politically difficult combination of rising expectations and continued hard times, the regime during this period of transition was able to limit imports and government expenditures. Changes in organization and the appointment of top technocrats to key posts contributed to the modest success of the transition.

Although oil for export did begin to flow in late 1987, the regime was forced in 1989 to reimpose austerity measures that it had relaxed prematurely the previous year. Nevertheless, at the same time that it wrestled with these politically hard choices, the government proceeded as fast as financing would allow with development of the oil and gas sector as well as with key infrastructure and agricultural projects.

In the 1980s, the increasing capacity of the Yemeni state for development also helped it to perform its more traditional functions and was partly understood and justified in these terms. This was especially the case when the regime stepped up efforts to extend its reach into NDF-influenced and tribal areas. Certain development efforts made the periphery more accessible and made possible the delivery of basic services to places where the state was regarded with suspicion or scorn. Hence the emphasis on pushing roads into such areas as soon as they were pacified. President Salih came to justify development efforts in terms of nation-state building—in terms of national integration—as well as economic gains. The development activities of the second half of the 1980s, as well as the content of the third Five-Year Development Plan adopted in 1988, reflected the continuing influence of these ideas.

This third period of YAR history, spanning the 1980s, ended with the creation of the Republic of Yemen, headed by President Salih. It was the political and economic turnaround of the YAR after the 1970s, as well as the sudden weakening of South Yemen in the late 1980s, that made possible the YAR-initiated merger.

BIBLIOGRAPHY

BURROWES, ROBERT D. *Historical Dictionary of Yemen.* Lanham, Md., 1995.

———. *The Yemen Arab Republic: The Politics of Development, 1962–1986.* Boulder, Colo., 1987.

DRESCH, PAUL. *Tribes, Government, and History in Yemen.* Oxford, 1989.

STOOKEY, ROBERT W. *Yemen: The Politics of the Yemen Arab Republic.* Boulder, Colo., 1978.

WENNER, MANFRED W. *The Yemen Arab Republic: Development and Change in an Ancient Land.* Boulder, Colo., 1991.

Robert D. Burrowes

Yemen Civil War

The long, bitter, and costly struggle in North Yemen fought by the republicans and royalists between 1962 and 1970.

The Yemen Civil War began with the 1962 revolution and dragged on intermittently until 1970. The second half of the war coincided with a long drought, and the two forces in combination caused hunger, economic hardship, social dislocation, and many deaths in most parts of the country. Without a doubt, the struggle remains as one of a few defining memories of one if not two generations of Yemenis.

In addition, the civil war forced the deferral of most major efforts at political and socioeconomic development in what would become the Yemen Arab Republic (YAR) until the 1970s. Indeed, it was not until after reconciliation that the Yemenis could really begin to take the destiny of YEMEN into their own hands. At the height of the struggle, the republicans, who were committed to creating a modern state and using it to overcome the weakness and "backwardness" of Yemen, controlled little more than the third of the country defined by the triangle

formed by the roads connecting San'a, Ta'iz, and Hodeida (al-Hudayda)—and much within the triangle was outside their effective control. Another third was controlled by the royalists and their tribal allies, and the last third by tribes and others either concerned with their own autonomy or willing to go either way if the price were right. If anything, the balance between the tribes and the state during these years was more in favor of the former than had been the case under the imamate just before the revolution.

The young imam Muhammad al-BADR survived the revolution on September 26, 1962, escaped from San'a, and went on to rally many of the northern tribes and other allies of the imamate for an assault upon the new republic. The civil war was quickly regionalized when Egypt came in strongly on the side of the republicans and Saudi Arabia sided with the imam and the royalists; it was internationalized when the Soviet Union and Eastern Europe supported Egypt and the new YAR, and the United States and the United Kingdom deferred to the Saudis and their interests. As a result, the Yemen Civil War became a microcosmic battleground for the "Arab cold war" between revolutionary Arab nationalist republicans and conservative monarchists and, to a lesser extent, between the Soviet Union and its socialist bloc and the Free World.

The Egyptians, who clearly saved the republic in those first years, took control of fighting the civil war and came to look over time more and more like an occupier; bogged down, they came to call the Yemeni civil war "our Vietnam." Seen as a puppet of Egypt's President Gamal Abdel Nasser, the regime headed by President Abdullah al-Sallal lost credibility and legitimacy. When Nasser withdrew his forces from Yemen on the occasion of the Arab–Israel War of 1967 (the Six-Day War), the Sallal regime collapsed in a matter of weeks, opening the way to the republican–royalist reconciliation that took another two years to consummate.

Although it put much state-building as well as socioeconomic development on hold and exacted a terrible price in human suffering, the civil war did open up an isolated and insulated Yemen to a flood of new ideas, institutions, and practices. The Yemen of the 1970s and later was able to grasp and utilize many of these new elements in a way that was impossible in the 1960s.

BIBLIOGRAPHY

BURROWES, ROBERT D. *The Yemen Arab Republic: The Politics of Development, 1962–1986.* Boulder, Colo., 1987.

DRESCH, PAUL. *Tribes, Government, and History in Yemen.* Oxford, 1989.

Robert D. Burrowes

Yemen Dynasties

Ruling families of the area known today as Yemen.

The Zaydi imamate in Yemen has its origins in 897, when al-Hadi ila al-Haqq Yahya became the first Zaydi imam (with his seat in Sa'da). His fame as an intellectual as well as a leader led to the invitation to Yemen; there he developed a multitude of policies that eventually became the basic guidelines for the religious as well as political characteristics of Yemeni ZAYDISM.

Yahya, however, was not able to consolidate his rule in all of Yemen; there were revolts as well as segments of the population that did not accept his pretensions to religio-political rule. Although he did not succeed in establishing any permanent administrative infrastructure, Yahya's descendants became the local aristocracy, and it is from among them that the imams of Yemen were selected for the next one thousand years.

Yemen throughout most of that period was only rarely a unified political entity; in fact, what was included within its frontiers varied widely, and it has not been governed consistently or uniformly by any single set of rulers. It existed as a part of a number of different political systems/ruling dynasties between the ninth and sixteenth centuries, after which it became a part of the Ottoman Empire.

After Imam Yahya's death, a multitude of smaller dynasties and families established themselves in the Tihama (the low coastal plain) as well as in the highlands. Among the better known of these are the Sulayhids, the Hatims, the Zuray'ids, and the Yu'firids. It was during this period, when the Fatimid state was influential, that a portion of the population was converted to ISMA'ILI SHI'ISM.

Beginning with the conquest of Yemen by the family of Salah al-Din ibn Ayyub (Saladin) in 1174, a series of dynasties exercised a modicum of control and administration in Yemen for roughly the next 400 years; these are, in chronological sequence, the Ayyubids, from 1173/74 to 1228; the Rasulids, from 1228 to 1454; the Tahirids, from 1454 to 1517; and the Mamluks, from 1517 to 1538, when the Ottoman Empire took the Yemeni Tihama.

During most of this period, the dynasties and their rulers were primarily engaged in familial, regional, and occasionally sectarian disputes. Ironically, the Sunni Rasulids, who eventually concentrated their rule in southern Yemen for precisely that reason, were the dynasty under which the region experienced the greatest economic growth and political stability.

Very little is known about the Zaydi imams and their efforts to establish themselves and develop some form of administration (including tax collection), or

their success in promoting Zaydi goals during this period. From the available evidence, there was very little continuity and a great deal of competition among the Zaydi families and clans. For example, in a presumably representative two-hundred-year period from the thirteenth to the fifteenth centuries, there appear to have been more than twenty different candidates for the imamate, representing more than ten distinct clans.

Eventually, as the Europeans entered the Middle East, specifically the Portuguese and then others in the effort to control the Red Sea trade, Yemen and its Zaydi imams were increasingly unable to maintain their independence. It was not until the ascendancy of Imam Qasim ibn Muhammad and his son al-Mu'ayyad Muhammad in the early seventeenth century that the Zaydi Yemenis were able to resist the Ottoman Empire's forces and become an independent political entity.

Manfred W. Wenner

Yemen Hunt Oil Company

U.S. company that discovered oil in Yemen and developed its export industry.

After a short search, the Yemen subsidiary of the Hunt Oil Company (YHOC) of Dallas discovered oil in commercial quantities in the Ma'rib/al-Jawf basin in North Yemen in 1984. It rapidly developed the production-for-export capacity of several fields in that basin. YHOC is also a member of the consortium of companies that signed an oil agreement with the new Republic of Yemen in the early 1990s for the promising neutral zone, previously the disputed borderland between the two Yemens and their respective oil fields in Ma'rib/al-Jawf and Shabwa.

Robert D. Burrowes

Yemeni Socialist Party

Yemeni political party.

The most important party in the former People's Democratic Republic of Yemen, the Yemeni Socialist party arranged the union with the Yemen Arab Republic and was one of the two major parties in the unified state until its leaders were exiled as a result of the 1994 civil war. Created in October 1978 as the "vanguard party" required by Marxist-Leninist theory, it superseded the United Political Organization of the National Front, which in turn had replaced the National Front for the Liberation of Occupied

South Yemen (the National Front), created in 1963. The latter, which was made up of seven smaller groupings (including the Arab Nationalist movement), eventually emerged as the strongest and best-organized of the various groups competing for leadership of Aden and the protectorates in opposition to the British presence. It was to the National Front that the British turned over independent South Yemen in November 1967.

Manfred W. Wenner

Yeni Mecmua

Ottoman literary magazine.

Published between 1917 and 1918, *Yeni Mecmua* (the New Digest) was an organ for the dissemination of Unionist thought. Ziya GÖKALP was a regular contributor, publicizing his ideas about Islamic modernism, Turkish nationalism, and social populism. In addition, *Yeni Mecmua* was a forum for discussions about the need to develop a native Turkish business class.

BIBLIOGRAPHY

Türkiye'de dergiler ansiklopediler, 1849–1984. Istanbul, 1984.

David Waldner

Yerevan

Capital city of Armenia.

Occupying a valuable location on the route used by trade caravans to cross Transcaucasia since ancient times, Yerevan (also Erevan) was a fortified city in the eighth century B.C.E., became part of the Armenian kingdom in the sixth century B.C.E., and was occupied by Romans, Arabs, Mongols, Ottoman Turks, and Georgians until it was incorporated into the Russian Empire in 1828.

Yerevan became the capital of the Armenian Soviet Socialist Republic of the USSR in 1920, and the capital of the Republic of Armenia after a referendum on independence on September 22, 1991. Yerevan is an important center of industry, and the Armenian State University and Academy of Sciences are located there. The 1986 population was 1,148,000.

BIBLIOGRAPHY

KURIAN, GEORGE THOMAS. *Encyclopedia of the Second World.* New York, 1991.
Webster's New Geographical Dictionary. Springfield, Mass., 1984.

David Waldner

Yerevantsi, Simeon   [1710–1780]

Armenian ecclesiastical leader and catholicos of all Armenians, 1763–1780.

Simeon Yerevantsi was born in Yerevan when it was the seat of a Persian khanate. Educated at the Holy See of Echmiadzin, where he later taught, Simeon was one of the most learned figures of the Armenian Apostolic Church. A wide-ranging intellectual, he wrote works on the theology, history, and administrative status of the church and catholicate at Echmiadzin. He traveled as a legate of the Holy See to Istanbul and to Madras, an important center of Armenian intellectual activity at the time.

Simeon was elected catholicos at Echmiadzin in 1763, and his pontificate marks a turning point in the importance of Echmiadzin for Armenians. While the Armenian patriarchate in Istanbul had become the most influential office in the Armenian Church, the remoteness of Echmiadzin in a frontier province of Iran left it isolated. Simeon labored to expand the role of the Holy See. In 1771, he established a printing press at the catholicate, the first on the territory of historic Armenia. He also organized against the spread of Roman Catholicism in eastern Armenia. He improved the school at the monastery, preparing the ground for when it would become a major center of learning in the nineteenth century with the establishment of a full-fledged academy in 1874 under Catholicos Gevorg IV.

Simeon codified the possessions and rights of the church by gathering and recording evidence documenting the privileges of the Echmiadzin catholicate. He also secured from Catherine the Great formal acknowledgment of his jurisdiction over the Armenian community and church in Russia, thus, with Iran and India already within his administrative competence, making Echmiadzin a focal point of the Armenian Apostolic Church and rival to the Armenian patriarchate in Istanbul. With the Russian conquests of the khanate of Yerevan in 1828 and the absorption of Echmiadzin into a Christian state, the ascendancy of Echmiadzin in Armenian ecclesiastical affairs became assured. In the twentieth century, with the founding of an Armenian state, its status was solidified in the eyes of Armenian people around the world.

Rouben P. Adalian

Yeshiva

A school in which the Talmud, Jewish legal codes, and rabbinic literature and commentaries are the primary subjects of study.

Although *semikha* (rabbinic ordination) may be an outcome of yeshiva study, yeshivas are institutions intended for all Jewish males who wish to advance their study of Judaism. Originally, it was the local place to sit and study texts. Yeshivas became places where scholars gathered, where each famous and learned teacher attracted his own students. In eighteenth-century Lithuania, where the modern form was developed, yeshivas drew students from a variety of European localities and provided the students with a formal curriculum, a place to stay, and often a stipend as well.

Yeshiva education consists of endless hours of vocal and intensive review of texts with fellow students (*khavruseh*). Usually once a day, after posting a bibliography and a series of textual glosses that students must explore in advance, a teacher will give a *shiur* (lesson in Talmud). Some modern yeshivas include secular studies as well (they are often called day schools in North America and *yeshivot tichoniyot* in Israel).

In Israel, yeshivas are numerous; some embrace the ideals of religious Zionism, and some deny them. The former encompass *hesder* yeshivas, whose students combine military service with study; the latter have students who are exempted from military service. Among the most prominent of the former are the Etzion Yeshiva, Mercaz HaRav Kook, and Kerem b' Yavneh. Among the latter are the Ponovez Yeshiva, in B'nai B'rak, and the Mir Yeshiva, in Jerusalem. The greatest growth has been in yeshivas connected with Sephardim.

BIBLIOGRAPHY

HELMREICH, W. *The World of the Yeshiva.* New York, 1982.

Samuel C. Heilman

Yeşilcam

Center of Turkey's film industry.

Yeşilcam (Green Pine) is the name of a street in Istanbul's Beyoğlu district where most of Turkey's film studios were founded in the 1940s and 1950s. The name came to be associated with Turkish Hollywood-style commercial cinema. The district's golden age was during the 1950s and 1960s, when dozens of studios churned out some two hundred films per year, often shooting two films at the same time with the same cast. Istanbul's movie theaters, first built in the district before World War I, were also concentrated there, making it a lively entertainment and arts area (akin to New York's Greenwich Village or London's Soho).

Turkish film studios, however, never attracted the continued capital investment or wielded the power of their Hollywood counterparts. The district declined with the economic downturn of the late 1970s and 1980s; production fell in 1980 to sixty-eight features. Erotic and martial-arts films dominated production in the 1970s. Government support, a growing video market among Turkish workers in Europe, and growing public interest in alternative cinema, however, fueled a revival of the industry in the late 1980s and early 1990s.

BIBLIOGRAPHY

WOODHEAD, CHRISTINE, ed. *Turkish Cinema: An Introduction.* London, 1989.

Elizabeth Thompson

Yiddish

A vernacular language used by certain Jewish groups.

A language based on Germanic dialects infused with Hebrew and loan words from areas in Europe in which it was spoken, Yiddish was the vernacular used by Ashkenazi Jews since the European Middle Ages. As Hebrew became primarily the language of liturgy and religious scholarship, Yiddish, by the end of the eighteenth century, emerged as the vehicle for the expression of secular literature, drama, poetry, and popular literature. By the nineteenth century, Yiddish was established as the language of a secular European Jewish culture focused primarily in Eastern Europe.

The Zionist ideology that stressed the return to the land and the use of Hebrew as the language of the nation was instrumental in the revival of Hebrew. The language controversy that ensued during the period of the YISHUV among those who advocated Hebrew, Yiddish, or German as the official language resulted in Hebrew becoming the established language of the Yishuv and, later, the State of Israel, with Yiddish relegated to the Jews of the Diaspora. Only after the Holocaust and the liquidation of Yiddish culture under Soviet rule has there been a resurgent interest in the language in Israel and the United States. As a spoken language, Yiddish has become the established vernacular of Orthodox Haredi Jews.

BIBLIOGRAPHY

LAQUEUR, WALTER. *A History of Zionism.* New York, 1972.

Reeva S. Simon

Yıldırım Army

Special Ottoman strike force, also known as the Thunderbolt, or Seventh Army.

The army was organized in early 1917 by Enver Paşa to defend the Eastern Front in World War I. It comprised fourteen Ottoman divisions headed by German General Erich von Falkenhayn and included six thousand German soldiers and sixty-five top Ottoman officers, including General Mustafa Kemal (Atatürk). Enver Paşa had originally planned this special army to recapture Iraq but, in March 1917, sent it to block the new British and Arab campaign in Palestine, where they joined the Fourth Army at Gaza and won an initial victory.

The Ottoman–German effort, however, was weakened by conflicts over jurisdiction, by Turkish nationalist dissent toward the German leadership, and by matériel disadvantages. In the autumn of 1917, the British and Arab offensive forced an Ottoman withdrawal to Damascus, with heavy losses on December 27. The Allied drive resumed the next autumn, and, on October 1, 1918, British General Edmund Allenby and the Arab nationalist revolt forced the Ottomans to evacuate the Syrian capital. Allenby's troops, aided by French forces landing at Beirut, nearly annihilated the Yıldırım Army as the Ottomans were driven back to Alexandretta within two weeks. General Otto Liman von Sanders gave command of the Yıldırım to Mustafa Kemal after the Mudros Armistice took effect October 31, and Kemal surrendered at Adana on November 13, 1918.

BIBLIOGRAPHY

SHAW, STANFORD J., and EZEL KURAL SHAW. *History of the Ottoman Empire and Modern Turkey.* Cambridge, U.K., 1977.

Elizabeth Thompson

Yishuv

The Jewish community in Palestine from the Ottoman period through the British mandate.

The Yishuv refers to the Jewish population living in Palestine before the State of Israel was proclaimed in 1948. The community was divided into old and new, based on economics, sociocultural background, and political aspiration. The Old Yishuv had its beginning in a religious revival among Jews in Eastern Europe at the end of the eighteenth century, which inspired increasing numbers to undertake the dangerous journey to Ottoman Palestine throughout the nineteenth century. Motivated by a desire to observe Jewish religious commandments, scholars and pious men came to pray and study as preconditions to salvation. They settled primarily in what they considered the holy cities: Tiberias, Safed, Hebron, and Jerusalem.

Jewish immigrants trying to enter Palestine illegally in 1946. (Institute for Palestine Studies)

As the grip of religious tradition began to loosen its hold on Jews in Europe and as assimilation began to become possible in some countries, concerned Jews began supporting the pious communities in what they called Zion or the Holy Land. Attempting to reinforce the daily religious life-style of Jews in Palestine, in 1810 the wealthy Dutch Jew R. Zvi Hirsch Lehren founded the Pekidim and Amarkalim of ERETZ YISRAEL (officials of *Eretz Yisrael* [The Land of Israel]) in Amsterdam, to centralize the collection and distribution of funds (called in Hebrew *halukkah*) used to support pious Jews and their religious institutions in Palestine. The system tied Palestine's Jews (often men who had left families behind) to their home communities.

Even with a sophisticated system of external funding, as the numbers of Jews in the Old Yishuv increased, their economic lot deteriorated. A few enjoyed economic security, but most lived in poverty. Attempts to coordinate additional financial aid and to distribute it equitably failed. The religious schools (*kollelim*) provided their own subsidies, sometimes offering rent, health care, and support for widows and orphans, but all charitable services depended on budgetary circumstances and on intellectual recognition; outstanding scholars received the highest payments.

By 1882, ZIONISM emerged in Europe, and Zionists began to sponsor immigration to Ottoman Palestine. Their goal was a self-supporting secular, egalitarian society based on productive labor and a Hebrew cultural renaissance; they named their community the New Yishuv. Proclaiming the need for social change, economic transformation, and political reform, Zionist activities threatened to rupture traditional patterns of pious Jewish life in Palestine.

Many leaders of the Old and New Yishuvs considered one another not just absolute rivals but implacable enemies. They were in competition for funds from Europe and the United States. The Old Yishuv continued a medieval European life-style, adopted for survival of Judaism in foreign lands; Zionists claimed a right to a new Hebrew-based culture that would evolve into a national tradition and a modern independent state. The Old Yishuv taught TALMUD and tradition in Yeshivas; Zionists taught secular subjects, liberal arts, practical sciences, and technology. The Old Yishuv spoke Yiddish but studied and prayed all day in liturgical Hebrew; the New Yishuv cut ties with ghetto Europe and spoke a revivified modern Hebrew that would provide one language for all Jews returning from a polyglot Diaspora.

In Zionist historiography the differences seem immense; in fact, Jews who studied Talmud daily established neighborhoods outside Jerusalem's Old City walls in the nineteenth century in an effort to raise their standard of living. Some bought land and tried to become farmers or to fashion basic necessities, often in the hope of creating a base for productive labor. Some negotiated the purchase of land for the first Zionist agricultural settlements; some advocated educational reform and contributed to the revival of Hebrew. A generation of Jews who matured in Jerusalem during the Ottoman reform era of the 1860s responded to the challenge of meeting daily needs as well as to the spirit of the age by calling for the creation of a productive Jewish economy. Yosef Rivlin, Yoel Moshe Salomon, and Israel Dov Frumkin, prominent cultural and religious figures, also became builders of new neighborhoods and founders of a new Jewish infrastructure. Among the housing projects outside the Old City that they developed or supported were Nahalat Shiva, Meah She'arim, Mishkenot Israel, Kiryah Ne'emanah, and Bet Yaakov. By 1880, two thousand Jews lived outside the Old City, and sixteen thousand lived within the walls. A similar impulse drove Jaffa's Jewish leaders to establish the new suburbs of Neve Shalom, Yefe Nof, and Ahva.

As for the Zionists, some came from traditional backgrounds and never gave up their faith or their observance of religious ritual. Permanent alliances across the two communities were generally short-lived, however; often they split over religious issues that constrained the establishment of a modern Jewish society. The first major controversy was over the application of the Jewish law of the sabbatical year, which provided for the land to lie fallow every seventh year; Zionists maintained that following this biblical injunction would cause the end of a viable agricultural base at a crucial point in their agronomy

schedule. Zionists also resisted any compromise formulas proffered by Palestine's Sephardic rabbis (the original injunction having come from the then-majority Ashkenazic rabbis, who represented the bulk of the European Jews at that time).

Although immigrants driven by piety continued to arrive alongside Zionists, it was the Zionist vision that created Palestine's new institutions. Schools, libraries, newspapers, workshops, cultural and commercial enterprises were established—even in Jerusalem, the heart of the Old Yishuv. The Old Yishuv principles, although honorable, seemed inadequate for the creation and functioning of an independent modern society, even before World War I severely undermined the community by disrupting communications and contact with Europe and its financial contributions.

After World War I and the dissolution of the Ottoman Empire, Palestine was ruled by the British under a mandate from the League of Nations. British doctrine recognized the Yishuv as a religious community within the region but, in practice, provided it with the opportunity to operate national-style institutions. Administered as a crown colony, Palestine had Zionist self-governing systems that often paralleled British mandate offices.

Zionists brought their political parties with them to Palestine. From the early years of the twentieth century, a number of Zionist–Socialist parties (Po'alei Ziyyon, Hapo'el Hatza'ir, Left Po'alei Tziyyon) as well as Mizrahi, the Religious Zionist movement, had adherents and activists in Palestine. Political parties opened employment offices and founded agricultural collectives, soup kitchens, loan funds, newspapers, and schools. They provided recreational and cultural activities for members. Many of these activities were absorbed in 1920 by the HISTADRUT, which became the central vehicle of state-building for the Yishuv. Histadrut operations—labor exchanges, construction companies, and an underground army—were similar to those of a sovereign state. The Histadrut became the base of power for David Ben-Gurion, who used his position as secretary-general to bring together several of labor's political parties in 1930 to form MAPAI, dominant in Yishuv politics and eventually in the World Zionist Organization. With backing from both the Histadrut and MAPAI, Ben-Gurion was able to outmaneuver political rivals such as Vladimir Jabotinsky and Chaim Weizmann.

Palestine's Jewish community organized itself in explicitly political structures, beginning with an assembly (Knesset Israel) elected by persons over twenty years with at least three months' residence in the region. Between sessions, the assembly delegated its powers to the Va'ad Le'umi (National Council), appointed from its ranks. The council nominated from among its members an executive (called the Jewish Agency) charged with the actual administration of the community. Policies generated by the self-governing institutions of the Yishuv covered matters of health, social welfare, defense, and education. Without authority to tax, however, Knesset Israel and its constituent institutions had limited power. Its funding depended on allocations from the World Zionist Organization. Many of Palestine's Orthodox Jewish residents remained aloof from the organization and did not participate in elections, since they objected to female suffrage and to the secular aims of Zionism. They insisted on their organizational separateness and retained an allegiance to the principles of the Old Yishuv.

Palestine was governed as a colony, but significant policies were often formulated by England's highest elected officials, including the prime minister, even Parliament. Yishuv politicians, such as Ben-Gurion, understood the pressing need to influence policymakers in London as much as those implementing regulations in Palestine. Hence, much power was assigned to international Zionist agencies and to their leaders, who attained global stature (e.g., Theodor Herzl and Chaim Weizmann).

Until the creation of an expanded Jewish Agency in 1929, the Zionist executive's political department was also the central mechanism for creating contacts with Arab leaders within and outside of Palestine. Founded and directed by Chaim Kalvaryski, this department initiated contacts with Palestinian personalities willing to sit with Jews in institutions established on the basis of the mandate's political framework. The department extended funds to village shaykhs, municipal leaders, and newspapers and movements deemed moderate on the issue of the establishment of a Jewish national home in Palestine. In 1929, the Jewish Agency and the National Council set up the Joint Bureau to handle relations with Britain in London and Palestine and with the League of Nations.

Two developments in the 1930s augmented the authority of Yishuv institutions. The first was a consequence of the increased number of Jewish immigrants to Palestine (fleeing fascist Europe), which increased the numbers who chose to participate in elections and other voluntary political activities. The second was the immediate effect of the outbreak of the Arab Revolt in 1936 and the need for a larger Yishuv defense force. The Yishuv assumed responsibility for helping to fund such a force through a voluntary tax levy. Yishuv institutions still primarily drew their authority from the networks created with various political movements and/or with the leadership of the Jewish Agency, but as the legitimacy of these institutions strengthened, they also began to function more effectively on their own.

When British rule began in Palestine, there were 56,000 Jews in a total population of 640,000. By the end of Britain's political tenure, the Jewish population had increased to 650,000 with substantial immigration occurring in the mandate's last decade. Undoubtedly, the rise of Nazism and the threat of war expanded both interest in immigration and the actual numbers of Jewish immigrants, despite Britain's attempts to control the number of Jews in Palestine.

The outbreak of the war in 1939 and the genocidal policies of the Nazis created enormous difficulty for the Yishuv. On the one hand, these policies substantiated the Zionist claim that Diaspora Jewry lived in fragile, untenable conditions; on the other, by slaughtering the movement's potential population, they threatened the possibility of achieving the Zionist dream of sovereignty. However, World War II ended with the beginning of the Cold War, and the dramatic shift in the balance of world power helped the Yishuv win necessary international support for Jewish statehood, especially from those interested in the dismantling of Great Britain's empire.

BIBLIOGRAPHY

HALPER, JEFF. *Between Redemption and Revival*. Boulder, Colo., 1991.

HUREWITZ, J. C. *The Struggle for Palestine*. New York, 1950.

LISSAK, MOSHE, and DAN HOROWITZ. *Origins of the Israeli Polity*. Chicago, 1978.

Donna Robinson Divine

Yizhar, S. [1918–   ]

Israeli novelist.

Born in Rehovot, Israel, the great-nephew of the Israeli author Moshe Smilansky (1874–1953), Yizhar was elected to the Knesset and served as a representative of the MAPAI and Rafi parties from 1949 to 1967. He also worked as a schoolteacher. In his novels, which deal with life in modern Israel, his characters struggle to reconcile contradictions between the norms of society and the dictates of personal conscience. Yizhar's most famous work is *Yeme Ziklag*.

BIBLIOGRAPHY

UKHMANI, A. *Le-Ever ha Adama*. 1953.

Bryan Daves

Yom Kippur War

See Arab–Israel War (1973)

Yön

An influential Turkish leftist journal.

A weekly paper founded in 1961 by a group of intellectuals in Turkey, *Yön* (Direction) quickly reached a circulation of thirty thousand. It attracted students and leftist groups after the government's 1962 crackdown on leftist political groups.

Yön espoused a non-Marxist policy that saw underdevelopment as Turkey's main problem and advocated a nationalist front of the masses to advance democracy, Kemalist state-led reform, and anti-imperialism. But *Yön*'s moderate stance was outstripped by the revolutionary atmosphere of the mid-1960s; it closed in 1967. It continued to influence students, however, who in the 1970s used its ideology but adopted radical reform tactics, including guerilla warfare.

BIBLIOGRAPHY

SAMIM, AHMET. "The Left." In *Turkey in Transition,* ed. by Irvin C. Schick and Ertuğrul Ahment Tonak. New York, 1987.

Elizabeth Thompson

Yöntem, Ali Canip [1887–1967]

Turkish poet and linguistic reformer.

Ali Canip Yöntem was raised in Salonika, where his father was in political exile. In Salonika, he was a member of the GENÇ KALEMLER (Young Pens) literary group, which espoused linguistic reform and the new language. Subsequently, he was appointed professor of Turkish at Istanbul University. Yöntem advocated purifying Turkish of Arabic and Farsi vocabulary and grammar and composed poetry in the Turkish *hece* meter rather than the Arabic *aruz*. His poetry reflects his belief that the poet performs a social function, not merely an aesthetic one.

BIBLIOGRAPHY

MITLER, LOUIS. *Contemporary Turkish Writers*. Bloomington, Ind., 1988.

David Waldner

Yosef, Ovadiah [1920–]

Israeli religious and political leader.

Born in Baghdad, Ovadiah Yosef moved to Palestine at the age of one with his parents. Educated at the Sephardic yeshiva Porat Yosef in Jerusalem, his intelligence and memory earned him recognition at an early age as a scholar. He served for a short time as the chief rabbi of Cairo and Egypt in the 1940s, then returned to Israel after 1948, where he became a religious judge. In 1966, he was appointed chief rabbi of Tel Aviv, then served as chief Sephardic rabbi of Israel and president of the Supreme Rabbinical Court from 1973 to 1983. His appointment as chief rabbi of Tel Aviv encouraged the establishment of many yeshivas and centers of learning for Sephardic youth.

After leaving the chief rabbinate, Yosef became involved in politics, founding the first ultra-Orthodox Sephardi party, SHAS, which won four seats in the National Assembly in 1984. Yosef has alternatively courted both the Labor and Likud parties, joining the National Unity government of 1988 and then allowing SHAS to support the Labor party's vote of no confidence in March 1990, which brought down the government. SHAS then rejoined the right-wing coalition formed by Yitzhak Shamir in June 1990. After the 1992 elections, in which SHAS received six seats, the party joined the Labor-led coalition but dropped out in 1994 over the peace process. At one time Yosef had been close with Ashkenazic rabbi Menachem Elazar Shach, but disputes between the two over politics have led to a deep rift between not only themselves but also between ultra-Orthodox Ashkenazic and Sephardic rabbis.

Yosef's most famous work, *Yabiah Omer,* for which he was awarded the Israel Prize, deals with halakic problems in daily life. Yosef's teachings stress the importance of yeshiva students learning to deal with practical problems, as opposed to theoretical halakic questions.

Julie Zuckerman

Young Algerians

A group of French-educated men who, early in the twentieth century, became the first Algerians to attempt reform within the colonial political system.

Estimated to number between 1,000 and 1,200, the Young Algerians *(Jeunes Algériens)* included intellectuals, members of the liberal professions, and individuals who had succeeded within French business circles. Most prominent among the group's members were Dr. Benthami Ould Hamida, Omar Bouderba, Fekar Ben Ali, Chérif Benhabylès, and—beginning in 1913—Khaled ibn Hashimi ibn Hajj Abd al-Qadir, grandson of Algerian patriot Abd al-Qadir.

While there were differences in the emphases of the Young Algerians, most were attempting to win for themselves rights approximating those of Frenchmen. Their agenda, before World War I, included exemption of at least some Algerians from the exceptive CODE DE L'INDIGÉNAT, more equitable distribution of taxes, easier access to French citizenship, and greater political participation for the educated. The agenda also included programs for the masses, including greater access to education, opening of grazing and forest lands, protections for property, and more careful monitoring of government abuse.

Despite support from many liberals in France, attempts to negotiate concessions failed in 1913 and 1914, largely because of colon opposition. During World War I, when thousands of Algerians served in the French armed forces, a grateful Prime Minister Georges Clemenceau promised reform. The resulting Jonnart Law of February 4, 1919, however, was viewed by most Young Algerians as being very far from what they had been promised. For a few years after the war, Khaled ibn Hashimi ibn Hajj Abd al-Qadir continued to lead the movement for reform within the system, but, by 1923, he gave up the effort and went into exile in the Near East.

BIBLIOGRAPHY

NOUSCHI, ANDRÉ. *La naissance du nationalisme algérien.* Paris, 1979.

John Ruedy

Young Egypt

A patriotic association of Egyptian youth established in October 1933.

In 1937, Young Egypt (Misr al-Fatat) became a formal political party in Egypt; in 1940, the name was changed to the Islamic Nationalist party (al-Hizb al-Watani al-Islami); in 1949, it became the Socialist party of Egypt (Hizb Misr al-Ishtiraki).

The dominant figure in Young Egypt throughout its history was the lawyer/politician Ahmad Husayn. In the 1930s, the movement's program combined a vehement, anti-British Egyptian nationalism, an antiparliamentary outlook, an emphasis on the paramilitary training and mobilization of youth, and a call for greater social justice. Politically opposed to the Wafd, Young Egypt aligned itself with the anti-Wafdist forces centered around the Egyptian palace;

its paramilitary squads of Green Shirts periodically fought with the Blue Shirts of the Wafd.

Although it was suppressed during World War II, it afterward dropped its paramilitary features while retaining, but relabeling, much of its prewar populism. Like all Egyptian political parties, it was abolished in January 1953, after the Free Officers, led by General Muhammad Naguib, seized power from the monarchy of King Farouk.

BIBLIOGRAPHY

JANKOWSKI, JAMES. *Egypt's Young Rebels: "Young Egypt," 1933–1952.* Stamford, Conn., 1975.

James Jankowski

Young Ottomans

Ottoman intellectuals and bureaucrats who constituted the first organized opposition to the pro-West modernizing elite of the Tanzimat.

Members of the group called themselves New Ottomans, while contemporary European observers referred to them as YOUNG TURKS. The latter term came to be used more specifically in reference to the next generation of liberal opponents of Sultan Abdülhamit as distinct from Young Ottomans, which has become the synonym of New Ottomans.

The Young Ottomans began their activities in Constantinople (now Istanbul). They faced repression and were forced into exile in Europe and other parts of the Ottoman Empire. Prominent Young Ottoman leaders were Namık Kemal (1840–1888), İbrahim Şinasi (1824–1871), Agâh Efendi (1832–1885), Abdülhamit Ziya Paşa (1825–1880), and Ali Suavi (1838–1878). The group received important financial and moral support from a disaffected member of the Egyptian khedival family who had entered the Ottoman service, Mustafa Fazıl Paşa (1829–1875). While these leaders were united in their opposition to the TANZIMAT elite, and to the autocratic ministry of Paşas Fu'ad and Ali, they had hardly been bystanders to the Tanzimat. They had matured intellectually and professionally during the Tanzimat period. Many had served in the Translation Bureau, a breeding ground for Tanzimat bureaucrats. Some were stimulated by the frustration of their career ambitions under the Tanzimat regime.

The Young Ottomans differed in social and professional background. Ziya Paşa, the oldest in the group, was a writer and poet and had served as third secretary to Sultan Abdülmecit II. Namık Kemal, also poet and writer, came from a distinguished bureaucratic family. Şinasi, an army captain's son who held a post in the imperial arsenal before he was sent to Paris to study finance, was the most innovative and versatile from a literary point of view. Ali Suavi was a middle-school teacher and a religious-minded writer, even agitator.

The forerunner of the group was the Alliance of Fidelity or Patriotic Alliance, a loose group consisting of literary men and functionaries, which first met in Constantinople in June 1865. Organization was secret and conspiratorial, apparently modeled along the Carbonari of Italy, Spain, and France and led by a French-educated agitator, Mehmet Bey. The group did not publicize a program. The members were motivated by recent Ottoman setbacks in the Balkans and Lebanon and fear of disintegration. They felt constitutional government was necessary to preserve the empire and to ward off Europe's economic domination and diplomatic interventions. The group's expanding membership included bureaucrats, *ulama* (Islamic clergy), and army officers.

In 1866/67 Namık Kemal and Ali Suavi published newspapers (*Tasvir-i Efkâr* and *Muhbir*) in which they vehemently criticized the government's policy regarding the insurrection in Crete and the impending surrender of Serbia. They published an open letter from Mustafa Fazıl, who had left the empire over issues pertaining to his political ambitions in Egypt, which addressed the sultan and amounted to a liberal manifesto. The government ordered Namık Kemal, Ziya, and Ali Suavi to domestic exile and closed their newspapers. Instead, they accepted an invitation from Mustafa Fazıl Paşa and fled to Paris. At this time, the government also uncovered the group's contacts with top security officials in preparation for a coup against Abdülaziz that was organized by Mehmet Bey.

The regrouping of the liberal-minded elements of the Patriotic Alliance as New Ottomans occurred in exile at the end of May 1867. In Paris and later London, they published the newspaper *Hürriyet,* edited by Namık Kemal and Ziya Paşa with financial support from Mustafa Fazıl. They promoted liberal political principles and demanded a parliament. At the same time, they denounced liberal economic policies and advocated measures to buttress indigenous trade and to promote industry.

Despite considerable variation in their outlook on politics, society, and religion, the Young Ottomans projected an Islamic modernist synthesis. They opposed Western political and economic interference and wholesale adoption of Western thought and culture. Nevertheless, they were sympathetic to Western political institutions. Their thought was premised on the existence in Islamic political traditions of the

concepts and institutions fundamental to a liberal political system based on representative principles. The Young Ottomans reinterpreted and popularized the concept of *watan* (homeland) to advance a political allegiance to the Ottoman state. They sought a contractual relationship between the subjects and the ruler, based on the Islamic principles of *shura* (consultation) and *ijma* (consensus), within the framework of an Ottoman watan. These views represented the first systematic expression of Islamic modernist ideas in the Muslim world.

The Young Ottoman movement was not the first expression of political protest against the Tanzimat. As early as 1859, a group of *ulama* and army officers had led a coup d'état aimed at Abdülmecit in resentment of Tanzimat policies that enhanced the status of the non-Muslim minorities vis-à-vis the Muslims, and—perhaps more importantly—had left the payment of officers in arrears (the KÜLELI INCIDENT). The Young Ottomans constituted the first opposition group that attempted to offer alternative programs, inspired by Western thought but consistent with Islamic political ideals.

The movement signifies the beginnings of a campaign for social mobilization and the forging of a public opinion in the Ottoman Empire, even though the group's propaganda remained restricted to a literate Turkish-speaking intelligentsia. Their ideas appealed to disfranchised Westernized groups, students, Muslim commercial associations, and religious conservative opponents of the Tanzimat. They propagated their views through newspapers and literature utilizing a simplified Ottoman-Turkish. They were influenced by contemporary Turkish discoveries, which reinforced the Islamist and anti-imperialist outlook, especially in the pen of Ali Suavi.

The Young Ottomans pioneered journalism and introduced new genres and themes to Ottoman literature. Indeed, future members of the group began their oppositional activity in the first privately published Ottoman journals that appeared in the early 1860s (such as *Tercüman-i Ahval* and *Tasvir-i Efkar*). They introduced the genres of the novel and the drama to Ottoman literature, popularized them, and effectively used them as vehicles of political propaganda. The pioneer in this journalistic and literary activity was Şinasi. The Young Ottomans also translated into Turkish the works of European Enlightenment philosophers and authors such as Rousseau, Montesquieu, Voltaire, Molière, and Lamartine.

The Young Ottomans did not constitute a party organization despite their espousal of political propaganda and promotion of political agendas. After the early 1870s, the group lost its cohesion. Ideological and personal differences led to estrangement in

European exile. Several leaders, including the bene-factor Mustafa Fazıl Paşa, accepted Abdülaziz's amnesty offer to return to Constantinople. Following the death of their nemesis, Ali Paşa, in 1871 the movement went into disarray in the capital. However, under the duress of the political and financial crises of the 1870s, progressive Ottoman statesmen started to look with favor upon Young Ottoman ideas about constitutional government. Midhat Paşa, known as the architect of the Ottoman constitution and parliament, emerged as the leading proponent of change and set out to give concrete expression to Young Ottoman ideas on constitutional government, drawing also on the services of Young Ottoman leaders. Namık Kemal and Ziya Paşa were members of the committee that drafted the Ottoman constitution of 1876. Namık Kemal's long struggle to promote the Young Ottoman cause, his refusal to compromise, his passionately patriotic poetry and drama, and his lucid political writings stressing the notion of popular sovereignty gave him a reputation as the most influential Young Ottoman activist and author, as well as making him a source of inspiration for later constitutionalists.

Due to the absence of a party organization and their dependence on literary forms for the propagation of their ideas, the Young Ottomans had no direct impact on non-Turkish-speaking parts of the empire. For instance, their Islamic modernist ideas did not have an appreciable influence on later and similar currents in the Arab-populated areas. The Young Ottoman movement, however, was the ideological forerunner and inspiration of the later and more broadly based Young Turk movement. The Young Ottomans may not have offered a coherent political philosophy, but they were the precursors of most modern intellectual and political movements in the Middle East.

BIBLIOGRAPHY

DAVISON, RODERIC H. *Reform in the Ottoman Empire, 1856–1876.* Princeton, N.J., 1963.
MARDIN, ŞERIF. *The Genesis of Young Ottoman Thought.* Princeton, N.J., 1962.

Hasan Kayali

Young Turks

Name given to groups in Ottoman society who demanded and strove for political and social change in the last several decades of the Ottoman Empire.

"Young Turk" is an expression coined in Europe that invokes three distinct phases of the Ottoman constitutionalist movement: the anti-TANZIMAT current better known to historians as the "Young Ottoman" movement; the constitutionalist opposition to Sultan Abdülhamit; and the Second Constitutional Period introduced by the reinstitution of the constitutional regime in 1908. There was at no point a distinct organization called the Young Turks; nor did the groups recognized as Young Turks generally embrace this name. Nevertheless, historians identify the last three decades of the empire in reference to Young Turks, while "the Young Turk period" corresponds more precisely to the decade of their political predominance from 1908 to 1918.

Young Turk activity began in the late 1880s. Until the revolution of 1908, their opposition to Abdülhamit manifested itself both within the empire and abroad. The two spheres of activity were linked together only loosely. When a group of medical students in Constantinople (now Istanbul) founded in 1889 the secret cells of what would develop into the COMMITTEE OF UNION AND PROGRESS (CUP), individual intellectuals in exile had already launched a political and journalistic campaign against the Hamitian regime. The best known in the latter group was Khalil Ghanem, a Syrian Christian, who published a journal called *La Jeune Turquie* (Young Turkey).

The Constantinople secret committee spread rapidly in the capital's higher schools and soon became known to the authorities. Reprisals forced many to exile, whereupon an expatriate liberal opposition came together around AHMET RIZA, a French-educated official in the Ministry of Agriculture. Influenced by European positivists, he failed to return from a mission in 1889 and turned into a vocal critic of the Hamitian regime. In 1895, he joined Khalil Ghanem, Alber Fua (a Jew), and Aristidi Paşa (a Greek) to publish *Meşveret*, which became the leading voice of Young Turks.

The next year, a member of the Constantinople secret committee, Murad Bey, fled to Cairo and later to Geneva. A Russian Turk who taught at the influential Mülkiye (civil service) school, Murad Bey was better connected with the liberal currents in Constantinople. His *Mizan* outshone *Meşveret*, both of which were smuggled into the empire. Murad was an Islamist-Turkist revolutionary, in contrast to Ahmet Rıza's elitist and gradualist outlook. The two men were united in their anti-imperialism and denunciation of the Hamitian autocracy. Murad, however, joined Abdülhamit in 1897. Rivalries within the Young Turk movement in exile continued with the publication in Geneva of *Osmanlı* by İshak Süküti and Ahmed Cevdet Paşa, founding members of the CUP in Constantinople. As repression increased in the empire, Young Turk activity shifted almost entirely to Europe and Egypt for a decade. The flight of Damad Mahmud Paşa, the brother-in-law of the sultan, to join the Young Turks in Europe opened a new phase in Young Turk activities.

Under the moral guidance and financial support of ailing Mahmud Paşa and the presidency of his son Sabahettin, the Young Turks held a conference in Paris in February 1902, which crystallized the divisions within the movement. Representatives of all major religious groups in the empire attended. The meeting revealed the separatist inclinations of Christian factions, while two groups around Ahmet Rıza and Sabahettin divided over the suitability of centralist versus decentralist policies in achieving the ultimate aim of preserving the integrity of the empire. Subsequently, Sabahettin formed the Society of Administrative Decentralization and Private Initiative, modeled along the teachings of economist Frédéric Le Play and Edmond Demolins and as a rival to the CUP. A second conference in 1907 aimed at a reconciliation failed to bring Greek, Albanian, and some Armenian factions to the table.

Meanwhile, domestic opposition and conspiracy against the Hamitian regime regrouped in Macedonia. Different oppositional groups coalesced to revitalize the CUP, which in 1907 contacted the Ahmet Rıza group in Europe. However, the exile communities had no role in the immediate circumstances that led to the Young Turk Revolution. If international events like the Japanese victory over Russia and the Russian and Iranian revolutions energized Young Turks everywhere, the nationalist activity among the Balkan peoples and the perceived threat to the empire by enhanced relations between Britain and Russia impelled the unionists in Salonika and Monastir to action.

Due to the role they played in the revolution, leaders of the Macedonian branches of the CUP eclipsed the other factions after 1908. They were, however, too inexperienced to take the helm of government and too insecure to embrace other Young Turk groups, including the CUP leadership in Europe. The differences within the Young Turk movement were now expressed in multiparty politics. The decentralists under Sabahettin formed the Liberal party before the 1908 elections. Even though they failed to block the election of a large majority of CUP candidates to parliament, the decentralists became an increasingly more potent opposition to the CUP, supported by autonomy-minded minority groups. Other parties that formed in 1910 and 1911 soon merged in the Ottoman Liberty and Entente party. The CUP's attempts to manipulate the elections to retain power undermined parliamentary rule, eliciting an ultimatum from a group of military of-

ficers called Saviors. Coupled with foreign preoccupations such as the Italian and Balkan wars, the Young Turk governments gave way to governments led by old-school politicians in 1912. In 1913 the CUP wrested power with a coup d'état. Despite conciliatory measures to the liberals, the CUP remained as that faction within the Young Turk movement that dominated Ottoman politics until the end of the empire.

The Young Turks promoted the ideology of OTTOMANISM in an attempt to foster in all peoples of the empire a commitment to the Ottoman homeland within the framework of a constitutional government. There were organizational similarities, some ideological continuity, and shared political goals between the YOUNG OTTOMANS and Young Turks. Despite what the ethnocentric term "Young Turk" suggests, the movement represented ethnically and religiously a much more diverse group than the Young Ottomans.

The Young Turk movement embraced varied ideological orientations (Westernism, Islamism, Turkism, positivism, centralism, decentralism), socioeconomic backgrounds (lower middle-class students and officers, high officials, members of Ottoman and Egyptian royal households), and ethnic-religious affiliations. It was unified in the conviction for the necessity of reform designed to preserve the empire. The Young Turks were responsible for instituting the beginnings of modern politics in the Middle East, for expanding education and journalism, and for realizing economic, social, and administrative reforms. The movement provided the political nuclei for the successor states of the Ottoman Empire.

BIBLIOGRAPHY

AHMAD, FEROZ. *The Young Turks: The Committee of Union and Progress in Turkish Politics, 1908–1914.* London, 1969.
AKSIN, SINA. *Jön Türkler ve İttihat ve Terakki* (The Young Turks and the Union and Progress). Istanbul, 1980.
RAMSAUR, ERNEST E. *The Young Turks: Prelude to the Revolution of 1908.* Princeton, N.J., 1957.

Hasan Kayali

Youth Aliyah

Organization that brought children to Palestine; today it educates needy immigrant youth in Israel.

Even before Hitler became Germany's chancellor (1933), Youth Aliyah (in Hebrew, Aliyat Hano'ar) had been established as a project by Recha Freier in response to the deteriorating condition of Jews in

Germany. It brought Jewish children to Palestine and provided them with vocational training. It was organized in Palestine by Henrietta Szold, with the cooperation of the Jewish Agency, the Va'ad Le'umi (National Council), and the Kibbutz movement. Originally, parents furnished the funds for their own children's transportation and room-and-board fees. For a number of years, British authorities did not count these children as part of the official immigration quota.

During the mid-1930s, the organization expanded its activities and rescued increasing numbers of children from Nazi Germany and later from Austria. Starting in 1939, with the outbreak of World War II, Youth Aliyah brought children from the battle zones to Great Britain, Scandinavia, Belgium, the Netherlands, and even to Palestine (such as the Polish children called "the Tehran children," who traveled in 1943 via the Soviet Union and Tehran). From 1945 to 1948, Youth Aliyah located orphaned children of the Holocaust and brought some 15,000 to Palestine as "illegals." With the independence of the State of Israel in 1948, Youth Aliyah has trained and rehabilitated needy immigrant children from countries of the Middle East, often in "youth communities." About 250,000 children have gone through Youth Aliyah programs, mostly financed by the Jewish Agency.

BIBLIOGRAPHY

GELBER, YOAV. "The Origins of Youth Aliya." *Zionism* 9 (1988): 147–172.

Donna Robinson Divine

Youth Movements

Social and political groupings and organizations formed for Middle Eastern adolescents and young adults.

Youth movements have played an important role in Middle Eastern politics and society. Until the late nineteenth century, the defense of neighborhoods was frequently ensured by FUTUWWA and other informal associations of young men operating as local militias. These "gangs" provided internal order and protection against outside threats and were often engaged in welfare and charitable activities; however, they sometimes preyed on the people instead.

Although in the twentieth century most of these groups disbanded, new kinds of youth movements developed that transcended residential loyalties. Between the two world wars, scouting and Young Men's Muslim associations made their appearance in many Middle Eastern countries. These nonpolitical youth groups frequently provided the nucleus from which full-fledged political movements developed. Initially, for example, the MUSLIM BROTHERHOOD relied heavily on the scouting movement to spread its religious message.

In the 1930s, several Middle Eastern countries spawned right-wing paramilitary youth associations and sporting clubs that were inspired by Hitler's Germany, Mussolini's Italy, and Franco's Spain. These intensely nationalistic groups recruited primarily among newly educated middle-class students disillusioned with Western-style liberal democracy. They drew their appeal from an admiration of fascist discipline, unity, militancy, organization, and power—and from the hope that Germany and Italy might eliminate Franco–British influence in the Middle East. Members of these groups wore uniforms and followed rituals patterned after those of the Hitler Youth and Franco's Falange. The Phalange party (al-Kata'ib) and the Helpers (al-Najjada), in Lebanon, and Young Egypt (Misr al-Fatat) developed out of such paramilitary groups. The youth groups called Beitar, which played an influential role in the development of revisionist Zionism in Europe and in Palestine under the British mandate, were also influenced in their organization and methods by the fascist youth movements.

In Palestine, from 1922 until the early years of the State of Israel, youth movements affiliated with the major Zionist political parties, the National Religious party (NRP) and the Histadrut (Israeli Federation of Labor Unions), played key roles as vehicles of socialization and integration into the Zionist polity and as agents of elite recruitment. He-Halutz (The Pioneer), a Zionist farming organization, trained young European Jews to join the agricultural movement in Palestine. The role of the youth branches of Israel's major political parties declined after the mid-1950s, except for B'nei Akivah, the NRP's youth branch, whose regular expansion since 1960 has contributed to the growth of religious nationalism in Israel.

In other Middle Eastern countries, governments have tried to prevent the development of autonomous youth movements. In one-party regimes, the ruling party usually has its own youth section. The most developed example of this is probably the Federation of Iraqi Youth, attached to the Iraqi Ba'th party. Under the auspices of athletic and cultural activities, the federation (which is itself divided into several programs catering to specific age groups) tries to diffuse the party's views among Iraq's younger generation.

Throughout the region, youth movements fueled by rapid population growth have played a leading role in antiregime activities. Student activism was a recurrent feature of political life in the 1970s and 1980s in countries as different as Morocco, Egypt, Lebanon, Iran, Turkey, Sudan, and Tunisia, where student associations sometimes joined forces with other social groups to participate in riots against the government. In particular, through a variety of Marxist and Islamic-leftist organizations, young people were actively involved in the 1979 downfall of the shah of Iran. More generally, the Islamic resurgence of the 1970s and 1980s has been primarily a movement of disaffected youth (particularly high school and university students of provincial origins and middle- and lower-middle-class backgrounds) who have organized themselves through informal religious associations.

Youth associations also contributed to the turmoil of the 1970s in Turkey, where the ultranationalist far-right National Action party used youth groups to spread its message and carry out its actions. Similarly, some of the organizational roots of the Intifada, the uprising of Palestinians that broke out in December 1987 in the Israeli-occupied territories, can be found in youth clubs formed in the 1970s and 1980s. These groups were initially created for cultural, social, and athletic activities, but they rapidly developed into a political movement of resistance to Israel's administration. Youth associations enabled a new generation—often the youth of Palestinian refugee camps, who had known only Israeli rule but who, unlike their elders, could no longer bear to live under such control and felt they had little to lose—to vent its anger, frustration, and hatred.

Middle Eastern youth movements also include scouting and Young Men's/Women's Christian associations in Egypt, Lebanon, Jordan, and the Israeli-ruled territories. In Israel, a Young Men's/Women's Hebrew Association is similar. In the 1970s, a Young Men's and a Young Women's Muslim Association were formed in the West Bank. Like scouting, these associations are concerned with organizing social, cultural, self-help, charitable, skill-training, and athletic activities.

BIBLIOGRAPHY

MARDIN, SERIF. "Youth and Violence in Turkey." European Journal of Sociology 19 (1978): 229–254.

EL-MESSIRI, SAWSAN. Ibn al-Balad: A Concept of Egyptian Identity. Leiden, 1978.

MUNSON, HENRY. Islam and Revolution in the Middle East. New Haven, Conn., 1988.

PERETZ, DON. Intifada: The Palestinian Uprising. Boulder, Colo., 1990.

Guilain P. Denoeux

Yücel, Hasan Ali [1897–1961]

Turkish educator, publisher, and writer.

Born in Istanbul, Yücel obtained a degree in philosophy from Istanbul University in 1921. After teaching philosophy for a few years, he worked in the new Republic of Turkey's education directorate and published poetry and books on Turkish literature in the late 1920s and 1930s. He also joined the Turkish language-reform movement and eventually became a protégé of Atatürk. Yücel served as minister of education between 1938 and 1946, when he became known as an active reformer and supervised the publication of hundreds of translations of world classics. He also fostered the development of Village Institutes, which trained local teachers. President İsmet İnönü promoted his strict and controversial language reforms in school textbooks.

In 1946, Yücel was accused by retired general Fevzi Çakmak of harboring communists in the Village Institutes. Although Yücel's name was cleared by a libel suit, during the trial accusations by Islam's religious right—that he supported subversive literature—cast a pall of self-censorship over public debate, and his successor undid many of his reforms. In the 1950s, Yücel worked for a publishing house and returned to writing, producing poetry and books of prose on citizenship, England, and Cyprus.

BIBLIOGRAPHY

HEYD, URIEL. Language Reform in Modern Turkey. Jerusalem, 1954.

Elizabeth Thompson

Yüksek Öğretim Kurulu

The Turkish Council of Higher Education (known as YÖK); policymaking and planning body founded in 1981 in accordance with a new law reorganizing and regulating all higher education in Turkey.

The 1981 council replaced an earlier, less centralized body; Professor Ihsan Doğramacı, chairman of YÖK as well as of the earlier Interuniversity Council, is fairly synonymous with the institution.

The council was originally established in 1973; in 1975, Turkey's Constitutional Court found YÖK's mandate to be incompatible with the constitutionally guaranteed principle of academic freedom and in conflict with the academic and administrative autonomy of universities. Constitutional changes made after the 1980 military takeover enabled the resurrection of YÖK.

The primary function of YÖK is to coordinate all resources allocated to higher education in the national budget, as well as to regulate academic and research programs. The council also acts as a conduit between state and government institutions and the universities. The chairman is directly appointed by the president of the republic, as are some of the council members. Other members are appointed by the president from among candidates proposed by the government, the chief of the general staff, and the interuniversity board. YÖK, as well as all but one of the twenty-nine universities in the country, is funded by the state budget. The only existing privately endowed university, Bilkent, was founded in 1986 by Doğramacı; it, too, is eligible for state financial support. YÖK also supervises the nationwide university entrance examinations through which, in 1990, about 900,000 applicants competed for admission to about 200,000 places in the higher education system, including 65,000 in the Open Education program.

Both in 1973 and much more urgently in 1981, authoritarian governments felt the need to keep student protests down—such as those at Istanbul University and Ankara University—and to depoliticize higher education. There has also been an increasing demand and pressure from high school graduates for university places. The main task of YÖK has been to ensure that all university administrators were of a similar mold—those who would keep politics out of campuses. To do this, the tradition of electing deans in faculties and rectors in universities was abandoned. According to the 1981 law, rectors are appointed by the president of the republic from among candidates submitted by YÖK. YÖK appoints deans from among candidates submitted by the rectors, and it also influences the appointment of all full professors.

In the early 1980s, YÖK supplied suggested curricula for all subjects to be followed in all universities and prescribed courses on the ideology of KEMALISM to be taught at all levels of higher education. Further standardization was hoped to have been achieved by the rule, later abandoned, that any academic promotion could only be effected at a university other than the candidate's own. This last rule was also designed to provide teaching staffs for the many universities opened in provincial centers to alleviate the pressure from the hundreds of thousands of high school graduates hoping to gain university places. The extreme centralization effected by YÖK has come under increasingly vociferous criticism. In the summer of 1992, the government had plans to democratize the university system through an overhaul of YÖK itself and through new legislation.

BIBLIOGRAPHY

"Higher Education in Turkey." UNESCO, European Centre for Higher Education. 1990.

WILLIAMSON, B. *Education and Social Change in Egypt and Turkey*. London, 1987.

World of Learning. 1990.

I. Metin Kunt

Yunis, Jabir Abu Bakr [1942–]

Libyan general.

A brigadier general and commander of the Libyan armed forces, Yunis was born in November 1942 in Zelaa, Libya. He was educated at the military college of Tripoli, where he was a classmate of Muammar al-Qaddafi and a member of the Free Officers movement. Yunis participated in the September 1969 coup that overthrew King Idris and became a member of Libya's Revolutionary Command Council (1969–1977).

Rhimou Bernikho-Canin

Yurdakul, Mehmet Emin [1869–1944]

Turkish poet and politician.

Known as the "national poet" for his patriotic verses (he published a famous collection in 1897, *Türkçe Şiirler*), Mehmet Emin was born in Istanbul during the Ottoman Empire, the son of a ship captain. He entered the civil service and was appointed governor of the Hijaz.

In 1912, Mehmet Emin was a founding member of Türk Ocaği (Turkish Hearth), and during World War I he joined the National Turkish party. After the war he became a member of parliament in the new Republic of Turkey, taking the surname Yurdakul (slave to the homeland). Although he was an admirer of Atatürk, Mehmet Emin expressed several disagreements with the ideology of the new government. His poetry, still memorized today by Turkish schoolchildren, was characterized by an unadorned style and unabashed praise for the Turkish nation.

BIBLIOGRAPHY

MITLER, LOUIS. *Ottoman Turkish Writers: A Bibliographical Dictionary of Significant Figures in Pre-Republican Turkish Literature*. New York, 1988.

David Waldner

Yusuf, Mulay

Alawi sultan of Morocco, 1912–1927.

The ouster by France of Yusuf's predecessor, Mulay Abd al-Hafiz, signaled the subordination of the Moroccan sultanate to French colonialism and a serious loss of prestige by the Moroccan ruling house. Mulay Yusuf's reign was marked largely by the implementation of the Treaty of Fes (March 1912) and the aggressive administration of French rule by the resident general, Marshal Louis LYAUTEY, who held office from 1912 to 1925. The period of Yusuf's reign also witnessed several significant movements against colonial rule, the most important of which was that of Abd al-Karim (al-Khattabi) in the Rif region from 1919 to 1926.

BIBLIOGRAPHY

BURKE, EDMUND, III. *Prelude to Protectorate in Morocco.* Chicago, 1976.
RINEHART, ROBERT, et al. *Morocco: A Country Survey.* Washington, D.C., 1985.

Matthew S. Gordon

Yusuf, Salah ibn

See Ben Yusuf, Salah

Yusuf, Yusuf Salman   [1901–1949]

Secretary-general of Iraq's Communist party, 1941–1949.

Yusuf, known as Comrade Fahd, was a Chaldean Christian. He attended the KUTV in Moscow (1935–1937). On his return to Iraq in 1938, he became a member of the Central Committee of the Communist party; he became its secretary-general in 1941. In 1947 he was condemned to death, but the sentence was commuted to penal servitude. He ran the party from prison until his retrial and execution in February 1949.

Marion Farouk-Sluglett

Yusuf Agah   [1744–1824]

The first permanent Ottoman ambassador.

Born in Morea (Peloponnesus) the son of an agha, Yusuf Agah Effendi went to Constantinople (now Istanbul) as a young man. He held numerous posts in the civil bureaucracy, rising to chief scribe in several offices. In 1793, he was named the Ottoman representative to London, the first of several diplomatic posts created by Selim I. Previous to Yusuf's appointment, the Ottomans had not maintained permanent missions in foreign capitals, preferring temporary assignments. Yusuf held the London post until 1797, when he returned to Constantinople and worked in the janissaries bureaucracy.

BIBLIOGRAPHY

MANTRAN, ROBERT, ed. *Histoire de l'empire ottoman.* Paris, 1989.

Elizabeth Thompson

Yusufian, Boghos   [1775–1844]

Armenian minister of commerce and foreign affairs in Egypt in the 1820s and 1830s.

Boghos Yusufian, better known as Boghos Bey, was born in İzmir to a family well connected to the Armenian merchant class involved with overseas commerce. He made his money in Egypt as a customs official and trader. He was skilled in languages and served the British as an interpreter in the campaign against the French. He was first hired by Muhammad Ali as an interpreter and rapidly progressed to the position of personal secretary. Consolidating his rule in Egypt, Muhammad Ali found in Boghos an instrument for pursuing policies independent of his Ottoman sovereigns. Having earned Muhammad Ali's trust during his service in the palace in Cairo, Boghos was made minister of commerce in 1826. He ran his office from Alexandria and proved an adept intermediary between Egyptian economic policy and European commercial interests. In a reorganization of the government in 1837, Muhammad Ali created the joint ministry of commerce and foreign affairs and appointed Boghos Bey head of the department, leading many foreigners to assume that Boghos was the "prime minister" of Egypt.

To help modernize the administration of the country and improve its economy, Muhammad Ali became a great patron of the Armenians. In his early bid for power in Egypt, Muhammad Ali, then a small tobacco merchant of no military repute, had found an Armenian, Yeghiazar Amira, who was willing to give him a loan. Muhammad Ali repaid Amira many times over. He also encouraged Armenian settlement in Egypt. With Boghos Bey as its leading figure, the Armenian community in Egypt grew from a few dozen to two thousand. Among them were many relatives of Boghos whom he had brought over from İzmir, including the Nubar and Abro families. Arakel Bey Nubar (1826–1859) followed in his uncle's footsteps and became Egypt's minister of commerce. Boghos Bey's more famous nephew, however, was Nubar Pasha, who served three terms as prime minister of Egypt in the last quarter of the nineteenth century. Dicran Pasha d'Abro was minister of foreign affairs in the 1890s.

Among his many assignments, Boghos had also been entrusted by Muhammad Ali with training new and capable administrators. Charged with sending the most promising to Europe for further education with the approval of the pasha, Boghos also sponsored the education of the sons of many Armenian merchants in the service of Muhammad Ali. Among them was his successor to the ministry of commerce and foreign affairs, Artin CHRAKIAN (1804–1859), whom Muhammad Ali appointed upon Boghos's death. It is reported that Boghos Bey died a man of modest means, all his resources having been placed in the service of his master.

BIBLIOGRAPHY

ADALIAN, ROUBEN. "The Armenian Colony of Egypt during the Reign of Muhammad Ali, 1805–1848." *Armenian Review* 33, no. 2 (1980): 115–144.

MARSOT, AFAF LUTFI AL-SAYYID. *Egypt in the Reign of Muhammad Ali.* Cambridge, U.K., 1984.

Rouben P. Adalian

Yusuf Kamil   [1808–1876]

Turkish translator and poet.

Yusuf Kamil was born in Arapkir and raised by his uncle, a customs officer. After finishing his education, he entered the civil service as a clerk for the Divan-i Hümayun (imperial council) in 1829; subsequently, he went to Egypt to enter the service of Muhammad Ali. In 1849, he returned to Istanbul and became grand vizier for a period in 1863. His translation of François Fénelon's *Les Aventures de Télémaque* appeared in 1862 as *Telemak* and was one of the first translations of a Western novel into Turkish. His poetry, written in the *divan* style, was collected and published in 1891 as *Eser-i Kamil Paşa* (The Works of Kamil Paşa).

BIBLIOGRAPHY

ÖZKIRIMLI, ATILLA. *Türk edebiyati ansiklopedisi,* vol. 4. Istanbul, 1982.

David Waldner

Z

Zab Rivers

Great Zab of Turkey and Iraq and Little Zab of Iran and Iraq; major tributaries of the Tigris river.

The Great Zab rises in the mountains of southeast Turkey and runs for 260 miles (420 km), flowing southwest into the Tigris below Mosul, Iraq. The Little Zab rises in the Zagros mountains and flows for about 230 miles (368 km) southwest into the Tigris, some 50 miles (80 km) below the Great Zab. Their violent seasonal spring flow contributes about half the flood crest of the Tigris.

BIBLIOGRAPHY

FISHER, SIDNEY N. *The Middle East*. New York, 1979.

John R. Clark

Zabul

Afghan province.

Located in southern Afghanistan on the Pakistan border, Zabul has a population of approximately 200,000, most of whom are Pakhtun, though some Hazara live in the north. The provincial capital is Kalat. Zabul, which is famous for its almonds, is in a very dry and windy region, where agriculture is limited to a few irrigated valleys. Approximately 60,000 refugees left Zabul during the war of resistance (1978–1992), but most of them have been repatri-

ated. The main highway from Kabul to Kandahar runs through Zabul.

BIBLIOGRAPHY

ADAMEC, LUDWIG. *Historical Dictionary of Afghanistan*. Metuchen, N.J., 1991.

Grant Farr

Zach, Natan [1930–]

Israeli poet and critic.

Zach, who had a profound influence on Israeli poetry and literature during the 1950s and 1960s, was born in Berlin and came to Israel in 1935. He studied at the Hebrew University in Jerusalem and later at the University of Essex, England, where he wrote his doctoral dissertation. In addition to his poems, Zach published critical essays and edited several literary publications. He won the Bialik Prize for his poetry.

One of his most instrumental contributions to the national literature was his conscious rejection of the national symbolism and ethnic sentimentality of mainstream Israeli poetry prior to 1948. Zach's early poems, *First Poems* and *Different Poems* (in Hebrew), exhibit a marked disassociation with the specifics of time and place, expressing instead the voice of the individual. Through emphasizing the more morbid aspects of human existence, Zach sought to undermine both the form and content of traditional Israeli poetry. To achieve that, he introduced new and unique poetic forms into Hebrew, including rhythm, rhyme, language, and metaphor. Other hallmarks of Zach's poetry are its intellectual detachment, emotional restraint, and subtle irony, all of which are employed against the excessive sentimentality and pathos of his predecessors. Zach influenced Hebrew poetry as well through his articulate and vociferous writings on its behalf. He published numerous essays promoting his modernist literary agenda both as a critic and as literary editor.

BIBLIOGRAPHY

CALDERON, NISSIM. *A Previous Chapter: On Natan Zach in the Early Sixties.* Hakkibutz Hameuchad, Israel, 1985.
ZACH, NATAN. *Against Parting.* Newcastle upon Tyne, U.K., 1967.
———. *All the Milk and Honey.* Am Oved, Israel, 1966. In Hebrew.

Yarom Peleg

Zaghlul, Sa'd

Egyptian nationalist and leader of the Wafd, the nationalist party founded in Egypt in 1919.

A lawyer by profession, Zaghlul served as Egypt's minister of education (1906), earning the praise of Lord Cromer. As vice-president of the Legislative Assembly (1913), Zaghlul attracted attention with his charismatic oratory. His wife, Safia, known in Egypt as "Mother of the People," was the daughter of Egypt's wealthy and pro-British prime minister, Mustafa Fahmi.

After World War I, Zaghlul led a delegation (Arabic, *wafd*) to Cairo to ask Britain's High Commissioner Reginald Wingate for permission to argue the case for Egypt's independence directly before the British government in London. Britain refused and in 1919 deported Zaghlul and other leading members of the WAFD to Malta. The deportations precipitated the 1919 uprisings, when Egyptians of all classes, throughout the nation, boycotted British goods and sometimes violently attacked British installations and personnel. In an attempt to halt the rioting, the British reluctantly permitted Zaghlul and others to present the Egyptian nationalist case to the great powers attending the PARIS PEACE SETTLEMENTS.

Although he enjoyed the support of the vast majority of Egyptians, Zaghlul failed to achieve independence from the British in these and subsequent negotiations. When he continued to demand the abolition of the protectorate over Egypt and nationalist agitation increased, the British deported Zaghlul again in 1921. The deportations only strengthened the Wafd and contributed to Zaghlul's popularity.

After the British had unilaterally declared the independence of Egypt in 1922 and King Ahmad Fu'ad had signed the new constitution in 1923, Zaghlul was permitted to return to Egypt where he promptly resumed leadership of the Wafdist nationalist forces. Following the Wafd's overwhelming victory in free elections, Zaghlul became prime minister in 1924.

Zaghlul's triumph was short-lived, for in November 1924 Sir Lee Stack, *sirdar* (commander in chief of the Egyptian army) and governor-general of the Sudan, was assassinated while visiting Cairo. The assassination, coupled with Britain's demands for apologies and reparations, precipitated a government crisis and forced Zaghlul's resignation. Although Zaghlul remained the most popular Egyptian leader, he was prevented by the British from becoming prime minister in subsequent governments. In 1927, he died quietly in his home.

BIBLIOGRAPHY

BISRI, TARIQ. *Sa'd Zaghlul.* Cairo, 1977. In Arabic.

Janice J. Terry

Zagros

Mountain range in Iran.

The Zagros mountain range is the largest in Iran, stretching for 1,400 miles (2,253 km) from Armenia in the former USSR in the northwest to the Persian/Arabian Gulf in the south, and thence eastward to Baluchistan. It consists of a number of parallel ranges, the highest peak of which rises to 14,000 feet (4,270 m).

Shepherd and his flock in a valley of the Zagros mountains. (Richard Bulliet)

It separates the Iranian plateau from the plains of Mesopotamia and Iraq in the west and the Persian/Arabian Gulf in the south. Together with the Elburz (also known as Alborz) ranges in the north, the Zagros was formed from the Paleozoic to the Pliocene period.

BIBLIOGRAPHY

EMBREE, A., ed. *Encyclopedia of Asian History.* New York, 1988.
WILBER, D. *Iran: Past and Present,* 4th ed. Princeton, N.J., 1958.

Parvaneh Pourshariati

Zāhawi, Jamil Sidqi   [1863–1936]

Iraqi poet.

Zāhawi, born in Baghdad to a Kurdish family, was tutored chiefly by his father, a Muslim scholar. He held a number of official posts, including editor of the government newspaper *al-Zawra* and judge on the Supreme Court of Appeals. In 1908 he was elected one of Baghdad's representatives in the Chamber of Deputies in Istanbul following the Young Turk Revolution. After the establishment of the British mandate in Iraq, he became chairman of the committee that translated Ottoman laws into Arabic. His political ambitions were thwarted after the establishment of the Kingdom of Iraq.

In his poetry, as in everything he wrote, Zahawi was an opponent of religious and social stagnation. He was one of the first Iraqi intellectuals to demand the emancipation of women and the development of a scientifically based society.

Zahawi's poetry is largely didactic, lacking in emotion, at times resembling versified articles. Social and philosophical arguments often overshadow the personal and emotive aspects. Like all the poets of his generation in Iraq, Zahawi composed his poetry in a basically neoclassical style, although his language was comparatively simpler and closer to modern written prose. As early as 1905 he experimented with blank verse, omitting the monorhyme. He also introduced the quartet form into Arabic poetry, in a 1924 volume titled *Ruba'iyyat al-Zahawi.* Four other volumes of poetry were published during his lifetime, and a sixth appeared posthumously in 1938. Twenty-five years later a seventh volume was discovered and published in Cairo by Hilal Naji.

[*See also:* Literature, Arabic]

BIBLIOGRAPHY

HAYWOOD, JOHN A. *Modern Arabic Literature, 1800–1970.* London, 1971.
IZZIDIEN, YOUSIF. *Modern Iraqi Poetry: Social and Political Influences.* Cairo, 1971.

Sasson Somekh

Zahedi, Ardeshir   [1928–   ]

Iranian foreign service officer, and former son-in-law of Mohammad Reza Shah Pahlavi.

Born in Tehran in 1928, son of General Fazlollah Zahedi, he married Princess Shahnaz Pahlavi, daughter of Mohammad Reza Shah Pahlavi from his first marriage to Princess Fawzia, sister of King Farouk of Egypt, in 1957. After pursuing his education in the United States, Ardeshir Zahedi returned to Iran, and, in 1950, was elected treasurer for the Iran-America Commission and served as deputy administrator of the Point Four Program in 1952. He was appointed civil adjutant to Mohammad Reza Shah Pahlavi in 1960, and ambassador to the United States from 1960 to 1962. In 1964, the year he divorced the shah's daughter, he was appointed ambassador to Britain and became minister of foreign affairs. He was once more appointed ambassador to the United States in 1969, with the inauguration of Richard Nixon as president, and retained this position until the Iranian Revolution of 1979. Zahedi was renowned for his personal flamboyance during his ambassadorship. After the revolution, he left Iran and took up residence in Europe.

BIBLIOGRAPHY

Iran Who's Who. Tehran, 1972.

Neguin Yavari

Zahedi, Fazlollah   [1892–1962]

Iranian general and politician.

Fazlollah Zahedi was born in 1892 in Hamadan. His father, Basir Divan-e Hamedani, worked as a deputy for Amir Afkham Qaragozlu, one of the province's most important landlords. After receiving a military education, Fazlollah began his career in the army in 1914. He was placed in the unit of Reza Khan (who became Reza Shah Pahlavi in 1923) and helped him quell many rebellions in the early days of his reign. In 1941, after the abdication of Reza Shah, Zahedi became the military governor of Isfahan. Accusing him of being a German agent, the British forces in Iran imprisoned him (1943) and held him until the end of World War II (1945). In the 1950s,

Zahedi befriended members of the National Front (see NATIONAL FRONT, IRAN). He was appointed minister of the interior in the government of Mohammad Mossadegh in 1951, but after a few months, disagreements emerged between them, and Zahedi resigned his post, obtaining an appointment to the senate. After he had played a decisive role in the CIA-supported coup d'état in 1953, the Anglo–American architects of the coup compelled the shah to appoint him prime minister. Zahedi's tenure as prime minister was marked by the persecution of the Soviet-backed TUDEH PARTY and by the receipt of prodigious amounts of financial and political support from the United States. In 1955, the shah accused Zahedi of corruption and excessive violence and forced him to resign. Some observers believe that the shah, weary of Zahedi's strong ties to the military, realized that the successful coup would result in dictatorial powers for Zahedi, not for him. After his resignation, Zahedi left Iran. He died in Europe in 1962.

BIBLIOGRAPHY

COTTAM, RICHARD W. *Iran and the United States: A Cold War Case Study*. Pittsburgh, 1988.

Neguin Yavari

Zahir

See Dahir

Zahir, Mohammad   [1914–   ]

King of Afghanistan, 1933–1973.

Born in Kabul, the capital of Afghanistan, Zahir attended Habibia and Istiqlal schools (1920–1924), then accompanied his father, Mohammad Nadir Khan, to France where he continued his studies. Zahir's father was the second eldest and most influential of five Musahiban brothers, members of the Muhammadzai royal clan of the Barakzai Pakhtun (or Pashtun) tribe, who enjoyed considerable power in court during the 1910s and 1920s. During the turbulent rule of the modernizing King Amanullah Barakzai (1919–1929), the Musahiban brothers fell into disfavor. In 1929, when popular rebellions forced Amanullah's abdication, followed by a nine-month interregnum of a non-Pakhtun ruler, Emir Habibullah II, Zahir's father returned to eastern Afghanistan from France. With assistance from the British in India, Pakhtun tribesmen, and religious leaders,

Nadir Khan claimed the Afghan throne, declaring himself Muhammad Nadir Shah on October 15, 1929—thereby establishing the Musahiban dynasty.

Zahir returned to Kabul in October 1930 and attended the Infantry Officers School for one year. In 1931, he married the daughter of Ahmad Shah, a court minister. The only surviving son of Nadir Shah, Crown Prince Zahir at age seventeen was appointed assistant war minister (1932), then minister of education (1933). On November 8, 1933, following the assassination of his father, he was proclaimed King Mohammad Zahir Shah, with the religious title al-Mutawakkil ala Allah (he who puts his faith in Allah). To ensure the continuation of Musahiban rule, his accession to the throne was unopposed by his three surviving uncles. For the next thirty years, Zahir Shah simply reigned while two of his strong-willed and autocratic uncles held actual power as prime ministers, Sardar (Prince) Muhammad Hashim Khan (1933–1947) and Sardar Shah Mahmud Khan (1947–1953), followed by Zahir Shah's cousin and brother-in-law, the dictatorial prime minister Sardar Muhammad Daud (1953–1963). During this period, although Afghanistan was officially a constitutional monarchy, power and decision making were monopolized by a few elder members of the Musahiban oligarchy; they maintained family unity through intermarriage, assuring continuation of their rule by stifling liberal expression and political freedoms with an oppressive police state.

Following a rift with Daud and his resignation as prime minister, Zahir Shah took power into his own hands in 1963 by appointing a nonrelative as prime minister. He then launched his program of *Demokrasy-i Now* (New Democracy)—a decade of experimentation with democratic liberalization that ended with his overthrow in 1973. During this decade, he encouraged the development of a new liberal constitution, supported relatively free elections, extended freedom of the press, and tolerated the formation of many political movements with diverse orientations. Indecisiveness and inaction on the passage of legislation governing political parties and his inability to prevent government interference by family members and friends undermined democratic experiments and by 1978 drove the country into communist hands (by Nur Muhammad Taraki's coup of April 27) and Soviet intervention.

Zahir Shah is considered a mild-mannered, soft-spoken, kindly gentleman who lacks energy and is devoid of initiative. Deposed by his paternal cousin (and sister's husband), Sardar Muhammad Daud, he lives in exile in Italy. He abdicated his throne without a fight and passively watched the suffering of his nation under Soviet occupation, communist rule, and civil war. Some Afghans, mostly his former associates and officials also living in exile, are advocating his return to Afghanistan, especially after the fall of the communist regime. Most Islamist groups, however, strongly oppose the return of the monarchy, and Zahir Shah, by showing no interest in the throne, continues to disappoint his supporters.

BIBLIOGRAPHY

AMSTUTZ, J. BRUCE. *Afghanistan: The First Five Years of Soviet Occupation.* Washington, D.C., 1986.
DUPREE, LOUIS. *Afghanistan.* Princeton, N.J., 1980.

M. Nazif Shahrani

Zahla

The capital of Lebanon's Biqaʻ valley and the center of its economic activity.

Under the mandate, Zahla was a small town growing silkworms for export to France; it has developed into a major economic hub for the BIQAʻ VALLEY. The city's geographic location makes it an important station for commercial trucks coming into or leaving Lebanon.

Zahla's main economic activity centers around the farming and poultry industries.

BIBLIOGRAPHY

Arab Information Center, Beirut.

George E. Irani

Zahrawi, Abd al-Hamid   [?–1916]

Syrian politician.

A native of Homs in present-day Syria, Shaykh Abd al-Hamid Zahrawi was president of a June 1913 congress in Paris. It was held to air Syrian Arab demands of the Ottoman Empire. Zahrawi was critical of the Committee of Union and Progress, which he felt only served to solidify the Turkish hold on Ottoman administration. Nonetheless, he was elected to the Chamber of Deputies. In 1916, for his criticism of Turkish authority, he was executed by Çemal Paça.

BIBLIOGRAPHY

KHOURY, PHILIP A. *Urban Notables and Arab Nationalism: The Politics of Damascus, 1860–1920.* Cambridge, U.K., 1983.

Charles U. Zenzie

Zaʻim

Title given to a military or political leader.

In Iraq after World War II, *zaʻim* was used to designate a colonel; in other countries, a brigadier general; and in Lebanon, a strong leader.

Marilyn Higbee

Zaʻim, Husni al-   [1889–1949]

Syrian military officer and politician.

Born in Aleppo to a Kurdish business family, Husni al-Zaʻim was captured by the British while serving in the Ottoman army and later joined the Troupes Spéciales in the French mandate forces. Promoted to lieutenant colonel in 1941, he was charged with embezzlement by the Vichy government and was later arrested by the Free French. He was promoted from director of public security to chief of staff of the army in May 1948. As a precursor to his coup d'état, al-Zaʻim defied President Shukri al-Quwatli's order to arrest Col. Antoine Bustani, the scapegoat of a minor scandal, and gave him a position in the defense ministry instead. In the spring of 1949, Colonel al-Zaʻim overthrew the government of Khalid al-Azm and arrested President al-Quwatli.

Supported by the future Syrian President Adib Shishakli, the Zaʻim coup marked the first comprehensive takeover by the military in regional politics. The Syrian military would never again be far from control of the political insitutions. Al-Zaʻim's short rule sought to forcibly strip many traditional customs that appeared to inhibit progress. His regime was overthrown on August 14, 1949, by Sami Hinnawi, and al-Zaʻim was executed.

BIBLIOGRAPHY

SEALE, PATRICK. *The Struggle for Syria: A Study of Post-War Arab Politics, 1945–1958.* London, 1958.

Charles U. Zenzie

Zakat

One of the five principal duties or "pillars" of Islam.

Zakat (obligatory almsgiving) is an act of service to God that must be rendered by all Muslims who have reached majority age and possess a minimum amount of personal wealth. *Zakat* should not be confused with voluntary and spontaneous charitable giving (*sadaqa*), which Muslim ethics strongly recommends as a highly meritorious practice to be undertaken as frequently as possible. Instead, *zakat* has traditionally been construed as an annual "tax" on all property—currency, commercial assets, agricultural produce, and livestock—to be paid for the benefit of the poor and others who have special financial needs, as well as in support of cultural, educational, and religious projects or institutions. Whereas in the medieval period *zakat* was often collected by the state and distributed to a schedule of legal recipients, in many modern contexts individuals are often responsible for selecting appropriate recipients and distributing their own obligatory alms. A special *zakat* collection (*zakat al-fitr*), in the amount of the cost of one day's food for each member of a donor household, is usually taken up in Muslim congregations toward the end of Ramadan to provide for the fast-breaking celebrations of the needy.

Scott Alexander

Zamir, Zvi   [1925–   ]

Israeli military figure.

Born in Poland, Zvi Zamir was educated at Hebrew University and served as the Haganah commander for the region of Jerusalem. After the State of Israel was proclaimed in 1948, he served in the Israeli Defense Forces in a variety of capacities and as military attaché to Britain. From 1968 to 1974, he was the chief of the Mossad, Israel's intelligence service.

Bryan Daves

Zamzam

The famous well of Mecca.

According to Muslim legend, Zamzam was opened by the angel Gabriel to provide for Hagar and Isma'il, who were in danger of dying of thirst after Abraham deposited them in what was then an unpopulated desert valley. History suggests that it was the coexistence of this well and the adjacent shrine (KA'BA) that led to the emergence of Mecca as an important commercial and cultural center in pre-Islamic Arabia. For centuries Muslims have cherished the brackish water of Zamzam as sacred and have sought to benefit from its reputed blessings. To this day, pilgrims to the Meccan sanctuary descend the enclosed staircase to the well and either draw water for themselves to drink, or bottle it and take it home for a relative or friend who is ill.

Scott Alexander

Zan-e Ruz

Iranian women's magazine.

Zan-e Ruz (Today's Woman) is a weekly journal published in Tehran, devoted to issues of women and families. Established in 1964, *Zan-e Ruz* is affiliated with the Kayhan News Institute. Its first editor was Majid Davami. *Zan-e Ruz* was a vanguard publication in propagating Western and modern values in women's issues, and its antitraditional stance enhanced its standing as the most widely read magazine of Pahlavi Iran. Even Ayatollah Mortaza MOTAHHARI occasionally contributed to *Zan-e Ruz*. By the mid-1990s the magazine was being published in Tehran, albeit with a modified stance, under the editorship of Ashraf Geramizadegan.

BIBLIOGRAPHY

BARZIN, MAS'UD. *Shenasnameh-ye Matbu'at-e Iran, 1315–1357* (Compendium of the Iranian Press, 1936–1978). Tehran, 1992.

Neguin Yavari

Zangwill, Israel   [1864–1926]

British novelist and playwright; early Zionist.

Zangwill was a sophisticated British wit whose reputation was established with his novel *Children of the Ghetto* (1892), which depicted Jewish immigrant life in the East London ghetto. He joined in the Zionist cause of Theodor Herzl in 1895, arranging for Herzl a series of community meetings with prominent members of English Jewish society. He introduced Herzl to the Maccabeans, a society of Jewish authors, artists, and professionals, and helped organize the Maccabean Pilgrimage to Palestine in 1897. He also helped and employed the wandering Hebrew poet Naphtali Herz Imber, author of the Zionist anthem Hatikvah, during his stay in England (1889–1892) and made him famous as a character in his writings.

During the period of the Uganda Project, Zangwill founded and led the Jewish Territorial Organization for the Settlement of the Jews within the British Empire (1905–1925); it pursued the possibility of an East African province for a Jewish settlement, a so-called provincial Palestine. Zangwill felt that "any territory which was Jewish [and] under a Jewish flag, saves the Jew's body and the Jew's soul." Many Zionists broke with him over this issue, since his group did not acknowledge any organic connection between Zionism and Palestine.

During the early 1900s, Zangwill scored tremendous success as a playwright in England and in the

United States. He also continued to write novels and produced his last play, *We Moderns* (1924), in New York City.

BIBLIOGRAPHY

LAQUEUR, WALTER. *A History of Zionism.* New York, 1972.
VITAL, DAVID. *The Origins of Zionism.* Oxford, 1975.
————. *Zionism, the Formative Years.* Oxford, 1982.

Miriam Simon

Zanzibar

Islands and coastal land in East Africa.

From the tenth century, many Arabs emigrated to Zanzibar, the 640-square-mile (1,658 sq. km) island of that name (also neighboring islands and the adjacent coast of East Africa). In 1698 Oman seized Zanzibar from the Portuguese, and in 1841 Oman's ruler, Shaykh Sayyid Sa'id, permanently moved his capital there from Musqat. Wealthy Omanis established an extensive plantation economy centered on clove production using African slave labor. After Sa'id's death in 1856, contention between his sons led to Britain's Canning Award (1861), splitting Oman and Zanzibar into separate sultanates. The latter declined, partly because of British suppression of the slave trade in 1873, and became a British protectorate in 1890.

Following Zanzibar's independence (1963) and union with Tanganyika (1964), the Arab population was severely mistreated by the Africans. Several thousand emigrated, mostly to the capital area of Musqat in Oman, after the accession of Sultan Qabus in 1970. The recent process of Omanization and the Zanzibaris' greater commercial sophistication have caused some friction between them and native Omanis.

BIBLIOGRAPHY

BENNETT, N. R. *A History of the Arab State of Zanzibar.* London, 1978.

Malcolm C. Peck

Zaqaziq University

University in Egypt.

Zaqaziq University was founded in the province of Sharqiya in the city of Zaqaziq in 1974 from branch faculties of Ayn Shams University in Cairo. The university employs 3,230 teachers and has 44,812 students.

BIBLIOGRAPHY

The World of Learning 1995, 45th ed. London, 1994.

Donald Malcolm Reid

Zaraniq Confederation

Tribal grouping on North Yemen's largely nontribal coastal desert, the Tihama.

The Zaraniq, the largest and most formidable tribal grouping of the Tihama, stood in the way of efforts by Imam Yahya to extend control of the imamate state and were compelled to submit to the imam only after a savage two-year campaign in the late 1920s. An important part of the history of the Tihama for many centuries, the Zaraniq were known in the past as the Ma'aziba tribe and, like other tribes on the Tihama, claimed descent from the Akk tribe.

Robert D. Burrowes

Zarhuni, al-Jilali ibn Idris al-

See Bu Hamara

Zaritzsky, Jossef [1891–1985]

Israeli artist.

Born in Russia, Zaritzsky studied at the Academy of Arts in Moscow and immigrated to Palestine in 1923. He painted landscapes in watercolor early in his career and later became a painter of abstract art. He was one of the founding members of the New Horizons group of Israeli artists.

Bryan Daves

Zarqa, al-

Jordanian city.

Lying some fourteen miles (23 km) northeast of Jordan's capital, Amman, al-Zarqa is Jordan's second-largest city (pop. 605,000 in 1992). The village witnessed tremendous growth since the 1950s through the presence of a major military base, the development of industry and a free trade zone, and the influx of Palestinian refugees (who constitute some 60 to 70 percent of the population).

BIBLIOGRAPHY

Statistical Yearbook 1992. Jordanian General Statistics Department, Amman.

Abla M. Amawi

Zarwal, Amin al-   [1941–   ]

President of Algeria since 1994.

Zarwal (or Zeroual) was born in Batna. In his teens he joined the Algerian resistance, the National Liberation Front (FLN), which sent him to Cairo to complete his education. Upon his return in 1962, he joined the army. By 1988 Zarwal had risen to the rank of general. He resigned in 1989 in a dispute with the commander in chief (later minister of defense), Khaled Nezzar, over restructuring the armed forces. In 1993 Nezzar resigned and named Zarwal to succeed him. In January 1994 Zarwal became head of state, officially for a period of three years. He was elected president in 1995.

BIBLIOGRAPHY

"Algeria: The Moves toward a Compromise." *Middle East Reporter Weekly* 73 (September 1994): 10–11.

Mia Bloom

Zawiya

Islamic compound.

Zawiya is Arabic for "corner" or "place of seclusion." In North Africa, it means the lodge of an Islamic brotherhood or the residence of a prominent marabout. In Libya, zawiyas were often located along trade routes and at the intersections of tribal territories. In Morocco, zawiyas often served to extend Islam and royal authority into tribal hinterlands.

BIBLIOGRAPHY

EICKELMAN, DALE F. *Moroccan Islam: Tradition and Society in a Pilgrimage Center.* Austin, Tex., 1976.

Dale F. Eickelman

Zaydan, Jurji   [1861–1914]

Early pan-Arab nationalist, author, and publisher.

Jurji Zaydan (also spelled Gurgi Zaidan) was born into a poor Greek Orthodox family in Beirut and, through self-education, obtained entry to the Syrian Protestant College in 1881. After a year in the medical school, he participated in a student strike and was expelled. As did many of his contemporaries, he went to Cairo, where he embarked on a career as a journalist, publisher, novelist, scholar, and pronationalist intellectual. He was a major contributor to Arab literature. During the thirty years of his life in Cairo, he produced twenty-one historical novels dealing with Arab history; a five-volume history of Islamic civilization (*Tarikh al-Tamaddun al-Islami,* Cairo, 1901–1906); a four-volume history of Arabic literature (*Tarikh Adab al-Lugha al-Arabiyya,* Cairo, 1910–1913); and a dozen other books on history, language, and literature. In 1892, he founded the magazine *al-Hilal,* which he authored, published, and distributed for the next twenty-two years practically singlehandedly. With *al-Muqtataf,* it became the most important forum of the Arab Nahda (Renaissance) for the discussion of history, nationalism, secularism, modern sciences, and political institutions. In addition, Zaydan was also the author of the first autobiography in Arabic (*Mudhakkirat Jurji Zaydan,* ed. by S. Munajjid, Beirut, 1966; English translation, *The Autobiography of Jurji Zaidan,* 1990).

At the end of the nineteenth century the European presence in the Middle East became ubiquitous and overwhelming in all its cultural, intellectual, political, and economic aspects. The task of the Arab intellectual was to respond to a twofold challenge: to adapt to life in the modern Europe-dominated world while continuing to assert the independent identity and viability of Arab society. It was exactly this twofold challenge that Zaydan made his life task to tackle. Less the political activist than the educator of the nation, he aimed at informing his Arab compatriots about the modern world as well as about their own past and national identity. Even as he familiarized his Arab readers with modern Europe and introduced them to European thought, he established the foundations for a pan-Arab national identity. He was the first to try in a scholarly and systematic fashion to reconstruct a history of the Arabs separate from Islamic history. By incorporating pre-Islamic Arabian and even Babylonian history into Arab history, Islam became only one phase. This perspective also made possible a future for the Arab nation independent from Islam. On the popular level, he tried to spread this idea along with national identity through his historical novels—a genre that he introduced to Arabic literature.

In addition to history, language assumed a central place in Zaydan's thinking. It was the symbol of national identity, a means of achieving such identity, and an expression of one's national culture and heritage. For him, the vitality of the language meant the viability of the nation. Drawing on concepts of evolution and progress, he attacked the classicist ideal and the religious rigor of archaic literary Arabic and insisted that developments and changes in the language were positive, proving its vitality. Especially through his magazine, *al-Hilal,* he contributed greatly to the simplification in style of formal literary Arabic and popularized new terms and concepts that reflected modern thought and knowledge.

His unceasing and successful effort to establish an Arab national identity defined by history and language created the foundations of political pan-Arab nationalism as it arose after the collapse of the Ottoman Empire.

BIBLIOGRAPHY

PHILIPP, T. *Gurgi Zaidan: His Life and Thought.* Wiesbaden, Germany, 1979.

Thomas Philipp

Zayd ibn Husayn   [1898–1970]

Hashimite prince and Iraqi ambassador.

Zayd ibn Husayn was the fourth son of former King Husayn ibn Ali of the Hijaz and half brother of King Faisal I of Iraq. Zayd substituted regularly for Faisal during the latter's absences from Iraq and was briefly considered as a possible regent for his great nephew Faisal II. Passed over in favor of Abd al-Illah, another of Husayn's sons, Zayd was appointed Iraqi ambassador to Great Britain several times between 1946 and 1958.

Peter Sluglett

Zaydism

The sect of Shi'a Islam that prevails in the northern highlands of North Yemen and the political system that has existed to defend and advance that sect almost continuously since the late ninth century.

The Zaydi sect takes its name from Zayd ibn Ali Zain al-Abidin, the fifth Shi'a imam and the grandson of Husayn, who was one of the two sons of Ali and Fatima, the cousin and daughter of the Prophet Muhammad. (Because Zayd was the fifth imam, Zaydis are sometimes called Fiver Shi'ites.) The doctrine of the sect as developed by Zayd and his followers was pragmatic, rational, and open to extension by critical examination and interpretation; and it rejected such features of other Shi'a sects as the ideas of a "hidden" imam, an occult explanation of the QUR'AN, systematic dissimulation, and mysticism. Often referred to as the "fifth school" of Sunni Islam, Zaydism differs from Sunni orthodoxy primarily in its insistence on the institution of the imamate and the right of the descendants of Ali and Fatima to rule the world of Islam through that religio-political institution.

The founder of the Zaydi imamate in Yemen was al-Hadi ila al-Haqq Yahya ibn Husayn. He did so in the year 897 after being invited by tribes in the area around Sa'da to come from his native Medina to mediate their disputes and govern them. Al-Hadi's fourteen-year reign established in the highlands of North Yemen the Zaydi imamate, a state and political system that was to persist with numerous changes of fortune and breaks in continuity for over one thousand years into the 1960s, all the while maintaining many of the features that he and his immediate successors had decreed for it. The strong imams of the first decades of the twentieth century, Imam Yahya and his son, Imam Ahmad ibn Yahya, served as the spiritual leaders, temporal rulers, and defenders of the community of Islam much as had their predecessors a millennium earlier. The Zaydi imamate was abolished on the occasion of the 1962 revolution that created the Yemen Arab Republic, but northern Yemen, and Sa'da in particular, is still known for its Zaydi population.

Robert D. Burrowes

Zaytuna University

Prominent university in Tunis.

Built as a mosque in the eighth century, Zaytuna was enlarged by the Aghlabids in 864 when the Abbasid caliph al-Mu'tasim ordered the addition of a wing. It continues to serve as a school mosque and houses a huge library that in the fourteenth century was administered by the Malikite theologian Muhammad ibn Arafa. One of Zaytuna's students was Abd al-Rahman ibn Khaldun, the well-known Arab historian and philosopher. In modern times alumni include the leader of the Tunisian Destour party, Abd al-Aziz Tha'labi. In addition many Zaytuna graduates staffed the cadres of the Neo-Destour party.

Although at first traditional, teaching at Zaytuna was gradually modernized. The last reform came in 1933, at the hands of its students. Upon Tunisia's independence the Zaytuna became the *Shari'a* (Islamic law) school of the University of Tunis.

In 1945, Zaytuna had five branches in various cities of Tunisia and three thousand students in the secondary and college levels combined. The regional branches were not very active, and their ties with Tunis were very weak. With the appointment of al-Taher ben Ashour as the director of Zaytuna, new branches were opened in Tunisia and even in Algeria, raising their number to twenty-five. All became very active. The number of students in the main and the regional branches jumped to twenty thousand.

The growing national role of Zaytuna University in opposing French colonialism and the leadership of its graduates in the nationalist movement, caused it to become the target of the French colonial government. The university gradually found itself at odds with the political powers, and its activities were curtailed. The great cultural support Tunisia received from the Arab League allowed it to pursue the spread of Arabic culture and language teaching through Zaytuna University as well as other centers of learning, thus counteracting the colonial cultural policy of promoting French at the expense of Arabic. Zaytuna University was instrumental in safeguarding Arabic culture in Tunisia and also helped its neighbor Algeria, a country that did not have a similar cultural center.

BIBLIOGRAPHY

ABU-NASR, JAMIL M. *A History of the Maghrib.* Cambridge, U.K., 1971.

HOURANI, ALBERT. *A History of the Arab Peoples.* Cambridge, Mass., 1991.

Aida A. Bamia

Zbiri, Tahar   [c. 1930–   ]

Algerian officer.

Born in the Annaba region, Zbiri joined Messali Hadj's movement and then the Armée de Libération Nationale (ALN; Army of National Liberation). He had a distinguished record during the Algerian War of Independence (1954–1962), participating in the initial attacks of November 1, 1954, escaping with "historic chief" Moustafa Ben Boulaid from the French, and breaching the Morice Line in 1960. Though he served as chief of staff of the Armée Nationale et Populaire (ANP; National and Popular Army) under President Ahmed Ben Bella, Zbiri's loyalties were to Houari Boumédienne, as demonstrated by his arrest of the president during the June 1965 coup. Zbiri remained chief of staff but grew averse to the new President Boumédienne's control over the army. In 1967, he organized a military revolt against Boumédienne that failed, resulting in his arrest and exile. He was subsequently pardoned by President Chadli Benjedid in 1980. Zbiri later joined other disaffected Front de Libération Nationale (FLN; National Liberation Front) members in opposition to President Benjedid.

BIBLIOGRAPHY

STORA, BENJAMIN. *Dictionnaire biographique des militants nationalistes algériens.* Paris, 1985.

Phillip C. Naylor

Zelda   [1914–1984]

Israeli poet.

Born Zelda Shneurson and also known as Zelda Mishkovsky, she signed her poems with her first name only. A devout Hasidic Jew, she was well versed in ancient sacred and traditional Jewish texts. In 1926 she immigrated to Israel from her native Ukraine. Her first publication, *Leisure*, appeared in 1968. Zelda published six additional volumes of poetry: *The Invisible Carmel, Be Not Far, Neither Mountain nor Fire, Tiny Poems, The Spectacular Difference,* and *Beyond All Distance.* Her work was acclaimed by secular Israeli readers for its gentle, transcendental, mystic quality. The main themes of her poetry are grief and loneliness, loss and disease. Nevertheless, a sense of acceptance and faith in glory, as well as an enchantment with the beauty and sanctity of life, mitigate her basically melancholic worldview.

Zvia Ginor

Zell al-Soltan, Mas'ud Mirza   [1850–1918]

The eldest son of Persia's Naser al-Din Shah.

Zell al-Soltan (Shadow of the Sovereign) was excluded from succeeding Naser al-Din because his mother was not of the Qajar dynasty. He became governor of Isfahan in 1874 and from 1881 to 1887 was the powerful and oppressive ruler of much of southern Iran. He had a large private army and kept the local tribesmen under control, killing an important Bakhtiari chief in 1882. He had contempt for the *ulama* (Islamic clergy). The rival of his half-brother and future monarch, Mozaffar al-Din, governor of Azerbaijan, Zell al-Soltan was opposed at court in Tehran by Ali-Asghar Amin al-Soltan. In 1888, because of his excesses, his power was restricted to Isfahan. During the Constitutional Revolution, he hoped to replace Mohammad Ali as shah and, consequently, aided the revolutionaries by supplying some financial support.

BIBLIOGRAPHY

CURZON, GEORGE N. *Persia and the Persian Question.* London, 1892. Reprint, 1966.

Lawrence G. Potter

Zeroual, Amine

See Zarwal, Amin al-

Zikhron Ya'akov

Village located in northern Israel on Mount Carmel.

In 1882, Romanian Jews founded Zikhron Ya'akov, one of the early settlements of the Hovevi Zion movement. Financially supported in part by the Baron Edmond de ROTHSCHILD, the settlement, shortly after its founding, was given its present name in memory of the baron's father, Jacob. Baron de Rothschild promoted the planting of grapes, and vineyards were established in the settlement as well as one of the largest wine cellars in Israel. In 1954, Baron de Rothschild and his wife were buried in Zikhron Ya'akov.

BIBLIOGRAPHY

SCHAMA, SIMON. *The Two Rothschilds and the Land of Israel.* New York, 1978.

Bryan Daves

Zili, Ridha   [1942–   ]

Tunisian poet and photographer.

Zili was born in Monastir, Tunisia. He received a bilingual (Arabic and French) education but writes in French. Zili's writing is greatly influenced by his work as a photographer, especially in his concept of the image. His only published collection of poetry, *Ifrikiya, Ma Pensée* (1967; Africa in My Thoughts), reveals his love for peace and his search for happiness. Zili rejects sadness and the nonsensical violence in the world and values his Tunisian African roots.

BIBLIOGRAPHY

FONTAINE, JEAN. *La littérature tunisienne contemporaine.* Paris, 1990.

Aida A. Bamia

Zilkha Family

Internationally known Jewish banking family originally from Iraq.

The name goes back to the ancestress Zilkha, who married a *cohen,* which automatically identified all their descendants in the male line as *cohanim*—hereditary priests descended from Moses' brother Aaron. The internationally known branch of the family was founded by Khedouri (1884–1956), son of Aboudi, a textile merchant. Khedouri married Louise Eliahu Bashi, who bore him four sons and three daughters. As a young man Khedouri went to Turkey where his maternal uncle, Yusef Shasha, introduced him to the world of business and finance. In 1902, when his uncle went to Manchester, England, Khedouri returned to Baghdad, and from modest beginings as a *sarraf* (moneylender-cum-banker), he became an important banker.

Threatened by the Black Hand Society (al-Yad al-Sawda), he moved to Beirut in 1927, leaving his Baghdad business in the hands of relatives.

The Beirut branch of the Zilkha bank opened in 1928 and by 1948 became the biggest private bank in the Middle East. The establishment of Israel and the Arab–Israel War of 1948 had adverse effects on the business; the Baghdad branch was closed in 1952, the Syrian in 1954; the Egyptian bank was sequestered in 1956 and nationalized by Egypt's President Gamal Abdel Nasser in 1958; the Lebanese branch was sold in 1957.

In 1941, Khedouri emigrated to the United States, where he established the American Banking Corporation, with activities extending to Europe and South America; ten more branches were added in other countries, including Hong Kong. He employed relatives in all his operations; his four sons were each stationed in a different city. Abdullah (born 1913), who had joined the bank at the age of fifteen in Baghdad, went to Switzerland; Maurice (1917–1964) was in Egypt and Paris; Ezra (born 1925) is in New York. Both Ezra and Selim (born 1927) had trained at Hambros Bank in London, and Selim had first settled there. Selim was the founder, chairman, and executive director of Mothercare (1961–1982) until it was taken over by Habitat. He then moved to the United States, started various ventures, and since 1987 has been the sole owner of the Zilkha Energy Company of Houston, Texas. The Khedouri A. Zilkha Chair for the Study of Jewish Civilization in the Near East was established at Princeton University by Ezra Zilkha in 1977 in honor of his father.

BIBLIOGRAPHY

TWENA, ABRAHAM. *Jewry of Iraq: Dispersion and Liberation.* Ramla, Israel, 1977, 1979.

Sylvia G. Haim

Z'inni, Omar   [1895–1961]

Popular Lebanese poet and ballad writer.

After leaving his government position to devote himself completely to his craft, Z'inni wrote biting political and social satire of the French mandate and the period following independence. He composed the music for most of his easily memorizable lyrics and sang them to the delight of his contemporaries.

BIBLIOGRAPHY

AL-JAMMAL, FARUQ. *Omar al-Zinni: Story of a People.* Beirut, 1979. In Arabic.

NUMAN, MAHMUD. *Omar al-Zinni: Poet of the People.* Beirut, 1979. In Arabic.

Bassam Namani

Zionism

The movement for the establishment of an independent nation in Eretz Yisrael for the dispersed Jewish people.

Zionism, a national liberation movement for a Jewish homeland based on the nineteenth-century European political model, was founded by European Jews. It defined Jews as a nation whose collective future depended on the establishment of a national territorial entity in Eretz Yisrael, from which most Jews had been dispersed by the Roman Empire at the beginning of the second century C.E. The movement's name was coined by the Viennese Jewish writer Nathan Birmbaum in 1885 and derives from Zion, one of the biblical names for Jerusalem, the focus of worldwide Judaism.

Zionists believed that anti-Semitism was endemic to the Diaspora; thus, the achievement of national and civil rights in host nations, while desirable, would be insufficient to secure economic and cultural interests for Jews in the long run. Few Zionists believed that the Diaspora would be swept away (as was attempted a century later by Hitler's Nazi Germany), but a Jewish homeland—which would serve as a cultural and political model and as a magnet for its finest sons and daughters—could help secure Jews a future.

Through the centuries of exile, ritual, prayer, and the study of sacred texts preserved for Jews the knowledge that, in Eretz Yisrael and Zion, Judaism had developed. In nineteenth-century Europe, during the Haskala (the Jewish Enlightenment), revival of the Hebrew language as a nonreligious, literary medium transmitted secular works and secularized versions of sacred histories to assimilated generations losing faith in religion and religious authority. If Zionism was to ensure the survival of the Jewish people, it could do so only by going through the modern European Jewish experience, not by denying it. Zionists were Jews who believed that only in Zion could Jewish culture and the Jewish people be reestablished and secure. At that time, however, Zion was located in the Palestine of the Ottoman Empire and was populated by Arabs under Ottoman jurisdiction.

Zionism had existed in fact before it was fully defined or before the word itself was coined. As a way of helping the indigent and scholarly Jewish populations in Ottoman Palestine, Western European philanthropists such as Edmond de Rothschild and Sir Moses Montefiore proffered aid to projects that later would come to be associated with the Zionist movement—the purchase of land for settlements, farms, and businesses from Ottoman officials and Arab landlords; the building of schools for vocational training; and the opening of medical facilities.

Jewish emigration to Eretz Yisrael also antedated the emergence of a Zionist movement. Jewish religious leaders had always endorsed the idea of living in the so-called Holy Land as a means of discharging religious duties and had actively promoted the expansion of Jewish communities in Safed, Tiberias, Hebron, and Jerusalem, creating financial mechanisms to meet the immigrants' material needs.

The wave of pogroms that followed the assassination of Russia's Czar Alexander II in 1881 turned an attachment for Zion into an ideology embraced by some of Russia's secular Jewish leaders and intellectuals. Newly promulgated regressive legislation and the resuscitation of anti-Semitic rhetoric dashed the hopes of those who had believed Russia's polity would evolve into a democracy, with basic rights granted to its population and the ideals of tolerance espoused. Although emigration to the United States and Britain was a popular way of escaping the immediate disabilities imposed by Russian policies, some educated Jews saw that moving to another land would neither end anti-Semitism nor secure a Jewish future. They argued that only a purposeful emigration with the goal of establishing a Jewish majority in a territory would achieve international respectability for Jewry and help protect Jews everywhere against discrimination. For those who called on Jews to liberate themselves, the Zionist idea supplanted the ideal of assimilation. Zionism was presented as resolving the Jewish problem by normalizing the conditions of Jewish existence.

While many rabbinical authorities opposed Zionism for its secular and humanistic principles, many rabbis—most notably Samuel Mohilever and Isaac Jacob Reines—welcomed Zionism; they affiliated with HIBBAT ZION, the first international Zionist organization to be founded, partly because they reasoned that in Eretz Yisrael a social and cultural environment could be created conducive to religious observance.

The Orthodox rabbinate did not, however, establish an entirely harmonious relationship with the secular leadership in Hibbat Zion. Many Orthodox rabbis could not abide the dynamics of a political struggle that effected compromises between the demands of Zionism's secular and religious constituencies. Nor were the Orthodox entirely comfortable in an organization that did not acknowledge the primacy of religious law and rabbinic authority. The first nonsecular Zionist group, the MIZRACHI, opened its office in 1893, but most rabbis, while comfortable with the nationalist claims of Zionism, were unwilling to accede to Zionist demands to share power and resources in local Jewish communities. As a consequence of the frustrating handicaps under which Hibbat Zion labored in the 1880s and 1890s, Zionism was at an impasse when Theodor HERZL undertook to lead the struggle for a Jewish state.

Unaware of developments in Eastern Europe, the Viennese journalist Theodor Herzl championed the idea of Jewish nationhood in response to the outbreak of anti-Semitism in France during the 1894/95 fraudulent espionage trial of Alfred Dreyfus. In 1896, Herzl published *Die Judenstaat* (The Jewish State), a book setting forth the argument that both the world and the Jews needed a Jewish state. In 1897, Herzl succeeded in drawing together representatives from the local and regional Hibbat Zion organizations in Eastern Europe and Jews from Western Europe, establishing and becoming president of a new Zionist framework, the World Zionist Organization (WZO). Authorized by the WZO to secure international recognition for Zionist political goals, Herzl pursued in the capitals of Europe and in the Ottoman capital, Istanbul, official sanction for Jewish colonization in Palestine, but his efforts, albeit feverish and intense, were unsuccessful. The Ottoman sultan Abdülhamit II was not persuaded that a larger Jewish population in Palestine was consistent with his imperial political objectives or that such a population would promote economic development.

Herzl's leadership did broaden the popularity of Zionism in Western and Eastern Europe and enlarge its Orthodox membership. Herzl focused the activities of the WZO on diplomacy and finances. This approach mobilized the support of a number of Orthodox rabbis concerned with easing the economic hardships in Palestine for East European immigrants and hopefuls, as well as with the creation of a hospitable political climate there. By permitting groups to shift the mode of their representation from regional affiliation to ideological, the WZO was also used advantageously by the Orthodox to influence the direction of policies and, for a number of years, to exclude Jewish culture from the scope of Zionist activities.

Zionism's preoccupation with political solutions and stratagems triggered opposition. Against the po-

Stamp showing Theodor Herzl, first president of the World Zionist Organization. (Richard Bulliet)

litical orientation associated with the leadership of Hibbat Zion, the writer Ahad Ha-Am argued that the purpose of Zionism ought to be to revive a modern Jewish culture through the medium of the Hebrew language and a renewed interpretation of classic religious texts; a new Jewish state could only be founded with new artifacts of Jewish culture. Cultural Zionist Ahad Ha-Am's insights on the problems besetting the Jewish people and the Zionist movement helped inspire a group opposing Herzl's leadership and political Zionism—the Democratic Faction. This group, led by the scientist Dr. Chaim WEIZMANN, did not repudiate political methods or consider them insignificant; rather, they insisted that just as legal titles (to land) could facilitate resettlement, so resettlement could lead to concrete political gains. Insisting that the structure of the WZO must be reformed to increase popular participation and broaden its agenda, the Democratic Faction defined its own priorities as the investigation of the physical, political, and social conditions of Palestine for purposes of increasing Jewish immigration.

Creating a Jewish community in Palestine was not simply the solution to continuing anti-Semitism but also the opportunity to establish a whole and vigorous modern Jewish life.

In the early years of the twentieth century, efforts to create a Youth Movement and to popularize Zionism among the young led several Zionist leaders to synthesize socialism with Zionism. No longer would Jews have to choose between socialism (popular in Russia and in the Pale of Settlement) and Zionism.

Some Socialist-Zionists promoted a non-Marxist socialism, emphasizing social welfare and justice; others insisted that even the Marxist version of socialism could be combined with Zionism. Branches of the first Labor Zionist party, Po'alei Zion, founded in 1906, opened in many towns and cities of Eastern Europe, attracting many educated Jewish teenagers. He-Halutz, the young pioneer farm movement, was nonpartisan and attracted many capable Austro-Hungarian Jewish youth, especially when it was funded by the WZO after World War I.

Before the conclusion of World War I, Zionists were unable to engage openly in mass mobilization in many countries. In the United States and Western Europe, where organizations could operate freely, Zionism did not hold the imagination of most immigrants, who were struggling to work their way out of grinding poverty. In Russia, where the majority of Jews presumably felt sympathy with Zionist aims, Zionist activities were hobbled by the Russian Revolution, Soviet dictatorship, and persecution. When at the Sèvres Treaty of 1920 Britain announced its endorsement for the establishment in Palestine of a Jewish national home, Zionism won its first major political victory. World War I changed the map of Eastern Europe as well as that of the Middle East, thereby providing Zionists an opportunity to engage in grass-roots political organization. Youth groups expanded, and camps were created to offer vocational and Hebrew-language training to prepare Jews for life and work in Palestine.

Throughout its history, the Zionist movement has made choices among several possibilities: Palestine versus any other territory, such as Uganda, Canada, Australia; nationalism versus a cultural center for world Jewry; nationalism versus binationalism, where Jews and Arabs create a co-polity; neutrality during World War I versus pro-British cooperation; activism versus noninvolvement during the World War I British campaign in Palestine; high political profile versus quiet political caucus; and unity versus diversity in political goals. Each decision was made after great debate during Zionist congresses, often triggering enmity and hard feelings, and even one serious split when Jabotinsky left the movement. The major rifts almost deteriorated into civil war before the mainstream of Zionism asserted itself, repeatedly. With increasing knowledge of the extent of the Holocaust during World War II, Zionism had to choose Jewish survival over British-mandate policy restrictions on immigration, so an anti-British militance attempted to provide free entry for Jewish refugees into Palestine from 1944 until 1948.

With the establishment of the State of Israel in May 1948, Zionism was incorporated into an international consensus endorsed by the United Nations, by the foreign policy of the world's nations, and by most Jews (religious Jews excepted). Zionism has meanwhile evolved into a movement extending immigration (ALIYAH) to as many Jews as possible, with political and economic support for Israel through institutionalized activity, and the acknowledgment of Israel's importance in sustaining Jewish identity.

BIBLIOGRAPHY

HALPERN, BEN. *The Idea of the Jewish State*. Cambridge, Mass., 1961.
HERTZBERG, ARTHUR, ed. *The Zionist Idea*. Philadelphia, 1959.
VITAL, DAVID. *The Origins of Zionism*. Oxford, 1975.

Donna Robinson Divine

Zionist Commission

Sole official representative of the World Zionist Organization in Palestine until 1921; a precursor of the Jewish Agency.

The Zionist Commission was an informal group established by Chaim WEIZMANN as president of the World Zionist Organization (WZO) to advise the British on policies regarding the establishment of the Jewish national home. It carried out initial surveys of Palestine and aided the repatriation of Jews sent into exile by the Ottoman Turks during World War I.

It expanded the WZO's Palestine office (established 1907), into small departments for agriculture, settlement, education, land, finance, immigration, and statistics. In 1921, the commission became the Palestine Zionist Executive, which acted as the JEWISH AGENCY, designated to advise the British mandate authorities on the development of the country in matters of Jewish interest.

BIBLIOGRAPHY

VITAL, DAVID. *Zionism: The Crucial Phase*. Oxford, 1987.

Donna Robinson Divine

Zionist Organization of America

American organization affiliated with the World Union of General Zionists; known as ZOA.

Founded in 1898 at a convention in New York as the Federation of American Zionists, the organization was only later renamed the Zionist Organization of America. Serving as the principal Zionist organization in the United States, it has had as its focus the support of political Zionism rather than practical or cultural Zionism. Its prominent leaders have included Richard Gottheil, Stephen S. Wise, Judah Magnes, Henrietta Szold, and Louis D. Brandeis.

Since the creation of Israel, the ZOA has been involved in fund-raising and educational and public-relations activities on behalf of Israel. It maintains the ZOA House in Tel Aviv and the Kfar Silver Agricultural training center near Ashkelon.

Bryan Daves

Ziwar, Ahmad   [1864–1945]

Egyptian lawyer, politician, and government minister.

Born in Alexandria to a family of Circassian origin, Ahmad Ziwar was educated in Jesuit schools in Alexandria and Beirut and awarded his law degree from Aix University in France. He became a judge, chancellor, provincial governor, cabinet minister, president of the Senate, prime minister, and head of King Fu'ad's office. He was well known for his opposition to the Wafd party, to popular participation in Egypt's political life, and to Egyptian nationalism generally.

BIBLIOGRAPHY

AL-SAYYID MARSOT, AFAF LUTFI. *Egypt's Liberal Experiment, 1922–1936.* Berkeley, Calif., 1977.
AL-ZIRIKLI, KHAYR AL-DIN. *Al-A'lam,* 4th ed.

Arthur Goldschmidt, Jr.

Ziya, Abdülhamit   [1825–1880]

Young Ottoman writer.

The son of a customs clerk, Ziya Paşa was educated in one of the first secular Ruşdiye schools in Istanbul. He began work in the translation office and, through the support of Tanzimat reformer Reşit Paşa in 1854, became a secretary to Sultan Abdülmecit I. He lost his palace job in 1861 with the accession of Sultan Abdülaziz and held several minor posts in the 1860s. By 1866 he had joined the Young Ottoman Society in Europe and, with Namık Kemal and İbrahim Şinasi, became a leading intellectual of the period. Under Abdülaziz's rule, Ziya's political satires and other writings were banned as seditious, and he was posted as governor of Syria, in virtual exile.

Ziya Paşa's greatest influence was through his writings. He warned against blind imitation of Europe and criticized autocracy and poor policies such

as the growing Ottoman debt. In 1868 he wrote a famous article, "Poetry and Prose" (Şiir ve Inşa), in which he criticized Ottoman literature as mere imitation of Arabic and Persian traditions and called on writers to seek inspiration in Turkish folk literature.

BIBLIOGRAPHY

DAVISON, RODERIC H. *Reform in the Ottoman Empire, 1856–1876.* Princeton, N.J., 1963.
LEWIS, BERNARD. *The Emergence of Modern Turkey.* New York, 1961.
SHAW, STANFORD J., and EZEL KURAL SHAW. *History of the Ottoman Empire and Modern Turkey,* vol. 2. New York, 1977.

Elizabeth Thompson

Zohar, Uri   [1935–   ]

Israeli award-winning actor and comedian who became a rabbi and teacher.

Zohar began his professional acting career in 1953 and quickly rose to fame as a satirist and humorist. He starred in Israeli films in the 1960s, including *A Hole in the Moon* and *Every Bastard a King.* He was the first cinema artist to win the Israel Prize, in 1976 (which he refused).

In the 1970s he became a sectarian Orthodox Jew and a rabbi/teacher in a yeshiva (religious school). He wrote an account of his religious transformation, *U-baharta ba-haim,* in 1983, subsequently translated as *Waking Up Jewish* (Jerusalem, 1985).

Chaim I. Waxman

Zohrab, Krikor   [1861–1915]

Armenian writer and deputy in the Ottoman parliament.

Krikor Zohrab, also known as Grigor Zohrap, was born in Istanbul. He was educated in his birthplace and practicing law by 1883. He distinguished himself as an attorney who defended cases against the government until he was deprived of his license in 1905 and went abroad to France and Egypt. With the end of the Hamidian autocracy and the restoration of the Ottoman constitution, Zohrab returned to Istanbul. From 1908 to 1915, he was a member of the Armenian National Assembly. He also was elected a deputy to the Ottoman parliament where he defended the cause of universal social justice and gained distinction as an orator. Shocked by the 1909 mass killings of Armenians in Adana, he published his findings in Paris under the pseudonym of Marcel Leart as *La Question Arménienne à la Lumière des Documents*.

Zohrab also earned fame as an author of short stories and novellas in the realist style. The subjects of social inequality, injustice, and prejudice preoccupied him. His more important works include *Anhetatsads Serunt Me* (A Vanished Generation, 1887), *Khghjmdanki Tzayner* (Voices of Conscience, 1909), *Kyanke Inchpes Vor e* (Life As It Is, 1911), and *Lur Tsaver* (Silent Sorrows, 1911). He also published essays on literature, politics, and the Armenian community. Before his own demise, he protested to Talat, the Young Turk minister of the interior, the summary arrest on the night of April 24, 1915, and subsequent execution of the Istanbul Armenian community leaders. His own immunity as a parliamentary deputy did not spare him from being arrested on June 3, deported, and killed near Diyarbekır.

BIBLIOGRAPHY

BALIOZIAN, ARA. *The Armenians: Their History and Culture.* Saddle Brook, N.J., 1980.

Rouben P. Adalian

Zonnenfeld, Yosef Hayyim   [1849–1932]

Rabbi; leader of ultra-Orthodox Jerusalem community.

Yosef Hayyim Zonnenfeld was born in Verbo, Slovakia, and educated in the yeshiva in Pressburg. Settling in Jerusalem in 1873, he actively opposed secular Zionist educational activities and became a leader of the Old City Jewish community, assisting in the founding of the MEAH SHE'ARIM community and others. A staunch sectarian, he opposed all cooperation between the Orthodox and non-Orthodox Jewish communities. He was one of the founders of the separatist rabbinic court in Jerusalem, and in 1920 he was elected rabbi of the separatist Orthodox community of Jerusalem. He was also a founder of the AGUDAT ISRAEL in Palestine. Despite their warm personal relationship, he opposed Rabbi Abraham Isaac Hacohen Kook as rabbi in Jerusalem and, subsequently, as chief rabbi of Palestine. However, he was a strong supporter of Jewish settlement in Eretz Yisrael.

BIBLIOGRAPHY

DANZIGER, HILLEL. *Guardian of Jerusalem: The Life and Times of Rabbi Yosef Chaim Sonnenfeld.* New York, 1983.
ZONNENFELD, SHLOMO ZALMAN. *Ha-ish al hakhoma* (Guardian of the Wall: The Life of the Chief Rabbi of Haredi Jewry in Eretz Israel), 3 vols. Jerusalem, 1971.

Chaim I. Waxman

Zoroastrianism

Pre-Islamic religion founded by the Iranian prophet Zarathushtra (Zoroaster).

Founded as early as 1400 to 1200 B.C.E., the faith spread from central Asia to Persia (now Iran) around the ninth century B.C.E., where it was propagated by priests called the *magi* or *mobeds*. Zoroastrianism remained the major faith in Persia until the Sassanian state fell to the Arabs in 651 C.E. Thereafter, the religion lost many followers through conversion to Islam between the eighth and the thirteenth centuries C.E. Zoroastrianism reached India in the tenth century C.E., when some Zoroastrians migrated from Persia to avoid adopting Islam. Descendants of these immigrants are called the Parsis (Parsees). Those who remained behind sought refuge from Islam by moving to sparsely populated regions in central Persia. By the thirteenth century, extensive contact between Parsis and Persian Zoroastrians had recommenced. In 1854, when the Parsis sent an emissary to the Qajar court in Persia, the poll tax levied from Persian Zoroastrians by the Muslim state was abolished. The community in India flourished, and in the mid-1990s it numbered around seventy-two thousand.

Zoroastrians in Iran encountered less success, though respite from financial hardship and pressure to practice Islam were experienced during the Pahlavi regime (Reza Shah Pahlavi, ruled 1925–1941; Mohammad Reza Pahlavi, ruled 1941–1979). Since the Iranian Revolution, despite being officially recognized as a minority of about thirty thousand, Zoroastrians in Iran are offered little protection from their Muslim neighbors, and many have fled that nation. International dispersion during the twentieth century has produced Zoroastrian communities in Pakistan (3,700), England (7,000), Australia (1,000),

Commencing of Jashan prayers of thanksgiving by Zoroastrians. (Jamsheed Choksy)

the United States and Canada (10,000), and other countries. As of the early 1990s, low birthrate in combination with widespread nonacceptance of converts contributes to an overall decline in the number of Zoroastrians.

The faith's central canon is the Avesta (Pure Instruction), a scripture that includes the Gathas (Songs)—probably composed by Zarathushtra himself. Prayers recited by the laity in daily religious observances are compiled in a text known as the Khorde Avesta (Shorter Avesta). Next in importance are religious exegeses written in Pahlavi, a Middle Iranian language; among these are the Zand, a commentary on the Avesta, and the Bundahishn (Book of Creation). There are more recent Zoroastrian texts in the New Persian, Gujarati, and English languages, which transmit to the general believers, who no longer understand the Avestan and Pahlavi languages, tenets of the faith and the meanings of rituals.

The religion proposes an ethical dualism—which later became a cosmic dualism—between righteousness and falsehood, personified by a pair of primal spirits: Ahura Mazda (Ohrmazd), the Lord Wisdom, and Angra Mainyu (Ahreman), the Destructive Spirit, respectively. Ahura Mazda, the supreme deity, is believed to have created the spiritual and material worlds completely pure. Evil, disease, pollution, and death are attributed to Angra Mainyu, the devil. According to Zoroastrianism, Ahura Mazda created six *amesha spentas,* or beneficent spiritual beings, and other minor good spirits to assist him in protecting the material creations. Angra Mainyu produced numerous *daevas,* or demons, to defile the spiritual and material worlds. Zoroastrian texts claim that human beings were created by Ahura Mazda as allies in the struggle against Angra Mainyu, and that humans entered into a covenant with their creator to combat the forces of evil through daily good deeds.

Between the ages of seven and twelve, each Zoroastrian child undergoes initiation into the religion. The ritual, which symbolizes a spiritual rebirth, is termed *sedra pushun* in Iran and *navjote* in India. At that time every initiate dons a white undershirt called the *sedra,* or *sudra,* and ties a sacred girdle known as the *kashti,* or *kusti,* around the waist. The girdle, which most Zoroastrians continue to wear, should be untied and retied with the recitation of prayers on awakening each morning, and prior to performing worship. Many rituals, such as the *Jashan,* or thanksgiving ceremony, are conducted within buildings known as fire temples. Fire is one of the seven sacred creations; the others are water, earth, metal, plants, animals, and human beings. Moreover, fire is believed to destroy evil, and thus it became the religion's icon. Sacred fires burn constantly in altars at major temples at Sharifabad near Yazd in Iran and Surat, Navsari, and Bombay in India. Smaller temples in both those countries and elsewhere do not maintain constantly burning fires; rather, a fire is lit in an altar prior to acts of worship. Since impurity is thought to arise from evil, Zoroastrians undergo elaborate rituals to ensure their spiritual purity. In addition to rituals of worship and purification, other acts of devotion include seven feasts, such as that celebrating Nav Ruz, the new year.

Zoroastrian doctrine holds that earth, fire, and water are polluted if a corpse is buried, cremated, or placed in water. Consequently, the corpse would be washed, then placed in a *dakhma* (funerary tower), which is open to the sky and accessible to birds of prey. Thereafter, the bones would be collected and disposed of. Exposure of corpses has been phased out in Iran since the 1940s, and replaced with interment (burial). Many Parsis in India and Pakistan continue the tradition of exposing bodies in funerary towers, particularly at Bombay and Karachi. However, most Zoroastrians elsewhere follow their Iranian coreligionists' adaptation. Certain Zoroastrian communities, particularly those in North America, now perform cremation. Zoroastrians believe that after death each individual's soul is judged by a triad of gods—Mithra the keeper of covenants, Rashnu the judge, and Sraosha the messenger—at the Bridge of the Separator, which connects earth to heaven over the pit of hell. If the soul's good deeds are greater than its evil deeds, it is led across the bridge into paradise. When its evil deeds outweigh the good, the soul is cast into hell until the day of universal judgment. In cases where a soul's good and evil deeds are equal, it is consigned to limbo. The faithful claim that the dead will be resurrected at the end of time by a savior (*saoshyant*). Thereafter, Ahura Mazda will descend to earth and separate the righteous individuals from the evil ones. Each sinner will be purified of his or her transgressions and granted immortality. Then Angra Mainyu will be forced back into hell, and the world will become free of evil and impurity forever, the religion's eschatology claims.

BIBLIOGRAPHY

BOYCE, MARY. *A Persian Stronghold of Zoroastrianism.* Oxford, 1977. Reprint, Lanham, Md., 1994.

CHOKSY, JAMSHEED K. *Purity and Pollution in Zoroastrianism: Triumph over Evil.* Austin, Tex., 1989.

WRITER, RASHNA. *Contemporary Zoroastrians: An Unstructured Nation.* Lanham, Md., 1994.

ZAEHNER, ROBERT C. *The Teachings of the Magi: A Compendium of Zoroastrian Beliefs.* Oxford, 1976.

Jamsheed K. Choksy

Zu'ayyin, Yusuf   [1931–   ]

Syrian politician.

Born in a Sunni Islam family in Abu Kamal, Syria, Yusuf Zu'ayyin was educated at the Damascus Faculty of Medicine. He served in the regional directorship of the al-Ba'th party and was appointed minister of agrarian reform under Amin al-Hafiz in 1963. He was selected as prime minister in 1965 by Salah Jadid and held the position through the radical takeover of the Ba'th on February 23, 1966.

Still supporting Salah Jadid through 1968, he lost that position in October 1968, because Hafiz al-Asad had become dominant in the party. He was arrested by President Asad in 1971 and jailed until 1981, when he fled to family members in Hungary.

BIBLIOGRAPHY

SEALE, PATRICK. *Asad: The Struggle for the Middle East.* Los Angeles, 1988.

Charles U. Zenzie

Zubara War

Eighteenth-century conflict on Qatar peninsula.

In the 1760s the al-Khalifa, one of the Utub clans that had settled Kuwait, migrated south. Following their ejection from Bahrain by that island's dominant Bani Madhkur tribe, they settled at Zubara on the northwest coast of the Qatar peninsula. The Bani Madhkur, disturbed at Zubara's rapid growth as an entrepôt, raided it; the al-Khalifa answered by seizing ships of Shaykh Nasr al-Madhkur, who ruled Bahrain in the name of the shah of Persia. The al-Khalifa defeated the shaykh's subsequent attack against Zubara, and their Al Sabah allies from Kuwait seized Bahrain, thus ending Persian influence on the Arab side of the Gulf.

In 1783 the al-Khalifa became the rulers of Bahrain, though initially Zubara remained their capital. In the late nineteenth century the Al Thani, another Utub clan, established their rule over Qatar, and in 1937, they took full control of Zubara. The al-Khalifa remain unreconciled to the loss of their former capital, a principal factor in strained relations between Qatar and Bahrain.

BIBLIOGRAPHY

CARTER, LARAINE NEWHOUSE, and P. A. KLUCK. "Qatar." In *Persian Gulf States: Country Studies,* ed. by Richard F. Nyrop. Washington, D.C., 1984.

LAWSON, FRED. *Bahrain: The Modernization of Autocracy.* Boulder, Colo., 1989.

Malcolm C. Peck

Zubayri, Qa'id Muhammad Mahmud al- [1919–1965]

Yemeni political reformer.

Born in San'a, Muhammad Mahmud al-Zubayri left North Yemen after a brief career as a government official. With Ahmad Muhammad Nu'man, he began his lifelong effort to reform Yemen's imamic government. He participated in the founding of the Liberal party and the Free Yemeni movement. At this time, his poetry, in particular, earned him a literary reputation. Zubayri strongly supported the revolution of 1962 but quickly became disillusioned with the policies of Abdullah al-Sallal. He founded the "Third Force" as an alternative to the royalists and republicans but was assassinated in 1965.

Manfred W. Wenner

Zubi, Mahmud al-

Syrian politician; prime minister.

Hailing from the southern city of Dera, Mahmud al-Zubi was a Ba'th party member in high school and studied agronomy in Cairo. He ascended in the party's agricultural bureaucracy to become head of the general authority for development of the Euphrates river basin and, in 1980, director of the *maktab al-fallahin* (the peasant office). Al-Zubi was continually responsive to agrarian concerns in his capacity as speaker of parliament and, later, as prime minister.

BIBLIOGRAPHY

HINNEBUSCH, RAYMOND A. *Authoritarian Power and State Formation in Ba'thist Syria: Army, Party and Peasant.* Boulder, Colo., 1990.

Charles U. Zenzie

Zurayk, Constantine   [1909–   ]

Syrian intellectual and educator.

Zurayk was born in Damascus. He received a B.A. from the American University of Beirut (AUB), an M.A. from the University of Chicago in 1929, and a Ph.D. from Princeton University in 1930. He was an assistant professor of history at AUB (1930–1945) and later distinguished professor (1958–1977). He also served as counselor to the Syrian legation and then as minister to the United States (1945–1947), AUB vice president (1947–1949, 1952–1954), rector of the Syrian University in Damascus (1949–1952), and AUB acting president (1954–1957).

Zurayk, a prominent Arab intellectual, wrote *Ma'na al-Nakba* (The Meaning of the Disaster; 1948), the first substantial critique of Arab society in light of the 1948 defeat in Palestine. An advocate of rationalism, scientific and cultural progress, and secular nationalism, he produced many other influential works, including *Nahnu wa al-Ta'rikh* (Facing History; 1959), *Fi Ma'rakat al-Hadara* (In the Battle for Civilization; 1964), and *Nahnu wa al-Mustaqbal* (Facing the Future), as well as translations and editions of European and Arabic works on cultural history.

BIBLIOGRAPHY

ATIYEH, GEORGE N., and IBRAHIM M. OWEISS. *Arab Civilization—Challenges and Responses: Studies in Honor of Constantine K. Zurayk.* Albany, N.Y., 1988.

NASHABÉ, HISHAM, ed. *Studia Palaestina: Studies in Honour of Constantine K. Zurayk.* Beirut, 1988.

Charles U. Zenzie

Zuwaya Tribe

A tribal group in Libya.

The Zuwaya probably originated, as a distinct group, as refugees from the Ottoman government. They left coastal pastures for the desert to escape taxation and control. To some extent, the Zuwaya continue to function as a tribal unit within the confines of the Libyan state.

BIBLIOGRAPHY

DAVIS, JOHN. *Libyan Politics: Tribe and Revolution.* Berkeley, Calif., 1987.

Stuart J. Borsch

Directory of Contributors

Nermin Abadan-Unat
Boğaziçi University, Istanbul

M. Morsy Abdullah
Centre for Documentation and Research, Abu Dhabi

Ervand Abrahamian
Baruch College

Kamal Abu-Deeb
University of London

As'ad AbuKhalil
California State University, Stanislaus

Rouben P. Adalian
Armenian Assembly of America, Washington, D.C.

Jamsheed Akrami
Cliffside Park, New Jersey

Scott Alexander
Indiana University, Bloomington

Hamid Algar
University of California, Berkeley

Calvin H. Allen, Jr.
Memphis State University

Roger Allen
University of Pennsylvania

Audrey L. Altstadt
University of Massachusetts, Amherst

Abla M. Amawi
Georgetown University

Hooshang Amirahmadi
Rutgers University, New Brunswick

Lisa Anderson
Columbia University

Walter Armbrust
University of Pennsylvania

Geoffrey Aronson
Hogan & Hartson, Washington, D.C.

Farhad Arshad
Columbia University

Ahmad Ashraf
Columbia University

Shimon Avish
Columbia University

Louay Bahry
Washington, D.C.

Raymond William Baker
Williams College

H. G. Balfour-Paul
Devon, England

Aida A. Bamia
University of Florida

Amatzia Baram
Haifa University

Larry A. Barrie
Fayetteville, North Carolina

Michael L. Bates
American Numismatic Society, New York

Yehuda Bauer
Hebrew University of Jerusalem

Lois Beck
Washington University in St. Louis

Tsilit Ben-Nevat
The Jewish Museum, New York

Elizabeth M. Bergman
Columbia University

Rhimou Bernikho-Canin
Tarzana, California

Robert Betts
American University of Beirut

Robert Bianchi
Chicago, Illinois

Dale L. Bishop
National Council of the Churches of Christ in the USA, New York

Gerald Blake
University of Durham, England

Khalid Y. Blankinship
Temple University

Mutlu Konuk Blasing
Brown University

Jonathan M. Bloom
Richmond, New Hampshire

Mia Bloom
Columbia University

Arnold Blumberg
Towson State University

Jerome Bookin-Wiener
Bentley College

Stuart J. Borsch
Columbia University

Selma Botman
College of the Holy Cross

Kamal Boullata
Rabat, Morocco

Rahma Bourqia
Mohamed V University, Rabat

Donna Lee Bowen
Brigham Young University

Henry S. Bradsher
Arlington, Virginia

Benjamin Braude
Boston College

Jack Bubon
Fairfax, Virginia

Richard W. Bulliet
Columbia University

Edmund Burke III
University of California, Santa Cruz

Kathleen R. F. Burrill
Columbia University

Robert D. Burrowes
University of Washington

Pierre Cachia
Columbia University

Byron Cannon
University of Utah

Neil Caplan
Vanier College

Stephanie Capparell
The Wall Street Journal, New York

Peter Chelkowski
New York University

Jamsheed K. Choksy
Indiana University, Bloomington

Kathleen M. Christison
Santa Fe, New Mexico

John R. Clark
Columbia University

William L. Cleveland
Simon Fraser University

Juan R. I. Cole
University of Michigan, Ann Arbor

Robert O. Collins
University of California, Santa Barbara

Hind Rassam Culhane
Dobbs Ferry, New York

Niyazi Dalyanci
Istanbul, Turkey

Virginia Danielson
Harvard University

Bryan Daves
Columbia University

Roderic H. Davison
Deceased

C. Ernest Dawn
University of Illinois, Urbana

Richard Dekmejian
University of Southern California

Walter Denny
University of Massachusetts, Amherst

Guilain P. Denoeux
Colby College

Shlomo Deshen
Tel Aviv University

Ali E. Hillal Dessouki
Cairo University

John C. Dewdney
University of Durham, England

Bradford Dillman
American University in Cairo

Donna Robinson Divine
Smith College

John J. Donohue
University of Saint Joseph, Beirut

Eleanor Abdella Doumato
University of Rhode Island

Michael Dunn
The International Estimate, Arlington

Evelyn A. Early
United States Information Service, Washington, D.C.

A. Chris Eccel
United States Information Service, Manama

Dale F. Eickelman
Dartmouth College

Tayeb El-Hibri
University of Massachusetts, Amherst

Michael Eppel
Haifa University

Mansoureh Ettehadieh
University of Tehran

Abdel Aziz EzzelArab
McGill University

Hani Fakhouri
University of Michigan, Flint

Marion Farouk-Sluglett
Deceased

Grant Farr
Portland State University

Yael Feldman
University of Oxford

Carter V. Findley
Ohio State University

Michael R. Fischbach
Randolph-Macon College

John Foran
University of California, Santa Barbara

Robert O. Freedman
Baltimore Hebrew University

F. Gregory Gause, III
University of Vermont

Irene Gendzier
Boston University

Jane Gerber
City University of New York

Fawaz A. Gerges
Sarah Lawrence College

Sabah Ghandour
University of Pennsylvania

Ashraf Ghani
Johns Hopkins University

Martin Gilbert
University of Oxford

Erika Gilson
Princeton University

Zvia Ginor
Jewish Theological Seminary, New York

Nili Gold
Columbia University

Ellis Goldberg
University of Washington

Arthur Goldschmidt, Jr.
Pennsylvania State University

Matthew S. Gordon
Miami University, Chicago

JoAnn Gross
Trenton State University

George E. Gruen
Columbia University

Peter Gubser
American Near East Refugee Aid, Washington, D.C.

Mahmoud Haddad
Columbia University

Sylvia G. Haim
Middle Eastern Studies, England

Majed Halawi
New York, New York

Wael B. Hallaq
McGill University

Robert E. Harkavy
Pennsylvania State University

Samuel C. Heilman
Queens College of the City University of New York

Marilyn Higbee
Columbia University

Michael C. Hillmann
University of Texas, Austin

Steven Holtzman
The World Bank, Washington, D.C.

Eric J. Hooglund
Critique Magazine, St. Paul

J. C. Hurewitz
Emeritus, Columbia University

Martha Imber-Goldstein
Jackson Heights, New York

George E. Irani
Lebanese American University

Charles Issawi
Princeton University

James Jankowski
University of Colorado

M. A. Jazayery
University of Texas, Austin

George Joffe
University of London

Benjamin Joseph
Philadelphia, Pennsylvania

Jon Jucovy
Ramaz School, New York

Albertine Jwaideh
University of Toronto

Ann Kahn
Brooklyn, New York

Zachary Karabell
Harvard University

Efraim Karsh
King's College

Hasan Kayali
University of California, San Diego

Nikki Keddie
University of California, Los Angeles

Nazar al-Khalaf
Montreal, Quebec

Rashid Khalidi
University of Chicago

Fred J. Khouri
Villanova University

Carolyn Killean
University of Chicago

Alexander Kitroeff
New York University

John F. Kolars
University of Michigan, Ann Arbor

C. Max Kortepeter
New York University

Joseph Kostiner
Tel Aviv University

Martin Kramer
Tel Aviv University

I. Metin Kunt
University of Cambridge

Aptullah Kuran
Boğaziçi University, Istanbul

Chris Kutschera
Paris, France

Ahmet Kuyas
Mount Holyoke College

Robert G. Landen
Virginia Polytechnic Institute and State University

Nico Landman
University of Utrecht

Michael M. Laskier
*Beit Berl College and the Ashqelon Regional College of
Bar-Ilan University*

Fred H. Lawson
Mills College

Ann M. Lesch
Villanova University

Rémy Leveau
Institut d'Études Politiques de Paris

Avigdor Levy
Brandeis University

F. T. Liu
International Peace Academy, New York

Charles G. MacDonald
Florida International University

Bruce Maddy-Weitzman
Tel Aviv University

Zev Maghen
Bar-Ilan University

Paul J. Magnarella
University of Florida

Gregory S. Mahler
University of Mississippi

Roshanak Malek
New York, New York

Martin Malin
Columbia University

Sumit Mandal
Ithaca, New York

Ruth Mandel
University College London

Abraham Marcus
University of Texas, Austin

Paul Martin
Columbia University

Philip Mattar
Institute for Palestine Studies, Washington, D.C.

Ann E. Mayer
University of Pennsylvania

Kenneth S. Mayers
University of California, Los Angeles

Justin McCarthy
University of Louisville

Mark Mechler
Washington, D.C.

Peter Mellini
Sonoma State University

John Micgiel
Columbia University

Laurence Michalak
University of California, Berkeley

Pardis Minuchehr
Columbia University

Mansoor Moaddel
Eastern Michigan University

Cyrus Moshaver
Columbia University

Muhammad Muslih
C.W. Post College of Long Island University

Edna Nahshon
Jewish Theological Seminary of America, New York

Emile A. Nakhleh
Mount St. Mary's College

Bassam Namani
Embassy of Lebanon, Washington, D.C.

Hisham Nashabi
Makassed Philanthropic Islamic Association, Beirut

Phillip C. Naylor
Marquette University

Benyamin Neuberger
Tel Aviv University

Francis R. Nicosia
Saint Michael's College

John D. Norton
University of Durham, England

Pierre Oberling
Hunter College of the City University of New York

Jean-Marc Ran Oppenheim
Columbia University

Les Ordeman
Columbia University

Nasser Ovissi
Reston, Virginia

Taha Parla
Boğaziçi University, Istanbul

David H. Partington
Harvard University

Malcolm C. Peck
Meridian International Center, Washington, D.C.

Yarom Peleg
Brandeis University

Thomas G. Penchoen
University of California, Los Angeles

C. R. Pennell
University of Melbourne

Don Peretz
Emeritus, State University of New York, Binghamton

Kenneth J. Perkins
University of South Carolina

Amos Perlmutter
American University

John R. Perry
University of Chicago

John E. Peterson
Office of the Deputy Prime Minister, Musqat

Thomas Philipp
Friedrich-Alexander Universität, Erlangen

Karen Pinto
Columbia University

Lawrence G. Potter
Columbia University

Parvaneh Pourshariati
Columbia University

Ayad al-Qazzaz
California State University, Sacramento

Donald Quataert
State University of New York, Binghamton

Mouin Rabbani
University of Oxford

Ali Jihad Racy
University of California, Los Angeles

Abdul-Karim Rafeq
College of William and Mary

Rasul Bakhsh Rais
Columbia University

Ruth Raphaeli
Columbia University

Sara Reguer
Brooklyn College of the City University of New York

Bernard Reich
George Washington University

Donald Malcolm Reid
Georgia State University

Nissim Rejwan
Jerusalem, Israel

Alan R. Richards
University of California, Santa Cruz

Paul Rivlin
Ramat Hasharon, Israel

Aleya Rouchdy
Wayne State University

Maurice M. Roumani
Ben-Gurion University of the Negev

Sara M. Roy
Harvard University

Barnett R. Rubin
Council on Foreign Relations, New York

John Ruedy
Georgetown University

James R. Russell
Harvard University

Ariel Salzmann
New York University

Uli Schamiloglu
University of Wisconsin, Madison

Jillian Schwedler
New York University

Aaron Segal
University of Texas, El Paso

Jean-François Seznec
Columbia University

A. Shahpur Shahbazi
Eastern Oregon State College

M. Nazif Shahrani
Indiana University, Bloomington

Zeva Shapiro
New York, New York

Yaakov Shavit
Tel Aviv University

William Shepard
University of Canterbury

Ahmad Abdul A. R. Shikara
United Arab Emirates University

Farhad Shirzad
New York, New York

Avi Shlaim
University of Oxford

Alain Silvera
Bryn Mawr College

Miriam Simon
Hebrew University of Jerusalem

Rachel Simon
Princeton University

Reeva S. Simon
Columbia University

Peter von Sivers
University of Utah

P. Oktor Skjaervo
Harvard University

Peter Sluglett
University of Utah

Oles M. Smolansky
Lehigh University

Reuven Snir
Haifa University

Sasson Somekh
Tel Aviv University

John P. Spagnolo
Simon Fraser University

Donald Spanel
The Brooklyn Museum, New York

Daniel E. Spector
University of Alabama, Birmingham

Denise A. Spellberg
University of Texas, Austin

Alison R. Steiner
Adelman & Steiner, Hattiesburg

Norman Stillman
University of Oklahoma

Will D. Swearingen
Montana State University

Frank Tachau
University of Illinois, Chicago

Kazuo Takahashi
University of the Air, Tokyo

Lawrence Tal
University of Oxford

Steve Tamari
Georgetown University

Abraham Terian
Andrews University

Janice J. Terry
Eastern Michigan University

Mary Ann Tétreault
Iowa State University

Elizabeth Thompson
University of Virginia

W. Kenneth Thompson
Department of State, Washington, D.C.

Karen A. Thornsvard
Madison, Wisconsin

Robert L. Tignor
Princeton University

Ehud R. Toledano
Tel Aviv University

Jenab Tutunji
George Washington University

Dirk Vandewalle
Dartmouth College

David Waldner
University of Virginia

Bernard Wasserstein
Brandeis University

Chaim I. Waxman
Rutgers University, New Brunswick

Walter F. Weiker
Rutgers University, Newark

Shalvah Weil
Hebrew University of Jerusalem

Marvin G. Weinbaum
University of Illinois, Urbana

Manfred W. Wenner
Northern Illinois University

Geoffrey Wigoder
Hebrew University of Jerusalem

Rodney J. A. Wilson
University of Durham, England

Clifford A. Wright
Arlington, Massachusetts

John L. Wright
Surrey, England

Nathan Yanai
Haifa University

Neguin Yavari
University of Oxford

Antoine Benjamin Zahlan
London, England

Shibolet Zait
Columbia University

Muhammad Zakariya
Arlington, Virginia

Mamoon A. Zaki
LeMoyne-Owen College

Ronen Zeidel
Haifa University

Charles U. Zenzie
U.S.-Indonesia Society, Washington, D.C.

Steve Zipperstein
Hebrew University of Jerusalem

Julie Zuckerman
Jerusalem, Israel

Genealogies and Lines
of Succession

Alawite Dynasty of Morocco, 1666–
Al Sabah Dynasty of Kuwait, 1756–
Al Sa'ud Dynasty of Saudi Arabia, 1735–
Hamid al-Din Family of Yemen, 1890–1962
Hashimite Family of the Hijaz, 1828–
Khalifa Family of Bahrain, 1782–
Muhammad Ali Family of Egypt, 1805–1953
Pahlavi Dynasty of Iran, 1925–1979
Qajar Dynasty of Persia, 1796–1925
Sultans of the Ottoman Empire, 1757–1922
Twelve Imams of Shi'a Islam

Note to the reader

In the following genealogies and lines of succession, an asterisk preceding a name indicates that the Encyclopedia contains an entry for that individual. Entries appear either under the given name or under the family or dynasty name, according to conventional usage. The names of those who ruled are indicated by boldface type. Titles such as *shah, pasha, amir, khedive,* and so on have been omitted.

Names in Arabic are arranged in a specified order, with lineage often indicated by *ibn* (son of), *bint* (daughter of), *umm* (mother of), or *abu* (father of). For example, the son of Egypt's Muhammad Ali was Ibrahim ibn Muhammad Ali (meaning "Ibrahim, son of Muhammad Ali"). Ibrahim's son was Isma'il ibn Ibrahim ibn Muhammad Ali, and so on. For simplicity, the following genealogies often use only the given name, the father's (or occasionally the mother's) name, and the family name. Thus, Ha-

mad ibn Isa ibn Sulman ibn Hamad ibn Isa ibn Ali al-Khalifa (where al-Khalifa is the family name) is given here simply as Hamad ibn Isa al-Khalifa. Occasionally the given name is dropped entirely in popular usage, as with Abd al-Aziz ibn Sa'ud Al Sa'ud, who is known simply as Ibn Sa'ud.

In the Middle East, the descendants in a single family line often number in the hundreds, particularly when a man fathers children through multiple wives. The following genealogies are therefore not exhaustive and include only well-known figures and those in the direct line of succession. Where possible, the existence of additional family members has been indicated with arrows. With a few exceptions, female descendants are not included because they are typically denied inheritance of a throne and, consequently, little information is available about them.

Alawite Dynasty of Morocco, 1666–

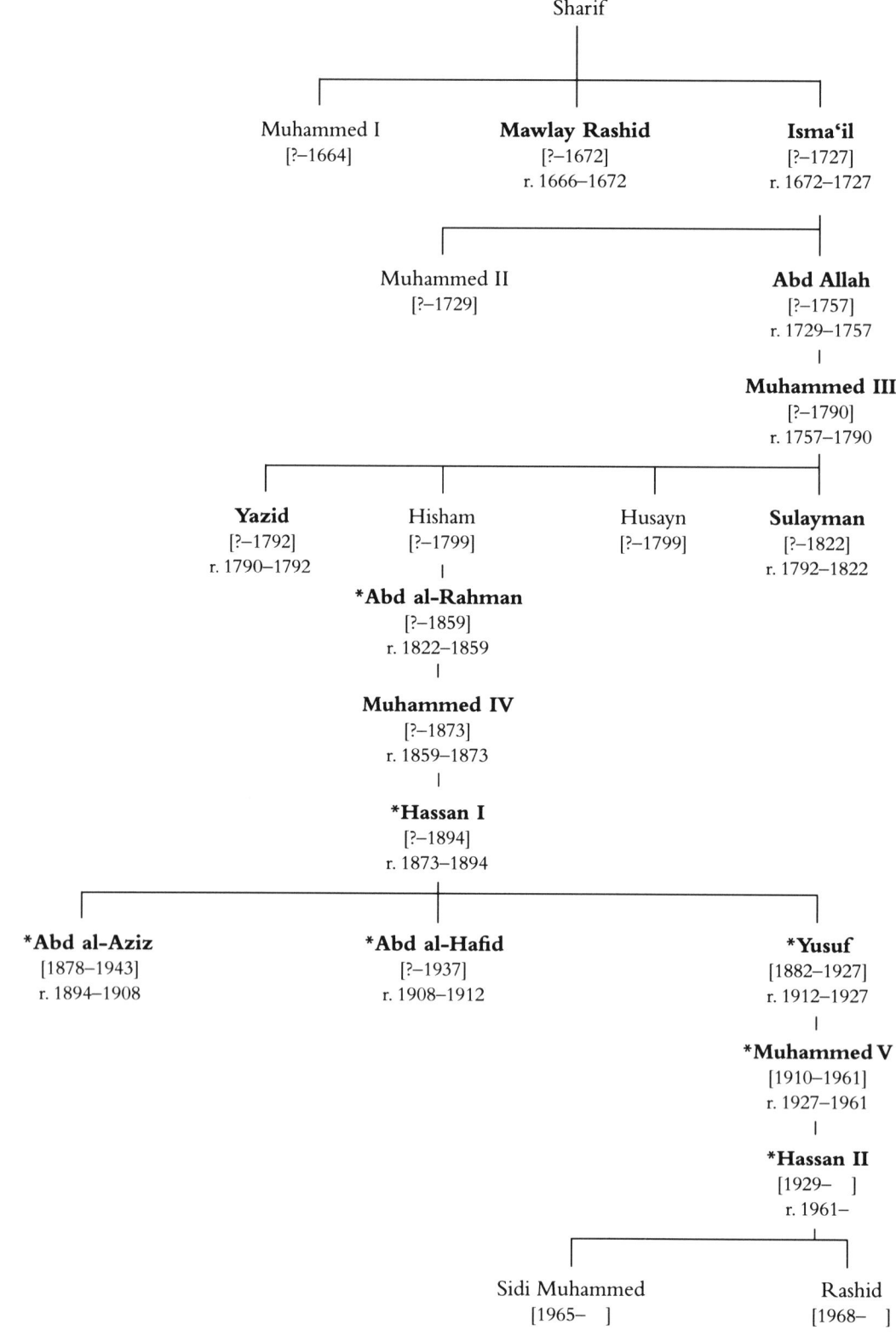

Al Sabah Dynasty of Kuwait, 1756–

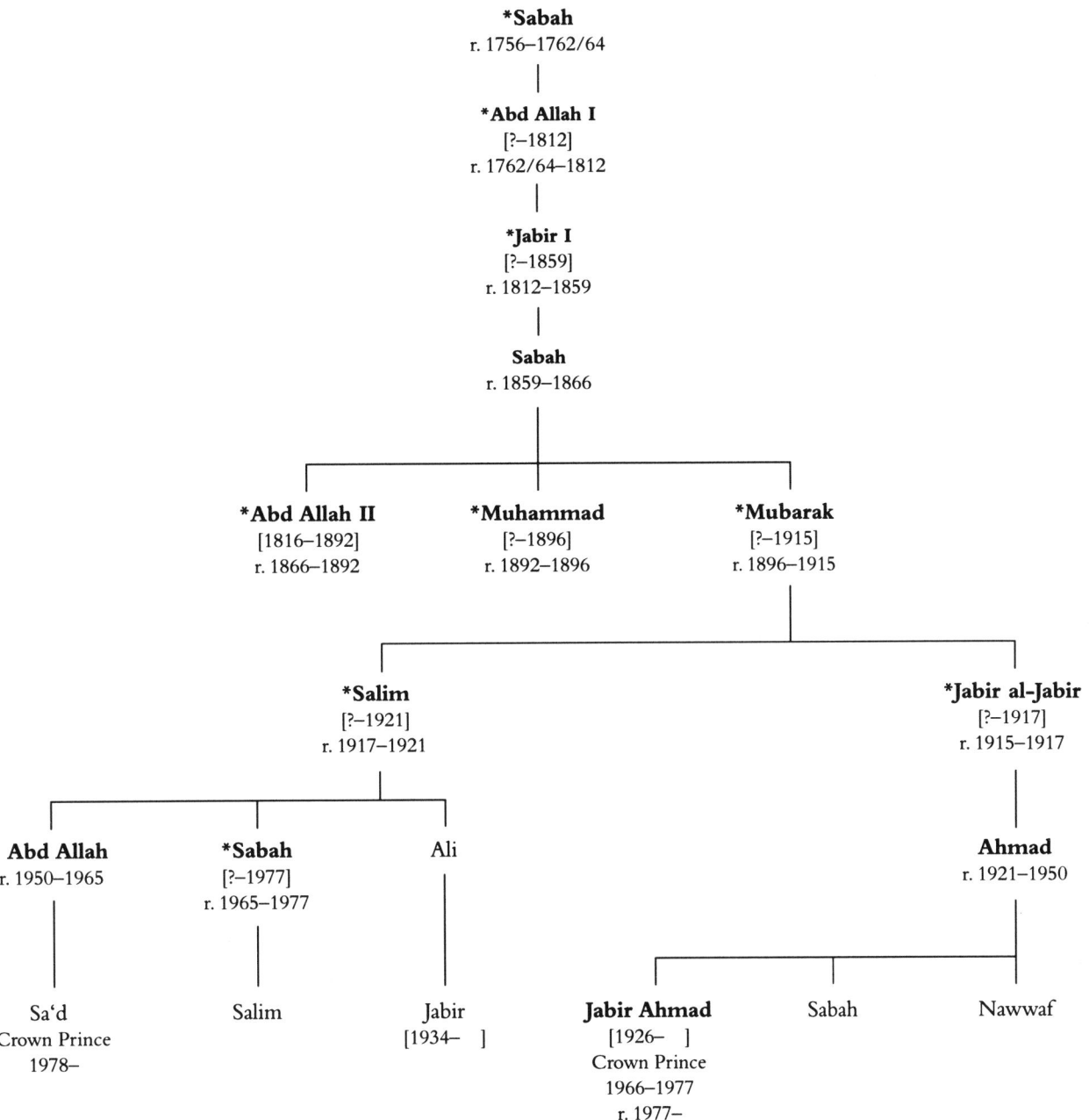

*Sabah
r. 1756–1762/64

*Abd Allah I
[?–1812]
r. 1762/64–1812

*Jabir I
[?–1859]
r. 1812–1859

Sabah
r. 1859–1866

*Abd Allah II
[1816–1892]
r. 1866–1892

*Muhammad
[?–1896]
r. 1892–1896

*Mubarak
[?–1915]
r. 1896–1915

*Salim
[?–1921]
r. 1917–1921

*Jabir al-Jabir
[?–1917]
r. 1915–1917

Abd Allah
r. 1950–1965

*Sabah
[?–1977]
r. 1965–1977

Ali

Ahmad
r. 1921–1950

Sa'd
Crown Prince
1978–

Salim

Jabir
[1934–]

Jabir Ahmad
[1926–]
Crown Prince
1966–1977
r. 1977–

Sabah

Nawwaf

Al Sa'ud Dynasty of Saudi Arabia, 1735–

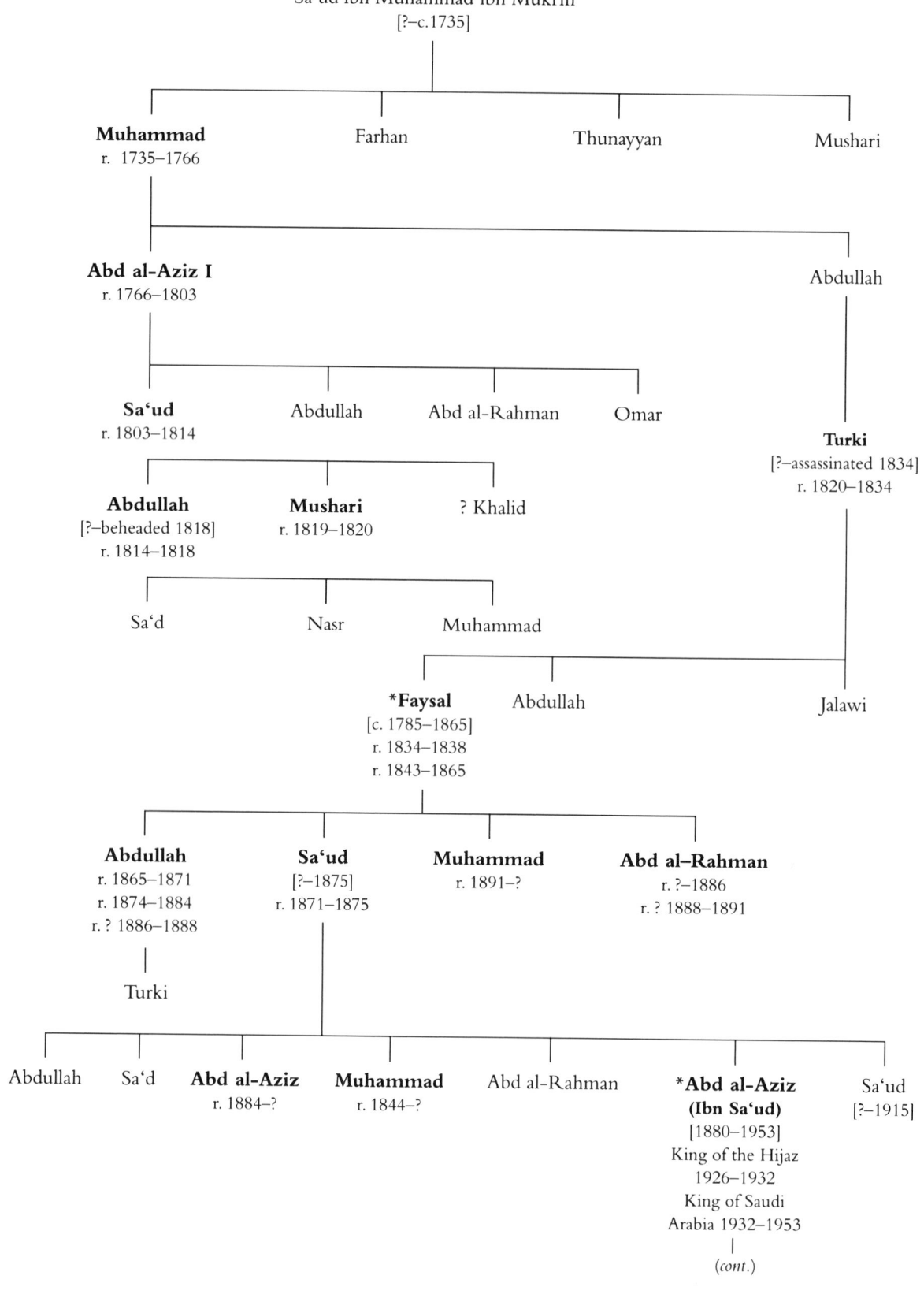

Al Sa'ud Dynasty of Saudi Arabia, 1735–   *(cont.)*

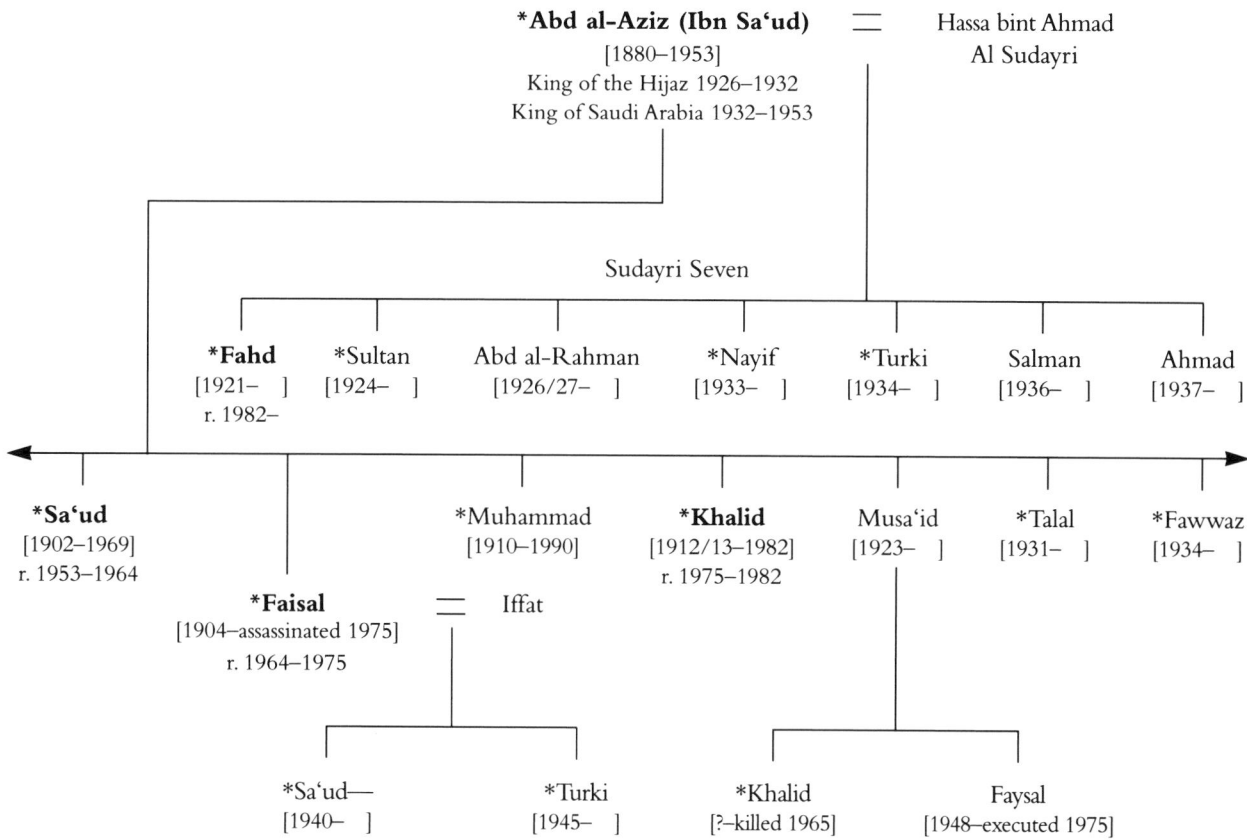

NOTE: Abd al-Aziz ibn Sa'ud Al Sa'ud (1880–1953) fathered forty-five sons and as many daughters by at least twenty-three different women. His wife Hassa gave birth to seven sons known as the Sudayri Seven, a reference to Hassa's descent from the Al Sudayri tribe. The descendants of Muhammad ibn Sa'ud, the founder of the Al Sa'ud dynasty, number in the tens of thousands and include the current king, Fahd, one of the Sudayri Seven.

Hamid al-Din Family of Yemen, 1890–1962

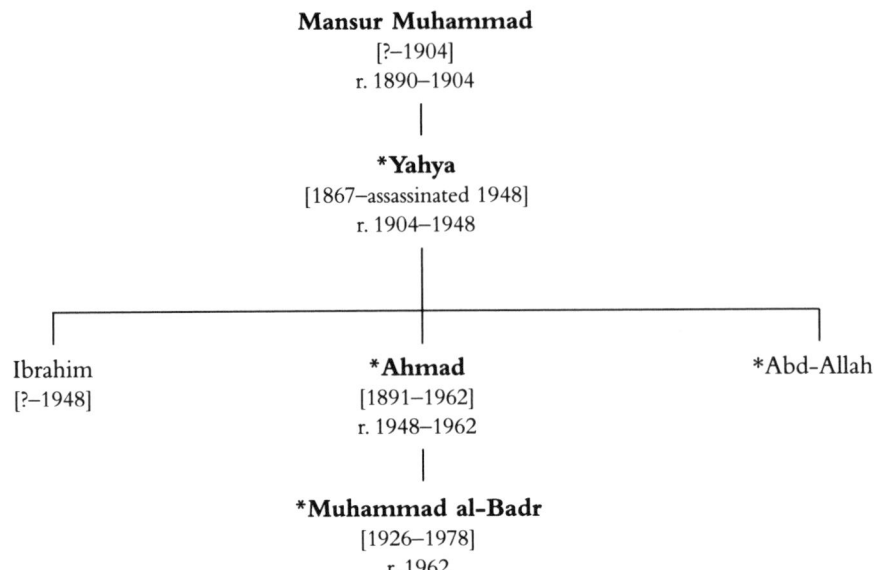

Mansur Muhammad
[?–1904]
r. 1890–1904

*Yahya
[1867–assassinated 1948]
r. 1904–1948

Ibrahim
[?–1948]

*Ahmad
[1891–1962]
r. 1948–1962

*Abd-Allah

*Muhammad al-Badr
[1926–1978]
r. 1962

Hashimite Family of the Hijaz, 1828–

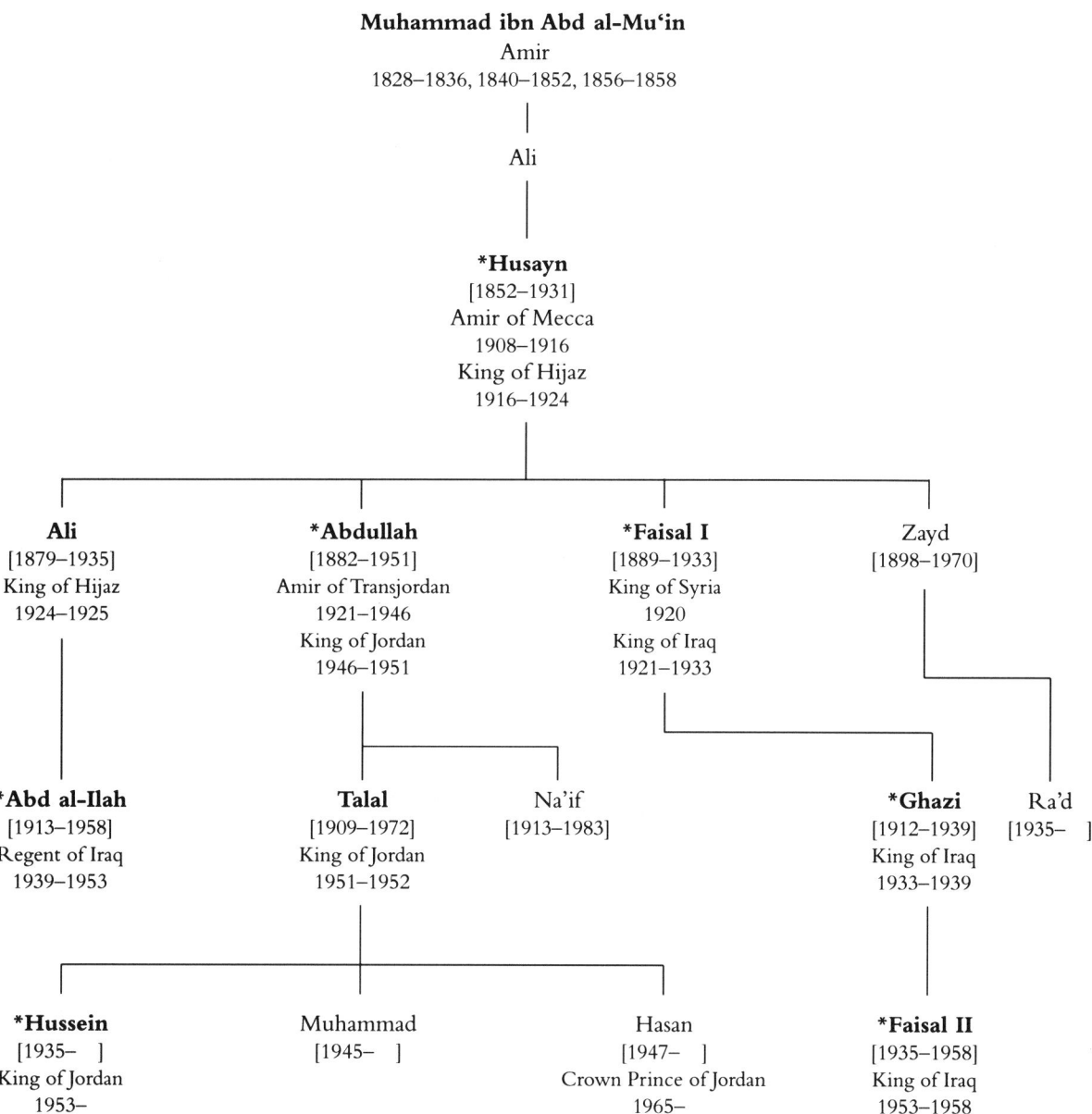

Muhammad ibn Abd al-Mu'in
Amir
1828–1836, 1840–1852, 1856–1858

Ali

*Husayn
[1852–1931]
Amir of Mecca
1908–1916
King of Hijaz
1916–1924

Ali
[1879–1935]
King of Hijaz
1924–1925

*Abdullah
[1882–1951]
Amir of Transjordan
1921–1946
King of Jordan
1946–1951

*Faisal I
[1889–1933]
King of Syria
1920
King of Iraq
1921–1933

Zayd
[1898–1970]

*Abd al-Ilah
[1913–1958]
Regent of Iraq
1939–1953

Talal
[1909–1972]
King of Jordan
1951–1952

Na'if
[1913–1983]

*Ghazi
[1912–1939]
King of Iraq
1933–1939

Ra'd
[1935–]

*Hussein
[1935–]
King of Jordan
1953–

Muhammad
[1945–]

Hasan
[1947–]
Crown Prince of Jordan
1965–

*Faisal II
[1935–1958]
King of Iraq
1953–1958

Khalifa Family of Bahrain, 1782–

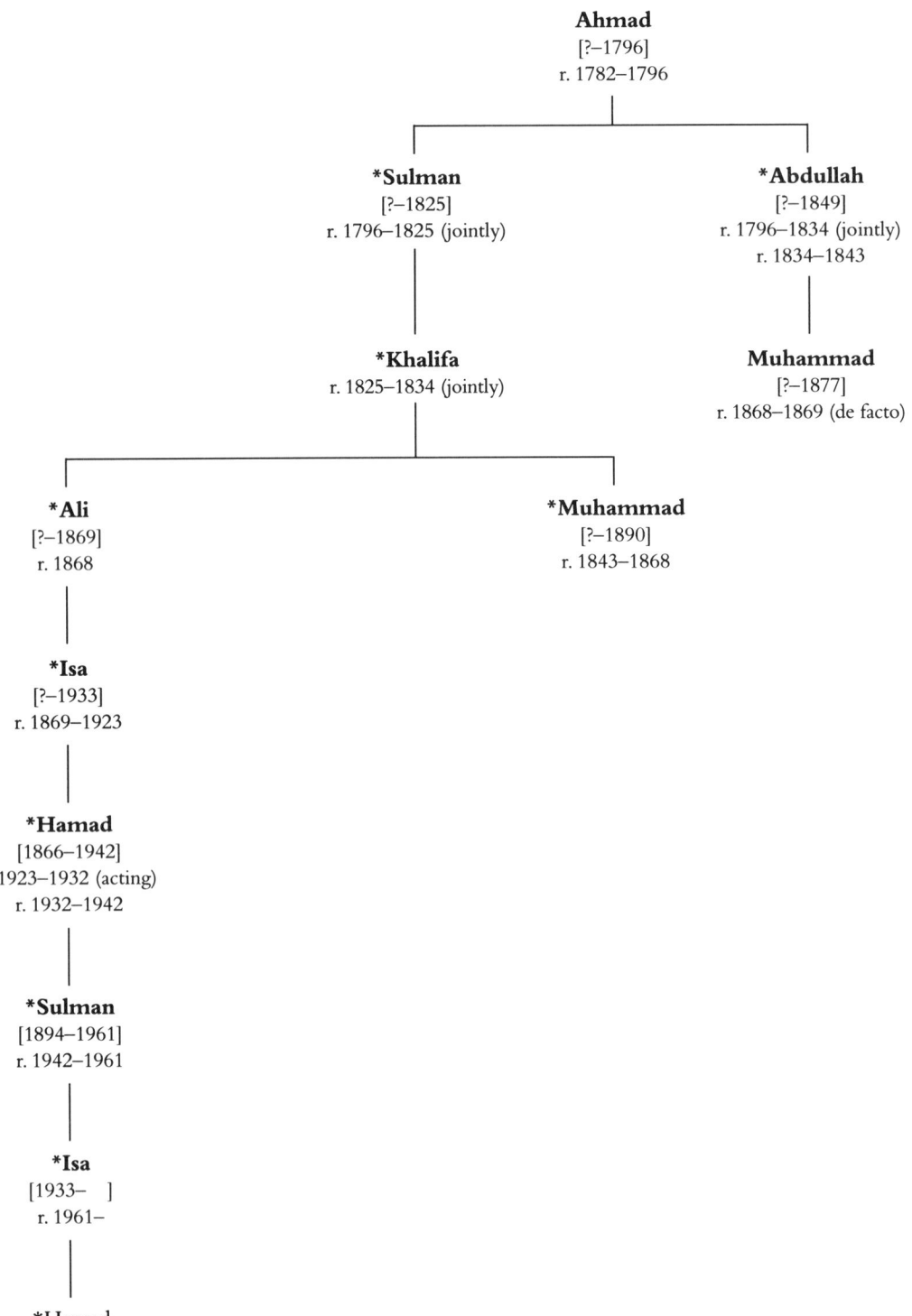

Muhammad Ali Family of Egypt, 1805–1953

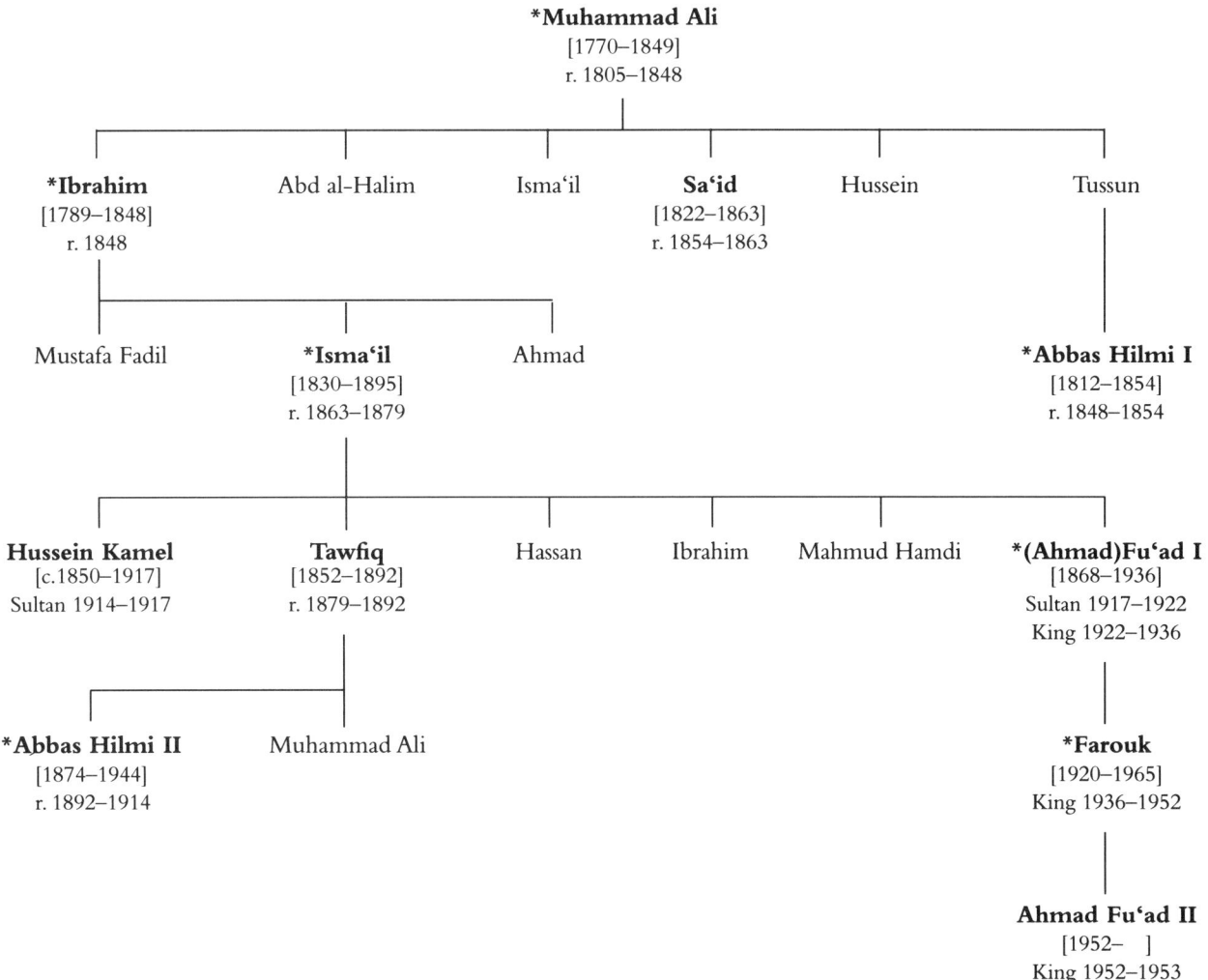

Pahlavi Dynasty of Iran, 1925–1979

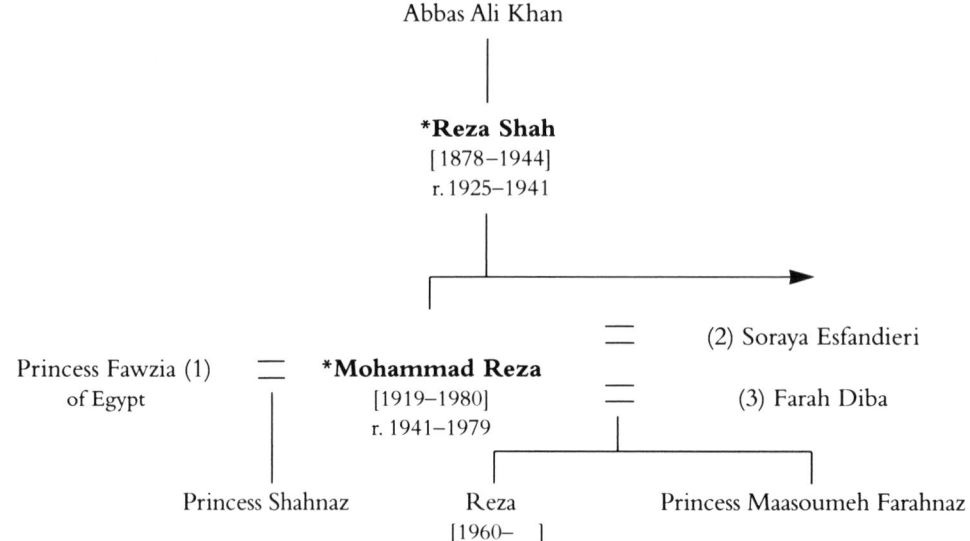

Qajar Dynasty of Persia, 1796–1925

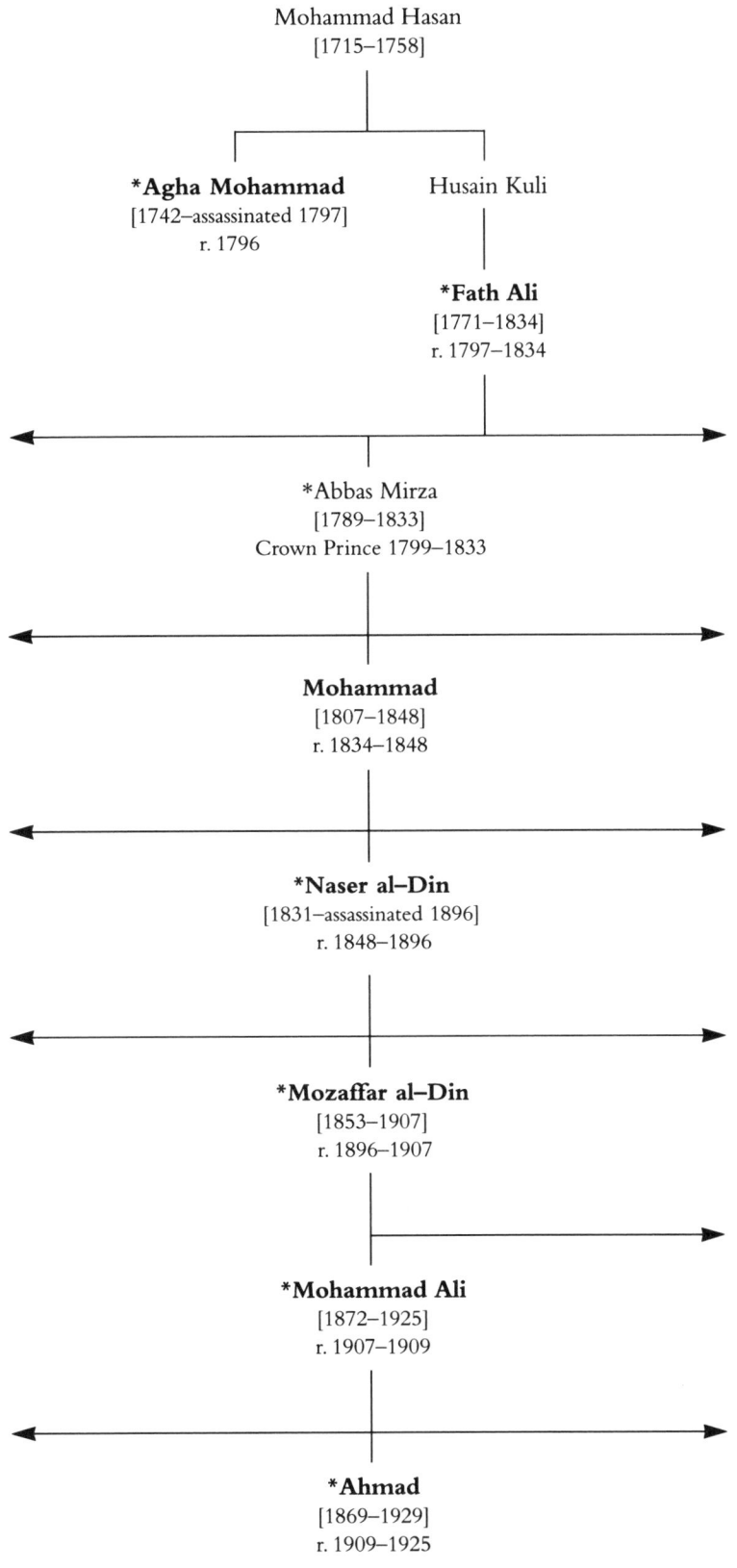

Mohammad Hasan
[1715–1758]

*Agha Mohammad
[1742–assassinated 1797]
r. 1796

Husain Kuli

*Fath Ali
[1771–1834]
r. 1797–1834

*Abbas Mirza
[1789–1833]
Crown Prince 1799–1833

Mohammad
[1807–1848]
r. 1834–1848

*Naser al–Din
[1831–assassinated 1896]
r. 1848–1896

*Mozaffar al–Din
[1853–1907]
r. 1896–1907

*Mohammad Ali
[1872–1925]
r. 1907–1909

*Ahmad
[1869–1929]
r. 1909–1925

Sultans of the Ottoman Empire, 1757–1922

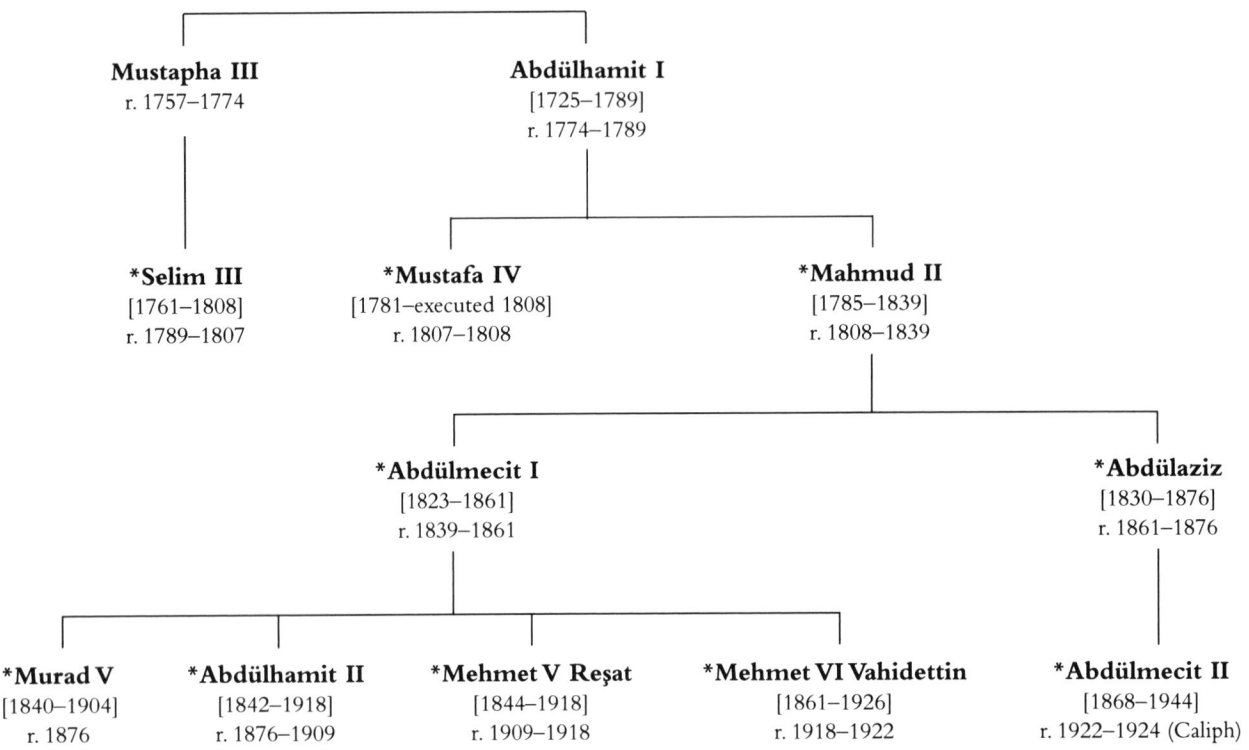

Twelve Imams of Shi'a Islam

Ali ibn Abi Talib (d. 661, al-Najaf)

Hasan (d. 669, Medina)

Husayn (d. 680, Karbala)

Ali Zayn al-Abidin (d. 712, Medina)

Muhammad al-Baqir (d. 731, Medina)

Ja'far al-Sadiq (d. 765, Medina)

Musa al-Kazim (d. 799, Baghdad)

Ali al-Rida (d. 818, Tus)

Muhammad al-Taqi al-Jawad (d. 835, Baghdad)

Muhammad al-Naqi (d. 868, Samarra)

Hasan al-Askari (d. 873, Samarra)

Muhammad al-Mahdi al-Muntazar (the vanished imam, 873)

Biographical Entries
by Category

This list organizes the Encyclopedia's biographical entries as well as entries on certain families and dynasties into the following categories. Some figures appear under more than one category, indicating that they participated in more than one profession or walk of life. Readers should refer to the general Index for page numbers of each entry and for additional references to these figures throughout the Encyclopedia.

Archeologists
Architects, Painters, and Sculptors
Civil Servants and Diplomats (European and American)
Civil Servants and Diplomats (Middle Eastern)
Civil Servants and Diplomats (Ottoman)
Distinguished Families
Educators and Scholars
Entrepreneurs, Economists, Industrialists, and Financiers
Explorers and Travelers
Fiction Writers, Playwrights, Poets, and Literary Essayists
Historians and Political Scientists
Journalists and Social Essayists
Labor Leaders
Lawyers and Jurisprudence Scholars
Medical Professionals and Scientists
Military Leaders
Musicians, Composers, and Singers
Nationalists (Eighteenth and Nineteenth Century)
Nationalists (Twentieth Century)
Philosophers and Religious Leaders, Thinkers, and Writers
Political Leaders (Nineteenth Century)
Political Leaders (Twentieth Century)
Rulers (Monarchs and Members of Dynasties)
Social Activists and Political Reformers (Nineteenth Century)
Social Activists and Political Reformers (Twentieth Century)
Theater, Film, and Dance Artists

Archeologists

Mariette, Auguste
Maspero, Gaston
Richmond, Ernest T.
Salim Hasan
Yadin, Yigal

Architects, Painters, and Sculptors

Abidin, Dino
Agam, Yaacov
Akbulut, Ahmet Ziya
Ali Rıza
Aral, Oğuz

Arseven, Celal Esat
Balyan family
Eldem, Sedad Hakki
Eyüboğlu, Bedri Rahmi
Fikret, Mualla
Güler, Ara
Hamdi, Osman

Hasan, Fa'iq
Hilmi, Kasımpaşalı
Kadishman, Menashe
Kemalettin Bey
Lifschitz, Uri
Mehmed, Hilmi
Mufide Kadri
Nazmi, Ziya
Qajar, Abd Allah Mirza
Ruhi Arel
Russi Khan
Salim, Jawad
Seker Ahmet
Tagger, Sioneh
Tek, Vedat
Zaritzsky, Jossef
Zili, Ridha

Civil Servants and Diplomats (European and American)

Acheson, Dean
Adenauer, Konrad
Allenby, Edmund Henry
Amery, Leopold Charles
Andrássy, Julius
Andrews, Lewis
Attlee, Clement
Baker, James
Balbo, Italo
Baring, Evelyn
Belgrave, Charles Dalrymple
Bentwich, Norman
Bernadotte, Folke
Bevin, Ernest
Bismarck, Otto von
Bruce, Thomas
Bunche, Ralph J.
Burton, Richard Francis
Cambon, Jules
Cambon, Paul
Canning, Stratford
Catroux, Georges
Cave, Stephen
Chancellor, John
Clayton, Gilbert
Cornwallis, Sir Kinahan
Cox, Percy
Creech-Jones, Arthur
Crossman, Richard
De Bunsen, Maurice
Deedes, Wyndham
Delouvrier, Paul
Dentz, Henri-Fernand
Dickson, Harold Richard Patrick
Dobbs, Henry
Dubs, Adolph
Dulles, John Foster
Durand, Henry Mortimer
Elphinstone, Mountstuart
Finn, James
Gambetta, Léon
Glubb, John Bagot
Gorchakov, Aleksandr Mikhailovich
Gorst, John Eldon
Grey, Edward

Grobba, Fritz Konrad Ferdinand
Guinness, Walter Edward
Habib, Philip Charles
Harriman, W. Averell
Helleu, Jean
Henderson, Loy
Hogarth, David George
Humphreys, Francis
Ignatiev, Nikolas Pavlovich
Jarring, Gunnar
Jernegan, John
Kirkbride, Alec Seath
Kissinger, Henry
Kitchener, Horatio Herbert
Kosygin, Aleksey Nikolayevich
Lacoste, Robert
Lampson, Miles
Lesseps, Ferdinand de
Lowther, Sir Gerald
Luke, Harry
Lyautey, Louis-Herbert Gonzalve
Lyttleton, Oliver
MacMichael, Harold
Malcolm, John
Marshall, George C.
Martel, Damien de
McMahon, Henry
Menou, Jacques François
Metternich, Klemens von
Nesselrode, Karl Robert von
Orlov, Aleksey Feodorovich
Ormsby-Gore, William George Arthur
Papen, Franz von
Pelt, Adrian
Pérez de Cuéllar, Javier
Peyrouton, Marcel
Philby, Kim
Plumer, Herbert Charles Onslow
Ponsot, Henri
Rendel, George William
Richmond, Ernest T.
Rogers, William Pierce
Roosevelt, Kermit
Samuel, Herbert Louis
Soustelle, Jacques
Stack, Lee
Storrs, Ronald
Sullivan, William
Sykes, Mark
Temple, Henry John
Thiers, Adolphe
Vance, Cyrus
Volpi, Giuseppe
Wauchope, Arthur
Webb, Sidney
Wilson, Arnold T.
Wingate, Reginald
Wolff, Henry Drummond

Civil Servants and Diplomats (Middle Eastern)

Abbas Hilmi I
Abbas Hilmi II
Abd al-Hadi, Awni

Ahmad al-Jazzar
Ahmad Bey of Constantine
Ala al-Saltaneh, Mirza Mohammad Ali Khan
Ali Nasir Muhammad al-Hasani
Al Sa'ud, Sa'ud ibn Faisal
Al Sa'ud, Talal ibn Abd al-Aziz
Al Sa'ud, Turki ibn Abd al-Aziz
Al Sa'ud, Turki ibn Faisal
Al Shaykh family
Al Sudayri family
Amin al-Dowleh, Mohammad Husayn
Amini, Abu al-Qasem
Antonius, George
Aranne, Zalman
Arens, Moshe
Aridor, Yoram
Arif, Arif al-
As'ad Wali
Atasi, Jamal al-
Attas, Haidar Abu Bakr al-
Ayn al-Dowleh, Abd al-Majid Mirza
Ayni, Muhsin al-
Ayyubi, Ali Jawdat al-
Aziz, Tariq
Azm, Abd al-Rahman al-
Azm, Haqqi al-
Baban, Jalal Rustam
Barazi, Husni al-
Bashayan, Burhan al-Din
Bayati, Abd al-Wahhab al-
Bazzaz, Abd al Rahman al-
Belgasem, Cherif
Ben Ammar, Tahar
Bin Ayad family
Bishara, Abdullah
Boulam, Benaïssa
Bouteflika, Abdelaziz
Boutros-Ghali, Boutros
Bugeaud de la Piconnerie, Thomas-Robert
Chalabi, Fadhil al-
Daim, Abdullah
Dashti, Ali
Dinur, Ben-Zion
Eban, Abba
Eddé, Henri
Eqbal, Manouchehr
Eshkol, Levi
Etemadi, Nur Ahmad
Faisal ibn Abd al-Aziz Al Sa'ud
Faiz Mohammad, Zikria
Farmanfarma, Abd al-Hoseyn Mirza
Fawzi, Mahmud
Ghali, Butros
Ghazzi, Sa'id al-
Ghorbal, Ashraf
Ghozali, Ahmed
Hadid, Muhammad
Hamedani, Mirza Abu al-Qasem Khan Naser al-Molk
Hani, Nasser al-
Harel, Isser
Hariri, Rafiq Baha'uddin al-
Harun, As'ad

Hashim Khan
Haytham, Muhammad Ali
Herzog, Hayim
Herzog, Ya'acov David
Heskayl, Sasson
Hillel, Shlomo
Humayd ibn Ahmad al-Mualla
Ibrahimi, Ahmed Taleb
Ibrahimi, Lakhdar al
Isma'il, Abd al-Fattah
Isma'il ibn Ibrahim
Jabri, Rashad
Jamali, Muhammad Fadhil al-
Jazrawi, Taha al-
Jundi, Sami al-
Kallas, Khalil
Kasim, Abd al-Ra'uf al-
Khaddam, Abd al-Halim
Khalidi, Husayn Fakhri al-
Kimche, David
Klibi, Chadli
Kollek, Teddy
Labaki, Naum
Lacheraf, Mostefa
Laraki, Ahmad
Lavon, Pinhas
Madani al-Glawi
Mahasin, As'ad
Mahmud Durrani
Makki, Hasan Muhammad
Maktum, Hamdan ibn Rashid al-
Maktum, Maktum ibn Rashid al-
Maktum, Muhammad ibn Rashid al-
Maktum, Rashid ibn Sa'id al-
Malik, Charles Habib
Malkom Khan, Mirza
Masharka, Zuhayr
Masmoudi, Muhammad
Modir al-Molk, Mahmud Khan Jam
Mohammad Ya'qub Barakzai
Mokhber al-Saltaneh, Mirza Mehdi
    Qoli Khan Hedayat
Moshir al-Dowleh, Mirza Hasan
    Khan Pirnia
Moshir al-Saltaneh, Mirza Ahmad
    Khan
Mostowfi al-Mamalek, Mirza Hasan
    Khan
Mutawakkil, Yahya Muhammad al-
Nabi, Belkacem
Namir, Mordekhai
Nammur, Musa
Naqqash, Alfred
Nazir, Hisham
Nezam al-Saltaneh, Mirza Hoseyn
    Qoli Khan Mafi
Nizam al-Din, Abd al-Baqi
Nu'man, Muhammad Ahmad
Nur, Nur Ahmad
Nusayba, Anwar
Osseyran, Adel
Oufkir, Muhammad
Pachachi, Muzahem al-
Pharaon, Rashad
Qavam al-Saltaneh
Qurai, Ahmad Sulaiman

Raslan, Abd al-Hasib al-
Razmara, Ali
Rimawi, Qassim al-
Riyad, Mahmoud
Riyad, Mustafa al-
Sa'd al-Dowleh, Mirza Javan Khan
Sadr, Muhsin
Sa'ed, Mohammad
Sa'id
Sasson, Eliyahu
Shami, Muhammad Abdullah al-
Sharabati, Ahmad al-
Sharaef, Ze'ev
Sharaf, Abd al-Hamid
Shawkat, Naji
Shuqayri, Ahmad
Solh, Kazem al-
Sulayman, Abdullah
Sulayman, Hikmat
Talfah, Adnan Khayr Allah
Taqla, Philippe
Tikriti, Hardan al-
Tutunji, Jamil Pasha
Twayni, Ghassan
Ubaydat, Ahmad
Uqayli, Abd al-Aziz al-
Uthman, Uthman Ahmad
Vazir Afkham, Soltan Ali Khan
Vozuq al-Dowleh, Mirza Hasan
    Khan
Ya'acobi, Gad
Yusufian, Boghos
Zahedi, Ardeshir
Zahedi, Fazlollah
Zayd ibn Husayn

Civil Servants and Diplomats (Ottoman)

Ahmad Rasim
Ahmet İzzet
Ahmet Vefik
Azm, Muhammad Fawzi al-
Bayrakdar, Mustafa
Bustani, Sulayman
Cavit, Mehmet
Cevdet, Ahmed
Chrakian, Artin
Da'ud Pasha
Esendal, Memduh Şevket
Faizi, Ahmad
Ferit, Damat Mehmet
Fuad, Mehmed
Halet, Mehmet Sait
Hüseyin Hilmi
Ibrahim Ethem
Kamil, Kıbrıslı Mehmet
Khalidi, Yusuf Diya al-
Khayr al-Din
Khaznader, Mustafa
Lutfi, Ahmet
Mahmud Nedim
Mehmet Emin, Kibrisli
Mehmet Emin Rauf
Mustafa Reşid
Naqib, Talib al-

Naum Pasha
Nazım, Hüseyin
Noradungian, Gabriel
Qiyomijian, Ohannes
Rustum Pasha
Saffet, Mehmet Esat
Sait, Küçük
Sait Halim
Şekip, Mehmet
Sham'a, Rushdi Bey al-
Talat, Mehmet
Tarhan, Abdülhak Hamit
Umar Pasha
Yusuf Agah

Distinguished Families

Abd al-Hadi family
Aboulker family
Alami family, al-
Al Rashid family
Al Saqr family
Al Shaykh family
Al Sudayri family
Arslan family
As'ad family
Assad family, al-
Atalla family
Azm family
Baban family
Balyan family
Baqri family
Barghuti family
Barzani family
Bin Ayad family
Busnach family
Capsali family
Cattaoui family
Chehab family
Corcos family
Curiel family
Dajani family, al-
Daniel family
De Menasce family
Eddé family
Farhi family
Franjiyya family
Ghanim, al-
Glawi family, al-
Haggiag family
Hajj Ibrahim family, al-
Hakim family
Hirsch, Maurice de
Husayni family, al-
Isa family, al-
Ja'bari family
Jalluli family
Jarallah family
Jumblatt family
Kadoori family
Kaylani family
Khalidi family, al-
Kikhya family
Mukrani family
Muntasir family
Musahiban brothers

Nahum, Halfallah
Nashashibi family
Nu'man, Ahmad Muhammad
Nusayba family
Olayan family
Qasimi imams
Rolo family
Saba family
Sassoon family
Sha'bi family
Shuqayri family
Solh family
Suarès family
Sursuq family
Suwaydi family
Tikriti family
Tuqan family
Zilkha family

Educators and Scholars

Abbud, Marun
Abovian, Khachatur
Adıvar, Abdulhak Adnan
Adıvar, Halide Edip
Aharonian, Avetis
Ahmet Vefik
Ahsa'i, Ahmad al-
Akl, Sa'id
Alusi, Mahmud Shukri al-
Amin, Ahmad
Antun, Farah
Arseven, Celal Esat
Awad, Louis
Ayyad, Kamal
Bahar, Mohammad Taqi
Baramki, Gabriel
Behar, Nissim
Belkind, Meir
Ben Badis, Abd al-Hamid
Bentwich, Norman
Ben-Yehuda, Eliezar
Bint al-Shati
Bliss, Daniel
Bliss, Howard
Boratav, Pertev Naili
Bowman, Humphrey
Brami, Joseph
Browne, Edward Granville
Bustani, Sulayman
Cevdet, Ahmed
Champollion, Jean-François
Cheikho, Louis
Dehkhoda, Ali Akbar
Dewey, John
Dinur, Ben-Zion
Fasi, Muhammad al-
Gaspirali, Ismail Bey
Gennage, Elias
Gökalp, Ziya
Grobba, Fritz Konrad Ferdinand
Hafız, Yasin al-
Harkabi, Yehoshaphat
Hoffman, Yoel
Husayn, Taha
Jabri, Shafiq al-

Jamali, Muhammad Fadhil al-
Kamal, Ahmad
Khalidi, Ahmad al-Samih al-
Khalidi, Walid
Khalidi, Yusuf Diya al-
Khatibi, Abdelkabir
Köprülü, Mehmet Fuat
Kurd Ali, Muhammad
Leibowitz, Yeshayahu
Magnes, Judah
Malik, Charles Habib
Midhat, Ahmet
Mubarak, Muhammad al-
Nasir, Hanna
Nimr, Faris
Nuqrashi, Mahmud Fahmi al-
Pagis, Dan
Rubinstein, Amnon
Sagues, Albert
Saimi, Shams al-Din
Sakakini, Khalil al-
Salim Hasan
Srvantziants, Garegin
Tahtawi, Rifa'a al-Rafi al-
Talebzadeh, Abd al-Rahman
Tanpınar, Ahmed Hamdi
Tarcan, Selim Sirri
Tekin Alp
Ter-Petrossian, Levon
Yadin, Yigal
Yaziji, Ibrahim
Yaziji, Nasif
Yehoshua, Avraham B.
Yöntem, Ali Canip
Yücel, Hasan Ali
Yusuf Kamil
Zaydan, Jurji
Zurayk, Constantine

Entrepreneurs, Economists, Industrialists, and Financiers

Abd al-Aziz abd al-Ghani
Al Saqr family
Amin al-Zarb, Mohammad Hasan
Amit, Meir
Amuzegar, Jahangir
Aqqad, Umar Abd al-Fattah al-
Atalla, Muhammad
Basri, Mir
Baydani, Abd al-Rahman
Chalabi, Fadhil al-
Crane, Charles R.
D'Arcy, William Knox
Eczacıbaşı, Nejat
Gennage, Elias
Ghanim, al-
Gülbenkian, Calouste
Gülersoy, Çelik
Hariri, Rafiq Baha'uddin al-
Hirsch, Maurice de
Holmes, Frank
Horowitz, David
Khashoggi, Adnan
Koç, Vehbi
Lajevardi, Qasem

Lamrani, Muhammad Karim
Lesseps, Ferdinand de
Mond, Alfred Moritz
Montefiore, Moses
Naftali, Perez
Nahum, Halfallah
Namazi, Mehdi
Nubar, Boghos
Politi, Elie
Qattan, Abd al-Muhsin
Qurai, Ahmad Sulaiman
Rutenberg, Pinchas
Sabanci, Sakıp
Sabbagh, Hasib
Sabeti, Habib
Sassoon family
Shammas, Ibrahim al-
Sharif-Emami, Ja'far
Shuster, Morgan
Sihnawi, Antoine
Sursuq family
Tariki, Abdullah
Uthman, Uthman Ahmad
Yamani, Ahmad Zaki

Explorers and Travelers

Barth, Henry
Beaufort, Charles-Marie-Napoléon d'Hautpoul de
Bell, Gertrude
Blunt, Wilfrid Scawen
Burckhardt, Johann Ludwig
Burton, Richard Francis
Chesney, Francis
Doughty, Charles
Elphinstone, Mountstuart
Foucauld, Charles Eugène de
Gordon, Charles
Habshush, Hayyim
Palgrave, William Gifford
Philby, Harry St. John Bridger
Stanhope, Hester
Stark, Freya
Thesiger, Wilfred
Thomas, Bertram
Wilson, Arnold T.

Fiction Writers, Playwrights, Poets, and Literary Essayists

Abasiyanik, Sait Faik
Abbud, Marun
Abd al-Aziz al-Maqalih
Abd al-Quddus, Ihsan
Abd al-Sabur, Salah
Abovian, Khachatur
Abu Risha, Umar
Adıvar, Halide Edip
Adonis
Agnon, Shmuel Yosef
Aharonian, Avetis
Ahmad, Muhammad Sulayman al-
Ahmet Rasim
Akhavan-Saless, Mehdi
Akhondzadeh, Mirza Fath Ali

Akl, Sa'id
Alavi, Bozorg
Al-e Ahmad, Jalal
Alishan, Ghevond
Almog, Ruth
Alterman, Natan
Altinay, Ahmed Refik
Amichai, Yehuda
Amir, Eli
Amrouche, Jean
Ani, Yusuf al-
Applefeld, Aharon
Aqqad, Abbas Mahmud al-
Araj, Wasini al-
Arslan, Adil
Arslan, Shakib
Avidan, David
Awad, Louis
Ayyub, Dhu al-Nun
Bahar, Mohammad Taqi
Ba'labakki, Layla
Bannis, Mohammad
Baraheni, Reza
Baron, Dvora
Basri, Mir
Bayati, Abd al-Wahhab al-
Bayburtlu, Zihni
Bejerano, Maya
Bekir Fahri
Ben Hadouga, Abdelhamid
Berkowitz, Yizhak
Berrada, Mohammad
Bialik, Hayyim Nahman
Bin Diyaf, Muhsen
Bint al-Shati
Bittari, Zoubida
Blunt, Wilfrid Scawen
Boudjedra, Rachid
Boumahdi, Ali
Bourboune, Mourad
Brenner, Yosef Hayyim
Burla, Yehuda
Bustani, Butrus al-
Camus, Albert
Castel-Bloom, Orli
Caylak
Cenap Sehabbettin
Cevdet, Abdullah
Charents, Yeghishe
Chraibi, Driss
Chubak, Sadeq
Dadaloğlu
Dağlarca, Fazıl Hüsnü
Daneshvar, Simin
Darwish, Mahmud
Dashti, Ali
Derdli
Devrim, Izzet Melih
Dib, Mohammed
Djaout, Taher
Djebar, Assia
Dou'aji, Ali al-
Dowlatabadi, Mahmoud
Ecevit, Bülent
Emin Nihat
Erbil, Leyla

Ersoy, Mehmet Akıf
Erzurumlu Emrah
Esendal, Memduh Şevket
Esfandiary, Fereydun
Faiz Mohammad, Zikria
Faraj, Murad
Farès, Nabile
Farrokhzad, Forugh
Fassih, Ismail
Feraoun, Mouloud
Frischmann, David
Galib, Şeyh
Ghallab, Abd al-Karim
Ghanim, Fathi
Gibran, Khalil
Gilboa, Amir
Goldberg, Leah
Golestan, Ibrahim
Golshiri Hushang
Greenberg, Uri Zvi
Guri, Haim
Gürpinar, Hüseyin Rahmi
Hacene, Farouk Zehar
Haddad, Malek
Hakim, Tawfiq al-
Halikarnas Balıkçısı
Hamzawi, Rashid al-
Hareven, Shulamit
Hawi, Khalil
Haykal, Muhammad Husayn
Hazaz, Hayyim
Hedayat, Sadegh
Hikmet, Nazim
Hoffman, Yoel
Huhu, Reda
Husayn, Taha
Ibrahim, Muhammad Hafiz
Idris, Yusuf
Ikhlassi, Walid
Jabal, Badawi al-
Jabotinsky, Vladimir Ze'ev
Jabri, Shafiq al-
Jamalzadeh, Mohammad Ali
Jawahiri, Muhammad Mahdi al-
Kabak, Aaron Abraham
Kanık, Orhan Veli
Kaniuk, Yoram
Karaosmanoğlu, Yakup Kadri
Kasap, Teodor
Kececizade, İzzet
Khal, Yusuf al-
Khatibi, Abdelkabir
Khatib, Kan'an al-
Khraief, Bechir
Knaz, Yehoshua
Kovner, Aba
Kuchek Khan-e Jangali
Laabi, Abdellatif
Lemsine, Aicha
Leskofcali Galip
Levin, Hanoch
Mahfuz, Najib
Mahmoud, Ahmad
Mala'ika, Nazik al-
Mammeri, Moulaoud
Ma'rufi, Abbas

Meddeb, Abdelwahhab
Meged, Aharon
Mehmed Rauf
Michael, Sami
Midhat, Ahmet
Mimouni, Rachid
Mir Sadeghi, Jamal
Muallim Naci
Müftüoğlu Ahmet Hikmet
Musahipzade Celal
Mutran, Khalil
Nabizade Nazım
Nasif, Malak Hifni
Nayır, Yaşar Nabi
Nesin, Nüsret Aziz
Nuri, Abd al-Malik
Ouary, Malek
Oz, Amos
Pagis, Dan
Parsipur, Shahnush
Pertev, Mehmet Sait
Qabbani, Nizar
Raab, Esther
Rabil, Mubarak
Raffi
Rasafi, Ma'ruf al-
Ratosh, Yonatan
Ravanipour, Moniro
Ravikovitch, Dahlia
Recaizade Mahmud Ekrem
Sadullah Paşa
Sa'edi, Gholamhossein
Safvet Ziya
Sa'id Aql
Salim, Ali
Sanu, Ya'qub
Sayfettin, Ömer
Sayyab, Badr Shakir al-
Sebbar, Leila
Sefriou, Ahmad
Sepehri, Sohrab
Seri, Dan-Benaya
Shabbi, Abu al-Qasim al-
Shahada, George
Shamir, Moshe
Shamlu, Ahmad
Shammas, Anton
Sharqawi, Abd al-Rahman al-
Sha'ul, Anwar
Shawqi, Ahmad
Shenhar, Yitzhak
Shidyaq, Ahmad Faris al-
Shlonsky, Avraham
Shufman, Gershon
Shukri, Mohammad
Şinasi, İbrahim
Smilansky, Moshe
Sobol, Yehoshua
Suissa, Albert
Süleyman Nazif
Tahir, Kemal
Tal, Mustafa Wahbi al-
Talebzadeh, Abd al-Rahman
Tammuz, Benyamin
Taner, Haldun
Tanpınar, Ahmed Hamdi

Tarhan, Abdülhak Hamit
Tchernichovsky, Saul
Tepeyran, Ebubekir Hazím
Tevfik Fikret
Tlili, Mustapha
Tunisi, Bayram al-
Tuqan, Fadwa
Ujayli, Abd al-Salam al-
Uşaklığıl, Halit Ziya
Vecihi
Wallach, Yona
Wattar, al-Taher
Wieseltier, Meir
Yacine, Kateb
Yaziji, Ibrahim
Yaşar, Kemal
Yehoshua, Avraham B.
Yizhar, S.
Yöntem, Ali Canip
Yücel, Hasan Ali
Yurdakul, Mehmet Emin
Yusuf Kamil
Zach, Natan
Zähawi, Jamil Sidqi
Zangwill, Israel
Zaydan, Jurji
Zelda
Zili, Ridha
Zinni, Omar
Zohrab, Krikor

Historians and Political Scientists

Adamiyat, Fereydun
Alishan, Ghevond
Altinay, Ahmed Refik
Alusi, Mahmud Shukri al-
Amin, Ahmad
Arif, Arif al-
Ataullah, Mehmed
Barkan, Ömer Lutfi
Cevdet, Ahmed
Chamchian, Mikayel
Champollion, Jean-François
Darwaza, Muhammad Izzat
Dinur, Ben-Zion
Ergin, Osman Nuri
Esad, Mehmet
Faiz Mohammad
Flapan, Simha
Jabarti, Abd al-Rahman al-
Koçu, Reşat Ekrem
Kurd Ali, Muhammad
Malcolm, John
Medani, Tewfiq al-
Moshir al-Dowleh, Mirza Hasan
    Khan Pirnia
Nasiri, Ahmad ibn Khalid al-
Sykes, Percy Molesworth

Journalists and Social Essayists

Abalioğlu, Yunus Nadi
Abbud, Marun
Abd al-Quddus, Ihsan
Abd al-Sabur, Salah

Adıvar, Halide Edip
Aflaq, Michel
Ahad Ha-Am
Ahmet İhsan To'kgoz
Ahmet Rasim
Ajilani, Munir al-
Akçura, Yusuf
Akhondzadeh, Mirza Fath Ali
Alavi, Bozorg
Al-e Ahmad, Jalal
Alishan, Ghevond
Ali Suavi
Altinay, Ahmed Refik
Amery, Leopold Charles
Amin, Qasim
Anderson, Terry
Antun, Farah
Aqqad, Abbas Mahmud al-
Arif, Arif al-
Arslan, Shakib
Arsuzi, Zaki al-
Asmar, Fawzi al-
Atay, Salıh Rifki
Avneri, Uri
Ayyub, Dhu al-Nun
Aziz, Tariq
Azm, Rafiq al-
Azuri, Najib
Bahar, Mohammad Taqi
Ba'labakki, Layla
Bayram V, Muhammad
Bazzaz, Abd al Rahman al-
Başiretci, Ali
Ben-Yehuda, Eliezar
Ben-Zvi, Yizhak
Berkowitz, Yizhak
Brami, Joseph
Brenner, Yosef Hayyim
Bustani, Sulayman
Castro, Léon
Cattan, Henry
Caylak
Cevdet, Abdullah
Churchill, William
Cohen, Ge'ula
Darwish, Mahmud
Dashti, Ali
Dehkhoda, Ali Akbar
Ebüzziya Tevfik
Ecevit, Bülent
Esad, Mehmet
Fanon, Frantz
Faraj, Murad
Frischmann, David
Ganim, Halil
Gaspirali, Ismail Bey
Ghallab, Abd al-Karim
Ghanim, Fathi
Gosn, Hanna
Gülek, Kasım
Güler, Ara
Guri, Haim
Gürpinar, Hüseyin Rahmi
Haddad, Tahir al-
Hadria-Cohen, Elie
Hakim, Tawfiq al-

Hamba, Ali Bash-
Hareven, Shulamit
Haykal, Muhammad Hasanayn
Haykal, Muhammad Husayn
Huhu, Reda
Idris, Yusuf
İleri, Celal Nuri
İpekci, Abdi
Isa, Isa al-
Isa family, al-
İshaq, Adib
Jabotinsky, Vladimir Ze'ev
Jawdah, Michel Abu
Kabbara, Sami
Kanafani, Ghassan
Kanbar, Ahmad
Kaniuk, Yoram
Karacan, Ali Naci
Karaosmanoğlu, Yakup Kadri
Kasap, Teodor
Kasravi, Ahmad
Katznelson, Berl
Keinan, Amos
Khalid, Khalid Muhammad
Kimche, David
Kisakürek, Necip Fazıl
Labaki, Naum
Luqman, Muhammad Ali
Madani, Abdullah al-
Maluf, Rushdi
Metni, Nassib
Midhat, Ahmet
M'Rabet, Fadela
Musa, Salama
Mutran, Khalil
Nadi, Yunus
Naftali, Perez
Namık Kemal
Nasir, Najib
Nimr, Faris
Politi, Elie
Qutb, Sayyid
Sa'dawi, Nawal al-
Saimi, Shams al-Din
Sanu, Ya'qub
Sarruf, Ya'qub
Sayyid, Ahmad Lutfi al-
Sfar, Bashir
Sha'arawi, Huda al-
Shafiq, Durriyya
Sha'ul, Anwar
Shidyaq, Ahmad Faris al-
Simavi, Sedat
Şinasi, İbrahim
Smilansky, Moshe
Smolenskin, Peretz
Sokolow, Nahum
Solh, Alia al-
Tabataba'i, Ziya
Tahtawi, Rifa'a al-Rafi al-
Tammuz, Benyamin
Taner, Haldun
Taqla, Bishara
Taqla, Salim
Tevetoğlu, Fethi
Turki, Fawwaz

Twayni, Ghassan
Uşaklıgıl, Halit Ziya
Yata, Ali
Ziya, Abdülhamit
Zohrab, Krikor

Labor Leaders

Achour, Habib
Arlosoroff, Haim
Ben Salah, Ahmed
Ben Seddiq, Mahjoub
Ben-Zvi, Yizhak
Borochov, Ber
Hached, Ferhat
Haddad, Tahir al-
Katznelson, Berl
Kessar, Israel
Luz, Kadish
Minz, Benjamin
Nir, Nahum
Remez, Moshe David
Shahabi, Hisham al-
Sprinzak, Joseph
Tabenkin, Yitzhak

Lawyers and Jurisprudence Scholars

Abd al-Raziq, Ali
Adalat-Khaneh
Antaki, Rizq Allah
Asyun, Fath Allah
Bazzaz, Abd al Rahman al-
Ben Simeon, Raphael Aaron
Brandeis, Louis Dembitz
Cattan, Henry
Cevdet, Ahmed
Ghali, Butros
Ghazzi, Sa'id al-
Golpayagani, Mohammad Reza
Ha-Cohen, Mordechai
Hakim, Yusuf al-
Haykal, Muhammad Husayn
Khalkhali, Mohammed Sadeq
Khoury, George-Paul
Kuzbari, Ma'mun al-
Nubar, Boghos
Paul-Boncour, Joseph
Rushdi, Husayn
Sayyid, Ahmad Lutfi al-
Siba'i, Mustafa al-
Tamir, Shmuel
Tayyara, Sami
Tekin Alp
Trad, Petro
Ziwar, Ahmad

Medical Professionals and Scientists

Adıvar, Abdulhak Adnan
Arafat, Fathi
Atasi, Jamal al-
Ataullah, Mehmed
Clot, Antoine Barthélémy
Fanon, Frantz

Jandali, Farhan
Karame, Elie
Khatib, Ahmad al-
Ne'eman, Yuval
Pharaon, Rashad
Ratebzad, Anahita
Sa'dawi, Nawal al-
Sartawi, Issam
Sati, Shawkat al-
Shumayyil, Shibli
Tchernichovsky, Saul
Tutunji, Jamil Pasha
Weizmann, Chaim

Military Leaders

Abbud, Ibrahim
Abd al-Rashid Doestam
Abd al-Razzaq, Arif
Abdelghani, Benhamed Mohammed
Abdullahi, Muhammad Turshain
Abu Asaf, Amin
Abu Mansur, Fadlallah
Abu Nuwwar, Ali
Ahmet İzzet
Ait Ahmed, Hocine
Allenby, Edmund Henry
Al Sabah, Mubarak al-Abd Allah
  al-Jabir
Alwan, Jasim
Amin, Abd al-Mutallib al-
Amir, Abd al-Hakim
Amri, Hasan al-
Andranik, Ozanian
Annab, Radi
Aoun, Michel
Arfa, Hasan
Argoud, Antoine
Asad, Hafiz al-
Askari, Ja'far al-
Assassa, Muwaffaq
Atatürk, Mustafa Kemal
Atfi, Abdullah
Auchinleck, Claude
Awdatallah, Tu'ma al-
Baghdadi, Abd al-Latif al-
Bakhtiar, Timur
Bakr, Ahmad Hasan al-
Bar-Lev, Haim
Bayrakdar, Mustafa
Beaufort, Charles-Marie-Napoléon
  d'Hautpoul de
Belgasem, Cherif
Bellounis, Mohamed
Benjedid, Chadli
Bizri, Afif al-
Bonaparte, Napoléon
Boumédienne, Houari
Boussouf, Abd al-Hafid
Bugeaud de la Piconnerie,
  Thomas-Robert
Bull, Odd
Bustani, Emile al-
Carmel, Moshe
Catroux, Georges
Cebesoy, Ali Fuat

Cemal Paça
Challe, Maurice
Chehab, Fu'ad
Clayton, Gilbert
Daghistani, Ghazi al-
Dayan, Moshe
Dayri, Akram al-
Deedes, Wyndham
De Gaulle, Charles
Delouvrier, Paul
Dentz, Henri-Fernand
Dlimi, Ahmed
Dunsterville, Lionel C.
Eisenhower, Dwight David
Eitan, Rafael
Enver Paşa
Fawzi, Muhammad
Galili, Israel
Garang, John
Ghanem, Iskander
Ghanim, Muhammad
Ghashmi, Ahmad Husayn
Ghaydan, Sa'dun
Giraud, Henri
Glubb, John Bagot
Goltz, Kolmar von der
Gordon, Charles
Goren, Shlomo
Graziani, Rodolfo
Grivas, Georgios Theodoros
Gur, Mordechai
Gürsel, Cemal
Haddad, Sa'd
Haines, Stafford Bettesworth
Halil Pasha
Hamdi, Ibrahim al-
Hashimi, Taha al-
Hashimi, Yasim al-
Hayari, Ali al-
Herzog, Hayim
Hiddaw, Husayn
Hinnawi, Sami al-
Hobeyka, Elie
Hunaydi, Ahmad al-
Husayni, Ibrahim al-
Hüseyin, Avni
Husrev, Mehmet Koja
Ibrahim ibn Muhammad Ali
Izzedine, Jado
Jadid, Ghassan
Jamil, Naji
Jibril, Ahmad
Jundi, Abd al-Karim al-
Jundi, Khalid al-
Kaid, Ahmed
Kallas, Bahij
Karabekir, Kazım
Karam, Yusef
Kassem, Abd al-Karim
Kisch, Frederick Hermann
Kitchener, Horatio Herbert
Kléber, Jean-Baptiste
Kuzbari, Haydar al-
Lahad, Antoine
Lawrence, Thomas Edward
Liman von Sanders, Otto

Lyautey, Louis-Herbert Gonzalve
Mahdawi, Fazil Abbas al-
Mahmud, Nur al-Din
Malcolm, John
Malki, Adnan al-
Ma'ruf, Muhammad
Maude, Frederick Stanley
Mehmet Ali, Damat
Menou, Jacques François
Mezzian, Muhammad
Mir, Ahmad al-
Misri, Aziz Ali al-
Moda'i, Yitzhak
Moltke, Helmuth von
Montgomery, Bernard Law
Mubarak, Husni
Muhammad Ali
Muhsin, Zahayr
Muhtar, Gazi Ahmet
Muhyi al-Din, Khalid
Muhyi al-Din, Zakariyya
Munassir, Qasim
Nafuri, Amin al-
Naguib, Muhammad
Nahlawi, Abd al-Karim
Nasser, Gamal Abdel
Ne'eman, Yuval
Nezzar, Khaled
Nizam al-Din, Tawfiq
Njeym, Jean
Numeiri, Muhammad Ja'far
Orbay, Hüseyin Rauf
Osman, Gazi
Oufkir, Muhammad
Oveisi, Gholam Ali
Pa'il, Me'ir
Peake, Frederick Gerard
Peled, Mattityahu
Pelly, Lewis
Peres, Shimon
Plumer, Herbert Charles Onslow
Qaddafi, Muammar al-
Qannut, Abd al-Ghani
Qawuqji, Fawzi al-
Qutayni, Rashid
Rabin, Yitzhak
Razmara, Ali
Rommel, Erwin
Sabbagh, Salah al-Din al-
Sabri, Ali
Sadat, Anwar al-
Sadiq, Yusuf
Safa, Muhammad
Salih, Ali Abdallah
Sarraj, Abd al-Hammid
Sebastiani, Horace
Şevket, Mahmut
Shakkur, Yusuf
Sharon, Ariel
Shawwaf, Abd al-Wahhab al-
Shazli, Sa'd al-Din
Shishakli, Salah
Shuqayr, Shawkat
Sidqi, Bakr
Süleyman Hüsnü
Sunay, Cevdet

Suwaydani, Ahmad
Sykes, Percy Molesworth
Tabaqjali, Nazim al-Kami
Tal, Abdullah al-
Talib, Naji
Templer, Gerald
Tikriti, Hardan al-
Tlas, Mustafa
Townshend, Charles
Trumpeldor, Yosef
Türkeş, Alparslan
Umran, Muhammad
Urabi, Ahmad
Wahhab, Abd al-Raqib Abd al-
Wavell, Archibald Percival
Weizman, Ezer
Wingate, Charles Orde
Wingate, Reginald
Yahya, Tahir
Yariv, Aharon
Yunis, Jabir Abu Bakr
Zahedi, Fazlollah
Za'im, Husni al-
Zamir, Zvi
Zbiri, Tahar

Musicians, Composers, and Singers

Arnita, Salvador
Asmahan
Atrash, Farid al-
Dadaloğlu
Darwish, Sayyid
Dede Zekai
Dellalzade, İsmail
Derdli
Fuleyhan, Anis
Haci, Arif
Hafiz, Abd al-Halim
Hammamzade İsmail Dede
Huda, Nur al-
Kemani, Sadi İsilay
Komitas
Muhlis Sabahattin
Rauf Yekta
Refik Fersan
Rhabani Brothers
Saadettin Kaynak
Şakir Ağa
Sanjari, Heshmat
Saygun, Ahmed Adnan
Selçuk, Munir Nurettin
Shemer, Naomi
Suphi Ezgi
Tanburi Cemil
Umm Kulthum
Vaziri, Qamar al-Moluk

Nationalists (Eighteenth and Nineteenth Century)

Abd al-Qadir
Ahmad Bey of Constantine
Ahmad Bey Husayn
Ahmad, Muhammad
Andranik, Ozanian
Bek, Davit

Bodenheimer, Max
Gaspirali, Ismail Bey
Herzl, Theodor
Hess, Moses
Kalischer, Hirsch
Kawakibi, Abd al-Rahman al-
Lilienblum, Moshe Leib
Mohilever, Samuel
Montefiore, Moses
Pinsker, Leo
Rothschild, Edmond de
Sapir, Joseph
Smolenskin, Peretz
Suwaydi family
Syrkin, Nachman
Urabi, Ahmad

Nationalists (Twentieth Century)

Abane, Ramdane
Abbas, Ferhat
Abd al-Aziz al-Maqalih
Abd al-Aziz ibn Sa'ud Al Sa'ud
Abd al-Hadi, Awni
Abu Da'ud
Abu Himara
Aflaq, Michel
Ahmad Hibat Allah
Ahmad ibn Muhammad al-Raysuni
Ahmad Shah Mas'ud
Ait Ahmed, Hocine
Akçura, Yusuf
Alami, Musa al-
Alawi, Mawlay al-Arabi al-
Andranik, Ozanian
Askari, Ja'far al-
Atasi, Hashim al-
Atatürk, Mustafa Kemal
Atrash, Sultan Pasha al-
Ayni, Muhsin al-
Azm, Rafiq al-
Azuri, Najib
Azzam, Abd al-Rahman al-
Balafrej, Ahmed
Banna, Sabri al-
Barzani, Mas'ud al-
Barzani, Mustafa
Barzani family
Baydh, Ali Salim al-
Begin, Menachem
Behar, Nissim
Bellounis, Mohamed
Ben Ammar, Tahar
Ben Badis, Abd al-Hamid
Ben Barka, Mehdi
Ben Bella, Ahmed
Ben Boulaid, Moustafa
Ben-Gurion, David
Ben Khedda, Ben Youssef
Ben M'Hidi, Muhammad Larbi
Ben Yusuf, Salah
Bitat, Rabah
Bodenheimer, Max
Borochov, Ber
Boudiaf, Mohamed
Boumédienne, Houari

Bourguiba, Habib
Boussouf, Abd al-Hafid
Brandeis, Louis Dembitz
Castro, Léon
Chenik, Muhammad
Dajani, Arif al-
Darwaza, Muhammad Izzat
Darwish, Ishaq
De Haan, Yaakov Yisrael
Didouche, Mourad
Eshkol, Levi
Fanon, Frantz
Farhat al-Zawi
Farid, Muhammad
Fasi, Allal al-
Fasi, Muhammad al-
Gailani, Ahmad
Garang, John
Ghuri, Emile al-
Goldmann, Nahum
Gordon, Aaron David
Grivas, Georgios Theodoros
Gruenbaum, Yizhak
Gruner, Dov
Guri, Haim
Habash, George
Haddad, Tahir al-
Haddad, Wadi
Hadj, Messali al-
Hadria-Cohen, Elie
Hakim, Adnan al-
Hamba, Ali Bash-
Hananu, Ibrahim
Hasan, Hani al-
Hasan, Khalid al-
Hawatma, Nayif
Haydar, Sa'id
Husayn, Ahmad
Husayni, Abd al-Qadir al-
Husayni, Jamal al-
Husayni, Muhammad Amin al-
Husayni, Musa Kazim al-
Husayn ibn Ali
Hut, Shafiq al-
Jabotinsky, Vladimir Ze'ev
Jibril, Ahmad
Jifri, Muhammad Ali
Kamil, Mustafa
Kanafani, Ghassan
Karaosmanoğlu, Yakup Kadri
Kassem, Abd al-Karim
Katznelson, Berl
Kaylani, Rashid Ali al-
Khalaf, Salah
Khalis, Mohammad Unis
Khattabi, Muhammed ibn Abd
    al-Karim al-
Khayr-Eddine, Mohammad
Khider, Mohamed
Kisch, Frederick Hermann
Kook, Abraham Isaac Hacohen
Kovner, Aba
Krim, Belkacem
Kubba, Muhammad Mahdi
Lacheraf, Mostefa
Lahouel, Hocine

Levin, Shmaryahu
Levin, Yizhak Meir
Levinger, Moshe
Levontin, Zalman
Lyazidi, Ahmad Muhammad
Mahmud of Sulaymania
Maimon, Yehudah Leib Hacohen
Makarios II
Makarios III
Manoogian, Vazgen
Mardam, Jamil
Mehiri, Taieb
Messaadia, Mohammad Cherif
Minz, Benjamin
Misri, Aziz Ali al-
Mond, Alfred Moritz
Mossadegh, Mohammad
Muhsin, Zuhayr
Mujaddedi, Sebghatullah
Mukhtar, Umar al-
Murat, Mehmet
Nadi, Yunus
Nasrullah, Maulawi
Nhaisi, Elia
Nordau, Max
Nouira, Hedi
Nu'man, Ahmad Muhammad
Nusayba, Sari
Pasdermajian, Garegin
Qaddumi, Faruq
Qahtan al-Sha'bi
Qasemlu, Abd al-Rahman
Qassam, Izz al-Din al-
Qawuqji, Fawzi al-
Qotbzadeh, Sadeq
Quwatli, Shukri al-
Rosen, Pinhas
Rothschild, Edmond de
Ruppin, Arthur
Rutenberg, Pinchas
Sab'awi, Yunis al-
Sabbagh, Salah al-Din al-
Sadawi, Bashir
Sapir, Joseph
Sartawi, Issam
Sfar, Tahar
Sha'arawi, Huda al-
Sha'bi family
Shahbandar, Abd al-Rahman
Shamir, Moshe
Shamir, Yitzhak
Shamlan, Abd al-Aziz
Shammas, Ibrahim al-
Shapira, Hayyim Moshe
Shawkat, Sami
Shazar, Shneour Zalman
Shuqayri, Ahmad
Shuqayri family
Silver, Abba Hillel
Sokolow, Nahum
Solh, Kazem al-
Solh, Taki al-Din al-
Stern, Abraham
Suwaydi family
Suwayhli, Ramadan al-
Syrkin, Nachman

Szold, Henrietta
Tabaqjali, Nazim al-Kami
Tabenkin, Yitzhak
Talabani, Jalal
Tamimi, Amin al-
Tekin Alp
Tevetoğlu, Fethi
Tharwat, Abd al-Khaliq
Trumpeldor, Yosef
Türkeş, Alparslan
Ussishkin, Menahem
Valensi, Alfred
Vratsian, Simon
Wazir, Khalil al-
Wazzani, Muhammad Hassan al-
Weizmann, Chaim
Wise, Stephen S.
Wolffsohn, David
Ya'ari, Me'ir
Yahiaoui, Mohmed Saleh
Yellin-Mor, Natan
Yurdakul, Mehmet Emin
Yusuf, Salah ibn
Zaghlul, Sa'd
Zaydan, Jurji

Philosophers and Religious Leaders, Thinkers, and Writers

Abd al-Aziz ibn Sa'ud Al Sa'ud
Abd al-Rahman al-Mahdi
Abduh, Muhammad
Abulafia, Hayyim Nissim
Abulafia, Itzhaq Moshe
Adıvar, Abdulhak Adnan
Afghani, Jamal al-Din al-
Ahmad, Muhammad
Ahsa'i, Ahmad al-
Alkalai, Judah ben Solomon Hai
Al Shaykh family
Alusi, Mahmud Shukri al-
Ardebili, Abd al-Karim Musavi
Bab, al-
Banna, Hasan al-
Beheshti, Mohammad
Belkind, Meir
Ben Simeon, Raphael Aaron
Bliss, Howard
Borujerdi, Hosayn
Brami, Joseph
Buber, Martin
Cyril IV
Cyril V
Cyril VI
Demetrius II
Faraj, Murad
Finn, James
Foucauld, Charles Eugène de
Gailani, Ahmad
Ghannushi, Rashid
Golpayagani, Mohammad Reza
Goren, Shlomo
Ha-Cohen, Mordechai
Haham Bashi
Hajri, Abdullah al-
Hakim family

Hayim, Yusef
Hazzan, Elijah Bekhor
Herzog, Izhak Halevi
Herzog, Ya'acov David
Ibrahimi, Bashir
John XIX
Kahane, Meir
Kalischer, Hirsch
Kashani, Abu al-Qasem
Kashif al-Ghita family
Kattani, Muhammad ibn Abd
al-Kabir al-
Khalid, Khalid Muhammad
Khamene'i, Ali
Kho'i Najafi
Khomeini, Ahmad
Khomeini, Ruhollah
Khrimian, Mkrtich
Kook, Abraham Isaac Hacohen
Kook, Zvi Yehuda
Leibowitz, Yeshayahu
Lilienblum, Moshe Leib
Ma al-Aynayn
Magnes, Judah
Mahdavi-Kani, Mohammad Reza
Maimon, Yehuda Leib Hacohen
Makarios II
Makarios III
Makarius III
Maratghi, Mustafa al-
Mark VIII
Meushi, Paul Peter
Modarres, Sayyed Hasan
Mohilever, Samuel
Montazeri, Hosayn Ali
Motahhari, Mortaza
Muhammad, Prophet of Islam
Musa Kazım Efendi
Nahum, Hayyim
Nerses
Nissim, Isaac
Nuri, Ali Akbar Nateq-e
Nuri, Fazlollah
Nursi, Said
Ormanian, Maghakia
Ouziel, Ben Zion Meir Hai
Peter VII
Qafih, Yihye ben Solomon
Qutb, Sayyid
Rafsanjani, Hashemi
Rida, Rashid
Sadr, Muhammad Baqir al-
Sadr, Musa
Salant, Samuel
Sanusi, Ahmad al-Sharif al-
Sanusi, Muhammad ibn Ali al-
Sebastatsi, Mekhitar
Shaltut, Muhammad
Shari'ati, Ali
Shariatmadari, Kazem
Shenouda III
Shim'un, Mar
Shirazi, Mirza Hasan
Shitreet, Bebor
Shuqayri, As'ad al-
Silver, Abba Hillel

Somekh, Abdallah
Srvantziants, Garegin
Suwaydi family
Tabataba'i, Mohammad
Taha, Mahmoud Muhamed
Turabi, Hasan al-
Uqbi, Tayyib al-
Vazhapetian, Nerses
Waite, Terry
Wise, Stephen S.
Yerevantsi, Simeon
Yosef, Ovadiah
Zohar, Uri
Zonnenfeld, Yosef Hayyim

Political Leaders
(Nineteenth Century)

Amin al-Dowleh, Mirza Ali Khan
Amin al-Dowleh, Mohammad
  Husayn
Amin al-Soltan, Ali-Asghar
Amir Kabir, Mirza Taqi Khan
Bonaparte, Napoléon
Chehab, Bashir
Curzon, George Nathaniel
Disraeli, Benjamin
Khayr al-Din
Khaznader, Mustafa
Makram, Umar
Temple, Henry John

Political Leaders (Twentieth
Century)

Abbas, Mahmud
Abd al-Aziz Abd al-Ghani
Abd al-Huda
Abd al-Karim, Ahmad
Abd-Allah ibn Yahya Hamid
  al-Din
Abd al-Masih, Georges
Abd al-Rahman al-Mahdi
Abd al-Raziq, Ali
Abd al-Razzaq, Arif
Abdelghani, Benhamed Mohammed
Abdesselam, Belaid
Abi Shahla, Habib
Abu Fadel, Munir
Abuhatzeira, Aharon
Accari, Nazim
Adli
Aflaq, Michel
Ahardane, Majoub
Aharonian, Avetis
Ahmad, Muhammad Sulyaman al-
Ahmad ibn Muhammad
  al-Raysuni
Ahmar, Abdullah ibn Husayn al-
Ajilani, Munir al-
Ala, Hoseyn
Alam, Amir Asadollah
Al Bu Sa'id, Tariq ibn Taymur
Ali Nasir Muhammad al-Hasani
Allon, Yigal
Al Sa'ud, Sultan ibn Abd al-Aziz
Amin, Hafizullah

Amini, Ali
Ammun, Dawud
Amuzegar, Jamshid
Antaki, Rizq Allah
Antar, Ali Ahmad Nasser
Arafat, Yasir
Arif, Abd al-Rahman
Arif, Abd al-Salam
Arslan, Adil
Arslan, Faysal
Arslan, Majid
Arslan, Shakib
Arsuzi, Zaki al-
As'ad, Ahmad
Asad, Hafiz al-
As'ad, Kamil
As'ad family
Asali, Faysal al-
Asali, Sabri al-
Asali, Shukri al-
Askari, Ja'far al-
Asnaj, Abdullah Ali
Atasi, Hashim al-
Atasi, Jamal al-
Atasi, Nur al-Din al-
Atatürk, Mustafa Kemal
Atrash, Mansur al-
Avneri, Uri
Ayn al-Dowleh, Abd al-Majid
  Mirza
Ayyubi, Mahmud al-
Azhari, Isma'il
Aziz, Tariq
Azm, Shafiq Mu'ayyad al-
Azzam, Abd al-Rahman al-
Baban, Ahmad Mukhtar
Baban, Jamal Rashid
Badran, Mudar
Baghdadi, Abd al-Latif al-
Bahnini, Muhammad
Bakhtiar, Shahpur
Bakhtiari, Najaf Qoli Khan Samsam
  al-Soltaneh
Bakkush, Hadi
Bakr, Ahmad Hasan al-
Balafrej, Ahmed
Bani Sadr, Abolhasan
Barazi, Husni al-
Barmada, Mustafa
Barondi, Fakhr al-
Baruni, Sulayman al-
Bar-Yehudah, Israel
Bayar, Celal
Bayat, Mortaza Qoli
Baydh, Ali Salim al-
Bazargan, Mahdi
Bazzaz, Abd al Rahman al-
Begin, Menachem
Beheshti, Mohammad
Ben Aharon, Yitzhak
Ben Ali, Zayn al-Abidine
Ben Bella, Ahmed
Ben-Gurion, David
Benjedid, Chadli
Ben Jelloun, Umar
Ben Khedda, Ben Youssef

Ben-Porat, Mordechai
Ben Salah, Ahmed
Bentov, Mordekhai
Ben Yusuf, Salah
Ben-Zvi, Yizhak
Berri, Nabi
Bilhayr, Abd al-Nabi
Bitar, Salah al-Din al-
Bitat, Rabah
Bouabid, Abderrahim
Boucetta, Muhammad
Boumédienne, Houari
Bourguiba, Habib
Brahimi, Abdelhamid
Brezhnev, Leonid Ilyich
Burg, Yosef
Bush, George Herbert Walker
Buzo, Ali
Carmel, Moshe
Carter, Jimmy
Cebesoy, Ali Fuat
Cemal Paça
Chader, Joseph
Chadirchi, Kamil
Chamoun, Camille
Chamoun, Dany
Chehab, Fu'ad
Chehab, Khalid
Churchill, Winston S.
Çiller, Tansu
Clemenceau, Georges
Cohen, Ge'ula
Curzon, George Nathaniel
Dabbas, Charles
Daddah, Mokhtar Ould
Daftari, Ahmad Matin
Dajani, Hasan Sidqi al-
Darwaza, Muhammad Izzat
Darwish, Ishaq
Daud, Muhammad
Dawalibi, Ma'ruf al-
Dayan, Moshe
De Gaulle, Charles
Demirel, Süleyman
Denktash, Rauf
Ecevit, Bülent
Eddé, Emile
Eddé, Raymond
Eden, Anthony
Ehrlich, Simha
Eisenhower, Dwight David
Eitan, Rafael
Eldad, Israel
Enver Paşa
Erbakan, Necmeddin
Eshkol, Levi
Etemadi, Nur Ahmad
Evren, Kenan
Fahum, Khalid Al-
Farhad, Ghulam Muhammad
Farraj, Ya'qub al-
Fathallah Khan Akbar, Mansur
Fayez, Akef al-
Foroughi, Mirza Mohammad Ali
    Khan Zaka al-Molk
Franjiyya, Hamid

Franjiyya, Sulayman
Franjiyya, Tony
Geagea, Samir
Ghali, Butros
Ghanim, Wahib
Ghannushi, Rashid
Ghaydan, Sa'dun
Guedira, Ahmad Rida
Gürsel, Cemal
Haffar, Lutfi al-
Hafiz, Amin al-
Hafiz, Amin Isma'il al-
Hajir, Abd al-Hoseyn
Hakim, Adnan al-
Hakim, Hasan al-
Hakimi, Ibrahim
Halabi, Muhammad Ali al-
Hamadi, Sabri
Hamdi, Ibrahim al-
Hamdun, Mustafa
Hammer, Zevulun
Hashim, Ibrahim
Hashim, Joseph
Hashimi, Yasin al-
Hawi, George
Hawmad, Abd al-Wahhab
Hawrani, Akram al-
Haykal, Muhammad Husayn
Hazan, Ya'akov
Hekmatyar, Golbuddin
Hilmi, Ahmad
Hilu, Charles
Hilu, Pierre
Hoss, Salim al-
Hoveyda, Amir Abbas
Husayn, Husayn al-
Husayni, Sa'id al-
Husayn Oweyni
Hussein, Saddam
Ibrahim, Abd al-Fattah
Ibrahim, Abdullah
Ibrahim, Izzat
Ibrahim ibn Yahya Hamid
    al-Din
Idris al-Sayyid Muhammad
    al-Sanusi
Ilyan, Mikha'il
İnönü, Erdal
İnönü, İsmet
Iryani, Abd al-Rahman al-
Isa, Isa al-
Isma'il, Abd al-Qadir
Ja'bari, Muhammad Ali
Jabiri, Ihsan al-
Jabiri, Sa'dallah al-
Jabr, Salih
Jadid, Ghassan
Jallud, Abd al-Salam
Johnson, Lyndon Baines
Joseph, Dov
Jumayyil, Amin
Jumayyil, Bashir
Jumayyil, Pierre
Jumblatt, Kamal
Jumblatt, Walid
Kabbara, Sami

Kahana, Kalman
Kahane, Meir
Kaid, Ahmed
Kalakani, Abd al-Majid
Kanna, Khalil
Karame, Abd al-Hamid
Karame, Elie
Karame, Rashid
Karmal, Babrak
Kassem, Abd al-Karim
Kaylani, Abd al-Rahman al-
Kaylani, Rashid Ali al-
Kayyali, Abd al-Rahman
Kayyali, Fakhir al-
Kennedy, John Fitzgerald
Khalaf, Abd al-Hadi
Khal'atbari, Mohammad Vali Khan
    Sepahsalar-e Tonekaboni
Khatib, Ahmad al-
Khatisian, Alexander
Khaz'al Khan
Khomeini, Ruhollah
Khrushchev, Nikita S.
Khulayfawi, Abd al-Rahman
Khuri, Bishara al-
Khuri, Khalil al-
Khyber, Mir Akbar
Kianuri, Nur al-Din
Kikhya family
Kikhya, Rushdi al-
Kol, Moshe
Kollek, Teddy
Koprülü, Mehmet Fuat
Kubbara, Sami
Kudsi, Nazim al-
Kuzbari, Ma'mun al-
Kzar, Nazim
Lansdowne, Henry Charles Keith
    Petty Fitzmaurice
Lawzi, Ahmad
Levy, David
Lloyd George, David
MacDonald, Ramsay
Madani, Abassi al-
Madani, Abdullah al-
Madani, Ahmad
Mahir, Ahmad
Mahir, Ali
Mahmud, Muhammad
Maiwandwal, Mohammad Hashim
Majali, Hazza' al-
Makarios III
Makhus, Ibrahim
Manoogian, Vazgen
Mansur, Hasan Ali
Mansur al-Molk, Rajabali
Maratghi, Mustafa al-
Maziq, Husayn
Meir, Golda
Menemencioğlu, Turgut
Mestiri, Ahmad
Midfa'i, Jamil al-
Minz, Benjamin
Mir, Juliette al-
Mollet, Guy
Mossadegh, Mohammad

Mubarak, Husni
Mubarak, Muhammad al-
Muhammad, Aziz
Muhyi al-Din, Khalid
Muhyi al-Din, Zakariyya
Mujaddedi, Sebghatullah
Mulki, Fawzi al-
Munla, Saadi
Mustafa Suphi
Mzali, Mohammed
Nabahani, Taki al-Din
Nabulsi, Sulayman al-
Naguib, Muhammad
Nahhas, Mustafa al-
Na'imi Mirza Nasr Allah Khan
    al-Dowleh
Najibullah
Nashashibi, Fakhri al-
Nashashibi, Raghib Bey al-
Nasser, Gamal Abdel
Navon, Yizhak
Netanyahu, Benjamin
Nir, Nahum
Nixon, Richard Milhous
Nouira, Hedi
Nubar, Boghos (Armenian)
Nubar, Boghos (Egyptian)
Nuqrashi, Mahmud Fahmi al-
Orbay, Hüseyin Rauf
Ozal, Turgut
Peres, Shimon
Qahtan al-Sha'bi
Qansu, Assem
Quwatli, Shukri al-
Raad, In'am
Rabbani, Burhanuddin
Rabin, Yitzhak
Rafsanjani, Hashemi
Raja'i, Mohammad Ali
Rajavi, Masud
Ratebzad, Anahita
Reagan, Ronald
Rifa'i, Abd al-Mun'im al-
Rifa'i, Nur al-Din al-
Rifa'i, Samir
Rifa'i, Zaid al-
Roosevelt, Franklin Delano
Rubinstein, Amnon
Russell, John
Saad, Habib al-
Saad, Ma'ruf
Sa'ada, Antun
Saade, George
Sa'd, Habib al-
Sa'di, Ali Salih
Sabri, Ali
Sadat, Anwar al-
Sa'dun, Abd al-Muhsin al-
Sahib ibn Isa
Sa'id, Nuri al-
Sa'id al-Mufti
Salam, Malik
Salam, Sa'ib
Salih, Ali Abdallah
Salim Rabiyya Ali
Sallal, Abdullah al-

Sanjabi, Karim
Sapir, Pinhas
Sarid, Yossi
Sarkis, Ilyas
Sarraj, Abd al-Hammid
Sayyid, Jalal al-
Sha'bi, Qahtan Abdal-Latif al-
Shader, Joseph
Shami, Ahmad Muhammad al-
Shamir, Moshe
Shamir, Yitzhak
Sharaf, Abd al-Hamid
Sharett, Moshe
Sharif, Aziz
Sharif-Emami, Ja'far
Sharon, Ariel
Shazar, Shneour Zalman
Shishakli, Abid
Siba'i, Hani al-
Sidqi, Isma'il
Sneh, Moshe
Soheyli, Ali
Solh, Rashid al-
Solh, Taki al-Din al-
Sprinzak, Joseph
Stalin, Josef
Sulh, Riyad al-
Sulh, Sami al-
Surur, Hail al-
Suwaydi, Tawfiq al-
Tabataba'i, Ziya
Tabet, Ayoub
Tal, Wasfi al-
Tamir, Shmuel
Tayyara, Sami
Ter-Petrossian, Levon
Thaalbi, Abd al-Aziz
Tharwat, Abd al-Khaliq
Tikriti family
Tlas, Mustafa
Toubi, Tawfiq
Trad, Petro
Truman, Harry S.
Türkeş, Alparslan
Ubayd, Hamad
Ulusu Bülent
Umari, Arshad al-
Umari, Mustafa al-
Uthman, Muhammad Ali
Venizélos, Eleuthérios
Wahrhaftig, Zerah
Weizman, Ezer
Weizmann, Chaim
Wilson, Woodrow
Ya'ari, Me'ir
Yafi, Abd Allah
Yata, Ali
Yazdi, Ibrahim
Yusuf, Yusuf Salman
Zahrawi, Abd al-Hamid
Zarwal, Amin al-
Zohrab, Krikor
Zu'ayyin, Yusuf
Zubayri, Qa'id Muhammad
    Mahmud al-
Zubi, Mahmud al-

Rulers (Monarchs and Members of Dynasties)

Abbas Mirza, Na'eb al-Saltaneh
Abd al-Aziz ibn al-Hassan
Abd al-Aziz ibn Sa'ud Al Sa'ud
Abd al-Hafid ibn al-Hassan
Abd al-Ilah ibn Ali
Abd al-Rahman ibn Hisham
Abd al-Rahman Khan
Abdülaziz
Abdülhamit II
Abdullah ibn Husayn
Abdülmecit I
Abdülmecit II
Ahmad Durrani
Ahmad ibn Rashid al-Mualla
Ahmad ibn Yahya Hamid al-Din
Ahmad Qajar
Alawite dynasty
Al Bu Sa'id, Faysal ibn Turki
Al Bu Sa'id, Qabus ibn Sa'id
Al Bu Sa'id, Sa'id ibn Sultan
Al Bu Sa'id, Sa'id ibn Taymur
Al Bu Sa'id, Taymur ibn Faysal
Alexander I
Alexander II
Al Jiluwi
Al Rashid family
Al Sabah, Abd Allah I
Al Sabah, Abd Allah II
Al Sabah, Jabir Ahmad
Al Sabah, Jabir al-Jabir ibn Mubarak
    al-Sabah
Al Sabah, Jabir I al-Sabah
Al Sabah, Mubarak
Al Sabah, Muhammad al-Sabah
Al Sabah, Sabah al-Salim
Al Sabah, Sabah ibn Jabir
Al Sabah, Salim al-Mubarak
    al-Jabir
Al Sa'ud family
Al Sa'ud, Fawwaz ibn Abd
    al-Aziz
Al Sa'ud, Khalid ibn Musa'id
Al Sa'ud, Muhammad ibn Abd al-
    Aziz
Al Sa'ud, Nayif ibn Abd al-Aziz
Al Sa'ud, Sa'ud ibn Faisal
Al Sa'ud, Sultan ibn Abd al-Aziz
Al Sa'ud, Talal ibn Abd al-Aziz
Al Sa'ud, Turki ibn Abd al-Aziz
Al Sa'ud, Turki ibn Faisal
Al Sudayri, Hassa bint Ahmad
Al Thani, Ahmad ibn Ali
Al Thani, Hamad ibn Khalifa
Al Thani, Khalifa ibn Hamad
Al Thani, Qasim ibn Muhammad
Al Thunayyan family
Alya
Amanollah Khan
Amin Bey, al-
Anaza tribe
Arfa, Muhammad ibn
As'ad, Ahmad
Aziz, Abd al-

Badr, Muhammad al-
Bahdinan family
Barakzai, Afdal
Barakzai dynasty
Cuza, Alexander
Dost Mohammad Barakzai
Fahd ibn Abd al-Aziz Al Sa'ud
Faisal ibn Abd al-Aziz Al Sa'ud
Faisal I ibn Husayn
Faisal II ibn Ghazi
Fakhr al-Din I al-Ma'ni
Farouk
Fath Ali Shah Qajar
Fath Jang Durrani
Fawzia
Faysal ibn Turki Al Sa'ud
Fu'ad
Ghazi ibn Faisal
Habibollah Khan
Hafid, Mulay
Hamid al-Din family
Hassan I
Hassan II
Husayn ibn Ali
Husayn Pasha
Hussein ibn Talal
Ibn Musa, Ahmad
Ibn Nasir, Husayn
Ibrahim ibn Muhammad Ali
Idris al-Sayyid Muhammad
    al-Sanusi
Idrisids
Khalid ibn Abd al-Aziz Al
    Sa'ud
Khalifa, Abdullah ibn Ahmad al-
Khalifa, Ali ibn Khalifa al-
Khalifa, Hamad ibn Isa al-
    (heir apparent of Bahrain)
Khalifa, Hamad ibn Isa al-
    (ninth ruler of Bahrain)
Khalifa, Isa ibn Ali al-
Khalifa, Isa ibn Sulman al-
Khalifa, Khalifa ibn Sulman al-
Khalifa, Muhammad ibn
    Khalifa al-
Khalifa, Sulman ibn Ahmad al-
Khalifa, Sulman ibn Hamad al-
Khalifa family
Mahd-e Ulya, Malek Jahan
    Khanum
Mahmud II
Mahmud Durrani
Maktum, Hamdan ibn Rashid al-
Maktum, Maktum ibn Rashid al-
Maktum, Muhammad ibn
    Rashid al-
Maktum, Rashid ibn Sa'id al-
Maktum family, al-
Mamluks
Mehmet V Reşat
Mehmet VI Vahidettin
Mohammad Ali Qajar
Mozaffar al-Din Qajar
Muhammad Ali
Muhammad al-Sadiq
Muhammad ibn Rashid

Muhammad ibn Thani
Muhammed V
Murad V
Mustafa IV
Mustafa Fazıl
Nadir Barakzai, Mohammad
Nahayyan, Khalifa ibn Zayid al-
Nahayyan, Zayid ibn Sultan al-
Nahayyan family, al-
Naser al-Din Shah
Nasir, Ahmed Sayf al-
Nicholas I
Nu'aymi, Rashid ibn Humayid, al-
Osman, House of
Pahlavi, Ashraf
Pahlavi, Mohammad Reza
Pahlavi, Reza
Pahlavi dynasty
Qajar, Agha Mohammad
Qajar dynasty
Qaramanli dynasty
Qasimi, Ibn Muhammad al-
Qasimi, Sultan ibn Muhammad al-
Qasimi family, al-
Sa'dun family, al-
Selim III
Shahpur Ahmadzai Amir
Sharifian dynasties
Sharqi, Hamad ibn Muhammad al-
Sharqi family, al-
Sulayman ibn Himyar
Sulaymani Sharifs
Suleiman, Mulay
Talal ibn Abdullah
Tawfiq
Thuwayni ibn Sa'id
Tuhami al-Glawi
Tuman Bey
Yahya ibn Muhammad Hamid
    al-Din
Yusuf, Mulay
Zahir, Mohammad
Zayd ibn Husayn
Zell al-Soltan, Mas'ud Mirza

Social Activists and Political Reformers (Nineteenth Century)

Abduh, Muhammad
Adamiyat, Abbasquli
Ahmad Bey Husayn
Ahmet Rıza
Ali Suavi
Amir Kabir, Mirza Taqi Khan
Cevdet, Abdullah
Cooper, Anthony Ashley
Fuad, Mehmed
Ganim, Halil
Khayr al-Din
Malkom Khan, Mirza
Matin-Daftari, Hedayatollah
Mehmet Bey
Murat, Mehmet
Mustafa Reşid
Namık Kemal
Sadik Rifat

Shahin, Tanyos
Tahtawi, Rifa'a al-Rafi al-

Social Activists and Political Reformers (Twentieth Century)

Adamiyat, Abbasquli
Ahmet Rıza
Al Sa'ud, Talal ibn Abd al-Aziz
Alusi, Mahmud Shukri al-
Amir-Entezam, Abbas
Arlosoroff, Haim
Atatürk, Mustafa Kemal
Banna, Hasan al-
Benvenisti, Meron
Bu Hamara
Cevdet, Abdullah
Chamran, Mostafa
Garang, John
Gökalp, Ziya
Kasravi, Ahmad
Kuchek Khan-e Jangali
Medani, Tewfiq al-
Mohammadi, Maulawi Mohammad
    Nabi
Nasif, Malak Hifni
Sabahettin
Sadat, Jihan
Sa'dawi, Nawal al-
Sattar Khan
Sha'arawi, Huda al-
Shafiq, Durriyya
Szold, Henrietta
Tabataba'i, Mohammad
Tekin Alp
Utaybi, Juhaiman al-

Theater, Film, and Dance Artists

Agop, Gullu
Ani, Yusuf al-
Aral, Oğuz
Arseven, Celal Esat
Asmahan
Atrash, Farid al-
Ertuğrul, Muhsin
Güney, Yılmaz
Hafiz, Abd al-Halim
Hamama, Fatima
Hamina, Mohammed Lakdar
Hayalı, Kücük Ali
Huda, Nur al-
Kel, Hasan
Kenter, Müşfik
Kenter, Yıldız
Kiarostami, Abbas
Makhmalbaf, Mohsen
Millo, Josef
Sabah
Salim, Ali
Salman, Muhammad
Sayyad, Parviz
Shahin, Yusuf
Sharif, Umar
Yasin, Isma'il
Zohar, Uri

Index

Numbers in **boldface** refer to the main entry on the subject; numbers in *italic* refer to illustrations.

A

Aba, **1**

Aba, Noureddine, 1113

Abadan, **1**, 328, 409
  closure of refinery, 417
  English-inspired urban plan, 1852
  Iranian control of Shatt al-Arab and, 885

Abadan-Unat, Nermin, *as contributor,* 477–478, 479–480, 553–554, 599–600, 638–639, 733, 813–814, 1226, 1328–1329, 1526–1527, 1532–1533, 1684–1685, 1810–1811, 1899–1900

Aba island, 63, 158, 159, 1356

Abalioğlu, Dogan Nadi, 2

Abalioğlu, Nadir Nadi, 2, 515

Abalioğlu, Yunus Nadi, **2**, 515

Ab Ali Road (Iran), *870*

Abane, Ramdane, **2**, 395

Aban river. *See* Barada river

Abasiyanik, Sait Faik, **2**, 1122, 1124

Abbas (uncle of the Prophet Muhammad), 1610, 1710

Abbas, Ferhat, **2–4**, 99, 100, 102, 145, 348, 357, 752
  Amis du Manifeste et de la Liberté (AML), 3, 143, 1018, 1433, 1459
  Blum-Viollette plan defeat (1936), 383
  as évolué, 626–627
  Manifesto of the Algerian Muslim People (1943), 1163
  Union Démocratique du Manifeste Algérien founding, 3, 1828

Abbas, Ihsan, 810, 1423

Abbas, Mahmud, **4**, 1472

Abbas ben Ali, 249

Abbas Hilmi I (viceroy of Egypt), **4**, 354, 483, 1187

Abbas Hilmi II (viceroy of Egypt), **4–5**, 320, 410, 683
  British deposition of (1914), 1903
  Ghali (Butros) as prime minister, 703, 719
  Gorst (John) friendship, 719
  Kamil (Mustafa) association, 978
  Kitchener (Horatio) policies and, 1034
  Liwa, al- (newspaper), 1125
  Mu'ayyad, al- (newspaper), 1264
  National party revival under, 1326
  Sayyid (Ahmad Lutfi al-) relationship, 1610

Abbasid dynasty
  caliphate, 437, 891, 1951
  calligraphy, 438
  ceramics, 456
  communication methods, 491
  Damascus, 527
  Islamic civilization at zenith under, 891
  rise of, 1653
  Samarra, 1592

Abbas Mirza, Na'eb al-Saltaneh (crown prince of Persia), **5–6**, 143, 642, 647, 871, 1559, 1560, 1817

Abbas mosque (Karbala), *984, 985*

Abbas II (Baring), 321

Abboud, Shafiq, 235

Abbud, Ibrahim, **6**, 270, 1693, 1695, 1826

Abbud, Marun, **6–7**

ABC. *See* Arabian Banking Corporation

Abcarius, Michael, 114

ABCFM. *See* American Board of Commissioners for Foreign Missions

ABCM. *See* American Board of Christian Missions

Abda, Fatma. *See* M'Rabet, Fadela

Abd al-Alim, Abdullay, 1589

Abd al-Azim shrine (Iran), 501, 502

Abd al-Aziz, Muhammad, 1466

Abd al-Aziz Abd al-Ghani, **7**

Abd al-Aziz al-Maqalih, **7**, 196

Abd al-Aziz ibn al-Hassan (sultan of Morocco), **7–8**, 84, 1135, 1246, 1642
  Abu Himara rebellion, 32
  civil war with brother, 12, 711, 754, 1138
  Ibn Musa (Ba Ahmad) regency, 840
  political resistance, 67, 991

Abd al-Aziz ibn Sa'ud Al Sa'ud (Ibn Sa'ud; king of the Hijaz and Saudi Arabia), **8–10**, 109, 131, 840
  Al Sabah (Salim al-Mubarak al-Jabir) feud, 119
  Al Shaykh family connections, 127, 128
  Al Thunayyan family and, 130
  Arab unification objections, 655
  British relations, 162, 476, 509, 711, 1294–1295
  broadcasting system, 1514
  caliphate claim, 437, 895, 1538
  favorite wife, 122, 127, 629, 633

Constantine (emperor of Rome), 262, 471, 816

R

BULGAR

GREECE

Tunis

Algiers

TUNISIA

Gibraltar

Valletta

Rabat • Fez

MALTA

Casablanca

Tripoli

MOROCCO

Ouargla

Benghazi

Marrakech

ALGERIA

30°

Sabhah

Reggane

WESTERN

El Aiun

LIBYA

SAHARA

Kufrah

Djanet

Fderik

Atar

MAURITANIA

Nouakchott

NIGER

MALI

15°

CHAD

SENEGAL

CENTRAL AFRICAN
REPUBLIC

45°

EQUATOR

ZAIRE